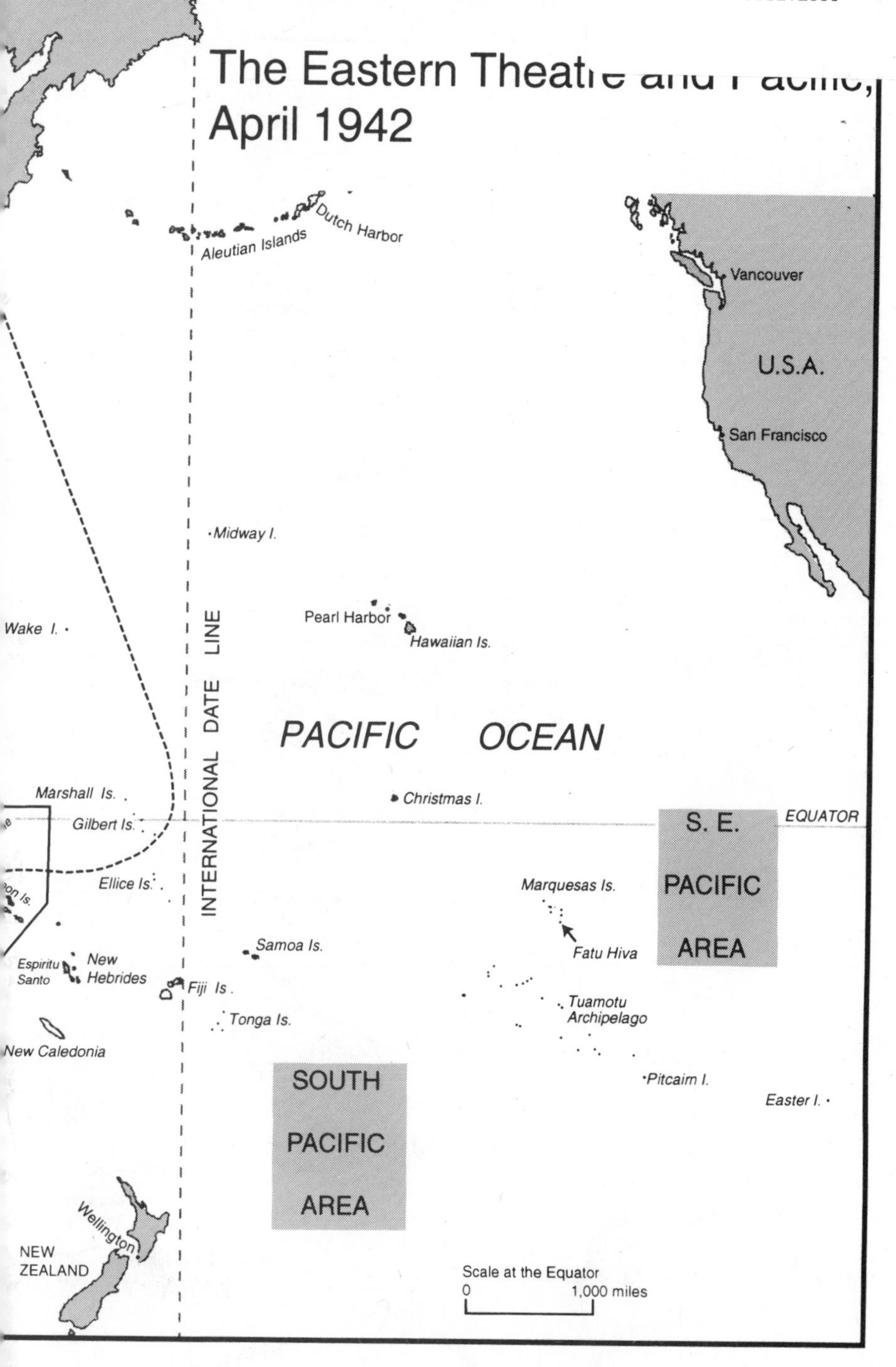
The Eastern Theatre and Pacific,
April 1942
Aleutian Islands
Dutch Harbor
Vancouver
U.S.A.
San Francisco
Midway I.
Wake I.
Pearl Harbor
Hawaiian Is.
INTERNATIONAL DATE LINE
PACIFIC OCEAN
Marshall Is.
Christmas I.
Gilbert Is.
EQUATOR
S. E. PACIFIC AREA
Ellice Is.
Marquesas Is.
Fatu Hiva
Samoa Is.
Espiritu Santo
New Hebrides
Fiji Is.
Tonga Is.
Tuamotu Archipelago
New Caledonia
Pitcairn I.
Easter I.
SOUTH PACIFIC AREA
Wellington
NEW ZEALAND
Scale at the Equator
0
1,000 miles

FAR EASTERN FILE

Given to mark the occasion
of your 60th birthday, Dad
lots of love
Sand + Steve xx

Also by Peter Elphick

Out of Norfolk -- Seamen and Travellers

Odd Man Out – The Story of the Singapore Traitor
(with Michael Smith)

Singapore: The Pregnable Fortress,
A study in Deception, Discord, and Desertion

Frank Carr – Ship Saver
(Booklet for The World Ship Trust)

FAR EASTERN FILE

The Intelligence War in the Far East, 1930–1945

Peter Elphick

Hodder & Stoughton

First published in 1997
by Hodder and Stoughton
A division of Hodder Headline PLC

10 9 8 7 6 5 4 3 2 1

British Library Cataloguing in Publication Data

A CIP catalogue record for this title
is available from the British Library

ISBN 0 340 66583 1

Typeset by Hewer Text Composition Services, Edinburgh
Printed and bound in Great Britain by
Mackays of Chatham PLC

Hodder and Stoughton Ltd
A division of Hodder Headline PLC
338 Euston Road
London NW1 3BH

This book is dedicated to the memory of
Colonel F. Hayley Bell
A.H. Dickinson
Brigadier H. Vinden
Mervyn Llewelyn Wynne

Contents

List of Illustrations

Section One

Section Two

Asama Maru boarded by British boat party, January 1940
Germans climbing aboard HMS *Liverpool*
SS *Automedon* and the German raider *Atlantis*, November 1940
Attack on Pearl Harbor, 7th December 1941
Admiral Yamamoto Isoroku
Prime Minister Tojo Hideki
General Douglas MacArthur and General Blamey
General MacArthur
Brigadier-General Willoughby
Gerald Wilkinson
'Twenty Curves' on the Burma Road
HMS *Formidable* under kamikaze attack, 4th May 1945
Group of kamikaze, 'Divine wind', pilots
Signals Intelligence officers at Wireless Experimental Centre, Delhi, July 1944
US Airways Listening Station, Harrogate

List of Maps

Author's Acknowledgements

A wide range of people have provided me with generous help during the research for this book. Sometimes the help has been extensive and has resulted in the discovery of important and previously unknown papers and memoirs held in private hands (copies of some of which, with the owners' permission, now reside in public archives). Sometimes the help has been in the form of a name which, when followed up, has resulted in the uncovering of valuable information. On occasion the help has simply prevented me going off on a wild goose chase. However, I alone am responsible for the way in which such information has been interpreted. My thanks to all those who have helped me. If any names have by accident been omitted from the list which follows, I offer my sincere apologies. As the list is a long one, I have arranged it alphabetically:

Tim Allen; Admiral A.M. Andrade e Silva (Portugal); Pauline Asbury, née Dickinson; Sir Harold Atcherley; Col. R.P. Baily; C. Baker; Sir Alexander Barrington; H.W.F. Baynham; Hugh Becker; Group Captain H.T. Bennett; Dr Robert Bickers; K. Bindoff; Gordon Blenkinsop; Anthony Brooke (New Zealand); Cedric Brown; Lionel A.C. Schuster Bruce; K.A. Brundle; M. Burkhardt; Mrs A.M.L. Buxton; Brian Cane; Dr Elizabeth Carmichael (South Africa); Dr Toby Carter; Professor John W.M. Chapman; the late Ursula Churchill-Dawes; John Clarkson; Leon Comber (Australia); Sonny Corbin; A.H. Cowling (Canada); George Crane; H.W.B. Croiset van Uchelen (Royal Netherlands Navy); H. William B. Croiset van

Uchelen (Holland); Baroness Sonja Croiset van Uchelen (Holland); James Cummins (assistant to Professor Charles Boxer); Major V.C.F. Davin; E.H. Dean; David Deptford; P. Dixon; Reg Eddington; Carole Edwards; Lt-Col. P. Emerson; Mrs Peggy Erskine-Tulloch; D.S.B. Ferguson (Singapore); the late Sir John Figgess; Gunner Finkemeyer (Australia); the late Dr O. Elliot Fisher; Jane Flower; L. Furness; A.J. Goddard; Basil A. Gotto; the Lord Greenway; Mrs Rosemary Grey; the late Lord Gridley; Christopher Hankey; R.W.E. Harper; Sam Harper; Anthony Hewitt (Australia); Liz Hewitt, née Hayley Bell (Australia); Professor F.H. Hinsley; W.J. Hitchins; Lt-Col. C.E.N. Hopkins-Husson; A.H.P. Humphrey; Johnnie Hunter; Peter Jamieson; Gerry Jenkins; Tony Jiggins (Singapore); Owen Jones; Jacques Jost (France); Allan Keet (Singapore); Dr John Keet; Group Captain J.N. Kentish; Michael Keon (Australia); Major-General Cliff Kinvig; J. Langstaff; Admiral of the Fleet Sir Henry Leach; Bill Lewis; G.D. Lewis; J.S.A. Lewis; Kathleen Lloyd (Australia); N.C. McClintock; the late Vice-Admiral Sir Hugh Mackenzie; Mrs Lavender Martin; Tommy Mellows; Charles Metcalf; Harry Miller (Spain); Mary, Lady Mills, née Hayley Bell; D. Molyneux; J.R. Munday; L. Newson-Davis; R. Parker; Commander A.F. Paterson; George S. Patterson, Lt-Col. P. Pender-Cudlip; Squadron Leader R.D. Phillips; the late Giles Playfair; Anthony Richards; Captain Philip Rivers (Malaya); J.F.M. Roualle; L. St John-Jones; A.E. Sale; Captain R.I.A. Sarell, RN; Elizabeth Scantlebury; Dr O. Schutte (Hoge Rood Van Adel, Holland); Walter Scragg (Australia); Charles Simon (Singapore); Mrs Winifrid Steel, née Hayley Bell; Keith Stevens; Alan Stripp; R.W.A. Suddaby; Squadron Leader D.A. Thomas; Dr P. Thwaites; Brigadier K.A. Timbers; Major J.W. Timbers; Bill Trotter; Virginia Valpy; Madame Rose Vinden (France); Mrs Winnie Vinden; Shamus O.D. Wade; Frank Walker; Squadron Leader D.W. Warne; John Waters; Douglas Weir; F.G. West; Mike West; the late Sir Gordon Whitteridge; the late Peter Wild; Professor R.H. Wilkinson; Geoffrey Wilson (Portugal); H. Wilson; Bill Wiseman; Ross Wood (Australia); H.J. Woolnough; John Wyatt-Smith.

Once again my especial thanks go to an ex-senior officer of the Special Branch, Straits Settlements Police Force who wishes to remain anonymous. I would have liked to have dedicated the book in part to him but, in the circumstances, this tucked-away reference to the great assistance he has given me, to say nothing of the friendship that has grown up between us, will have to suffice.

Author's Acknowledgements

My grateful thanks to John Bright-Holmes, the publisher's editor, and to Alan Palmer who read the book in manuscript and made many valuable suggestions.

I also owe a debt of gratitude to the staff of the following organisations: Imperial War Museum (especially to Roderick Suddaby); Shell Pensions Trust Ltd; University of Sheffield (W.J. Hitchins and Miss Lulu Landale); Australian Archives (Barbara Court); Royal Signals Museum, Blandford Forum (Dr Peter Thwaites); Royal Marines Museum (Matt Little); John Swire & Sons Ltd (Charlotte de Havilland); National Army Museum (Dr Peter Boyden); Oriental and India Office Collections and the Newspaper Library (both of the British Library); Indian Army Association; Essex Regiment Association (Major David Thorogood); Essex Regiment Museum (Ian Hook); Eastern Daily Press (Steve Snelling); Merseyside Maritime Museum (M.K. Stammers and J. Gordon Read); Eton College Register (Neil Flanagan); Public Record Office, Kew; Australian War Memorial; Blue Funnel Association; HMS *Liverpool* Association; HMS *Mauritius* Association; Foreign and Commonwealth Office Library, London (Carole Edwards); The Royal Artillery Historical Trust; The Commonwealth Forces History Trust; School of Oriental and Asiatic Studies; Johanniter Orcle in Nederland, The Hague; Rhodes Library, Oxford: Overseas Development Administration, Glasgow; Liddell Hart Centre, King's College London; National Archives, Washington; Royal Commonwealth Library, Cambridge; Registrar-General of Ships and Seamen, Cardiff; The *Times* Newspaper archives; Hampton Court Palace 'Grace and Favour' Staff.

Quotations from documents under Crown Copyright in the Public Record Office and in the Oriental and India Office Collections appear by permission. Quotations from documents in the Royal Commonwealth Society Collections appear by permission of the Syndics of Cambridge University. Quotations from documents in the Liddell Hart Centre appear by permission of King's College, London. Quotations from documents in the Imperial War Museum and Sheffield University appear by permission.

The author's special thanks go to Sir Harold Atcherley, Hugh Becker, Mrs A.M.L. Buxton, Dr T.C. Carter, H. William B. Croiset van Uchelen, Baroness Sonja Croiset van Uchelen, Basil G. Gotto, Mrs Liz Hewitt, Sam Harper, Lt-Col. Peter Pender-Cudlip, Mrs Virginia Valpy, Madame Rose Vinden, Mrs Winnie Vinden, F.G. West and Geoffrey Wilson, for access to private papers and photographs.

Author's Note

In this book the words 'code' and 'cypher' are used indiscriminately, although there is a technical difference between them. My excuse is that this is not a treatise on cryptography and that, anyway, many of the official documents quoted from also use the words as though they were synonyms. Technically, however, a code is a method of replacing plaintext elements such as phrases and sentences by groups of letters or numbers, whereas, in a cypher (or cipher), the original letters are replaced by other letters or by numbers, or are transposed.

Chinese place names and personal names are shown with the anglicised spellings in use at the time. For example, the capital, Peking, is now Beijing, and Mao Tse-Tung is now spelt Mao Zedong.

Japanese personal names are given in the Japanese way, that is, surname first: e.g. Admiral Yamamoto Isoroku and Major Fujiwara Iwaichi.

Thailand is called by that name throughout except where direct quotations use the old name of Siam. The change was promulgated in Bangkok on 24th June 1939.

Introduction

✦

The dinner at Chequers on Sunday evening, 7th December 1941, was almost an all-American affair. Half-American Winston Churchill was entertaining John Winant, US ambassador to the Court of St James, together with Averell Harriman, President Roosevelt's special envoy. Even the radio perched on the table close to Churchill's hand was an American set; it had cost $15 and had been a gift from Harry Hopkins, Roosevelt's personal adviser and confidant.

Churchill switched on the radio shortly before the nine o'clock news and at the end of the bulletin the news reader spoke a few sentences regarding an attack by the Japanese on American shipping at Hawaii and also about Japanese attacks on British shipping in the East Indies. In his description of that evening's events in his *The Second World War*, Churchill noted that he 'did not personally sustain any direct impression', but that Harriman said there was something about the Japanese attacking the Americans. Then the butler, Sawyers, came into the room to say that he too had heard it. The Japanese had attacked the Americans.

Apart from that most apposite choice of guests on that particular night, the notable point about this anecdote, or at least the way Churchill recorded it, was that the only glimmer of surprise and excitement in that room seems to have arrived with the butler.

Over on the other side of the Atlantic Harry Hopkins was lunching with the President in the Oval Room of the White House, when at about 1.40pm the Secretary of the Navy, Frank Knox, telephoned and said they had picked up a radio from Honolulu advising 'all our stations that an air raid was on and that it was "no drill"'. Hopkins expressed the belief that there must be some mistake, that surely Japan would not attack Honolulu. The President thought the report was probably true, it was just the sort of unexpected thing the Japanese might do. Confirmation came at 2.28 and Roosevelt called a meeting of his departmental heads and advisers half an hour later. Wrote Hopkins:

> The conference met in not too tense an atmosphere, because I think that all of us believed that in the last analysis the enemy was Hitler and that he could never be defeated without force of arms; that sooner or later we were bound to be in the war and that Japan had given us the opportunity.
>
> Churchill called from England. The President told him we were all in the same boat now, and that he was going to Congress tomorrow. Churchill apparently told him that the Malay States had been attacked and that he, too, was going to the House of Commons in the morning and would ask for a declaration of war.

John Winant later gave Harry Hopkins a description of the London end of the story which rather differs from Churchill's. He said that when the news reader announced that the Japanese had attacked Pearl Harbor, Churchill jumped to his feet and was about to call the Foreign Office to give instructions to declare war within the minute, but Winant suggested that it would be better to get confirmation from the White House first, which Churchill did.

Churchill, too, notes that he made such a call to Washington and records that at the end of it he said, '"This certainly simplifies things. God be with you," or words to that effect.' Later he wrote of the great joy he felt because the United States was in the war. 'So we had won after all!' were the words he used to end that passage.

Whatever the exact facts of those two happenings on either side of the Atlantic, it is clear that no one seemed too surprised that the Japanese had struck. The attitudes of all concerned, and probably Churchill's choice of guests that night, indicate that some Japanese move was expected. The reason for the lack of surprise, was that the Americans and the British had been intercepting and reading Japanese messages sent in their diplomatic codes, and these messages had for some weeks indicated that Japan was building up to some major move. Recent messages had ordered Japanese embassies and consulates world-wide to destroy their codes and burn all records. All those on the Allied side who were within the limited group given access to this 'Special' intelligence knew that some move was imminent though not when or where it might fall.

Intelligence was to play a vital part in the Allied victories in the Far East during World War Two. For the Japanese, intelligence and all the functions associated with it had played an important role in their earlier conquest of Manchuria in 1931, their victories in China, and in their preparations for the world war that was to come.

Japanese pre-war undercover penetration throughout the Far East area was of the most comprehensive nature. They had agents and fellow-travellers all over. From the reports of these people Japan was enabled to build up profiles of the lands and peoples of the area, their communications and defences, and just about everything else of importance. As all but one of the countries of Southeast Asia, the exception being Thailand, were colonies of western nations, and China itself was covered in a rash of International Settlements and foreign-dominated Concession Areas, Japan perforce also built up considerable intelligence information about the western nations too.

Japan's use of the traditional methods of intelligence was excellent. Their fishing fleets roamed the Southern Seas, spied on naval manoeuvres, kept a check on shipping movements, and surveyed the sites of likely landing beaches. They had spies looking down on Pearl Harbor from the hills behind it. Other agents worked in the vicinity of the Singapore Naval Base, whilst at least one worked inside the Base. All over Southeast Asia, and beyond into India, Japanese officers under guise of being something else, were busy making notes.

Japanese agents and sympathisers did not neglect the associated fields of subversion and fifth-column, indeed, to their minds and ways of operating, there was little to separate plain outright spying from the others. They used for their own purposes the nationalist aspirations of the people in the various colonial empires; and to fan the irredentist aspirations of the Thais who, in the previous century, had lost lands to those colonial powers, they supplied them with funds and sometimes with arms. From very early days they planted agents in remote places, agents who one day would act as guides to Japanese armies. Japan's Axis partners-to-be also aided them in many ways. Even the Falangists in Spain sent a man to the former Spanish colonial territory of the Philippines who, with the aid of Filipinos who wanted the Americans out of their islands even earlier than had been agreed, so thoroughly infiltrated the Civil Administration there that it broke down completely after Japan attacked.

Japan's pre-war use of traditional or 'ground' espionage methods was thus excellent. In contrast, they neglected the use of signals intelligence, or what one author has called 'spying on the airwaves'. Their use of cryptanalysis was rather perfunctory, although they did have a few successes with Chinese and Russian codes. Possibly because they were always the surprise aggressor and had such excellent ground intelligence sources, they did not see much need to be good in this field too.

In contrast to the Japanese, pre-war Allied ground intelligence tended to be amateurish, and in Japan itself was almost non-existent. Immediately pre-war Japan was almost a closed society, especially in the immediate areas surrounding naval bases and military installations. During those years the British had cut back generally on intelligence spending, and these cutbacks fell especially hard on the Far East, where the British Secret Service actually had to close down two of its offices. The Americans at that time tended to look on spying as not quite gentlemanly, so their efforts were scrappy too.

In contrast to the Japanese however, the western nations did set store by signals intelligence. Britain, for example, set up a huge listening station at Hong Kong in 1935 under what it called the Far East Combined Bureau. Even so, it took the Japanese attacks of December 1941 to start Britain pouring resources into breaking Japanese codes. Those same attacks caused the Americans to pour in resources too.

British Far East intelligence efforts received no coverage at all in F.H. Hinsley's monumental official publication, *British Intelligence in the Second World War*. In a letter to this author dated 1st May 1995, Professor Hinsley said that the reason for the omission was that when he compiled his volumes from 1979 onwards, only about a quarter of the Far East material was available in the United Kingdom, and that no authoritative account could be provided unless intelligence material is co-ordinated with operational decisions, of which most in the Far East were made by the Americans. There was probably another reason which Professor Hinsley did not mention. Although he had permission to look at everything, however secret, he did not necessarily get permission to quote from it, for it is only in very recent years that some of the material he perhaps saw, has been released into the public domain.

This book makes no pretence to fill the gap in Hinsley's authoritative work. It covers matters outside his 'British' remit and also contains much information on matters pre-dating World War Two. But it will help to fill that gap.

One

The Rise of Japan

The last years of the sixteenth century brought an unsuccessful Japanese attempt under Hideyoshi, their *kampaku*, or civil dictator, to conquer Korea. Hideyoshi's successor, Ieyasu, secured for himself the title of 'Shogun', or military leader of the country, in 1603, and he began the process of cutting Japan off from the rest of the world. There were several reasons for this, but basically it was to prevent the disaffected elements in Japanese society from using foreign influences and technology to undermine the shogunate. Few breaches were permitted in Ieyasu's screen. He himself made use of the services of the 'first Englishman in Japan', Will Adams, as an adviser on maritime and trade matters, and Ieyasu and his successors allowed Chinese merchants to trade through the port of Nagasaki and also permitted the operation of a small Dutch trading factory on Deshima Island off that same port. Otherwise the country was virtually closed. Japanese were not allowed to visit foreign lands and foreigners were forbidden to enter Japan.[1]

Two centuries later all this was to change, a change that came about because of what was happening to China, Japan's immediate mainland neighbour.

By the early 1800s the once powerful Chinese Empire had grown weak and was in a state of decay. China was thus ripe for exploitation by the colonial nations of Europe. The British, who had taken over the lead in opium importation into China from the Portuguese in 1773, were now to lead the way in making territorial gains and forcing extra-territorial rights. All came to a head when in 1836 the Chinese emperor decided to stamp out the illegal opium trade which, based mainly on Canton, had thrived under the general but arm's-length guidance of Britain's East India Company until it lost its monopoly of the China trade in 1834, and the direct involvement of so-called 'country traders' such as William Jardine.*

As a result of the East India Company's loss of its monopoly, officials of the British Crown replaced the Company's men at Canton, so that as the Chinese continued to pressure for the close down of the trade, although commercial interests continued to dominate British policy, considerations of national honour and prestige had now entered the picture. Chinese ultimatums to the British Superintendent of Trade at Canton, and then his detention and other such 'slights', finally led to the First Opium War in 1840. The Treaty of Nanking in 1842 brought the war to an end; under its terms the British gained legitimate footholds at Canton, Amoy, Shanghai and other places along the Chinese coast. China also ceded Hong Kong to the British 'in perpetuity'. By 1844 some seventy British or Anglo-Indian companies were operating from these original Treaty Ports. The Second and Third Opium Wars of 1856 and 1857, the latter being a combined Anglo-French operation, led to the establishment of other Treaty Ports, Tientsin becoming the sixteenth in 1860. In that same year Kowloon on the mainland opposite Hong Kong became

* The East India Company perfected the technique of growing opium cheaply in India – the actual farmers receiving a pittance for the product of their efforts – but officially disengaged itself from the task of illegally importing it into China by licensing 'country ships' to carry it. The Company's hypocrisy was compounded by: 1) the issuance of public sailing orders for each vessel involved in the trade which stated that there was a prohibition against the carriage of opium; 2) the fact that each opium chest was stamped with the Company's chop which was taken by the Chinese merchants involved in the trade as a guarantee of quality; and 3) in the early days it was the Company's representative in Canton who recorded the transactions, the opium being paid for by Chinese silver which was then used to buy Chinese tea and silks for the British market. The trade was a sort of Eastern equivalent of the 'triangular trade' centred about slave-trafficking in the Atlantic, and was equally as objectionable. The British government countenanced the East India Company's involvement, and later its own, mainly because the revenue accruing to the Company prevented India becoming a financial burden on Britain. (The Duke of Wellington was to declare in May 1838 that Parliament had not only refused to frown upon the opium trade, 'but had cherished it, extended it, and promoted it'.) It is interesting to reflect that the activities of country traders like William Jardine, a name still perpetuated in the most famous of Hong Kong's trading companies, would nowadays have resulted in long prison terms or even the hangman's noose.

British territory together with Stonecutters Island in Hong Kong harbour. The latter part of the century brought an international scramble for other footholds along the Chinese coast, with France, Germany, and other nations joining in, while to the north Russia's gradual colonisation of Siberia resulted in her taking an interest in the adjacent provinces of China. In June 1898 Britain took a 99-year lease on the 'New Territories' adjacent to Kowloon.

While all this was taking place international interest in the nearby hidden kingdom of Japan grew. This interest was led by the United States which had become a Pacific Power with the opening up of California in 1846 followed by the Gold Rush years of 1848–49. The United States, which was already trading with China, began developing whaling interests in the Pacific and, during their voyages, many American ships sailed close to the forbidden coasts of Japan. Some sailed too close, and shipwrecked mariners who landed on her shores were repatriated through the good offices of the Dutch at Nagasaki, but often only after being maltreated by the Japanese.

On the pretext of demanding good treatment for future shipwrecked mariners, an American fleet of four ships under Commodore Matthew Perry arrived off Japan in 1853. What the Americans really sought was access to Japanese ports as a source of bunkers for their ships, and a general opening up of trade. Perry demanded agreement on an exchange of plenipotentiaries, and sailed away promising to return for an answer the following year with an even larger fleet; which is exactly what he did.

These flagrant acts of gunboat diplomacy were soon followed by others. In fact, within days of the Perry expedition sailing away, a Russian fleet sailed in. In consequence, in the following year the Japanese government, fearing that the motherland might go the way of China, agreed to sign a treaty – the Treaty of Kanagawa – with the Americans under which the United States was granted the right to trade with designated Japanese ports and to station a representative in the country.

The arrival seven months later of Admiral Stirling's British fleet – he came in search of the Russian Far Eastern Fleet, for the Crimean War had begun – pushed the bamboo screen further aside. The Japanese came to an agreement with Britain similar to their one with the United States.

With this forcible breaching of its insularity came a rise in the power of Japan's merchant class, to whom many of the ruling *diamyo* class were already in debt. Internal pressures built up, and finally, after a decade of dissension and political in-fighting, an army fighting in the name of the Emperor Meiji overthrew the shogunate in 1868. But the new rulers of Japan were pragmatists, so, although the uprising had been associated in the minds of ordinary Japanese with the desire to throw out the 'white barbarian', there was to be no return to the old feudal and insular ways. Instead, in the knowledge of how far they had fallen behind the rest of the world during the centuries of isolation, the new leaders embarked upon an intensive and quite remarkable catching-up exercise. The race to modernise – given extra impetus by fear that the colonial powers might take further advantage of her comparative weakness – was pressed ahead with extraordinary speed, special attention being given to building up a modern army and navy. By the late 1870s, for example, Japan was sending naval cadets to Greenwich for training.

As she modernised, and her manufacturing industries grew, Japan found herself short of raw materials and of overseas markets for her products. She began to cast covetous eyes on the large deposits of iron ore and coal in Korea, a kingdom over which China held suzerainty. Impressed not only by the western technology they were so busy copying, but also by the success of western imperial practices, Japanese leaders began to think seriously of emulating those as well. Apart from any other considerations, taking control of nearby mainland territories would provide them with a buffer against the imperialist nations.

In the early 1870s the Japanese tried some Commodore Perry treatment of their own against the Kingdom of Korea. However, not being strong enough yet, they found themselves rebuffed. But in 1876, under threat of military invasion, Korea was forced to sign the Treaty of Kanghwa under which she had to open her doors to Japanese trade, surrender some extraterritorial rights, and hand over control of its customs' revenue. The Japanese were excellent learners, for this treaty bore all the hallmarks of the similarly unequal ones forced upon themselves a few decades earlier. Furthermore, Japan did this against the background of seeking to abrogate the earlier treaties and saw no inconsistency in forcing upon another country terms which she was trying to get out of herself. Professor Saburo Ienaga has written, 'Japan perceived the international arena as a dog-eat-dog struggle where the devil and colonialism took the hindmost.'[2]

Japan nurtured her aspirations as she grew in strength, being careful not to antagonise the nations of the West too much. By the 1890s she

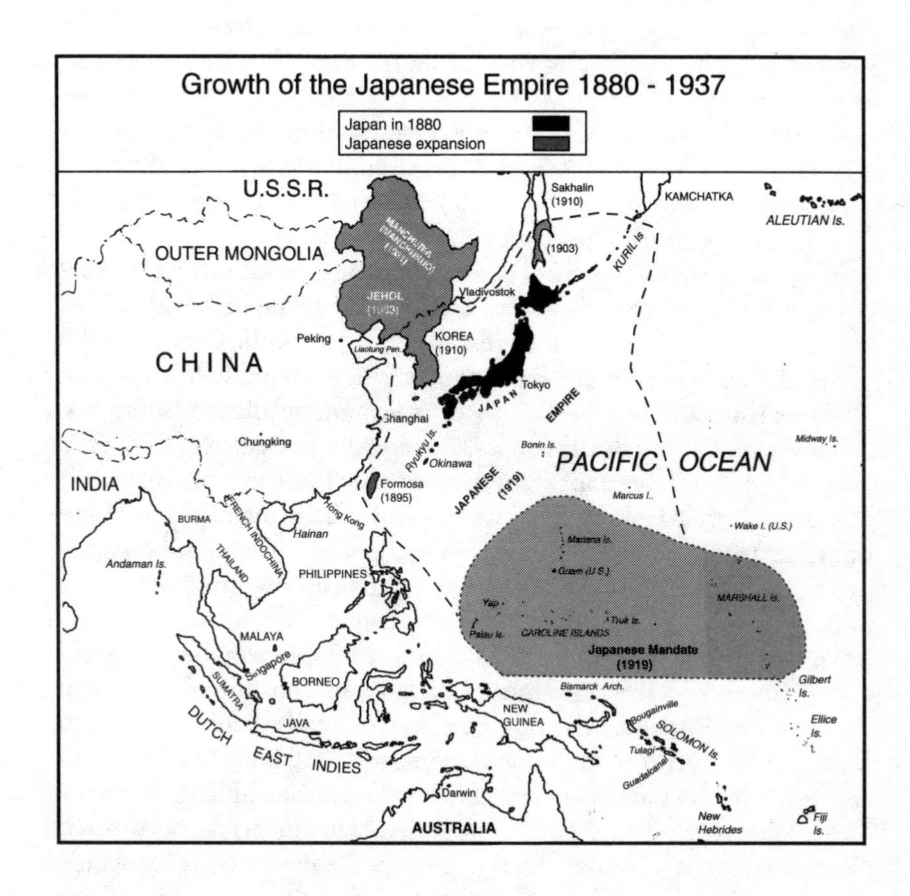
Growth of the Japanese Empire 1880 - 1937
Japan in 1880
Japanese expansion
U.S.S.R.
OUTER MONGOLIA
MANCHURIA
(MANCHUKUO)
JEHOL
Sakhalin
(1910)
(1903)
KAMCHATKA
ALEUTIAN Is.
KURIL Is
Vladivostok
Peking
Liaotung Pen.
KOREA
(1910)
CHINA
Tokyo
JAPAN
EMPIRE
Shanghai
Chungking
Ryukyu Is.
Okinawa
Bonin Is.
PACIFIC OCEAN
Midway Is.
INDIA
Formosa
(1895)
JAPANESE
(1919)
Marcus I..
BURMA
FRENCH INDOCHINA
Hong Kong
Hainan
THAILAND
Wake I. (U.S.)
Mariana Is.
Guam (U.S.)
Andaman Is.
PHILIPPINES
Yap
MARSHALL Is.
Truk Is.
Palau Is.
CAROLINE ISLANDS
Japanese Mandate
(1919)
MALAYA
Singapore
BORNEO
Bismarck Arch.
Gilbert
Is.
SUMATRA
NEW
GUINEA
Bougainville
Ellice
Is.
DUTCH
JAVA
SOLOMON Is.
Tulagi
EAST
INDIES
Guadalcanal
Darwin
New
Hebrides
AUSTRALIA
Fiji
Is.

felt ready to take the next major step, one that was presaged by the activities of members of some of her secret societies. She despatched agents to stir up unrest among the Koreans, and then sent in troops to put down the unrest. The Korean government, unable either to restore order or force the Japanese to withdraw their troops, called on China for help, and Chinese troops were sent in.

As she was to do again in 1904, and once more in 1941, Japan struck without formal declaration of war.* Her warships sank a Chinese troopship and captured one of the escort vessels. During the following nine months the Japanese army drove the Chinese from Korea, seized Manchuria's Liaotung peninsula including Port Arthur, so affording protection to Korea's western flank, and farther south seized the port of Weihaiwei on the coast of Shantung Province. The Japanese navy went on to sink a Chinese fleet off the Yalu River. China sued for peace and, under the Treaty of Shimonoseki of April 1895, yielded up the island of Formosa to Japan as well as the Liaotung peninsula. China also recognised the independence of Korea, which resulted in de facto control of that country by the Japanese.

All of this came as an unpleasant surprise to most Westerners. Within a short time of the signing of the Shimonoseki treaty, Russia, France and Germany, under what came to be called the 'Triple Intervention', forced Japan to give up the Liaotung peninsula on the grounds that her presence there would disturb the peace of the Far East. Japan, with no allies, was forced into face-losing submission, and from that day on viewed the actions of Russia, her giant neighbour to the northwest, with dislike and suspicion.

This suspicion was confirmed when, in the following year, Russia and China agreed the Manchuria Convention. The most direct route from central Russia to the Siberian port of Vladivostok lay through Manchurian territory, and Russia persuaded China to agree to the construction of a railway line across Manchuria, linking with the Trans-Siberian railway and passing through Harbin. But Russian interest was not confined to the proposed railway corridor which their troops occupied and which gave them virtual control of the country. They sent their Eastern fleet south to winter at ice-free Port Arthur in 1897, a move that provoked Germany to occupy

* Japan has been thoroughly criticised for this practice – vide Roosevelt's speech on 8th December 1941 in which he coined the phrase 'day of infamy' – but in fact this has been common throughout history. It is easy to argue that it does not really make sense to give a prospective enemy notice of one's intentions.

Kiachow Bay in November of that year, taking out a 99-year lease from China and building there the naval base of Tsingtao. Thereupon Russia formally leased Port Arthur in the following March, a move that drove Britain to counter it with the leasing of nearby Weihaiwei in July. It seemed to Japan that any act of colonialism was acceptable in the world's corridors of power providing it was not carried out by a nation from the East.

The next worry for Japan came in 1900 when Russia used the Boxer Rising in China as a pretext for moving large armed forces southwards through Manchuria into China. Now it seemed to the Japanese that Korea, their 'special interest' area, was under threat.

Britain had stood aloof from the 'Triple Intervention', as indicated in the *Punch* cartoon (below) but when in 1902 France and Russia grew closer together in face of the prospect of the renewal of the Triple Alliance between Germany, Italy and Austria-Hungary, the tocsin began to toll in London. Ever mindful of its self-imposed role of holding the balance of power in Europe, and conscious of the Far Eastern Empire it had to protect, perhaps from the old enemy France or from the encroaching Russian bear, Britain sought an ally, a search made more important by the rising German naval menace. In that

[Reproduced by permission of the Proprietors of "Punch"]

JOHN STANDS ALOOF

Russia: "Is he to have all *this*?"

John Bull: "Well–he's played a square game–*I* don't see any call to interfere!"

same year Britain signed a Treaty of Alliance with Japan, which she hoped would permit her to bring ships back to home waters and cut naval expenditure in the Far East in anticipation of the new naval base at Rosyth, begun in 1903.

Britain gained from the treaty, but the Japanese gained much more. To them it meant that they had entered the league of most powerful nations. Furthermore, it went a long way towards wiping out the loss of face caused by the 'Triple Intervention'.

The occupation of Port Arthur had given Russia virtual control of the Gulf of Chihli. Russia now dominated Tientsin, Peking's sea-gateway, on one side, and created a threat to the approaches to Inchon, the port of Korea's capital Seoul, on the other. This was not just galling to Japan, it was alarming. Seeing it as a threat to her special interest, she began to prepare for a struggle with Russia.

Once again following up subversive operations conducted by members of secret societies, Japanese agents penetrated the area around Port Arthur and into the heart of Russian defences in Manchuria, to probe the strength there. Whilst these covert operations went on Japan opened negotiations with Russia in an attempt to negotiate a buffer zone in Korea and gain access to the resources of southern Manchuria. The Russians would have none of this, though, and Japan broke off negotiations on 6th February 1904.

That very day the Imperial Japanese Navy sailed from Sasebo and during the night of 8/9th February struck at the Russian fleet anchored off Port Arthur, not formally declaring war until 10th February which caused Russia and other countries to complain that Japan had broken international usage. However, *The Times* in London, probably reflecting British government opinion, declared, 'The Japanese Navy has opened the war by an act of daring which is destined to take a place of honour in naval annals'.

The Russo-Japanese war lasted a year and a half, with the Japanese gaining decisive victories on both land and sea. A distinctive feature of the war was the mainly chivalrous manner in which both sides fought; in striking contrast to the Japanese armies a few decades later in China, and after that in Malaya and the Philippines.

In October 1904 a Russian fleet of some forty vessels set out for the Far East from the Baltic. It received material aid from the French who provided coaling facilities at Madagascar and Indo-China; conversely it was regarded with hostility by Great Britain, Japan's ally. The fleet arrived in the east in May 1905 and was engaged by a Japanese fleet under Admiral Togo on 27th May at the Battle of Tsushima. For the loss of only three torpedo-boats, the Japanese sank or captured every Russian ship except one in the most decisive and dramatic sea-battle for a century. The British Admiralty's contemporary assessment of the battle was that 'Tsushima is the equivalent of Trafalgar'. In fact, as the Japanese fleet had been largely built and equipped in England, and as most Japanese naval officers had been trained by the Royal Navy, the British felt almost as pleased and proud of the victory as did the Japanese themselves.

The cost of the war to both sides in manpower, materials and funds was high. A week after the Battle of Tsushima the USA was asked by Japan to propose peace talks with the Russians, and on 5th September the war was brought to an end by the Treaty of Portsmouth (in New Hampshire). Under its terms Russia recognised Japan's special interest in Korea, transferred the lease of Port Arthur to Japan – which the Chinese accepted only with the greatest reluctance – and agreed other concessions in southern Manchuria. This was not enough for many Japanese, however, for they were largely unaware of the dire financial straits their country was in. There were riots in Tokyo stirred up by nationalist groups and the secret societies. Martial law was proclaimed, and when the Foreign Minister returned from America he had to land secretly for fear of assassination. For all that, in the eyes of the world Japan's success in the war had brought her much kudos. Nor was thus all, for by replacing Russia in southern Manchuria, Japan had joined the company of nations exploiting China.

It is from this date that we can see a great expansion in the activities and membership of the Japanese ultra-nationalist secret societies and an increase in their influence over the armed forces, more especially the army. This was important, for out of the activities and influence of these societies was to grow the modern Japanese intelligence services.

In the next quarter of a century Japan continued to grow as an industrial and military nation. In 1910 she annexed Korea which then became part of the Japanese Empire and was called Chosen. When, in 1911, the people of China revolted against their emperor and established a republic and in the process became riven by civil war, Japan took advantage of the situation to strengthen its position in China.

By now Japan was losing any chivalrous image it had gained in the Russian war. It acted ruthlessly against signs of resistance in the annexed regions. Professor Saburo has written, 'policies towards Taiwan and Korea became more ruthless as pressure increased on China; resistance to annexation in both areas was mercilessly crushed'.[3] One of the reasons for this change in attitude was that Japanese army lines of communication had become over-extended and it could not afford to show leniency to those causing trouble in the rear. More importantly, perhaps, was rising jingoism, based on racism, back in the homeland. The Japanese had a word for the Chinese which equated with the disparaging 'Chinks' in English. It was used in popular songs which fanned hatred for the Chinese. Again, in both Korea and Taiwan, the people were treated as second-class citizens and were not represented in the Japanese Diet (Parliament). Much Korean land was confiscated and handed over to Japanese settlers; landless Koreans were then sent to Japan to become labourers on the lowest of wages and to find themselves confronted with racial aggression.

World War One provided Japan with further opportunities to enhance her international position. In accordance with her treaty with Britain she entered the war on the Allied side. From Penang in Malaya her navy patrolled the Indian Ocean, so protecting Australia and New Zealand; she sent a fleet into the Mediterranean consisting of a cruiser and fourteen destroyers; along part of its sea-route it fell to the Japanese to protect the Great Convoy of ANZAC troops travelling to the European war zones. In 1915 marines from some of her ships helped put down an Indian army mutiny in Singapore.[4] Part of the Japanese fleet protected Hong Kong and the International Settlement at Shanghai. She sent troops to occupy German possessions in the Pacific and to take control of the German Treaty Ports in China including the important naval base of Tsingtao. It was the size of the Japanese naval contribution during World War One that was later to give Japan such high standing at the Paris Peace Conference.

But in respect of China, Japan then overplayed her hand. Within months of taking over the Treaty Ports she made her notorious 'Twenty-One Demands' on the Chinese government. This was an 'ill-conceived and clumsily handled diplomatic offensive' that 'can be summed up as an opportunist and maladroit attempt by Japan to bring China under her supervision, if not control', wrote Richard Storry in *A History of Modern Japan*.[5] The demands included the permanent transfer of the German Treaty Ports to Japan, an extension of her rights in Manchuria, the employment of Japanese military and financial advisers, and that China must in future purchase all her war materials from Japan.

Acceptance of the Twenty-One Demands would have made China a virtual Japanese protectorate. What saved China was sustained international indignation, especially from the United States. Britain protested too, and the Japanese action was to become one of the factors that led to the abandonment of the Anglo-Japanese Treaty a few years later. Some members of the Japanese aristocracy even weighed in to curb what they saw as an abuse of power by the Japanese Cabinet. Nevertheless, China had to agree to a watered down set of demands from which Japan still gained much.

Although later the Japanese tried to appease China by granting huge loans and by bribing key officials, Japan in Chinese eyes had become the most loathsome of all the foreign interlopers on her soil. But the most important consequence of the Twenty-One Demands was that they created hostility against Japan and, conversely, great sympathy for China in the United States.

At the end of World War One the situation in the Far East was to grow yet more complex. The so-called Siberian Intervention of 1918 grew out of the chaos that was Russia after the Revolution of 1917. It seemed that Bolshevism might spill over into Manchuria and Korea, and, after some argument between the Allies, it was decided to land an Expeditionary Force at Vladivostok, partly to stem the spread of Communism and partly to help extricate the Czech Legion. This Legion, raised from prisoners-of-war and deserters in Russia, had fought the Germans until the Revolution but then found its only avenue of escape was to cross the continent on the Trans-Siberian Railway, and had to fight Bolshevik troops in order to do so. British troops landed at Vladivostok in August 1918, followed by Americans, French, Canadians and Japanese. The Japanese sent by far the largest force, consisting of 70,000 men, and this time their soldiers were not noted for chivalrous behaviour.

In the spring of 1920 the Czechs finally extricated themselves and all the Allied troops withdrew except for the Japanese. Not only did the Japanese army stay against the directions of its government back home, but it also extended its military operations into the Sakhalin peninsula. This major disobedience was to set an evil precedent, but on this first occasion the Japanese military did not have significant public support in Japan, and the army had to return home in October 1922.

Meanwhile the Paris Peace Conference had opened in January 1919. Japan, at the top table, emerged from the Conference with control over the former German concessions in China together with a Mandate over the German islands – the Marianas, Caroline and Marshall islands – which she had seized in the Pacific at the outbreak of the war. She also came away with one of the permanent seats on the Council of the League of Nations. What she did not win was the insertion of a clause in the League's Charter which would have established the principle of racial equality, a clause most strongly opposed by the United States and Australia. Despite the value Britain placed on its friendship with Japan, it too eventually opposed the clause. The clause might have had a greater chance of inclusion in the Charter had Japan's own racial record in Taiwan, Korea, and China been better. However, that did not stop the Japanese using the racial card against the West at every opportunity in the future.

World War One had irrevocably altered the balance of world naval power. Britain was still the leading country but was in imminent danger of being overtaken by the United States because of the vast shipbuilding potential that country had built up, and because Britain was financially exhausted after four years of fighting. As Germany's navy now scarcely existed, Japan became number three in the pecking order. In effect, the centre of gravity of world naval power had shifted from the Atlantic to the Pacific.

As each of the naval powers reflected upon the huge costs involved in a naval arms race, the rumblings of great political changes began to be heard in those countries both on the giving and the receiving end of imperialism. In no country was this more evident than in China, the most populous country in the world. Out of this, in the West though not in Japan, there grew a greater 'readiness to treat China as other countries were treated'.[6]

The boom of the war years had passed in Japan by the end of the 1920s. There was much unemployment and industrial unrest. There came a significant increase in what the police called 'dangerous thoughts' and, slowly and mainly covertly, contempt for the Diet and for big business was growing. The seeds of military fascism, lying mainly dormant but never far below the surface of Japanese society, began to germinate.

At the British Imperial Conference held in London in 1921 special

[6] As quoted in Martin Gilbert's *Winston S. Churchill*, Volume IV.

attention was paid to Japan's manifest intention to expand its influence in China and the effect this might have on the strategic situation in the Far East, especially over the defence of Australia and New Zealand. Britain took the view that her treaty with Japan, which was due for renewal, could be a possible moral check on Japan's expansionist policies. The antipodean Dominions tended to agree, but not Canada which backed the stated American view that the treaty must be terminated. Two of Winston Churchill's comments at this time are worthy of note: 'Japan is the danger to be guarded against'. On the subject of treaty non-renewal, he remarked: 'Getting Japan to protect you against Japan is like drinking salt water to slake thirst.'*

The American attitude, aggravated by the Twenty-One Demands and by Japanese brutality in the annexed territories, was born out of the race hatred that had erupted in California and then in other states west of the Rocky Mountains between the turn of the century and World War One. 'It is impossible to exaggerate the outrageousness and popularity of the xenophobia and race hatred so manifest on the Pacific slopes during that period', wrote the authors of *Total War*.[7] By 1921 most of that hatred was directed at Japan, and the Anglo-Japanese Alliance had become a major obstacle in the way of Anglo-American friendship and of disarmanent. An American writer of the time, H.W. Elson, even wrote that 'until that alliance was broken it would have been folly for America to disarm on the sea; for at any time those two powers might have joined against us in the Pacific Ocean'. Quite apart from the inconceivability of such an event, the revised treaty of 1911 had been framed to exclude that possibility. Nevertheless Elson was expressing a view widely held then in the United States.

Towards the end of 1921 the Washington Conference on the limitation of arms was held, and the future of the Anglo-Japanese Treaty became a central feature of it. An indigent Britain, needing a limitation on arms and especially on naval shipbuilding, was faced with making a choice between American goodwill and that of Japan. It was a fateful decision but ultimately no contest. 'Few such . . . have been made with so little national debate, and with such small public realisation of what had been done, and what it meant for the future'.[8] The Conference agreed to a ratio of capital ship tonnage at 5:5:3:1.75:1.75, as between the British Empire, the United States, Japan, France and Italy respectively, and these ratios were confirmed

* As quoted in Martin Gilbert's *Winston S. Churchill*, Volume IV.

in the Naval Treaty of 1922. This was a momentous decision, but in the light of what happened during the next two decades, perhaps the most fateful decision made at the Conference was the termination of the Anglo-Japanese Treaty announced on 10th December 1921. It was to be replaced by a Four Power Treaty between Britain, the United States, Japan and France. This was basically a non-aggression pact and a device to save Japanese face, but was of considerably lower status to the treaty it had been designed to replace. Professor Richard Storry has written that the termination of the Anglo-Japanese Alliance 'removed . . . the possibility of friendly and effective British influence on policy-making in Tokyo, while it did nothing to strengthen the security of the United States; and of course it greatly weakened the whole strategic situation of Australia and New Zealand, to say nothing of Hong Kong and other British possessions east of the Bay of Bengal'.[9*]

Admiral of the Fleet Lord Chatfield wrote of the termination of the treaty, 'however politically wise, we had weakened most gravely our Imperial strategic position. We had turned a proved friend . . . into a potential and powerful foe'.[10] Some more informed American opinion was also critical of the change. Frederick Moore, who had been an adviser to the Japanese government for many years and who was one-time US Acting Secretary of State, wrote in his book, *With Japan's Leaders*:

> I felt strongly that it was a mistake in foreign policy for the United States to press Britain for a termination of their Alliance with Japan. The Alliance could not menace us. The charge that it could was, I thought, false. The Japanese were shocked by its termination . . . This was the beginning of the nation's turn towards independent action . . . It opened the way psychologically for co-operation with Germany. It is, I think, even probable that had the Alliance been permitted to continue there would have been enough restraint kept upon the Army by civilian and naval influence in Japan to prevent its going to China. There would also have been, I believe, enough of such influence to prevent the alignment of Japan with the Axis Powers.[11]

* US involvement in the decision is perhaps best illustrated by the fact that it was Senator Henry Cabot Lodge who, at the Washington Conference, recited the four articles of the 'Four Power Treaty of the Pacific'. At the end he said, 'This agreement shall be ratified as soon as possible . . . at Washington, and thereupon the agreement between Great Britain and Japan concluded at London on 13th July 1911, shall terminate.'

Major-General F.S.G. Piggott, who served for many years in Japan, first as a language officers,* then as Assistant Military Attaché and finally as Military Attaché, and who had been a member of the British army delegation at the Washington Conference, entitled his history of his years in that country *Broken Thread*, a reference to the parting of the ways of Britain and Japan on 10th December 1921. He wrote that its effect 'was felt far more in Japan than in England . . . in Japan there was a dull glow of resentment, which every now and again showed signs of bursting into flames'. Relations between Britain and Japan were never to be the same again.†

Japan gained a major concession at the Washington Conference. Agreement was reached that no new naval bases were to be constructed in the Western Pacific, although Singapore was specifically excluded from that proviso, as was Pearl Harbor. The exclusion of Singapore was important for Britain, for earlier that same year it had been decided to build a huge new naval base there after consideration had been given to several other possible places. In the following year, 1922, the actual site for the base was selected on the north side of the island on the Johore Strait, a little to the east of the causeway which joined the island to the mainland. Planning and construction of the base began in 1923.

However, although the new naval base was designed to house and service a large fleet, it was never the intention for a permanent Far Eastern Fleet to be based there. Britain could not afford to maintain such a fleet on station, so instead the government decided to send such a fleet there only when the situation in that part of the world became critical. A phrase was coined to cover the period between the coming of such a time and the fleet's actual arrival at the base. It was called the 'period before relief', and in the 1920s was taken to be seventy days. The theory was that during this interim period the defence of the base would be the responsibility of the RAF and the troops of the garrison. As early as 1924 General Smuts, the South African premier, pointed out that tensions in the Far East were only

* Language officers were attached to embassy staffs, not only to learn a particular foreign language, but to help foster good relations between the armed services of the countries concerned. They came under the appropriate attaché but, unlike the attaché, did not enjoy diplomatic immunity.

† It was on the twentieth anniversary of the day of the cancellation of the Anglo-Japanese Treaty, on 10th December 1941, that the Japanese sank the pride of the Royal Navy, HMS *Prince of Wales* along with HMS *Repulse*.

likely to arise after troubles in Europe made it impossible for the British to send a fleet to Singapore, but no one took any notice of his or of any other criticism of the policy. Furthermore, over the years, the period before relief grew longer, until by 1941 it was one hundred and eighty days – that is, six *months*.

Pearl Harbor had also been exempted from the 'no development of naval bases' policy. The Americans continued to develop this fine base, which was situated west of Honolulu on Oahu, one of the Hawaiian Islands. Although some 3,400 miles away on Japan's eastern flank, it and the outlying bases at Wake and Guam, the American-held islands in the West Pacific, posed definite threats to Japanese lines of communication in the event that they should decide on a move south.

Two

Supreme in Eastern Asia

Despite the lasting rankle left by the treaty events of 1921, the first half of the 1920s seemed to be a period of prosperity for Japan in the field of foreign relations. Relations with China improved and Japan exchanged ambassadors with the Soviet Union. Only in 1924, when Congress passed a law prohibiting immigration from eastern countries, including Japan, did Japanese ire rise. As with their failure to have the racial equality clause inserted in the League of Nations Charter, this had a hurtful and lasting effect on Japanese pride.

When in 1926 a new emperor, Hirohito, came to the Japanese throne, taking as the title for his reign the characters meaning 'enlightened peace', or *Showa*, it seemed that a new, more liberal attitude had been born in Japan. But this was largely a show. As early as 1921 Prince Higashikuni, who was 'studying' in Paris at the advanced age of thirty-six and was suspected by the French Sûreté of running the Japanese Intelligence network in Europe, organised a meeting at Baden Baden of Japanese Military Attachés, almost certainly with Crown Prince Hirohito's consent.[1] This group produced an outline programme to make the Japanese army and navy the most efficient in the world, and created an inner council of young officers called 'the eleven reliables' to implement it. Amongst them were Tojo and Doihara, both Manchurian specialists.

Even at the time of Hirohito's coronation clouds were gathering on Japan's western horizon. Kuomintang forces under Chiang Kai-shek were beginning the long task of unifying warlord-ridden China. In

1927 they gained control of the heart of the nation, the great Yangtze river basin, and began fanning out to the north and east. They attacked the communists under Mao Tse-tung who retreated and set up a base in the mountains on the Hunan-Kiangsi border, and who themselves then began the task of clearing their own 'liberated' zone. One of Chiang Kai-shek's expressed aims was the abolition of all extra-territorial arrangements in China, including those of Japan.

In that same year Japan experienced a depression, a precursor of the world-wide one to come in 1930. Three dozen banks failed, and the government fell with them. The new dynamism in China and the internal problems in Japan fomented extreme nationalist and economic ideas in the junior officer ranks of the Japanese army. One symptom of this was the creation of a secret society within army ranks dedicated to planning a *coup d'état* and to establishing a military dictatorship.

The new Prime Minister, General Tanaka, adopted a tough stance against China and sent in troops to stem the Kuomintang's move north and to protect Japan's special rights in China and its position in Manchuria. Professor Saburo has condemned this move in radical terms:

> If Japan had been a champion of Asian nationalism, had really desired independence and progress for its neighbour, and had joined with China to liberate Asia from Western imperialism, the subsequent history of the region would have been vastly different . . . Unfortunately, Japanese leaders chose the opposite course. They competed with the west for a place at the imperial table and a slice of the Chinese melon.[2]

The Japanese army based in the southern part of Manchuria, which called itself the Kwantung army, at first set out to appease the warlord there, Chang Tso-lin, but in 1928 some army Staff and Intelligence officers conceived a plan to seize all of Manchuria and kill Chang in the process. As a train carrying Chang passed over a crossing it was blown up by explosives laid by Japanese army engineers, after which it was arranged for bombs to be thrown at Japanese offices in Mukden. The plotters then had three Chinese vagrants arrested for these events and took them to the site of the explosion for execution. However, one managed to escape and the nature of the plot leaked out. Though the officers had intended the events to provide an excuse for occupying all of Manchuria, on orders from home the movement of troops was blocked by the Japanese consul in Mukden.

Chang Tso-lin's death also backfired on the plotters, for his son, known as the 'Young Marshal', pledged allegiance to the Nationalists, and everywhere Chinese resistance increased. In Japan the Tanaka government was forced to resign.

But out of all those events grew an extra determination on the part of officers of the Kwantung army to seize the whole of Manchuria, whatever the government back home might think about it. As in 1919 in Siberia, the Japanese army was getting out of political control. More secret plans were laid, and on the evening of 18th September 1931, the Kwantung army struck. Again an explosion on the railway at Mukden was arranged, and this time the army did move in. It was widely reported that the Chinese had set off the explosion, but many years later one of the plotters, Hanaya Tadashi, was to tell the true facts. (See Chapter 4.)

Covertly sympathetic to the aspirations of the Kwantung army before the fact, certain senior army officers in Tokyo approved of the troop movements in Manchuria after the fact, and from that moment, one by one, the agencies of the Japanese state, some more enthusiastically than others, joined the warmongering cabal. Now the liberal element in Japan, who came to call the period of the 1930s *kurai tanima* or 'dark valley', had to tread very carefully in a country beset by reaction and revolution.

The army moved quickly to extend its operations in Manchuria and set up a puppet government there under Henry Pu-yi, the heir to the Manchu dynasty, an affair stage-managed by Colonel Doihara Kenji, by now a senior intelligence officer. In January 1932 the occupation of Manchuria was complete, and the Japanese changed its name to Manchukuo.

This subjugation of Manchuria fanned the fires of Chinese nationalism. Japanese goods were boycotted all over China and especially in Shanghai. In retaliation the Japanese manufactured more incidents as an excuse to attack other parts of China, and in January 1932 came the first of the so-called Shanghai Incidents as the Japanese landed first marines there and then the army. Fighting was extremely fierce, with repeated Japanese air attacks on the densely populated city. Finally an Anglo-American peace proposal for the Shanghai area was agreed.

Back home in Japan there was a string of political murders, some carried out by a secret society calling itself the League of Blood; but the most important one, the assassination of Prime Minister Inukai on 15th May 1932, was carried out by a group of young officers. The latter event, as Professor Storry has pointed out, effectively put an end to party cabinets in Japan for the next thirteen years, for from now on the army would carry on the old tradition of filling the Minister of War position in the cabinet only when that cabinet was led by a naval or military man; not when it was led by a civilian.

In February 1933, after Lord Lytton's Manchuria Commission had reported to the League of Nations, that body voted 42 to 1 (Japan) on a resolution condemning Japan's take-over of that country. The Japanese responded by walking out of the League for ever. In the eyes of western nations she had now become an outlaw state.

As Japan advanced into northern Manchuria the Soviet Union had stood back. Its first Five Year Plan was just beginning and the Soviets were not ready for a showdown despite this encroachment into their field of influence. They even offered to sell the Chinese Eastern Railroad to the Japanese, a sale that was concluded in March 1935, and after which the Russians withdrew their last troops from the railway zone.

In 1934 the Japanese abrogated the Washington and London Disarmament Treaties, and withdrew from the London Naval Conference the following year. Back home in that year Japanese police uncovered a plot, a civilian one this time, to liquidate the entire cabinet. Then, in 1936, came a military mutiny, the immediate cause of which was the removal of the popular – with the military, that is – General Mazarki from the post of Inspector-General of Military Training. The man who brought about the change, Major-General Nagata, was cut down in his office by an obscure lieutenant-colonel. During this officer's subsequent court-martial, parties of sympathisers from the Tokyo garrison made attacks on the homes of the Prime Minister and others. Although the Prime Minister escaped death, several other senior politicians were shot. The mutineers, numbering about 1,500 and including no one more senior than the rank of captain, proclaimed that they were doing their duty as the emperor's subjects. The emperor did not agree with them, however. Martial law was proclaimed and troops were brought into the capital from outside. After a four-day stand-off the rebels surrendered. Secret courts-martial were held and thirteen officers were executed, along with Nagata's assassin.

This affair created revulsion against the army among the general populace, but paradoxically this revulsion led to the army tightening its grip on the state machine, the military leaders considering it essential that they not lose any more credibility.

The abrogation of the Disarmament Treaties meant that Japan was free to engage in naval and military expansion limited only by its resources, and this she commenced to do. In December 1936 she signed the Anti-Comintern Pact with Germany, the negotiations for this being carried out by the army and not by the Foreign Ministry. With but one or two minor setbacks in the future, the army was now firmly in control of Japanese politics.

In July 1937, in an incident engineered by the Japanese, fighting broke out near Peking between Japanese and Chinese troops. This clash widened into a full-scale invasion of China. In the following month fighting began in and around Shanghai, and this time Japanese might prevailed. International attempts at peace-making were ignored by Japan. In December they took Nanking, committing widespread atrocities there against the civilian population, a fact not allowed to appear in the Japanese press. Once again the Japanese army was out of political control, which resulted in the sinking of the USS *Panay* on the Yangtze and the shelling of a British gunboat HMS *Ladybird*. The Americans obtained an apology and compensation from Japan, but British protests were treated with disdain.

If the Japanese ever believed that Chiang Kai-shek would sue for terms after the fall of Nanking, they were disappointed. The Japanese made some approaches themselves through the German ambassador in China, but the Generalissimo turned the conditions down, with only a minority faction led by his lieutenant, Wang Ching-wei, favouring acceptance. The war went on with heavy losses on both sides.

In the summer of that year Japanese and Soviet forces clashed in an area where the borders of Korea, Manchukuo and the Russian Far East met. There were elements in the Japanese army quite prepared to take on China and Russia simultaneously, but political common sense prevailed and the border dispute was settled. However, within a year a much more serious Soviet–Japanese clash was to occur in Outer Mongolia.

In the autumn of 1938, Hankow fell to the Japanese. They followed up that victory by landing just east of Hong Kong and advancing upon Canton in southern China, which they quickly captured. Chiang Kai-shek, from his new capital in Chungking, vowed to carry on the struggle, a decision not even the hawks in the Japanese army could have been happy with, for although they held the towns and the major installations, including the railways, in the areas they had occupied, they did not hold the countryside. It is not true to say the Japanese were bogged down in China, but the vastness of the countryside made it ideal territory for the operation of Chinese guerrilla forces, and they often played havoc with Japanese lines of communication. Nevertheless, it seemed that, given time, the Japanese would prevail in China. Certainly Wang Ching-wei thought so, for in due course he went over to the Japanese who set him up in Nanking as their puppet ruler in north China.

Once Japan, pushed by the military, had embarked upon a policy of carving out an empire for herself in China and beyond, she was bound to collide sooner or later with those Western powers who, for one reason or another, felt obliged to oppose her. Not yet ready to take on Great Britain and/or the United States, nevertheless she adopted a policy of confrontation with Britain over that country's concession areas in China, especially now that war was looming in Europe.

In June 1939 Britain's Tientsin Concession became the scene of one such confrontation. Using as a convenient excuse the British refusal to hand over four Chinese 'criminals' seeking refuge in the Concession, the Japanese sealed off both the British and French areas of the city. Many Britons passing through the barricades suffered indignities at the hands of Japanese soldiery. Goods were held up, food and milk became scarce, and British ships stopped calling at the port. Britain protested, but the Japanese again took scant notice. An Anglo-Japanese conference was held in Tokyo, the two sides headed by Foreign Minister Arita and the British ambassador, Sir Robert Craigie. Japan demanded nothing less than British recognition of its hegemony in China, and got it. Bearing similar hallmarks to the Munich accord, or appeasement, of only ten months earlier, the Craigie–Arita agreement read:

> His Majesty's Government . . . fully recognise the actual situation in China where hostilities on a large scale are in progress and note that as long as that state of affairs continues to exist, the Japanese forces in China have special requirements for the purpose of safeguarding their own security and maintaining public order in regions under their control and that they have to suppress or remove any such acts or causes as will obstruct them or benefit their enemy.
>
> His Majesty's Government have no intention of countenancing any act prejudicial to the attainment of the above mentioned objects by the Japanese forces, and they will take this opportunity to confirm their policy

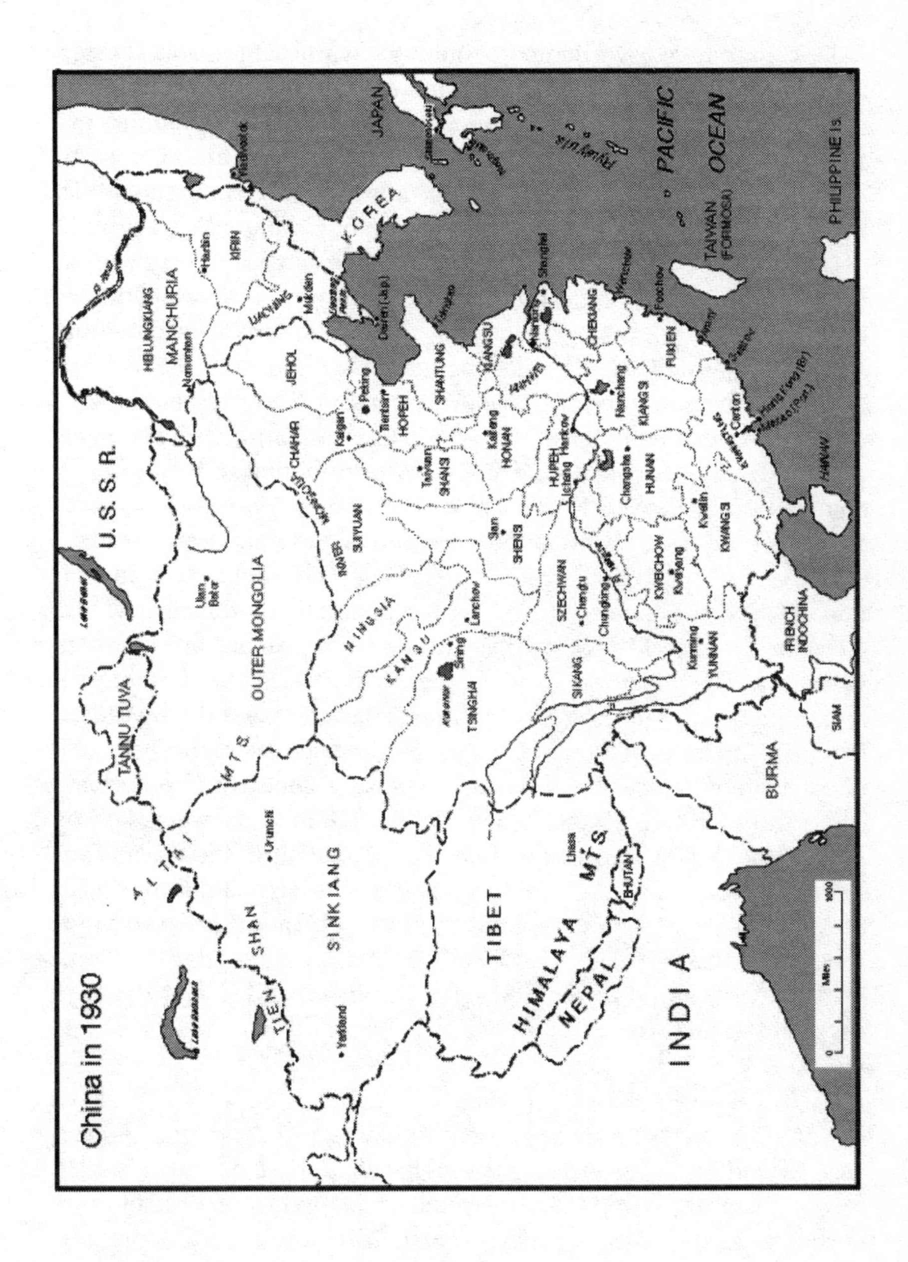
China in 1930
U.S.S.R.
MANCHURIA
HEILUNGKIANG
KIRIN
Harbin
Mukden
JEHOL
KOREA
JAPAN
PACIFIC
OCEAN
TAIWAN
(FORMOSA)
PHILIPPINE Is.
OUTER MONGOLIA
TANNU TUVA
Ulan Bator
SINKIANG
Urumchi
Yarkand
TIBET
Lhasa
HIMALAYA
MTS
NEPAL
BHUTAN
INDIA
BURMA
SIAM
FRENCH
INDOCHINA
YUNNAN
Kunming
KWANGSI
Kweilin
KWEICHOW
Kweiyang
SZECHWAN
Chengtu
Chungking
SIKANG
TSINGHAI
Sining
Lanchow
SUIYUAN
CHAHAR
Kalgan
HOPEH
Peking
Tientsin
SHANSI
Taiyuan
SHENSI
Sian
HONAN
Kaifeng
HUPEH
Hankow
HUNAN
Changsha
KIANGSI
Nanchang
FUKIEN
Foochow
CHEKIANG
KIANGSU
Shanghai
SHANTUNG
Canton
Miles
0
1000

in this respect by making it plain to the British authorities in China that they should refrain from such acts and measures.[3]

This agreement reverberated around the world. 'It was another step in the disintegration of the British Empire', said newspapers in Berlin and Rome. Chiang Kai-shek 'could not conceal his disappointment', and the Soviets denounced the agreement as a betrayal of China. In Washington it was admitted that Britain had very little choice. In Britain itself, Chamberlain told the House of Commons that this did not mean that Britain was taking Japan's side or that she recognised Japanese sovereignty over the occupied territories in China. Britain's Foreign Minister, Lord Halifax, in an even finer piece of verbal dissembling, said that the Tokyo agreement 'recognised' but did not 'condone' the presence of Japanese troops in China. Even so, that agreement eventually led to the evacuation of the British regiment stationed in Tientsin, a move which had a detrimental effect on British Signals Intelligence in North China.

The situation in Europe now began to have an ever stronger influence on Japanese strategic thinking. Throughout 1938 and into 1939 the Japanese flirted with the idea put forward by the German Foreign Minister, Ribbentrop, for a military alliance with Germany. The Japanese army wanted it, but the idea was opposed by the navy and by the Foreign Ministry on the basis that, with the looming situation in Europe, Japan might become embroiled with Great Britain before she was ready. Then suddenly, out of the blue, came the German–Soviet Pact of August 1939. This was taken by the Japanese as a slap in the face, for at that time their army was being severely mauled by the Russians on the disputed border area of Manchukuo with Outer Mongolia, over which, in theory at least, Japan could have called upon Germany's assistance under the terms of the Anti-Comintern Pact. She felt betrayed, and in consequence determined that, for the moment at least, she would steer a middle course in the forthcoming war in Europe.

That attitude did not last long. When the European war began in September 1939 the success of the German *Blitzkrieg* on Poland was lauded in Japan. Then, through the period of the so-called 'phoney war' in Europe during which it seemed the Germans were in stalemate, the Japanese again became lukewarm towards Germany. All that changed, however, when Germany overran Norway and the Low Countries. June 1940 brought the collapse of France, and in that same month Italy entered the war on Germany's side. It now seemed to Japan that there was no way the British could withstand the German juggernaut, and in September she signed a Tripartite Axis Pact with Germany and Italy.

For a long time the Japanese had cast envious eyes southward in the direction of French Indo-China, British Malaya, and the Netherlands East Indies, rich in natural resources, especially in oil, rubber, tin and rice. As Holland and France fell to the Germans and it looked likely that Britain would go the same way, the Japanese worried lest these eastern lands fall under German influence despite various assurances from Berlin that there was no such intent.

On the fall of Metropolitan France the Japanese began to plan a move to the south. They increased and upgraded their intelligence effort throughout Southeast Asia. They forced the Vichy French in charge of Indo-China to accept Japanese military observers in Hanoi, a move soon followed by the establishment of Japanese army and air bases throughout the northern part of the colony which effectively cut off one of the routes over which Chiang Kai-shek's forces were receiving supplies. This occupation took place peacefully, for the French were in no position to resist.

Nor was Britain in any position to resist Japanese pressure. When in September 1940 Japan demanded that the Burma Road be closed, over which the Chinese were also receiving supplies, she too acquiesced, albeit temporarily.

The most strategically placed country in Southeast Asia was Thailand; in London it was called the key to the south, for it was the landward doorway into both Malaya and Burma. Despite reports to the contrary issued by Sir Josiah Crosby, Britain's envoy in Bangkok, many of Thailand's top leaders had for long been sympathetic to the Japanese, and they became even more so after the success of their Japanese instigated war against the French in Indo-China at the end of 1940 and beginning of 1941. The Japanese 'mediation' which followed this resulted in Thailand regaining much of the territory it had lost to the French over the years.

Early in December 1940 the German Naval Attaché in Tokyo handed over to the Japanese copies of secret British documents obtained in one of the great intelligence coups of the war,* which made it clear that Britain could not spare forces to save the island

* See below, Chapter 14.

'fortress' in the event of a Japanese attack. This information sealed the Japanese intent to move south, for even Admiral Yamamoto, Commander-in-Chief of the Imperial Navy, who had previously been opposed to any such undertaking, now came round to agree with it.

Early in 1941 Foreign Minister Matsuoka Yosuke visited Rome and then went on to Berlin where Ribbentrop urged that Japan commit herself to an immediate attack on Singapore. Matsuoka travelled back to Japan via the Soviet Union, on the way concluding a Neutrality Pact with Stalin, thereby safeguarding Japan's northern flank.

Still the Japanese hesitated. The country had stocks of oil for only two years, and war would deny them oil supplies from the Netherlands East Indies, at least until they conquered them. Then, in June 1941 Germany launched its offensive against Russia. Within a month, the Japanese army embarked on further territorial adventures, marching into southern Indo-China to occupy it. Joseph Grew, the American ambassador in Tokyo, noted in his diary for 25th July 1941:

> The official spokesman in Vichy announced . . . that a request had been presented by Japan to occupy bases at strategic points in Indo-China, he said that negotiations were going on both at Vichy and Hanoi and that there had been no ultimatum from Japan nor any German pressure . . . no inconvenience in temporarily extending the military agreement with Japan was seen so long as there was to be no change in French sovereignty over Indo-China.[4]

Grew went on to note that when a newspaper correspondent asked the Vichy spokesman whether France had sought American assistance in preserving the *status quo* in Indo-China, the spokesman said that France had not bothered to do so at this time since no satisfaction had been received when American assistance had been sought during the dispute with Thailand in 1940. Vichy France, it seems, held a grudge for the non-involvement stance adopted by the Americans at the time of the Thai attack.

The occupation of southern Indo-China created an immediate response from America, Great Britain and the Dutch government in exile in London, which Konoye, the Japanese Prime Minister, had not foreseen. They slapped an economic embargo on Japan, in the face of advice from both the US and British ambassadors in Tokyo who foresaw the possible consequences of such a move.

For some time talks had been going on in Washington between the Japanese ambassador, Admiral Nomura, and Secretary of State Cordell Hull. The Americans demanded that the Japanese withdraw from China and Indo-China, whilst the Japanese required a recognition of their hegemony in East Asia and a cessation of American support for the Chinese government in Chungking. The talks now gained new urgency. To the Japanese, who were not prepared to vacate China, it seemed that war with Great Britain and Holland and probably with the USA was inevitable, short of accepting economic strangulation.*

Japan was now supreme throughout eastern Asia. More from the fact that Russia was embroiled with Germany than from the effect of the Soviet–Japan Neutrality Pact, her northern frontier was safe. The Thai leaders were in her pocket, and her air forces in Indo-China were within flying distance of Malaya. Japanese troops lay in wait around Hong Kong. Her navy was planning the most audacious naval attack in history. Her army and her air force had been conditioned by years of fighting in China. On top of all that, in every country which was schemed to become part of her Greater East Asia Co-Prosperity Sphere, her agents had, ever since the turn of the century, been sending home intelligence reports.

Japan was ready to strike.

* In these Washington talks both Britain and Holland seemed prepared to leave all the talking on the Allied side to the Americans, despite the fact that matters were being discussed which affected the safety of not only Malaya, Hong Kong and the Dutch colonies, but also Australia and New Zealand.

Three

The Japanese Secret Services

Before World War Two little was known of the organisation and methodology of the Japanese Secret Intelligence Services. This was in spite of the fact that they had been operating in many countries, and particularly in the Far East, since the beginning of the century.

The Japanese definition of what constituted intelligence differed from that used by western nations. In the West, intelligence is usually defined as 'The product resulting from the collection, evaluation, analysis, integration and interpretation of all available information which concerns one or more aspects of foreign nations or of areas of operations and which is immediately or potentially significant to military planning and operations.'[1] This definition does not cover fifth-column activities, nor subversive functions such as economic, political and psychological penetration, including propaganda. Nor does it cover sabotage. In the West these are treated as separate, albeit connected functions. This was not the way of the Japanese, who regarded all these functions as being so closely related that in practice they often became inseparable in their concept of total war. It is, therefore, difficult to differentiate, for example, between those organisations designed for the collection and collation of economic intelligence, and those engaged in purely military, naval or political matters.

This lack of clear compartmentalisation is perhaps surprising in view of the fact that Japanese military thought had always been profoundly influenced by the ancient Chinese treatise called *The Art of War* in which its author, Sun Tzu, advocated such compartmentalisation and the need for multi-level operations. Perhaps the answer to this seeming paradox lies in the written Chinese character used in the title of the chapter in Sun Tzu's work which translates as 'Use of Spies'. The character means 'the space between' two objects – such as the crack between double-doors – and thus 'cleavage', 'division', or 'to divide'. It also means 'spies', 'spying', or 'espionage'.[2] The verb 'to divide' can thus be said to cover the activities of agents engaged in all forms of divisive espionage and subversion.

The concept, whereby the maximum number of agencies and agents were utilised to assist Japanese expansionist policy, called the 'mass method' by one authority, led to an enormous overlap and duplication of effort.[3] However, the Japanese regarded this as a virtue; it was a means by which information received and the activities of agents involved in obtaining it could be double-checked and controlled.

This overlap of responsibilities sometimes caused strain and dissension between various Japanese agencies; but such dissension and strain was also apparent, for instance, in the British Intelligence system, which did work under more compartmentalised arrangements. Robert Cecil has recorded that Section D of the British Secret Intelligence Service (SIS – to be called MI6 after 1942), which was set up in 1938 for planning sabotage and subversion behind enemy lines, met with so much internal hostility that Churchill made a new start in 1940 by setting up a new organisation, the Special Operations Executive (SOE). But that too caused problems: 'There were built-in causes of friction between SIS, which aimed to preserve intelligence channels undisturbed, and SOE, which was committed to wreckage and resistance, regardless of consequences.'[4] SIS also set up its Section V for counter-espionage activities – Kim Philby being an early member of it – which rather trod on the toes of MI5, the internal security organisation. The creation of Section V did not lead to the massive friction between SIS and MI5 that some writers have suggested, but it did breed jurisdictional and other disputes.

In accordance with the concept of using every possible medium for penetrating foreign countries in peacetime, the Japanese made use of their many nationals scattered throughout the world. These expatriates were required to serve as part of a subversive network which could be put to any purpose the authorities back home thought fit. Given the Japanese national psyche, most overseas Japanese were deeply honoured and proud to conduct this work; they were serving their emperor.

Since its emergence in the 1850s from self-imposed seclusion, Japan had been involved in three wars: the war of 1894 with China, that of 1904–05 with Russia, and the war in China which commenced on a grand scale in 1937, though augured by fighting that began in 1931. Japan never regarded World War One, in which she participated on the Allied side, as her own war, although she gained much from it. Before the three earlier wars, and before 1941, she made massive preparations in the intelligence field in which the creation of fifth columns, Quislings and propaganda networks formed an integral part. A man who knew Japan and the Japanese well, Captain Malcolm Kennedy, has written 'What . . . is specially striking is that the particular methods employed were almost identical for each war. A study of these methods can, in fact, lead to but one conclusion – "*Plus ça change, plus c'est la même chose.*"'[5]

As Kennedy went on to point out, in each instance there was close co-ordination and interdependence between Military Intelligence and extreme nationalist elements in Japanese society, and with business interests, especially those engaged in import/export trades. In each case it was the nationalists and the secret societies they formed which set and forced the pace, and gave the lead to the army and commercial interests. They did this by setting up intelligence systems of their own and using them to exploit nationalistic and malcontent elements in the countries they deemed of importance to their Greater Asia expansionist schemes. To a nation determined to follow such a policy, one that could never be carried out solely by peaceful means, subversive activities and espionage, were prerequisites.

This concept was easily understood by the Japanese since the fundamentals of spying had existed within its own borders since the 1600s in the form of the so-called *Hoko* System, a system of communal spy-hostages. Under it *Tonari Gumi*, or Neighbourhood Associations, were established, in which a designated member of each household was held responsible for the words and deeds of the rest of the household. From every ten households one 'warden' was elected to be responsible for the group, and from every hundred wardens one was elected to overall responsibility, and so on. By ruthless enforcement of the hostage principle, the Japanese government was able to keep track of words and actions of every member of the community. 'A person had to be very careful of everything he said and did', wrote Saburo

Ienaga. 'It was dangerous to confide one's real feelings in a diary.' He went on to point out that there was no need for concentration camps, and that executions were rare. 'Every aspect of life was so regimented and controlled that no one could plan a treacherous act worthy of the death penalty!'[6] As Japan extended her conquests, similar systems were introduced into the conquered territories.

The earliest of the nationalist secret societies to send agents overseas was the 'Black Ocean Society'. Formed in 1881, it sent agents into Korea and China. One of over a hundred agents sent into China in 1882 was a remarkable young man called Arao Kiyoshi who can be described as the father of modern Japanese espionage. Arao graduated from the Japanese Military Academy after his return from China and was then attached to the Army General Staff as Chinese Affairs specialist. At his suggestion a special bureau was set up to deal with intelligence from China, and in time this grew into a system of branch bureaux covering all parts of the Far East and Central Asia.

Arao returned to China in 1886, setting up branches of the *Rakusendo*, or 'Hall of Pleasurable Delights', in Shanghai and Hankow. In a sort of dress rehearsal for the cover system of barber shops, dental surgeries, bordellos and photography establishments to be set up throughout the East in the following century, Arao's agents, disguised as Chinese and based at these Halls, travelled far and wide peddling 'medicine' and 'literature' in the form of aphrodisiacs and pornographic pictures. Those who came back returned with information on economic and agricultural developments, on personalities – particularly those likely to be sympathetic towards Japan – on roads and communications, on Russian, Chinese and Indian defences, and on the prospects for utilising Moslem and Buddhist clergy for Japanese intriguing. Some of the agents did not return; a number, apprehended by the Russians in Turkestan, were never heard of again.

When Arao returned to Japan in 1889 he conceived a more ambitious enterprise to accelerate his country's penetration of China. He began touring the country urging business leaders to enter the China trade. He selected over a hundred men from the world of business and sent them to Shanghai and formed around them the *Nisshin Boeki Kenkyujo*, or Sino-Japanese Commercial Research College. The students were taught Chinese and other subjects, and they and their successors at the College were then sent out to all parts of the Far East and South Seas.

Out of the Black Ocean Society there grew, in 1901, the Black

Dragon Society or *Kokuryukai*, which in Japanese is the equivalent of 'The Society of the Amur River', for the characters used in the name of this river mean Black Dragon. As the Amur River formed the border between Russian and Chinese territory, the name of the society was an expression of its aims, which was preparation for the coming war with Russia. So comprehensive was the intelligence provided by the Black Dragon Society to the Japanese Military party, that it virtually became the overseas secret agency of the War Ministry. The society opened a Russian Language Institute in Tokyo which was really a school for spies and whenever the State itself could not very well execute some particular piece of overseas dirty work, the society gladly stepped in.

Before each of the earlier wars, organisations were set up for espionage and subversion under the guise of being harmless commercial, cultural or educational institutions, whilst seemingly religious bodies sent out Buddhist and Moslem missions to intrigue with and collect information from their co-religionists.

Arao Kiyoshi died in Formosa shortly after the war of 1904–05, leaving behind a legacy from which evolved the official Japanese Secret Services, with methodologies based on an intimate tie-in between the Japanese military, extreme nationalist societies and business interests. The legacy began evincing itself within a year of Arao's death, for in 1905 both French Indo-China and Thailand were, according to Lieutenant-Colonel Picard of the French Army, 'swarming with Japanese Agents'.[7]

Subsequently, three separate intelligence services developed in Japan which, by the 1930s, were controlled respectively by the army, the navy and the Foreign Office. From 1937 onwards the activities of the first two were to some extent co-ordinated by the Imperial General Headquarters. All three still made use of the services of what might best be described, in view of the number of top Japanese who were members of them, as the quasi-official secret societies.

Army Intelligence Organisations

The army's Special Service Organisation, or *Tokumu Kikan*, which operated abroad, was established in the late 1920s, its activities then centred on China, Manchuria and Mongolia. As the Pacific War loomed in the 1930s, it set up offices in French Indo-China, Thailand, Malaya, the Netherlands East Indies, and Burma. For security reasons such branch offices operated under a variety of cover names some of which underwent frequent changes, although the word *kikan* (organisation) nearly always appeared in the title. Some *kikans* took their names from the leader involved – for example *Fujiwara Kikan*, which engaged in 1941 in subverting Indian army troops in Malaya, was named after Major Fujiwara Iwaichi. Others were called after businessmen or business firms involved in the operations; yet others took the names of birds, trees or animals, for example *Kame Kikan*, or Tortoise Organisation, which was also engaged in subversion in Malaya. In general the use of individuals' names fell into disuse on the outbreak of the Pacific War as the system caused confusion whenever commanders were changed.

These organisations came under No. 2 Department (Intelligence) of the General Staff, Tokyo, although in practice they possessed considerable autonomy. Some of this autonomy was granted from the centre but much more was simply assumed, the amount assumed often being entirely dependent upon the strength of character of the unit's commander or that of his immediate superior in the field. This self-granted autonomy was particularly noticeable in Manchuria where operations were often conducted without any authority from home, and sometimes even against express orders.

Some *kikans* were more or less permanent and operated within the Intelligence Department of the army formation within whose territory it operated. The functions of these can best be described as being of a strategic nature. Others, of a tactical nature, were formed in forward areas for specific purposes and with limited objectives.

The functions of these organisations covered all clandestine intelligence work, excluding straightforward Military Intelligence duties, but including in peace time, espionage, propaganda and subversion. In wartime, fifth-column activity and sabotage were added. After subjugation of an area, such organisations were often used in internal security, which included 'pacification' of the local population and liaison between the Japanese military and local government officials.

Agents of a particular *kikan* rarely stayed together after arrival in the country where they were to work. They arrived under the guise of immigrants, students or businessmen, then spread out and established various covers for themselves. Not only did they collect intelligence material themselves, they acted as contacts for more itinerant agents and as information conduits for the Japanese Consular Service. They distributed propaganda, wrote articles for local publications, and sometimes launched newspapers. They made contact with dissidents and in certain areas arranged smuggled arms and ammunition for them. They trained fifth-columnists and saboteurs for forthcoming operations.

In a few respects the Special Service Organisation resembled the German *Abwehr*, for the Japanese army tended to model itself on the German army just as the Japanese navy tended to model itself upon the Royal Navy. There was one important and fundamental difference between the two organisations, however. The *Abwehr* had its own independent worldwide wireless network, whereas the Japanese organisation did not. Instead it relied upon either military wireless circuits and codes, or upon diplomatic ones. Another point of difference was that the *Abwehr* was organised mainly by countries, whereas a Japanese *kikan* sometimes operated across several borders. An example of this was *Hikari Kikan* whose task it was to train Indians in espionage and sabotage, and which had branches in Burma, Malaya and the Netherlands East Indies.

The importance the Japanese placed on these organisations is shown by their personnel policy. Pre-war leaders were often retired army officers with excellent qualifications. Some had been members of the Young Officers' Clique which had committed several political assassinations in 1936. They were called 'Young Officers' to differentiate them from the top brass, though in fact all were majors or lieutenant-colonels. They formed the original backbone of the system, but were supplemented by selected graduates from Officers' Training Schools. Only about three per cent of graduates were offered the chance to volunteer for Special Service duty, and not all of those passed the rigorous entrance examinations. Civilians were also used, most of them specialists in either engineering, oil refining, languages, shipping or finance. Some non-Japanese were recruited, and selected ones from among them were sent to Japan for extensive training and indoctrination; some of these were returned to their countries pre-war but others were retained in Japan until allotted to the invading armies as liaison officers.

Candidates from the army underwent training at the Nakano School near Tokyo. There they donned civilian clothes, changed their names, and were required to estrange themselves from their families. The course – it would be euphemistic to call it just rigorous – lasted three years. The curriculum covered espionage, the use of explosives, wireless, codes, propaganda techniques, the political sciences and foreign languages. Candidates were set initiative tests such as gaining access, unseen, to heavily guarded military installations.

Fellow trainees at the school were from the Japanese Military Police, the *Kempetai*. Unlike such organisations in other countries, the *Kempetai* had a policy of its own, which stood for the extreme of reactionary nationalism. Unlike in other countries, the preservation of discipline in the army was not its main function. Its main task covered Field Security – carried out in the British army by a branch of Military Intelligence – and that was defined by the Japanese in the very broadest of terms.

At Nakano, as in other Japanese army training establishments, cruelty towards subordinates was an accepted psychological technique. It provided an outlet for pressure, and it allowed each rank to shift oppression to the one below. Saburo Ienaga has written, 'The oppression snowballed as it rolled down the ranks, till all the tensions and abuse landed on the recruits. They were the lowest of the low; they had no outlet, no one they could mistreat.'[8]*

Over the years 'language officers' from the British and Indian armies and other armies of the world were stationed in Tokyo. As part of their training they were permitted to visit various military establishments in Japan, but none was ever permitted to visit the Nakano School.[9]

Naval Intelligence Organisations

Japanese Naval Intelligence was never as important, comprehensive or powerful as its army counterpart. It was divided into the Department of Naval Intelligence and the Naval Special Service Organisation.

Departments 3 and 4 of the Naval General Staff were responsible for intelligence, the former concerning itself with 'ordinary' or ground

* No one, that is, within their own army. They were to find many to abuse and maltreat during and after battle.

intelligence and the latter with signals intelligence. Department 3 was itself divided into various sections on a geographical basis. For example:

No. 5 Section – North America
No. 6 section – China
No. 7 Section – Europe
No. 8 Section – South Seas.

The Naval Special Service Organisation (called *Kaigun Tokumu Bu*) originated about 1930 in China with a system of Resident Naval Attachés at some of the major ports. The most important office was the one in Shanghai. Its functions, generally speaking, were similar to those of the Army Organisation with which it was supposed to liaise closely. However, there was much friction between the two services, and Australian Intelligence picked up a report which showed that the Japanese naval representative in Tientsin was not above reporting on the activities of his army opposite number to his own superiors in Tokyo.[10]

Perhaps the most important work conducted by *Kaigun Tokumu Bu* was the intelligence-gathering carried out by its agents on board Japanese fishing fleets which ranged throughout the South China and Southern Seas.

Except off the immediate coasts of China, the Japanese fishing fleets were by far the largest in the area. The fleets roamed east, and south as far as the coasts of Australia. From a very early date it was known that personnel in the fleet were engaged in collecting intelligence, and that included conducting unauthorised hydrographic surveys. So rife did this become around the coasts of Malaya and Singapore that, in 1937, the government decided to limit the number of annual licences issued to the Japanese for fishing the coastal waters, and, furthermore, to operate a system of inspection. More is known about the fishing fleet based at Singapore than those based in other places, for the existence of the mighty naval base made the authorities take particular notice. But it is likely that the Singapore experience was duplicated elsewhere.

In 1914 the Japanese government despatched a three-man team to Singapore to investigate and report on the local fishing grounds and markets. A member of the team was Tora Eifuku, who eventually became the head of the largest fishing company based in Singapore.

This company, *Taichong Kongsi*, was heavily subsidised by the China and Southern Bank of Japan, and the loans granted were probably guaranteed by the Japanese government. Its fleet of fifty-two boats operated as far north as French Indo-China and North Borneo, throughout the Netherlands East Indies, and voyaged as far west as Rangoon and the Andaman Islands.

Many of the officers on these vessels were naval officers, and some were inclined to be intransigent when their vessels were boarded for inspection. In one case Singapore Special Branch thought it likely that the boat concerned was carrying explosives, arms, or some other form of contraband. The boat, the *Taisei Maru*, was boarded by a Malay Assistant Superintendent of Customs on 18th June 1935 off the coast of Johore. The captain, a man called Hamakawa, promptly threw the Malay officer overboard and sailed away. The following day the boat called at Pulo Aur, and this time it was boarded by a British Superintendent of Customs. He was allowed to search, and found each fish compartment full of ice except for one which was 'suspiciously empty'. Even on this visit the captain's attitude was so truculent that it was decided not to arrest him for the previous assault.[11]

The largest Japanese fishing boat to visit Singapore was the 473-ton *Shinkyo Maru*. She made her first call there in the same month, June 1935. So smartly did her officers and crew conduct themselves that it was thought they were almost certainly naval reservists. Singapore Special Branch reported that she gave the impression of being more of a naval patrol boat than a trawler. She carried two wireless sets, one medium-wave and one short-wave, and the latter had a transmission range of ten thousand miles at night. Intercepted messages showed that she kept in regular contact with Japan. Later she was discovered to be conducting 'experimental fishing' off Calcutta and then off Colombo.

In that same year too, another British customs officer out on sea patrol in the launch *Artemis* boarded several Japanese boats and reported that they had on board modern equipment quite unnecessary for fishermen's purposes, and 'carefully prepared' charts in addition to British Admiralty ones. That officer's reception was hostile too, and he recommended that such boardings should in future only be made in the presence of a squad of armed police.

There can be little doubt that the success of the Japanese landings on the coasts of Malaya in 1941, not to mention the landings in

Thailand, the Philippines, Borneo and the Netherlands East Indies, was in no small part due to the detailed knowledge of the littoral waters built up by the men of these fishing fleets. René Onraet, Singapore Police Chief until 1939, wrote of these fishermen: 'They were operating all the way back to Japan – in reality a permanent standing patrol'. He described them as 'South Seas *Ronin*' or 'wave men'.[12]

Japanese Naval Intelligence did not confine itself to activities in the Far East. A few examples will indicate how wide it spread its tentacles.

In the early years of the century the Japanese had established a 'Naval Centre' in London, originally at No. 1 Lygon Place, Ebury Street, and latterly in Broadway Court. This was a matter that seems, by 1934, to have begun to exasperate Rear-Admiral (later Admiral Sir) G.C. Dickens, Director of Naval Intelligence (DNI), as the officers of the Centre, twenty-one in number, were known to be involved in espionage. He pointed out that Japan was the only country to have been granted this privilege by Britain and, furthermore, that not only had the British not been granted similar facilities in Tokyo but 'the Japanese were doing everything possible to prevent the few naval officers we have in Japan i.e. Naval Attaché, Assistant Naval Attaché, and three or four language officers from acquiring the most ordinary information.'[13] He went on: 'Though not directly under diplomatic privilege it [the Centre] was presided over by the Japanese Naval Attaché and thus to all intents and purposes was sheltered by diplomatic privilege.'

The Japanese Naval Attaché at that time was Captain Oka Arata, and from his period in that post comes the following curious and previously unpublished story.[14]

In the early 1930s a British businessman, Herbert Greene, who had served as an officer in the Suffolk Regiment in World War One, was a passenger aboard a Japanese ship, the *Rio de Janeiro Maru*, from the Cape to Montevideo. A fellow passenger was a Japanese called Inouye. The pair struck up a friendship after Greene had been in an altercation with an American banker on board during which, in the heat of the moment, he had expressed some anti-American views. Greene told Inouye that he would shortly be returning to England and that he would be looking for work there. Before they parted Inouye presented Greene with a card on which he had written the name of Captain Oka Arata, and he advised Greene to contact Oka when he reached London.

Greene met Oka, but only after speaking with someone from British Naval Intelligence, and with the US Naval Attaché in London, Captain Bristol. The initial meeting was made in the Tokiwaya Japanese Restaurant near Cambridge Circus. Oka asked many questions and, apparently satisfied with the answers, said he would be in touch again. Greene reported the meeting first to Captain Bristol, who 'seemed very pleased', and then to Colonel Washington (Royal Marines), an Assistant Director of Naval Intelligence. Colonel Washington advised Greene against taking the matter further on the grounds that personal danger was involved. However, when three weeks later Oka contacted him again, Greene made another visit to the restaurant. He met Oka there and was told to report to the latter's flat in Campden Court Mansions at four that afternoon. There he was handed an envelope containing two hundred pounds. That bundle of notes, wrote Greene, 'was to lead me into and show me strange places and strange men . . . to hectic parties in Mayfair and great hotels in Scotland, to Paris during the Stavisky Riots, to the BBC in Langham Place, and to the great tragedy of Madrid'.

In a letter dated 19th August 1947, Greene wrote, 'in London in the early thirties I worked for Capt. Arata Oka [*sic*] . . . who was running a spy bureau . . . I wangled my way into his employ . . . the authorities knew, Admiral Dickens (DNI) and Col. Washington (ADNI). Also Capt. (now Admiral) Bristol, American Naval Attaché.'[15]

Exactly how long Greene 'worked for' Oka, and what he achieved, if anything, for either British or American Intelligence, is not known. But by 1938 all such connections must have been severed, for Greene published in a British tabloid a warning about the extent of the Japanese spy service in Britain. It may have been this article that caused Greene trouble when he joined the British army at the beginning of World War Two. Enlisting as a private, he was soon recommended for a commission in the Royal Army Service Corps, but at the last minute this was turned down. He was then recommended by two Military Intelligence officers for a commission in a 'security force'. That too was turned down on the grounds that he 'was unreliable'. Still a private, Greene was finally transferred to the Pioneer Corps and saw out the war in that capacity.

Even earlier than the Greene affair, in 1928, it was discovered in London by the interception and decoding of messages sent by the

Japanese Naval Attaché, that a Labour Member of Parliament, Cecil Malone, was being paid a regular retainer for providing information about defence matters. The decoding of the messages was carried out by Eric Nave of the Royal Australian Navy who was on secondment to the British Government Code and Cypher School (GC&CS).[16] Malone had joined the Royal Navy in 1905 but transferred to the Royal Naval Air Service in 1911. He had commanded the seaplane carrier *Ben-My-Chree* at the Dardanelles and was responsible for sending off the seaplanes which torpedoed three Turkish vessels at anchor during 14th–17th August 1915.* This was the very first engagement of aircraft using torpedoes. At the time Malone claimed that this was 'a development which will tend to revolutionise warfare'. He ended the war with the rank of lieutenant-colonel and was awarded the OBE. He may have felt that this was insufficient reward for his enterprise.

In 1918 Malone was Air Attaché at the British embassy in Paris, after which he embarked upon a political career. Elected as a Coalition Liberal MP in December 1918, he soon afterwards joined the British Socialist Party which became the Communist Party in July 1920. He was then imprisoned for six months under the Defence of the Realm Act, for agitating against sending supplies to the White Russians, and deprived of his OBE. In 1928 he returned to Parliament as the Labour MP for Northampton. There can be little doubt that such a man could have passed on much useful information to the Japanese, but it was decided not to arrest him as any such action would have compromised the British ability to read the attaché's codes, and anyway, Britain was not then at war with Japan. Malone's pro-Japanese sympathies are perhaps best illustrated by the title of one of the books he wrote. It was called *Manchoukuo, Jewel of Asia*.[17]

Eric Nave's work at this time also led to the discovery that an ex-British army officer, Major Frederick Joseph Rutland, was working for the Japanese and that they had ordered him to California. Rutland was not arrested either, but was kept under surveillance by an SIS officer during the voyage to the States. Rutland there opened an

* The *Ben-My-Chree* had not been purpose-built as a seaplane carrier. She had been constructed in 1908 to the order of the Isle of Man Steam Packet Company and was chartered in by the Admiralty during World War One. She was sunk by shore shell-fire on 11th January 1917 off Kastelorgio Harbour in Greece. At that time she was under the command of Wing Commander C.R. Samson of the Royal Navy Air Service.

investment brokerage company, which was kept under surveillance by the FBI.

By 1936 Rear-Admiral Dickens had more cause for complaint. The British ambassador in Tokyo had reported that, 'The Naval and Air Attachés especially have been treated in a manner that is little short of discourteous.'*

The Commander-in-Chief, China Fleet reported in the same year that the visit of HMS *Dorsetshire* to Yokosuka Dockyard had been unwelcome. Then, in October, three British sailors from HMS *Medway* were beaten up by Japanese police at Keelung, Formosa, and the officer sent to gain their release was insulted. After that Britain suspended all courtesy naval visits and the Japanese navy followed suit. The only breach in this state of affairs was Japanese attendance at the Coronation Review in 1937.

Admiral Dickens also noted that in the previous year, 1935, the Japanese had permitted only twenty-nine visits to naval establishments by nine British officers. He compared that with the seventy-one visits to British naval establishments by sixty-three Japanese officers over the same period. On top of that, fifty-three Japanese civilians had made forty-three visits to British firms with naval contracts.

Dickens demanded that suitable action be taken when, in December 1937, two Japanese naval officers, Lieutenant-Commander Suzuki and Engineer Commander Miyagawa, paid visits to Portsmouth and Devonport Dockyards without prior clearance. This almost developed into a major diplomatic incident, with the navy demanding that the two men be ordered from Britain. After suitable apologies had been made by the Japanese ambassador, though, the matter was closed and the officers permitted to stay.[18] However, the British Security Services knew exactly where the two officers had stayed and the precise length of their sojourns in both ports, and had full details of their journey arrangements.

In the late summer of 1937 Japanese Naval Intelligence established another centre of great interest to the British. The purpose of the Intelligence Centre at Port Said at the northern end of the Suez Canal was to collect information on ships and cargoes proceeding to Chinese ports.[19]

* The Military Attaché was not mentioned in the ambassador's report. This probably reflects the Japanese regard for and attitude towards Major-General F.S.G. Piggott, the Attaché. Piggott held strong pro-Japanese views, so much so that in London his reports were labelled 'Piggottry'.

Japanese Government Intelligence Agencies

The Japanese Intelligence Services did not work in watertight compartments, indeed there was a good deal of overlapping and duplication. Ambassadors and Service attachés at diplomatic posts collected intelligence that was of interest not only to their own departments, but also to others. Japanese embassies, legations and consulates were loaded with officials whose main task was intelligence-gathering.

In addition to the Foreign Office several other ministries were engaged in intelligence and propaganda activities. Closely connected with these ministries at times, were the overseas branches of Japanese secret societies.

Japanese embassies and consulates everywhere had the covert function of directing secret activities within the countries to which they were accredited. From official premises they organised the undercover operations of commercial firms, Japanese associations and clubs and they made contact with nationalist movements and seditionists. They operated as clearing houses for information, and were a double conduit, passing information to Tokyo via wireless, diplomatic bag or by the hand of ships' captains, and in the other direction instructions and funds for secret purposes received from Tokyo.

Embassy and consulate officials took full advantage of their diplomatic privilege status in collecting information. There was nothing new in this, for every country did (and does) it.

However, the Japanese used the cover of their embassies more extensively than most for covert operations. Although officially assigned as 'attachés' to the ambassador, it is known that in the pre-war embassy in Washington, to give but one example, the Military and Naval Attachés carried out their intelligence-gathering functions entirely independently of the ambassador. Nor did they make their reports through him.

The information flowing in was multifarious in nature and arrived from many sources. In the United States, for example, Japanese banking concerns were a special source of intelligence, as were the Japanese shipping lines that had offices in every major American port. One important piece of information supplied by the latter in 1940 was in respect of Liberty Ship construction.[20]

The use of Japanese consulates before the war in planning and developing fifth-column and other subversive work is illustrated by what happened in the Netherlands East Indies. A Dutch report indicates that activity in these fields began in the early 1930s and then carried on without let-up. Well planned and well executed, it concentrated principally on the exploitation of nationalist elements among the native population. Consulate officers and floating agents made regular contacts with the leaders of these indigenous factions, and acquired for them several newspapers which not only served as a means of spreading nationalist views but also pro-Japanese propaganda. In western Java, in the vicinity of the capital Batavia, the chief architect of subversion was Saito Ototsugu, later to become consul-general in the capital. One vice-consul on Java, Naojiro Takagi, was especially active in underground activities. He had set up a business in Surabaya and under its cover imported illegal weapons for the nationalists.[21]

Offshoots of the Black Dragon Society operated throughout the Far East and often concerned themselves with aiding nationalist groups. The Society's interest in such matters was a long-standing one, for it had accepted Rash Behari Bose under its wing when he took up residence in Japan following his escape from India after his attempt on the life of the British Viceroy, Baron Hardinge of Penshurst, in 1912. In Japan Bose married a Japanese lady. As a member of the Society he worked avidly throughout the 1930s in fostering anti-British sentiments among the Indian community in Japan.

The Society's most important offshoot was home-based. It was called the East Asia Economic Investigation Bureau (*Toa Keizai Chosa Kyoku*). Originally built up under the guise of being a subsidiary of the South Manchuria Railway Company, it became a clearing house for overseas intelligence of such importance that eventually it was taken over, lock, stock and barrel by the Foreign Office, and Dr Okawa Shumei was made its director. After the take-over it received incoming intelligence from embassies and consulates, passing on anything of military and naval interest to the requisite departments.

Dr Okawa, a spy himself, was a revolutionary who was responsible for several political assassinations. It was he who created the Showa School of Foreign Languages – sometimes called the Okawa School after him. It taught English, French, Hindustani, Malay, Siamese, and other languages, but that was a front for its spy-training activities. 'Graduates' of the two-year course were sent abroad under consular or commercial cover, and many of them became long-term residents of the countries they were sent to. Some of the school's graduates, the pick of the bunch, were allotted permanently to the Army *Tokumu Kikan*, whilst others were borrowed from time to time by various operational *kikans*.

Commercial Espionage

Almost all Japanese firms operating abroad were engaged in some form of intelligence work. Most firms were members of government-sponsored development boards and trading associations, which were funded or subsidised from central funds. If one adds to that the fact that most Japanese citizens were willing to die for their emperor and country – a willingness stressed and inculcated in them from their schooldays – they even had a name for the concept, *chukun aikoku* – then it is also reasonable to say that nearly every Japanese employee of firms working overseas engaged himself or herself in espionage whenever it was required of them.

Some firms' sole raison d'être was carrying out espionage and other subversive activities, whilst others were genuine commercial firms indulging in espionage on the side. Among the former category was the Nippon Trade Agency, which was almost certainly a section of the Army Special Service Section. It had branches in Calcutta, Karachi, Singapore, Bangkok, Sydney, Alexandria, Baghdad, and elsewhere including China, where it was known as the 'Japanese Detective Bureau'. The Indian Police Special Branch had collected much information on its spying activities.

Another such firm was the South Manchurian Railway Company (SMR) which gave birth to the Economic Research and Investigation Bureau. SMR had close links with the army in Manchuria, and had many intelligence-gathering operatives. Three of their officials, when searched in Singapore, were found to be in possession of documents and reports on the railways of Thailand, Indo-China, and the Netherlands East Indies (NEI), together with a confidential book on the Malayan railway system of which there were only a few copies with restricted circulation.

The tentacles of Japanese pre-war espionage in the Pacific and

Indian Oceans stretched south to Australia and New Zealand, westward into Burma and India, and in the east to Pearl Harbor and almost everywhere in between.

René Onraet, as Inspector-General of the Straits Settlements Police until 1939, knew as much about the development and operational methods of the Japanese Secret Services as any Westerner. In the following passage he comments on Japanese activities in Malaya, but what he said could be applied to their activities anywhere:

> For twenty years after the Great War the Japanese expanded their trade in and increased their knowledge of Malaya. They were ubiquitous. Europeans in the East who witnessed the activities of travellers, photographers, prospectors and orchid collectors from close quarters, considered them all to be spies – and, of course, as men who travelled about, they were a menace, but the real villains were the directors of firms and banks, of the semi-official commercial museum, and members of the official consulate.

He went on:

> I look back at Japanese activities in Malaya with the conviction of having witnessed a patient and confident preparation for ultimate occupation, all the more easy to organise as no one thought a military success, on which such an occupation depended, was possible.

It had been Onraet who, in the year prior to his retirement, had urged upon the Governor of Singapore the need to introduce legislation that would limit the number of Japanese working for Japanese companies in the colony. His advice was not accepted.

Four

Undercover Operations in China in the 1930s

In China by the 1930s there existed two home-bred intelligence services, those of the Kuomintang (KMT) and the Communists (CCP). In addition there was an extensive operation run by the Japanese, for China, including Manchuria, had become the main testing ground for Japanese Special Services Organisations.[1] The Russians, the British and other nationalities also conducted undercover operations in China.

The two Chinese Secret Services developed from the same stock, the Intelligence Service set up in the 1920s by Dr Sun Yat-sen upon the advice of his 'senior adviser', Mikhail Borodin, the Comintern's representative to the Kuomintang in those years.[2] Under Dr Sun the communists had been well represented in his Government of National Unification, but that had changed when Sun died in 1925 and Chiang Kai-shek came to power. Chiang began a series of purges which resulted in a split between the two sides in 1927. Later there was fighting between them, which culminated in Mao Tse-tung's famous Long March of 1934–35 and the setting up of a separate communist state in the remote region of Shensi centred around the city of Yenan. Out of this split grew the two separate intelligence services.

The fledgling intelligence service of the CCP had but one primary task in the early days, and that was 'simply to ensure the survival of the tiny communist state remote in the heart of China'.[3] The KMT's intelligence service on the other hand, had a far wider scope.

Ostensibly providing the government of all China, the KMT had not only to cope with internal security against Chinese communists and warlords, but with matters of labyrinthine difficulty caused by the actions of the many countries which had over the years, and by one method or another, gained control of parts of mother China. In the 1930s this applied especially to Japan. It also applied to the Soviet Union which was busy aiding the indigenous communists, though never to the extent of really rocking the KMT boat, for the Soviet leaders were pragmatists and knew a powerful man when they saw one; they saw one in Chiang Kai-shek.

An important aspect in the development of both Chinese Intelligence Services was the influence upon them of non-Chinese. Several Russians in addition to Mikhail Borodin, who had advised Dr Sun on the creation of the original service, were involved in this development.

However, the foreigner whose actions perhaps brought the most long-lasting benefits to the KMT intelligence service was an English-born Jew called Morris Cohen. Born in 1889, Cohen had left Britain for Canada whilst in his teens and had made good there. In Edmonton, Alberta, he was able to get on good terms with the city's large Chinese community, to such an extent that, and unusually for a foreigner, he was made a member of the local branch of a Chinese secret society called Tsing Chunghui. Through this contact he was to meet Dr Sun Yat-sen who was travelling the world expounding his vision of a new China.

Cohen must have impressed Sun for he was made the doctor's bodyguard in Canada. After Sun's departure, and still only in his early twenties, Cohen then made several arms-buying trips for Sun. In between these he created an army cadet corps from among the Edmonton Chinese, and it was from this time that he gained the sobriquets 'Two-Gun' and 'General Ma'. During the Great War Cohen served in the British army in France, and was wounded. After that he returned to Canada, but in 1922 travelled to China to become one of Sun's ADCs.

A year later at Canton, Cohen met Charles Drage, First Lieutenant of HMS *Bluebell*, and struck up what was to become a life-long friendship. It is through this contact that we know a good deal about Cohen, for Drage eventually wrote a book about him.[4] In the 1930s Commander Drage, as he had become, served with British Naval Intelligence and then with the British SIS in the Far

East. Drage made use of Cohen's wide knowledge of the Chinese situation, though his main interest was in intelligence concerning the Japanese.

First under Dr Sun, and then under Chiang Kai-shek, Cohen was given the task of studying the tactics of Chinese warlord armies. He once told Drage, who recorded it in his book, that he had to keep a special eye on the emissaries of the warlords from the north who kept turning up at headquarters even though the KMT were at open war with them: 'I came to realise that every civil war in China proceeds simultaneously on two fronts, military and political, and of these the political is the most important. While two groups of armies were fighting – not very hard – the two sets of leaders were constantly trying to come to terms with some faction on the other side. If they succeeded, they'd join forces and turn on the ones who'd been left out of the deal.'

Under Chiang, Cohen negotiated several undercover arms deals. He also persuaded Chiang to make extensive use of overseas Chinese, especially the large numbers living in the United States and Canada, in the field of political propaganda. This is one of the reasons why the 'China Lobby' became so powerful an influence in the United States in the late 1930s.

Living in Shanghai in 1927 were two Chinese men of diametrically opposed political persuasions, both of whom were destined to rise to head their own party's intelligence service. One was called Tai Li, a captain in the Chinese Military Police in Shanghai, who was to rise to be Chief of Intelligence under Chiang Kai-shek. The other was K'ang Sheng, who was Organisational Director for the Shanghai District Communist Party; he was to rise to head CCP intelligence.

There is some evidence to suggest that Tai Li may have been some sort of double-agent early in his career, playing both ends against the middle. He finally made up his mind which way to go when he handed over a list of active communists in the Shanghai area during one of Chiang Kai-shek's periodic purges; many of those featured on the list were eliminated.

Tai Li was a man of striking personality with an ability to mesmerise subordinates and scare them half out of their wits. Clever but not particularly brilliant, he probably owed his rise to the peak of intelligence ranks to his extreme ruthlessness. He earned the nickname 'The Butcher' by inventing a new way of disposing of people deemed to be political enemies:

> He lined up some locomotives in a siding, got the fireboxes red hot, opened their doors, tied down the whistles to shut out the screams, and one after another threw his living victims into the fiery furnaces. According to tradition, thousands of labour leaders and students and intellectuals were killed in a few days.[5]

Under Tai's guidance the KMT Intelligence Service gained credibility, and it was to work well with its American counterpart in the Pacific War that was to come, but not with the British for Tai Li was passionately anti-British. In internal security it became especially 'efficient' by adopting interrogation techniques borrowed from the German Gestapo, techniques probably imported by one or more of the German advisers who had been brought in to advise and train KMT forces.

One of Tai Li's greatest successes came in 1938 when one of the most beautiful of his female agents persuaded a leading communist, Chang Kuo-tao, to defect to the other side. Han Suyin has written of this event that the turncoat 'was greeted with honour by Tai Li, the number one hatchet man of Chiang Kai-shek, and began working as an informer against the Communist Party'.[6]

The man who was to become Tai Li's opposite number on the communist side, K'ang Sheng, was actually arrested for subversion by the KMT authorities in Shanghai in 1930 but somehow not only avoided liquidation but managed to get himself released. He went underground inside the French Concession there, where, it is said, he acquired a wide knowledge of French intelligence methods.[7]

In 1933 K'ang was sent to Moscow to study Soviet intelligence practices. This visit was made against the background of the Soviets' long held view, and one they officially continued to hold until 1949 despite one or two wrinkles along the way, that Chiang's KMT was the legitimate government of China. This is one reason why K'ang never fully trusted the Russians. While in Moscow he published a series of propaganda leaflets concerning Chinese Communism, and from that time on always regarded propaganda as an essential part of espionage operations, a view shared of course by Japanese spymasters. After four years of learning as much about Soviet intelligence as they wished him to know, K'ang was recalled to China having built up many unofficial contacts inside the Soviet Union that were to prove of value to him later on. Back home he was placed in charge of the CCP Secret Service, but unlike Tai Li on the KMT side, worked very much undercover and did not publicise his role.

K'ang Sheng was still in Russia when the Chinese communists hatched a plot to kidnap Chiang Kai-shek in December 1936. The communists were to argue that this undertaking took place against a groundswell of public opinion throughout all China to combine together to fight renewed Japanese encroachment on Chinese territory. There is little evidence that there was any such general groundswell of public opinion in the country; nevertheless, it was a good ploy to use in the communist scheme to dominate the country.

The plot began early in 1936 when CCP agents all over the country began espousing a grand alliance of all factions in China against Japan. Slogans appeared on city streets urging that 'Chinese must not fight Chinese'. Chiang Kai-shek's KMT was having none of this however, for it was set on domestic consolidation before taking on the Japanese.

Chiang Kai-shek now made a gross error, probably caused by poor intelligence. Unaware of the low morale of the Nationalist Northeastern army under Chang Hsueh-liang – known as the 'Young Marshal' – and apparently forgetting the hatred in which that commander held the Japanese for the assassination of his father in 1928, Chiang ordered that army to attack the communists in their mountain hideaway instead of sending it against the Japanese. The ensuing fighting was ineffective, and communist agents made contact with the disaffected Young Marshal and won him over to the idea of a United Front against Japan.

On 3rd December 1936 Chiang Kai-shek flew to Sian where Chang had his headquarters, with a view to sorting matters out but within days there was a mutiny and Chiang found himself a prisoner. In her biography of Mao Tse-tung, Han Suyin states that 'the whole of Chiang's kidnapping was engineered by the Communists', although she did not specify whether she was referring to the CCP, the Soviets, or to both.[8] At the time of the kidnapping, the American journalist and communist sympathiser, Agnes Smedley, was in Sian, and was at the very least, a peripheral member of the Shanghai-based Russian spy network which had been created by Richard Sorge. The International Settlement at Shanghai had, by the 1930s, become a hotbed of intrigue, for the city was playing host to undercover operations by the secret services of many countries. It seems likely, therefore, that the kidnap coup, although organised by Chinese communists, received at least some egging-on by Soviet agents, although this may not have been with the approval of Moscow who disapproved of the Young Marshal. Smedley's sympathies in fact lay mainly with the Chinese communists rather than the Russian communists, and she may well have been a double-agent, working also for the CCP Secret Service.

The KMT leaders in Nanking retaliated by sending planes to attack Sian in a show of strength, and for a while it looked as if a new civil war was about to break out. 'The Sian mutiny and the kidnap of Chiang stunned the country and the world', says Professor Immanuel Hsu.[9] What was equally stunning was the consequent remarkable turnabout in the policy of Chiang Kai-shek.

Immediately following the kidnapping the Young Marshal issued a set of eight demands which included the reorganisation of the Nanking government to include all factions in the fight for national salvation. Then he went too far by setting up a Military Commission with himself as its head. The Chinese communists, now sensing that the Young Marshal had ambitions to lead the United Front and concluding that any large-scale KMT attack would inevitably involve them, decided that the release of Chiang Kai-shek was the lesser of two evils. Moscow, too, realised that further disorder in China could only benefit the Japanese. So Chou En-lai came out of the communists' mountain retreat to offer mediation and to finalise the release of Chiang who, by now all sweet reasonableness, signed an accord agreeing to switch to a policy of resisting Japan.

The loser in the deal was the Young Marshal who was court-martialled and given a long period of house arrest. This meant that the Japanese gained too, for they had lost an avid enemy. The Young Marshal later ended up in Taiwan.

Despite the signed accord, open fighting was still to break out from time to time between KMT and CCP forces. Undercover war between the two factions went on as well. Tai Li expanded the connections that the KMT had always had with Chinese Triads, and used the Triad networks for intelligence purposes, not only behind Japanese lines but in CCP controlled areas too. Individual Triad members were used as spies and saboteurs. This use of the Triads by Tai Li should be compared with K'ang Sheng's attitude; he made no use of them and always purged his organisation of anyone thought to have such links.

Throughout this period, confusion was the most obvious characteristic of the Chinese scene, and it applied in intelligence as it did in every other field. Although from an ideological point of view the Soviets were far closer to the CCP than to the KMT, it was the KMT they backed in those years. They saw Chiang Kai-shek as posing more of a threat to Japan, the ancient enemy, than did their Chinese communist comrades. That is why they signed the USSR–China Non-Aggression Pact in 1937 and supplied Chiang with aid and supplies several times larger than those given by the United States and Britain.

As with all the other military operations in their modern history, the Japanese opened their campaign to dominate China by sending in agents and by activating others already residing there. By the 1930s they had a well-established system of Resident Officers, called *Chuzai Bukan*, in most of the important cities of North and Central China including Manchuria. These officers were all of senior rank, ranging from colonel to general if they were from the army, and from captain to admiral if from the navy. In addition, and as was their wont, Japanese commercial firms, educational and cultural institutions, were loaded with their agents.

The first step in the conquest of China, the army insisted, must be the conquest of Manchuria, the southern part of which was already garrisoned by Japan's Kwantung army, the army which had been prevented by politicians back home from launching an all-out attack in 1928 after its agents had arranged the assassination of warlord Chang Tso-lin, the Young Marshal's father, which, together with its aftermath, came to be known as the first Mukden Incident. But this time there was more support in Japan for such adventure, not least because by then three-quarters of foreign investment in Manchuria was Japanese. On top of that, a certain sense of urgency had arisen in the Kwantung army because the two main plotters behind the 1928 plot, Colonel Itagaki Seishiro, who was to become Japan's War Minister in 1938, and Lieutenant-Colonel Ishiwara Kanji, were due to be reassigned elsewhere. Secret army conferences were held in Tokyo and in Manchuria, and soon rumours were rife that a Manchurian expedition would take place in the late summer of 1931. One of the rumours concerned the construction of a huge gun emplacement close to Mukden. Surrounded by a high wooden fence, the area was kept strictly out-of-bounds, a rather strange degree of security for what was officially said to be a swimming pool. The foundations completed, the Japanese then smuggled in two 9.5-inch guns.

In preparation for the coming attack, teams of spies were sent to various places in and around Manchuria to stir up trouble. Many of these agents were members of the *Sakura* or Cherry Blossom Secret Society with a membership restricted to 150 officers of the ranks between captain and colonel and which was a focal point of extreme nationalist ideology within the military. One team of four posing as agricultural experts and led by Captain Nakamura Shintaro, was sent in to disaffect the Inner Mongolians on Manchuria's western border. They were killed there, an unplanned event but one that provided a welcome excuse for Itagaki and Ishiwara and their fellow adventurers, high among whom were Hanaya Tadashi and Doihara Kenji, to make their move.

Hearing of the possibility of an army move in Manchuria, the Japanese emperor sent General Tatekawa to Mukden ostensibly to restrain any such operation. However, as Hirohito, when still Crown Prince, and together with an inner circle of advisers known as 'the eleven reliables', had begun planning the take-over of Manchuria as far back as 1921, it is likely either that he did not consider 1931 to be a particularly propitious year to make the attempt at conquest, or that his 'restraining order' was merely a device to impress the international community.[10] Be that as it may, after reaching Manchuria, Tatekawa was either tricked into delaying delivery of the message, or was party to the delaying tactics used to make it look like a trick. The conspirators merely moved forward the target date they had set for blowing up part of the Southern Manchurian Railway at Mukden (an echo of the earlier Mukden incident) to 18th September.

The damage done by that explosion was minimal, but the Japanese reported that one of their patrols had been fired upon by Chinese troops in the area and then blamed the explosion itself on those troops. The untrue version was widely reported around the world, the facts being concealed from the Japanese people for many years until one of the plotters, Hanaya Tadashi, revealed the truth after the Pacific War ended.[11]

Armed with these 'excuses' the Kwantung army under the command of field officers but with the tacit consent of their seniors, struck, and with the aid of the two large guns outside the city, Mukden had fallen to the Japanese by the following morning. In less than five months they had overrun the whole of Manchuria.

Colonel Doihara Kenji, Japan's most able agent, came into his own during this period. Doihara had spent many years in China and was one of 'the eleven reliables' hand-picked to fulfil his emperor's dream of annexing Manchuria. Doihara's sister was in fact First Concubine to an Imperial prince. Doihara himself had befriended Henry Pu Yi, the heir to the Manchu throne, and in many ways had taken the place of Pu Yi's former mentor, Sir Reginald Johnston, who left the royal employment in 1925. Johnston, in almost his last duty to his charge, had been involved with some of Doihara's agents in getting Pu Yi to safety in the Japanese legation in Peking after the heir had been ejected from the Forbidden City by KMT forces. Pu Yi was later spirited away to Tientsin to take refuge in the Japanese Concession there.[12]

It was said of Doihara that he could speak four Chinese dialects and nine European tongues, including Russian and English. His knowledge of Chinese and Russian certainly proved useful at the start of his career in subversion which began in Manchuria when, at the head of a gang of Chinese bandits, he held up and harassed Russian trains on the Harbin to Vladivostok railway.

His spymaster career had begun later in the 1920s when he set up a network of agents throughout Manchuria which included a number of turncoat Chinese. He operated a chain of brothels in Mukden and Harbin, manned, if that is the right word, by girls from among the 100,000-strong White Russian community who had fled south via Siberia into Manchuria and China after the Russian Revolution. The girls' secondary use was the gathering of intelligence.

Doihara also set up a chain of illicit opium-dens and engaged in drug trafficking, the drugs coming into the country disguised as military supplies. Among those 'supplies' was a type of cigarette marketed under the brand name 'Golden Bat', and manufactured in Japan where their sale was forbidden. They had capsules of opium in their mouth ends, and were highly addictive. Doihara believed that not only could selected addicts be easily persuaded to become spies and informants, but that widespread use of drugs would undermine the population and make subsequent conquest that much simpler. Besides which, there was gain to be made from the traffic: 'To kill with bullets costs money, but to kill with drugs and to reap large profits thereby, is not only good business but also brilliant military strategy', is said to have been his philosophy regarding the poppy trade. According to Australian Military Intelligence, Doihara's drug trafficking was not confined to Manchuria, but spread throughout Southeast Asia and to South America, Australia and New Zealand.

Doihara's chief aide in Manchuria was a Japanese who, perhaps in order to get closer to the White Russians in Harbin where he was a barber by trade, had become a convert to the Russian Orthodox Church. He gloried in the name Konstantin Ivanovich Nakamura, and had the worst kind of reputation with the Chinese police for his barber shop being a cover for subversion, drugs and prostitution. When the Japanese finally took over Manchuria, Nakamura became an adviser to the Kempetai, the Military Police.

Clearly Doihara was a ruthless man. Prior to the capture of the city of Harbin he and his agents promised the large White Russian community there a measure of self-government in return for their collaboration. Not only were these promises not kept, the Russians found themselves treated cruelly, and many of their womenfolk were raped by Japanese soldiery.

At least one of the foreign agents Doihara employed, a man of Italian birth called Amleto Vespa, was forced to work for the Japanese on pain of something nasty happening to his wife and family if he did not. To convince the Italian that he meant business, Doihara reminded Vespa of the fate of a man called Swineheart who, according to Tokyo newspapers, had died from accidental drowning in Japan, but who in fact had been murdered. Vespa wrote that Swineheart was an American; but he was not, he was English. Swineheart had been an agent in the pay of the warlord Chang Tso-lin who had met his death in the train explosion at Mukden in 1928. Vespa did not know, or at least did not record, that prior to the assassination, Swineheart had sent a message to Chang warning him not to travel on the train. Putting all this together, it seems Doihara was almost certainly involved in Swineheart's death. According to Vespa, Doihara held a violent dislike for the British and Americans, so much so that he refused to speak English unless he had to.[13]

As the cities of Manchuria fell to Japanese arms, Doihara began to work towards the next stage of the Japanese plan, the setting up of a puppet government in the country under Henry Pu Yi. He organised 'public support' for Japan among the Chinese in Mukden. 'Combining threats with bribery, Doihara got together a group of mainly unknown Chinese and placed them in nominal charge of the city and forced them to issue manifestos to their nationals that extolled the virtues of the Japanese,' wrote the American journalist Mark Gayn.[14] Hard on the heels of the army Doihara moved on to other cities, placing Chinese adventurers ready to do his bidding in charge of each, and through them, organising sabotage, assassinations, and strikes wherever these appeared to help his country's cause. Behind the screens erected by these Chinese puppets the Japanese did, in fact, much as they pleased.

Meanwhile Doihara had sent one of his most trusted henchmen, Major Tanaka Takayoshi, together with a beautiful Manchu princess spy called Eastern Jewel, to Tientsin in an attempt to persuade Pu Yi to go to Manchuria.

Tanaka and Eastern Jewel made an excellent spy team. They had met several years before in Shanghai and became lovers. He set her up in the style to which she was accustomed, and began to use her avid bisexuality and her aristocratic connections to good purpose. 'Being a Chinese princess she could move in Chinese circles closed to any other [spies].'[15] Eastern Jewel, in fact, was a distant relative of Pu Yi's, but had been adopted as a child by the Japanese General Kawashima Yoshiyuki and she sometimes used her adoptive name of Kawashima Yoshiko.

Tanaka and Eastern Jewel reported to Doihara that Pu Yi did not want to leave Tientsin where he had become something of a playboy in a city that, after Shanghai, was the most cosmopolitan in China. Pu Yi's reluctance probably stemmed from a desire not to exchange his present lifestyle for the less worldly one he might find in Manchuria. Another reason may have been that his wife despised the Japanese.

Doihara set about arranging for Pu Yi to change his mind. Japanese agents organised large-scale 'anti-Pu Yi' riots in Tientsin, using Chinese agitators together with soldiers from the local Japanese garrison. The British-run Municipal Police Force there were unable to control the consequent outbreak of violence, and several Chinese policemen were killed. Much Chinese property was destroyed. Some arrested rioters confessed to having been armed and paid by the Japanese, but the general populace, and Pu Yi himself, were convinced by Japanese disinformation that the rioters were out to kill him. By car, and then by ship, he allowed himself to be smuggled from the city to Japanese-held Dairen. Six weeks later Eastern Jewel finally managed to persuade Pu Yi's wife to follow him.

The Japanese set up a puppet government in Manchuria, now

Manchukuo, under Pu Yi and in March 1934 he was officially proclaimed Emperor.

On 18th June 1935 a British newspaper correspondent, working for London's *Evening Standard*, dubbed Doihara the 'Lawrence of Manchuria'. Although Lawrence was in the news at that time, as he had been fatally injured in a motorcycle accident four weeks earlier, the correspondent, should have known better, for there was little resemblance between Doihara's activities and those of Lawrence of Arabia. But the sobriquet caught on, not least with Doihara himself who gave an interview to the journalist concerned. Doihara was small and round, a roundness that grew with the passage of years, and by no stretch of the imagination did he look the part of a romantic hero.

Doihara flitted here, there, and everywhere. Captain Malcolm Kennedy, officially in Japan as the Reuters Correspondent but who was also working for British Intelligence, wrote the following about Doihara in his diary entry for 27th January 1932, at about the time Harbin was falling to the Japanese army. Kennedy had lunched in Tokyo that day with Colonel Hugh Simson the British Military Attaché:

> Half-jokingly I remarked to Colonel Simson that this latest development would seem to indicate that Colonel Doihara must be somewhere in the background, to which Simson replied that he *is* in Harbin now! It would hardly be too much to say that a knowledge of Doihara's whereabouts is the best guide as to where trouble is to be expected. Mukden, Tientsin, and now Harbin. Always he has been on the spot on the outbreak of trouble!

Less than three weeks later, on 15th February, Kennedy had more to say about Doihara:

> Had an interesting talk with Babb* on the subject of Doihara . . . according to Babb . . . the real brains behind Doihara is Colonel Itagaki. Subsequently, talking with Iwanaga [one of Kennedy's many Japanese contacts] on the same subject, Iwanaga maintained that Lt. Colonel Ishihara is the real moving spirit behind the scenes. Be that as it may, it is Doihara who figures most prominently in the news and generally seems to appear in the role of a stormy petrel.[16]

* Joseph Glenn Babb, American journalist who worked for Associated Press in Tokyo. He was also working for American Intelligence.

Doihara's efforts went on unabated. He branched out into China proper, into Inner Mongolia, and even into parts of Russia. With the annexation of Manchuria, a buffer between Japan and Russia had been removed, and friction developed between the two nations. In 1934 White Russian units armed and organised by Doihara were infiltrated through the border defences into Soviet territory. These and other more direct incidents caused the Soviets to force the pace of development in Siberia.

By the time the Sino-Japanese war began Doihara had been promoted to major-general, and in 1938 he was in charge of the *Tokumo Kikan* in China which had the special task of directing Chinese puppet rulers. But he maintained other interests. Some of his agents penetrated Chiang Kai-shek's High Command, and some Chinese divisional commanders were in his pay. Doihara's greatest achievement at this time was in enticing Huang-sen, personal assistant to Chiang, into spying for him. Perhaps the most important information Huang-sen handed over was a detailed Chinese plan to entrap Japanese ships trading on the Yangtze River. When Huang-sen's treachery was eventually discovered, he was executed.

Doihara's star agent, Eastern Jewel, went back to Shanghai with her Major Tanaka after the Pu Yi affair. By that time, just as they had done with Doihara, the foreign press had found a name for her. She was dubbed the 'Joan of Arc of Manchuria', one imagines more for her penchant for donning masculine garb than for any saintly virtue. In Shanghai she added two more names to her list of lovers. One was a British officer serving as a Military Attaché at the consulate-general's office. From him she gleaned the information that, despite Britain's condemnation of Japanese aggression in Manchuria, Britain intended to take no practical measures against Japan. Her other new lover was the son of Dr Sun Yat-sen, who presented her with much information on KMT plans. In 1937, and by then no longer needing to conceal her pro-Japanese activities from her fellow Chinese, Eastern Jewel was living in the area of north China where Japan had set up another puppet state. There she became wealthy by blackmailing Chinese with the threat of reporting their 'anti-Japanese' sentiments. Little is known of her activities after the Pacific War began in 1941. After the war she managed to evade capture for three years but was finally caught and beheaded on Chiang Kai-shek's order in 1949.

Doihara himself was executed as a war criminal in 1946.

* * *

Because of its concessions at Shanghai, Tientsin, and other places, and also because of its colony of Hong Kong, Britain was strongly interested in China and in Japanese activities there. Throughout the 1930s British agents were sent into China on spying missions either from the legation at Peking or from the consulate at Shanghai. Mandarin-speaking Robert (later Sir Robert) Scott was sent from Peking on one such mission in 1931.[17] His intelligence-gathering mission covered Mongolia and included traversing the entire length of that country's border with Siberia. Scott found himself 'assisted' and 'closely escorted' by the Kempetai, the Japanese Military Police, in some Japanese-occupied areas. In the following year he was to come face-to-face with the Kempetai again during the so-called Shanghai Incident, but no details are available about what caused the confrontation.[18]

The British set up a wireless intelligence listening station, called the North China Signals Section, at Tientsin in 1935, which in the hot summer months moved north to the British Summer Camp at Shanhaikuan. The section usually comprised between fourteen and twenty-four men from the Royal Corps of Signals under a captain or lieutenant, and included a few of what the British army called 'high-speed operators'. An administration staff of four, Chinese chosen for their trustworthiness, was also attached.

The section had several tasks. Its wireless station monitored frequencies which could not be picked up by the much larger installation situated on Stonecutters Island, Hong Kong, and paid special attention to local Japanese consular and army traffic. At one time a cryptographer was attached to the unit, but most intercepted material was relayed to the Far East Combined Bureau (FECB) at Hong Kong where it would be processed and evaluated (see below, page 70). The section also acted as the W/T station for the British battalion based at the Tientsin Concession and was in contact with the GOC Hong Kong and the Officer Commanding the Shanghai Defence Force, and directly with the War Office in London. Additionally it provided back-up for the W/T station at the British legation in Peking, kept regular wireless contact with British guardships off Chingwantao and off Taku Bar, near Tientsin, and was in direct contact with the British China Fleet. The station also had landline connections with Peking, but these were mainly unworkable during rainy weather.[19]

An indication of the effect the Sino-Japanese conflict had on the volume of wireless traffic passing through the North China Signals

Section is given by the number of messages it handled before that conflict began and afterwards. In 1935 messages averaged 21,400 a month, a figure that rose by only 10 per cent in 1936. However, by early 1937 'the traffic on circuits had more than trebled'. It increased even more when the Japanese cut the telegraph line between Tientsin and Peking at the end of July that year.

In 1938 the section was confronted with further Japanese-created difficulties.

> In August Tientsin Telephone exchange situated in British Concession was being more or less amalgamated with the Tientsin City Telephone Administration under the auspices of the New Provisional Government [Japanese].
>
> In view of this changeover it was at once realised that all conversations were liable to be censored in the telephone exchange, also, in the event of further political trouble essential communications could easily be disrupted. As a means of safeguarding against this, the British Municipal Council installed at this HQ a 20-line CB Board complete with lines to British Consulate, Consul-General's Residence, Brigadier's Residence, British Municipal Council Offices, British Municipal Police HQ, etc.

The Japanese were flexing their muscles all over northern China by this time and most of the flak not reserved for China itself, was directed at British interests. The Japanese were no longer prepared to put up with any 'nonsense' from their erstwhile ally, especially now that the former friend was preoccupied with events unfolding on the other side of the world.

During the winter of 1937–38, Berkeley Gage (later Sir Berkeley, and Britain's ambassador to Thailand from 1954–57), who at the time was an agent of Britain's Secret Intelligence Service, was chased from northern China by Japanese counter-intelligence officers. They followed him right across the country, the extent and urgency of the chase probably indicative of the importance the Japanese placed on whatever information Gage had obtained. He reached northern India in late February 1938, and boarded the Imperial Airways flying-boat at Allahabad on the 28th of that month.* On board Gage fell into conversation with an English lady, Mrs Victoria Wilkins, who was

* Allahabad, at the conjunction of the Ganges and Jumna rivers, was the middle one of the three flying-boat stops in India, and that particular flight happened to be the return journey of the first Far East flight of the 'Empire' flying boat.

flying home with her young son from Singapore. He told her he had 'just been chased right across China one step ahead of the Japs'. He must have lost some weight during the marathon journey for he added, 'I left broad gage, now I'm narrow gage.' It was a pun Mrs Wilkins always remembered, and she reminded Sir Berkeley of it when she met him again in 1954 in Penang. Gage was then attending a Far East Security Meeting with officers from MI5, a meeting held in the offices of District Commissioner R.P. Bingham.[20]

Another incident occurred in August 1939 when the Japanese arrested the British Military Attaché in China, Lieutenant-Colonel C.R. Spear. Spear was travelling behind Japanese lines from Shanghai to Peking, and was in mufti when arrested. The Japanese accused him of spying, which was almost certainly true for 'the route he had taken was tortuous'. The Japanese had an extensive dossier on the route and Spear's activities along it, the latter sworn to by Chinese witnesses. After Spear had endured ten weeks of solitary confinement, Major-General Piggott, British Military Attaché in Tokyo, was able to secure his release. One of the accusations made by the Japanese against Spear was that he had made anti-Japanese remarks to Chinese troops. Piggott pointed out that Spear could hardly have made pro-Japanese statements to them. Full details of the agreement that resulted in Spear's release are not known, but the colonel returned to England a few weeks later.[21]

The North China Signals Section, which had been a source of continuous aggravation to the Japanese, was closed down during the winter of 1939–40. During the preceding spring and summer the Japanese had made life extremely difficult for the British in and around its Tientsin Concession area. The city was blockaded in retaliation for Britain not handing over some Chinese fugitives on Japan's wanted list, and British people were subjected to a series of humiliating incidents. The New Zealand government representative in the city, Cecil Davis, was forced to strip naked in public to be searched, for instance, and something similar happened to a British lady. These provocations and the subsequent negotiations to end them, finally led to the withdrawal of the British battalion from Tientsin. Along with the battalion went Major P.G. Parker, who was not only its official Japanese interpreter but was also the British Military Intelligence man in Tientsin. Along with the battalion also went the Signals Section.

The United States was also concerned with wireless interception in

China. The American Peking Station had been established even earlier than the British one at Tientsin. Operational in 1927, it was the third station in a string designed to intercept Japanese diplomatic messages in the Japan–China area, the other two being at Shanghai, established in 1924 with the additional responsibility of intercepting Japanese naval traffic, and at Wailupe, Hawaii, established in 1925.[22] Perhaps foreseeing the difficulties to come, the Americans closed down the Peking Station in July 1935, transferring its duties to Shanghai.

Five

Hong Kong, 1930–1941

For many years Hong Kong had been an important but rather small British naval base. It was one of the several ports considered in 1921 by Britain's Committee of Imperial Defence for the site of a huge new naval installation. However, it was soon decided that there was no possibility of making Hong Kong sufficiently secure against attack, and Singapore was chosen instead. In the following year Britain had no hesitation, therefore, in signing a treaty with the United States, France, Italy and Japan, which contained a clause in its Article XIX specifically stating, in deference to Japan's wishes, that no extensions to the existing naval facility at Hong Kong were to be made, though normal repairs and replacements were permitted.

From that moment, although Hong Kong was still to be regarded as an outpost of Imperial defence of middling importance, and as a symbol of British prestige in the area, there was never any intention of doing very much to save it if it should ever be attacked by the only conceivable aggressor, Japan. It was an outpost that in the event of war was to hold out as long as possible. Even if its garrison was able to hold out indefinitely the port would be of little use, for it could be neutralised by Japanese air forces operating from Formosa. When Japanese forces landed just thirty-five miles northeast of Hong Kong to take nearby Canton in October 1938, and in February of the following year occupied the island of Hainan to the south, the indefensibility of the colony became even more apparent.[1]

In addition to its naval base, Hong Kong possessed another,

but more important, military facility, for it was the site of one of the world's major Signals Intelligence (Sigint) operations, and except for the years of Japanese occupation, was to remain so until 1995.

The Royal Corps of Signals had established a small Sigint operation there in the early 1920s. Shortly afterwards the British Admiralty and the Government Code & Cypher School (GC & CS) established a similar operation on the flagship, China Station which had, according to Commander A.G. Denniston, facilities for local interception: 'Thus a start was made on Japanese naval traffic.'[2] The naval side of the operation had grown in size and in importance by the early 1930s when a powerful intercept station was built on Stonecutters Island, close to the Kowloon shore of Hong Kong harbour.[3]

The tall wireless masts on Stonecutters, a 'closed' island which also played host to a Royal Navy Armaments Depot and to three of the colony's twenty-nine sea defence guns, were a familiar sight to anyone crossing the harbour by boat. After World War Two the Stonecutters installation was rehabilitated, and other sites were developed over the years, as new port construction, especially container-handling wharves, grew in the vicinity of the island. The new Sigint sites were at various times sited at Tai Po Sai in the New Territories, at Little Sai Wan on the north coast of Victoria Island, at Tai Mo Shan, the highest point in the mountains of the New Territories, and finally at Chung Hom Kok on Victoria Island's southern shore. The latter operation, run by the British Government Communications Headquarters (GCHQ) and manned by the RAF, was code-named Operation Kittiwake. The installations became progressively larger and more powerful: 'The gleaming white domes and tall radio mast . . . of Tai Mo Shan', wrote Leon Comber, 'are visible from miles away.'[4] With the handover of Hong Kong to China due to take place in 1997, the Chung Hom Kok operation was transferred to Geraldton, Western Australia, in January 1995.

In 1934, following an earlier exploratory visit by Captain Campbell Tait, Deputy Director Naval Intelligence (DDNI), the Admiralty sent Paymaster Captain Arthur Shaw to Hong Kong to set up the Far East Combined Bureau (FECB), a body designed to collect, collate and evaluate Naval and Military Intelligence relevant to the possibility of war with Japan.

The establishment of FECB at Hong Kong had come about as something of a compromise between the wishes of the Royal Navy and those of the British Army. The latter, from 1927, maintained what was known as the Shanghai Intelligence Office as part of Shaforce (Shanghai Defence Force), Britain's contribution to the defence of the International Settlement there. This Intelligence Office was headquartered in the building of the British consulate-general in Shanghai and was staffed by a Japanese-speaking officer of GSO2 rank, usually a major, and a Chinese-speaking officer of GS03 rank, usually a captain. The office had close contacts with the Naval Staff Officer, Intelligence, or SO (I), in Shanghai, with officers of the Special Intelligence Service (SIS, or nowadays more frequently called MI6), and with the Special Branch of the Shanghai Municipal Police. The army wished to maintain this 'forward' position.

The Royal Navy had different ideas. As well as its SO (I) in Shanghai, the navy maintained others in Hong Kong and Singapore. One of the main tasks of these officers, who in the early 1930s were usually 'passed over' lieutenant-commanders – i.e. officers of that rank who, for one reason or another, could expect no further promotion – was to keep a check on the shipping movements of likely belligerent countries. They did this through a system of unpaid Reporting Officers, often Customs Officers who were ideally situated to cover such movements. Officers of the Imperial Chinese Maritime Customs Service, a huge organisation whose senior ranks were staffed mainly by Britons, were used for this purpose throughout China. By 1934, with the growing danger from Japan, the navy decided that this system needed to be expanded, and with the Singapore naval base in the process of construction, the navy wished to concentrate its intelligence-gathering capability within the confines of that 'impregnable' fortress.[5]

As a compromise, and since by 1934 Hong Kong was already home to the wireless intercept installation on Stonecutters, London decided on Hong Kong as the site for FECB. It came under the aegis of the Commander-in-Chief, China Fleet, and was manned mainly by the Royal Navy but with some Army and Royal Air Force personnel attached. At a later date it also employed civilian operatives.

The FECB's main tasks were defined as giving timely warning of impending hostilities in the area and, in time of war, a) to supplement intelligence sent from London to the local C-in-Cs, and b) to keep London informed of events in the area. It serviced the Pacific

Naval Intelligence Organisation,* Far East Military Intelligence, and Far East Air Intelligence. Later it also incorporated a replica of the Admiralty's Operational Intelligence Centre.[6] At this time the organisation's contacts with His Majesty's Embassies in the region were through the various Naval, Military and Air Attachés, and with certain diplomatic and consular officers. The British ambassadors in the region seem to have been unaware of the Bureau's existence, at least officially. This was no doubt a deliberate policy which enabled the ambassadors to plead ignorance had the Bureau's activities ever come to light. At no time did FECB run agents of its own.

FECB began operations in 1935 from premises situated within Hong Kong's Naval Dockyard, the Sigint station at Stonecutters being an integral part of it as the interception side of what was called its 'Y' Service section. This 'Y' section acted as an outstation of the Government Code and Cypher School in London which was later moved to Bletchley Park. At that time 'Y' covered signals interception, traffic analysis and the breaking of cyphers, although later, during World War Two, 'Y' took on a different meaning, covering only interception and radio direction-finding. Captain Arthur Shaw was in charge of this section, with an Australian navy commander as his deputy and with a staff that included three lieutenant-commanders; a complement that shows the importance placed on the section. Intercepted material picked up by Stonecutters was passed for processing to the 'Y' room at the Naval Dockyard where the cryptanalysis section had direct communication with GC&CS in London.[7]

The task of running the whole FECB set-up fell to Captain J.W.A. Waller, RN, whose official title was Captain on the Staff, C-in-C, China Fleet. His confidential title was Chief-of-Intelligence-Staff (COIS); that title and its abbreviation being used only in secret communications.[8] He was responsible not only to the Admiral, China Fleet, but also, as far as the naval part of his charge was concerned, to the Director of Naval Intelligence (DNI) in London. Dual lines of responsibility are rarely good practice, but there is no

* The Pacific Naval Intelligence Organisation collected information from naval sources in the area lying between the east coast of Africa and the west coast of North and South America. It embraced the whole of China, the East Indies, Australia, New Zealand, and American and West Indies Naval Commands and also the South Atlantic Station east of Capetown.

evidence to suggest that this had a detrimental effect on Waller's performance or on those of his successors. Waller's Deputy COIS was Commander McDonald, RAN, and it is noteworthy that from its very inception FECB contained a number of Australians. The SO (I), who in 1935 was a Major Bramwell, Royal Marines, became part of the FECB set-up, although he also had duties for which he was responsible directly to the Admiral, China Fleet.

Throughout the existence of this 'combined' bureau it was always predominantly navy-oriented. With the benefit of hindsight this could be seen as a mistake, but FECB was the first major attempt in any theatre of operations to co-ordinate the intelligence arms of all three services.

The army representatives in the beginning were Colonel V.R. Burkhardt, GSO1, a Chinese speaker,[9] and Captain C.R. Boxer, GSO3, who spoke Japanese. Charles Boxer had in earlier years been a language officer attached to the office of the Military Attaché at the British Embassy in Tokyo.[10] An official file in the Public Record Office at Kew is incorrect in naming the RAF officer at FECB, at the time of its inception, as Squadron Leader H.T. Bennett. 'Alf' Bennett was a language officer attached to the office of the British Air Attaché in Tokyo from 1935 to 1938, and followed that with a course at Bletchley Park before arriving for the first time at FECB in March 1939.[11] His predecessor at Hong Kong was in fact Wing Commander 'Rosie' Warburton who, after Bennett's arrival, went on to join the staff of the Air Attaché at the British embassy in Chungking.

The FECB organisation inevitably suffered some initial problems. One of these concerned the siting of the HQ within the confines of the Naval Dockyard. This was all very well from a security point of view, for the dockyard and the offices of the FECB within it were policed by armed Sikhs. This show of military force, however, proved a strong deterrent to visits by those civilians who had hitherto supplied the SO (I) with much of his information. These included representatives of commercial firms returning from business trips deep into either Chinese or Japanese-held territory, or officers of the Merchant Navy back from Chinese and Japanese ports, and other informants of a more clandestine nature. All had previously been in the habit of dropping in to the former office of the SO (I) for informal but informative chats whenever they pleased. Now that was more difficult. However, the problem was partially solved by the SIS providing an office in the city 'where informants whom it was not desirable to introduce into the dockyard could be interviewed'.[12] This office was in the Hong Kong & Shanghai Bank Building, the SIS man involved being Commander Charles Drage.

The army had graver concerns. When Colonel Burkhardt joined the organisation he discovered that

> no great intimacy existed between the heads of the Naval and Military sections. Each service ran its own work on its own lines, though all were under the same roof. Visits to the 'Y' room were distinctly discouraged, and very little information was handed out to the Army on the grounds that it did nothing to contribute to production in this line.[13]

If this was truly the reason for the navy holding back information, and it was not merely the application of the 'need-to-know principle', then it was another example of the navy's well-known tendency to do its own thing vis-à-vis the other services. Wesley K. Wark has pointed out that the Admiralty, with its tradition of independent action firmly established since World War One, had cultivated a high degree of autonomy in the intelligence field because there was no real co-ordination of the specialised intelligence reporting of the three services.[14] It may be that the early situation at FECB, which was always at least eighty per cent manned by the navy, was a result of this attitude, and that the navy tended to treat the officers from the other Services as mere liaison officers.

The writings of Brigadier E.E. Mockler-Ferryman contain a passage which seems, however, to point to a more profound field of internal friction than that mentioned by Burkhardt. He wrote:

> Though there was not much inter-service friction there was a considerable amount between the Sigint group and the COIS on the Station, through whom, from 1937, all the group's output was handled operationally, and this friction was to continue throughout the war.[15]

Mockler-Ferryman's comment is important. FECB came in for much criticism at the time of Japan's entry into World War Two, and several accusations of failure were made against it. It is possible that this friction between the 'Y' boys who, though they held naval and military ranks, were often intellectual 'boffin' types and perhaps not much given to military-style discipline, and their local superiors, might have been a contributory factor, if indeed failures there were. Of equal importance perhaps is that 'Y' room personnel had a dual responsibility, working in part directly with GC&CS in London. The various COISs may not have liked some of their staff having an additional line of reporting. It might also be that some of the brigadier's comments refer to the attitude of Major P. Marr-Johnson who was attached to FECB at Hong Kong some time in 1939. 'Marr-Johnson adamantly refused to work under the Admiralty umbrella – went over the top about this', reports Alf Bennett. Marr-Johnson was a Japanese speaker and indeed, held a special commission later in Singapore. It may be that he held a similar one in Hong Kong, but if so, Bennett did not know of it.

Another major problem was that of finance. Memoranda of 1937 from the DNI in London showed that the gravity of the Far Eastern situation was fully realised, but 'to get the necessary sanction for a proper intelligence service in that part of the world was a matter of extreme difficulty'.[16] The British Treasury's purse-strings had by that date been somewhat loosened after years of austerity following World War One, but new expenditure tended to be concentrated on matters back home.

In an attempt to overcome the naval monopoly of 'Y', four army signallers were sent out by the War Office to assist with reception on Stonecutters, but the effect of their introduction was only gradual for they had first to be trained in Japanese morse. It seemed to Colonel Burkhardt that any intelligence doled out to the army would continue to be proportionate to its contribution to the task of reception unless the mutual interservice suspicion could be broken down. He decided that the best means to this end was the personal one, and he used the Army Entertainment Fund allocated to his office for a series of weekly Chinese dinners for FECB staff at his house. This, he later reported, did much to break down interservice barriers and to knit the intelligence staff together as a corporate body with its own special identity.

Colonel Burkhardt also noted that the British community in Hong Kong was in general happy with the military and naval presence in the colony, and that full co-operation was given by the Governor and the Hong Kong Civil Service. This was in marked contrast to the attitude, around this time of the Governors of Signapore and of the Malayan Civil Service under them. In Singapore the military presence was resented, not least because some of the costs of building the Singapore Naval Base and some of the expenses of protecting it, were expected to be borne locally.*

By 1937 the 'hush-hush' intercept station on Stonecutters Island, known to senior local military and naval commanders as 'Q' Station, had the capability to eavesdrop on all transmissions from Japan, no matter how faint, according to Eric Nave, one of the naval officers stationed there.[17] Indeed, by the end of that year, Admiral Sir Percy Noble, C-in-C, China Fleet, was able to report that FECB had fully justified its existence and, 'amid the turmoil of Shanghai and the wild rumours of Hong Kong', he had received 'unfailingly reliable information from the COIS and it is impossible to speak too highly of the work of the Combined Intelligence Bureau at Hong Kong'.[18]

From an early date cryptographers based at FECB, Hong Kong, achieved considerable success in breaking Japanese cyphers. Eric Nave was one of these men. An Australian, he had so impressed the British Naval Attaché with his ability whilst serving as a language officer in Japan that Canberra had been asked to lend him to the Royal Navy. In consequence he joined HMS *Hawkins* on the China Station in 1925 and, on board that ship and afterwards when ashore in Hong Kong, set about the task of breaking Japanese cyphers. 'At the end of two years, in 1927, Nave's Sigint work in Hong Kong had laid bare the entire Japanese naval radio organisation. Additionally all the Japanese naval codes then in use had been broken, so that GC&CS could read every message sent from Tokyo and those sent from one warship to another.'[19] The decrypts from this work were at that time known as 'Special'. Nave did not do all this on his own, of course, for other officers in the Japanese section of GC&CS in London were also working on the codes. GC&CS, headed by Commander A.G. Denniston, was divided into operational sections, and the section dealing with Japanese naval codes was under the then Paymaster Lieutenant-Commander Arthur Shaw, who had been a fellow language officer of Nave's in Japan. Nevertheless, it appears that Eric Nave's role was pivotal, so much so that in 1928 he was

* In earlier years when the Singapore garrison had consisted only of one infantry battalion and a regiment of gunners, all the modest cost involved had fallen upon that colony and the soldiers were regarded as the property of the civilians. This intimacy was lost with Singapore's expansion into a 'fortress' and the increased costs on the local business community.

sent to join GC&CS in London where he and his fellows continued to work on Japanese cyphers.

The political situation in China grew ever more grave throughout the thirties; the situation was in a state of great flux, with many interwoven, often conflicting strands. But in December 1936, when Japan signed the Anti-Comintern Pact with Germany, the situation took a distinct downturn. It began to look very dangerous for Britain as well as for other nations with interests in the region. Already worried lest Chinese nationalism at any time take another anti-British trend like the one which, in 1927, had resulted in her having to surrender her concession on the upper reaches of the Yangtze River, Britain now became concerned that Japan's signing of the Pact – which had the Soviet Union as its main target, thus giving protection to Japan's north-western flank – might presage further Japanese encroachment into southern China, a move that could result in full-scale war between the two Asiatic countries and have repercussions on the colony of Hong Kong. Intelligence reports reaching the British indicated a stepping-up of Japanese fifth-column intrigue and subversion operations throughout China.

Britain's worries caused her to permit Chiang Kai-shek's Kuomintang secret service to set up a radio intercept station of their own in the New Territories area of Hong Kong in 1937 to monitor Japanese army signals. This station was run by the Chinese Bureau of Investigation and Statistics, or *Diaocha Tongzhi*. It was closed down before Hong Kong fell to the Japanese in December 1941, and its staff escaped back into China.[20]

It was not only a possible war between Japan and China that Britain feared. Her own direct relationship with Japan had been deteriorating fast. One sign of this was the ugly incident that took place at Keelung on the island of Taiwan in which British ratings from visiting warships were arrested and beaten up. Relations between the British and Japanese navies, once so friendly had reached rock bottom. There were growing signs that the Japanese dislike of foreigners, and especially of the British, made an outbreak of war with the West a distinct possibility.

Captain E.G.N. Rushbrooke relieved Captain Waller as COIS at the beginning of 1937, by which time the 'responsibility for keeping track of political trends in Japan, of military and strategic developments, and of any secret preparations for a military blow to be delivered without warning . . . had devolved upon FECB'.[21] The most serious problem confronting the C-in-C, China Fleet, was that, as Captain Rushbrooke reported, 'an expedition against Hong Kong or Singapore might well be undertaken without having recourse to the Japanese overseas Mercantile fleet'. One of the more important tasks of Rushbrooke's organisation was collecting information from Reporting Officers and the masters of British merchantmen about the distribution of naval ships and merchant vessels belonging to potential belligerents, information augmented and confirmed by the Sigint operation. But this tracking, and the plots made from the information, had given no warning signs of the transportation of Japanese forces sent to North China during 1937 and 1938. The conclusion was that the Japanese had mobilised only their coastal shipping for the purpose and, because such ships normally only sailed home waters, including the vast Inland Sea of Japan, they were much harder to track. 'That increased the value of "Special" [in this context, intercepts and Direction Finding (DF) made by Stonecutters and other listening stations]and of any kind of information from Japan.'

Nevertheless, the Reporting Officer system was gradually improved and became steadily more sophisticated as information was fed into the plotting room from such sources as the New York Maritime Register, and the Panama and Suez Canal Transit Lists. Admiral Noble felt able to comment in 1939 that 'it is the most valuable shipping, plying regularly on normal routes which should give the first indication of impending hostilities by the appearance of irregularities. This type of shipping is more easily returned [to Japan] and more worth watching than tramp tonnage, only a marked withdrawal of which would be noticeable.' Noble was right.

Eric Nave returned to Hong Kong as part of the FECB organisation from October 1937 until August 1939 when FECB was relocated in Singapore. During those two years much of the Japanese wireless traffic intercepted by Stonecutters concerned the invasion 'without warning' of China. In a book which Nave co-wrote with James Rusbridger in 1991, the following description appears:

> FECB read all the Japanese messages with ease and had prior knowledge of every operation they planned. The first advice usually came after a War Cabinet meeting in Tokyo and would be sent in the Commander-in-Chief's code. A typical message would read, 'Instructions have been issued for the capture of Canton. This will

be known as Operation Y. Further details will be given by Chief of Naval Staff.' This immediately helped FECB identify the much longer passages that would shortly be intercepted . . . These would give precise details of the number of transports, escorting warships, the Army units involved, landing place, route to be taken, and so forth. Not a single message escaped the listening post in Hong Kong. The powerful intercept station at Stonecutters sucked up everything transmitted from Japan and by any ship at sea. However, none of this information was passed on to the Chinese . . . presumably because GC&CS could not risk letting the Japanese become aware that their codes were compromised. China was the first major overseas military operation the Japanese had embarked on, and for FECB and GC&CS in London it was the perfect Signit training ground . . .[22]

Nave, or more likely his co-author Rusbridger who was rather given to exaggeration, was certainly indulging in hyperbole when he said that not a single message escaped the listeners on Stonecutters. Nevertheless, many messages were intercepted, and equally important of course, deciphered and read. Commander Denniston, Head of the Naval Section of GC&CS in London at the time, probably described the situation more accurately. Writing in 1986 he had this to say:

It can be maintained that in early 1939, GC&CS had full control of diplomatic and attaché traffic, were reasonably fluent in their reading of all main naval cyphers and knew quite a lot about Japanese army cyphers used in China.

In a summation of his department's abilities, Denniston added: 'To sum up the situation of the Naval Section in 1939, including the Japanese branch in Hong Kong: they exercised a very fair measure of control of all Italian and Japanese naval cyphers.'[23]

Certain members of FECB had noteworthy adventures during their service in Hong Kong. Captain Charles Boxer, who had been a language officer in Tokyo in the early 1930s, was often given the task of escorting visiting Japanese army officers around the colony. Early in February 1938, at a time when anti-Japanese feeling was running high among the Chinese in Hong Kong, he was escorting two of them around when he and they were set upon by Chinese and badly beaten up.[24]

Boxer was periodically sent to Shanghai to liaise with various British Intelligence organisations, and also took 'local' leave there. On one of these trips he met the American writer, Emily Hahn, who later became his second wife. Miss Hahn was something of a personality being well-known for her cigar-smoking and for attending parties with a monkey perched on her shoulder. By 1940, after the war in Europe had begun, Miss Hahn was with Charles Boxer in Hong Kong and was in his company when she was introduced to several Britons engaged in clandestine activities of one form or another. She wrote of them in a book published in the United States in 1943 after she had been repatriated in a civilian 'exchange' of personnel in late 1942.[25]

One of the Britons was Ian Morrison, 'something to do with The *Times* . . . had taught in Tokyo . . . then secretary to the British Ambassador in Tokyo'. Emily Hahn went on to record of Morrison that,

> all . . . his contacts, I decided, must add up to something; the usual something known among the British as 'Intelligence'. They would never let a man like him slip through their fingers. Besides, Ian was awfully mysterious and thrilled about his work. Whenever he was asked what he was doing he hesitated palpably before replying, and when he replied it was with a palpable lie. I teased him about it when I knew him better.*

Emily Hahn got to know well Boxer's fellow FECB officer, Alf Bennett. She also met Robert Winter, who may have been working for SIS and was definitely working for the Chinese against the Japanese. She wrote: 'I am giving away no secrets when I tell this, because Bob wasn't like Ian Morrison and the other British Intelligence boys; he advertised himself directly instead of by implication.'

* Ian Morrison, 1913–50. Born in Peking, he was the eldest son of Dr George Ernest Morrison, the *Times* correspondent 'Chinese' Morrison. It is not generally known outside Far Eastern circles that Ian Morrison was the true hero of Han Suyin's autobiographical work, *A Many Splendoured Thing*. For the purposes of her book and probably because Morrison was already married (to a Czech lady named Marie Therese), Han called him 'Mark Elliot'. The character gained a further metamorphosis in the film of the book, becoming an American played by the actor, William Holden. Both book and film became very popular due to the highly romantic content. However, the truth is that Morrison, according to his aunt, was a ladies' man with paramours all over the Far East and in Australia. As in the book, Morrison was killed in the Korean War whilst serving as Special Correspondent for *The Times*. He was travelling in a jeep near the front-line when it struck a mine. Killed along with him were Christopher Buckley of the *Daily Telegraph* and Colonel Unni Nayar of the Indian army.

She also mentioned two other 'out-of-town' intelligence officers as visiting Hong Kong. One was Robert Scott who had been sent on an intelligence mission along the Siberian border in 1931. His official title now was Director of Information, Singapore. The other was Kenneth Miller who may have worked for SIS in Shanghai.

If Emily Hahn, an American citizen, could so easily learn the names of several British Intelligence officers, it is not surprising that, on 6th January 1941, the British C-in-C, Far East, Air Chief Marshal Sir Robert Brooke-Popham, found it necessary to report in a cable home that the identities of the principal SIS officers at Shanghai and Hong Kong (he also included Singapore) were known to many.[26] Perhaps Winter and Miller were among 'the chief subordinates' mentioned in that same cable of Brooke-Popham's whom he described as being 'in general local amateurs with no training in intelligence duties nor adequate knowledge of military, naval, air or political affairs'.

Eric Nave recorded an event that shows a rather strange lapse of security on the part of the Head of FECB, Captain Edmund Rushbrooke. It happened som etime in 1937, early in Nave's second term in Hong Kong. Nave had made arrangements with the manager of the Eastern Telegraph Company, a subsidiary of Cable & Wireless Ltd, which ensured he received copies of all cables sent or received by the Japanese consul-general. It was not long before Nave decoded one that informed Tokyo of his own arrival in the colony together with other information about the Stonecutters operation. As this was all 'top secret' it indicated a high-level leak. Keeping the information to himself, Nave began feeding disinformation into the FECB system, and it was not long before decryptions of further cables narrowed the range of suspects down to an Italian lady who was a close friend of Captain Rushbrooke's new, second, wife, Marjorie. Nave's suspicions of the Italian had, in fact, been first aroused when she questioned him closely during a dinner party soon after his arrival in Hong Kong. The opportunity soon arose to prove the source of the Japanese consul-general's reports when the lady left the colony with her businessman husband to go home on leave. The reports ceased at once.

When Rushbrooke was confronted by Nave with the evidence he at first refused to believe it. It was only after the Italian couple's return and the consul's reports, based on information deliberately fed to Marjorie Rushbrooke began again, that Rushbrooke was convinced. British Naval Intelligence afterwards ascertained that the Italian lady had been recruited as a spy by Contessa Edda Ciano, Mussolini's daughter, during the time Ciano had been the Italian consul-general at Shanghai.

Italian Intelligence had other successes in Hong Kong. In the spring of 1939 their agents somehow gained access to a Royal Navy establishment where they obtained a copy of a secret report dated 5th May 1939 from the C-in-C China Fleet, Sir Percy Noble to the First Sea Lord. Part of the report stated that Britain would be unable to defend both the Middle East and Far East simultaneously, and could be forced into making a choice between one or the other, and that Singapore could be defended only with American help. A copy of the Noble report was handed over to the German ambassador in Rome who sent it on to Berlin.[27] At about the same time Italian agents also managed to break into the governor's residence in Hong Kong, though it is not known what information, if any, they procured.

All this was hushed up. The 'Rushbrooke affair' did not harm that officer's career. During 1939 he went on to command the first of several ships including the aircraft-carrier HMS *Eagle*, and in 1942 he was promoted Commodore and then took over Rear-Admiral John Godfrey's position at Whitehall. The job Godfrey vacated for Rushbrooke was that of DNI, Director of Naval Intelligence, a position Rushbrooke held for the remainder of the war.[28]

During 1938 the possible removal of FECB to Singapore came under discussion. The Japanese had taken Canton, only seventy miles from Hong Kong, and Canton's large airfield and its direct rail contact with the colony underlined how Hong Kong was no place now for an important Sigint operation. Contingency plans were put in hand to move the major part of the operation; a move that required the expansion of the existing wireless station at Kranji on Singapore Island which had to be made ready to conduct all the Stonecutter operations immediately should the worst come to the worst. Throughout the winter of 1938 and the spring of 1939 these plans were pushed ahead, the matter made ever more urgent by what was happening on the other side of the world. By the summer the Bureau, now headed by Captain F.J. Wylie, RN, who had relieved Rushbrooke in January, was ready to move, and in August was brought to twelve-hours' notice. On 24th August the cruiser HMS *Birmingham* arrived for a routine dry-docking, but instead found herself inundated with 'Y' ratings from Stonecutters with their equipment, who set about turning the ship into a floating 'Y' station. They were followed by other operatives and 'about twenty long loads of office equipment'. The ship sailed for Singapore at noon the following day. The Stonecutters installation was kept in operation with a reduced staff, and a few FECB officers remained at Hong Kong, the three senior ones being Charles Boxer, now promoted to Major, Squadron Leader Bennett, and the Royal Marines Major R.G. Giles, with the latter continuing to double as SO (I).

Alf Bennett says that, for a time in late 1939 or early 1940, he was transferred to Singapore, but did not like it there and asked to be sent back. During the brief period he was away his position in the FECB 'rump' at Hong Kong was taken by 'Art' Cooper. Cooper, whose older brother worked at Bletchley Park, spoke no oriental languages, though he was fluent in Icelandic and Swedish, attributes of little value in the East.

The senior SIS officer in Hong Kong in the immediate pre-war years was Commander Charles Drage, RN. His cover was that of Commercial Adviser to the governor and he had offices in the Hong Kong & Shanghai Bank Building. 'But many of us knew he was the head of MI6 in South China', reported George Wright-Nooth, who arrived in Hong Kong in 1939 as a newly appointed Assistant Superintendent of Police. Drage was responsible to the senior SIS man in the Far East, Harry Steptoe, whose own cover was that of British consul in Shanghai.

Wright-Nooth, who lodged in the same 'chummery' as did Drage, writes:

> I vividly recall the ritual when Charles Drage had his first gin in the evening. After a bath and a change of clothes he would slump down in the most comfortable of our armchairs. Then his personal boy, who looked like a pirate, would enter with a tray on which was a bottle of Plymouth Gin, several squashed fresh limes, and a silver bucket of ice, and, most prominently of all, a pint glass. The 'Pirate' would fill a third of a glass with gin, followed by fresh lime and topped to the brim with ice, which he would stir gently. Charles would then take a large swig and settle down to his homework. This entailed reading the newspapers and snipping out articles of interest. These, we were convinced, formed the basis of his intelligence reports to the government. Whatever his sources, he anticipated by a few months the Japanese attack on Hong Kong. When he said goodbye to us before leaving hurriedly on a cruiser for Singapore, we were more concerned that he settled his household bills before he left.[29]

Charles Drage had previously been in British Naval Intelligence in the Far East. In that service from the mid-1930s he seems to have had something of a roving commission in the area. He is known to have touched variously at Shanghai, Hong Kong and Singapore. He was in the latter place in September 1939 where he witnessed the round-up of German nationals at the outbreak of the war in Europe, and again in 1941 by which time he was the SIS man based there. He was well known to officers of the Far East Combined Bureau and officers of Singapore Special Branch.

Drage first arrived in the Orient in 1923 as an officer aboard the sloop HMS *Bluebell* at Canton. While there he was introduced to and was befriended by Morris Cohen, the Briton at the heart of Chiang Kai-shek's Intelligence Service. Keeping in contact with Cohen from about 1932 onward, and trying to discover Chinese plans vis-à-vis the Japanese, seems to have been Drage's principal intelligence task until he became an SIS officer. Drage must have been high up on the Japanese wanted list, for when Cohen was captured by the Japanese in Hong Kong at the start of the Far Eastern war, he was first placed in a cell with Elston Shaftain who had been in charge of Hong Kong Police Special Branch. Cohen wrote later that, 'Elston had a high forehead and a big moon-face like Charles, and the Japanese at first thought they had caught Drage'. Drage's other main contacts in China were Captain Walther Stennes, a German serving on Chiang's staff, and the Chinese General Gaston Wong Keung.

Of his own intelligence efforts during 1932–36, Drage wrote:

> Life had not been easy for me since my arrival in the Far East a few years earlier on a mission of which it is sufficient to say that my interests were centred exclusively in Japan. I had made every kind of mistake and met with every sort of setback, while progress of any kind had been heartbreakingly slow. But gradually – one by one, with intervals of many months when nothing seemed to happen at all – I had found two or three powerful allies. They came from widely different walks of life and from backgrounds as diverse as could well be imagined; one thing only had they in common, a clear and steadfast loyalty to the new China . . . whose very existence was threatened by the Japanese Army. The first of these had been 'Two-Gun' Cohen, the second, General Wong, and the third, Captain Walther Stennes.[30]

Perhaps among Drage's mistakes was the fact that his status in the British Intelligence Services was widely known. He made little attempt to make a secret of it during his many perambulations around the Far East.[31] But Wright-Nooth need not have worried about Drage's ability to pay his household bills; his maternal grandfather was Thomas Ismay, founder of the White Star Line, and he had a substantial private income.

After Drage left the colony, Alex Summers became SIS's chief agent in Southern China. His number two was George Merriman. Both became internees when the Japanese captured Hong Kong at the end of December 1941. The Japanese did not discover their pre-war intelligence connections, nor did they discover that the pair had a radio hidden in the wall of their quarters in the internment camp. It is thought that Summers used the radio to keep in touch with the British Army Aid Group (BAAG) based at Kweilin in Chinese-held territory in Hong Kong's hinterland; BAAG was an 'escape' organisation which also conducted some espionage. On more than one occasion Summers and Merriman were nearly caught with the radio. It was a capital offence to have one; however, both survived internment.

Up to September 1939, when all the Germans left in the colony were rounded up and interned, the *Abwehr*, like the Italian Secret Service, was actively engaged in espionage in Hong Kong. Its tasks were probably facilitated by the number of German advisers employed in Chiang Kai-shek's armies across the border. One of these advisers was Captain Walther Stennes. He is known to have met Colonel Irwin, GSO1, as well as Charles Drage, in 1938. Stennes, who was no Nazi, may not have passed any information on to *Abwehr* agents, but the incident shows it would have been possible for him to have done so.

A German adventurer called Carl Jochheim managed to escape from internment in Hong Kong in October 1939. Two years previously he had been deported from Japan because of accusations of swindling made against him. He then went to the Philippines where again he was involved in criminal activities. After his escape from Hong Kong he somehow managed to re-enter Japan in November and was employed by the German Naval Attaché. His good knowledge of English was used to extract information from the crewmen of visiting British ships, and he was later transferred to Shanghai to do the same job there.

Of the Axis partners, however, it was the Japanese who were most active in espionage in Hong Kong, and as the Rushbrooke affair showed, the Japanese consul-general was up to his eyes in such matters. 'The Japanese consular staff can have had little difficulty in making a full and accurate survey of the whole defensive position', said the authors of the British Official History of the war against Japan.

In Hong Kong, as throughout the rest of the Far East, many Japanese were engaged in espionage, feeding information through the local consulate. Japanese firms were fronts for espionage activities and subversion, as were educational and cultural institutions. Japanese-run drinking halls in the Wanchai red-light district were considered better by British troops than the Chinese ones; cheaper beer was on offer, and pretty 'hostesses' even offered credit facilities, whilst the proprietors sat and listened. The top men's hairdresser was a Japanese who had been there for seven years during which time he had cut the hair of the governor, senior army and police officers and civil administrators; he proved to be a commander in the Imperial Japanese Navy. Another man called Mizuno ran a sports shop in Wanchai; he turned out to be a lieutenant in the Japanese army.

The Japanese made use for subversive purposes of organisations set up by Wang Ching-wei, their puppet ruler in North China. In February 1939 Wang Ching-wei had formed and directed an organisation in Hong Kong called National Salvation Through Peace which, in reality, issued pro-Japanese propaganda and concerned itself with fifth-column work, sabotage, subversion and espionage in the colony. It also sent agents to Malaya, the Netherlands East Indies, Indo-China and the Philippines. There were at least three other 'puppet' companies involved in these activities, and each had a set of aims that included disaffecting Chinese of both the Kuomintang and Communist factions throughout the Far East.[32] From 1940 onward rumours circulated that Wang Ching-wei's army, which he dubbed the 'National Peace and Regeneration Army', was preparing to attack the colony.

According to the British official historians of the war in the Far East, little was done to stop the activities of these agents:

> The special branch of the Hong Kong police was weak, and the civil administration was slow to arrest or deport suspicious characters, some of whom were known to be enemy agents. The normal unrestricted movement of all and sundry between the island and the mainland

> facilitated the activities of enemy agents, who passed unnoticed in the guise of Chinese coolies or traders.
>
> The case of Colonel Suzuki, a Japanese language officer, illustrates well the attitude taken over the question of security. He lived in Hong Kong and, when the British military authorities pointed out that he made no attempt to take English lessons, the Japanese Consul-General admitted that the Colonel was really an intelligence officer who had contacts with Chungking and southern China. The question of issuing an expulsion order was referred to the Foreign Office, who thought . . . Japan might regard this as an affront [and] it would be better to wait until Suzuki went on leave . . . Thus Colonel Suzuki eventually departed for Tokyo via Canton on New Year's Day 1941 . . . at his own convenience.[33]

When Suzuki was questioned by a British Intelligence Officer about his failure to learn any English he replied, through an interpreter, that he regretted the fact exceedingly but that his intelligence duties took up most of his time.

The official historians were perhaps being a little hard on the Hong Kong Police and the civil administration. The governor, Sir Geoffrey Northcote (who was to be relieved by Sir Mark Young in September 1941) through the Colonial Office, and supported by the General-Officer-Commanding (GOC) through the War Office, strongly urged Suzuki's expulsion. Furthermore, Suzuki's secretary had been arrested, convicted and heavily fined under local alien laws in April 1940 for posing as a Chinese while engaged in suborning Chinese labour and certain Chinese societies.[34] The police believed they had enough evidence to convict Suzuki himself for subversive activities had there not been diplomatic intervention from London. But the British Foreign Office had the final word on most matters dealing with Japan, and vetoed any action against Suzuki. It was the season for appeasing Japan.*

In the summer of 1941, the Hong Kong Police uncovered a Gestapo-like organisation that had been set up by Tai Li, the Kuomintang's Chief of Intelligence. It has been described as a merciless band of thugs. Members of it had begun rounding up

* The Colonial Office did manage to get its way on one important matter. The Foreign Office thought that evacuating European and Indian women and children from Hong Kong might be regarded by the Japanese as a 'panic measure' and thus encourage their aggressive policy. However, from July 1940 no fewer than 1,646 service families and over 1,800 wives and children of civilians were sent away from the colony.

and executing both communist and Wang Ching-wei sympathisers. It was hustled out of the colony, a move that added fuel to Tai Li's burning hatred of the British.

Immediately after the Japanese attack came on 8th December 1941, Chinese Triads took advantage of the situation to extort money from the government. According to Superintendent George Wright-Nooth, word was spread that the Triads were banding together to kill all Europeans but that 'money might persuade them to change their minds'. Senior police officers, including Commissioner Pennefather-Evans and Superintendent F. Shaftain, who as Head of CID was responsible for the Force's small Special Branch, and assisted by a senior Kuomintang Intelligence officer, Colonel S.K. Yeo, held a meeting with 'Triad mediators'. One of these was a man called Chang Ji Lin, who was 'visiting' the colony from Shanghai where he was the master of the underworld. A sum of HK$20,000 was paid over as an initial payment, and the threat was called off on the understanding that further moneys would be paid after the war. Shaftain is reported to have said post-war that the debt to Chang Ji Lin was settled.

During the battle for the colony, Superintendent Shaftain led the fight against enemy agents. He and his men discovered several transmitters that were being used to send information about British defences, and he took upon himself the responsibility for having the perpetrators shot.

Hong Kong's large Indian resident community, together with the two Indian army battalions and the Indian gunners of the Hong Kong and Singapore Royal Artillery (HK&SRA) stationed there, ensured that the colony became a prime target for Japanese subversive agents; the agents set about the task of working on the desires of many Indians to wrest independence from Britain. Japan had provided safe haven for disaffected Indians for many years and its Secret Services were well versed in the ramifications of the independence movement. In Hong Kong, as elsewhere, this was a cause of considerable concern to the British.

After serious trouble with an Indian army battalion at Singapore in 1940, the then Secretary of State for India, Lord Zetland, wrote to Lord Linlithgow, the Viceroy, that, 'following . . . the trouble . . . after the Indian brigades reached Egypt and the serious episode*

* See below, page 194–195.

which took place on the [Northwest] Frontier some time ago . . . gives one cause for anxiety'.[35] The British were extremely worried over the loyalty of some Indian army regiments, especially those now mostly officered by Indians.

Zetland had left his post by the end of 1940. Had he still been there in December his anxieties would have increased. Trouble began in Hong Kong when eighty-five of the Sikhs who made up the 800-strong HK&SRA, refused to don tin-helmets during training exercises. Led by a senior Havildar Major, the group continued to refuse and it 'then became evident that concerted action on the part of all 800 Sikhs had to be anticipated'. This might have been an 'outward manifestation of subversive influences in the background', and there were fears that the incident could spill over to disaffect the Sikhs of the 2/14th Punjab Regiment of the Indian Army stationed in the colony. (The other regiment of the Indian army in the colony was the 5/7th Rajput Regiment.) In fact there were strong though unproven rumours that the Sikhs of the Indian army were plotting a mutiny.[36] The eighty-five men were arrested and held for General Courts Martial; whilst being held they went on hunger strike.

The MI5 man in Hong Kong who held the cover title of Defence Security Officer (DSO), was Colonel Holt, and he was convinced that the trouble had been instigated by local Indian dissidents spurred on by the Japanese, and this was later confirmed by the Hong Kong Police Special Branch. This was the first and most serious of a series of similar incidents that caused the GOC, Hong Kong, Major-General A.E. Grasett (soon to be relieved by Major-General C.M. Maltby) to suggest, with the governor's support, that Holt, who was on the point of vacating his appointment, be replaced by either an Indian army officer or by a police officer from the Punjab; the Punjab being the home of the Sikhs. In fact, a Major Kilroy together with a police interrogator had already been sent from India 'to investigate subversive activities amongst Indian troops here'.[37] They were soon followed by Superintendent Bill Robinson of the Indian Intelligence Bureau, together with another Indian army major and a Sikh Superintendent of Police. A widespread and covert inquiry was carried out, made all the more urgent because of the disappearance from Hong Kong of a large number of the unarrested Sikh soldiers. 'They seemed, literally, to have been spirited away in the night from their barrack rooms, even from their units on exercises.'[38] Further arrests were made and eventually all the arrested men were shipped back to India.

The British Commander-in-Chief, Far East, Air Chief Marshal Sir Robert Brooke-Popham, took these matters very seriously indeed, for Indian army battalions formed the major part of the troops in his command. In a cypher message dated 28th March 1941 to the C-in-C, India and copied to the War Office for the attention of MI5, 'regarding the protection of Indian troops from enemy agents', he described the situation in Singapore where, less than a year before, there had been a serious mutiny in a regiment of the Indian army, as 'probably less dangerous than in Hong Kong'.[39]

As a result of these Hong Kong incidents, several Indian civilian dissidents were arrested by Special Branch and jailed for anti-British activities. Three managed to escape to reach the Japanese 21st Army HQ at Canton. There they met the Japanese expert on Indian affairs, Major Fujiwara Iwaichi, and persuaded him to ship them south to join their Indian Independence League comrades already working in Malaya and Thailand.

As war with Japan grew ever more imminent, the Far East HQ of the British Special Operations Executive (SOE) set up in 1941 a small seven-man operational unit in Hong Kong with an associated reconnaissance force. The leaders of the unit were M.H. Turner and G.F. Swettenham, both serving members of the Hong Kong Volunteer Force and three members of the unit received training at the SOE training base in Singapore. Turner was given a secret military commission as acting captain, and SOE funds in the Hong Kong & Shanghai Bank were placed at his disposal under the fictitious name of Leonard Brown. Turner, it was reported, had 'got quickly off the mark once we had started him in his activities, and at the time war was declared was already beginning to perform useful work'. Some of this 'useful work' included organising contacts with the Chinese communist representatives on Hainan Island, and supplying them with funds and smuggled-in stores. This suggests that some of the SOE operatives must have been Chinese.

The reconnaissance force had in fact predated the formation of the SOE unit with which it afterwards worked. The GOC, Hong Kong, had set it up with officers of the Volunteers and some civilians in July 1939 when it was code-named 'Z Force'. In early 1941 it set up food and ammunition dumps in various places in the New Territories, including one in the Tai Mo Shan caves high up in the mountains. The stores were transported there by mules belonging to the HK&SRA, the expedition being led by Lieutenant Bill Wiseman, RASC, with an escort of Hong Kong policemen under the command of Assistant Superintendent Geoffrey Wilson. 'It was no easy task,' Wiseman relates. 'On top of the fact that the Indian muleteers spoke no English and I spoke no Urdu, I had a wooden leg.'[40] Another policeman, George Wright-Nooth, was also an early member of 'Z Force', but both he and Wilson soon had to leave the force to concentrate on police duties.

After the Japanese attacked Hong Kong, two members of the reconnaissance group sank a Japanese transport ship in the harbour with a limpet mine, and other members of the force, using the caves as a base, mined a road and destroyed several lorries. Subsequently some of them escaped across China to reach safety in Chungking.[41]

In February 1941, after visiting Hong Kong, Air Chief Marshal Brooke-Popham and his staff concluded that the colony could hold out against a Japanese attack for at least four months – in the event the defence lasted only seventeen days. A few weeks later he urged that it be reinforced by two additional battalions, bringing the total to six, and that a policy be adopted of holding the port against the Japanese until it could be relieved. His idea was that it could then be used as a base for offensive operations. (In addition to the two Indian regiments already mentioned, there were two British battalions in Hong Kong, 2nd Royal Scots and 1st Middlesex.)

The Chiefs-of-Staff in London disagreed; so did Mr Churchill who declared there was 'not the slightest chance of holding Hong Kong or relieving it'.

Then came a new development. Brooke-Popham's idea of a prolonged defence had at least in part been due to discussions he had held with Major-General A.E. Grasett, the outgoing GOC, Hong Kong. On being relieved in July 1941, Grasett returned to England by way of Canada. In Ottawa he informed the Canadian General Staff that two additional battalions in Hong Kong would make it strong enough to withstand an attack for a long period.[42] When he arrived in London he gave an optimistic report there as well, declaring that such a reinforcement would show Japan that Britain intended to fight for the colony despite her commitments elsewhere, adding that Canada, in view of her interests in the Pacific, might be prepared to supply the battalions.

The upshot was that the British Chiefs-of-Staff approved the reinforcement, coming as it did 'from a hitherto unconsidered source'.[43] The Canadian government then agreed to a formal British request for the troops. The Winnipeg Grenadiers and Royal Rifles of Canada arrived in Hong Kong a little over three weeks prior to the Japanese attack. Most of their equipment never did arrive.*

In the summary of Brooke-Popham's secret despatch on the Far East printed in London in July 1942, the following paragraphs appeared under the heading 'Defence of Hong Kong':

> Hong Kong was regarded officially as an undesirable military commitment. General Chiang Kai-shek had accepted the withdrawal of [British] troops from Peking, Tientsin and Shanghai as inevitable, but a withdrawal from Hong Kong at the time the Burma Road was closed might have seriously affected his determination to fight on. The policy to defend Hong Kong may be said to have played an important part in the Chinese war effort during this critical period. Sir Robert also suggests that the de-militarisation of Hong Kong might have led to the Americans taking the same action in the Philippines. For these two reasons he feels the loss of six battalions and other troops was justified.
>
> The arrival of the two Canadian battalions on the 16th November 1941, made possible the defence of the mainland.

After that, a quote from the Swedish writer Karolina Sofia Key (1846–1926) might not be out of place: 'Everything, everything in war is barbaric'.

For several weeks before the Japanese onslaught, which came in the early hours of 8th December 1941, Major Charles Boxer of FECB had been in the habit of slipping over the New Territories frontier to visit Japanese officers in their HQ close to the Sham Chun River which formed part of the frontier. He became particularly friendly with the golf and whisky-loving Major-General Ito Takeo, taking him gifts of golf balls and Scotch. However, the Japanese were canny and gave away little information, and Boxer was not

* In view of the content of a Canadian television documentary shown around the world in 1995 in which Britain alone was castigated for allowing the two battalions to be sent to Hong Kong, it is worth while mentioning that Grasett was a Canadian, having been born in Toronto in 1888. Grasett's involvement in the decision was not mentioned in the documentary.

permitted to see anything outside the immediate bounds of the headquarters.

Early in November an agent reported that Japanese military activity around Canton and the Pearl River, some seventy miles away, was above normal. Then came a report from a Japanese army deserter that tanks, armoured cars, motor transport and massed troops had arrived near the frontier. The deserter, named as Private Yashinoa, had walked over the border and been closely interrogated by British Military Intelligence. When asked why he had deserted, Yashinoa replied that he was fed up with the Japanese army. Tim Carew, in his book *The Fall of Hong Kong* which was based on post-war interviews with officers who had served there, explained the incident:

> Yashinoa . . . had joined the Army because a friend of his in Tokyo had told him that it was a life of glory, honour and unbridled rape. None of these things had come Yashinoa's way; instead he had been abused by officers and slapped around by brutal noncoms. His leaves had been cancelled, he seemed to have walked the length and breadth of China and he hadn't raped a woman yet. There seemed little future in such an existence, so, in search of co-prosperity, he slipped across the frontier by night and presented himself with a courtly bow to the nearest British unit.[44]

As no sign of these movements had been detected by British forward observation posts, these reports coming from a lowly private were not believed. Carew blamed the FECB for this, but such a matter is more likely to have been handled directly by Military Intelligence.

On 29th November, in answer to a request from the War Office, General Maltby sent an estimate of the size of Japanese forces in the region of Canton that was grossly in error; he underestimated them by one division and by a large quantity of artillery.[45]

Whatever new troop dispositions the Japanese were making it seems they were carrying them out without the airwaves' eavesdroppers on Stonecutters learning of them. So successful were the Japanese in this, that about a week before the attack came, FECB Hong Kong, according to Captain Anthony Hewitt of the Middlesex Regiment, was able to issue an Intelligence Summary to the effect that war with Japan was less likely than it had been for some months past.[46] That, however, must be compared with a post-war statement made by Major R.G. Giles, RM, the SO (I), Hong Kong. He reported that 'Intelligence had known for at least ten days [before the attack] that some form of action by Japan was imminent'. But he went on to say, 'It was anticipated that the Japanese would by-pass the Colony for the time being and occupy Siam.'[47] It is Group Captain Alf Bennett's recollection that the GOC was given plenty of warning of the attack on the colony, although its exact timing was not known.

Bennett's comment is supported by a note in an official British file on General Maltby's post-war despatch on the campaign.[48] Maltby said the weakness of his intelligence service was a contributory cause leading to the fall of the colony, but since the author of the note was not so sure, he supplied himself the comments given in round brackets below:

> Hong Kong was warned well before the attack by FECB that an attack by one Japanese division, supported by a second, might be expected.
>
> It was known at Headquarters that great activity had taken place in the preceding month in the Canton area, where the Japanese had been reinforced by the equivalent of three divisions.
>
> The Japanese withdrew their outlying garrisons into a perimeter close around Canton city, and no news of their doings filtered out. (Comment: Absolutely typical of an intention to attack . . .)
>
> This great increase of the Japanese garrison was attributed (obviously by wishful thinking on the part of the Operations Staff, and certainly not by the Intelligence Bureau) to:
> (i) An intention to attack Kunming!
> (The General might as well have suggested Lhasa as an objective . . .)
> (ii) That they were constructing a base for an attack on Siam.
> (This is an even greater absurdity . . . [there was] her occupation of Indo-China, and it was known that Hainan was being stocked as a base . . .)
>
> (Comment: One can only attribute the General's attitude to his Intelligence as tinged with that form of wishful thinking which infected our politicians between the two wars. It is evident that the branch of FECB which was left to him under Major Boxer was taking no risks, for it kept a twenty-four watch on the wireless and gave him the warning at 0445 hours on the 8th December.
>
> According to Major Giles, the view of the Office was that the attack on Malaya was certain, but that it was on the cards that the Japanese would not think Hong Kong worth mopping up, but would simply mask it, while they were getting on with the bigger job.)

Whatever intelligence failings, if any, there were over reports about the dispositions and actions of Japanese forces prior to the attack, the authors of the British Official History had no right whatsoever to record that 'information on the quality of the Japanese forces was no better than the information about their dispositions'. That statement flies in the face of information FECB in Singapore had published in a booklet in late 1940, and which was republished with additions and modifications in India in March 1942. The booklet, entitled 'Japanese Army Memorandum', which gets no mention in the Official History, gives the lie to several of the myths in circulation at the time about Japanese inadequacies.

In spite of the confused intelligence situation in Hong Kong, at the end of November 1941 certain precautionary measures were implemented. British and Allied merchant shipping was diverted to Manila and Singapore, and the harbour was closed by night. Vital installations were closely guarded, and the coastwatch organisation mobilised. The Hong Kong Volunteers were not mobilised yet, as within the confines of the small colony, exercises had shown they could be at their allotted posts within six hours.

On 3rd December it seemed that the Japanese were withdrawing from the frontier area, which was probably a feint. On the following day, General Maltby, 'from information received', reckoned that the Japanese had insufficient forces in south China to launch a major attack on the colony. Then, on the evening of 6th December, three Japanese divisions were reported to be within eight miles of the frontier. Despite this, and what the Official History calls 'other indications', Maltby was not yet convinced that war was imminent. On 7th December he reported to the War Office that reports that between ten and twenty thousand troops were massed to attack the colony were certainly exaggerated and had the appearance of being deliberately fostered by the Japanese. He considered that the Japanese around Canton and the frontier area were distinctly nervous about being themselves attacked. (One can only wonder who by?) He also considered that the Japanese were disseminating reports to cover up their numerical weakness in south China. 'The four divisions in the area', commented the Official Historians, 'could hardly be described as numerical weakness.' In fact the intelligence report of 7th December proved to be surprisingly accurate, for on that date the Japanese 38th Division with attached troops was positioning itself for an attack.

When the attack came, Major Giles of FECB said:

> The New Territories were rapidly overrun and Fifth-Column activity handicapped our resistance. Formosans had since 1938 been seeping

> into the Colony in the guise of Fukienese whom they resemble in appearance. They acted as guides for the Japanese and reported British troop and other movements.

Major Giles went on to say that, 'Demolition of oil supplies was not very effective and tanks at Laichikok (where considerable damage was done) and at Gindrinkers Bay (Texaco) were captured by the enemy.' That example of badly carried out denial schemes was mirrored over and over again in the Malayan campaign 1,400 miles to the south.

A feature of the battle for the mainland part of the colony, and afterwards for the island of Hong Kong itself, was the incidence of sabotage and sniping carried out by followers of Wang Ching-wei, the Japanese puppet-ruler in northern China. The British often had to clear houses in their rear of such adherents before retreat was possible.[49]

The colony fell on Christmas Day 1941, and on that very day Lieutenant-Colonel Iguchi of the Imperial Japanese Army established a *kikan* there named after him. It had various sections, including espionage, counter-espionage, and a special department known as the 'Pacification section'. The latter's main task was to keep a close watch on Allied prisoners-of-war, and to do so it employed Indians as observers.[50]

Major Charles Boxer of FECB was badly injured in the arm during the fighting.* He and the other members of FECB were taken prisoner, but avoided interrogation. Major Giles reported in 1946 that three of the staff had been 'removed to Saigon but were returned to Hong Kong a month later to be interned in Stanley PoW Camp'. Giles's memory was at fault here. The only FECB staff member taken to Saigon was Squadron Leader Alf Bennett. The two men sent with him were Wing Commander Sullivan, Commanding

* Bill Wiseman, who had lost a leg in a civilian accident some years earlier, was wounded in his good leg during the fighting. He was placed in a hospital bed next to that of Charles Boxer's. He woke up one day to find the ward crowded with hissing and bowing Japanese officers, Major-General Ito foremost amongst them. Ito was returning the earlier favours, and had brought Boxer several bottles of whisky. After some minutes of chat in Japanese around Boxer's bed, General Ito bustled over to hiss and bow exceedingly low in front of the recumbent Wiseman before leading his officers from the room.

'What was all that about?' enquired Wiseman of his bedfellow.

'Oh,' Boxer replied with a smile, 'I told the General you had lost your leg at Dunkirk when you stopped a German tank by thrusting it through its tracks. It mightily impressed him.'

Officer of Kai Tak aerodrome, and a Flying Officer Grey. The Japanese believed that the three RAF men had information about the airfields in northern Malaya, but by the time the men reached Saigon the Japanese had already captured the airfields in question.

Six

'The Paris of the East'

During the 1930s there were several large centres of international intrigue in the Far East – Manila, Hong Kong, Singapore and Batavia (present-day Djakarta) fell into that category – but as hotbeds of conspiracy and espionage none of them surpassed Shanghai.

By 1930 Shanghai was known variously as 'The sixth city of the world', 'The Paris of the East', and 'The New York of the West'.[1] It had all begun with the 1842 Treaty of Nanking which ended the First Opium War and under which Shanghai became one of the so-called Treaty Ports. The place then began its transformation from a mere fishing village on a mudflat lying to the north of the old Chinese walled city into the most cosmopolitan city in the world and the home of some 3,000,000 souls.

The British were the first to open a factory there under the provisions of the Treaty which also permitted merchants and their families to reside there. Settlers from other countries soon followed, in particular the Americans and the French. In 1863, the British, American and other foreign zones in Shanghai merged into the International Settlement, though the former zonal distinctions were retained for a few purposes, except for the French Concession which remained independent. Concomitant with the development of Shanghai and the other Treaty Ports in China came the reorganisation under the supervision of Britain, the United States, and France, of the Chinese Customs Service. This was carried out with the 'concurrence' of the Chinese and the new service was renamed the Chinese Maritime

Customs Service. As the senior officers of it were nearly always British, it became a good source of shipping intelligence for Britain.

The International Settlement and the French Concession formed only a fraction of the much larger city, the Chinese part being administered by the Chinese Special Municipality of Shanghai, a body established in 1927 after Chiang Kai-shek's Nationalists conquered Southern China. This Municipal Council, set up in what was then China's only metropolis of note, was something of a test case for Chiang Kai-shek's ability to run China; he was striving to prove to the world that, under his leadership, the Chinese were quite capable of ruling themselves and so were deserving of recovering their sovereignty over the Treaty Ports, including all of Shanghai itself.

'Foreign' Shanghai was not a colony although many colonial attitudes prevailed among the non-Chinese population. The French Concession under a *Conseil d'Administration Municipale*, and the International Settlement under the Shanghai Municipal Council, were both self-governing bodies elected by a comparatively small number of merchants, property owners, and ratepayers. The President of the *Conseil* was always the French consul-general, which resulted in that body coming under a measure of French governmental control. So, up to 1927 when the Chinese Nationalists began pushing for more power, the 'foreign' parts of Shanghai were controlled exclusively by what has been called a 'Taipan Oligarchy'. By the 1930s the Chinese Nationalists had broken into this capitalists' paradise, and in 1934 provided five members of the elected fourteen-man ruling body of the Shanghai Municipal Council, the same number as Britain. The other four members were two Americans and two Japanese. Though the number of Chinese members was limited by agreement to five, the composition of the foreign contingent had come about by tradition, a sort of unwritten law. Indeed, later on in the decade the Council was expanded in numbers and other countries gained representation on it.

In addition to Britain, the United States and Japan, who all had representatives on the Shanghai Municipal Council, and France with its separate Concession, ten other countries enjoyed favoured nation treaties with China and exercised some extra-territorial privileges and rights within the International Settlement. These were Belgium, Brazil, Denmark, Italy, the Netherlands, Norway, Portugal, Spain, Sweden and Switzerland, each with its own Consular Court in Shanghai. The British had His Britannic Majesty's Supreme Court, and the Americans their United States Court for China. Chinese courts also operated within the Settlement, dealing not only with matters concerning their own nationals, but also with the nationals of other countries which, although represented in Shanghai, had no extra-territorial rights. Those countries were Austria, Germany, Hungary, and Russia.

There were some 25,000 White Russians in the city with no allegiance to any country. These refugees had, over the years since the Russian Revolution, made their way southeastward through China via Harbin to settle in the city. Most had arrived with little more than the clothes on their backs, and now eked out precarious and obscure livings. Many were ex-military men, and some of these were used by local shipping magnates aboard their vessels as armed guards against the pirates that abounded in the China Seas. They were trained and armed by the Shanghai Police. The White Russian community also became an important source of recruits for the intelligence services of many nations. By the mid-1930s too, as a result of purges in Nazi Germany, many German Jews had taken up residence there.

In the early days of the Settlement some of the principal consulates ran their own police forces, but that situation soon evolved into the establishment of the Shanghai Municipal Police force (SMP) with responsibilities throughout the Settlement and on some of the roads leading into it from the Chinese-controlled parts of the city. The French looked after their own Concession through the French Concession Police (FCP). The Japanese with a force of Consular Police, sometimes estimated as being 250 in strength and including within its ranks members of the Japanese Secret Service, on occasion arrested their own nationals without reference to the SMP. A US Marshal attached to the US Court for China was empowered to do the same for American citizens. On top of that, the countries that maintained military and naval presences in the area operated military and naval police patrols. From 1927 the parts of the city controlled by the Nationalist Chinese were policed by the Public Security Bureau (PSB), into which after 1930 were drafted officers trained at the Central Officers School of the Chinese army. The PSB had close connections with Chiang Kai-shek's Secret Service. Indeed, Tai Li, one day to be the Head of that Secret Service, was in Shanghai from 1927 as a captain in the Military Police. The man who was to become his counterpart in the Chinese Communist Secret Service, K'ang Sheng, was also in Shanghai at about the same time.

In the 1930s Shanghai offered all the pleasures and vices that one would expect of the most cosmopolitan city in the world, as the guide book of 1934, entitled *All About Shanghai*, indicated:

> Shanghai flames with millions of flashing jewels at midnight.
> The centre of night life is a vast crucible of electric flame.
> The throb of the jungle tom-tom; the symphony of lust;
> the music of a hundred orchestras; the shuffling of feet;
> the swaying of bodies; the rhythm of abandon; the hot smoke
> of desire – desire under the floodlights; it's all fun; it's life.
> Joy, gin, and jazz. There's nothing puritanical about Shanghai.

In fact, that was but the half of it. Beneath the thick mantle of affluence in this single most important piece of real estate in the Orient – American investment in the city alone was estimated to have been $250,000,000 in 1937 – lay a vast underworld of pimps and prostitutes, spies and seditionists, traitors and touts, drug addicts and drug pedlars, Triad gangsters and gunmen.

Many of the prostitutes were White Russian girls who apparently made a good living out of it. Sergeant Maurice Tinkler of the Shanghai Municipal Police Force, in a letter to his sister in England, wrote:

> Some of the Russian girls here, young, amazingly beautiful, clever and well educated, are worse than libertines. To start with conditions are abnormal. White women have an inflated value because of the fact that the greater part of the white population consists of males, and, if a woman with any looks whatever leaves the narrow path of virtue, you bet your life she lives at about $500 a month, with automobiles, jazz and everything. Shanghai is nothing but jazz.

Tinkler knew what he was talking about. In another letter to his sister, who one imagines must have been rather broadminded for the times, he made it clear that he had partaken of the wares of some of these Tsarist beauties.[2]

Shanghai had become the crime centre of the Orient, a fact that can partly be attributed to the prevalence of warlord armies in China, as such armies provided fine training for gangsters. It also proved a profitable haven for international criminals.[3] The many nationalities and factions represented there also made it, in the words of Major-General Charles Willoughby, who was General

MacArthur's Chief of Intelligence from 1941 to 1945, 'a veritable witch's cauldron of international intrigue'.[4]

At one time or another, elements of the criminal fraternity in Shanghai were made use of by both the Chinese Nationalist and Chinese Communist Secret Services, and the Japanese also used the services of the underworld's drug network. The dominant Triad in Shanghai was known as the Green Circle, with a membership of some 100,000. From time to time, neither the SMP nor the FCP were loath to seek the help of this Triad in solving crimes, always of course, those in which the Triad had no direct interest.

Policing the city was one of the toughest police operations in the world, and the three police forces involved had suitably robust reputations. The Chinese Public Security Bureau, operating in its own part of the city, had a special reputation for taking extreme action. Acting without the constraints set by at least a veneer of civilised police behaviour imposed on the other two organisations, PSB officers often resorted to torture to gain confessions, and as its senior officers were from the Chinese military and opposed to Communism, they tended to act harshly against members of communist cells they unearthed.

The veneer of civilised police behaviour of the SMP sometimes cracked under pressure. In 1923 six of its detectives, two British, three Chinese and one Japanese, were arrested and charged with torturing a prisoner. The charges were later dropped, but the officers concerned were dismissed from the service.

The French Concession Police, like the British-run SMP, was imbued with attitudes created by being part of a global system of imperialism. The senior French police officers, often Corsicans, a traditionally tough race, had served in French colonial armies or police forces in North Africa and Indo-China. Many of the lower FCP grades were Annamese from Indo-China – Annam is one of the states which make up present-day Viet Nam.

Some senior officers of the SMP had previously served in the Indian or Straits Settlements Police Services, or in the British or Indian armies. Captain W.G. Clarke, for example, had served in the Indian Police before becoming head of the SMP Sikh Contingent. He later rose to be Deputy Commissioner in charge of CID in Shanghai, and if an article in the *China Weekly Review* in October 1929 is correct, he was considered by many Shanghai residents to be the top British Secret Intelligence Service man in China at that time. Generally speaking, SMP officers who had held military titles tended to retain them. Hence the last British Commissioner of Police before the city was taken over by the Japanese in December 1941, was always known as Major K.M. Bourne. His British Deputy was an ex-Gurkha officer, Captain H.M. Smyth.

The SMP was a multi-national force and in 1938 had a total strength of 4,774 of which 3,550 were Chinese, with 502 Sikhs, 270 Japanese and another 452 lumped together under the heading 'foreign'.[5] This force policed an area of about nine square miles and operated from fourteen police stations. One of these, at Louza, had the dubious honour of being the busiest in the world as far as handling crime was concerned.

A measure of the toughness of members of the SMP is that several of them during World War Two, and in places far removed from Shanghai, were given exacting war roles. At least four were used as Field Security Officers during the battle for Malaya and Singapore. One of these, Detective Sub-Inspector E.M. Golder, who had been given the rank of captain in the British army, is known to have been a member of the 'death squad' that arbitrarily dealt with suspected fifth-columnists on Singapore Island. Golder became a PoW in Changi, and was one of those who 'kept their heads down' during those days for fear of Japanese reprisals. Two other SMP officers whose services were used in Singapore were the Canadian-born 'Snowy' Whittaker, and one-time London policeman Reg Bloor. Another ex-Shanghai man was William Stafford. Previously a sailor, Stafford had served on the Shanghai River with the Admiralty police where he worked closely with the SMP river branch. He had then transferred to the Admiralty police in Singapore, and managed to escape on one of the last ships to leave that island prior to its surrender in February 1942. He then became a member of Force 136 and worked with guerrillas in the Burmese jungle. After the war he joined the Singapore police, and, during the Malayan Emergency became known as 'Two-Gun' Stafford, or the 'Iron Broom', and was famous as the man who shot Lau Yew, a top communist terrorist in an ambush in which Stafford had disguised himself as a Russian communist.

Two other ex-SMP men, Major W.E. Fairbairn now with the rank of colonel, and Sergeant Sykes, taught at the Special Operations Executive School at Arisaig in Scotland in the early years of the war. They were specialists in weapons and unarmed combat, and together invented the commando knife. Fairbairn had written two books on unarmed combat, one of which was called *Scientific Self-Defence*. Published in Shanghai in 1931, it became the standard textbook on the subject for both the SMP and the Hong Kong Police. His silent killing methods, for which he had coined the word 'defendu', were a fusion of the more extreme actions of ju-jitsu and karate with the even more lethal arts he had learned in order to keep himself alive on the Shanghai waterfront. Fairbairn must have impressed the Americans for they borrowed him later in the war to train some of their Office of Strategic Services (OSS) operatives at the Oshawa training camp near Toronto.

At sergeant rank and above, most SMP men were British, but some were Chinese, Japanese, White Russians, a few Americans, and a handful of other nationalities, including at least one Dutchman.

Unlike candidates for British colonial police forces who were recruited by the Crown Agents, SMP men recruited in Britain were dealt with by a commercial firm, John Pook & Company of 168 Fenchurch Street, London. Interviews were conducted by John Pook himself sitting with any senior SMP officers who happened to be on leave in England at the time. Some candidates were recruited directly in Shanghai; this applied especially to men who had served in the British army there and who wished to stay on. The standards required of applicants, especially physical standards, were exceptionally high. Candidates came from many walks of life, including British police forces, the army and the Merchant Service – the latter no doubt chosen because in their visits to some of the less salubrious ports of the world they would have learned some of the methods of self-preservation adapted by Major Fairbairn. Some successful candidates, however, came from backgrounds which were not manifestly tough. One of these, Ted Quigley, who joined in 1937/38, had been a furniture-maker.[6] A sense of adventure was a requirement, but any candidate who showed too much of a bent for a Sax Rohmer-type role, or who showed signs of being over-keen on the known pleasures of Shanghai, was soon weeded out. On arrival at Shanghai recruits received their initial training at the Ping-Liang Depot, where one of the weapons they were trained to use was the tommy-gun, the favourite weapon of the SMP's famous riot squads. All were taught 'quick-draw' pistol techniques, and were ordered to have the safety-catches of their weapons in the 'off' position whenever they were on patrol. A requisite for promotion was passing an examination in the Shanghai dialect.

SMP had its own Special Branch (SB) which was divided into six sections. S1 had a supervisory role and covered general enquiries together with Russian, Japanese and Jewish affairs. S2 looked after Chinese liaison matters, and S3, film censorship. S4 dealt with Indian affairs, primarily the collecting of information on subversive activity of British Indians. S5 held a purview over newspapers and translations, whilst S6 was concerned with boarding-houses, shipping and general licence applications. A measure of the influence of British imperialistic attitudes in Shanghai, and of the concern in London and Delhi over the rise in Indian nationalism, is that the most secret of these sections was S4, for there were many Indians in the city.

SMP's multi-national make-up must often have provided SB with some special internal problems. The rank and file were mostly Chinese with a fair proportion of Indians, and the force had some Chinese and Japanese officers. As SB's main tasks in the pre-war years was dealing with Chinese communist and associated Russian Comintern activities, with Indian seditionists, and with Japanese intriguing, it is clear SB must have had its work cut out. Stanley Knowles, formerly of the SMP, says that 'Japanese officers made life difficult . . . they were mischief makers'.[7] One Japanese, C. Akagi, held the rank of Special Deputy Commissioner of Police in 1938, and one can surmise that it must have been difficult to keep him from seeing reports that were 'Japan sensitive'.

Despite these difficulties SB managed to do some excellent work in surveillance and reporting on these matters. It had close contacts with Indian Police CID in Delhi which had an obvious interest in the Indian nationalists living in Shanghai, and with the Singapore Police. But in the early 1930s it was over communist activities that the SMP's Special Branch met with their greatest successes. In 1933 SB uncovered within SMP's own ranks a communist Red Brigade cell that had been set up three years earlier, and arrested several of its members. An early success illustrates the close working relationship that existed between SMP and the Singapore Police. A message intercepted by the Singapore Police from an organisation calling itself Shanghai Central, and addressed to the Singapore Communist Party, was passed to SMP through the office of the British consul-general, Shanghai. It mentioned a certain bookstore in the city as being a meeting place for subversives. The shop was placed under surveillance and later arrest warrants were issued for all found on the premises.

As a matter of routine SMP and the French Concession Police exchanged information and worked closely together, for there were few restrictions on people passing between the International and French sectors. Many foreigners worked in the International Settlement but had homes in the more elegant parts of the French Concession. Both police forces had regular contact with British, United States and French military intelligence officers attached to their respective consulates, and with Military Attachés at the embassies in Nanking. The French were particularly concerned with communist-inspired anti-imperialist propaganda being distributed among their Annamese police officers and garrison troops.

Perhaps the greatest anti-communist success achieved by this co-operation – a success aided by a valuable contribution from Singapore – was in the so-called Hilaire Noulens case. In the late 1920s the Comintern had set up its Far East Bureau to control its agents throughout the East. The Bureau maintained a courier system between Shanghai, Berlin and Moscow and developed a system of coded letters, postal boxes rented under assumed names, and safe houses. It was responsible for distributing in various currencies to agents throughout the east a sum amounting to $55,000 per annum. Noulens, who had arrived in the city using a stolen Belgian passport, was in charge of these communications, and worked under the cover of being the secretary of the Pan-Pacific Trade Union. He was a man of many aliases: Paul Ruegg, Charles Alison and Dr W. O'Neill being just a few of them. Even Hilaire Noulens was an alias, for he was in fact a NKVD (forerunner of the KGB) agent called Luft.[8] It was the French Concession Police who gained the first inkling of the existence of the Far East Bureau after Annamese communists arrested in the Concession divulged its existence under interrogation in April 1931. The FCP were unable to track the Bureau down although they did obtain further confirmation of its existence. Then in June 1931 Singapore Special Branch arrested a French Comintern agent called Joseph Decroux who had on his person papers giving telegraphic code and post-box addresses in Shanghai. Through the British consulate-general's office, this information was passed to SMP Special Branch which, working in conjunction with the French Police, identified Noulens as the box holder. After a period of surveillance Noulens was arrested and three steel boxes found at his address proved to be the Bureau's archives. Other addresses were raided and Noulens was arrested. Many other documents were seized, including code-books and lists of cover organisations and agents' names. Like the Japanese Secret Service, but not on the same scale, the Russians used a number of commercial organisations as fronts. One in Shanghai that was on Decroux's lists was the *Centrosojus* Russian Tea Company. The discovery of these lists led to a number of arrests throughout the region. One of Noulens's many correspondents was Nguyen Ai Quoc, who was arrested in Hong Kong on 31st July 1931 and sentenced by a military court there to two years' imprisonment. He was also known as Ho Chi Minh.

The Far East Bureau's archives also identified some Japanese communists operating in Shanghai. Their names were handed to the Japanese Consular Police and several were arrested, most of them being students. Another facet of co-operation with the Japanese was that the Japanese Secret Service aided the overall investigation by identifying some of the couriers and routes involved in transporting Bureau funds north through territory occupied by them.

Noulens and his wife were handed over to the Chinese authorities who decided they were to be tried by a military court. The couple were transferred to Nanking and were brought to trial there in October. Meanwhile a committee to help 'the secretary of the Pan-Pacific Trade Union' had been set up in Shanghai; its members included the editor of one of the city's English language newspapers, and the American journalist called Agnes Smedley.

Noulens was condemned to death and his wife to life imprisonment, but the 'help committee' raised an international clamour. In face of it, Chiang Kai-shek ordered a new trial in a civilian court which took place in July 1932. The Noulenses were found guilty again, and this time both were sentenced to death. However, under a general amnesty the sentences were commuted to life imprisonment. They were to serve only five years, for the Japanese released them after taking Nanking in 1937. It is believed they went back to the USSR and eventually perished in one of Stalin's purges.

Despite Chiang Kai-shek's desire that the world see the Chinese could run their own affairs in the form of the Chinese Municipal Council, the nationalistic zeal of the Chinese Public Security Bureau was soon tempered by a measure of pragmatism. Their increasing fear of a communist take-over caused them to request co-operation from both the SMP and FCP, and gradually a flow of information on these matters developed between all three forces. Sometimes this co-operation had deadly results. In January 1931, for example,

SMP received through British intelligence sources information that Moscow was concentrating its financial and personnel resources in the area on fostering antagonism against 'imperialist' nations. In consequence SMP Special Branch raided a clandestine meeting of communists being held at the Eastern Hotel in Thibet Road. Thirty-six men and women were arrested, to be promptly handed over to the PSB. Less than two weeks later twenty-three of them, including three women, were secretly shot and two months were to pass before the residents of Shanghai got to know of the event. The PSB did not show the same keenness in regard to co-operation over Indian nationalist matters, however. These Indians, after all, were but pursuing the same anti-imperialist aims as the Chinese themselves.

Surviving SMP records show that in the 1930s the force was on the track of a Chinese communist-inspired conspiracy to overthrow Chiang Kai-shek and his Nationalist government, though the full extent of the intrigue was not known. Not all SMP records survived World War Two. Some were no doubt weeded out by the Japanese during the occupation years 1941–45, and others were interfered with when the Chinese gained control of the city at the end of the war. Those that did survive – some of which had been tampered with – were collected together and micro-filmed in 1945 after a search headed by General Willoughby, the American Chief of Intelligence in Occupied Japan. The micro-films are now in the US National Archives.

SMP had extensive files on a number of foreigners conducting activities in the city for the Comintern in Moscow and for Red Army Intelligence. Indeed, as a matter of course SMP and the French police kept records on most foreigners. Amongst these was Agnes Smedley, the American who had been a prime mover in forming the 'help committee' for Hilaire Noulens. Smedley had arrived in Shanghai in 1929 and finally left in 1937. She was heavily engaged in propagating the communist ethic in those years and was involved with many social and cultural organisations that facilitated her main reason for being in the city. A chart in the SMP file on Smedley showed her many associations, including those with Indian nationalist groups, among them the Hindustan Association of Berlin, the Indian Youth League, and the Indian Revolutionary Society. Special Branch knew her to be in the service of the Eastern Division of the Communist International.[9]

Other American communists involved in the Shanghai scene were Paul Eugene Walsh and Leon Minster. Walsh's real identity was

Eugene Dennis who, after World War Two, led the American Communist Party. He was in Shanghai during 1933 and 1934, propagating communist ideas especially among labour unions within the dock area. He was also reported to be engaged in 'penetration of various armed forces stationed in the Settlement'. Leon Minster was a naturalised American, having been born in Russia. He was in Shanghai throughout 1934 and 1935, where he set up a shop selling radios, a cover for operating his long-range radio equipment. His wife was the sister of V.M. Molotov who from 1939 became the Soviet Union's long-term Foreign Minister.

Other foreign agents espousing Moscow's ideals in Shanghai at various times in the 1930s were a man called Koenig around 1934, and Joseph Walden from 1935. But there were many others.

SMP's successful surveillance of Walsh and Koenig, which culminated in raids on the places where they lived, caused Harry Steptoe, who under the front of being the British consul in Shanghai was Britain's top Secret Service man there from around 1934* to write the following to the then Deputy Commissioner of Police, T.P. Givens, on 19th January 1935:

> Broadly speaking the function of the Comintern is to act as the mainspring of an illegal conspiracy against international law and order. The function of the Police is to preserve that law and order . . . it is very often the case, that we do not except in outstanding cases, like the Noulens case, see the results of painstaking enquiry and watching . . . In watching Koenig as the Special Branch officer so successfully did . . . caused a complete breakdown in the liaison services of the Comintern of which he was head.[10]

Many communist agents in Shanghai in the early part of the decade met regularly at the Zeitgeist Bookshop run by a German, Fräulein Irene Weidemeyer. She had married Wu Shao-kuo, a Chinese communist, but retained her former name. The shop was a clearing house for communist information. She had ties with Mrs V.N. Sotov, the wife of the Head of the Russian News Agency TASS in Shanghai.

Some of the communist agents mentioned were mainly engaged

* Harry Steptoe had served in an SIS capacity in China since at least 1927. His original cover was as a reporter on an English-language Shanghai newspaper.

in political matters, but the activities of others in Shanghai lay solely in the field of military intelligence. One such group was called the 'Lehman group'. Its head arrived in Shanghai in late 1929 or early 1930 and reported to the 4th Bureau of the Red Army, and his prime duty was a preparatory one in establishing radio communications between Shanghai, other parts of China, and with Moscow. One of the radio technicians involved was called Max Klausen. Another Shanghai-based group engaged in collecting military intelligence was called the 'Frolich-Feldman group'. Its head was Major-General Frolich of the Red Army, and its task was to make contacts with the Chinese Red Army and to gather intelligence concerning it. Lieutenant-Colonel Feldman was the group's radio expert. It met with little success and left Shanghai during 1931.

However the Russian spy who is arguably the most successful agent in the history of espionage was Richard Sorge. Kim Philby, a man who knew a successful spy if anyone did, expressed to his biographer a great admiration for Sorge. 'He felt that Sorge was the only secret agent beyond reproach.'[11] Shanghai became Sorge's espionage training ground from 1930, but later he went on to much greater things in Japan. SMP had a file on him but it seems not to have been an extensive one. If that is so, then it must be regarded as a measure of his success as an undercover agent. On the other hand the file may have been subjected to a weeding process by the Japanese when they took control of the city in December 1941.

Richard Sorge was born in Baku, Russia in 1895, the son of a German father working in Russia with an oil firm, and a Russian mother. When he was still a child the family moved back to Germany. His paternal grandfather, Adolf Sorge, had once been secretary to Karl Marx.

Sorge joined the German army in 1914 and was wounded twice. During extended convalescence, and again after the war, he studied at universities in Berlin, Kiel and Hamburg, ending with a Doctorate in Political Science in 1920. His political bias may have stemmed either from his paternal grandfather or from his days in Hamburg, the seat of early German Communism. He became a schoolteacher, and sometime coalminer, and in 1922 began writing for left-wing newspapers, introducing many of his pupils and fellow miners to Marxism. Besides being bilingual in German and Russian, in later years he could converse well in English, French, Japanese, and possibly Chinese. By 1924 his activities in German Communism had attracted the attention of Moscow and he was summoned there to become a Comintern agent. From 1927 to 1929 he was in Scandinavia and Britain as a special representative of the Comintern's Intelligence and Organisation Bureau. According to Peter Wright in his book *Spycatcher*, while he was in London Sorge met Captain Charles 'Dickie' Ellis, a senior SIS officer. Wright was convinced that Ellis was in the pay of the Russians but his evidence for saying so is extremely flimsy.

Back in Moscow in 1929, Sorge urged upon his superiors the need to split espionage from Party activity, arguing that whenever Party activists were arrested overseas, intelligence agents associated with them tended to be arrested as well. Red Army Intelligence was sympathetic to this view, and Sorge transferred to the 4th Bureau of the Red Army Staff, the Army's top intelligence agency, also known as the GRU. Henceforth in his overseas postings Sorge had little to do with local Party activists, a fact that almost certainly contributed to his success as a spy.

Sorge was sent to Shanghai in January 1930 with the cover of correspondent for the German *Soziologische Magazin*, and travelling under a German passport. He developed a spy ring of about twenty agents throughout China, and seems to have been guided by three principles in his selection of agents: 1) there was not a Russian among them; 2) every agent was a Party member or fellow traveller but avoided association whenever possible with the Chinese Communist Party; 3) the group worked on a need-to-know basis, some being unaware of the existence of the others. Agnes Smedley was of the group, and so was the radio technician Max Klausen. There were at least three Chinese and five Japanese agents amongst the others. Sorge's most successful work was to be conducted in Tokyo, but the foundations for that success were laid in Shanghai.

According to Sorge's own testimony, his duties in China included: a) making analyses of the Chinese classes supporting the Nationalist government and investigating that government's military strength; b) studying and assessing the strengths of the anti-government factions and analysing the actions of the British, the Americans and the Japanese towards these factions (the British, for example, with the security of Hong Kong in mind, were seeking *rapprochement* with such factions in South China); and c) keeping a close watch on foreign garrison forces and fleets in China, especially of changes to them.[12]

There was an increasing number of German military advisers

arriving in China at that time, and Sorge produced a detailed study for Moscow of their activities. He was able to get close to many of the Germans as they considered him to be one of themselves. Germany was endeavouring to increase its political prestige in China and, through its military advisers' recommendations, hoped to supply China with war materials. China, in fact, became something of a proving ground for the German aeronautical industry, and Sorge's reports on that must have been extremely valuable to the Russians.

Sorge was in Shanghai in 1932 during the first of the two so-called 'Shanghai Incidents' – the second and major one was to take place in 1937 as part of the broader 'China Incident'. It was the year after the conquest of Manchuria by the Japanese who, in an attempt to divert international attention from their northern activities, opened a second front in Shanghai. The Japanese occupied the Chinese part of the city and the surrounding countryside, only to agree to evacuate them again four months later after international negotiations. Moscow 'viewed the new Japanese activity with new eyes and, perforce, with new apprehension', said Sorge. 'It goes without saying that I devoted the closest attention to these new problems.'

A prominent Japanese member of Sorge's spy-ring in Shanghai, and later in Japan itself, was Ozaki Hozumi. He was a journalist in Shanghai serving as special correspondent for the *Osaka Asahi* from 1928 to 1932. He had developed leftist leanings as a boy and was hostile to Japanese militarism and in China associated with several left-wing groups. Agnes Smedley introduced him to Sorge in 1930. All members of the group had code names, and Ozaki knew Sorge only as 'Johnson', and it was not until 1936 in Tokyo that Ozaki found out Sorge's true identity. From that time on Ozaki was a Soviet agent, and he began to supply Sorge with information on Japanese policy towards China.

Max Klausen, the radio operator, was another member of the ring. He, who had the rank of major in the Red Army, was a German born in Schleswig-Holstein in 1899. He became interested in Communism after joining the German Seamen's Union in Hamburg. He went to Moscow in 1929, and then to Shanghai as part of the Lehman group.

One member of the ring was an American journalist with the cover name 'Jacob', who has never been firmly identified. This author has been given information that indicates the journalist was Mark Gayn, one-time member of the staff of the Japanese Domei News Agency, and Far East correspondent for *The Washington Post* from 1934 to 1939. Gayn certainly was of a leftist persuasion.[13]

A bizarre and shadowy character living in Shanghai at the time does not fit easily into any particular facet of the espionage scene there, though with his record he was almost certainly involved, especially if there was financial gain to be made. SMP had an extensive file on him. In Shanghai he was known as 'Abbot' Chao King, but his real name was Trebitsch Lincoln. A Hungarian Jew, he had arrived in England in 1902 and became, of all things, a Church of England curate at Ashford in Kent. He gained British citizenship, and in 1909 was elected Liberal Member of Parliament for Darlington. Finding himself in financial difficulties he did not defend the seat and was subsequently made bankrupt. During World War One he spied for the Germans on the continent. He then went to the States but was extradited to Britain to face charges of forging Seebohm Rowntree's signatures, and was sentenced to three years' imprisonment. After his release and several other adventures in the espionage field, he arrived in China in the 1920s and entered a lamasery. He attempted a return to Britain in 1926 when his son Natzl was about to be executed for murder, but was refused admission, something that aggravated his already deep-seated hatred of Britain. There is little doubt that such a man would have been involved on at least the fringe of espionage in China, and that his efforts would likely have been against British interests. Trebitsch Lincoln died in Shanghai on 9th October 1943 during World War Two.

Although the Soviets were prepared to spend considerable amounts of money on intelligence and subversion in the Shanghai area, Britain was much more frugal.

The Director of Naval Intelligence (DNI) in London was one senior member of the British Intelligence Services who recognised the importance of Shanghai as 'the sounding board for the Far East'. As the 1930s progressed and the situation in that part of the world grew ever more grave, pressure grew for an upgrading of British intelligence-gathering in the area to support the work of the Far East Combined Bureau. But getting sanction and proper finance from a parsimonious Admiralty and its political masters for such upgrading proved extremely difficult, even in what appear now to have been matters requiring comparatively minor financial adjustments. This is evidenced by the two-way flow of letters, signals and memoranda around 1936 and 1937 between the C-in-C, China Fleet, and Admiral

Dickens, the DNI in London, regarding the status of the Staff Officer (Intelligence) in Shanghai who held the comparatively low rank of Lieutenant-Commander.[14]

Members of the British community in Shanghai, and officers of the Merchant Service calling at the port, were in a position to supply 'most valuable information about shipping movements, the Japanese armed forces, and the trends of Chinese and Japanese policy and public opinion. It was a matter of getting hold of this intelligence', and Lieutenant-Commander Ryder, the SO (I) in 1937, complained that he had neither the means nor the status to facilitate this. He could not, he said, mix on equal terms with business and official magnates of the city, nor, as a mere passed-over lieutenant-commander, was he likely to rate membership of the prestigious and highly selective Shanghai Club, located at No. 3, The Bund, in the heart of the Shanghai business area and overlooking the River Whampoa.[15]

If Ryder ever held hopes of gaining the promotion previously denied him, or of obtaining an appropriate allowance, he was to be disappointed. Despite the C-in-C's efforts to get his appointment extended, he was replaced by a serving officer of the Royal Marines, Major R. Neville, who had previously served as SO (I) Jamaica. This was in fact an upgrading concession, for Marine majors serving ashore were always treated as if they were a rank higher, that is, lieutenant-colonel, the equivalent of a navy commander. This change occurred after Admiral Dickens in London had vehemently turned down what he called 'the most improper suggestion that an officer of private means might be selected for the post'.

Such changes in personnel did not seem always to result in an immediate rise in efficiency. An Admiralty file notes that:

> It is impossible not to feel extreme sympathy with the SO (I's) of Shanghai, Hong Kong and Singapore who were apparently expected to come out new from England and at once become conversant with the complexities of eastern life and politics, which baffle those who have spent years in China and the adjacent countries. That they tackled the task with energy and ability is shown by the fact that Sir Percy Noble, C-in-C, China Fleet, was able to report that FECB had in 1937 fully justified its existence, and 'amid the turmoil of Shanghai and the wild rumours of Hong Kong' the C-in-C received 'unfailingly reliable information from the Chief of Intelligence Staff and it is impossible to speak too highly of the work of the Combined Intelligence Bureau at Hong Kong'.[16]

In 1938, at the time of the Shanghai crisis, Major Neville convened a meeting of all retired RN and RNR officers in the city. About a dozen attended to hear Neville explain that the Admiralty required volunteers to set up a Naval Control Service. He got his volunteers, and the organisation was headed by Commander J.B. Woolley, RN (Retd). Woolley and his assistants, one of whom was Lieutenant-Commander P.C. Gilmour, were housed in a room close to Neville's in the British consulate-general's buildings. This was a large complex which occupied *the* prime site on The Bund, and which stretched far back from the river.

The Naval Control Service began keeping plots of shipping movements in the area, but it seems that the Admiralty soon lost interest in the project for plans to send the volunteers to Hong Kong for training fell through and the unit was disbanded. On 26th August 1939, a week before the war with Germany broke out, the organisation was resurrected and fortunately Woolley, Gilmour and some of the other retired officers were still available to take part in it.

Over the years the Chinese Maritime Customs Service (CMCS), with its main office in Shanghai and controlled mainly by the British, provided cover for several Britons engaged in the collection of intelligence. One of these was Colonel Francis Hayley Bell, who was a CMCS Commissioner until he retired in 1931. His official job was a roving one, and he travelled the coasts and river estuaries of China in a small customs' gunboat. At one time or another he was based at most of the main ports along the Chinese coast. He spoke several Chinese dialects, and although he did not speak their language, made many contacts with Japanese businessmen and traders. During his years in China, Hayley Bell worked for British intelligence in an unofficial sort of way, passing on the many scraps of information he picked up during his travels.[17]

The Japanese conquests along most of the Chinese coast after 1937 resulted in their gaining de facto control of many aspects of the CMCS. This was a blow for the British who had used it as an excellent source for shipping and general intelligence. Even so, after 1939 Commander Woolley was still able to rely upon getting a good deal of information on Japanese shipping movements from that source.

Naval Intelligence was not the only British intelligence organisation busy in Shanghai. In 1929 it was general knowledge in the city that Captain W.G. Clarke of the SMP was the senior Secret Intelligence

Service man in China. Later, SMP Deputy Commissioner T.P. Givens became SIS's man in the SMP, a fact that was also well-known in the city. There are references to his being in the British Secret Service in the files of the French Concession Police.[18] As in other places in the Far East it seems that in Shanghai it was impossible for the British to maintain much secrecy over these appointments, a symptom perhaps of the difficulties involved when Europeans attempt to work undercover in eastern lands, and aggravated in a few cases by an apparent inability of some agents to be discreet.

British Military Intelligence maintained a Shanghai Army Intelligence Office as an adjunct to 'Shaforce' (Shanghai Defence Force) which had been sent in to secure the International Settlement in 1927 at the time of the Nationalist capture of the city. The GSOI with that force was John Vereker, later Field-Marshal Viscount Gort. The Military Intelligence Office was located at the British consulate-general, and towards the end of the 1930s was manned by a Japanese-speaking GSOI and a Chinese-speaking GSO2. The office kept in close touch with the SO (I) and with SIS officers in the city, which was not difficult to do as all were housed in the same building. The senior of the two military officers was always the Japanese speaker, no doubt an indication of the War Office's opinion of the relative importance of the two nations.

During the 1930s, and due to the movements of the Chinese Nationalist Government forced upon them by the actions of Japanese military forces, the British consulate-general was upgraded almost to embassy status, the International Settlement being considered a safe haven for diplomats.

There was nothing unique about its involvement in intelligence; staff at embassies and consulates of nations everywhere have always engaged in intelligence work, and in Britain's case this is one reason why full consular records have never appeared in the public domain. Nevertheless, the Shanghai experience provides some idea of what went on in important and strategically placed consulates at the time.

Examples of how the consulate acted as a two-way conduit between the SMP Special Branch and its counterparts in India and Singapore have already been mentioned. SMP records show that even earlier than the examples given, in 1929, C.M. Halland, the Military Intelligence Officer then based at the consulate, passed information from New Delhi to the SMP regarding Indian nationalists and suspected communists. In 1931 Halland was pooling similar information with his opposite number in the US consulate, this time the information deriving from Singapore. Much of this information would have been received over the consulate's own radio communications system, a system no doubt used at various times by each of the intelligence branches housed inside the consulate premises.

But consular involvement did not end with communications and the supply of offices. A letter from Consul Harry Steptoe, in 1935, to T.P. Givens, policeman and SIS agent, concerning communist conspiracies, has already been quoted (page 109). Other portions of the same letter indicate that Steptoe had a wide knowledge of intelligence in such matters. 'In the case of Walsh *we know* that part of his functions was the penetration of various armed services stationed here', he wrote. Near the end of the letter we read, 'The cumulative effect of the blows dealt . . ., *I know*, is great and is causing much uneasiness in Comintern circles'. [Author's italics in both instances.] His 'we know' and 'I know' are informative, for Steptoe was not only an SIS man himself, but the top SIS man in southern China.

One of two Military Intelligence officers based at the consulate in 1936, was Major A.K. Ferguson.[19] The other was Major E. Ainger, of the 3rd Hussars. Early that year an Australian Member of Parliament, Hon. Charles Hawker, on what can only be described as an intelligence-gathering tour of Japan, Manchuria and China, visited Shanghai and had discussions with Ferguson and later with the Commodore, Hong Kong. Hawker wrote an extensive report in which he noted that Japanese troops in the field seemed superior to European troops. However, his conversations with Ferguson and the Commodore led him to write that the Japanese navy was ten years out of date, an observation that was not true even in 1936. Later in 1936 V.G. Bowden, an Australian with many years' experience in China, was appointed Australian Trade Commissioner, China, based in Shanghai. He was both a Chinese and a Japanese speaker. He began remitting diplomatic and trade intelligence reports home to Canberra, which in fact contained many observations on military matters.[20]

The office of the US consulate-general in Shanghai was also a centre for the collection of intelligence. The Americans set up a wireless intercept station in the consulate as early as 1924. Intelligence officers based there kept in close contact and exchanged information with SMP Special Branch. These contacts at one time resulted in an attempt to muzzle the ebullient American Emily Hahn who, from about 1937, worked on the *North China Daily News* in Shanghai. She took great delight in teasing any SMP officer she met about their undercover work and this resulted in the police file on her being rather more weighty than those of most of her compatriots in the International Settlement. She records in her book *China to Me* that she was paid a visit by a friend in US Intelligence, who told her about the file and warned her to be careful.

Japanese intelligence efforts in Shanghai, like those of the British, were based around their consul-general's office. It was the main conduit for intelligence, and the police attached to it were engaged in espionage activities.

Early in the century the Japanese had established one of their *Tung Wen* ('same language') colleges in the city. There were three others in China proper, and one was opened in Singapore although it remained dormant. Ostensibly joint schools for Japanese and Chinese, by the 1930s it had become evident that they were schools devoted to the training of Japanese agents in propaganda, espionage, and subversion, and so were largely boycotted by the Chinese.

An integral part of Japanese subversion activities was their use of drug smuggling throughout the east; such involvement of course also providing funds that could be used for other subversive activities. Ted Quigley records the following from Shanghai in 1939:

> On one search I seized 19lb of high-grade Yunnan opium in one pound blocks from a car driven by a Chinese. It was one of the biggest hauls on record and I had visions of a commendation for my vigilance. Alas, my hopes were dashed when a high-ranking officer of the Japanese Gendarmerie claimed the opium was the property of the Japanese military authorities. It was handed over and driven away in a Japanese staff car.

Earlier, in 1937, when they took control of the Chinese part of the city, the Japanese had attempted to place their own man at the head of its drug network.

The Southern Manchurian Railway company (SMR) so heavily involved in military events in northern China, had a branch in Shanghai. The SMR 'was an important branch of Military Intelligence besides being a powerful commercial concern.'[21] It even had an internal department called the Investigation Bureau. In the Japanese occupied areas of China no attempt was made to disguise the connection between the company and the army, but in Shanghai the connection was not so obvious. Because of their 'legitimate' presence in the city, there was no need for the Japanese to use commercial firms as elaborate fronts for their Secret Service on quite the same scale as they did elsewhere.

Some White Russians in Shanghai were closely involved with Japanese Intelligence. An offshoot of the Russian Fascist Union, headquartered in Harbin, existed in the city and its members had known anti-British, and so pro-Japanese, sentiments.

There was close liaison between Japanese and German nationals in East Asia, and this applied in the intelligence field and especially at Shanghai. The leading Nazi in the city in the late 1930s was Dr Beck who openly conducted pro-Japanese work from the Nazi HQ there, and this work continued even after the war in Europe began in September 1939, for China was not at war with Germany. In the early part of the decade a Nazi called Dr Muck had been police adviser to the Chinese Nationalist Government and he had some influence on the development of the Shanghai PSB.[22]

A similar close relationship existed between the Italians in the Settlement and Japanese Intelligence. Indeed, the Italians seem to have had one of the largest Military Intelligence presences in the city, for along with the British, Americans, French and Japanese, the Italians kept troops there as part of the international force. Latterly these were the Savoia Grenadiers, who were to be stranded in the Settlement for the duration when Italy entered the European war. Italian agents were known to be working closely with Commander Otani, the Japanese Naval Attaché in Shanghai, who also headed the Naval Intelligence unit there.

The Japanese, encouraged by their easy conquest of Manchuria and by the lack of international sanctions over it, wished to turn north China into a second Manchukuo. On 7th July 1937, a group of so-called Young Officers, urged on by the Japanese Secret Service, manufactured an incident at the Marco Polo Bridge, ten miles east of Peking. This precipitated a clash with Chinese troops and, despite attempts to defuse the situation, fighting between Japanese and Chinese troops soon broke out in many other places. A month later, the Japanese extended the conflict by attacking in the Shanghai area.

At Shanghai Chiang Kai-shek threw in his best German-trained troops and succeeded in stalling the Japanese advance for three months. This Chinese resistance, while it lasted, was a tremendous morale booster throughout China. Chiang was hoping that Japanese aggression so close to the International Settlement would result in intervention by the Great Powers, but in this he was disappointed. Driving up the Yangtze River, the Japanese bypassed the Chinese force around Shanghai and took Nanking in December.

By the end of 1937 Japanese troops had captured the Chinese parts of Shanghai in battles watched with perturbed interest by many residents of the International Settlement as the fighting raged around them on the ground and over their heads. The fighting went on with little concern from either side for the safety of non-combatants. Percy Chen tells of one incident involving two Chinese intelligence agents whose escape from the Japanese was watched by on-lookers crowding all the available windows along The Bund and waterfront. The two men were seen attempting to escape by jumping into the river. As they made for the far shore they disappeared behind a sampan being rowed by a woman standing in the stern. Japanese soldiers on the shore opened fire on the sampan, and, as it passed Japanese ships moored in the river, they opened up on it too. Miraculously the boat was not hit, and not once did the woman stop rowing. Then, to cheers from the crew of the USS *Augusta*, also moored in the river, and the crowds on the shore, boat and swimmers disappeared among moored Chinese craft higher up the river.[23]

Even after the Nationalists had vacated the city their agents there managed to settle some old scores. Several hundred known or suspected collaborators of the Japanese were assassinated. Amongst them was a man, one Zhang Xiaolin, who, it had been planned, would take over the drugs network in the city with the help of the Japanese. Two senior SMP Chinese police officers were also killed. One of them was Superintendent Tan Shao Liang, known by the Chinese Nationalist Secret Service to have been an agent of the Japanese since 1932. They had previously left him alone because of his expert knowledge of Chinese communists. Several times he had helped PSB in their battle against Communism, an activity with which Tan's Japanese masters were in complete agreement. But they had no further use for him after the loss of the city, and he was killed by Chinese Secret Service men in May 1938.

The other policeman who met a similar fate was Lu Lian Kui, Chief of Chinese Detectives with the SMP. According to his obituary in the *China Weekly Review*, Lu was considered 'the best Chinese police official in the annals of Shanghai police history', yet he, too, had been a Japanese agent for several years. He was shot by three gunmen in August 1938, and his funeral procession was attended by the SMP Commissioner of Police, K. Bourne, and by the Special Deputy Commissioner, C. Akagi. One can speculate that Akagi's presence was as much because he was Japanese as that he was a senior serving officer of the SMP.

Seven

Singapore, Malaya and British Borneo, 1930–1939

The importance of the trade of the Malay Peninsula and Singapore during the third and fourth decades of this century is not usually recognised. In 1926 when the value of the trade peaked, it exceeded that of all the other British colonies put together. It diminished after that, mainly due to a fall in the price of rubber during and after the world slump, but in 1938 its trade still exceeded that of New Zealand, or the combined trade of all seventeen British African colonies, and was more than half the trade of British India.[1] No wonder Japan looked greedily upon the country, not only as a gateway into the oil-rich Netherlands East Indies to the south, but as a desirable conquest in its own right, producing as it did over half of the world's rubber and a third of its tin, not to mention the iron-ore deposits which Japanese companies had been so assiduously mining for a number of years. Near the top of the catalogue of attractions was the thriving entrepot port of Singapore, whilst over on the other side of the South China Sea, and lying within Britain's political control in one way or another, were other attractive states: Sarawak and Brunei with their oil-wells, and British North Borneo with its timber.

Prior to February 1942 Singapore was described in the world press as an 'impregnable fortress'. British politicians made no attempt to correct the image the journalists wrote of even if they themselves, as Captain Russell Grenfell once wrote, 'may not actually commit themselves to using the word impregnable'.[2] Vast sums had been spent on the new Singapore Naval Base and nothing suited the politicians better than for the public to conceive that the money had been spent to good purpose. Furthermore, the politicians reasoned, it did no harm to British Empire security for Japan, the only likely aggressor in the Far East, to read of this impregnability, conveniently forgetting that Japan had taken two 'impregnable fortresses', Port Arthur and Tsingtao, earlier in the century. It also suited those British Dominions most closely concerned, Australia and New Zealand, to accept as virtual fact that Singapore was an invulnerable bastion of Imperial defence, the Gibraltar of the East.

After World War One Britain saw the need for a fleet to be permanently based in the Pacific to protect her eastern colonies and dominions. However, after four years of total war she had not the funds to spend on the many extra ships such a policy required, so it was decided to plan instead around sending a fleet out from Home Waters if and when it was needed. Both alternatives called for a base in the Pacific area large enough to service such a fleet, and after long discussion Singapore was chosen by the Committee of Imperial Defence (CID). During its deliberations the CID coined, as mentioned earlier, a phrase for the lapse of time between the moment the situation arose necessitating the sending of the fleet out from home and its actual arrival in the Far East. This was the 'period before relief'. In 1921 it was estimated as being 70 days; by the end of the 1930s – such were the other tasks that had fallen upon the Royal Navy and so parsimonious had been government spending on new ships – the period had grown to 180 days. The concept required a sufficient garrison and air force to be on hand in Singapore to hold out until the arrival of the fleet.

Several facts should be remembered about the Singapore Naval Base project. First, the original decision was made in the days when air power was still in its infancy, and sea-air power was still only in the experimental stage. With the benefit of hindsight it is easy to argue that not enough notice was taken of air power at any stage of the base's construction. Second, the building of the base, which was not formerly opened until 1938, was bedevilled by the stop-go attitude of successive British governments mainly due to financial constraints. Third, and this is important in that it helped to colour Japanese attitudes towards Britain, Japan took the building of the base as an affront second only to Britain's abrogation of the

Anglo-Japanese Alliance in 1921.* Major-General F.S.G. Piggott, the British Military Attaché in Tokyo at the time, has recorded what a pro-British Japanese general said to him in 1922: 'You had an Alliance with us on Sunday; broke it on Monday and started a base on Tuesday. Surely the inference is obvious that you no longer trust us.'[3]

Lastly, the military garrison and air force strength in Singapore and Malaya, their respective roles, and whether mainland Malaya, to which Singapore Island was connected by a causeway, should be protected as well as the fortress itself, all became subject to perennial argument between the local commanders and colonial administrators, and between each of those and their respective government departments back in Britain. Some of these arguments had not been sorted out by the time of the Japanese attack.

It was against this background of British inter-service and inter-departmental wrangling, and the reluctance of the British government to spend much money on such matters as intelligence and counter-intelligence, that the Japanese were enabled to build up an extensive espionage network in Singapore and Malaya, and to set the ground-work of a subversive campaign among nationalists that was, in at least one respect, to bear spectacular results when war came.

After China, it was Singapore and the Malay Peninsula which together hosted the largest concentration of the Japanese espionage effort, for the peninsula was the bridge to the oil-rich Dutch East Indies, and Singapore by far the largest naval base in the Far East.

This Japanese effort was made in what was probably the most complex constitution within the British Empire. The Governor of the Crown Colony of the Straits Settlements, which consisted of Singapore, Penang, the Province of Wellesley and Malacca, was also High Commissioner for the nine Malay States, each of which had its own Ruler. The complications did not end there. The Malay States were divided – by British policy – into two separate entities, the Federated Malay States and the Unfederated Malay States. The Rulers of the four Federated States – Perak, Selangor, Pahang and Negri Sembilan – each had a British Resident. The Rulers of the five Unfederated States – Johore, Kedah, Kelantan, Trengganu and

* Ships of several nations including the United States, and Holland attended the 1938 opening of the base. The Royal Indian Navy was represented. The Japanese were not invited to send any ships. The consul-general of Japan in Singapore attended the opening ceremony but left before the reception, a fact noted in the local newspapers as an indication of Japanese displeasure.

Perlis – had British Advisers instead of Residents. The Governor of the Straits Settlements also controlled two dependent territories, Labuan off the North Borneo coast, and Christmas Island in the Indian Ocean. He had official duties in regard to Brunei, and to a lesser extent with Sarawak and North Borneo, the former ruled by 'White' Rajah Sir Charles Vyner Brooke, and the latter by the North Borneo Company.

The Straits Settlements were policed by one force – for ease of presentation called in this book the Singapore Police – and the Federated Malay States (FMS) by another. Each of the states constituting the Unfederated Malay States (UMS) had its own police force. Most of the senior officers in all the forces were British, and there were fairly frequent interchanges between them of personnel. The head of the Singapore force had long been, in common with most other parts of the Colonial Empire, called Inspector-General of Police (IGP). Up to 1938, when the FMS force followed suit, the top man there was called Commissioner, which must have been rather confusing as the top policeman seconded to each of the UMS forces also held that title, although his substantive rank in the overall set-up may only have been Assistant Superintendent. Every senior police officer, however, appeared in the police section of the all-embracing Malayan Establishment List published every six months, which was then and remains now, the best means of following a particular officer's career through his different postings and titles.

All British police officers had to learn the Malay language, plus at least one Chinese or Indian dialect for which they were sent away as language officers for eighteen months. Some officers went further than this basic requirement either because they had a bent for linguistics or because there happened to be a language bonus system in operation. In 1936 several officers were sent to Tokyo to learn Japanese.[4]

The Rulers of the Unfederated States jealously guarded the 'independent' status of their police forces. One result of this was the standing rule that neither of the IGPs before 1939, when the IGP Singapore was appointed Civil Security Officer for the entire peninsula, could enter a UMS state in his official capacity without the prior permission of the Ruler concerned.

Both the main forces had Special Branches (SB). Important sections of these from the mid-1930s specialised in matters concerning the

Japanese. Other sections dealt with Malay and Indian nationalism. From a much earlier date a major preoccupation was Chinese Communism.[5]

The task of administering and policing His Excellency the Governor's domains was made no more simple by the ethnic mix of the people. On mainland Malaya the Malays were the largest ethnic group but the Chinese were growing in numbers. In the Straits Settlements the Chinese were in preponderance, so much so that, by 1941 and taking the country as a whole, they formed the largest group overall, a fact which the Malay rulers did not much care for. There were also many Indians in the country, most of them originally brought in to work the rubber plantations. A substantial number of Eurasians lived in the larger conurbations, and there was a small but influential community of Arabs found mostly in Singapore. There was a similarly small but influential community of Jews. About 30,000 Europeans lived in the country, most of them engaged in government or in management posts in commerce and industry. In addition there were smaller communities of other nationalities ranging in size from a few hundreds to a few thousands. Included amongst them were the Japanese residents, estimated in 1940 as being around 6,000.

Chinese had been arriving legally and illegally in the country for many years, and as their numbers grew so did their influence. They tended to dominate trade wherever they settled and most shops and trading concerns were owned by them. To the rulers this was a cause of continuous concern, indeed of aggravation. In November 1937 at a Durbar held at Klang, 'the Rulers expressed grave anxiety at the continued increase in the Chinese population, which already outnumbers that of the Malays themselves in Selangor, Perak and Negri Sembilan . . . consequently [they] suggested that the emigration of Javanese labourers . . . should be encouraged . . . in preference to Chinese and others'.[6] At that same Durbar the Ruler of Negri Sembilan said he 'did not want Indians coming in either'.

In the late 1930s, based on political sympathies the Chinese could be divided into four groupings. First, there were the adherents of the Kuomintang which governed most of those parts of China that had not been overrun by the Japanese. At the centre of that faction in Malaya was the so-called Hung League. Second, there were those who supported Mao Tse-tung's communists. They were not so numerous as the Kuomintang supporters but were more vociferous and politically active, to such an extent that some of their leading lights had been imprisoned for sedition. At the centre of the Communist Movement was the Han League. A third and much smaller group were supporters of Wang Ching-wei, the Japanese puppet-ruler of occupied north China. The fourth and by far the largest group were those Chinese who had either pro-British leanings or who were politically independent. Their main interests were in trade and making money; members of this group were prone to being dragooned by the other three, each of which had its own underground network of agents. All Chinese were anti-Japanese except for the adherents of Wang Ching-wei.

Chinese communist agents had been active in Malaya since 1925, and were soon followed by Russian Comintern agents. Ho Chi Minh, representing Indo-China, attended a secret meeting of communist organisations at Singapore in April 1930, where a Malayan Communist Party was established responsible to the Far East Bureau of the Comintern at Shanghai. One Comintern agent, who seems to have been used mainly as a courier, was a Frenchman called Joseph Ducroux, who arrived in Singapore on 27th April 1931. The twenty-six-year-old Ducroux had previously visited Shanghai, where he had dealings with Hilaire Noulens (see above, page 106), then Hong Kong, Shanghai, and Manila. By the time he landed in Singapore the Frenchman was already a man marked down by British Intelligence to be watched, and the watching brief fell to René Onraet, who at that time headed the Criminal Investigation Branch of the Singapore Police. It is possible that Onraet, who had been born in Mauritius and had dark skin-tones, might have carried out some of the surveillance on Ducroux himself for it was not unknown for him to dress up as a coolie, and even pull a rickshaw.

Ducroux set up office in Winchester House on Collier Quay in Singapore's main business district, ostensibly representing a French company selling timber equipment. He took on an Indian employee who in fact was being run by Onraet. It is probable that this Indian was Prithvi Chand, an undercover agent used extensively by Onraet and by other senior members of the Singapore Police. The Ducroux operation might have been the first of many collaborations between Onraet and Prithvi Chand.

Ducroux's mail was intercepted, copied and translated before being sent on. The recipient of one letter was alleged to have been Ho Chi Minh under a pseudonym. Some of the letters were in cypher. His visitors were watched, especially two known communist agents, Fu Tai-keng and Wong Muk-han; the latter had clandestinely crept back into the colony after being banished in 1929 for running a bomb factory in Balistier Road. After telegraphic contact with the police forces in Shanghai and Indo-China, Onraet struck, and Ducroux was arrested on suspicion of being a communist on 1st June 1931, after barely a month in the colony. Arrested along with him were fourteen others, including Fu and Wong. There can be little doubt that these arrests were part of a concerted international effort against Communism being waged about this time all over the Far East. As Laurent Metzger has pointed out in an article in the *Journal of the Royal Asiatic Society*, high-level anti-communist talks had been going on since January 1930 when the governor of Singapore visited Hanoi. Another important round of talks took place in February 1931 when the governor of the Netherlands East Indies visited Singapore and North Borneo.[7]

Ducroux was not the mastermind behind the Malayan Communist Party that some authorities have suggested: he was far too young, and he had scarcely any knowledge of the Far East. His importance lies mainly in that names contained in his address book led to the arrest of Hilaire Noulens in June at Shanghai and possibly later in the year to the arrest of other leading Malayan communists including Jamaluddin Tamin in Singapore and Tan Malaka in Hong Kong. His trial became important in that the British made much anti-communist capital out of it. Ducroux was sentenced to eighteen months' rigorous detention for assisting in the management of an unlawful organisation and spreading subversive propaganda. Wong Muk-han got life imprisonment and died in prison the following year.[8]

By 1931, Singapore Police Special Branch had uncovered in some detail Moscow's plan for Colonial Revolution in Malaya. The first violent disorders as part of that plan had come with an armed clash in 1927, and from then on, and despite many other arrests like those of 1931, the fight against Communism was a continuous one. There were other disorders, the worst being the prolonged ones in the State of Selangor in 1936/37. Throughout the period there was a continuous exchange of intelligence between the British, the French and the Dutch, which made possible the holding in check of Moscow's original plan. Anti-communist measures were the one field in which the colonial countries were in complete agreement.[9]

The average Malay was not at all politically minded; he left that to the intelligentsia of whom a large proportion were schoolteachers. Many of these teachers were trained at the Sultan Idris Training College, a school noted for producing nationalist-minded graduates. Malay nationalism had been rising in this group for a number of years.

Although the great majority of Indians in Malaya, most of them Tamils, traditionally sought nothing but a quiet livelihood, now, mirroring the situation back home, many were falling under the influence of the Indian Independence League (IIL), a militant offshoot of the Congress Party which sought the end of British rule in India. The Inspector-General of Singapore Police from 1939 was A.H. Dickinson who was a Tamil speaker. He recorded that the 'IIL movement was becoming dangerous'. He considered that the most dangerous grouping was that among the numerically small but strongly organised Sikh community which he seemed to hold in small regard. They were, he said, susceptible to anti-British propaganda emanating from the Punjab and from Sikh exiles in America and Japan. He said they 'contributed nothing to the welfare of Malaya, and . . . could only be regarded as parasitic, stupid and likely to be openly anti-British in the event of disaster overtaking British arms'.[10]

Japanese espionage in Malaya began on any appreciable scale when, during World War One, Britain granted naval facilities at Penang to her then ally. By the 1920s Japan had infiltrated agents into Malaya and Singapore who were able to link up with their counterparts operating in the Dutch territories to the south, and with others in Thailand to the north. The Japanese espionage system in Malaya was a very complex affair with agents mainly involved in collecting commercial intelligence but with cells actively engaged in subversion, and with both resident and itinerant agents engaged in military espionage. From early on the actions, both overt and covert, of the Japanese in the country caused senior police officers much concern.

The main nerve-centre of this Japanese network was the consulate-general's office in Singapore. The office was used not only as a conduit for passing information back to Japan, but officers based there, including the consul himself, were actively engaged in espionage and subversion. Abuse of diplomatic privilege in this way was never the sole confine of the Japanese, but with them it was almost commonplace and they were very successful at it. As a matter of geographical convenience agents based in northern Malaya passed their information through the Japanese legation – later raised to embassy status – in Bangkok, the capital of Thailand. From

Singapore and Bangkok collected intelligence went by diplomatic bag, or was smuggled out on ships, or was transmitted over radios based in the official buildings or perhaps on ships in the harbour. From early in the decade some of these wireless messages were being intercepted by the British and decyphered.

With Singapore as the network's main base, it is not surprising that it was the Singapore Police who took the lead in counter-intelligence activities against the Japanese. From 1914 successive IGPs in Singapore – from A.R. Chancellor who was appointed in that year through to A.H. Dickinson appointed in 1939 – were well aware of the build-up of the Japanese spy network. There was a continuity of reporting on the Japanese menace and, whenever higher authority permitted them to do so, the police took action against it. Had sufficient funds been made available for counter-espionage purposes much more could have been done even within the confines of an overall policy instigated by the British Foreign Office which required that all matters pertaining to Japan be treated with kid gloves.

Chancellor was IGP from 1914 to 1923, a period that included both the abrogation of the Anglo-Japanese Treaty and the decision by the British government to build the Singapore Naval Base. This period brought the initial build-up of the Japanese spy network under the cover of

> banking, mining, fishing, and agricultural enterprises . . . developed by Japanese immigrants in almost bewildering profusion. Commercial enterprises, official agencies, social organisations, private individuals, and secret political associations, became indissolubly linked to form the close network of the Japanese intelligence fabric which covered every aspect of Malayan life.[11]

In 1918, the South Seas Society, subsidised by the Japanese government, founded the Singapore Japanese Commercial Museum, which in later years became a sort of secondary control centre for that part of espionage and propaganda work it was thought better not to conduct directly from the office of the consul-general. It was in this early period too, that two leading figures in Japan's so-called 'advance to the south' movement came to reside in Singapore. They were Ishihara Koichiro and Yoshida Seisuke. The former owned iron mines on the coasts of Trengganu and Johore, and ran subsidiary companies in Singapore and other places, one of which was the Southern Godown Company known by the police to be indulging in 'undesirable activities'. Yoshida also built up a mining organisation, whose employees were strongly suspected of collecting military intelligence.

The next IGP was G.C. Denham, borrowed from the Indian Police from 1923 to 1925. Godfrey Denham, together with a man coyly described in official documents as 'Mr Petrie' also from the Indian Police, set up the Malayan Political Advisory Bureau in 1924.[12] 'Mr Petrie', later Sir David, was to become Head of MI5 in London in 1940. The Bureau was designed to provide information to relevant government departments and to the military, about all matters pertaining to internal security in Malaya. At its head was a Director, and standing members of it were the IGP himself, the Secretary of Chinese Affairs, the Army GSO (I) and the Navy SO (I).[13]

It was during Denham's time as IGP that a spy called Ishigai Kosaki, who had earlier been secretary to the Director of the Japanese Commercial Museum and who before that had worked for a Japanese shipping line in San Francisco, was suspected not only of spying, but of drug smuggling. When his house in Trengganu was searched, documents were discovered giving precise descriptions of many parts of Malaya's east coast.

Denham was followed as IGP in 1925 by Harold Fairburn who was to hold the post for ten years. Fairburn's counterparts in the FMS Police, with whom he worked very closely on all matters dealing with internal security, were C. Hannigan, from 1926 to 1931, followed by C.H. Sansom. The middle years of Fairburn's reign brought some relief from Japanese penetration for, in 1931 and 1932, most of Japan's interests and energies were directed towards the conquest of Manchuria.

It was in 1930/31 that the Malayan Political Advisory Bureau was replaced by a Standing Committee on Intelligence (SCI). The exact details are not known, but it seems that this creation of the Malayan Civil Service did not go out of its way to co-operate with the Army Command in Malaya, an early sign of the lack of co-operation between the civil and the military arms that still bedevilled the situation in Malaya at the time of the Japanese victory in 1942. Nevertheless, every month the SCI issued what were called Malayan Combined Intelligence Summaries which included some input from the army and from MI5's man in Singapore.[14]

The devaluation of the yen in 1932 brought a vast increase in

Japanese trade with Malaya in spite of a boycott of Japanese goods by resident Chinese over the Manchurian invasion. This commercial expansion was followed by considerable Japanese penetration in other fields, especially propaganda and espionage. During this period many 'sleeper' agents were introduced into the country to take up jobs as barbers, masseurs, photographers, waiters, and the like, a favourite ploy of Japanese Intelligence. In India they added dentists to the list, dental surgeons setting up practices in several garrison towns.

Another favourite ploy adopted in Singapore, Penang, Kuala Lumpur, Taiping and other large urban centres, was the opening of Japanese-run brothels. Originally staffed by *mama-sans* and girls specially brought in from Japan, information was collected from British soldier and sailor clients along with the fee for services rendered, or perhaps as the fee itself. An associated ploy was the use of Japanese mistresses kept by some Europeans and rich Asiatics. Japanese women, renowned for their docility and compliancy, made excellent mistresses. These ladies 'were not a negligible source of information', reported René Onraet, the IGP from 1935.

In 1932 Japanese agents used bribery to obtain information about the Singapore Naval Base, and in that same year a leading aircraftsman named Graham sold them information about RAF facilities. In the following year the Japanese obtained drawings of parts of the naval base from a man called Roberts for the sum of Straits $1,300 (over £5,000 at 1997 values). Japanese spy interests were wide-ranging. FMS Police discovered that agents had obtained drawings of the important Guillemarde Railway Bridge over the Sungei Kelantan, only twenty miles south of Kota Bharu, which was to be one of the invasion places in 1941. They also purchased drawings of the Causeway linking Singapore to the mainland and of its lock which operated as a sluice-gate. They acquired plans of the crucial Woodlands Railway switch on Singapore Island.

Japanese companies were active in buying up rubber plantations, especially those in strategic positions. They purchased several in the Batu Pahat area of Johore, later to be the scene of an outflanking landing by Japanese troops.

By 1933, the growth in Japanese clandestine and not so clandestine activities was so disturbing that both the Singapore and FMS Police Forces formed Japanese Sections in their Special Branches. These Sections began to keep extensive files on all resident and itinerant Japanese. Many of these files were taken out of Singapore in late

January 1942, about three weeks before Singapore fell, by an officer specially selected for the purpose, Assistant Superintendent E.A.G. Blades, one of Special Branch's specialists in Japanese matters.

One of the most blatant acts of intelligence-gathering at this time revolved around the attempt in 1933/34 by a Japanese salvage team to raise the wreck of the Russian cruiser *Jemtchug* in Penang harbour. In the attempt, which failed, Japanese salvage men took photographs and soundings all around the harbour to an extent not justified by the operation itself.[15]

In Malaya, and elsewhere, special passports were issued to Japanese travellers engaged in espionage. These were not diplomatic passports – which give their holders special status under international law – but passports stamped with the word 'official', and designed to indicate some sort of intermediate status entitling the holders to disregard such requirements as registering with the local authorities. Many of these passports were also issued under false names.

An example of this latter practice was discovered in December 1934. A Japanese named as Kashima Teizo had arrived at Singapore the previous month aboard the *Rio de Janeiro Maru*. He was supposed to be an employee of the Southern Godown Company. In fact he was Lieutenant-Commander Kaseda Tetsubiko of the Japanese navy. Travelling with Kaseda was Kizaki Katsujiro, described in his passport as an author. During their brief time in Singapore they stayed at a famous geisha house at Katong from where they were in regular touch with their consul-general. Their stay was organised by one Nishimura Yoshio of the Southern Godown Company. SB arrested the pair after they had unsuccessfully attempted to obtain a copy of a signal code from an RAF warrant officer. They were found to have about S$6,000 in their possession, a large sum of money in those days. Under questioning both admitted to being on an espionage mission, Kaseda admitting to his true name and rank. It was found that Kizaki was a member of a secret society much given to the use of violence. Under orders from London both were deported on 5th December without any charges being brought against them. On that same day Nishimura, the man who had made the arrangements for the agents' visit, was called to SB offices for questioning, for the police had evidence that he sought to purchase the plans of the RAF base at Seletar. Nishimura took a dose of strychnine on the way, timing it with the precision of a Japanese tea-making ceremony, and dying just as his interrogation was about to begin.

That was not the end of the Kaseda–Kizaki affair, however. On the same ship that took that pair away, three other Japanese fled, all of them on SB's suspect list. One of them was Yoshida Seisuke who was the owner of mining companies suspected of military espionage. A few days later two other Japanese were arrested on banishment orders. A search of the house of one of them, Kokubo Hiromichi, revealed information that connected him with four men of the Royal Artillery serving on Blakang Mati Island where some of Singapore's big guns were sited. Other information on the shore defences at Changi was discovered, some of it so secret that the authorities took great care that not a whisper of the affair got out at the time. Kokubo and his confederate were placed aboard a ship for Japan in March 1935.

A man believed by SB to be a key figure in Japanese espionage in Malaya – indeed for a time he was almost certainly at the head of the entire operation – was Dr Ouchi Tsuni. Ouchi had arrived Singapore in 1929 as the representative of the League of Nations Health Bureau for Singapore, a position that afforded him diplomatic immunity.[16] Assistant Superintendent L.F. Knight, SB's Chief in 1938, reported that Ouchi had been part of the Japanese network since 1934, and had been involved in the Kaseda–Kizaki affair. Knight went on to report that three police undercover agents acting independently and unaware of each other's existence, had reported that Ouchi was the chief spymaster in the area.

On Fairburn's retirement in 1935, René Onraet, the man who had arrested Joseph Ducroux four years earlier, became IGP Singapore.[17] He was to oversee the period that brought with it the most active Japanese penetration in the area. After his retirement in 1939 he wrote:

> I look back at Japanese activities in Malaya with the conviction of having witnessed a patient and confident preparation for ultimate occupation, all the more easy to organise as no-one thought a military success, on which such an occupation depended, was possible.[18]

In 1936 two men of very different character arrived in Singapore to help in the battle against Japanese espionage and subversion. They were Major K.S. Morgan from the Indian army who arrived first, and Colonel Francis Hayley Bell. Unfortunately, the two found it impossible to get on with each other.

It was René Onraet who arranged the secondment of Major Morgan to Singapore SB as the first head of its Japanese Section. Kenneth Morgan was then forty years of age. Commissioned into the British army in 1915, he had transferred into the Indian army two years later. In 1921 he became one of nine Indian army officers sent that year to Japan as language officers. In 1925 he became a language officer in Russia. The Indian Army Lists show him as being an Interpreter 1st Class in both languages. At one time he served on the Indian Army Intelligence Staff at Simla.[19]

Morgan proved to be good at his job in Singapore although he had some rather strange ideas and personal characteristics. He suffered from emphysema which brought on bouts of acute breathlessness and he had a habit of dropping off to sleep in mid-sentence. He considered, perhaps rightly, that his position in the Japanese Section of SB made him a target for assassination. This, reported his private secretary, Miss Barbara Brown, resulted in both of them leading a strange cloak-and-dagger style existence. The oddest fact of all was that, on joining the police, Morgan was permitted to become something of a law unto himself: he did not subscribe to normal police procedures. For 'security' reasons he insisted on having an office of his own, refused to use the Central Office and its filing arrangements or its clerks, and jealously guarded his own voluminous files by building into the retrieval system certain personal idiosyncrasies that ensured that no-one but himself or Miss Brown could easily get at them.[20]

Colonel Hayley Bell arrived in Singapore as the MI5 officer on station with the title Defence Security Officer. Then in his fifty-eighth year, he had had a remarkable career. Born in Shanghai, he was schooled at Oakfield and Rugby before returning to China in 1892. Four years later he joined the Imperial Chinese Maritime Customs Service and eventually rose to the rank of Commissioner. He taught himself seven Chinese dialects and could also speak Russian. On leave of absence from China in 1905 he went to South Africa and joined the Mounted Police. The following year he fought with the Natal Carabineers during a Zulu insurrection. He returned to China, and after 'fluttering every heart in the drawing-rooms on the coast', according to Enid Saunders, he married a missionary's daughter in 1910.[21] He returned to England in 1913 and spent a year with the XI Hussars. In 1915 as a Territorial Captain in the 10th Queen's Royal Regiment he went to France and was badly wounded near Passchendale. A friend from those early war days was Colonel Frank

Rennick of the Indian army who was serving in Military Intelligence at the time. Rennick instilled in Hayley Bell's mind warnings which he never forgot, about future Japanese aspirations and the tactics they might use.[22]

Awarded the DSO in 1918, Hayley Bell was then wounded again. The year 1919 saw him back in China where he served as Commissioner of Customs in various places including Macau, Canton and Chefoo. During this period of his career says Lady (Mary) Mills, the eldest of his three daughters, 'his job was very like MI5 . . . and he had the use of a small gunboat'.[23] Tony Hewitt, married to Elizabeth Hayley Bell, the youngest of the daughters, says of his father-in-law, that he 'was a splendid man, courageous but impetuous . . . [Only] men of exceptionally fine character were chosen as commissioners for the Chinese Maritime Customs'.[24] Hayley Bell was an officer in the Shanghai Volunteer Force during the troubles there in the early 1930s, and served for a time as an official of the Shanghai Municipal Council where he often came into contact with Japanese officials. He ended his Chinese Customs career as Commissioner and Non-resident Secretary in the London Office of the Service.

In his capacity as Defence Security Officer, Singapore, Hayley Bell was responsible directly to Colonel Vernon Kell, Head of MI5 in London, and only indirectly to General Dobbie, GOC Malaya Command. It may have been resentment over this chain of responsibility that caused his views to be mainly disregarded by the military hierarchy in Singapore, or it may have been the fact that he was not in the regular army; in 1936 and for a few years afterwards, territorial officers tended to be looked down upon by regulars.

Hayley Bell was well briefed in London about the Japanese menace, and he knew the Japanese well from his years in Shanghai and other parts of China. So, when soon after his arrival in the colony he presented his credentials to the governor, Sir Shenton Thomas, it was not long before the subject of Japan came up in discussion. Wyn Steel, the second of Hayley Bell's daughters, and who with Elizabeth and their mother arrived with him at Singapore, well remembers her father quoting Sir Shenton after that meeting. 'Who but a fool, Hayley Bell,' quoth the governor, 'thinks Japan wants Singapore!'*

* When A.H. Dickinson, the last pre-war Inspector-General of Police in Singapore heard of this remark some years later, he commented, 'This could not have been said on the advice of the IGP. For years we had been building up our anti-Japanese section. Who in this case misled him [Thomas] so grievously?'

The remark set the tone for the four years of Hayley Bell's tenure in Singapore. Wyn Steel goes on to relate that 'General Dobbie didn't like my father or his views. Neither did Air Vice Marshal (later Marshal of the Royal Air Force, Lord) Tedder, the AOC Malaya. Dobbie Junior, the General's son and ADC, said of my father, "He has Japan in his hair". Admiral Sir Percy Noble was the only senior officer to listen.'[25]

Perhaps it was the fact that Morgan was a regular officer of the Indian army, and a passed-over major, whereas Hayley Bell was 'only' a territorial but two ranks senior, that caused the friction between the two. Or it may simply have been that Morgan had been brought in as the Japanese expert and did not like others trespassing on his patch. Whatever the cause, Morgan found Hayley Bell anathema, a feeling soon reciprocated, and he denied Hayley Bell all access to information in his files. This made life extremely difficult for Barbara Brown, who remembers:

> HB used to wander aimlessly into my office and try to get me to show him the files without Morgan knowing, but I couldn't do it, although personally I thought it very odd and was obstructing HB in his job.

Miss Brown's comments show that there was little or no co-operation between the Japanese Section of SB and MI5 at this time; but even stronger evidence exists that Morgan was withholding important information from MI5 and directly from the military authorities in reports made by General Dobbie's GSO1, none other than Colonel A.E. Percival, who later was GOC, Malaya Command, at the time of the Japanese attack.

Malaya Command had established, together with the Royal Navy and Royal Air Force, a body called the Joint Intelligence Bureau (JIB). Like its civilian counterpart, the Standing Committee on Intelligence, it produced Monthly Intelligence Summaries, but the JIB were far more wide-ranging. The distribution list of these Summaries included the War Office, military attachés in Japan, China and Thailand, and British consular offices throughout the Far East. The Joint Intelligence Bureau was small, each of the three services providing one representative. From April 1937 the army man, a member of General Dobbie's staff, was Major (later Brigadier) Herbert 'Jo' Vinden.[26] Vinden had other intelligence tasks too, one of which was being the link with Colonel Hayley Bell. In fact

Vinden is on record as saying that his link with MI5 was a direct one 'without passing through the GOC'.

It may have been Vinden who drew Colonel Percival's attention to the situation that existed between Morgan and Hayley Bell. In subsequent meetings in the autumn of 1937 between Dobbie, IGP René Onraet, Percival, and some of their subordinates, it was discovered that Morgan had information about potential sabotage of military installations on Singapore Island that he had not seen fit to tell the army about. In an attempt to rectify this situation an office was made available for Hayley Bell at Police Headquarters. Onraet went on record as saying that the police 'are always ready to supply the Defence Security Officer with information on any subject, and that he would [henceforth] be supplied with a monthly précis of the security work undertaken by the police'.

Despite this undertaking Morgan continued to hold out. Onraet, under considerable pressure himself, at last leant heavily on the Head of his Japanese Section, and at a meeting held on 12th October 1937 an extraordinary statement prepared by Morgan was read out which detailed a great deal of information on the activities of Japanese agents all with regard to military targets, information which Morgan had neither passed on to MI5 nor directly to the army. In his official report of that meeting Colonel Percival said Morgan had information that explosives had been buried under defensive works in both the Kranji and Changi areas of Singapore, and that explosives had been placed on wrecks in the harbour by Japanese salvage companies. Morgan said he had not previously reported the matter of the hiding of a quantity of explosives in the Kranji area – 'enough to blow up the whole of Singapore', commented Percival – because there were so many explosives legitimately stored by Japanese mining companies in Malaya, 'that the enemy would not need to use this hidden store, and that it was impossible to find by search anyway'. Morgan added the comment that he believed the Services were trying to tell him how to run his operation, and that he was not going to have it.

Onraet, apparently in an attempt to cover Morgan's intransigence, noted that under ordinary circumstances none of this information would have been disclosed to anyone outside the police 'because none of it had been confirmed', though he went on to state that in Morgan's opinion 'the information concerned can be accepted as being correct'.

Colonel Percival's summing up of the situation was a masterly piece of understatement. 'There has', he wrote, 'been a lack of frankness.' He went on to say that he appreciated the desire to pass on only *proven* information but 'considered that the items of information about Kranji and Changi should most certainly have been communicated to the Defence Security Officer, particularly as the police considered the information sufficient to take action to intercept the explosives'.

In a later memorandum to General Dobbie, and by that time obviously seeing no further need to dissemble, Percival wrote: 'Major Morgan is lacking in ability and is not fitted for the appointment which he holds. This view is supported by information as to his past history and antecedents . . . On the other hand, he appears to be on a 7- or 10-year contract, so there may be difficulty in removing him from his appointment.'

No record has been found of what Percival had discovered about Morgan's 'past history and antecedents'. Percival is known to have held a poor view of the Indian army, and perhaps it was that and the fact that Morgan had been passed over for promotion in that army, that made him write what he did. Morgan's playing of his cards so close to his chest certainly bordered on the bizarre. Maybe, as the only Japanese-speaking officer in the Singapore Police at that time he hoped to make a name for himself by catching some spies in the act.* Yet, despite his odd behaviour, Morgan carried out some good counter-espionage work. He set up channels of communication with his opposite numbers in French Indo-China and the Netherlands East Indies, and after the war Alan Blades, who rose to be Singapore's top policeman, played generous tribute to him.

One example of Morgan's work came with the detention and final deportation of Goma Shohei, one of the most important Japanese agents in the area, whose case shows the many interlinking tentacles of Japanese espionage. Goma Shohei arrived in Singapore on his first officially recorded visit in 1936. He was then forty-two years of age. The name was an alias, for he was the younger brother of the Japanese transport minister of the time, Nakajima Tsunekichi. Goma worked for the East Asiatic Economic Investigation Bureau in Tokyo, the body at the heart of Japanese Intelligence. One of his acquaintances in Tokyo had been Rash Behari Bose, the Indian nationalist and renegade who

* Assistant Superintendent E.A.G. Blades had been selected in 1936, in his own words, 'at the eleventh hour', together with C.M.J. Kirke of the FMS Police, to undergo a Japanese language course. But at this time neither of them had returned.

had become a naturalised Japanese citizen. Earlier, after being trained at the Japanese spy training school, he travelled to China and then to Formosa, where he became an expert on all aspects of the opium trade. In 1928 he spent some time in Bangkok, before illegally crossing the border and entering Malaya and then Singapore for the first time. He stayed in Singapore unknown to the authorities for three years working at the Dr Nakano Dispensary in Victoria Street, believed to have been a centre for Japanese espionage and for drug smuggling until it closed down in 1932. Goma then left for India, the Middle East and finally Burma. He returned to Japan in 1936 and, after various briefings from naval officers, re-entered Singapore on 27th October that year, this time legally but with certain illicit plans in mind.

Goma seems to have been something of a linchpin in Japanese intelligence in the area, for agents in French Indo-China, Burma and Hong Kong soon made contact with him. One of those was Captain Endo Etsu of the Japanese General Staff who was engaged in espionage in Indo-China. Soon after contacting Goma, Endo was arrested by the French when caught red-handed whilst spying on defence installations. Endo was deported by the French in January 1937.

Special Branch somehow intercepted some of Goma's correspondence with the Bureau in Tokyo or managed to obtain copies of them. They found that he lived off funds sent to him by the Bureau. Through other agents he was in contact with a notorious Sumatran revolutionary called Josef (or Joseph) Hassan who had close links with Rash Behari Bose in Japan. Goma also had dealings with Dr Ouchi Tsuni, who used his League of Nations status as a cover for clandestine work. Goma's principal contact, however, was a man called Nakamura Yobei, who seems to have acted as some kind of go-between between Goma and several other agents. Nakamura was connected with a Japanese department store in Middle Road, Singapore, called K. Baba & Company, known by SB to be a collecting agency for intelligence. There was some evidence that the firm acted as a distributor of secret funds, and it was actually raided by SB in February 1938.

Another of Goma's contacts was Tsujimori Tamizo who had left the Netherlands East Indies in August 1935 'at the request of the Dutch authorities' for being in contact with Josef Hassan, the Sumatran revolutionary mentioned above. In an earlier visit to Singapore he had worked at the Japanese Commercial Museum. Other contacts of Goma's were Hosaka Masaji, Kai Ippei and Shirai Sakahiko.

Hosaka had come to Malaya after World War One, working first as a photographer. Between trips to Japan he later worked in places all over Malaya, and had been one of the leading lights behind the attempt to salvage the *Jemtchug* at Penang. In a raid on his house at the time of his arrest, documents were found linking him with many persons and firms believed by the police to be engaged in espionage in Southeast Asia, and in particular with a Captain Adachi of the Japanese Naval General Staff who, during an earlier visit to Singapore was himself thought by SB to be engaged in spying. Kai Ippei appears to have been some sort of courier.

Goma was arrested on a banishment warrant in the latter part of 1937, along with Tsujimori, Hosaka, Kai and Shirai. Of the five only Shirai Sakahiko provided a clear case of espionage in its restricted and generally accepted connotation, for he was found to have been copying official photographs made by the RAF.

Goma was interrogated at Pearl's Hill Jail by Kenneth Morgan. During one of these sessions, Morgan fell asleep in mid-sentence. Barbara Brown, who was there, reported: 'Goma and I looked at each other – he, I suppose, thinking he might escape, I, thinking of what he could do to me – so I quickly kicked Morgan under the table and the interrogation went on.'

Accused of trying to obtain information about the naval base through Chinese employees working there, and of using Malays and Tamils to monitor the movements and locations of British troops, Goma denied everything although papers found during various police raids at the time, linked his name with just about every suspected spy and subversive in Malaya. Goma and the other four were deported in February 1938.[27] These deportations resulted in a diplomatic row between Tokyo and London, with Tokyo complaining bitterly of the treatment the five had received whilst being held in prison. It is more likely that Japanese anger was caused by the loss of the services of Goma and his colleagues.

In November, Assistant Superintendent J.S.H. Brett of Singapore Special Branch took it upon himself to board the Japanese *Hakone Maru* where, acting on a tip-off, he searched the baggage of a passenger called Akiyama Motioichu. It is not known what Brett discovered; but it is known that Akiyama was travelling on a diplomatic passport. This resulted in another row with Tokyo,[28] and from that moment on Britain's attitude towards Japan bordered on appeasement at almost any cost. Deportations of suspected spies from Malaya still went on, but they were conducted without publicity; only rarely now was the kid-glove approach not followed.

Throughout this period the Japanese continued to send migrants into the country. A Malayan Combined Intelligence Summary of May 1937 dealt with Japanese settlement in the Cameron Highlands in northern Malaya and to a visit made there by Mr Inoue Masaji of the South Seas Society. This Japanese government-funded society was primarily interested in the opening up of Malaya, the Netherlands East Indies and other parts of the Far East to Japanese goods and Japanese migrants, and operated through a system of apprentices, many of whom were known to be espionage agents. The following is an extract from the Summary:

> *Penetration into the Cameron Highlands.*
>
> Mr Inoue, Managing Director of the South Seas Society, stated in Tokyo:
>
> That there are only 13 Japanese families in the Cameron Highlands and that he required greater efforts made in exploiting this district. He considered the Highlands were a central spot in Malaya and added, 'The vegetable growers of the Cameron Highlands must form the base for our advance North . . . From this base our advance to Pahang and thence Siam is not empty talk.'

The Summary went on to report what Assistant District Officer W.J. Peel had to say about the Japanese in his district. Of the thirty-one adult Japanese in the Cameron Highlands, he said, only four actually owned the land they cultivated. He pointed out that one of the four was the President of the Japanese Commercial Museum in Singapore, known by Special Branch to be a front for espionage activities. There followed a note by the governor, Sir Shenton Thomas, to the effect that not much could be done about the Japanese because the terms of the 1911 Treaty with Japan, 'require that the subjects of Japan should enjoy rights of owning houses and of leasing lands in the same manner as native subjects'.[29]

It was not only the police who were active over matters concerning the Japanese. The British army and MI5 were also busy, and this author has obtained copies of previously unpublished documents, papers, and information from the families of Major Vinden the Intelligence Officer on General Dobbie's staff, and Colonel Hayley Bell, the Defence Security Officer, which indicate a degree of collaboration between the two men.

When Vinden arrived at Singapore in April 1937 to join General Dobbie's staff, he found Colonel Percival ensconced as GSO1. In view of Percival's later appointment as GOC, Malaya Command, it is worth mentioning that Vinden found Percival to be 'very intelligent' with 'warmth in his personality'. However, he goes on:

> I must admit, however, that he had not been particularly worried about the possibility of a Japanese invasion and the defence problems. I think he accepted the home government's view that Japan was fully engaged in China and lacked the resources for a southward move. However, he was most sympathetic to my appreciation of the situation, which I recount later, in contrast to his successor who regarded me as a bloody nuisance.[30*]

Vinden noted that there were a fair number of Japanese in the country and that 'these became of concern to me'. He pointed out their ubiquitousness and that many ran photographers' shops in numerous villages. 'As the Muslim religion prohibits images, their businesses could not have been lucrative,' he remarked. He commented on an unknown number of Japanese fishermen working on over a hundred fishing boats licensed by the government and operating all around Singapore, adding, 'Shortly before my arrival one of these fishing boats had been arrested on some technical ground and it was discovered that the captain was a captain in the Japanese Navy'.

Vinden's first tasks were 'to study the defence plan laid down by the Committee of Imperial Defence, to carry out a thorough reconnaissance of Malaya, and to see how this small force [the standing garrison] could hold out . . . in the event of an attack by Japan.' He was soon convinced that if Japan attacked she would do so without warning and only when Britain was embroiled in a war in Europe.

As a first step he asked the Malayan navy to take him, his deputy, and the police officer in charge of counter-espionage, up the east coast

* Percival's successor as GSO1 was Colonel E.G. Miles who did not stay long in the post. After about a year he was succeeded by Colonel K.S. Torrance, OBE, MC. This illustrates one of the problems of military service in that area of growing strategic importance. Military commanders and their staffs came, served their allotted span – or less – then went, taking with them any local knowledge and experience they had built up and leaving their successors to build anew contacts with local residents and officers of the Malayan Civil Service.

of Malaya. Vinden does not name the policeman, but it was almost certainly Superintendent Mervyn Llewellyn Wynne. The object was to land on all the beaches and to visit the Japanese-run iron mines along that coast.

> We landed on several beaches from a dinghy and came close inshore all the way along the coast. The beaches presented no difficulty to any landing party. I was particularly interested in the beaches around Kuantan from which town there was at that date the only lateral road from the east coast to the main Singapore-Penang road and railway. The defence scheme, as laid down by the CID, considered that any attack during the period of the northeast monsoon from November to February was impossible due to rough seas. To show how misleading this belief was, from the police officer I learned that during this period several thousand Chinese landed on the east coast every year. They came from Hainan in junks to avoid the Malayan Government's immigration quota. The police usually picked up a token thousand of these illegal immigrants and returned them to China. It was disconcerting to find that the CID had based this part of the defence scheme on inadequate information.

This is an important statement. It shows that in 1937 a Malayan Command Staff Officer had become convinced that landings in the northeast monsoon on the east coast of Malaya were feasible, something the naval authorities in Singapore were still refusing to believe in 1941. Had Vinden delved further into the relevant police knowledge, he would have discovered that the junk masters bringing in the illegal immigrants, rarely came at any time other than during the monsoon season when the rough seas and poor visibility made detection by both sea and shore patrols extremely unlikely. He would also have discovered that this practice had been going on for many, many years; the number of illegal arrivals was one cause of the rapid rise in the size of the country's Chinese population.*

* Only a small percentage of the illegals were ever picked up. Those discovered were sent to Singapore and then shipped back to China via Hong Kong in batches of about 150. Each group was escorted by a European police officer, a Chinese detective and two armed policemen from the Sikh Contingent. On board the ships the deportees were kept in specially constructed security cages. They were properly fed and not ill-treated. These voyages were considered something of a junket by the British police officers involved, and there was a rota system in

Vinden terminated his sea trip at Kota Bharu and, with his deputy, journeyed over the border into Thailand and up to Singora where they found a good harbour and adequate buildings 'which were suitable for the establishment of an invasion base'. There they hired ponies and travelled on a dirt road to Kroh, a small town on the Malayan side of the border, and then made their way to Jitra and Alor Star both in northern Malaya. Some four years later the Japanese used Singora as one of their landing places, and another Japanese force which had landed at Patani in Thailand tore down that Kroh road to occupy a dominant point on it called The Ledge before a British column coming from the opposite direction could reach it.

Back in Singapore, Vinden had discussions with the Netherlands consul-general who was receiving regular intelligence reports from General Pabst, the Dutch Military Attaché in Tokyo. Through the consul, arrangements were made for Vinden to visit General Boestra, Commander-in-Chief of the Netherlands Indies army headquartered at Bandung in the mountains behind Batavia. Vinden travelled in mufti and under a false passport because of the Dutch attitude of 'strict neutrality'. He was flown around various military installations on the island of Java in one of the Dutch airforce's 'newly-received American Glen Martin bombers'. Vinden got on well with Boestra who invited him to come back later to attend army manoeuvres – an invitation also extended to Colonel Percival.

Vinden's next overseas visit, in early 1938, was to French Indo-China. At that time 'we had no idea of the strength and disposition of the French forces', he wrote. In preparation for his visit he and his staff built up a card index based on information carried in newspapers published in the French colony about the 'arrivals and departures of officers, paragraphs about farewell parties and notices

(cont'd)
operation. On 13th November 1939, a batch of 146 was placed aboard the P&O ship *Sirdhana*. On sailing, the ship strayed off the track and struck a mine in the protective minefield. She sank in under twenty minutes, but not before the escorting officer, Inspector S.W.R. Marsden, the Chinese detective, and a Sikh corporal, risked their lives to go below, shoot the lock off the grill and release the prisoners, all of whom managed to swim the three miles to St John's Island, although twenty Asiatic deck passengers lost their lives in the incident. Stanley Marsden was awarded the King's Police Medal. Detective (No. 112) Ng Kim Bok and Corporal (No. 3508) Mustan Singh were awarded Colonial Police Medals. The two latter awards were made by the governor at a ceremony called 'The First Review of the Police of the Straits Settlements' on 12th April 1940. As it turned out, that was also to be the last such pre-war Review.

of births, marriages, and deaths amongst the French forces'. By this means he was able to build up an order of battle.

> I showed this to the French Staff in Hanoi and found, to the surprise of the Colonel in charge of their Intelligence, that it was 95% correct. Intelligence is not always an affair of spies looking through keyholes or of seduction by charming ladies with big black eyes.

He found himself welcomed by the French C-in-C, General Martin, and his Staff. He was taken to inspect the garrison regiment of the Foreign Legion, 'the majority of them were German by birth'. He found that there was no concern in Hanoi about the possibility of Japanese expansion southwards.

Vinden travelled back to Singapore by ship from Haiphong and General Dobbie, who had been spending a holiday at the temples of Angkor Wat, joined the ship when it called at Saigon. Vinden wrote: 'This gave me the opportunity for a deal of discussion about the defence of Malaya during which I expressed my apprehensions. General Dobbie asked me to write an "appreciation of the situation".' Major Vinden went on to produce his appreciation.

> It was a longish paper, but the gist of it was that a Japanese attack would come when Britain was involved in Europe and without a declaration of war. Initially, it would be directed to capture Songklha [*sic*; another spelling for Singora] as a base and Kota Bharu as a subsidiary, destroy the airfields and capture Penang as the first objective. Further advance would be via the west coast road and railway, and a landing would then take place at Kuantan which would join up with the main advance. Singapore would be attacked from the land side with no attempt at landing on the island from the sea.
>
> It was quite impossible to defend a country the size of England with four battalions of infantry. Our engagements in Europe would prevent any reinforcement after the initial Japanese attack and the defence depended on having adequate and well trained forces in the country before war broke out. I considered that the minimum force required was six divisions with all the necessary ancillary troops including at least a tank brigade. The whole would have to be trained in jungle warfare . . .

Vinden went on to advocate the cancellation of the order for the fourth and fifth 15-inch guns of Singapore's sea defences which had not then been installed. The cost of installation of these guns, which he estimated at £15,000,000 should, he said, be spent instead on aircraft 'in which Malaya was pitifully deficient, not only in numbers but with obsolete machines'.

Vinden concluded: 'General Dobbie sent this appreciation to Air Commodore [*sic*] Tedder who returned it with the following notation: "Any attack on Malaya will be prevented by the Royal Air Force". This was a surprising assessment.'

Jo Vinden noted that events turned out almost exactly as he had forecasted, adding, 'I am not trying to give the impression that I was a strategic genius or a medium reading the thoughts of the Japanese government. The situation in 1938 was plain to any intelligent person, civilian or soldier. What was distressing was the complacency everywhere.'

His appreciation, 'not under my own name of course', was sent to the War Office by General Dobbie, and was probably incorporated in Dobbie's 'New Proposals for the Defence of the Far East' dated October/November 1938. [31]

It is not known exactly how fully Vinden co-operated with Colonel Hayley Bell, the MI5 man on station, nor how much background information for Vinden's 'appreciation' came from that source. After the comment about his appreciation not being sent under his own name, Vinden went on to say that 'it so happened that through my link with MI5, I sent a copy of my appreciation to the War Office'. It is not clear whether he meant that he sent it through Hayley Bell, or directly to MI5 at the War Office in London; but what is known is that Hayley Bell's small organisation produced some significant intelligence information and that this information played a part in Dobbie's proposals for the defence of Malaya made in both 1937 and 1938.

One occasional member of Hayley Bell's team was the then Lieutenant Ivan Lyon of the Gordon Highlanders, which was part of the Singapore garrison. A great sailing man, in 1937 Lyon and a colleague voyaged up the east coast of Malaya and into Thai waters in a small sloop-rigged craft and returned with a comprehensive intelligence report.

Another member of the team, then a civilian, was John Becker who had arrived in Malaya in 1920. Except for a three-year spell in India, Becker had served in Malaya, Thailand, and the Netherlands East Indies ever since. He was something of a linguist, being fluent in both Malay and Thai. His job with the general trading firm of Frazer & Neave – known throughout the East as 'F & N' – caused him to travel the length and breadth of Malaya and often to cross into Thailand. In both countries whenever he could he 'went native', dressing as one of the local populace. He seems to have fancied himself as a sort of latter-day Lawrence of Arabia. Be that as it may, his willingness to associate with both Malays and Thais made him many friends, including some among the Royalist Party in Thailand, a country then ruled by a military dictatorship.[32]

Another agent used by Hayley Bell was a shadowy figure named Bavier or Baviot, a Swiss national, half-Swiss and half-Japanese by blood.[33] He too travelled between Thailand and Malaya, and in 1937 somehow came up with details of provisional Japanese plans for the invasion of Thailand and Malaya.[34]

> Hayley Bell himself travelled throughout Malaya, sometimes in the company of his two youngest daughters whom he used as part-time secretaries. On one occasion he turned up with them at Kuantan, half-way up Malaya's eastern seaboard. Guy Madoc, the Officer Commanding Police Department (OCPD) there, remembers the visit well, but perhaps not primarily for the business in hand. 'Hayley Bell turned up at Kuantan some time between June and October 1938 with his two striking daughters. He stayed at the Rest House [a government-run hotel] and phoned me one evening. Said he wanted to brief me on something highly confidential. We arranged to meet under a distinctive tree on the golf-course at the back of the Rest House. The meeting was brief. He said he had been investigating some conjectural military preparations by the Japanese on the east coast of Siam. He asked whether I knew anything, and I answered "no". He told me that he had an agent currently in Siam and that he might travel south down the east coast and requested that I help him if he arrived in the area. I agreed, and afterwards the colonel invited me to breakfast. I remember the tall and dishy daughters.'

The agent Madoc was asked to look out for may have been the Swiss.[35]

Documents seen by Brigadier Ivan Simson in the 1960s and mentioned by him in correspondence regarding his book *Singapore: Too Little Too Late*, copies of some of which have been unearthed by this author, clearly reveal that Hayley Bell carried out excellent intelligence work in the years 1936–39. The original documents were of copies of letters and reports between Hayley Bell, and Vernon Kell of MI5, Sir John Brennan at the Foreign Office and the Singapore IGP, René Onraet. The papers also indicate that Hayley Bell's later reports were not favourably received by the governor, Sir Shenton Thomas, nor by General Bond who succeeded Dobbie as GOC. The reports touched upon sensitive areas and were deemed to be sensationalist. Sir Josiah Crosby, the long-serving pro-Thai British Minister in Bangkok, disliked them too, for some contained warnings of Thai involvement with the Japanese.

One report was critical of certain aspects of the military leadership in Singapore. In it Hayley Bell commented on the 'transient nature of our leaders and their staffs'. He said that officers no longer travelled much, and did not spend their leaves exploring the countries they were stationed in, as once they used to do. In a private letter he wrote: 'a couple of years in the country is scant time for mediocre intelligences to absorb abstractions well outside routine and recreation; in which to propound to unwelcoming ears theories inopportune and embarrassing.'

He went on to comment upon the 'thousands of quietly nosing Nippon fishers, surveying, sounding, in creek and inlet; the constant intense, and penetrating espionage; the impersonation of harmless immigrants by military and technical experts; the steady acquisition of tactical sites.'

One of his reports was especially embarrassing to the local military commanders. In 1938 the army held manoeuvres which Hayley Bell described as a grand affair of combined operations:

> To furnish transport facilities for innumerable staff officers, umpires, commanders, and what not, numbers of taxis and cars were hired under tender, issued some time before, to all the local garages. The great days passed; it was a huge success. But long after, it was discovered that the cars had been driven by Japanese. One is left to picture their innocent interest in our diversions; the overheard discussions over sandwiches and beer; behind a sleepy, ignorant native of sorts, the left-about maps, schemes, operation orders . . .

He reported on the existing security safeguards concerning the thousands of people of all races engaged in work on government contracts, including the naval dockyard and military fortifications. All these people were finger-printed, photographed, and their antecedents looked into. He found it strange, therefore, that certain people holding the highest offices in the Colony, adamantly refused to permit their house-servants to be included in this process. He commented, 'so, private letters and memoranda may be read, conferences and conversations at table reported'. He added, 'Be sure that it is so.'

Perhaps Hayley Bell's greatest indictment of Singapore authority came towards the end of his tenure there; indeed it may have played an important part in his dismissal a few months later.

In late 1938 he, together with Major Jo Vinden and a group of 'like-minded' officers and specialists, decided on a mock sabotage exercise designed to put out of action and play havoc with all of Singapore. Amongst the officers enlisted either as ersatz saboteurs or as umpires to test the feasibility of each operation, were Major John Westall RM, the SO (I), and Ivan Lyon of the Gordon Highlanders.

This is how the pseudo-operation went:

> On a lorry laden with building material for the naval base, half a dozen disguised enemy drove in . . . to the dockyard and on to the very dock-gate where they detonated their concealed charge of explosives and destroyed the . . . caisson or plug of the great graving dock, thereby letting in a wall of water 48 feet high.

Hayley Bell commented that it would have made a great sight had it actually happened.

> At the same time a dozen swam from the Johore shore to the floating dock moored in the Roads, guarded only by a couple of dockyard police. They opened the sea-cocks and sank it.
>
> At the depot, ten miles outside Singapore town, that contained the entire stock of RAF aviation fuel . . . another lorry, manned by ten technical desperadoes, crashed suddenly from the main public road through the particularly flimsy gates; the single Indian policeman who constituted the entire garrison of the place by night was suitably dealt with and the telephone kept occupied with random converse, while the crew, working in perfect security and in their own time, systematically blew up and fired the only supplies of aviation spirit in the Colony.
>
> A dozen 'Japanese Loochow islanders' swimming under water to the fleet of flying-boats moored off the RAF HQ simultaneously perforated the float on one side of each boat, thereby causing each one to turn over and go to the bottom.
>
> At the civil telephone exchange – particularly vulnerable inasmuch as it was without any pretence of protection or more than the most

> casual guarding – the switchboards were bombed out of existence or the possibility of repair.
>
> At the great main Power Station of the island a manhole – situated, strangely enough, bang in the middle of the main public road from the docks – was levered up with crowbars, and a couple of medium-sized bombs, accompanied by a few bottles of sulphuric acid, were dropped on to the seventeen cables that comprise the entire lighting and power connections of Singapore. Repair to these would take not less than a fortnight.
>
> Many other subsidiary operations were carried out . . . all perfectly synchronised to produce a maximum effect; smaller affairs not worthy of special mention, but causing fires, floods from the reservoirs, and explosions at magazines, each confidently looked-to to occasion general confusion and alarm throughout the fortress and among the population.

Each and every one of these operations, Hayley Bell commented, was well within the competence of undercover agents within the Japanese community. He kept his most devastating statement to last:

> After the scheme, nothing whatever was done by way of making such a holocaust an impossibility. I except here only the Royal Navy. The proven perils to the still unfinished naval base were immediately taken in hand. A single Indian watchman continues to be responsible throughout the dark hours for the aviation spirit. The challenged civil utilities slumber on.

Hayley Bell's reports and activities were not received favourably by either the military or the civilian authorities in Malaya; they rocked the boat in the still waters surrounding the 'impregnable' fortress. Moreover, his reports that the Thais were in bed with the Japanese, offended Sir Josiah Crosby, the British Minister in Bangkok. So when, early in 1939, Eric Holt Wilson, the Deputy Chief of MI5, toured the Far East, he was urged from all sides to get rid of Hayley Bell. Wilson accepted the criticisms in good faith and, after he arrived back in London, a summary of his report was made and circulated by his superior, Colonel Sir Vernon Kell. The summary stated that, 'It is generally considered that the organisation for defence security [in Malaya] is unsatisfactory at present and that drastic and energetic action is now necessary to remedy the defects.' The major problems were identified as lack of funds and 'poor co-operation between the Services and the Defence Security Officer, and a Defence Security Officer who was incompetent'. The report went on to say that Hayley Bell must be replaced as he was 'ill-qualified for such an important position. He lacks energy and tact and cannot appreciate the Service side of the problem. He considers himself qualified to interfere widely.' It was noted that Hayley Bell was a recipient of certain Secret Intelligence Service reports emanating from China, although strictly speaking his actions should have been confined to internal Malayan matters.

The end-result was that Hayley Bell was ordered home in May 1939. He was convinced that his dismissal was engineered by an unholy alliance between the governor, Sir Shenton Thomas and General Bond. He died in Chelsea in 1944; a death hastened, according to Lady Mills, by the bad treatment he had received in Malaya and in the knowledge that many of his unbelieved warnings had come true.

John Becker had preceded Hayley Bell home by about three months. He was to join Military Intelligence and return to Malaya at a later date.

Late in 1938 Major Vinden made a second visit to Hanoi, before going on to Hong Kong and Shanghai. He was in the latter place in time to witness the final stages of the Japanese occupation of the Chinese part of the city and the adjoining countryside.

He left Malaya for good in early 1940. One of his last tasks had been to travel to Sarawak to initiate, in conjunction with the police, plans for the destruction of the Shell oilfields at Miri and Seria in the event of a Japanese attack.

Eight

The Far East Combined Bureau moves to Singapore

During the early part of 1939 the naval authorities at Singapore busied themselves in preparing for the arrival of the Far East Combined Bureau from Hong Kong. Quarters and offices for the staff were constructed on the 'living on the job principle' in a reasonably secluded part of the Seletar Naval Base. Preparations included the installation of sealed telephones connecting with the separate headquarters of the navy, the army, and the air force, as well as with the expanded 'Y' and H/F-D/F (high frequency, direction finding, colloquially named 'Huff-Duff') station at Kranji with its very powerful wireless equipment under the technical care of Lieutenant-Commander S.W. Francis. Two teleprinter circuits were provided between the Bureau premises and Kranji, but there was some delay in supplying the instruments.[1]

HMS *Birmingham* duly arrived at Singapore with almost the entire FECB organisation on Monday 28th August 1939; the start of the war in Europe was now only a week away. Kranji immediately took over most of the 'Y' work – the interception of wireless signals – previously carried out on Stonecutters Island, Hong Kong, though that station continued to operate with a much-reduced staff. Also left behind in Hong Kong were three FECB officers – Major Boxer, Group Captain Bennett and Major Giles – to assist Major-General Maltby, the GOC there, with his Intelligence requirements.*

* At about this time Britain also had smaller 'Y' stations at Kuching in Sarawak, and at Penang, according to information contained in file ADM 1/21145 at the PRO.

Within a remarkably short space of time FECB, under Captain F.J. Wylie, was up and running at its new site. However, as the war with Germany developed, staffing problems were experienced, especially in the 'Y' and Direction-Finding departments which Wylie was anxious to expand. The problems were, he reported, 'the effect of having to expand during a crisis, train staff and keep abreast of current work – all with a transplanted organisation'. The Bureau's secretariat, under Paymaster Commander Shearburn, was expected with a staff of only six to cope with 'all outgoing signals and cypherings as well as with over a hundred a day coming in of which 30% required back references, 15% had errors or queries, and 20% were in cypher.' Wylie's correspondence at this time contained many references to these staffing difficulties, and he was especially concerned about the effect of the tropical heat on some of the older officers sent out to join him. 'Retired naval officers so far sent out are not able to stand up to watchkeeping and energetic duties . . . in this climate, and several important aspects of intelligence are not covered.'

At this stage Wylie's deputy was Commander Palmer of the Royal Australian Navy. Other naval officers holding important positions on the 'Y' staff were Paymaster Captain Shaw, Commander Eric Nave, and Lieutenant-Commanders W.W. Mortimer and M. Burnett.

The army officers attached to FECB were: Colonel G.E. Grimsdale, GSO1; Major A.K. Ferguson, GSO2; and Captain P. Pender-Cudlip, GSO3. One of the tasks of Gordon Grimsdale, who spoke neither Japanese nor Chinese – he had the help of a Chinese-speaking NCO on his staff – as 'Director of Military Intelligence' at FECB, was to present lectures on security matters at various military establishments, and he was at Alor Star aerodrome in northern Malaya for this purpose on 23rd July 1941. Both Ferguson and Pender-Cudlip were fluent in Japanese, having been language officers in Tokyo. Another member of the army team was Major J.G. 'Porky' Ewens, who was responsible for intelligence from French Indo-China, Thailand and the Netherlands East Indies.[2] In the case of Indo-China, up until the fall of France in June 1940 when the colony came under Vichy control, Ewens was assisted by two French liaison officers.

The two RAF Intelligence officers at the Bureau at this time were Wing Commander Walser and Flying Officer Terrell. One highly competent lady civilian member of the staff who dealt with 'Special' – later called 'Ultra' – material, seems to have been a certain Mrs Wingfield, who left a big gap in the organisation when she returned to join her husband in the UK in May 1941.

The Royal Navy's SO (I) at Singapore was Captain (soon to be promoted Major) J.C. Westall, Royal Marines. Westall was not strictly speaking part of FECB – he was on the staff of, and responsible to the Rear Admiral, Malaya – but his duties called for him to be in close contact with that organisation. One of his more important tasks was to run the network of Reporting Officers in the region. Westall's man at Port Dickson on the west coast of Malaya, for example, was Customs Officer John Lewis who also acted as Harbour Master. His reporting work is probably typical of all the others. Supplied with naval code books, he reported over Post Office cable lines on the movements of Japanese vessels visiting the port, and kept his ear to the ground for any other useful information. Lewis says that the codes were intricate, and that using the Post Office lines created delays. Also the system was liable to errors. 'Westall told me it would be easier if I just rang up!'[3]

Apart from the French, other nations posted liaison officers at FECB. An Australian navy captain provided a direct link with Naval Command at Melbourne, and the Dutch had an observer. Colonel F.C. Brink was the US army's representative, and the US navy provided, successively, Captains A. Archer and John 'Jack' M. Creighton – Archer was in Singapore from November 1939, two years before America entered the war.

One of the difficulties in sorting out the responsibilities of the British officers involved in FECB after the passage of over fifty years, is that several of them seem to have enjoyed dual roles. Colonel Grimsdale, for example, was closely involved with Military Intelligence at Malaya Command HQ at Fort Canning, and Major Ewens was actually stationed at that HQ, where his secretary was the wife of Captain Pender-Cudlip. Mrs Pender-Cudlip must have proved very useful to Ewens, for not only had she a BA degree in modern languages – French and German – she had learned to speak Japanese whilst staying with her husband in Japan after they married there. She was also well used to typing up military reports, having typed her husband's after his various attachments to Japanese army units during his service in Japan.

Information from 'ground' intelligence agencies was soon being received by FECB at Singapore from all over the Pacific Basin, the Indian Ocean, and from as far afield as the West Indies Station. 'Contact with Secret Intelligence Service was satisfactory and telegrams from all Far East posts were repeated to Hong Kong and Singapore.' Contact with the French authorities in Hanoi and Saigon was established through the interchange of naval liaison officers, the French naval officers based in Singapore being in direct contact with the French Naval C-in-C in the Far East aboard the cruiser *Lamotte Picquet*. FECB, until the fall of France, co-ordinated the sending of Naval Intelligence from Singapore to all the French equivalents of SO (I) in the area. Existing contacts with the Dutch intelligence authorities were expanded, and in their case this included exchange of 'Y' material, for the Dutch had their own wireless intercept station on Java and a decyphering unit which had considerable success in breaking Japanese cyphers.

What Captain Wylie termed 'local sources for FECB information' included several offices of the Singapore government, including the Censorship Department, the Director of Information, the Custodian of Enemy Property and the Police Special Branch. Other sources were from MI5 (Defence Security Officer) and from contacts within certain firms in the private sector, more importantly Cable & Wireless and Reuters. 'Cable & Wireless faithfully tapped through cables and supplied "Y" intelligence', say the authors of an official internal history of British Naval Intelligence.[4]

The 'Y' station at Kranji, under Paymaster Captain Shaw, employed thirty Chief Petty Officer Telegraphists from the WRNS (Women's Royal Navy Service, or Wrens), trained in the special meanings given by the Japanese to the otherwise universal morse symbols. Civilian wireless telegraphy operators were also employed, mainly on the D/F, direction-finding, side.

'Y' and D/F operators acted in tandem in regard to the identification of ship signals. Whenever 'Y' intercepted a signal from an 'enemy' vessel, its frequency was passed to the D/F stations which then tuned in and obtained bearings of the point of origin of the transmission. Two or more bearings together provided a 'fix' on the exact position of the transmitter. Information on the position of German vessels in the area covered – mostly Armed Merchant Cruisers, but also the occasional submarine – were relayed to the Admiralty. Fixes of Japanese vessels were kept on an FECB plot to which were added visual sightings made by British merchant vessels. Positive identification of ship call-signs were made, and from early in 1941 were confirmed by use of 'radio finger-printing', or RFP, equipment. This was an ultra-secret technique using a very high-speed cine-camera with specially sensitive film. It was the invention of Professor (later Sir) Alistair Hardy of zoology and oceanography fame, who was sent out from England to instruct operators at Kranji in its use.[5] The camera was designed to film visual presentations of wireless transmissions as presented on a cathode-ray tube. Examination of the film not only allowed the design of the transmitter to be determined, but microscopic examination of the split-second of film as the transmitter operator pressed his key, allowed the actual transmitter itself to be identified. By the middle of 1941 FECB had what was virtually a dictionary of transmissions of radio sets aboard major Japanese ships. This meant that ships could be identified without the necessity of identifying their call-signs which might be changed from time to time. At Kranji in 1941 the RFP system was under the charge of Captain J.W. McClelland who headed the steadily growing D/F network and who promulgated a daily summary of ship positions.

The DF receivers at Kranji were very powerful indeed. Group Captain Bennett, one of the FECB people left behind in Hong Kong but who for a brief time was transferred to Singapore, says that either the Kranji or Stonecutters installations, or perhaps both, were part of the British D/F network which in November and December 1939 helped track the *Admiral Graf Spee* when it made its foray from the Atlantic into the Indian Ocean. This was shown by Admiral Sir Percy Noble's report on FECB for 1939: 'Admiral Noble . . . mentions that they were able to fix the German pocket battleship . . . with four cross bearings at ranges between 3,000 and 5,600 miles'. These distances indicate that FECB's involvement came when the German pocket-battleship was operating south of Madagascar in November. Later, bottled up in the River Plate by British ships, she was scuttled by her crew.[6]

Admiral Noble also commented on the speeding up of the production of W/T intelligence: 'since June 1939 [it has made it] possible for me to know with reasonable accuracy the whereabouts of the Japanese Combined Fleet.'*

Captain (later Lieutenant-Colonel) Peter Pender-Cudlip – who may now (1997) be the only permanently Singapore-based FECB

* At this time the C-in-C, China Station, still had his HQ at Hong Kong, which made for not inconsiderable communications problems with FECB.

officer still alive – cannot recall much about his work at Singapore after fifty-odd years, but he does remember preparing a short report on Japanese twin-keeled landing-craft, the construction of which followed the design of the majority of their wooden-hulled fishing fleet – 'Hence a large stock of potential landing craft.'[7] That report sticks in Pender-Cudlip's mind because Captain Wylie sent for him one day to pass on an Admiralty commendation for it.

A précis of that landing-craft report appeared in a booklet called the 'Japanese Army Memorandum' prepared by FECB in late 1940 or early 1941, a booklet which, in March 1941, was reprinted with additions and modifications by the General Staff, India. It was distributed, not under a 'Secret' caveat as one might suppose, but under a general statement that it was 'not to be communicated, either directly or indirectly, to the Press or to any person not holding an official position in His Majesty's Services'. This suggests that the Memorandum was intended for wide circulation. Indeed, a printer's code mark on the only copy of the document this author has managed to trace, indicates that the reprint ran to 1,500 copies. Furthermore, as the introduction to the booklet states that its object was to give regimental officers a general idea of the characteristics, organisation, armament, tactics and training of the Japanese army, this suggests that it was intended as a guide to a wide range of officers.[8]

No officer, having read this FECB Memorandum, be he general or subaltern, could have been in the dark about many of the capabilities of the Japanese army, the army air service, or the naval air service. Yet most authorities, including the commanders in charge of British forces in the Far East in their reports and official despatches – some of them made post-war – wrote that they were surprised by the expertise shown by the Japanese and by the excellence of their equipment, especially their aircraft when compared with those the British had in the area in 1941. Yet, amongst other matters, the FECB Memorandum had noted the Japanese 'most marked' preparedness for combined operations, their training in night operations and river crossings, and that in morale they were 'singularly well equipped in this respect'. It went on to note the military's training in opposed landings and stated that 'the initial landing is usually carried out in the dark or shortly before daybreak', in other words, exactly what was to happen when the Japanese landed in Malaya and Thailand. The Japanese army's fondness for the tactic of envelopment was commented upon, plus their use of vigorous pursuit and the employment of tanks to maintain momentum; again, exactly what was to happen throughout the Malayan campaign. Most important of all was a listing of the qualities of the aircraft available to the Japanese; their qualities far outstripping those of the largely obsolete and obsolescent types of aircraft available to the RAF in Malaya with the exception of the few Blenheims.*

The FECB Memorandum was, and is, important. However, over the past five years, this author has interviewed well over one hundred officers who served in either the British, Indian, or Australian armies in Malaya, and he has yet to meet one who had any knowledge of this FECB booklet's existence.†

The Admiralty-run FECB found itself in trouble whenever it was considered to have trodden on the toes of other Departments of State. An example of this came in December 1939 when FECB established the Far Eastern Security Section, or FESS for short, as an integral part of the organisation. FESS was formed 'to collect, co-ordinate and pass to the authorities concerned reports of anti-British activities in the area'. This included building up a black-list of persons working against British security. Under the authority of the C-in-C, China Station, Captain Wylie circulated FECB's intentions about this to all Naval Intelligence stations in the area, to Reporting Officers, and to the British envoys in Japan, China and Thailand, asking them to submit any relevant material they might have. The proposal met with a major stumbling block in the person of 'our man in Bangkok', Sir Josiah Crosby.

Apparently Crosby was not aware of FECB's existence, although his fellow envoys in the east were, for members of *their* staffs had for some time been sources of information coming into FECB.[9] Crosby may have been deliberately left in the dark as both the military and the naval authorities regarded him as too pro-Thai.

Crosby copied the FECB request to the Foreign Office in London in January 1940, pointing out in a covering letter that the request for such information should have come to him through proper channels, that is via the FO itself. Furthermore, in that letter and in the immediate answer to FECB written on his direction, he said that if his officers became involved in such matters and this was discovered

* See also pages 166–168 below.
† See also page 95.

by the Thais, then relations would be strained, and that in any case his officers had not the time for this new work. He added: 'In so far as the desired information may come within the scope of the work performed by the SIS, the acquisition of it is, of course, strictly "taboo" for Diplomatic and Consular Officers alike.'

From this it appears that Crosby's legation and consular staff must have been the only part of the Foreign Office representation in the area which did not have SIS operatives operating under cover of being consular officials. Either that, or he chose to be or was deliberately kept unaware of the existence of any SIS agent, or agents, within his staff. (Nominally SIS came under the aegis of the Foreign Office.)

Crosby's covering letter included a postscript: 'You will see that Captain Wylie's letter to me is headed "MOST SECRET". The use of this superscription causes me some misgiving.' Crosby's own letter to the Foreign Office, which included a copy of Wylie's, was marked merely 'SECRET'.

Some officers at the Foreign Office also seemed unaware of FECB's existence. One of them recorded the following on 29th February 1940. 'A thorough search through our archives back to 1934 has been made but we can find nothing about the Combined Bureau. Possibly the Bureau is the author of the "Combined Intelligence Summary" which we receive regularly from Singapore.'

The matter was finally sorted out when Berkeley Gage became involved. Gage had been working in the Far Eastern section of the Foreign Office at Whitehall ever since his own SIS days in China and his escape from Japanese hands there (see above page 60). Gage worked out a compromise in which Crosby's staff communicated 'all information of the type desired' that was picked up 'in the course of their duties'. In other words they were not required to go out ferreting around for it. Gage thought that Crosby's objections on this sort of reporting applied with even greater force to Japan where the British ambassador, Sir Robert Craigie, was already co-operating with FESS. This was disputed by other officials who thought that Japan could have 'no real grounds for objecting to the collection by H.M. Consular Officers of information about purely anti-British activities'. (Surely, that also applied to Thailand?) In the end, as far as Japan was concerned, it was decided to leave the matter to Craigie's discretion.

A memorandum from Admiral Godfrey, Director of Naval Intelligence, to Mr Henniker-Major of the Foreign Office dated 30th

March 1940, went some way to explaining FECB's role. It included a reference to the fact that amongst FECB's 'Y' personnel were some 'Foreign Office people', a case of the left hand not knowing what the right was doing. In fact the situation in Singapore mirrored the situation at Bletchley Park, which also had Foreign Office representation. Possibly in an attempt to pre-empt any request from these FO officials for more information, Admiral Godfrey added that FECB's 'Y' section produced 'much Intelligence, some of which cannot be acted upon for fear of compromising the source'.

A more detailed description of FECB but one which contains no mention of 'Y' though much about FESS, is to be found in Australian Archives.[10] The information is contained in a secret communication from Captain Wylie to the Director of Naval Intelligence, Melbourne, dated 9th March 1940 in which, as Wylie admitted, 'the organisation and status of the Bureau is somewhat complex'. He hoped that the document would clear up any difficulties that Melbourne had on the subject.

Wylie wrote that FECB was officially representative of the three Services, with the naval side of it controlling the Naval Intelligence organisation on the China Station: 'The Military side of it represents the HQ of Military Intelligence in the Far East, and the Air side has approximately the same scope. Each of the three sides is responsible to its own senior officer, e.g. C-in-C, China Station; the GOC; Malaya Command; and the AOC, Far East, and is also responsible to the HQ of its Service in London.'

Wylie went on:

> So far as is possible, in every matter which is of combined Service interest the Bureau acts as a single unit. Typical of this is the Security Intelligence Section [FESS] . . . In fact, when it deals with the question of enemy organisations in Far Eastern countries which are inimical to Security, the issue is obviously broader than a 'Service' one, it is Imperial.

Information came to FESS, he wrote, from a number of sources outside of the Services' own intelligence organisations, including the SIS, Police, censors, and diplomatic and consular officials. With regard to the problems raised mainly by Sir Josiah Crosby, Wylie made a gentle side-swipe at one or two 'of the more conservative-minded authorities [who] thought that I was trying to urge the Consuls to do espionage'.

More details about FESS are contained in the FECB secret memorandum No. 305/069 dated 2nd May 1940. After a preamble it describes the four provisional lists and summaries to be prepared and distributed.

(a) *Far Eastern Black List.*
(Short title: F.E.B.L.)

Will contain the names, personal details and activities of persons *known by direct evidence* to be active enemy agents or potential agents of any nationality, who are engaged in espionage, sabotage, propaganda or other subversive activities against Allied interests. Each person will be given a number preceded by the initials 'BL'.

N.B. It will be essential to confine this list to really dangerous persons about whose subversive dealings there is sufficient evidence to justify drastic action.

(b) *Far Eastern Security Suspect List.*
(Short title: F.E.S.L.)

Will contain names and records of persons of any nationality *suspected* of subversive activities of any kind against Allied interests. Each person will be given a number preceded by the initials 'SL'.

N.B. Possession of enemy nationality is not a sufficient qualification for this list. There must be some evidence in addition.

(c) *Postulated Foreign Intelligence Organisations in the Far East by Areas.*
(Short title: F.E.P.O.)

These summaries will contain a description of the relevant organisation, objects, general activities, main contacts and personnel, but will not give information regarding particular activities of individuals. Each person will have a number indicating his or her area: (vide FECB Summary 5102A of 9th April 1940). If the individual is on either FEBL or FESL, the 'BL' or 'SL' number will also be given.

(d) *Far Eastern Periodical Summaries of Security Intelligence.*
(Short title: F.E.P.S.)

Will consist of two parts. Part I will cover recent information concerning activities of organisations, while Part II will deal with activities of individuals. Cross references to FEBL, FESL, or FEPO will always be made in the case of individuals. Amendments to FEBL and FESL will be issued as appendices to these summaries.

The distribution list for this particular document included the French Intelligence Service in Hanoi. Strangely it did not include the

Police Special Branch in Singapore, but possibly MI5's representative in Singapore, who was on the list as 'DSO Singapore', was required to liaise with the police on this. SB had, in fact, been compiling its own 'black lists' for years. One of the SB lists, an extensive one, contained information on homosexuals in the region, for at that time – and until recently – homosexuals were considered security risks as being particularly liable to blackmail. The names on the list included those of several senior officials of the Malayan Civil Service, and at least one senior officer in the FMS police. The most illustrious name on it however, was that of Sir Josiah Crosby; perhaps this was another reason why Crosby was not trusted by the authorities in Singapore?

Certain persons known to have featured on FECB's Security Suspect List were:

J.B. David. A member of a Singapore Jewish family, David was well known for throwing parties at which subversives gathered. He was also on SB's suspect list.*

Arbenz. The Swiss Consul in Singapore who was for some unknown reason virulently anti-British. Also on SB's list.

G. MacBryan. An officer of the Sarawak Civil Service, and a close confident of Rajah Sir Charles Vyner Brooke. He had become a Muslim. He was suspected of fomenting nationalism.[11]

O.W. Grut A Scandinavian rubber-planter in northern Malaya. Probably under suspicion because he had a Japanese wife. He in fact served in the Malayan Volunteer Air Force and escaped from Singapore.

Magnus G. Streyffert. Another Scandinavian. Worked at the Ford assembly plant in Singapore. It was vaguely noted 'that there had been concern over some of the things he had said'.

FESS recruited some people with local knowledge to its staff. One of these, from the Singapore Volunteers, was Arthur Cramsie, who says that from early 1941 he spent much time collecting information from various sources on Japanese espionage activities in Malaya and Singapore.[12]

* During the battle for Malaya in December 1941, a German employee of David's, who had somehow escaped internment in September 1939, was involved in a Japanese ambush of a unit of the Argyll & Sutherland Highlanders. The German was shot and killed by Corporal Jock Hogan who then slung the body on to his armoured car and brought it out. Hogan was awarded the Military Medal. (See Report No. 175, Malayan Research Bureau, CO980/217 at the PRO.)

Not many copies of FECB reports and Intelligence Summaries are to be found in 'open' files at the Public Record Office. The few that are available lie scattered under Admiralty, Foreign, Colonial, and War Office references. Some of the available ones seem to have been subjected to an official weeding process. A few also survive in Australian Archives.

The consecutive numbers of the open documents indicate that the total number of reports was large. Their content was wide-ranging, as evidenced by the following extracts.

Secret Notes on Preventive Security issued by
FECB (No. 5907) 4th September 1941.

> The case is cited of a recent investigation at the Netherlands's Legation, Bangkok. The finding of a broken key in the lock of the principal safe led to the discovery that a native employee had duplicate keys to all the safes in the Legation. Furthermore, the native in question was known to have been in indirect contact with the Japanese Military Attaché.
>
> *Sources of Intelligence*. A consideration which is perhaps not always appreciated is that the value of a *source* of intelligence is almost invariably greater than any given piece of information which that source produces, bearing in mind the dividends which it is hoped to reap from it in the future. The authority of a source is normally a 'Most Secret' subject, even if the information itself may be promulgated as merely, 'Confidential'.[13]

FECB report No. 5401 (1st Ed. A), dated November 1941 was on the subject of Japanese espionage in Thailand, and refers to three earlier reports on this subject dating back to December 1940. It made mention of a visit to Thailand in April by Rear Admiral Maeda, Chief of Japanese Naval Intelligence, and how there had been an intensification of Japanese intelligence activities since. In an appendix it listed all the Japanese Service attachés there who were deemed to be spies, and went on to give an estimate of the amount of money Japan was expending on espionage in that country. It commented upon contacts between Japanese and German agents in Thailand, reporting that 'It can be taken for granted that if Japanese occupation of Thailand is in Germany's interest, any plans which have been made for this eventuality will receive the active support of the German General Staff through their representatives in the country.' It mentioned the presence of German 'intriguers' in the country, including Baron Leopold von Plessen, Lieutenant-Colonel Scholl and Major Franz Hueber, a Gestapo officer.[14]

In 1995 the British government began to release some of the 'Y' intercepts concerning the Far East that had been decyphered at either FECB or Bletchley Park. The files containing the released documents are by no means complete, as is shown by either the consecutive numbering of the intercepts, or by the appended cover sheet which listed the original contents of a particular file; even some of the cover sheets are missing. Much of this newly released material is shown and commented upon in this book. However, it must be said that no proper summation of FECB's overall performance can be given unless and until *all* the relevant material about it that survives in certain British government departments is released into the public domain. However, even on the basis of the incomplete information presently available, it can be said that the commanders and staff officers who in their despatches and reports tended to castigate FECB for not providing sufficient and timely warning of Japanese intentions, were likely using FECB as a convenient scapegoat. It was easy to blame an organisation whose members were bound by secrecy at the time and for a long time afterwards, and who therefore were not in a position to speak up for themselves.

The official despatch of Air Chief Marshal Sir Robert Brooke-Popham at the end of his tenure as C-in-C, Far East – from the autumn of 1940 until the end of December 1941 – is typical of all the reports containing criticisms of FECB, and as his was the first to be written – having been produced in July 1942, only six months after he was relieved of command – we shall deal only with the points made by him.[15] The summary of his despatch stated that:

> The efficiency of the Japanese Army and Air Force was particularly underestimated on the following points: their disregard for weather conditions; their mobility, due to the small reliance they placed on mechanisation and artillery and the fact that the men only required simple food; the initiative of the individual Japanese soldier; the performance of the Zero single-seater fighter; the rapidity with which they repaired bridges and aerodromes.

Brooke-Popham had the grace to add that these errors in judgement must not be attributed to the FECB only. It appears, indeed, that

FECB may have been at fault on only one of the points he mentioned, and that is by no means certain.

Let us take the Air Marshal's 'particular' points one by one and relate them to the information in FECB's 'Japanese Army Memorandum' of December 1940/January 1941, remembering that a further twelve months were to elapse from the date of publication until the Japanese attack on Malaya in December 1941. No doubt in the intervening period other important information was received by the British and promulgated.

On Japanese 'disregard for weather conditions', the authors of the FECB Memorandum stated particularly, in regard to opposed landings from the sea which are among the most difficult military operations to conduct in bad weather, that 'Periods of rain or stormy weather are chosen for these operations when possible so as to achieve surprise.'

On Japanese mobility and the requirement for only simple food, 'Flying columns . . . are used to threaten the flank and rear of the enemy, disrupt communications, carry out surprise attacks, harass large formations and for reconnaissance duties', and, 'the following are the arrangements for rations . . . in the field, one day's field ration and one iron ration on the man'. The use of bicycles by these flying columns, a feature of the Malayan campaign, is not mentioned although motor-cycles are.

On the initiative of the individual Japanese soldier the Memorandum likens the Japanese army to the Samurai, and says that in Japanese training manuals 'emphasis is laid on morale and offensive action'. On the expertise of their engineers, 'Technically, the work of engineers in bridging and in the maintenance of roads and tracks is of a high order'. Brooke-Popham also mentioned repairs to aerodromes. We can give him the benefit of the doubt and assume that, at the time he left Singapore at the end of December 1941, he was unaware that the British efforts to destroy the aerodromes they had vacated during the retreat down the peninsula, in most cases when they were under no close attack from Japanese land forces, were very largely ineffective, and that in all cases the Japanese were using them within a day or two of capturing them.

Only on the performance of the Navy Type 'O' fighter, the Zero, may Brooke-Popham have had a valid criticism of FECB. 'This aircraft proved the greatest surprise of the campaign,' said the authors of the Official History of the RAF in World War Two.[16] It had a top speed of some 350mph, and was highly manoeuvrable. With an additional petrol tank (capable of being jettisoned, however) its range could be appreciably increased. It was more than a match for the Brewster Buffalo fighter with which the RAF in Malaya were initially equipped, and, except at heights above 20,000 feet, even for the comparatively few Hurricane Mark IIs that arrived in Malaya when the campaign was nearly over. The official historians wrote:

> The Japanese had made use of the Navy Zero against the Chinese in the spring of 1940. Some details of its performance had been divulged by American newspaper correspondents stationed in Chungking, who had seen it in action at that time, and in the *same* year more details had reached the Air Ministry from other sources . . . On 2nd September *1941* this information was duly forwarded to FECB for transmission to Air HQ. It never arrived there. Moreover . . . a detailed description of it, written in Chinese, reached Singapore in July and was duly translated. What happened next is a matter for conjecture for all records have been destroyed; but it seems probable that this very important report formed part of the mass of accumulated files with which the makeshift Intelligence Section, set up at Air HQ in October 1941, attempted to deal. When war broke out they had by no means completed their task and the report remained undiscovered. The result was a disastrous surprise causing many casualties to pilots who had been informed that the Buffalos they were flying were faster and better than any Japanese fighter – not one of which, it was reported, could reach 20,000 feet – and who in consequence evolved a system of air tactics based on this ill-founded assumption. [Emphasis added.]

That must be compared with Professor Arthur Marder's statement that in May 1941 details of the armament and tankage of a Zero shot down in China in May 1941 also reached Singapore, and that in September further information on the aircraft's performance was sent to both Singapore and London by the Air Attaché in Chungking. Marder says that London and Singapore therefore had a pretty good idea of the Zero's capabilities but that faulty organisation at Headquarters, Far East Air Command resulted in the technical information not being passed to the RAF squadrons.[17]

Whether it was FECB or Headquarters, Air Command, who were at fault over this matter, it is impossible to say. Whichever of them was responsible for this 'gross negligence', as Marder calls it, it is unlikely, given the superiority of the Zero over the Brewster Buffalo, that any air tactic would have saved the latter in the long run, apart from an early and as fast as possible departure from the area. But that would not have been in keeping with the traditions of the RAF.

Brooke-Popham did not lay all errors of judgement solely on FECB. It is as well he did not, for a close member of his own staff was involved in some of them. That person was Group Captain Lawrence Darvall, the senior air member on the staff.

Vice-Admiral Sir Geoffrey Layton, who relieved Admiral Noble as C-in-C, China Station in 1940, in a secret supplement to his official despatch that was not made public until 1994, probably because it contained criticisms of many of his fellow commanders and of political figures in the Far East, commented that Brooke-Popham was not the man for the job he had been given:

> He was unfortunate in losing his first Chief of Staff – Major-General Dewing – from sickness before he was well in the saddle, but it seemed to me even more unfortunate in the extent he was swayed by the extremely optimistic advice given on the Air side by his principal Air Staff Officer, Group Captain L. Darvall.[18]

In a letter dated 7th January 1962 to Professor J.R.M. Butler, the author of *Grand Strategy, Vol. III* of the British Official History of World War Two, General Percival wrote:

> Although it was apparent to most of us, including apparently the C-in-C, Far East and the AOC, that our Air Force was too weak to do much damage to a seaborne expedition before it could establish a bridgehead, yet at a Joint Staff Defence Conference held, I think, about August 1941, the view was officially expressed by the C-in-C's air representative (Group Captain Darvall) that we could rely on the Air Force destroying, I think, about 70% of the ships of an invading force before it landed. The trouble all along was that most of the Naval and RAF senior officers were *far* too optimistic as to what they would be able to do.

Commenting on this in his book *Singapore, 1941–1942*, Louis Allen calls this 'ill-considered optimism on Darvall's part'. However, it seems that Darvall has more to answer for than just ill-considered optimism. Commander (later Captain) A.N. Grey was also on Brooke-Popham's staff. After recording that the strength of the force employed by the Japanese when they attacked Malaya had been correctly forecast many weeks before by Colonel Ferguson of FECB, in an appreciation made soon after Japanese infiltration into French Indo-China had become effective, Grey wrote:

> This appreciation was considered 'alarmist and defeatist' by Group Captain Darvall on whom the Air Chief Marshal relied for advice on Intelligence matters. The appreciation was not accepted by the Air Chief Marshal or his Chief of Staff [Major-General Playfair], nor was it forwarded to London.

Darvall's influence on his C-in-C at this critical time, his dismissal of the FECB report, and his misconception of the RAF's capabilities, has not been previously recorded in full. Flight Lieutenant (later Wing Commander Dr) Toby Carter, who was engaged on top secret radar work in Singapore, met Darvall once in Britain, and met him again in Singapore. 'The impression he made on me,' says Carter, 'was of a rather dull, conventional, regular RAF officer who probably accepted received teaching without question and did everything by the book'.[19] The least one can say about Darvall at this stage in his career is that in matters concerning intelligence, he was purblind. None of this, however, seems to have affected his career. Darvall transferred to General Wavell's staff when Wavell later took command of Allied forces in Southeast Asia. By the end of the war he had reached the rank of Air Vice-Marshal and was later knighted.[20]

It is likely that FECB's *apparent* underestimation of Japanese military capabilities may have in part been due to a desire to maintain local morale. FECB's own Japanese Army Memorandum had clearly indicated some of the strengths of that army. Yet, when Colonel J.H. Thyer, Chief of Staff of the Australian Division in Malaya, met with some senior British Staff officers, he was told by 'an army man who had been in Shanghai and Hong Kong that the Japanese Army is a bubble waiting to be pricked'. British senior officers seemed dead set on permitting an underestimation of Japanese military prowess to permeate all levels of Malaya Command. This is indicated by the experience of Colonel G.T. Wards, one-time language officer and later Military Attaché in Tokyo, who was considered *the* expert on Japanese military matters. He came to Malaya to lecture officers, and was insistent that a Japanese battalion was, in training, discipline and intrepid efficiency, as good as a crack battalion of the Indian army and that meant as good as any battalion anywhere in the world. His listeners shook their heads over what they considered the defeatism of Wards's words, and he was not invited again.

In a letter dated 8th March 1942 from his new base at Chungking, to General Ismay, Churchill's Chief of Staff, Colonel Grimsdale had this to say of FECB:

> Although, God knows, our sources of information were nothing like as good as they should have been, they were the best available, and Dicky [Major-General R.H. Dewing, Chief of Staff, Malaya Command, until sent home sick in mid-1941] invariably relied on us. Directly he went the rest of GHQ staff never believed us and always called us 'alarmists' when we told them how many divisions or aeroplanes the Japs could use. As it happens, our estimates were more accurate even than we had suggested they were. On the day before the war started one of the GHQ staff said publicly that he couldn't understand why the Governor had got the wind up and mobilised the volunteers! If that was the attitude of GHQ, you can understand why people lower down adopted a complacent attitude.[21]

The sources of information Grimsdale referred to were agencies not controlled by FECB itself, for FECB ran no agents of its own. The organisation can scarcely be blamed for lack of or for poor information coming in from these outside sources.

Mid-1940 was a critical period in the Far East. Holland and then France, both with large colonies in the East, had fallen under the heel of the Germans in June. July brought a change of government in Japan with anti-Western elements there, including General Tojo as War Minister, now in complete control. Japan demanded that Britain close the Burma Road along which supplies were reaching Chiang Kai-shek, and made vigorous approaches to the Netherlands East Indies government for oil and other raw materials. There was also successful Japanese pressure on the Vichy French governor of Indo-China to allow them use of airfields and to station troops in the north of that colony, something that brought them closer to 'fortress' Singapore. The move into Indo-China caused the United States government to freeze all Japanese assets in the USA, a move which, according to Joseph Grew, the US ambassador in Tokyo, caused serious concern and bitter resentment in the Japanese cabinet. Throughout the Far East tension was rising.[22]

This was also the time when, because of the situation in Home Waters and the Mediterranean, Britain was actually reducing its naval forces in the Far East. Between February and June 1940, all fifteen submarines on the China Station were ordered to the Mediterranean. In December 1941, on the outbreak of war with Japan, there was only one British submarine in the eastern theatre, HMS *Rover* at Singapore, and she was only there refitting from the Middle East.[23] In fact Admiral Layton had invented non-existent submarines as part of an elaborate deception scheme in which FECB was involved. FECB 'leaked' information about these bogus submarines over the airwaves, and was subsequently rewarded when an intercept revealed the information had been sent to Tokyo.

At such a critical period, it was really no time to change the man at the head of FECB, but that is what happened. Captain Wylie was relieved by Captain K.L. Harkness who had no experience whatsoever of intelligence work; he was a gunnery specialist and had had command in destroyers.[24] The appointment came as a complete surprise to him. Professor Marder says in his *Old friends, New Enemies*, that because Harkness was too pleasant and not sufficiently ruthless when he needed to be, he was unable to inspire the full confidence of the commanders in Singapore.

There were other changes in the FECB staff during 1940. The most important was the loss of Eric Nave who was invalided back to Australia in February 1940; (he stayed there to run the Royal Australian Navy's radio interception centre at Melbourne.) Group Captain (later Air Commodore) R.W. Chappell came to head the air section, perhaps as a result of what Air Chief Marshal Brooke-Popham found in October when he arrived to become C-in-C, Far East. He reported then that FECB was 'somewhat unbalanced', with too much attention 'concentrated on Naval Intelligence, and the Air Intelligence was quite inadequate'.[25]

Some civilian officers joined, though exactly what they did in FECB is not known. Two were Asiatic Petroleum Company (Shell) employees, taken on for their knowledge of the oil industry and perhaps for their specific knowledge of Japanese oil stocks. One of them was R.J.F. Kalberer and the other was named Tate or Tait. Kalberer, who was born in 1911, died in March 1942 in the Dutch islands south of Singapore during an attempt to escape from the Japanese. The fate of Tate/Tait is unknown.

It may have been FECB reports prepared by these men that were used as the basis for the estimates of Japan's oil stocks which the Joint Intelligence Committee (JIC) placed before the Joint Chiefs of Staff in London. The JIC Report of 24th May 1941 demolished the widely held idea that, as Japan was not an oil-producing nation, she was in no position to wage war. It was estimated that she had stocks of between 6.3 and 7.5 million tons at the end of 1940, although the report added that Japanese secrecy made it difficult to estimate stocks accurately. Nevertheless, the stocks were sufficient for war and civilian purposes to last for eight to twelve months.

Nine

'Special' Intelligence

Early in 1940, one of Bletchley Park's Special Liaison Units, or SLUs, was stationed at Singapore, a fact not previously published. The SLUs were formed to handle and control all Special Intelligence from 'Y' sources, and were the brainchild of Group Captain F.W. Winterbotham. A pre-war SIS agent, Winterbotham, was now based at Bletchley Park and in charge of security and communication of all intelligence gathered from decyphering Axis signals – signals which later fell under the popularly known codename 'Ultra'.[1] An SLU was formed of a small group of officers and technicians, the latter all being sergeants. The officers appointed, usually from the RAF though not in the case of Singapore, were never of high rank in order to avoid speculation about what they were up to. So secret was their work that, even after the war, very few received any kind of official recognition for their services.

'Special' or 'Ultra' Signals Intelligence was so vital that Winterbotham devised what are probably the strictest security arrangements ever conceived for such material, and the SLUs attached to field command headquarters were crucial to these arrangements. It says much for Winterbotham's foresight and organising ability that the principles he early laid down for governing the operations of the SLUs did not vary throughout the war. In *The Ultra Secret* he wrote:

> The SLU officer was responsible for personally delivering the Ultra message to the commander or to a member of his staff designated

to receive it. All messages were to be recovered by the SLU officer as soon as they were read and understood. They were then destroyed. No Ultra recipient was allowed to transmit or repeat an Ultra signal. Any action taken by a commander on the information given by Ultra was to be by way of an operation order or command or instruction which in no way referred to the Ultra signal or could lead the enemy to believe his signals were being read.

The system, in short, was built around the need-to-know principle, and in practice a commander could not act upon Ultra information unless there was another possible source that the enemy could 'blame' for the leak.

The SLU at Singapore was in situ prior to 5th January 1940, which means that it predates the earliest of those in other theatres of war that have been mentioned in published references. This indicates the importance which Whitehall placed on Japanese 'Special' Intelligence. At the very least it proves that, from early 1940, Japanese 'Special' was being handled in Singapore, for under the strict Ultra rules there was no other reason for the unit to be there.

The identities of only a few officers forming SLUs have become known over the years. The existence of the unit and the identities of all three officers in the Singapore party, where it was officially known as the 'Military Special Intelligence Party' and unofficially amongst the few who knew of them as the 'Bletchley Park people', would not be known now had it not been for what appears to be some form of administrative cock-up between FECB, Malaya Command, and Whitehall, over which part of the War Establishment they belonged to. In other words, whose pay-roll they were on.

Colonel Grimsdale sent the following message to the War Office on 11th June 1941:

MOST SECRET

From GSO1 (Intelligence) Far East, Singapore.

No. 19798 11/6/41

It appears that military special intelligence party (Captain Marr-Johnson etc.) are not regarded by the War Office as part of War Establishment of FECB. This is anomalous situation since they should surely appear on some establishment. Suggest this be rectified by inclusion in FECB. Present number includes 3 officers 3 RASC clerks and 2 T.W.Ss.[2]

The three officers were Captain P. Marr-Johnson, Captain G.G. Stevens and Lieutenant N.F. Webb. Marr-Johnson had earlier fought

(*Above*) The young Prince Hirohito's visit to Buckingham Palace in 1921, during the late years of the Anglo-Japanese accord. Colonel F. S. G. Piggott, the British Military Attaché, is third from left, back row; his predecessor, Brigadier-General C. R. Woodroffe, eighth from left.

(*Below*) The marriage in 1920 of A. H. Dickinson who became Inspector-General of Police in Singapore in 1939. He and his predecessor, René Onraet (second from right, standing), were actively engaged in Intelligence work against the Japanese and the communists. (*Courtesy Pauline Asbury*)

(*Above*) The Royal Navy delegates to the Washington Conference of 1921, which resulted in the international Naval Armament 'Limitation' agreement of 1922. Rear Admiral Eonle, later Admiral of the Fleet Lord, Chatfield (third from left) was the author in 1924 of *It Might Happen Again*.

(*Below*) Return visit of the Prince of Wales (sitting seventh from left) to Tokyo in 1922. Standing almost directly behind him is Lieutenant Lord Louis Mountbatten.

(*Right*) The Electric Code machine invented by Edward Hebern in the early 1930s, the forerunner of the US 'Purple Machine' which produced 'Magic', the US equivalent of 'Ultra' or 'Special'.

(*Above*) Stonecutters Island, Hong Kong, The site of the Radio Interception and Direction-finding Station, set up in 1935. The station's appearance had not generally altered by the late 1940s when this photograph was taken. (*Below*) The North China Signal Section – Peking Signals, Peking 1934 (*Royal Signals Museum*).

(*Above, left*) Colonel Doihara Kenji, an outstanding and unscrupulous agent for Japan whom the British press dubbed the 'Lawrence of Manchuria'. (*Right*) Richard Sorge, German-born Soviet master spy, arguably the most successful spy in history. (*Below*) Group photo, taken in 1931, of the Shanghai Police at 'Bubbling Well' station. It shows the international make-up of the Shanghai Municipal Police at that time. (*Courtesy Superintendent Frederick West*)

(*Above*) Colonel and Mrs Francis Hayley Bell in 1939, when he was Defence Security Officer in Singapore. With them are two of their daughters, Winifred (*right*) and Elizabeth. (*Courtesy Mrs Elizabeth Hewitt*). (*Below, left*) Senior Superintendent M.Ll. Wynne, 1936, who headed, before the war, the Japanese Section of Singapore Special Branch. (*Right*) Captain Malcolm Duncan Kennedy, an oil executive who later became Reuter's correspondent in Japan. He had close connections with MI6. (*Courtesy D. Kippford*)

(*Above*) A gathering of military attachés hosted in 1936 by the Japanese Minister of War. Major-General Piggott is sitting fifth from right, and the British Air Attaché, Wing Commander R. W. Chappell, at the right-hand end.

(*Below*) A party for Japanese officers at the British Embassy. The ambassador, Sir Robert Craigie, is wearing a hat, and third from left is Sir George Sansom, commercial councillor, but with connections with British Intelligence.

(*Above*) Major-General F. S. G. Piggott, the long-serving Military Attaché in Japan, whose reports sympathetic to the country and its traditions, were sometimes referred to as 'Piggottry'.
(*Below*) Lieutenant Pender-Cudlip, a language officer in Japan, was in the War Office on attachment with 1st (Independent) Mountain Artillery Regiment in Takata in 1937. He annotated this photograph.

(*Right*) René Onraet, the Inspector-General of Police in Singapore who created the Japanese section of the Singapore Special Branch. (*Below*) Major-General William Dobbie, GOC Malaya, 1936-39, and his staff, which includes Colonel Percival, later GOC, and Colonel Shakspear (right and left of front row respectively), and Major H. Vinden, standing second from right, who dealt with intelligence matters, and has left in his papers some shrewd contemporary assessments.

a running battle in Hong Kong with the naval head of FECB and had refused point blank to work under the Admiralty umbrella. That Marr-Johnson apparently got away with this refusal seems to indicate his importance in the Special Intelligence field. It is not known, however, whether he was part of an SLU in Hong Kong. If he was, that makes the Far Eastern SLU connection an even earlier one.

After being commissioned into the Royal Artillery, Marr-Johnson quickly showed an ability in learning languages, and in 1932, along with J.D.P. Chapman of the Royal Engineers and Charles Boxer of the Lincolnshire Regiment, he was sent to Japan as a language officer. All three men were to reach an exceptionally high standard. Marr-Johnson was in his last year in Japan when Peter Pender-Cudlip arrived, and he was, says Pender-Cudlip, 'one of the best Japanese linguists there had ever been among the language officers'. After leaving Japan Marr-Johnson received training in cryptography at GC&CS in London. He was sent to Hong Kong early in 1939. Ten days after the Japanese attacked Malaya in December 1941, newly promoted Major Marr-Johnson was sent to India to command a new unit of cryptographers being set up there, though there is a possibility that he was in Java for a few weeks early in 1942 as a one-man SLU to General Wavell.[3]

The second member of the team was Captain Geoffrey Stevens of the Essex Regiment. He had been with Marr-Johnson in Hong Kong. The fact that Stevens spoke fluent Italian – he knew no Japanese – suggests that the British were intercepting a range of Italian messages in the Far East. After leaving Singapore, Stevens took up an intelligence job in Washington DC.

Unlike his colleagues, N.F. Webb, always known as 'Webbo', was a war-commissioned officer who had earlier worked for a subsidiary of the Shell Company in Yokohama called the Rising Sun Oil Company. He spoke fluent Japanese. At the outbreak of the war with Germany he travelled back to the United Kingdom to join up. After the war Webb rejoined Shell, and later became the Secretary of the Japanese Association in London.

This then was the group of officers who were responsible, amongst other things, for advising the C-in-C, Far East on whether or not he could act upon any Special Intelligence received.

The arrival of FECB in Singapore and the sacking of Colonel Hayley Bell were not the only changes in the security scene in Malaya in

1939. Both René Onraet and Charles Sansom, Singapore and FMS Inspectors-General of Police respectively, retired that year, to be replaced by A.H. Dickinson and E. Bagot.

Arthur Harold Dickinson is arguably the finest policeman produced by the Singapore/FMS branch of the British Colonial Police Service. He arrived in Malaya as a Cadet in 1912, and then went to Madras for two years to study Tamil. During his spell in India he caught the eye of David (later Sir David) Petrie, a senior officer of the Indian Police Service. The pair renewed their acquaintance in 1922 when Petrie worked with G.C. Denham to form the Malayan Political Advisory Bureau. In 1915, Dickinson was involved in action against the 5th Light Infantry of the Indian Army when it mutinied in Singapore.

Dickinson seems early on to have been destined for high office. A measure of this perhaps, is that when in 1920 and still only twenty-eight years old, he married Ethel Kitchen in Singapore, the wedding was attended by the IGP, A.R. Chancellor, and by two future IGPs, Charles Hannigan (FMS) and René Onraet. Dickinson was awarded the King's Police Medal in 1928, and ten years later the OBE for his part in putting down a communist-inspired armed insurrection by strikers at Batu Arang when he was Chief Police Officer, Selangor.

In 1938 MI5 in London produced a Fortress Defence Scheme for Singapore that provided for a Civil Security Officer (CSO) to work alongside MI5's own man there, the Defence Security Officer (DSO). In 1939, with the coming of the war with Germany, the Scheme was implemented, and Arthur Dickinson as IGP became the CSO. He at once recommended the setting up of the Malayan Security Service, in order to:

> co-ordinate the work of the various police organisations in the Peninsula, to establish a central control and uniform legislation for aliens, to provide security control of the Northern Border [with Thailand], and pan-Malayan direction from a central office in all police civil security affairs, which covered a very wide field.[4]

As with all other schemes and legislation which concerned pan-Malayan matters, agreement for this measure could only be reached after discussion between representatives of the nine constituent members of the Federated and Unfederated Malay States, the Straits Settlements, Brunei, Sarawak and British North Borneo, a total of thirteen separate authorities. Not surprisingly, agreement for the scheme took a long time, in this case almost two years, but, said Dickinson, '"Malayan Security" was up and running some time before the outbreak of the Malayan Campaign [December 1941], giving aid in local state intelligence and executive action, and assisting the Governor and High Commissioner.'

Under the scheme a police officer in each Malayan state became the 'Security Officer'. The one for Johore, for example, being Assistant Superintendent H.B.J. Donaldson. In a report made in 1954 Donaldson wrote; 'it must be remembered that I was only made local security officer, Johore, on November 1st 1941'.[5] This was less than six weeks before the Japanese army landed in Malaya.

Also set up was the Malaya Defence Security Committee consisting of Staff Officers (Intelligence) from each of the Services, together with the Defence Security Officer and the Inspector-General of Police. It is in regard to this latter body that this author has discovered the only contemporary criticism of Dickinson. Major J.C. Westall, the SO (I), has recorded, 'This committee functioned well and obtained results when we were once able to persuade the IGP to forward definite recommendations instead of long treatises'.[6] The criticism was a little unfair. Dickinson was a policeman trained to present thoroughly documented cases that would stand up in court. He was also subject to a civil service environment that required every innovative proposal to pass through various departments and committees, and for that to be done successfully, the proposal and all its ramifications had to be fully documented and explained. It was not Dickinson's fault that the Malayan Civil Service system was long-winded and incapable of quickly adjusting to a wartime footing. Only the man at the head of that Civil Service, Governor Sir Shenton Thomas, had the power to shake the Service from long-established routines and procedures, and this he signally failed to do.

Matters outside Singapore and Malaya with which Dickinson was actively involved were security in Sarawak, Brunei and British North Borneo, including 'oil-denial' plans for the two former territories in the event they were attacked by Japan. One Dickinson-run agent was the mysterious Indian called Prithvi Chand who had been involved in political security matters with René Onraet, the previous Inspector-General of Police. 'That pair', reports a Singapore police officer, 'were probably as expert in Far East politics as anyone around at the time'.[7] With Dickinson, Prithvi Chand was involved in investigations into Japanese clandestine activities in the Borneo territories, and from time to time he was even loaned to the police in Hong Kong. In Singapore itself, he managed to get himself into the good graces of J.B. David, one of the men on Special Branch's Black List of subversives, and was able to supply SB with much useful information.

The Defence Security Officer, Singapore, appointed by MI5 to follow Hayley Bell, was a Colonel Green. Not much is known about him except that he did not stay long in the position. Green was succeeded by Colonel J.G. Johnston about whom A.H. Dickinson was to write:

> The Defence Security Officer latterly in Malaya was handicapped by the fact that he was not personally equipped, and was consequently not regarded as an expert. There was insufficient appreciation of the importance which should have attached to his appointment, insufficient realisation of the wider implications of his work. His office in practice was overwhelmed with elementary and pettifogging detail, insisted upon by the Services, which cluttered up the machinery both of the Services themselves and the Civil Police in particular. Nor did his position appear to be defined sufficiently firmly in relation to the Services to give him that authority which war conditions demanded, if there was to be firm control. In effect, this office became largely a post-box which, in the stress of affairs, had to be circumvented as frequently as it was used, both by the Services and the Civil Police, if wheels were to be kept turning.

Dickinson believed that DSOs should be young and highly qualified officers with a flair for political assessment. In his view such posts were no places for elderly retired officers:

> It is a matter for regret that MI5 was unable, through the immense pressure of events in Europe, to spare more time for criticism and control of its security responsibilities in Malaya. From its birth, the post of DSO, Malaya [*sic*], had been an ailing and ill-developed child.[8]

In a move which mirrored that of FECB, the headquarters of the British Secret Intelligence Service for Southeast Asia was also shifted from Hong Kong to Singapore sometime during 1939, leaving Charles Drage behind in charge of the local operation. Drage himself left Hong Kong in 1941, and for a time joined the SIS team in Singapore.

Air Chief Marshal Sir Robert Brooke-Popham, as C-in-C, Far East, made a tour of his domains around Christmas 1940, returning to Singapore with none too high a regard for the British Intelligence community. We have earlier seen that he had singled SIS out for special criticism in a message dated 6th January 1941 to the Air Ministry. He ended that message:

> I am aware that a representative is being sent out to investigate but consider that action is required at once. Suggest immediate appointment of Head of SIS organisation in Far East to supervise and co-ordinate work of existing three sections [probably China, Japan and Southeast Asia sections] and with power to make changes in personnel without delay.[9]

That this was not London's first intimation of problems with the SIS is clear from the Air Ministry's reply dated 21st January:

> No. X.470. . . . Defects and also inherent difficulties of this essential link in our Intelligence Organisation are fully appreciated here as is also urgency of problem. These were explained in detail by Admiral Noble in report received last November. Latter had close personal knowledge of individuals concerned during his period of Command.
>
> As a result of Admiral Noble's report suitable experienced officer was sent out by 'C' to investigate and report by telegram on suitability of personnel, method of improving co-operation between representatives and organisation generally.
>
> This officer who is representative referred to by you, is shortly due at Singapore and will contact you on arrival. 'C' proposes to take immediate action on his recommendations.*

The unnamed Inspecting Officer, who in fact was G.C. Denham, finally made a report to Brooke-Popham who sent a message to the War Office on 17th May 1941 summarising the findings.

> No. 63/3.
> Defects in organisation here derive from following. (A) Personalities. (B)

* 'C' was the codename for the Head of SIS in London, at this time Colonel Stewart Menzies.

Lack of adequate training of personnel. (C) Lack of central direction and co-ordination out here. (D) Ineffective criticism by Service Authorities of information obtained and insufficient trust and use of SIS sources. (E) Lack of an organisation in Burma which will become a principal centre in war.

2. Defects in (A) (B) and (C) can to great extent be overcome by appointment of central co-ordinating officer here. Defects under (D) which have been serious are in process of being put right already. I most strongly recommend the immediate setting up of a Co-ordinating Head for Far East to be located here. Your Inspecting Officer may be prepared to undertake task of setting up office and acting as co-ordinating authority so long as he can give occasional time to his local business interests in Java. I strongly recommend that he should be appointed and consider his business interests would provide good cover for his work. Proposal did not originate from him. C-in-C, China [Fleet] concurs.

A day earlier Brooke-Popham had urged the War Office to agree to the setting up of an independent office of the Ministry of Economic Warfare (MEW) in Singapore, to control and co-ordinate 'anti-Axis measures between the Dutch, Americans and ourselves'. He went on:

> The setting up of MEW organisation in Malaya might be expensive and take time to be effective but failure to do so is even more costly in permitting supplies to reach the enemy . . . But economic pressure is only one aspect of non-belligerent action to control Japanese pro-Axis activities. Other important fields are intelligence and security, propaganda and information and shipping control. Some action on all these heads is already being taken but it cannot be really effective unless it is centrally controlled.[10]

Many of the points made by Brooke-Popham were answered in a telegram from the War Office on 7th June. It was pointed out that important economic warfare decisions could only be made after consultations with other departments, and that was only practicable in London. The MEW was considering however, the appointment of a representative to FECB. The message went on:

> No. 70866.
> Following points have been agreed and where necessary action is being taken here:
> (a) FECB to be co-ordinating authority for all intelligence in Far East.

(b) SIS are nominating a head to co-ordinate all SIS agencies in the Far East. This officer will be a member of FECB but responsible to 'C'.
(c) Foreign Office have been invited to consider issue of direction to HM Consular Officers in Far East instructing them to encourage British subjects in collection of intelligence. Proposal is to issue questionnaire for guidance of these officers and to specify certain areas in which consuls will be intimately connected with all aspects of intelligence work including SIS particularly in providing quick means of inter-communication.
(d) Australian Naval authorities have been approached with a view to increasing our sources of information in the Japanese Mandated Islands.
(e) Intimate co-operation with American officials in Far East as regards complete exchange of intelligence on countries in which British Empire and USA have a mutual interest. Instructions in this sense are being telegraphed separately to you, also to Hong Kong and to British Military attachés in Tokyo, Chungking, and Bangkok, and to the Consul-Generals at Manila and Peking.

The message went on to ask the C-in-C, as if he had not done so already, to 'indicate any special points which are causing you anxiety'. That resulted in a joint reply from the C-in-C, Far East and the C-in-C, China Station which is recorded here in full not only because it shows the measure of the chief commanders' concerns, but, much more importantly, because it is evidence that, at the time of the reply in June 1941, FECB (and consequently GC&CS) was reading Japanese Consular codes but not Naval ones. The significance of this will be made clear.

MOST SECRET.
AIDAC 714. 14.6.41
Following for War Office from C. in C. Far East and C. in C. China . . . Following are the points on which anxiety is principally felt in regard to security arrangements in Far East.
(i) Lack of information regarding Japanese Espionage and of effective counter-measures. Almost our only means at present of gauging extent and success of Japanese espionage is derived from Special Intelligence sources, which may for technical reasons dry up at any moment, and are in any case *limited to Intelligence transmitted through consular channel*.
(ii) Information received as in (i) reveals continuous stream of Military and Shipping Intelligence through consuls, but this cannot be controlled as withdrawals of cypher facilities would be followed by similar action

by Japan, and source cannot be revealed in order to furnish evidence against Japanese consul.
(iii) No evidence of German Espionage Organisation or of co-operation between German and Japanese organisations has been detected though something must exist.
(iv) Arrangement to detect illicit W/T transmissions are incomplete. Solid liaison with American Security organisations is an urgent requirement. With Dutch it is already good.
2. Consider best way of instituting inquiry would be to send an experienced Officer as Inspector of Defence Security in Far East.[11] [Emphasis added.]

This message, sent jointly to the Admiralty by Air Chief Marshal Sir Robert Brooke-Popham, a recipient of 'Special Intelligence', and by Admiral Sir Geoffrey Layton under whose command FECB came, is strong evidence, if not incontrovertible proof, that in June 1941 the British were not able to read Japanese naval codes.

Ever since the last war 'conspiracy theories' have been advanced about the circumstances behind the unpreparedness of the American army and navy commanders and their forces at Pearl Harbor when it was attacked by Japanese carrier-based aircraft on 7th December 1941. It has been argued that President Roosevelt, who definitely wanted to enter the war in the face of the isolationism that was still a strong force in the United States, deliberately withheld from those commanders some of the Sigint material he had received regarding Japanese intentions, thus encouraging an attack that would unite his nation behind him. Then, in 1991, James Rusbridger in *Betrayal at Pearl Harbor*, co-authored by Eric Nave, added a significant new dimension to those conspiracy theories by asserting that, through British ability to intercept and read the main Japanese naval code – called JN-25 by the Allies – which had been broken in the autumn of 1939, Churchill had foreknowledge of the Pearl Harbor attack but failed to warn the Americans of it, and thus ensured that the United States was well and truly in the war. This rather oversimplifies the case which Rusbridger made, but it is correct in essence.

Rusbridger's case largely rested upon information which he indicated had been supplied by his co-author, cryptographer Captain Eric Nave. However, in an interview in 1991 for Japanese television, Nave repudiated a large slice of what Rusbridger had written, calling it speculation. In addition, Nave had apparently forgotten that on 1st December 1940, a year before the attack on Pearl Harbor, the Japanese had replaced code JN-25, which was being at least part-read by Britain, with another the Allies called JN-25b. No mention of this new code, which the American navy cryptographic section in Washington (OP-20-G) was also working on, was made by Rusbridger.

This new code proved a very hard nut to crack. So much so that when the Royal Australian Navy's Director of Signals Communications, Commander J.B. Newman, visited FECB in March 1941, he reported home that most Japanese codes were still unable to be read, and that at that time FECB was almost wholly dependent for naval information on traffic-analysis and direction-finding.[12]

The Brooke-Popham/Layton message, from a source even more authoritative than Commander Newman's, now advances the date of the Allies' inability (by then the British, Americans and Dutch were co-operating on these matters in the Far East) to read the new Japanese naval code, to at least the middle of June 1941. This fact in itself goes a long way towards undermining Rusbridger's theory which was based on the continuity of the British ability to read the code the Japanese navy was using. (See also page 288 below.)

G.C. Denham, the unnamed Inspecting Officer, with business interests in Java, mentioned in Brooke-Popham's message of 17th May, and who was recommended by him for the post of Co-ordinating Officer, was formerly of the Indian Police and the man who had taken the top police job in Singapore for two years in the 1920s. Since retiring from the Indian Police in 1933 Denham had been Managing Director of the Anglo-Dutch Plantation Company which had its Head Office at Surabaya in East Java.

In London 'C' took Brooke-Popham's advice and duly appointed Godfrey Denham to head the SIS organisation in the Far East. The area of Denham's responsibility was vast, stretching from Tokyo in the north down to the Netherlands East Indies, and from Burma in the west across to the Philippines in the east. On top of the problems of distance, the appointment came far too late. According to Brooke-Popham some improvements were made, but as Denham had to rely mainly on agents already in situ, he was not able to accomplish many changes in what turned out to be the short time available to him.

So SIS had donned a new cloak but most of the daggers were held in the same old hands. Apart from those operatives already mentioned such as Charles Drage, and Harry Steptoe in Shanghai, two other senior SIS men inherited by Denham were G.H. Wilkinson in Manila, given the honorary rank of Lieutenant-Colonel by the British to give him some status with his American hosts, and H.A. Graves, His Britannic Majesty's Consul-General in Kobe, who was Britain's top agent in Japan.

As A.H. Dickinson pointed out in 1946 in an essay on Malayan Security, it is doubtful whether non-Asiatics can operate effectively in intelligence in Asiatic countries. By the time Denham arrived, there was little time to select and place 'local' agents, let alone train them, and that applied equally to new European agents. For that matter, if the sort of training that might have been given then bore any resemblance to the sort given by SIS in London in 1946 to European Far Eastern specialists, it is unlikely to have done much good. Of what use is it for a Briton selected by SIS for training for placement in a country in Southeast Asia, and selected because his entire working life had been spent in that area and because he spoke several of the local languages, to learn the art of 'contacting' another European agent on the steps of St Paul's Cathedral? At St Paul's the trainee, and the SIS lady he met, may have been lost in the crowd, but that would not have been the case at, say, the entrance to the Wat Phra Kaeo, or the Temple of the Emerald Buddha, in downtown Bangkok.

Denham set up his office in the Police CID building alongside that of MI5's Colonel Johnston, with the local cover of being Johnston's assistant. In his papers A.H. Dickinson always referred to Denham as the 'Foreign Office representative', a reference to the paymaster organisation behind SIS. Denham, with his earlier experience of using 'native' agents in India, made a start on creating a similar network in Southeast Asia. For this he used the services of the Chinese Communist Party in Singapore which had connections everywhere.[13]

Probably because of his police background Denham was able to work successfully with the Singapore Special Branch. It was SB that introduced him to Loi Tek, the Chief Secretary of the local Communist Party, who was on the police unofficial payroll. Of Denham, Dickinson was to write, 'This officer's interests lay outside Malaya but his work necessitated the closest liaison with the Civil Police.' Denham also managed to keep his cover intact, in sharp contrast to Drage. The true nature of Denham's work was known on the police side only to Dickinson and to his deputy M. Ll. Wynne. Even Dickinson's personal secretary, Mrs Thompson, made no mention of Denham in her notes, although she mentions Johnston and several others engaged in intelligence. Peter Pender-Cudlip of FECB also knew nothing of Denham although he had met Charles Drage on three or four occasions at the FECB offices. He says, 'the reports we had from Drage's organisation were not much use, as I remember, but a few were of new or confirmatory value.'

Mervyn Wynne, Singapore's number two policeman, had a hornet rather than a bee in his bonnet about Japanese clandestine activities in Malaya. Over several years his reports on Japanese subversion and espionage and their links with Chinese Triads, especially in relation to opium smuggling, were so voluminous and so frequent that many persons high up in the Malayan Civil Service dismissed them as signs of paranoia. H.P. Bryson, of MCS, wrote in 1972, after Wynne was long since dead, 'I can still see Wynne creeping silently into my room with some blood-curdling information that the authorities wouldn't listen to.'[14]

Harry Harper, who was serving as the Officer Superintending Police Circle at Kuala Kangsar in Malaya in 1939, recalls one of Wynne's visits: 'I remember Mervyn bursting into my office and, looking at the large wall map of Malaya hanging behind my desk, strode up to it and with a blue pencil drew a line around Siam and with large letters wrote JAPAN, so even at that distant date he seemed to have an idea of what we were in for.'[15]

It was to Wynne, called the 'great expert on Japanese spy methods' by one of Brooke-Popham's staff officers, that an 'Asiatic' was brought in the summer of 1941 after he had been arrested for spying on the defences around Kuching, the capital of Sarawak. The alleged spy carried documents that no one in Sarawak could decypher. No useful information was obtained, and it is not known what happened to the spy, or if indeed he proved to be one.[16]

Wynne, who had served with distinction in the 5th Battalion, Rifle Brigade, in 1917–18, was a brilliant police officer. His book *Triad and Tabut* is still considered a standard work on Chinese Triads and Muslim secret societies. He was also an expert on the irredentist movement in the Malayan State of Trengganu, and had extensive files going back many years on the significant number of people in that State who sought a return to Thai rule. But it was on Japanese matters that he began writing directly and frequently to Sir Vernon

Kell, head of MI5 in London, without the knowledge of his superiors, action no doubt fuelled by the lack of serious interest given to his reports locally. In December 1941, when the Japanese landed and Wynne saw his worst fears realised, a close colleague says, 'I saw Mervyn break up and grow old before my very eyes'.

Ten

Japanese Infiltration and Indian Nationalism

Just as she had an appeasement policy over Germany in the years prior to 1939, Britain developed a similar policy with Japan especially after the war in Europe began. One sign of it was the closing of the Burma Road, one of Chiang Kai-shek's primary supply routes, in early July 1940 after sustained pressure from Japan. It remained closed until 18th October, and the fact that the closure period coincided with the rainy season which made the road impassable anyway, does not hide the fact that Britain was forced into closing it. Only rarely did Britain adopt a strong stance against Japan, and whenever Japanese spies were uncovered in a part of the Empire the cases seldom ended in any way other than a quietly arranged deportation of the men involved.

However when, at the end of July 1940, a number of British subjects were arrested in Japan on charges of spying, for once Britain acted firmly, an attitude made politically necessary by the fact that one of those arrested, Reuters' Representative in Tokyo, M.J. Cox, either committed suicide during interrogation by throwing himself out of a window at Japanese Kempetai headquarters, or, was thrown out.

Sir Alexander Cadogan, Under-Secretary of State at the Foreign Office at the time, recorded in his diary on 29th July:

> These Jap savages have arrested 11 Britishers. One has committed suicide. We can't stand this . . . Halifax [Foreign Secretary] will ask Cabinet tomorrow for authority to 'pick up' a number of Japanese

in India, Malaya and here. We really *must* stand against them now. Surely even Winston [Churchill] will realise that we can't 'appease' any further.

The Cox case led to a temporary toughening of Britain's attitude towards Japan. One result of this was the arrest of Shinozaki Mamoru, press attaché at the consulate-general in Singapore on 21st September 1940. The uniqueness of the British stance caused the resulting trial to become something of a cause célèbre.

Shinozaki had been under surveillance by Singapore SB for some months, and on his arrest a search of his living accommodation produced evidence which established that he and a girl accomplice, Yamakawa Atsuko, who was also arrested, had been collaborating in suborning certain members of the British Services in Singapore. The case against the girl was not proceeded with, but on 22nd November Shinozaki was found guilty on two charges of acting for a purpose prejudicial to the interests of the British Empire. Specifically it was found that between December 1939 and August 1940 he had obtained from Gunner Frank Gardner of the Royal Artillery and Corporal Crompton of the RAF, information regarding troop and troopship movements, and about military and RAF installations on the island. Gardner, who 'lacked friends in the Army and kept much to himself, and was short of money', had been arrested on 25th August at the Japanese-owned Sakura Hotel, and became the main witness against Shinozaki, from whom he admitted receiving a series of sums ranging from $10 to $40. Miss Yamakawa, who met Gardner at the YWCA Sports Club, was used to escort him to various parties organised by Shinozaki.*

Shinozaki's most significant spying role had nothing, however, to do with his British informants, and it was not one of the charges brought against him. In September 1940 he had conducted Lieutenant-Colonel Tanikawa Kazuo and Captain Kunetake Teruhito, both of the Japanese Imperial Army Staff, around military installations in southern Malaya and Singapore. This pair subsequently prepared a report for Colonel Tsuji Masanobu who had been given the task of

* In Britain all court-martial records are kept closed for one hundred years. However, it is understood that Gardner was court-martialled on 7th February 1941. It is not known what happened to Corporal Crompton, whose name is published here for the first time. One of the items Crompton supplied to Shinozaki was a book of silhouettes of British aircraft.

planning the attack on Malaya. Tsuji was to become Chief of Staff to General Yamashita during that attack, and Kunetake was also on that staff.

At his trial Shinozaki denied all the charges, and in a statement said he could not have been a spy because if he had have been he would not have been so open about town in his contacts with servicemen and, furthermore, that had he been guilty he would have disappeared during the four weeks that elapsed between Gardner's arrest and his own. In response the judge in his summing-up said, 'a spy is no less a spy because he is bad one'. Shinozaki was fined $1,000 and sentenced to three years' rigorous imprisonment.[1]

The arrest and conviction of Shinozaki did not reduce the scale of Japanese espionage in Malaya. In fact it increased it, for Toyoda Kaoru, the Japanese consul-general, was ordered home in November 1940, to be replaced by Tsurumi Ken, a much more dangerous character who involved himself even more deeply than his predecessor in espionage and subversion matters.

The Shinozaki case proved no more than a temporary cessation in Britain's appeasement policy. When in March 1941 the Governor of Singapore reported to the Colonial Office that a known Japanese agent called Takasuki had travelled all over Singapore and Malaya before crossing the border into Thailand, no attempt was made to detain the Japanese although 'he was under unobtrusive surveillance throughout and we know he visited many places where troops are stationed and defence measures have been taken'.[2]

Neither was any action taken on the report of Captain C.E. Collinge of the Straits Settlements Volunteer Force who, during an exercise at Endau on the east coast of Johore with his armoured car company, actually saw a man dressed in the uniform of a colonel of the Japanese Imperial Staff, who boarded a motorised sampan to disappear seawards. After reporting the incident Collinge was told to keep quiet about it 'as the policy at that time was one of appeasement'.[3] Whether that incident was connected with the reports that, in August 1941, two Japanese submarines were seen berthed alongside the wharf at Endau owned by a Japanese iron-ore mining company, is not known. The submarines were seen to land several men and some crates of equipment. It would have been easy for them to evade detection by the few patrol boats the Royal Navy had in the area.

At some time during 1941 the Japanese supplied a Malay nationalist named Ibrahim bin Haji Ya'acob, a teacher turned journalist, with Straits $40,000 with which to purchase an anti-government Malay newspaper called *Warta Malaya*. Another of Ya'acob's activities was recruiting suitable Malays for a subversive organisation called *Kematuan Malaya Muda* (KMM). The KMM was a front for an even more esoteric organisation, the members of which were trained in fifth-column techniques and sabotage, which operated from early November 1941 under the code-name *Kame*, the Japanese word for 'tortoise'. The existence of *Kame* was known to Special Branch because of intercepted messages sent in consular codes from the Japanese consul-general to Tokyo, and possibly because Ya'acob was a double-agent who was also working for the British. Until his arrest under the Defence (Emergency) Regulations when war began, Ya'acob was unaware that the British knew of his double role. During his interrogation by SB officers, Ya'acob admitted that he was the controller of various associations and had obtained much information which he had passed on to the Japanese. During post-war interrogations of Japanese intelligence officers, it was discovered that the information Ya'acob had passed on included the dispositions of British troops, suitable landing places at Kota Bharu, and the fortifications at places along the Perak River.[4]

A man much more deeply involved with *Kame* than Ya'acob, was Bachtiar Effendi, an Indonesian member of a touring theatrical company. He was arrested on the outbreak of war and was interrogated by Assistant Superintendent H.B.J. Donaldson, the Malayan Security Officer for Johore. Effendi denied any connection with the Japanese, although his touring company had been a front behind which he had spread nationalist and pro-Japanese propaganda. He had also been in contact with other subversives. He was interned in Outram Road jail in Singapore and, after being released by the victorious Japanese, appeared in the uniform of a Japanese officer and made inquiries about Donaldson's whereabouts. Perhaps fortunately for Donaldson, Effendi did not discover that he was in the civilian internment camp.

Over the years Japanese agents managed to infiltrate the most unlikely of places. The Asian Chief Steward of the Officers' Club in the Naval Base was a man called Shawan whom everyone assumed to be Chinese. It was part of his job to select other servants of the club. About a month before the Japanese attack came, when only a few people at the top of the navy hierarchy in Singapore knew that

HMS *Prince of Wales* was on its way to the colony, Shawan must have heard some loose talk, for a piece of paper was found on him indicating the vessel's arrival. Interrogation revealed Shawan's true identity as Colonel Kadomatsu Tsugunori of the Japanese army who had once attended America's West Point Military Academy.

Another Japanese agent well-connected with the Singapore Naval Base was a man called Nakajima, a resident of Singapore for many years. He was a photographer whose services were often used to take official photographs of events within the base. His studio, situated just outside the Sembawang gate to the base, was a popular choice for many British servicemen who wished to have a pictorial record of their stay in the colony. Nakajima's 'chop' appears on the reverse side of many pre-war photos. He, too, was a colonel in Japanese Intelligence, although in his case this was not discovered until after the war began.

Colonel R.R. Baily of the 1st Battalion, Malay Regiment, recalls that pre-war he regularly had his haircut at 'Violets', a barber's shop close to an army camp at Seremban in central Malaya. He writes, 'after the surrender I saw a group of three Japanese officers at Changi, and one of them was Captain Violet!'[5]

As espionage and subversion are by definition secret clandestine operations about which few records are kept and even fewer made public within the lifetimes of those most interested, it is difficult to gauge, in anything but the broadest terms, the success of Japanese efforts in these fields in Malaya. Furthermore, the Americans and the British weeded out information from surviving Japanese archives after the war. It is even more difficult to attribute achievements to specific individuals. In fact, this is possible with only one man. His efforts, albeit carried out on a base of earlier solid work by others, was to have a significant effect on the campaign in Malaya.

Major Fujiwara Iwaichi, who had been trained at *Nakano Gakko*, the Japanese Intelligence School, arrived at Bangkok with his aide, Lieutenant Yamaguchi, in October 1941. He had been sent there from his previous posting as an intelligence officer with the Japanese 21st Army in Canton, in south China. In Canton he had headed the team that interrogated three civilian Indian nationalists who had escaped from jail in Hong Kong where they had been imprisoned for instigating anti-British activities, most importantly, among the Indian troops serving there. The three men desired to be sent to Thailand and Malaya to carry on their subversive work there – no doubt they had another word for their activities – and Fujiwara obliged them.*

The Japanese had been paying considerable attention to the views of Indian nationalists for years. Japan, as with her Axis partner Germany, became a haven for many Indian dissidents during pre-war years. In the 1930s, in Hong Kong, Malaya and Singapore, all with sizeable Indian communities, the Japanese began providing funds and encouragement to the Indian Independence League (IIL), a militant offshoot of the Indian Congress Party. Whatever amount of money was spent in this way, it was to produce huge dividends.

The IIL had an extensive network of cells and agents in Malaya. Some of the agents used the guise of hawkers of religious books. One IIL cell, which called itself the Central Indian Association and which received direct funding from the Japanese, was behind a serious outbreak of unrest during a strike of Tamil rubber estate workers at Port Swettenham (now called Klang) in May 1941. Fighting broke out between strikers and estate managers, and when the police were unable to cope with it, the 1/13th Frontier Force Regiment of the Indian army was sent in. It might have been better to have sent in a British regiment, for setting Indian against Indian in a foreign land could have done little for the morale of the Indian army units in Malaya.

In fact, the IIL's greatest successes were achieved within the ranks of those units of the Indian army and Indian States Forces serving in Malaya, and this is important because the Indians comprised at the time of the Japanese attack 49 per cent of the combined British/Indian/Australian/Malayan force.†

Indian army battalions in India, based in their self-contained cantonments and garrison towns, were largely – though not wholly – insulated from the growing aspirations for Indian independence. 'Pride in the regiment' lay at the core of these regiments, a concept fostered over many years by the continuity of regimental service of British officers and Indian non-commissioned officers. Even in India itself by 1939 this had begun to change in consequence of

* There was a rumour in Hong Kong at the time these men escaped that the break-out was engineered by Sikh prison guards. The author has not managed to uncover any evidence that this was so.

† The total Commonwealth force in Malaya at the time of the attack was 87,000. Reinforcements of 20,800 men of the British 18th Division, 12,000 Indians, and 3,550 Australians arrived later.

the huge expansion of the Indian army that began on the outbreak of the war with Germany. Battalions were 'milked' of experienced officers and NCOs who found themselves posted to form the nuclei of new battalions. Many of the 'emergency commissioned officers' brought in as replacements knew little about India or Indians, and few of them could speak Urdu, the *lingua franca* of the army.

The insulation of the regiments was further breached when they were sent abroad. In Malaya, the fifteen battalions of the Indian army – there were also three battalions of Gurkhas – and the five battalions of Indian States Forces, came into contact with influences scarcely met with in the garrison towns back home. In Malaya the protective barrier of tradition, usage and regimental family spirit was less effective, and there was another factor. Since the 1920s the Indian army had been 'Indianizing' part of its officer corps. Back home in the garrison towns these Indian officers were treated in exactly the same way as British officers, except by a handful of die-hard Colonel Blimps of the old school. This was not the case in Malaya where regiments were stationed in close proximity to ordinary towns, the European communities in them tending to restrict social invitations to British officers. This attitude was not entirely racially inspired, for many Europeans did not like the army, any army, being in the land at all, and Australian officers were often ignored as well.

This was the background against which the Indian Independence League operated, and they took full advantage of it. One important incident in which IIL influence was involved was the near-mutiny in May 1940 of part of the 4/19th Hyderabads at Tyersall Park camp in Singapore. When resentment against racial bias becomes mixed with nationalist tendencies, it produces a highly volatile mixture.

The trouble began when the censor intercepted a letter containing seditious material written by Lieutenant Mohammed Zahir-ud-Din to an Anglo-Indian lady called Mrs Grantzer back home in Patna. In it, Zahir expressed the wish that the war in Europe last for ten years so that the British Empire became so exhausted that Indians could turn the British out of their country. Zahir had also been passing his pro-nationalist views on to the Ahir sepoys in his company, as well as to fellow Indian officers. Another matter held against him was that he was living with a white woman in Singapore, which, given the mores of the time, may have been considered even worse than the alleged sedition. The lady was said to be German, although there is no explanation in the official file for why a German national was being allowed to live free in Singapore in May 1940.[6]

When Zahir was ordered home his Ahirs mutinied, refusing to load their kit on to lorries due to take them on exercise. No doubt with the mutiny of the 5th Indian Light Infantry in Singapore in 1915 in mind, the military authorities placed the Argyll & Sutherland Highlanders, stationed in the same camp, on standby, but only the company commanders were told the real reason. The Hyderabads were disarmed, and this annoyed the Jats of another Hyderabad company who had not been involved in the Ahir incident, and trouble started with them as well. The mutiny was only brought to an end when Zahir was permitted to say farewell to his men at a company parade.

The GOC at the time, General Bond, recommended that the whole battalion be sent back to India, but this was not done. It was this incident that caused Lord Zetland, the Secretary of State for India, to write a letter to Lord Linlithgow, Viceroy of India, dated 9th May 1940, in which he described the incident as 'a somewhat serious matter', following upon other trouble with Indian brigades in Egypt, 'and the serious episode which took place on the [Northwest] Frontier some time ago when a number of English officers were shot.'

The incident on the Northwest Frontier to which Lord Zetland alluded has received no attention at all from the authors of the several modern books written on the history of the Indian army, although an outline of it is given in the official history of the regiment involved, the 2nd Punjabis.[7] The regimental officer author of the book was either unaware of the Indian *police* inquiry into the affair, or chose, in the interests of the regiment, to record only the verdict of the internal Indian Army Court of Inquiry. The incident is recorded here for it indicates how even in India, regiments were not entirely immune from the influences of the independence movement.

The battalion concerned was the regiment's 4th Battalion, and the tragedy took place in the early hours of 24th November 1938 at a training camp at Walai, near Nowshera. According to the regimental history a Punjabi Mussulman sepoy of the battalion ran amok, shot the CO, Colonel E.H. Gray, dead, 'and then went through the camp firing at every British and Punjabi Mussulman officer he met'. There were seven British officers serving or attached to the battalion that morning, four of whom, including the CO, were killed outright or subsequently died of their wounds. Two of the other three were wounded, one so seriously that his leg had to be amputated. Three Punjabi Mussulman officers were also killed outright or died later from wounds. 'The murderer was shot dead outside the perimeter while attempting to flee the camp.'

The Court of Inquiry noted that the sepoy had 'selected' only officers for his victims, and that he shot only British and Punjabi Mussulman officers and not those officers from the 'other classes serving with the regiment'. The Inquiry was unable to 'arrive at any reason for the man's activities'.

The Indian Police, however, most certainly did. Their investigations uncovered an extremist nationalist cell of which the dead sepoy had been a member. It seems highly possible that it was because of the police report that seven months later, in January 1939, the disbandment of the Punjabi Mussulman part of the battalion was ordered, to be followed soon afterwards by the disbandment of the entire battalion.

In Malaya, the IIL-bred trouble did not end with the Hyderabads. Of especial interest to its cells were the officers and men of the five Indian States Forces battalions in the country. These were not parts of the Indian army proper, but units raised and paid for by Indian princes. Most of the officers were Indians, although their COs were British officers seconded from the Indian army. In general, these battalions were not considered first-class troops.

One of these battalions, the 1st Bahawalpurs, arrived in Malaya in March 1941. It had a new CO in Lieutenant-Colonel Roger Fletcher, who apparently considered his secondment a demotion; a short-tempered man, he found fault with everything and everyone, and was not above lashing out at people with his cane. Even before sailing from home, there were among its Indian officers several who held nationalist views, including the most senior among them, Lieutenant-Colonel Qasim Gilani. Another such was Captain A.D. Jahangir. Given this, plus Fletcher's character, and the fact that the battalion was given the menial task – menial, that is, from the military point of view, of guarding airfields, it is not surprising that the battalion provided a fine field for IIL subversion. Serious unrest broke out among the officers, and it was only temporarily relieved when Brigadier (later Major-General) D.M. Murray-Lyon, the local commander, was brought in. He sacked Fletcher who was relieved by Major (later raised to Lieutenant-Colonel) H.E. Tyrell from the 2/16th Punjabis. But the unrest persisted and resulted in four Indian officers being sent home, and despite Tyrell's efforts, the battalion was still in disarray at the time of the Japanese attack.

Throughout 1941 there were persistent disciplinary problems with Indian regiments in Malaya. Both in number and in nature, they were out of the ordinary for the relatively small force there. Many trouble-makers were sent home without charges being brought, but during the four-month period May to September 1941, at least sixteen Indian soldiers were court-martialled for serious offences. The problem was so great that the scarcity of officers with sufficient service to act on courts-martial was considered acute, and time which could have been more valuably spent, was wasted on training officers in court-martial procedures.

This was the situation into which Major Fujiwara sailed. He and his aide entered Thailand under the assumed names of Yamashita Koichi and Yamada Hajime, to set up *F-Kikan* – 'F' for Fujiwara, *kikan* for organisation – designed to speed up the process of subverting Indian troops in Malaya. He met with a leading Indian nationalist, Pritam Singh, who reported on the present extent of the IIL's activities among Indian troops in Malaya. Soon, upon Fujiwara's advice there was an increase in number and intensity of propaganda broadcasts in Urdu from a station on Formosa which related incidents, some of them true, of unrest among Indians troops in Malaya.

Although the British, through an intercept picked up by FECB, knew of Fujiwara's arrival at Bangkok, they did not know what his duties were until secret Japanese documents were captured in January 1942. By that time his subversive efforts had been successful beyond even his own wildest dreams.

When, at the eleventh hour, in 1941, the British authorities in Whitehall decided to improve and increase its espionage, counter-espionage, and other 'ground intelligence' activities in the East, there was a general shake-up of that part of Military Intelligence which was not part of FECB. Officers were transferred from one posting to another and additional ones were sent out from home. One of the new arrivals was Major (soon to be Colonel) A. Chamier, who had just time enough to introduce some improvements, according to the C-in-C, Brooke-Popham, but he did not specify what the improvements were.

In May the Ministry of Economic Warfare (MEW) set up a Singapore section of the Special Operations Executive (SOE). The unit was known as the Oriental Mission, or OM. The opening of it had been presaged in January by an exploratory visit made by A.E. Jones, travelling under the guise of being a representative of the Asiatic Petroleum Company, for whom he had indeed worked for a number of years. It was further presaged in March by the arrival of Lieutenant-Colonel A.G. Warren, Royal Marines, sent out by London to study the scope for special operations in the area.*

In retrospect, and in view of the fact that the civilian appointed to lead OM, Valentine St J. Killery, was unable to get on with the military authorities in Singapore, it seems a pity that the post did not go to Warren. At the very least Warren would not have made the mistakes in 'military etiquette' that were made by Killery, which included not keeping General Percival, the army commander, informed of his intentions, many of which impinged on military matters.

As an expert, if not *the* expert, on all things Japanese, Sir George Sansom, previously attached to the British embassy in Tokyo, was brought down to Singapore to advise Killery.

Part of Oriental Mission's remit was the organisation and training of 'stay-behind' parties to work behind enemy lines if and when an attack came, and for this purpose No. 101 Special Training School was set up at Jurong on Singapore Island. Although Brooke-Popham knew of Killery's plans, apparently General Percival only found them out by accident. The ensuing arguments resulted in delays that at that late hour should not have been tolerated.

The governor, Sir Shenton Thomas, was not too pleased with Killery either. He agreed with Percival that the formation of stay-behind parties implied that an invasion was likely to take place and that if news of that got around, it would damage morale.

Killery's remit covered all of Southeast Asia, including Thailand, and in that country his plans fell foul of Sir Josiah Crosby who demanded to vet any plans which Killery put forward. One of those plans, one which barely got beyond the preliminary stages, was to create a pro-British coup d'état in Thailand. Even the thought of it made Crosby see red, and when in October 1941, leaflets of an extreme anti-Japanese nature were discovered circulating in Bangkok and the Thai Prime Minister blamed Britain for it, Crosby in turn blamed Killery. In London, the

* Warren's advance party included Captain K. Gerhold, RA, who had once been in the FMS police. Gerhold was not permitted to stay in Malaya after it was pointed out to Brooke-Popham that he had been sacked from the police for actions that would have gained him a place on one of Special Branch's black lists.

Foreign Secretary, Anthony Eden, jumped in on Crosby's side: 'I must know about this organisation that makes our ambassador's life a misery and vitiates my policy, and they must come under direct Foreign Office control. The present situation is intolerable.'[8]

In fact Killery's organisation was almost certainly not to blame for the leaflets. They were probably the work of John Becker, originally part of Hayley Bell's team and now back in Malaya as a captain in Military Intelligence. According to Becker, he too was working towards a coup d'état in Thailand with the backing of certain royalists there. He did this with the full knowledge of General Percival, and it is likely that Brooke-Popham knew of it too; he certainly knew of Becker's presence in the area having been the recipient of a letter recommending Becker to him as someone who would be ideal in an intelligence role being well versed in knowledge of, and the languages of, the whole area.

But Becker went too far from the point of view of his superiors. The embarrassment he caused Crosby, who was no admirer of the Thai royal family, on top of some other peccadilloes, caused Percival to order not only the calling-off of the coup plan but also Becker's arrest in Singapore; he was finally sent home to England a few weeks before the Japanese attack on Malaya. When Becker met Percival in London after the war, Percival disclaimed all memory of these pre-war events.

New information has recently come to light which indicates that one Thai supporter of the royalist cause, who worked either on the Becker or the Killery plan for a coup was a man called Luang Sarabhaya. Sarabhaya fled to Singapore after the calling-off of the plans, and spent the rest of the war in Australia working in an intelligence capacity and broadcasting over the Thai service of the Political Warfare radio network. Whilst in Australia he was befriended by Michael Keon who was working in the same branch of Intelligence. Keon says that Sarabhaya denounced Josiah Crosby as being hostile to the Thai royal family and for being 'the cause of the breakdown of a plan he, Sarabhaya, had been involved with in Singapore along with someone on the British side, which was to have been in support of the British military position'. It was Sarabhaya's opinion that 'had the plan succeeded, Yamashita would never have got his troops ashore at Singora'.[9]

Michael Keon says that he helped Sarabhaya return to Thailand after the war and then lost touch with him. Then, in the 1960s, when

Keon was working for the United Nations Food and Agriculture Organisation in Bangkok, his Thai adviser, Surathoen Bunnag, 'a member of Thailand's second family and King Bhumibol's Man Friday, being married to Queen Sirikit's Chief Lady-in-Waiting', came to him with the news that Sarabhaya was dying and wished to see him. At that meeting Sarabhaya told Keon a little more about his pre-war escape from Thailand and mentioned that he was spirited away by an 'Englishman who was Thailand's best friend'. Keon cannot now recall if John Becker's name was mentioned in this context, but the 'best friend' sobriquet certainly fits in with what other Thais called Becker in post-war years. Also in attendance at that death-bed meeting was a pre-war veteran of the Thai Cabinet, Chao Phya Sri Thammathibet. He confirmed to Keon that Sarabhaya had indeed been part of a British underground operation, and had been the Thai mastermind behind the plans for a coup.

Killery's pre-war OM organisation, however, seems to have accomplished little save in one respect. Colonel Warren, who had stayed in Singapore as part of the organisation, together with Captain Ivan Lyon, like Becker another of Hayley Bell's old associates, had the foresight to set up an escape route through the Dutch islands to the south of Singapore by which, in the event, many official escapees and also many deserters, were able to escape from Japanese clutches.

The British ministry in charge of propaganda, euphemistically called the Ministry of Information, also set up an operation in Singapore. It was called the Far Eastern Bureau (FEB, not to be confused with FECB), and it worked closely with SOE. At its head was Robert Scott, and one of his part-time staff members was Ian Morrison, both of whom Emily Hahn had named as being in intelligence when she met them in Hong Kong. Morrison's other work in Singapore was as the *Times* correspondent. An Australian liaison officer attached to FEB was Lionel Wigmore who, after the war, became the author of the official Australian history of the Malayan campaign.[10] Morrison and Wigmore and other members of the Bureau managed to make successful escapes from Singapore in February 1942.

In his executive capacity as the Head of FEB, Scott was to become a member of the War Council set up in Singapore, which must either indicate the importance attached to the work of his Bureau or, much more likely, the importance of Scott himself in the Intelligence field. It is not clear how close Scott's organisation was to being involved in actual intelligence-gathering. But as FEB was in charge of all British propaganda affairs in the Far East – its area of operations covering China, Thailand, the NEI, French Indo-China and Japan itself where Vere Redman at the embassy was 'their man' – and in Singapore it also dealt with all kinds of censorship, it definitely had some such connection. FEB worked closely with the propaganda arm of the Oriental Mission, known as the Economic Research Bureau (ERB), and also with the Police Special Branch.[11]

In a similar category to members of Scott's organisation, and again closely associated with it, were some of the men working for the Malaya Broadcasting Corporation (MBC). Giles Playfair was sent out to run the Corporation late in 1941. He escaped from Singapore three days before the island fell to the Japanese, and ended up in the United States where he worked more directly for British Intelligence as a member of William Stephenson's British Security Co-ordination team.[12] An OM report notes the close relationship between Scott's organisation, its own propaganda arm, and the official broadcasters.[13]

Someone else who worked on British propaganda in Singapore was a young lady named Doris Lim, who had been brought up in Shanghai and spoke English with an American accent. She had worked for a branch of British Intelligence in north China, escaping from Tientsin just before the city was overrun by the Japanese, on whose 'wanted' list her name appeared. She was also one jump ahead of them in escaping from Shanghai and then from Hong Kong. Keeping up her record, she also escaped from Singapore shortly before it fell. But her luck finally ran out when she boarded the Dutch *Rooseboom* at Padang in Sumatra. When the ship was sunk by a torpedo she was among those aboard the only surviving lifeboat. After days at sea watching others in the lifeboat die one by one, including Brigadier Archie Paris of the Indian army, she, Sergeant Walter Gibson of the Argyles, and three native seamen, the only ones left alive, reached a Sumatran beach where they fell into Japanese hands. Doris Lim did not survive the war years. It is said she suffered interrogation by the Japanese, was imprisoned but then released. She married a Chinese in Sumatra called Chong Teck Lim, but was murdered by him on 7th March 1945. Walter Gibson survived to write of his, and her, experiences in a book called *The Boat*.[14]

Whatever the extent of Robert Scott's involvement in intelligence matters, to the Japanese 'information' equated with 'intelligence', so that when Scott was captured in the Banka Strait in 1942 after his own late attempt to escape from Singapore, they gave him a very hard time indeed. Some of the treatment meted out to him may well have been as a result of his earlier contacts with the Kempetai in China. It was a Kempetai officer, Sumida Haruzo – hanged in 1946 for war crimes – who pin-pointed Scott as the mastermind who had instructed Chinese agents in acts of sabotage.

The fall of France in June 1940 and the setting up of the Vichy Government had several important side effects in the Far East. Because the Royal Navy in the Mediterranean now had to take on many of the duties previously carried out by the French Navy, it was even more difficult for Britain to send ships to the Far East if danger threatened there.

Admiral Sir Percy Noble, the then C-in-C, China Fleet, invited Admiral Jean Decoux, the French naval commander in Indo-China, to transfer his fleet to Singapore, but the invitation was turned down. Soon afterwards, the pro-Vichy and anglophobic Decoux was promoted Governor-General of the French colony, and subsequent Vichy agreements with Japan enabled the Japanese to move their forces much closer to Singapore. Decoux's attitude was particularly unfortunate from an intelligence point of view in that before the fall of France, he had been the recipient of considerable information concerning the Allied Combined Defence Scheme for the area. Another effect of Decoux's appointment was that any plans for setting up a major Free French movement to frustrate the designs of the Japanese in Indo-China had to be abandoned.

An almost surreal situation now developed between the British in the Far East and the Vichy Government of Indo-China, which fell increasingly under Japanese influence. Even while a British-sponsored Free French organisation was being formed in Singapore, agreements were reached with Decoux which allowed some local trading links to be maintained, and provided for some restraint in anti-British propaganda by the Vichy authorities. Britain agreed not to interfere with French shipping providing no French reinforcements were sent to Indo-China. Capitaine René Jouan, Decoux's go-between, later described by an officer on Brooke-Popham's staff as 'a very untrustworthy character', even agreed on 28th December 1940 for visits to be made to the colony by British officers providing they went in mufti and the visits were kept short.

In May 1941, Britain received a request from Decoux to permit the passage of repair materials for the French cruiser *Lamotte Picquet*. On 13th May Vice-Admiral Sir Geoffrey Layton, the new Commander-in-Chief, China, advised the Admiralty against this 'though it is desirable to appear to view the request sympathetically'. The list of required materials, which included 116 tons of steel, 42,000 boiler tubes, 50,000 condenser tubes and 82,000 metres of electric cabling, indicates that the French ship was in a bad way. There is no indication that this 'order list' was ever filled. It seems very unlikely that it was, as Japanese penetration of Indo-China gained momentum. Moreover, Vichy did its best to circumvent British controls over strategic materials reaching Germany from Indo-China. The *Françoise LD*, carrying 6,700 tons of rubber, sailed from Saigon on 15th August 1941 ostensibly for Kobe in Japan. Instead, she ended up in Casablanca, having been refuelled on the voyage by a German supply vessel.

Around mid-1941 Capitaine Jouan became involved in the 'Madame Breguet affair'. This lady, married to the son of the famous French aircraft designer, was granted permission by the British government to pass through Singapore on her way back from Indo-China to France. However, when she arrived in Singapore she made contact with the head of the Banque du Indo-Chine there, the Comte de Courseilles who, though professing to be anti-Vichy, had an Italian wife who was known to be strongly pro-Fascist. Her name was Lyra, and she featured on one of FESS's black lists. The lovely Lyra had spent most of her life in Shanghai and had fallen to the amorous attentions of Count Ciano when he had been Italian consul-general there. The Shanghai Municipal Police also held a file on this lady who had come under suspicion of spying in the early 1930s during her frequent visits to Weihaiwei in North China, where Britain based part of her China fleet. In Singapore, Lyra was known to be on close terms with the Vichy-inclined French consul-general, M. Pingaud. All this meant that anyone going near Lyra or her husband automatically became suspect.

Despite her protestations Madame Breguet's exit permit was held up. The Singapore authorities were certain that she carried papers from Decoux to Vichy, and reasonably sure that she was also being used as a courier by Italian agents in the Far East. Jouan became embroiled in the ensuing three-cornered diplomatic arguments between Saigon, Singapore and London. Finally, the British Foreign Office decided she could depart, a decision at least partly due to the fact that her father, Pierre Etienne Flandin, was a man of some influence in France, having once been Prime Minister. He was always close to Pierre Laval and Admiral Darlan, and from December 1940 to February 1941 was Foreign Minister in Marshal Pétain's Vichy Government.

The SOE in Singapore took particular care to ensure security of their tentative plans for a branch of the organisation in Indo-China. This was on account of the presence of the Vichy-minded consul-general in Singapore, who had complete freedom and diplomatic immunity. SOE reported that there was evidence of him misusing consular-bag privileges, and that on one occasion the Free French intercepted a safe-hand letter addressed to him from the Vichy consul-general in Batavia which contained German espionage material. The report went on: 'The experts at the Naval Base were never able to crack his high-grade cyphers in Singapore, and the volume of his cypher traffic was too great for us to ask for it to be submitted to London for analysis.'[15] So it seems that FECB was not only having trouble with Japanese codes at this time, but also with French ones.

The headquarters of the Free French movement in the Far East was in Singapore under C.F. Baron. The various sub-branches and leaders were: Singapore (Brizay), Malaya (de Langlade), Thailand (Charleaux) and the Dutch East Indies (Ricard). It seems that the out-stations obeyed Baron's instructions only when it suited them to do so.[16] The organisation – which seemed to wield power out of all proportion to its size and importance to the Allied cause – had taken upon itself, or been granted, perhaps by de Gaulle in London, the right not only to purge Vichy sympathisers, but actually to court-martial and shoot some of them. In Singapore any Frenchman not known to be an active Free Frenchman, was considered to be Vichy.

Brizay's secretary in Singapore was Gabrielle, the French wife of Captain Ivan Lyon of the Gordon Highlanders, who was on attachment to the security services. It was she who acted as interpreter when a Vichy officer from Indo-China, Commandant Maurice Lenormand, was picked up by Singapore Special Branch. He was subsequently handed over to the Free French who tried and sentenced him to death, but was rescued from death-row in Outram Road jail by the victorious Japanese.

To the British, after the fall of France and before the Japanese war began, the value of the Free French movement in the Far East lay mainly in the possibilities it gave to develop intelligence regarding French Indo-China. The Deputy Director of Military Intelligence in

London stated in an undated memo that there 'are obvious possibilities which are being developed . . . which should be of considerable value in the event of war with Japan'. It is not known how successful these 'developments' were.

One liaison officer at Baron's HQ was Second-Lieutenant Pierre Boulle. After special training in demolitions, he was sent into Indo-China by the SOE in October 1941. That operation was aborted after a message was received from French agents within Indo-China that the situation there was dangerous. On a subsequent operation Boulle was captured by the Japanese and was interned for the duration of the war. He survived to write *The Bridge on the River Kwai*.

Eleven

Subversion in the South

Thailand – or Siam as it was known until its name was officially changed by the Thais in 1939 but still called Siam thereafter in many official British documents – was the key to the south. For an attack on Malaya and Singapore by the 'backdoor' route to be successful, attacking forces must come via Thailand; through that country, too, must pass troops to attack Burma, the gateway to India. To the south of Singapore lay the oil-rich island of Sumatra and the other highly desirable islands that made up the Netherlands East Indies. Thailand was therefore a major focal point of Japanese subversive and intelligence operations in that part of the world, and drawing the Thais closer to them was an important part of pre-war Japanese diplomatic effort.

Thailand had much in common with Japan. They were the only two countries in the Far East that were not under some form of political domination by Western nations, and they were both monarchies, although by the late 1930s the King of Siam was mainly a figure-head 'ruling' by grace of a military junta.

Thailand had close links with Britain, links that had been there even before 1862 when Anna Leonowens arrived in the land to teach the royal children. By 1930 three-quarters of Thai exports passed through Singapore and other British ports in the area. Rice, her major export, was shipped in bags manufactured from gunny from British India. The country's foreign debt was held in London, and there were British advisers to several Thai ministries.

The country therefore formed a confrontation ground for Japanese versus British interests. Field Marshal Luang Pibul, the Thai leader, had much in common with the Fascist leaders of Germany, Italy and Japan, but he was a realist with his own country's interests at heart. It is more than possible that, had Britain been able to convince the Thai military leader that she had the power to protect the eastern country's independence, then Thailand would have remained within the Western camp. But Britain had no such power, especially after the war with Germany began in 1939.

Pibul had come to power after a military coup in 1934 and was Prime Minister by 1939. Sir Josiah Crosby, Britain's long-serving envoy in Bangkok, who tended to see everything Thai through rose-tinted glasses, remained convinced until it was too late that Pibul was pro-British. Crosby's views became the officially held views of the Foreign Office in London, but were in sharp contrast to those held by the War Office working on information sent to them by Military Attachés and from other sources including pro-British elements within the Thai royal family and the Thai Cabinet. This divergence of views was so great that by 1941 Lieutenant-Colonel D.L. Mackenzie of the General Staff in London was writing to the Deputy Director, Military Intelligence, advising that all future messages from Crosby 'be interpreted with the utmost care'.[1]

According to British secret sources, and contrary to Crosby's expressed views, Japanese policy towards Thailand was from an early stage 'based on the unreserved approval of Field Marshal Pibul'.[2] As in all other countries in the area, Japan penetrated Thailand with commercial firms and small traders. All were concerned with picking up intelligence, or subversion, or persuading Thais after the Japanese attack on China in 1937 to restrict the activities of the large Chinese community in the country. The American journalist Mark Gayn, who as editor of the English Department of the Japanese Domei News Agency in the Far East from 1935 to 1940 was in a unique 'inside' position to observe Japanese policies, observed that it was under Japanese pressure that Pibul began introducing anti-Chinese measures. Gayn, a closet sympathiser of the communist Chinese, presented a strong case. Chinese schools were closed, and immigration from China banned. The number of Chinese employed in any firm was strictly controlled, and all business accounts had to be kept in Thai. The largest Chinese companies in the country, those in the rice and tobacco industries, found themselves nationalised virtually overnight, and some Chinese newspapers were closed down.[3]

In the spring of 1940 the Japanese began extending their propaganda network in Thailand by paying subsidies to local newspapers. One Thai-language newspaper, the *Khao Phap Press*, was virtually owned by the Japanese; and by supplying it with scarce newsprint they gradually changed the anti-Japanese stance of the Thai-owned English-language newspaper, *Bangkok Chronicle*.

Pibul, at heart an irredentist, wanted to regain all the old Thai provinces lost over the years to the French in Indo-China and to the British in Malaya and Burma. With the fall of Metropolitan France in June 1940 he saw the chance of getting back the former. Long-standing disputes, mainly of a verbal nature, had been going on over border issues along the 2,000 mile Thai/Indo-Chinese frontier, but now the Thai tone changed. By the autumn they were demanding that the Vichy Government hand back parts of Laos, demands that were at first indignantly refused.

Sensing its chance, Japan sent in a crack agent, Lieutenant-Colonel Saito Jiro. Saito, a protégé of Colonel Doihara Kenjichi, the so-called 'Lawrence of Manchuria', had been educated in Honolulu and was a noted linguist. Earlier he had been Military Attaché at Bangkok and knew the Thais well. He set about fanning the irredentist flames within the Thai Cabinet, and as a result the Thai demands grew even stronger. With no reaction coming from either London or Washington, in late November 1940 the Thais urged on by Saito, struck across the border. Initial skirmishes soon developed into a small-scale war, with planes, artillery and tanks. Inside two weeks Thai troops had occupied several frontier districts and bombed the Laotian capital, Vientiane. The French were surprised not only by the standard of equipment used by the Thais, but also at the expertise shown by Thai pilots who had not fought in battle for over twenty years. Admiral Decoux, the Vichy French governor, recorded that Thai planes seemed to be flown by pilots with plenty of war experience and when the Japanese offered their mediation services in the dispute, he made the insinuation even more clear not only by vehemently refusing it, but commenting that mediation by a *neutral* country would however be welcome.

Reports from the British Military Attaché, Bangkok, and other secret sources, confirmed that not only were Japanese arms and equipment coming into the country in large quantities, but that Japanese officers had been arriving to 'advise' on their use.[4]

Under further Thai pressure the French land forces caved in, and with a strong Japanese naval force now anchored off Saigon, the Vichy Government instructed Decoux to accept Japanese mediation. Both sides got something out of the resulting agreement, although the Thais gained less territory than they expected. In a secret deal with the French, the Japanese obtained access to airfields in southern Indo-China in exchange for watering down the Thai demands.

Major-General I.S.O. Playfair, Chief of Staff to Air Chief Marshal Brooke-Popham in Malaya, has memorably written, 'Singapore fell when France fell'; but an even more proximate French connection with the fall of Singapore was this secret Vichy–Japan deal signed early in 1941.

The Vichy–Japanese agreement was not the only bit of conniving that went on over the dispute. The British consul-general in Saigon somehow got his hands on a letter dated 1st February 1941 from the Japanese legation in Bangkok to Tokyo, and sent a secret message to FECB about it. It showed that there had been an understanding between Prime Minister Pibul and the Japanese dating from August 1940, three months before the Thais struck into Indo-China, that Japan would act as arbitrator in the dispute.[5] If other reports are to be believed, Sir Josiah Crosby may have been directly involved, too. A secret message to the Foreign Office from the British consul-general in Tangiers dated 10th February 1941 contained information from an agent code-named 'André'.

> Franco-Thai conflict.
> 'André' tells me that there is great pessimism at Vichy over this question and that it is widely rumoured that HM Minister at Bangkok is responsible for having urged the Thais to take this hostile action. 'André' himself realised that Thailand had been incited by Japan to take action against Indo-China.[6]

Sir Robert Craigie, the British ambassador in Tokyo, reported similarly. In a message dated 15th April 1941 to the head of FECB, Singapore, and copied to the Foreign Office, he reported a conversation he had held with the Counsellor of the French embassy in Tokyo. Apparently French delegates from Indo-China had brought with them 'certain proof' that Great Britain had supported Thai claims to French territory. Craigie followed that up less than a fortnight later with another message saying that the 'proof' had come from Hanoi, that it was considered there was no possibility of it being either a Japanese or a German forgery, and that the evidence purported 'to prove that Sir J. Crosby, in an effort to counter Japanese influence in Thailand, had secretly but formally supported Thai territorial claims in Indo-China'.[7]

The Japanese followed their successful mediation, which had been conducted by their grandiosely named 'Boundary Commission', by packing their embassy in Bangkok with extra 'attachés', some of them officers left over from that Commission. Their main tasks were five-fold:

(i) To win over leading personalities in Thai government;
(ii) direction and training of Thai army;
(iii) to obtain war material for Japan;
(iv) to collect intelligence information;
(v) to collect topographical information.[8]

At the Japanese embassy Colonel Tamura Hiroshi was in overall charge of intelligence-gathering and subversive activities, and under him were experts with specialist responsibilities, including signals. He was involved in the creation of *Kame*, the pro-Japanese youth movement across the border in Malaya. In October 1941, Tamura supplied an agent called Karimoto with funds to set up a rubber factory at Haadyai in southern Thailand; not only was this factory a cover for subversive activities, but its position close to the important Haadyai rail junction made it important during the coming Japanese offensive. Colonel Tamura also sent a Malay-speaking agent called Tashiro into Malaya with funds amounting to 5,000 yen; Tashiro was later known to be a member of *F-Kikan*, the organisation behind subversion in the Indian army in Malaya.

Holding a job of special importance was Tamura's deputy, Lieutenant-Colonel Yahara Hiromiti. His main concern was Burma. He collated information coming across the Thai border from that country, and liaised with *Minami Kikan*, a subversive organisation set up by Colonel Suzuki Keiji for operations within Burma in December 1940.

The Thai Prime Minister, Pibul, his hopes of regaining land along the Burma border kindled by his success in Indo-China, attended in February 1941 a meeting at the Japanese legation in Bangkok where a number of Burmese nationalists were present, and at which the subject discussed was a planned uprising against the British in Burma. As 1941 progressed, some prominent Burmese nationalists were evacuated by *Minami Kikan* through Thailand, with or without Pibul's cognisance. In August the headquarters of this *kikan* was moved from Burma into Thailand as British security had become aware of its operations and were closing in on it.

Japanese Intelligence in Thailand was not concerned solely with anti-British matters. Certain sections of the Thai armed services were known to be supporters of the Thai royal family, several of whom were pro-British in stance; other military officers supported Pibul's bitter rival, the left-leaning Luang Pradit who, with Pibul, had led the 1932 uprising which had toppled the power of the throne. Colonel Tamura and his staff busily collected everything they could on the Thai situation. Japanese Boundary Commission officers had already gathered a great deal of intelligence during the course of their activities, all of which was, of course, made available to Tamura. On top of that, an agent working for the commercial firm Showa Tsusho, a man called Utagawa, managed to get on extremely close terms with members of the Thai Cabinet and with Army leaders. He was aided in this by a Scandinavian who also worked for the firm, a man called Andersen, a great friend of an officer of the Kempetai working in Thailand.

In mid-1941, in an apparent bid to squeeze the last ounce of intelligence from Japanese residents all over the Far East, a Major Iino was made responsible for this in Thailand. His travels took him to every corner of the land to visit those Japanese who could not make it to Bangkok for 'interrogation'.

When the Japanese began taking virtual control of Indo-China in the summer of 1941, they were concerned that Thailand might take this as a threat to its own sovereignty. The Foreign Office in London informed Sir Josiah Crosby on 17th July that from a 'secret and reliable source that should on no account be quoted or compromised', they had learned that the object of Japanese propaganda in Thailand was now to convince the Thais that their own independence was not threatened and that Japan's actions in Indo-China were purely defensive and, indeed, that Japan had no intention of encroaching even upon the sovereignty of Indo-China. The Japanese ambassador in Bangkok had been ordered to tell the Thais that the Japanese action 'constitutes no threat to Thailand, but on the contrary . . . enables Japan to protect Thailand from threats from other countries'. Crosby was ordered to burn this message after perusal. The information had clearly come from the interception and decryption of a Japanese diplomatic message.[9]

Interception of other Japanese diplomatic messages during 1941 provided the British with indications of proposed Japanese–Thai collaboration. In a secret communication dated 15th October the Foreign Office advised Crosby that 'the Japanese had decided to supply . . . Thailand with 12,000 tons of crude oil provided the Thais agreed to reserve for Japanese use the whole of the refined product.' This gesture would not only provide Japanese forces with a supply of oil when they entered the country, but would 'keep the Thai oil refineries going', thus making them immediately available to the Japanese when they arrived.[10]

Burma, the land that provided a route into India and which was also the southern terminus of the Burma Road over which the Kuomintang in China were receiving supplies, was of special interest to the Japanese. Geographically Burma occupied a position about halfway between Malaya and India, while politically it was about halfway between the rather quiescent nationalism of the Malays and the much more active nationalism of the Congress Party in India. When the British separated Burma from India in 1937, made it a separate colony, and later made Dr Ba Maw the Premier despite his known anti-British sentiments, the Japanese saw a chance of influencing him in their favour. In 1939 they made approaches which included the offer of a substantial sum of money, if he would stop the traffic of arms and munitions passing along the Burma Road. These approaches were made through a Japanese, Dr Suzuki, who was Ba Maw's physician. Ba Maw was unable to help as any closing of the Road was a British decision, and most Burmese were at that time in no mind for armed insurrection.

The Japanese, determined to change all that, in 1940 sent in Colonel Suzuki, not to be confused with Ba Maw's physician, Dr Suzuki. Colonel Suzuki was of the same swashbuckling mould as Colonels Doihara Kenjichi and Saito Jiro – it says much for the excellence of the Japanese Intelligence training system that it produced at least three officers who proved themselves so highly adept in the field of subversion.

After service in Shanghai, in which he had been a central figure in a dispute between the intelligence arms of the army and navy,

Suzuki had returned to Tokyo and there became the secretary of the Japan–Burma Association, one of several cultural organisations formed, as Louis Allen has written, because they 'might later have a political pay-off'.[11] Suzuki, who was to end the war with the rank of Major-General, threw himself into his new task with enthusiasm. When Thein Maung, politician, newspaper editor, and friend to Premier Ba Maw, visited Tokyo in late 1939, Suzuki cultivated him, so that when he himself arrived in Rangoon in 1940, he already had a powerful link with the political parties there.

One of Suzuki's most important agents in Burma was a Japanese Buddhist monk called Nagai, who had resided there for many years. As with all Buddhist monks, Nagai's subsistence came from itinerant begging, a useful cover for an intelligence agent. He provided contact between Suzuki and several members of the nationalist movement, known as Thakin, and, through Thein Maung, with Ba Maw.

Suzuki's initial aim was simple. It was to close the Burma Road, and the best way to do that, he thought, was to promote a Thakin insurrection. He became an ardent believer in Burmese independence per se, and not just as part of Japan's political plans for the Far East. So close did he get to the Burmese, indeed, and so imbued with their nationalist aspirations, that this later got him into trouble with his superiors. The sobriquet 'Lawrence of Burma' was never used, but would have suited him comfortably.

Whilst Suzuki supplied Thakin with funds and tried to foment trouble, the Japanese consul-general in Rangoon, Kuga, made direct contact with Ba Maw in the summer of 1940. Ba Maw told him that if there was to be a Burmese insurrection, then 5,000,000 rupees, 5,000 rifles and Japanese instructors would be required.[12]

The British, aware of some of the intriguing going on, imprisoned Ba Maw under the Defence of Burma Act in August, and this caused a man at the centre of the Thakin movement, Aung San, one day to become the leader of a free Burma, to flee the country aboard a Norwegian freighter. In November Colonel Suzuki flew to Tokyo to meet Aung San who, after some adventures on the way, had ended up there. As a result of that meeting *Minami Kikan* was formed the following month.

The *kikan* began to spirit leading Thakin adherents across the border into Thailand, from where they were taken to Hainan Island for training in subversion. Then they were spirited back in again. About thirty Thakins were so trained. From the *kikan's* bases set up at strategic places along the Thai border, Japanese agents were sent in to survey possible invasion routes into Burma. From Ranong one officer, pretending to be a forestry expert, surveyed the area leading to Victoria Point. This village, the most southerly in Burma, was important for one reason only; it was the site of a British airfield on the air reinforcement route to Singapore.

As war neared, the thirty trained Thakin, together with Suzuki, took an oath at a blood-drinking ceremony which bound them together as the 'Thirty Comrades'. They were to form the nucleus of the officer corps of an army to be formed to fight for Burmese independence in the process of supporting the Japanese army. On 31st December 1941, two weeks after Japanese armies had crossed the Kra Isthmus into Burma, the Thirty Comrades with some 300 other Burmese, recruited either from the border areas or from among the Burmese community in Bangkok, went through another ceremony before leaving for the front. At this ceremony the *kikan*, which had not achieved its original purpose of closing the Burma Road, was dissolved, and the Burma Independence Army (BIA) inaugurated in its place. Divided into six units, the BIA then headed for the border. Three units were to act as liaison units with attacking Japanese forces, another two became combat units. The sixth unit under Bo Ne Win and a Japanese lieutenant became a sabotage unit.

Colonel Suzuki might have been the most colourful Japanese agent working in Burma, but he was far from being the only one. In September 1938 a dental surgeon calling himself Mr Iida arrived at Rangoon to take up residence in a Japanese hotel there. He was not seen to do much in the way of dental work, but several times he travelled up the Irrawaddy to the riverhead at Bhamo close to the Chinese frontier and to Lashio on the Burma Road itself. Amongst the Chinese he posed as a merchant on the lookout for possible markets.

Iida was in fact a Colonel Sugasawa, sent to collect what intelligence he could on the shipments destined for China. Sugasawa did not bother with codes, but sent his reports to Tokyo in plain language either through the Japanese consul or through passengers or crew members of Japanese ships. By the spring of 1939 he came to realise that he was being watched, and asked to be recalled to Tokyo, a request granted in August.

A British report noted that a man called Yasuda, who was working for the Rangoon Daishin Company, was particularly close to several

Burmese ministers, and that it was intended to use these ministers in the event of war to organise riots, looting and sabotage. When Rangoon fell in March 1942, there was indeed widespread looting and rioting, though how much of this was politically inspired and how much was merely a result of the breakdown in order as the British left, will never be known. British Field Security was very busy in those last days, some rioters were shot and killed, and there were many reports of snipers at work in the city.[13]

Vichy-French Indo-China was practically an open field for Japanese Intelligence activities. In other territories the Japanese were usually discreet enough to operate in mufti, but in Indo-China Military Intelligence agents frequently did not trouble to change out of uniform.

Up until the time the Japanese began stationing troops in the country, their consulates had been the main centres of subversion and espionage. After July 1940, a 'special service' unit was set up called *Sumida Kikan*, also known as *Nishihara Kikan* after the Major-General who created it. Its headquarters were at Hanoi, in the north, and its initial purpose to watch and report on supplies passing across the Chinese border to Chiang Kai-shek's troops. That purpose soon changed. When Japanese troops were 'permitted' to land in the north, those supplies stopped moving, and were kept in the *kikan*'s own 'safe-keeping'.[14] Its task then changed again, and it came to be used as a sort of liaison unit with the local Vichy authorities. In between times, it was busy encouraging the local anti-French Annamese Independence Movement, a body that provided a useful source of intelligence. The Japanese had adopted a long-term view and had no intention of allowing a European nation, even one of the Vichy variety, to maintain a hold on any part of the Far East.

There were other *kikans*, who though headquartered in Indo-China – the Japanese Southern Army, which was to control all operations from Burma eastward to New Guinea when war came, had its HQ in Saigon – spread their tentacles into other countries. Most of these *kikans* had a military purpose, but a few were used for economic purposes. One, *Yamane Kikan*, although created by an army colonel of that name, was solely engaged in buying non-military goods from local firms.

When, on 25th November 1941, a bomb wrecked the American

consulate in Saigon, the British consul-general there reported to London that the Japanese were thought to be responsible.

Britain's Intelligence in Indo-China seems to have been poor. France was an ally until it fell in June 1940, but prior to that the British had not seen the need to put in much intelligence effort of their own, though the consuls at Saigon and Hanoi would have kept their ears to the ground. After June 1940 British official policy was to keep on good terms with the Vichy administration of Indo-China, and this meant largely ignoring the Free French element there who might well have formed the basis of a good intelligence network.

A report of 4th August 1941 made by that section of Britain's Special Operation Executive (SOE) known as the Oriental Mission (OM) and based at Singapore, said that the Admiral Layton–Admiral Decoux agreement made on 15th February that year – which 'regularised' relations between Britain and the French colony – 'was a constant obstacle and embarrassment to OM. So anxious was the C-in-C, China [Layton] to have it maintained that the French were allowed to perpetrate flagrant breaches of the agreement without serious objections from Singapore.' One of the French breaches was to permit ever-increasing anti-British propaganda to be printed in local newspapers and to be broadcast over Radio Saigon.

Nevertheless SOE had a French section in Singapore which did keep in touch with Free Frenchmen in Indo-China, including the captains of French ships trading between Saigon and Singapore, but what of value resulted from these contacts is not known. This French section had the part-time services of Captain Ivan Lyon and his French wife, and the full-time services of a French surgeon called Meyer May who had left Saigon early in 1941. They also employed another Frenchman, Frederick Marie Jocosta, but he was not permitted to handle certain confidential material.[15] Amongst SOE's proposals for Indo-China in the months before the Far Eastern war began was the blocking of the Saigon River and action against naval vessels in Camranh Bay, but these came to nothing.

G.C. Denham, who headed the British Secret Intelligence Service in the Far East from about mid-1941, had some agents in the French territory, but who they were and how long they had been there is not known. The SOE report dated 4th August 1941 noted that 'one of Denham's people is prepared to do something for us, but this must be balanced by the importance of his maintaining his own cover.'

Whether there was a British Secret Service involvement in the destruction of a Japanese oil dump of 1,600 drums stored in barges near Thuduc on 21st November is not known. The British consul-general reported that he had strong indications that the fire was caused by sabotage by private French persons.[16]

In the Netherlands East Indies (NEI) Japanese subversion and espionage efforts were run by consul-general Saito in Batavia. Taking full advantage of his diplomatic immunity, Saito was involved in issuing propaganda, inciting nationalists and setting up fifth-column organisations. He made use of anybody and any organisation with a grudge against the Dutch administration, including local cells of the Communist Party. For printing propaganda leaflets he bought up a private printing shop.

His vice-consul, named Takagi, did not carry out any normal consular duties, but set himself up as a potato dealer in the dock area of Surabaya, the most important naval port in the NEI situated at the eastern end of the island of Java. Using Formosans as agents, for they looked much like the Chinese who abounded throughout Java, he set about creating provocations and acts of terrorism, using the slogan 'Asia for the Asiatics'. His warehouse was used as a store for smuggled weapons.

Throughout Java native traders were induced by offers of financial credit and other forms of support to sell Japanese goods. This provided opportunity for those traders to be imbued with anti-Dutch sentiments.

One Japanese stratagem, notable mainly for its failure, was to provide finance for Javan youths to study in Japan with the view of preparing them to undermine the government on their return. Not many youths apparently took up the offer.

As in nearby Malaya, the Japanese bought up or bought into certain local newspapers. The Dutch took retaliatory action, in the form of withholding newsprint, against one called *Sinar Selatan*, or Star of the South, based in the port-town of Semarang. A naval officer spy, Keizo Kaneko, a resident in the Indies for many years, was found to be involved in a proposal to publish a new Malay daily in Batavia in 1938. Fortunately for the Dutch, who were mostly as chary as the British in Malaya over offending Japanese sensibilities, it was discovered that the Indonesian director fronting the scheme was involved in embezzling the funds. On his arrest, the scheme collapsed.

Another Japanese, Tomegoro Yoshizumi, editor of the Japanese language newspaper, *Tohindo Nippo*, was deported from the NEI in February 1941 for 'subversive activities', but apparently he did not go far. On 8th December, the day the Japanese attacked Malaya, during the Dutch operation to round up all Japanese in the country, Tomegoro was discovered on the island of Banka disguised as a native; he had been clandestinely brought back on a Japanese fishing boat. He was found to be in possession of 57,000 guilders which he admitted he had received from the consul-general.

The authorities estimated that there were about 4,000 Japanese fishermen and at least 500 vessels in NEI waters towards the end of 1941. The boats, established at strategic places covering the Torres and Maccasser Straits and other prime routes into the archipelago, were often seen taking soundings and bearings instead of fishing. Unlike in the waters around Malaya and Singapore, where some kind of control at least could be kept over their activities, those using the waters of the vast NEI archipelago with its many remote islands, could do much as they pleased. The crews were unruly, and terrorised the native residents of some of the islands.

The fishing fleets were often visited by naval officers sent down from Palao, the capital of the Japanese Mandated Islands to the north. Sometimes, instead of fishing, Japanese craft were seen making contact with passing Japanese merchantmen, and intelligence sources revealed that in some cases these contacts concerned opium smuggling. In 1938, in the Rhio Strait just south of Singapore, a Japanese submarine was sighted taking aboard supplies from a fishing craft.

The organising company for the majority of the fleet in 1940 was the Japan Ocean Bonito & Tunny Fish Company at Batavia, considered to be a front for espionage. Its outlying offices were all in strategic places.

Amongst many other Japanese companies known to be fronts for espionage activities in the NEI was the Nanyo Warehousing Company – also known in the same context in Singapore. Its Batavia branch was under a former naval officer, Aratama Naoju, who had been dismissed the Japanese navy for his role in the military rebellion in Tokyo in February 1936. He was now trying to rehabilitate himself by engaging in espionage work. After the war in Europe began, Aratama is known to have had regular contact with the German consulate in Batavia. Another naval officer working for the Nanyo company was Ohta Mamoru, who in mid-1940 was ordered to look for suitable landing places on the west coast of Java, some of which were later used by Japanese troops.

There seems to have been an organisation in the NEI very similar to *Kame* in Malaya. It was run by a spy called Kobayashi, whose front was that of being a planter in North Celebes. He was known to be in regular touch with Tokyo and with Palao, personally handing his reports to the masters of Japanese vessels using the port of Menado in the Celebes. Kobayashi controlled many Indonesian nationalists by promising them they would retain their status in the community when the Japanese took control of the country.

The Japanese worked closely with German intelligence in the NEI, for the Germans had had a significant presence in the islands from well before the war. In May 1940 there were around 7,000 Germans and Austrians there, including 400 who had reached high positions in the Dutch army, the police, and in the civil administration. Based at the German consulate itself, in the capacity of Trade Commissioner, was Julius Ruckenbrod, who in reality was an officer of the Gestapo. He was responsible for the formation of an organisation similar to the Hitler Youth Movement. When the Germans marched into Holland the NEI authorities arrested a number of Germans and their Dutch collaborators. Amongst the latter was Police Commissioner U.J.A. Piepers, a fanatical member of the Dutch Nazi Party.

By the time the Japanese made their attacks at various places in the Indies, they had a full and thorough knowledge of Dutch military dispositions, which were not impressive, and about their airfields and naval bases. Those pre-war subversion operations nullified any small chance there might have been of native uprisings in support of the Dutch, who in fact had very little support from any section of the local community. The British had constructed two airfields near the southern end of Sumatra but, rather strangely the Japanese did not discover the existence of one of these until after the war had started.

Twelve

Australian Diplomatic Intelligence in the Far East

It is the traditional view that, prior to World War Two, Australia had not taken up her right to have her own diplomatic representation overseas, but instead relied upon Britain's embassies and consulates for her overseas contacts and representations. The Australian historian David Day contrasted the Australian attitude regarding foreign service representation to the more independent attitudes adopted by two of the other British Dominions, Canada and South Africa.[1] 'Australia', he wrote, 'resolutely chose not to exercise that right until her precarious wartime position made it unavoidable.' He goes on, 'Until then, she had only a High Commissioner in London . . . and from 1937, a Counsellor at the British Embassy in Washington.'

This view is not strictly true, for it did not apply in the Far East where, from 1934 onward, the Australians established, albeit somewhat discreetly, a network of diplomatic intelligence officers. These officers were stationed in Japan, China, the Netherlands East Indies, Portuguese Timor and Singapore.

At this time Australian Military and Naval Intelligence existed only on a small scale. Apart from a liaison officer in London who was attached to the staff of Sir Maurice Hankey, the Secretary of the Committee of Imperial Defence, and some officers loaned to FECB in Hong Kong, Australian Intelligence was mainly concerned with internal security matters. For external intelligence it had to rely on any crumbs that London allowed it.

In the early 1930s there was a rising fear of Japan amongst Australian politicians. Internal intelligence reported growing Japanese espionage and penetration of the country. There was concern over the number of reports coming in about the activities of naval personnel on board Japanese fishing craft and merchantmen who were busy photographing and surveying parts of the north and east coasts. Reports of this nature had begun indeed as early as 1908 when pearling luggers had been discovered surveying parts of Queensland and the Great Barrier Reef. That resulted in an Act of Parliament being passed making it, in certain circumstances, an offence for ships to take unauthorised soundings. Surveying marks were discovered, and the Japanese made so many surveys of Stockton beach, a few miles north of Newcastle and only eighty miles north of Sydney, that army intelligence considered it the most likely invasion site.[2] In 1937 the Japanese survey vessel *Zuiho Maru* was surveying within Australian territorial waters whilst ostensibly on a goodwill cruise. In that same year an Australian patrol craft, the *Larrakia*, actually opened fire on a fleet of Japanese fishermen off Darwin who were offending against the 1908 Act.

An Australian mission was sent around the Far East in 1934 under J. Tonkin of the Department of Commerce. The mission's major aim was to seek out markets for Australian products, but a large part of the report presented on its return concerned defence and political matters. The Tonkin mission was followed in that same year by the Australian Eastern Mission (AEM). Though it travelled as a 'goodwill' mission its leader, John Latham, had a background in intelligence. In 1916 as a lieutenant-commander with the Royal Australian Navy, he had headed a political intelligence unit formed to combat the influence of the communist-inspired International Workers of the World after an incident of sabotage aboard HMAS *Brisbane*. In 1918 he became naval adviser to the Australian delegation at the Versailles peace conferences, and while in London attempted rather unsuccessfully to improve Australian access to Admiralty intelligence. By 1925 he was Australian Attorney-General, and he built up its Investigation Branch to have strong links with MI5 in London and with Special Branch, New Scotland Yard.

The AEM visited Japan, China, Singapore and the NEI, and Latham submitted three reports on his return, one of them a secret strategic survey.[3] Anticipating Australia's present-day efforts to draw closer to her Asian neighbours, Latham called the area he visited the 'Near

East'. His report gave a pessimistic view of China, a view opposite to that of Britain which at the time looked upon China as a breakwater against Japan. He did not subscribe to the current view of British Intelligence that Japan was second-rate and inefficient, and that the worst Australia could expect should Japan decide to make war on the West was harassment by cruiser raids. He was highly critical of the British stop-go attitude over the Singapore Naval Base, and made the prophetic statement that its defences might be adequate provided it was allotted sufficient fighter protection.

During the next two years other missions were sent out, and each resulted in confidential reports being made on strategic matters. A mission in 1936 was headed by Charles Hawker, a Member of Parliament from South Australia. It travelled to Japan, Manchuria and China. Although some of Hawker's assessments of the physical characteristics of the Japanese are risible from a present-day outlook, he noted that the Japanese troops in China were superior to the European troops stationed there. He predicted that the Japanese military were capable of pushing Japan into war, and that a 'penetration and commercial percolation policy' in a southward direction might pave the way for territorial claims. He warned that such claims might be made on parts of Northern Australia.

All of these reports indicated a possible threat by Japan against Australian territory. In consequence, by mid-1935 steps had been taken to implement a trade commissioner service, ostensibly to deal with trade matters and to provide a measure of Australian diplomatic representation in the countries concerned, but also to provide intelligence. The designated places for these commissioners were Tokyo, Shanghai and Batavia. Then, in 1938, a Government Commissioner was appointed to Singapore, and three years later Australia sent out another overseas representative, this time to Portuguese Timor, a territory strategically placed to the north of the island continent.

The commissioner appointed to Tokyo was Edwin E. Longfield-Lloyd, and his previous history points to the true nature of at least part of his task there. He had been a member of the 1934 AEM and was a major in the Intelligence Corps of the Australian Militia (the equivalent of Britain's Territorial Army or the US National Guard); he was also a senior officer of the Attorney-General's Investigation Branch.

The man selected for Shanghai was Vivian G. Bowden, who had

been a major in the Royal Engineers during World War One. Prior to that he had joined his father's business in Yokohama, and after the war established his own business in Shanghai. He was fluent in Japanese and Chinese and could also speak French, Russian and German.[4] Charles R. Critchley, the man chosen for Batavia had also been a soldier.

David Ross, the man sent to Timor in early 1941, had been a naval pilot. He went to Timor as representative of the Australian Department of Civilian Aviation. His job dealt with the establishment of air and landing rights, but he was also required 'to send intelligence reports, especially about what the Japanese were doing there'[5] Ross's number two was Lieutenant Whittaker RAN, a Naval Intelligence officer.

Each of the Trade Commissioners reported directly to the Chief Investigating Officer of the Australian Commercial Intelligence Service. In Tokyo Longfield-Lloyd took particular interest in the unofficial but influential Southwards Expansion Movement whose declared aim was economic expansion linked with migration, and in 1938 he sent home copies of Japanese maps which depicted Australia as an integral part of the Japanese Imperial Empire.

A good example of the convoluted espionage scene in the Far East is that one of Longfield-Long's sources for economic intelligence was a journalist named Gunther Stein. A left-winger and half-Jewish, he had been driven out of Germany. He then proceeded via Russia to Japan, arriving there in 1935, and became something of an expert on Japanese trade and industry. As well as his contacts with the Australian, Stein became particularly friendly with Sir George Sansom, Trade Counsellor at the British embassy. He then went to Hong Kong and launched an English language newspaper, the funding for which remains a mystery to this day. He travelled to China and befriended Sir Archibald Clark Kerr, the British Minister there, who for some reason arranged British citizenship for him. After Japan entered the war, Stein became a war correspondent in China. Stein's contacts with Longfield-Lloyd, Sansom and Clark Kerr, probably proved more profitable to him than to them, for ever since 1935 he had been a member of Richard Sorge's Soviet spy ring in Tokyo.[6]

Vivien Bowden commenced his duties as Trade Commissioner, China in 1936. His despatches included little in the way of useful intelligence but that was probably a reflection of the difficulties involved in travelling around a country at war with the Japanese. It might also have reflected the fact that having no 'closed' radio link, he had to rely on ordinary telegraph communication with Australia. In his annual report for 1938 however, Bowden included much intelligence material, covering such matters as Japanese troop movements and troop capabilities. He thought the Japanese troops were of above average quality.

In late 1938 Bowden was transferred to become the Australian Government Commissioner in Singapore, leaving his assistant, a man called Nutt, in Shanghai. Bowden sent intelligence reports home from Singapore, and after the Japanese attack on Malaya warned that the impregnability of the 'fortress' was a sham. In December 1941 he became the Australian representative on the War Council in Singapore, an appointment which showed Duff Cooper, Britain's Resident Cabinet Minister there, to be two-faced. To the Australian government Duff expressed his opinion of the soundness of Bowden's views, whilst to Churchill he said that he was of no account.[7] The former opinion was much fairer to this highly capable man. Bowden attempted to escape from the Japanese a few days before the fall of Singapore, but was captured in the Banka Strait and executed at Muntok.[8]

Charles Critchley was Trade Commissioner in Batavia from 1936 to 1938. From the start his despatches included intelligence material regarding Japanese penetration of the Netherlands East Indies. He had close contacts with the Dutch colonial government, and was even supplied by them with a copy of the official anti-Japanese penetration policy. Critchley also had a good rapport with the British consul-general in Batavia.

In 1941 it was estimated that there were 2,000 Japanese in Australia. Many of them were not residents but tourists and visiting businessmen according to an official Australian report,[9] while those who were residents were mostly of the merchant and official classes. Others, mainly employed as laundrymen and gardeners, had arrived in Australia prior to the Immigration Act of 1908, sometimes called the White Australia Act, and were consequently permanent residents. Some of them had married Europeans.

As in other Far Eastern lands the Japanese community in Australia was the most consolidated block of any foreign nationals, and even in the case of the long-time residents it was considered that the loyalties of most lay 'unquestionably with Japan'. The Australian internal intelligence services reported that 'there is ample evidence . . . that the Japanese, silent partners in the Axis, were most active in acquiring information on Australian economic development and defence preparations'. Certain items of information were passed on to the other Axis partners. Prior to the outbreak of the war in Europe, the then vice-consul in Sydney, Miyake, was known to have been a close friend of his opposite number in the German consulate, Dr Hoops, and also of Arnold von Skerst, the editor of the German weekly *Die Brücke*, who was a member of the Nazi Party.

Japanese consulate officials were known to be collecting intelligence material and 'were directing agencies for espionage and and 5th column'. In November 1937 information was received that Mr Wakamatsu, the consul-general at Sydney, was the head organiser of a Secret Service Agency in Australia, but even though countermeasures were taken there was never enough information to build up a detailed picture of his organisation. However, the chancellor at the consulate, named Yanase, was interested in mapping and shipping movements, and a man called Inoue was responsible for transmitting information and documents via Japanese ships. It was also clear that the Japanese, as throughout the East, were making use of commercial firms, Japanese residents, individuals with pro-Japanese sympathies, and organisations such as the Japan Chamber of Commerce, to collect information which was then channelled through the consulates.

The semi-official Domei News Agency was involved, and Australian intelligence authorities were aware that its head J. Toyada, was active in spying. Domei had 'a complete set of aerial photos of positions on the New South Wales coast clearly showing defence installations'. Just before Toyada left Australia in May 1940, he received a letter from the Chief of Naval Information in Tokyo thanking him for information supplied and requesting more naval intelligence. The letter was opened by Australian Intelligence. The replacement for Toyada, who was sent to Shanghai, was called Kurata. Unlike his predecessor he was not a trained journalist and made little pretence of being one. He had served in the Japanese army in China. There were indications that he was sending documents to Japan in diplomatic bags and by safe hand of masters of Japanese ships.

Despite their abhorrence of Communism back home and in China, towards the end of 1937 the Japanese showed interest in the activities of, and made contacts with members of the Communist Party of Australia. They were also interested in Jewish organisations, to learn whether any such organisation was in need of funds.

After the European war began, the personal secretary to the Japanese Minister who had been appointed to Australia, kept a notebook in which he recorded details of such items as Australia's war effort, munitions and aircraft production and manpower problems, and so on. This was discovered when the secretary left the notebook in a taxi whilst being driven around the port city of Melbourne.

Two Japanese working in Australia, whose main purpose was spying and subversion, were called Amano and Ikeda. Amano worked for the Mitsui Shipping Line in Australia, but was actually a lieutenant in the Japanese army. Ikeda, an extra assistant secretary on the legation staff, was the eldest son of the Marquis Ikeda, and it was his task to spread pro-Japanese propaganda. Australian intelligence discovered in November 1941 that the Japanese Minister had received special funds from Tokyo for use by these men.

Amano was not the only Mitsui Line employee whose principal purpose for being in the country was espionage. In September 1939 it was discovered that the company's chief wool buyer, Takahashi, was a leading spy in Australia, and that one of his most important informants was one of the long-term resident laundrymen, a man called Umino, who lived in North Sydney.

Another business resident, Miura, was manager of the Brisbane branch of F. Kanematsu (Australia) Pty. Ltd. In July 1940 he made extensive enquiries about the disposition of Australian troops, and Australian Intelligence marked him down as the head man behind Japanese Intelligence in Queensland.

There were other short-stay agents, men sent into Australia for a specific purpose and for relatively short time. Major Hashida entered the country in January 1941 as Mr Hashida, and it was not discovered until later that he was a member of the Japanese Imperial General Staff. The stated reason for his visit was to purchase wheat, wool, and scrap iron. During his three month stay – he left in March 1941 – he kept a journal, which some time later, probably post-war, fell into Allied hands. Hashida's visit to Brisbane, where he met up with a laundryman spy called Suzuki, resulted in him recording details of the airfield there and the seaplane landing facility. In Sydney he recorded notes about the Harbour Bridge and the naval flying-boat base. He made contact with the Japanese consul-general in Sydney, and it may have been as a result that he was granted an interview with a man he described as the 'Australian Minister of War'. Hashida wrote in his journal, 'How far can I lead him up the garden path?' He went on to travel to Adelaide and Perth. Other items he recorded concerned a delivery of arms to the Netherlands East Indies, the movement of a battalion of New Zealand soldiers, the sailings of the troopships *Aquitania* and *Queen Mary* and the departure of Australian troops to Singapore. Apparently fearing a search as he left the country, Hashida handed his journal to Captain Orihara of the *Canberra Maru* to take home.

Aboard the next trip of the *Canberra Maru* to Sydney, and appearing on the crew list as a cabin boy, was another successful short-term agent. He was Lieutenant Ogawa of the Japanese army. He arrived in May 1941 and was permitted to land as a sheep attendant. Before he left on the same ship in June he had carried out a systematic reconnaissance of the Sydney Harbour area which included taking photographs. Ogawa turned up again later in New Guinea as head of a Japanese Special Services Organisation known as *Taka*. His survey at Sydney might well have helped the planning of the Japanese midget submarine raid there on the night of 31st May/1st June 1942.

All Japanese residing in Australia were rounded up on the outbreak of the Pacific War. In August 1944 it is likely that either personnel or cargo was landed near Cape Leveque on the northwest coast from a Chinese junk that may have been on a spying mission. The craft was intercepted, and its Chinese master claimed he had been blown off course voyaging between Java and Koepang, a story the navy thought unlikely given the weather conditions at the time. A search of the craft revealed copies of Japanese charts of the Australian coast from Albany in the south to Darwin in the north. Also found were a British flag and some Australian currency. On board were seventeen Chinese crew members. One of them held a British Seaman's card, another an Alien's Registration Card issued in Melbourne, and a third had a pass that once would have gained him entry into the Royal Navy Dockyard in Hong Kong.

After the fall of Singapore in February 1942, when the Australians feared that their country was next on the Japanese list for conquest, there were signs of spy-fever in the land. One such led to the arrest of a Briton who, with his family, had been evacuated from Japan in the spring of 1941 and had ended up at Brisbane. Claude Vane Ross had been a schoolteacher for ten years at the Mita Gakho School in Japan. He was arrested in April 1942 and interned at the Gaythorne

Internment Camp. He was detained, according to an official document issued by the Commonwealth Investigation Bureau, 'because he is regarded as being of pro-Japanese sentiments and sympathies'.[10] He had been living at Caloundra and by 'his inquisitive nature and suspicious activities has aroused considerable suspicion in the minds of local residents'. The rather flimsy evidence against him included 'the sound of a typewriter being used at his house at all hours', and that his eight-year-old daughter had told a schoolfriend that her father wrote with invisible ink between the typewritten lines. Other information came from anonymous sources. It is possible that another reason for Ross's internment was that, by living in Brisbane, he was close to the headquarters, or planned headquarters, of several Allied intelligence organisations; it was a particularly 'sensitive' area. The allegations against him were not substantiated, and Ross was released from internment in November 1942.

Thirteen

Inside Japan Pre-war

The tentacles of the Japanese intelligence effort stretched everywhere throughout the Far East and to many places farther afield. By the late 1930s their agents were ubiquitous, and, given the 'appeasement' attitude of Britain, France and Holland during the years when trouble was brewing in Europe, the Japanese were largely able to get away with it. The United States, in her endeavour to stay out of a new war, and despite having a large colony of her own in the Far East – though she would not have described the Philippines as that – also did little to stem Japanese espionage activities.

Reports from agents enabled the Japanase to build up comprehensive economic and military profiles of many countries. In particular, by 1941, they possessed excellent information on the defence capabilities of all the lands constituting Southeast Asia. However, because ships and fleets are not static but tend to move around and so make long-term surveillance difficult, they had less information on naval matters. This was a cause of concern to the Imperial Japanese Navy.

In the case of the Royal Navy the Japanese knew that in primary armament only the 16-inch guns of *Nelson* and *Rodney* came near to matching their own in range. But in January 1941 *Life* magazine published some aerial photographs of HMS *King George V* entering Chesapeake Bay and when copies reached Tokyo in early February, the Japanese were worried to see the ship had been fitted with anti-aircraft rocket launchers. In fact that particular type of rocket launcher was not a success and later that year was replaced by Vickers pom-poms, but the Japanese did not learn of that until much later.

Of even greater concern was British radar. The *Life* magazine feature clearly showed the external signs of a comprehensive radar system, far in advance of the rudimentary system the Japanese had achieved since 1940. The Japanese navy had perfected night operations but were worried lest radar give the British an advantage. British asdic detection equipment, against submarines, was also rightly considered to be far in advance of the Japanese model.

The Japanese were less impressed with the intelligence they received from the Germans about the attack by carrier-based British Swordfish biplanes which crippled the Italian battle fleet in Taranto harbour on 11th November 1940. Despite this success the Japanese considered the Swordfish obsolete, its performance not outstanding, and quite rightly attributed the triumph to the bravery of the pilots.

Despite Japanese concern about the lack of intelligence on certain naval matters, overall their intelligence-gathering was excellent. Furthermore, they were even cleverer in 'ground' – as opposed to Sigint – intelligence matters than the flood of information pouring into Tokyo indicated; for they had also taken steps to see that there was no corresponding outflow. They did this largely by clamping down on the activities of every foreigner in the country. All foreigners, including embassy staffs, were kept under surveillance, phones were tapped and cables intercepted. Even the citizens of Japan's Axis partners were watched. The Japanese often took exception to the activities of the German Gestapo representatives in the country and Japanese ire in this direction was stirred up occasionally by British embassy staff engaged in propaganda.

All this was in sharp contrast to earlier years when the Japanese were building up their armed forces and modelling them after European counterparts. Because the worst Allied misjudgement and underestimation of Japanese military preparedness in those pre-war years proved to be over the size and efficiency of Japanese naval air power, the change from an open-to-learning process to one of the utmost secrecy, is perhaps best illustrated by the Japanese fleet air arm.

This had begun in April 1921 when W.F. Forbes-Sempill (Lord Sempill to be), late of the Royal Naval Air Service and of the RAF, arrived in Japan at the head of a thirty-strong party of British officers and warrant officers with similar experience to his own, to organise, supervise, equip and train the Imperial Japanese Navy Air Service. Probably because international moves were already afoot to abrogate the Anglo-Japanese Treaty – it was to end in December – Sempill's mission, although called the British Aviation Mission and having the blessing of the British government, was classified as unofficial.

An air station had been constructed at Lake Kasumi-ga-ura, a huge stretch of inland water close to the sea some forty miles northeast of Tokyo. The British group stayed there for almost three years, all members of it being given acting ranks in the Japanese navy, Sempill's own being that of captain. 'The value of the technical assistance rendered to the Japanese Navy . . . and to the advancement of aeronautics in both its military and civil phases was naturally considerable under such specially qualified instructors', wrote Major-General F.S.G. Piggott.[1]

At the end of that period Sempill was to record that Japanese 'air ability is perhaps higher than we are accustomed to find in the West; the pilots ever ready to undertake the most difficult manoeuvres'. In the last year of Sempill's tenure at the air station, and on to 1925, the Executive Officer at the base was Captain Yamamoto Isoroku who, as an admiral, was to be the brains behind the attack on Pearl Harbor in 1941. Later, in 1925 to 1928, whilst serving as Naval Attaché in Washington, Yamamoto was also influenced by that avid proponent of air power, Brigadier Billy Mitchell.

After Sempill's departure in 1923 the Japanese drew blinds around the air station, so much so that in 1930–31 when Wing Commander R.W. Chappell, previously a language officer and later British Air Attaché in Tokyo, was on loan to the Japanese navy, he noted Japanese proficiency in torpedo-bombing though stating he was not allowed to see any of it for himself. He obtained his information from listening to conversations of navy pilots.

The air station was not the only part of the Japanese navy around which fell a bamboo blind. Few foreigners were allowed anywhere near naval installations. One of the few exceptions was the Englishman, Cecil Bullock, who was allowed to teach English at Etajima, the Japanese Naval College on an island near Kure, the giant Inland Sea naval base. In his book published in 1943 Bullock said much about the college curriculum but little about Japanese ships, for he was not permitted to see many.[2]

Admiral Sir Frederic Dreyer, writing in 1939 but basing what he had to say on his experience as C-in-C, China Fleet in 1934 – when he witnessed Japanese aircraft which he had seen in other exercises, landing on an aircraft-carrier – urged in a memorandum that the Japanese fleet should not be underrated. The First Sea Lord noted that, because of Dreyer's experience, 'his views are of great value'. However, the Director of Plans at the Admiralty, Rear-Admiral V.H. Danckwerts, noted that Dreyer 'had a bee in his bonnet about Japan', and advised that no action should be taken on Dreyer's memorandum.[3] One of Dreyer's successors, Admiral Sir Charles Little, saw units of the Imperial Japanese Navy at sea exercises in 1937, and although in his report to the Admiralty he was disparaging about the general performance of that navy, he excepted the air arm from that criticism.[4]

In spite of these early reports, and because foreigners were never permitted to see the Japanese naval air service in operation, the Admiralty felt able to advise the British Joint Intelligence Council in May 1941 that the estimated efficiency of the Japanese naval air force was no higher in quality than that of the Italians.[5]

The Japanese took positive deception measures to prevent knowledge of their naval preparations falling into foreign hands. At Kure, behind the twenty-foot fence that surrounded the Navy Yard, a fence that Cecil Bullock and no other foreigner was ever allowed to pass through, the Japanese laid the keel of the battleship *Yamato* in 1937. She was the first of a proposed class of four dreadnoughts of 64,000 tons, each carrying nine 18-inch guns that were to make them the most powerful in the world. Only two were in fact built, a third, the *Shinano*, being converted during building into an aircraft-carrier. So secret was their construction that only those navy officers deemed to hold a need-to-know position were aware of them. And only in Japan, with its restrictions and close surveillance over foreigners travelling in the country, and its hold over its own subjects, could such a secret have been successfully kept for so long.

As a deception device the Japanese put about rumours that new battleships under construction were of only 40,000 tons and would carry only 16-inch guns. They even gave a name to one of these fictitious ships, *Nissin*. Japan's ally, Germany, knew nothing about the *Yamato* which was launched in 1940 and commissioned a week after the Far East war began.[6] FECB knew nothing about it either, until told by United States Naval Intelligence in 1942.*

* *Yamato* was sunk on 7th April 1945 by carrier-based American planes about fifty miles off the southwest coast of Kyushu. Her sister ship *Musashi* had been sunk on 25th October 1944 in the Battle of Surigao Strait. The half-sister ship, the carrier *Shinano*, was sunk off the entrance to Tokyo Bay on 29th November 1944 by the US submarine *Archerfish*.

In the long run, for the day of the battleship was almost over by the time *Yamato* was commissioned, it was British and American underestimation of the quality of Japanese navy planes that was more important than lack of knowledge of Japanese battleship construction.

The Type 97 carrier-borne bomber, which the Allies called 'Kate' had a much greater range, though it was slower, than either its British or American counterparts. Kates were to succeed in firing torpedoes into the shallow waters of Pearl Harbor and hit their targets. The Japanese navy's land-based bomber, Type 96 and dubbed 'Nell' by the Allies, was also an excellent aircraft. Nells were the main aircraft used in the successful attacks against *Prince of Wales* and *Repulse* on 10th December 1941. The other land-based aircraft used in this battle was the Type 1, called 'Betty' which was faster than the Nell. As a comparison, the standard carrier-based British torpedo-bomber, the Swordfish, had a speed of only 121 knots, about half of that of the Japanese planes mentioned.

The Japanese also managed to keep from Western eyes and ears most of the technical details of their oxygen-propelled torpedo; the West knew the Japanese had developed one, but were not aware of its full capability. Britain had experimented with this means of propulsion in the 1920s, but had given it up as too dangerous. In 1927, however, a Japanese officer on a visit to Portsmouth mistakenly thought that he had seen the necessary equipment for producing oxygen, and his subsequent report set the Japanese off on developing one of their own at Kure Naval Arsenal.* By 1935 they had developed the Long Lance oxygen-propelled torpedo which had a maximum range of 33,000 yards and a maximum speed of 50 knots. In both range and speed it was significantly better than anything the British and Americans had, and could carry a greater explosive charge. In trials and exercises the Japanese always recovered any torpedoes used, and

* The three main Japanese naval bases were at Kure, Sasebo and Yokosuka. In addition to being bases, they had extensive shipbuilding and ship repair facilities, and were also naval arsenals. Near to Kure was the main naval college, and from around 1930 Kure could be likened to Portsmouth, the Clyde and Greenwich rolled into one. It was still very much a naval port in the 1950s when it was being used by the Royal Navy and as 'home-base' for the British and Commonwealth forces fighting in Korea. The author, who was then a junior officer aboard a British Landing Ship (Tanks), or LST, visited the port often at that time, transporting men, tanks and vehicles back and forth between Japan and Inchon in Korea. By that time the twenty-foot fence had disappeared.

on top of that discounted both its range and speed even in official documents. Its performance was to come as a nasty shock to the Allies at the start of the war.

For technical reasons the oxygen-torpedo was not used by torpedo-bombers.[7] But even the hot-air aerial type the Japanese developed was better in some respects than the one available to the British in 1941. Its specifications must have impressed the Germans, for in mid-May 1941, seven months before the Japanese entered the war, their Air Attaché in Tokyo, Colonel von Gronau, negotiated the purchase of a hundred of them. A month earlier the Germans had even sent an unidentified agent known only as 'Toni' to Japan via the Trans-Siberian railway to receive specifications of these aerial torpedoes, but he got stuck in Tokyo after the Germans invaded Russia in June. So important did the Germans consider these torpedoes that forty were shipped aboard the blockade-runner *Anneliese Essberger*, utilising loading space previously allocated for a shipment of rubber, a valuable strategic commodity that was in very short supply in Germany.

To keep this shipment away from the eyes of British Intelligence, the torpedoes were loaded on the ship in a secluded bay near the port of Sasebo on 23rd June, just prior to the ship's sailing. Information about the shipment might have reached British ears, for on 9th July the German Naval Attaché in Tokyo informed Berlin that the ship's radio operator, Neuwald, had passed information about the ship's departure to a Japanese woman who may have been a British agent although all crew members had received strict orders to keep their mouths shut. The Attaché requested that Neuwald be indicted when the ship arrived at Bordeaux, the port that most blockade-runners made for as they could make use of Spanish territorial waters during the last part of their run to safety. Despite this breach in security the *Anneliese Essberger*, under her commander Captain Bahl, successfully ran the British blockade and reached Bordeaux on 10th September. For part of the voyage she had disguised herself as an American freighter.[8*]

Captain J.G.P. Vivian, the British Naval Attaché in Tokyo in 1935, made a number of misjudgements over the capabilities of

* The *Anneliese Essberger* ran out of luck in attempting a return journey to Japan a year later. She left Bordeaux on 4th November 1942, and at daybreak on 21st November was intercepted by British warships and sunk by gunfire about four hundred miles east of St Paul Rocks which lie off the coast of Brazil.

the Japanese navy in his reports to the Admiralty, misjudgements no doubt caused by the paucity of intelligence he was receiving. With regard to the efficiency of Japanese naval gunnery Vivian quoted a Japanese admiral as saying that 'not one in five attacking torpedo planes would be disabled by gunfire', a remark that Vivian took to be a slight on the efficiency of Japanese naval gunnery. The remark could have meant that Japanese torpedo-bombers were so fast and so well-handled as to stand a good chance against defensive guns, much as they did six years later in real operations at Pearl Harbor and in the *Prince of Wales* battle.

Technical misjudgements were not the only ones made by Captain Vivian. He also wrote a report on Japanese national characteristics, accusing them of being slow of mind and of being a nation of saké drinkers. One cannot help wondering whether, had Vivian been Attaché in the busily re-arming Germany of that day, he would have dismissed them as a nation of beer-swillers. He concluded that the average efficiency of the younger Japanese officer was not of a high order. He went on to say that he thought the Japanese navy was second-class. It was his views that seemed to have prevailed in the corridors of the Admiralty.

Vivian's comments should be compared with the later ones of the then Lieutenant Peter Pender-Cudlip of the Royal Artillery who, as a language officer, did two attachments with the Japanese army, and between them took part in a conducted tour of the north China battlefields. The first of the attachments lasted five months during 1937, and was spent with 1st (Independent) Mountain Artillery Regiment at Takata (now more commonly anglicised as Takada), south of the city of Niigata on the west coast of Honshu Island.

The language officer system had been adopted by many nations. Not only did the mutual exchange of officers afford an excellent way for them to learn a particular foreign language, it also fostered good relations between the armed services of the nations concerned. And like the Military, Naval and Air Attaché system itself, it also provided, within certain prescribed bounds of course, a method of picking up intelligence. The attaché system also provided an avenue for the *exchange* of intelligence information. In the years from 1936 to 1938, for example, a period during which Britain, in common with other countries in the West was roundly condemning Japanese actions in China, Britain was exchanging intelligence information with Japan regarding the Soviet Union, though on a strictly quid pro quo basis.[9] Professor Bradley Smith supplies a graphic example of the convoluted nature of the international intelligence-swapping scene in his book *The Ultra-Magic Deals*. In 1937 whilst the British were exchanging intelligence about Russia with the Japanese army, the American and British navies were exchanging secret intelligence about the Japanese navy.

In Japan at least, the bounds within which attachés and language officers worked, became either more rigid or more flexible with changes in the international situation. They were sometimes also affected by the character of the officer involved. Lieutenant Pender-Cudlip for example, got on excellently with his Japanese hosts, who also had a high regard for his superior, the British Military Attaché, Major-General Piggott.

British language officers sent on attachments in Japan were required to make reports on their experiences, and these went via the appropriate attaché to the Directors of Operations and Intelligence in London. If Peter Pender-Cudlip's reports are anything to go by, these reports covered every aspect of military life and were of a high standard.[10]

Pender-Cudlip's Takata report gave a rather different summing up of Japanese officers' efficiency than that of Captain Vivian, albeit Vivian had been writing about sailors and not soldiers. 'Officers' professional knowledge and ability left little to be desired', wrote Pender-Cudlip. He then went on to say of the ordinary soldier, 'their standard of intelligence was surprisingly high, and for keenness and efficiency I think this Regiment would compare favourably with any in the Japanese Army.' Although he too remarked upon the 'national characteristic' of slowness of thought – it was considered to have something to do with the many characters of the written language that had to be learnt by rote at school – and said the Japanese 'would find itself at a disadvantage if faced by a first-class modern European army', he thought them 'generally keen and knowledgeable . . . hard-working, conscientious, fit, and high in morale.'

He picked up an interesting piece of intelligence from a church missionary based in Takata, that poison gas was almost certainly being manufactured in the area where so-called nitrate fertiliser factories were 'going full blast'. He noted that the North China Incident, during which there were several reports of Japanese use of poison gas, had broken out shortly before this.

In 1939 Pender-Cudlip went on another attachment, this time to the 15th Cavalry Regiment at Narashino. It lasted for three months and was the very last such attachment permitted by the Japanese army which, by then, had grown as secretive as the navy. This attachment was probably only permitted then because Major-General Piggott, the British Army Attaché, was so highly regarded. The other major feature of this attachment was the area it took place in. For not only was Narashino, some eighteen miles east of Tokyo, the Japanese equivalent of the British Army's Salisbury Plain, it was also the home of the so-called Narashino School, a highly secret place where chemical weapons were tested and men trained in their use.

In the report he made after this attachment, Pender-Cudlip seemed to have revised his opinion of the 'national characteristic'. He wrote:

> Whether the defects which are commonly attributed to Japanese officers, viz. slowness in making up their minds . . . really existed to any great extent among the officers of this Regiment I can neither confirm nor deny. My comparatively limited acquaintance with them gave no grounds for such belief.

He went on: 'I consider that many people are liable in their appreciation of various aspects of Japan, military and economic as well as moral, seriously to underrate her strength and efficiency.' This report was shorter than the previous one for, as the Colonel of the Regiment pointed out to Pender-Cudlip in a farewell speech in his honour, it had on this occasion only been possible to vouchsafe little information. Pender-Cudlip had obviously been briefed to keep his eyes and ears open about matters concerning the Narashino School, and he reported: 'The activities of this school were kept as secret from me as they are from everyone else not connected with it.' However, on one parade occasion he did see about two hundred men from units all over the country who were attending the school, and sometimes saw officers and instructors who 'probably belonged to the Army Special Service Section'. He was asked to keep clear of certain parts of the plain where the School was liable to carry out technical work. All he ever saw were a few horse-drawn carts carrying boxes of white powder which was spread about the plain, and some exercises which involved the use of 'smoke-candles'.

* * *

Only one man, and the organisation he created, managed any continuous and major breach in the security fence the Japanese built around themselves. That man was Richard Sorge, the Russian master spy. After he left Shanghai for Moscow in 1932, he spent a period in Germany establishing the cover he intended to use in Japan, and arrived in Tokyo in September 1933 as a newspaper correspondent. He was well-armed with letters of introduction to officials at the German embassy there, and also with credentials as a member of the Nazi Party.[11]

The sending of Sorge to Tokyo was based on an acceptance by the Kremlin that Japan was likely to attack whichever one of the Great Powers was weakest and that it therefore behoved Russia to build up her defences in the Far East. The first line of defence was an intelligence network. This appreciation of the situation was in fact based on Sorge's earlier reports from Shanghai.

Sorge's network of agents in Japan was eventually about forty strong. The majority were Japanese, the most important one being Ozaki Hosumi. He was an adviser on China to the Japanese Cabinet and acted in a similar capacity to the South Manchuria Railway Company, the cover organisation behind several intelligence *kikans*. An educated and knowledgeable man, Ozaki did not pass on 'raw' intelligence to Sorge, but evaluated any information that came his way before doing so, thus enhancing its value.

Two of Sorge's foreign agents were a Yugoslav named Voukelitch, who was working in Tokyo as correspondent for a French newspaper, and Max Klausen who had previously worked for him in China. Their main task was the setting up and operation of a secret wireless station.

Sorge soon befriended Colonel Eugene Ott who became the German Military Attaché in 1934 and four years later, as Major-General Ott, was raised by Hitler to the post of German ambassador to Japan. Sorge became a part-time press attaché to the embassy and Ott, both as attaché and later ambassador, got into the habit of discussing many matters with him; furthermore Sorge was often shown copies of secret reports sent to Berlin. Sorge also cultivated Ott's successor as Military Attaché, Lieutenant-Colonel Friedrich von Schol. Every scrap of information Sorge picked up, not only about German–Japanese relations but also sometimes on German plans world-wide, was sent to Moscow. His discussions with Ott enabled Sorge to keep abreast of German attempts to persuade the Japanese to attack Russia, and this information was passed to Ozaki who was busy advising members of the Japanese Cabinet not to attack Russia; it made for a perfect pitch.

One of Sorge's major intelligence coups came with the so-called Changkufeng Incident of July–August 1938. At the place of that name on the Tumun River – where the frontiers of Korea, the USSR and Japanese Manchukuo met – there was a major clash of arms between Japanese and Russian forces, the exact circumstances of which are still shrouded in mystery. A short while before the fighting began General G.S. Lyushkov of Stalin's secret police, the NKVD, came over resplendent in uniform and medals and surrendered himself to the Japanese. Apparently he thought it likely that he would soon be a victim of the purge of senior officers which Stalin was conducting that summer. There is a strong likelihood that Lyushkov had been acting as a Japanese spy before that. An immediate result of Lyushkov's defection was a general tightening up of Soviet border security.

Then Japan's monitoring of Russian military wireless communications – a Sigint operation probably facilitated by information about Russian codes Lyushkov had brought with him – gave warning of impending trouble. Suddenly, and it is still not clear who fired the first shot, a pitched battle developed for control of the surrounding heights. Over 40,000 men were deployed and both sides suffered heavy casualties.

From Sorge, who was using information passed to him by Ozaki, Moscow soon learnt that the Japanese generals in the area had been acting without the consent of the Imperial General Staff, and that Emperor Hirohito himself was against any kind of incident with the Russians whilst Japanese troops were so heavily engaged with China to the south, and especially while the Japanese air force was still passing through its development stage. As always, the problem of the Russian bear on their vulnerable flank figured prominently in Tokyo policy-making, and, although the Japanese army won the fighting by taking the heights, so urgent was Tokyo's desire to reach a peaceful conclusion that the rapid settlement of the matter transformed military victory for the Japanese into a Russian political triumph, for under the terms of the settlement all troops were ordered to return to their pre-incident positions.

Meanwhile, back in Tokyo General Lyushkov was pouring out his heart to Japanese interrogators who passed some of the information on to von Schol, the new German Military Attaché, who obligingly told Sorge. Sorge's remitting of this information to Moscow led directly to the execution of Marshal Blyukher, the Russian commander in the area of the incident.

Then came a new development. When it became apparent that Lyushkov was willing to talk about the internal situation in Russia proper, Berlin requested permission to send a team to Japan to interrogate the general themselves, and the request was granted. At the end of their task the German team produced a report of several hundred pages of which a copy was given to von Schol. He showed it to Sorge who somehow managed to photograph much of it, and sent the films to Moscow in the spring of 1939, rather aptly at blossom time in Japan for Moscow was thus provided with two bites at the same cherry.

The 1938 incident and its aftermath did nothing to diminish the propensity of the young turks in charge of the Japanese armies in Manchukuo to act without reference to Tokyo; in fact it had the reverse effect, for they felt in honour bound to reverse the humiliation brought about by the political settlement.

In May 1939 another incident developed, this time at the border town of Nomonhan. It began with excursions across the border by Japanese cavalry units, presaged by the actions of, and then urged on by, local secret service units. Sorge was again privy to the Japanese Cabinet's desire to avoid a major conflict with the Soviets, and not only that, obtained information on the Japanese order of battle and about troop movements. Stalin was not convinced that the Japanese would not use this new incident as a pretext for a full invasion, and ordered more troops and equipment in. This conflict lasted until September. The Soviets set a trap for the Japanese, and after artillery barrages, tank engagements, and air battles the Japanese were soundly defeated. Sorge had once again proved his worth.

It is rather strange that Sorge carried out his clandestine work while under suspicion from the Japanese. Not only that, he knew he was under suspicion. All foreigners in Japan were to some extent kept under surveillance, but in his case his house-servants were often interrogated and his house was searched whenever he was away. He threw the security authorities off the scent by making contact with his agents only under cover of the noisy parties he threw at home. Towards the end he also came under suspicion from the Gestapo, a suspicion no doubt aroused by his close association with the senior staff at the German embassy. In Berlin the file on Sorge was examined and it provided enough information to indicate at least the possibility that he might be a Soviet agent, and when Colonel Joseph Meisinger of the Gestapo arrived in Tokyo as Police Attaché, he had orders to keep an especial eye on Sorge. It seems that, when the two men met, they got on well. Both enjoyed a tipple, although they were completely different in character. Sorge was considered a pleasant person by most people who knew him, whereas Meisinger has been described as 'one of the most evil creatures among Heydrich's bunch of thugs'. His previous record had been too much for even the Gestapo Chief, Himmler, to bear; he had once ordered Meisinger to be court-martialled and shot, but his situation was saved by the intervention of Reinhard Heydrich, Himmler's protégé.

It may have been a tip-off from Meisinger that resulted in the Japanese taking more interest in Sorge, an interest that finally led to his arrest in October 1941. But earlier that year, in April, he had warned Moscow that 150 German divisions were poised to attack across the Russian border, a warning he followed up by giving 22nd June as the exact date of the invasion. Stalin ignored these warnings, just as he did others received from Winston Churchill that were based on a reading of Ultra decrypts. Later, a few weeks before his arrest, Sorge provided Moscow with the priceless information that the Japanese intended to attack south, information that enabled Stalin to withdraw forces from the Far East to defend Moscow. One of Sorge's messages to Moscow, almost his last one, informed the Russians that Japan would first attack the 'United States, then Malaya, Singapore, and Sumatra', but it was no more specific than that and he provided no dates. He had, however, been able to reassure Stalin that Japan was not going to rush to Germany's aid by attacking Russia.

Most members of Sorge's ring were rounded up with him. Sorge and Ozaki were sentenced to death and were hanged on 7th November 1944 after over three years in prison. Voukelitch and Klausen were jailed, the former dying in prison in 1945, the latter being released that same year. In 1964 Sorge was made a posthumous Hero of the Soviet Union.

Professor John Chapman has written that the Japanese navy was constantly obsessed with the legendary capabilities of the British Secret Intelligence Service, or SIS.[12] An indication of this was given on 8th January 1941, when Captain Nakamura, adjutant to the Navy Minister and the go-between for the Japanese navy and the German embassy, reported that not a single anchorage existed in Japan that was not under surveillance by British agents. On another occasion Nakamura said that, before the port of Hachinohe in northeast Honshu could be used for loading a German blockade-runner, the home of a Canadian missionary there would have to be sealed.

In fact, the Japanese need not have been too concerned about SIS operations in Japan itself. Although the SIS had some agents in the country and useful local contacts in harbour masters' offices and in the customs service, they were none too thick on the ground.

As with all British government institutions between the two world wars, the SIS, funded from the Foreign Office secret vote, was starved of money, and what money was available was not usually spent in the Far East but in areas much closer to home. In fact, during those years some SIS Far East Stations were closed down, notably those at Vladivostok and Yokohama. This relegation of the Far East area to a sort of second division status in British intelligence, can also in part be attributed to the views held and expressed in 1928 by the then Colonel F.S.G. Piggott. He was of the opinion that, in regard to Japan, the collection of Military Intelligence was 'best left to above board methods', that is by Military Attachés and language officers. Piggott also cited the difficulties that agents of European stock would have in operating in a relatively closed society such as Japan's.[13] Had sufficient funds been made available, no doubt more agents from within the local populace could have been recruited and trained.

Towards the end of the decade, when Britain opened its intelligence purse-strings a little, SIS operations in Japan picked up, but there was little time to accomplish much organisationally before the start of the war with Japan's Anti-Comintern Pact partner, Germany, a partnership that was to draw even closer with the signing of the Axis Pact in September 1940. What the SIS did accomplish was built around the small but strategically placed British business community in Japan, some of whose firms had been there for decades. They could have been used far earlier, at least on peripheral intelligence-collecting, despite Piggott's statement. These Britons would not have been allowed within miles of any Japanese naval base, but most of them lived near ports and some had houses with sea views, and if they had been trained in what to observe, could no doubt have come up with valuable intelligence during the barren years.

Members of the German embassy in Tokyo in 1941, and especially Colonel Meisinger of the Gestapo, apparently believed that the head of SIS in Japan was Herbert Vere Redman, and this was passed on to the Japanese. Redman had arrived in Japan in 1927 as a Lecturer in English at Tokyo University. During his six years at the university he was also an associate editor of the *Japan Advertiser*, a job he was to keep until 1938 along with being the Tokyo correspondent for London's *Daily Mail* and *The Sun* of Baltimore. In 1939 he was made press attaché at the British embassy in Tokyo.[14]

German suspicions of Redman's role in British clandestine affairs apparently came to a head over the case of Carl Lenz. Lenz was a German national who, as a press associate in the German embassy, had worked closely with Richard Sorge. Meisinger claimed that, in November 1941, Redman approached Lenz through an intermediary for information about the ramifications of Sorge's arrest. In December, immediately upon the start of the war in the Far East, the Japanese raided Redman's house and arrested both him and his French-born wife. His wife was soon 'released' into internment with other British diplomats, but Redman was kept in jail until he became part of the exchange of diplomatic personnel that took place at Lorenço Marques in the summer of 1942.

Meisinger had made a reasonable stab at guessing the identity of the head of SIS in Japan. Redman certainly worked for the organisation, and he was the representative in Japan of Robert Scott's Far Eastern Division of the British Ministry of Economic Warfare which had its headquarters in Singapore. He was behind several British propaganda coups, and involved in attempts to undermine the influence of Indian nationalists in Japan. Even so, Meisinger and his colleagues had guessed wrongly. The top SIS man in Japan, here revealed for the first time, was Hubert Graves, His Britannic Majesty's Consul-General at the port of Kobe.[15]

Graves (later Sir Hubert) was a Far East expert, having spent all his years in the Consular Service in that area. So valuable was his experience, after taking part in the official exchange of diplomats in mid-1942, he was sent to Australia as the British Foreign Office Adviser to the Political Warfare Department there. He made it known to his colleagues in the department that he had been 'Britain's main spymaster in Japan'.[16]

Graves had done his best to build up a SIS network under the very difficult conditions that prevailed in Japan. He concentrated most of his efforts in the country's major ports where the majority of foreigners likely to be of assistance to him lived. He built up a network of people in these ports whose main tasks were, after the war with Germany began in September 1939, to keep watch on the arrivals and sailings of German ships, obtain information from their crews, and wherever possible get crew members to defect. The work can perhaps be best described as a port-watch system. It proved a great worry to the Germans, for not only were some of their blockade-runners using Japanese ports, as were also supply vessels servicing their armed merchant cruisers, but Japan was also used as a staging post to get merchant seamen and other Germans vital to their war effort back home via the Siberian railway system.

There are many references to these concerns in the diaries of the German Naval Attaché in Tokyo. An entry for 3rd October 1939 states:

> It was reported that the British Vice-Consul at Nagasaki could spot the harbour area from his windows and would certainly be kept informed of the movements of the two [German] vessels because their shipping agent was the British-owned firm of Holme, Ringer & Co.[17]

Holme, Ringer & Company is mentioned elsewhere in the diaries, for it was involved in the absconding of a Lithuanian crew member called Martin Markowski from the German freighter *Anneliese Essberger* at Nagasaki in November 1939. The Lithuanian, according to the diary entry, was assisted by the British consul and by the local agent of the company, who supplied him with papers and funds.

That 'local agent's' name was Vanya Ringer. His family firm, known to the Japanese as the Uriu Shokai Steamship Agency, had been founded by Vanya's grandfather at Nagasaki around 1860, another branch being opened in 1890 at Shimonoseki on the southwestern tip of Honshu Island. Both Vanya, who in 1940 was twenty-five years old, and his brother Michael, who was two years older and ran the Shimonoseki branch, were born in Japan and were fluent Japanese speakers. The Ringer brothers were therefore 'naturals' for recruitment into SIS's port-watch.[18]

So concerned were the Germans about British secret activities in Japanese ports that they used an English-speaking agent called Carl Jochheim to haunt various waterfronts to see what he could discover about them, with the additional task of picking up any other intelligence he could. In January 1940 he reported that the British and French consul-generals in Kobe had set up an organisation of

British, French and Japanese volunteers to keep German vessels under surveillance – there were some thirty of these ships bottled up in various Japanese ports at the outbreak of the European war. The volunteers included officers of British merchantmen in port who were sometimes persuaded to break the seals on their radio transmitters, seals placed there by the Japanese authorities, in order to send information about departing vessels. The French part of the Kobe organisation, headed by Paul Duboll, had rented a house overlooking the harbour, whilst the SIS had a Japanese in its pay who spied on the provisioning of German ships. Jochheim followed up that report with a similar one on British activities in Yokohama. The Germans preferred their ships to use Kobe rather than Yokohama for the latter place, being close to Tokyo, was home to a larger British community.

In February 1940 the Germans were concerned that the travel arrangements of Admiral Wenneker, their new Naval Attaché to Tokyo, might be discovered by the British Secret Service. Wenneker, who travelled via the Trans-Siberian railway, then to Pusan in Korea, and by ferry from there to Shimonoseki, in fact arrived safely.

The port-watch's reporting system did not directly lead to the sinking by the Royal Navy of any of the German blockade-runners which sailed from Japanese ports, although several were sunk in the Atlantic before they reached a 'friendly' port. Not only were the British unable to spare at any one time more than a ship or two to patrol off the Japanese coast, to have placed more in position would have annoyed the Japanese. In fact the patrol was usually maintained by one cruiser only, from time to time backed by an Australian Armed Merchant Cruiser.[19] In the early days, British patrol ships were occasionally joined by a French ship from Indo-China. These ships were periodically replenished at sea with stores by ships of the Blue Funnel and Glen Lines, which must have caused the Japanese some annoyance because the supply ships carried out this task on their way to visit Japanese ports.

What is certain is that port-watch reports, together with others from outside sources, formed the basis of the many complaints made to the Japanese naval authorities during 1940–41 by the British Naval Attaché in Tokyo, Captain D.N.C. Tufnell, about the types of German merchant ship being permitted to enter and leave Japanese ports. Tufnell argued that some were auxiliary naval ships in disguise and that for the Japanese to permit them to stay more than twenty-four hours and then leave, was a transgression against international maritime law. He also complained about the number of German seamen and technical experts being conveyed by Japanese ships from North and South America to Japan and then being allowed to depart for Germany via Siberia. There was indeed a great deal of connivance between the Japanese and Germans on naval matters, the most important being the granting of secret bases – called 'sheltering places' and given code-letters by the Germans – in the Japanese Aleutian Islands in the north and their Mandated Islands in the south, at which German commerce raiders and their supply ships could hide. They also allowed German supply ships to service these sheltering places from Japanese ports. Some German vessels, with or without permission, sailed under the Japanese flag and used Japanese names.

The matter of the transportation of German seamen aboard Japanese ships came to a head in an incident involving the cruiser, HMS *Liverpool*, which took place in January 1940. Before describing that incident it is worth looking at some details of that vessel's preceding voyage, for not only does it show an international exchange of intelligence information, but it also reveals that not all the conniving was taking place on the Axis side.

HMS *Liverpool* had been on a protracted 8,000-mile patrol that had taken her as far north as Vladivostok. In late December 1939, low on bunkers, she was making back for Hong Kong when she received instructions to intercept the Russian freighter *Selenga* which had loaded a cargo of wolfram from a German ship sheltering from the Royal Navy in the port of Manila. The *Selenga*, being a neutral ship, was being used to transport the extremely valuable cargo – wolfram is the ore of tungsten, the steel hardener – to Vladivostok where it would go by rail to Germany, a cargo route much used by Germany until she attacked Russia in June 1941. Working on signals received from the Americans in Manila via Hong Kong, giving the Russian ship's time of departure, course and speed, *Liverpool* sailed to intercept in the knowledge that her patrol range was now limited by her fuel situation. In bad visibility the Russian ship managed to slip by, and it was decided to try a ruse. According to Professor G.R. Steele,

> *Liverpool* had advanced D/F equipment . . . An emergency transmitter was used to fake low grade merchant ship signals, and to give the call sign of a vessel known to be well clear of the area. *Selenga* was called

> up ostensibly to pass a message and, when she replied, it was claimed that her signals were unclear. She was enticed to radio three times, in so doing, gave a bearing upon which *Liverpool* could sail . . . she was soon overtaken, boarded and turned for Hong Kong.[20]

The Russians exerted considerable diplomatic pressure and *Selenga* was eventually allowed to refuel and sail with her cargo intact. But the British had warned the French in Indo-China – France still at that time being an ally – and they, 'having fewer diplomatic scruples', sent a warship from Saigon. *Selenga* was taken to that port where her cargo was unloaded before she was sent empty towards Vladivostok.

Whilst *Liverpool* was involved in this adventure in the South China Sea, over on the other side of the world, and due to intelligence co-operation between the United States, which was still neutral, Canada and Britain, the fast German liner *Columbus* was meeting her fate. She had sailed from Vera Cruz with the intention of racing across the North Atlantic for Oslo in an attempt to evade the British blockade, but was intercepted by the USS *Tuscaloosa* who began tracking her, relaying her position to Washington every two hours. This information was passed to Ottawa, and the Canadian destroyer HMCS *Hyperion* was ordered to the area. To avoid capture *Columbus* made for US territorial waters and her crew scuttled her on 19th December 1939 when some 420 miles southeast of New York. The crew were picked up by *Tuscaloosa* and taken to Ellis Island. At first they were detained under international law, with Britain arguing that *Columbus* had been used for naval auxiliary purposes and that therefore the crew were belligerents. This was never properly established and the United States released the men as shipwrecked mariners at Christmas time. Then, on 6th January Japan stepped in to 'assist' in their repatriation.

Britain, in a rare foray into confrontation with the Japanese, warned that it would stop any ship carrying *Columbus* crew members as passengers, take them off and intern them as belligerents. The Japanese advised the German embassy in Tokyo that, while they considered the implications of the British threat, it would be better not 'to make use of the vessels already planned', but rather 'divide up those being transported into very small groups on a large number of ships'.[21] The all-round connivance was far from over yet.

The British, from information supplied to them by the Americans either through SIS agents in the United States or direct to London, learnt that a 21-strong party from the *Columbus*, together with some other Germans who had been employed on tankers belonging to the Standard Oil Company, had boarded the Japanese liner *Asama Maru* at San Francisco. The British were even supplied with a list of the names of all the Germans, including those of a captain and several officers. The British Admiralty decided to follow through with the threat, apparently with the consent of the Far Eastern Department of the Foreign Office, though not with that of Sir Alexander Cadogan, the Under-Secretary of State.

The *Liverpool*, now back on station off Japan, was ordered to intercept the *Asama Maru*, and used her D/F equipment to keep track of the Japanese vessel as she crossed the North Pacific. It added some insult to the huge indignation soon to be felt by the Japanese, that the 17,000-ton *Asama Maru* was the pride of their merchant fleet. But further insult was to follow, for the interception took place within sight of Japan's sacred mountain and so was considered a personal affront to the Emperor of Japan.

Whilst lying in wait HMS *Liverpool* was approached by a Japanese freighter, and in an apparently successful attempt at disguise, ran up the Japanese naval ensign at the yard arm, a disguise complemented by quick thinking on the part of Leading Stoker Smith, in charge of the Walrus aircraft catapult crew who hastily covered up the red, white, and blue bullseye markings on the aircraft. Professor Steele writes:

> On 21st January, visual contact was made just 35 miles off the coast of Japan and within sight of Mount Fujiyama. *Asama Maru* was directed by flag signals to stop, which she failed to do until a shot was fired across her bows. A launch was sent over with an armed party of thirteen officers and men, and her Captain was given a list of the individuals required. Fifty-one Germans were on board but only twenty-one, whose names were on the British official list, were removed with their luggage. Two others who were wanted had concealed themselves. The Germans were placed under Marine guard for their passage to Hong Kong, during which time a microphone was placed in a vent to eavesdrop on their conversation.
>
> *Liverpool* arrived at Hong Kong on 28th and, having exceeded her previous speed record in order to evade Japanese destroyers sent to intercept her, handed over the prisoners to the military authorities.

The incident caused a major diplomatic row. On the day after it happened and a week before *Liverpool*'s arrival at Hong Kong, the

Japanese handed a note of protest to Sir Robert Craigie, the British ambassador in Tokyo. What is more, a formation of Japanese aircraft based in China violated Hong Kong airspace by flying over the colony in a show of strength. Then, in a more direct reprisal, the Japanese stopped and searched the British SS *Wing Sang* off Foochow.

Sir Alexander Cadogan, later to become more opposed to appeasement of the Japanese, wrote in his diary for 23rd January 1940: 'Talked to H[alifax, Foreign Secretary] about trouble over removing Germans from Jap ships – which looks ugly. (Far Eastern Dept. very unlucky: they never refer things to me and always get into trouble.)'

That was followed two days later by the entry: 'H. saw Shigemitsu [Japanese ambassador to Britain] about 'Asama Maru' and tried to patch up an agreement. It is really tiresome that at critical moments we always get let down in the Far East. But tempers have cooled a bit.'[22]

The British apparently decided that they had made their point, for when the *Tatsutu Maru* was intercepted off Honolulu by a British destroyer, no attempt was made to take off the five Germans on board. Finally an agreement was hammered out, according to Cadogan 'with undue difficulty'. Nine of the Germans were handed over to the Japanese, with the Japanese promising to refuse passage on their ships to Germans on their way home to join the armed services. As the later entries in the diary of the German Naval Attaché show, that was an undertaking the Japanese did not keep.

One intelligence coup by the Royal Navy which resulted in important information being handed to FECB in Singapore, came from an extraordinary voyage made by HM Submarine *Regulus* in October 1940. The exact details are not known as the submarine's log books are missing from the official records; she was lost in a minefield in the Taranto Straits in the Mediterranean two months later.

In October the submarine had approached Shibushi Bay on the south side of Kyushu Island, a bay often used by the Japanese as a base for their fleet. As the bay is shallow *Regulus* must have sent in a small boat that somehow managed to make itself look like a Japanese fishing craft. However it was done, photographs were taken of the Japanese flagship *Nagato* and of other naval craft, and details were noted about the speed and training ability of the flagship's main battery. That was not the end of the operation, for the submarine then entered Japan's Inland Sea, a much more dangerous undertaking, and slipping into

Osaka Bay, spent several days submerged there while the captain made more notes and took more photographs.

All this was discovered by Commander Kukui of the Imperial Japanese Navy when, after the fall of Singapore in February 1942, he examined the contents of the Royal Navy's Operations Room there. This find shows a lamentable lack of security on the part of the Royal Navy in not having destroyed these important documents, and it was a lapse that cannot be blamed on FECB for they had moved to Colombo a month before Singapore fell.

Three months earlier than that epic voyage of *Regulus* an event occurred in Japan that soured Anglo-Japanese relations yet again, which this time resulted in retaliation by the British in the form of the action taken in Singapore against the Japanese spy Shinozaki (see above, page 188).

On 27th July 1940, in concerted raids in Tokyo, Yokohama, Shimonoseki, Nagasaki, and Kobe, the Japanese arrested fifteen Britons who, they alleged, were spies. One of them, Melville James Cox, was the Reuters correspondent in Tokyo. Cox, fifty-six years of age, had taken over the Reuters post from Captain Malcolm Kennedy in 1934. Kennedy had also been working undercover for SIS in Japan. As British Intelligence Services hardly ever make known the names of their agents, it cannot be said for certain that Cox also worked for the SIS, but it seems likely that he did, especially in view of what was to happen to him and the cover-up that followed it.

The Japanese had issued an immediate ban on press releases after the arrests, but this was suddenly lifted by the Minister of Justice on the 30th July;[23] almost certainly this was due to the fact that at 3.45 on the previous afternoon, during interrogation at Kempetai headquarters in Tokyo, Cox had met a violent death. The police alleged that Cox committed suicide by jumping from a window, an explanation that was finally officially accepted by the British, apparently in an attempt to damp down any further inquiry. The official Japanese report stated that Cox had 'sprung' on to the window sill and that a warder grabbed his foot but could not hold on. A British Foreign Office official, Patrick Dean, was later to record that the window concerned was only a yard square and that the sill was a yard from the floor, and that Cox's body, after a fall of some thirty-five feet, was found twenty feet from the wall of the building. 'On these facts', commented Dean, 'it appears to me most peculiar that his body should have been picked up so far from the wall.' On the facts given, and assuming that Cox was not killed somewhere else and his body just placed there, the only way Cox's body could have landed so far from the wall is if he was propelled through the window.

Mrs Cox, who identified her husband's remains, claimed that he had been tortured. The Foreign Office file on this matter indicated a desire to pay Mrs Cox compensation, amounting to £5,000, a princely sum in those days, and one is left with the thought that it might have been paid to keep her quiet.[24] One thing is certain; Cox's death has never been satisfactorily explained. However, some new information has come to light that tends to support the theory that Cox was thrown from the window.

Of the fifteen arrested Britons, and excluding Cox, ten were indicted and eventually tried and found guilty. One, Vincent O. Peters, who was arrested in Kobe, was sentenced to eight years' imprisonment for being a member of a spy ring which had been under police surveillance following suspicions aroused by activities centred on the Seamen's Mission, an unnamed Blue Funnel Line ship being used to relay messages from Kobe to Hong Kong. Peters, who had been in Japan since October 1938, was, said the Japanese, involved in naval and economic espionage, including obtaining information on the nature and quantities of shipments from Japan to Germany.

Also among those arrested, indicted and found guilty were Vanya and Michael Ringer. In an unpublished memoir Vanya states that the family house at Shimonoseki overlooked the strait of the same name, and that through that narrow strait from 1937 onward sailed the troopships carrying the Japanese army to China. 'It was our misfortune to be close eye-witnesses . . . we were for this reason regarded as spies by the local gendarmes.' The family, at both Nagasaki and Shimonoseki, regularly entertained the masters of Norwegian, Dutch and British merchant ships, and this resulted in more suspicion, and their houseservants and local office staff were regularly interrogated by the police.

Vanya was arrested on 27th July 1940 at Nagasaki and his interrogation began almost immediately. Amongst other matters he was asked about the use of the company launch around the harbour area. The interrogation went on day after day, and between sessions he was kept in an extremely unpleasant cell with other local prisoners. On 29th July he was told that Cox had committed suicide by jumping from a window. He wrote in his memoir: 'However, ten minutes later one of the men questioning me told me that if I did not tell the truth I should get the same treatment as Mr Cox, and he could not say what might happen to my wife and child.'

Vanya goes on: 'It was obvious to me that Mr Cox was pushed out of the window, as from my first moment in the gendarmerie to the time I left, I was never left with fewer than two gendarmes in the room.'

At a later date Vanya learnt, perhaps from Mrs Cox who left Japan on the same ship as he, that the post-mortem examination on Cox had revealed twenty injection marks in his arm, something not mentioned in the documents in the Foreign Office file.

On one occasion during over a month of questioning Ringer was told he might be shot as a spy. This was after the Japanese had opened up some intercepted consular mail and discovered that he had been reporting movements of military transports to the British consul. 'This', he said, 'was the most serious charge they had against me.' On other occasions he was made to watch several members of his local staff being beaten up. In the third week of August the fifty-year-old Englishman, William De Trafford, a lecturer at the Higher Commercial College, Nagasaki, also a victim of the original day of arrests, was thrown in with him.

Later Vanya was kept in solitary confinement in a six-foot by seven-foot cell which was full of mosquitoes and had a temperature of 110° Fahrenheit. He was tried on 12th September and a week later was fined and sentenced to eighteen months' hard labour, suspended for five years. The family firm was forcibly closed down. On 28th September Vanya, with his wife and two daughters, together with his brother who had received a similar suspended sentence, sailed from Moji aboard SS *Nankin*. He left, he said, holding a hatred for the Japanese as a nation.

After they arrived in India, both Vanya and Michael were commissioned into the Indian army, Vanya into the 5/14th Punjab Regiment, Michael into the Dogras. Both went to Malaya where Michael became an intelligence officer, and was ordered out of Singapore two days before it capitulated on 15th February 1942, it being considered that, with the suspended sentence hanging over his head he was in particular danger from the Japanese. Vanya, during fighting with his regiment in the Malayan jungle in January, was posted missing, believed killed.

One Briton thought to be in danger of being arrested in July 1940 was Lewis Bush, a lecturer in the Japanese Higher School in

Tokyo. He and his Japanese wife, Tsujimura Kane, took refuge in the British embassy. Kane, under the pseudonym 'Kaneko', had written anti-German propaganda articles published in the *Japan Times* and *Japan Advertiser* since September 1939. Bush left Japan for Hong Kong in September, and Kane followed him in January 1941. Bush joined the RNVR there, whilst Kane assisted the SO (I) Major Giles, and Major Boxer of FECB, in translation work. Husband and wife were both to suffer solitary confinement when captured by the Japanese when Hong Kong fell.[25]

That spate of arrests of British subjects in Japan in July 1940 which had resulted in the death of Melville Cox and the imprisonment of others, was not to be the only one.

The British believed that the Gestapo in Tokyo was behind the arrests in September 1941 of Day Mason, secretary of the Tokyo Club, and a man called Graham Martyr. They were arrested along with Doctor Frantisek Havlicek the former Czech Minister to Japan, who, not being able to return home when his legation was closed down in 1939 after his country had come under the control of the Germans, had stayed on. Havlicek was probably on the Gestapo's 'most-wanted' list.

Those arrests led to an increase in the already active anti-German British propaganda efforts in Japan. In a secret message of 31st October 1941 to the Ministry of Information in London, Sir Robert Craigie, the British ambassador, noted that the newspaper articles planted abroad about clandestine German activities in Japan had borne fruit. 'I now feel that this witch-hunt can be left to the Japanese themselves', he said.[26]

There is little doubt that the Japanese, with their paranoia over secrecy, were as concerned about German clandestine activities as they were about those of the Allies. In the early 1930s a German called Franz Huber had become an adviser to the Japanese Home Office on police matters, whilst on the side he organised a branch of the Nazi Party; by 1937 every German resident in Japan had been persuaded to become a member of it. That Huber's extra-curricular activities did not meet with Japanese approval is evidenced by a FECB Intelligence Summary dated 22nd November 1940, which pointed out that Huber was now having difficulty in gaining access to secret documents in the Home Office, 'owing to reluctance on the part of the Japanese'.[27] On top of everything else, the Japanese knew that Richard Sorge, the recently arrested Russian spy, had been *persona grata* at the German embassy for years.

Despite Craigie saying that the witch-hunt could be left to the Japanese themselves, he apparently agreed with proposals made by Vere Redman that more such propaganda projects should be launched outside Japan. In that same message of 31st October 1941 Craigie outlined 'ingenious projects . . . suggested by Mr Redman', which involved the planting of articles in overseas newspapers designed to undermine Japanese confidence in their German ally.

On the first day of the Pacific War most, but not all, British residents in Japan were either interned or arrested. Amongst those arrested was Vere Redman, who on German advice the Japanese mistakenly assumed to be Britain's top SIS man in the country. Another man arrested was Frank Hawley, Director of the British Library of Information and Culture in Tokyo, which had been opened under the auspices of the British Council. It is not clear how involved Hawley was in the British propaganda effort, but the Japanese believed he was up to his ears in it. Like Redman, Hawley was kept under arrest until he became part of the 'exchange' of diplomatic personnel in late summer 1942.

Some Britons were not interned at all, but stayed in their homes under a loose form of house-arrest. One such was John Morris who, as Professor of English at Keio University, had doubled as an adviser to the Japanese Department of Foreign Affairs. He was kept on pay until he was exchanged but in the interim had not been required to carry out any duties.[28]

According to the Tokyo English-language newspaper *Japan Times*, on 17th December 1941, George Thomas May, Cypher Officer at the British Embassy and his family were excluded from the list of designated foreigners whose assets in Japan had been seized. The article referred to May as 'a friendly foreigner'. It is not known what Mr May had done to deserve such special treatment. What is known from the post-war interrogation of an operative of the Japanese Intelligence branch dealing with cables, a man called Takayamagi Yotaro, is that cables between the Foreign Office in London and the British ambassador in Tokyo were being intercepted and in part read.

Two other Britons not arrested were Dr Thomas Baty and his sister. Baty, a world authority on international law, had arrived in

Japan during World War One as an adviser to the Japanese Foreign Office. He was a strange character; shy and effeminate, he loved dressing up in Japanese women's kimonos, and was unabashed when seen in that garb by visitors. In his entry in *Who's Who* he described himself as an 'extreme feminist'. He was a pacifist, and scared stiff of the number thirteen. Despite being a vegetarian he, and his sister who lived with him, gave some of the best dinner parties in Tokyo. According to General Piggott, the foreign community in Tokyo owed much to Baty for forming, in 1923, the *Kohakubaikai*, or Red and White Plum Blossom Society, which arranged meetings with influential Japanese, and visits to places of interest. Though he claimed to be a Scot and formed the Scottish Circle in Tokyo, he came from Cumberland. Despite his pacifism his friends included members of the notorious Black Dragon Society.

Baty stayed free in Japan throughout the war. After the war he was accused of being a traitor. However, he was not arrested by the British although he was deprived of 'British protection', whatever that might mean. He died in Japan in 1954 at the age of eighty-four.

Fourteen

SS *Automedon*

↟

As early as 1930, when they opened a listening station on their main home island, Honshu, the Japanese had begun to develop their own Sigint capability. More stations were opened after the Shanghai Incident of 1932, when it became clear that it was necessary to monitor the movements of foreign ships-of-war. Their cryptographic capability grew in tandem, and by the middle of the 1930s they were able to read some foreign diplomatic codes, but not operational military or naval ones. By the end of the decade, however, they were successfully monitoring and reading some low-grade Chinese army codes. That, and their earlier success in reading Russian codes, which was aided by the defection to them of General Lyushkov in 1938, was almost the sum total of their Sigint successes, a poor performance when compared with their ground intelligence operations. Alan Stripp says: 'they went about the whole business of code-breaking in a half-hearted way, assuming from the start that their only hope lay in attacking low-grade signals, and even in this their approach was scrappy and unmethodical'.[1] He partly put this down to the fact that the aggressor's need for first-class intelligence is not so desperate as the defender's, and Japan had already been a notably successful aggressor.

Professor Chapman shows that collaboration in both Sigint and non-Sigint intelligence matters between the Axis partners began in 1932 and expanded in stages from then on. The Italian navy played a pivotal role in the latter stages of this collaboration. This joint effort is no better illustrated than by an incident which occurred in November 1940 that brought about one of the greatest, possibly *the* greatest, non-Sigint intelligence coups of World War Two, and one that fell to the Axis partners.

The British Blue Funnel cargo liner *Automedon* – on a voyage from Liverpool via Durban to Penang, Singapore, Hong Kong and Shanghai – was at daybreak on 11th November 1940 about three hundred miles off the coast of Sumatra and a day-and-a-half's sailing from Penang, when she fell in with the German Armed Merchant Cruiser *Atlantis*, commanded by Captain Bernhard Rogge. The *Automedon*'s track across the Indian Ocean had been monitored by the Italian Sigint unit based in East Africa, which passed the information on to Rogge.

The details of the action that followed came from a report made by Samuel Elsby Harper, *Automedon*'s 4th Engineer, and was based on what he saw for himself or obtained from other officers immediately afterwards.[2]

> The Raider had the appearance of a Dutch merchant vessel, for which I understand she was mistaken . . . She was first sighted about 7 a.m. . . . going slow in the same direction as ourselves and we were overtaking her on her starboard side.
>
> As we approached she opened up to full speed and closed us on our port bow. The first shot fired by her was at 8.20 a.m. when she was about 350 yards distant. She put this shot across our bows.

Automedon's Wireless Operator was able to send a part signal 'RRR Automedon 0416N' (RRR being the signal for raider alert) which was picked up by the radio station in Colombo and by another Blue Funnel ship in the area, *Helenus*, before the transmission was jammed.* Shells exploded on the bridge, killing Captain W.B. Ewan

* There is the best possible evidence that *Helenus* not only picked up the message but relayed it smartly to the Blue Funnel Head Office in Liverpool. Frank Walker, at that time a deck-boy aboard *Automedon*, discovered after the war that his 'allotment' to his mother was cut off fifteen days after the loss of the ship. 'Allotments' were that part of a merchant seaman's wages paid regularly to a nominated next-of-kin whilst the seaman was on pay, or 'on articles' as it was called. Wages, and allotments, came to an end at the closing of the 'articles' when the voyage ended at a home port or was lost at sea. To put it another way, a British merchant seaman could have his ship blown from under him and then spend days or even weeks in a lifeboat, knowing he was off pay from the time of the sinking and that no allotment was going to his family. One can imagine the added element of distress this cancelling of the allotment caused Mrs Walker, who did not learn for many months that her sixteen-year-old son had in fact survived and was a prisoner-of-war.

and six others, and wounding twelve including First Mate P.E. Evans. Everything happened so quickly, and so devastatingly accurate was the raider's fire, that there had been no time for Captain Ewan or anyone else to throw overboard the weighted contents of the Master's safe, let alone the secret contents of the ship's strong-room and, most secret of all, a 'long narrow envelope enclosed in a green bag, a bag equipped with brass eyelets to let the water in to facilitate its sinking'. So reported Commander Mohr, Rogge's second-in-command who led the boarding party of armed Germans and who found the bag in the wrecked chartroom where it had been handy for jettisoning.[3]

The surviving crew members, including the wounded, and the ship's passengers, were transferred to *Atlantis* except for the only deck officer still able to walk, the slightly wounded Second Mate Donald Stewart. He had been knocked out by the explosions on the bridge and came to and found himself surrounded by dead companions. He knew nothing of the green bag in the chartroom, the existence of which was probably only known to the captain and first mate, but he did know about the weighted bags in the strong-room. So he made for the captain's cabin where the key to the strong-room was kept. The cabin was a wreck, and slumped across the threshold was the badly wounded First Mate Evans, who had obviously had the same idea. Stewart was still searching in the shambles for the key when the Germans collared him.

There were two second mates on board, the other one, designated Extra Second Mate, being T.G. Wilson, who was amongst those killed. The carrying of an extra officer on board a merchantship was usually for a specific purpose, for example, to fill a vacancy on another ship at a future port of call or, in the case of engineer officers, when the ship was carrying frozen meat, to look after the freezer machinery. But given the exigencies of war, and the severe shortage of qualified officers, and ratings, in the Merchant Navy after over a year of losses to U-boats, raiders, and minefields, there must have been a special reason to warrant the *Automedon*'s carrying the extra officer. The intriguing possibility is that he was there because of the secret consignment of papers; and it may have been his task in an emergency to dispose of the bags in the strong-room, for the consignment was above average in size.

Mohr led a search of the ship taking Stewart with him as guide. Frozen meat, whisky, and cigarettes in the cargo were transported across to the raider. On reaching the strong-room Stewart passed it off as the Bosun's Store, and to his relief the Germans accepted that. Captain S.W. Roskill, in his book *A Merchant Fleet at War*, had this to say about what happened next:

> There now took place a most unfortunate mischance. The three first-class passengers (one woman and two men) . . . were among those first transferred to the raider . . . and the woman requested that her two trunks which were in the baggage room should be sent across.
>
> The raider captain granted her request and [Mohr] demanded Stewart should show him where the trunks were stowed. The Second Mate knew only too well that the baggage room was identical to the strong-room. He tried to bluff the enemy but his bluff failed.[4]

In point of fact there were six first-class passengers on board, not three. Mr and Mrs Ferguson were newly married and were proceeding to Singapore where Mr Ferguson, a marine engineer, was to join a ship belonging to the Blue Funnel subsidiary, Straits Steamship Company. The others were a Mr McBride, another man, and two ladies, one of them a nursing sister described as 'a good-looking bird'. It is not known which of these ladies inadvertently gave the game away by asking for her trunks.[5]

The upshot was that the Germans blew the strong-room door and transferred fifteen mailbags and the passengers' luggage to the raider. *Automedon* was then scuttled, after which *Atlantis* raced from the scene and made for a rendezvous with two Norwegian tankers it had previously captured, *Teddy* on 8th November and *Ole Jacob* on the 10th.[6] (It says something about the standard of conduct of Captain Rogge and his crew that after four years of internment Mrs Ferguson was reunited with her luggage, including some wedding presents, at war's end. The nursing sister died of dysentery as an internee.)

In his report made in Liverpool on 27th June 1941, Sam Harper wrote:

> The raider had captured two ships previous to us, the *Teddy* and the *Ole Jacob*, both Norwegian tankers sailing under the British flag. Part of the crews of both vessels were on board . . . but were soon transferred to *Ole Jacob* and sent to a neutral port with six German guards. The *Teddy* was sunk.

Sam Harper and the crews of eight British ships previously sunk by *Atlantis* were transferred to another captured Norwegian ship and taken to Bordeaux. During a train journey across France towards Germany, he and three other British engineer officers jumped off the train. After many adventures Harper and one companion got back to England via Barcelona and Gibraltar. During their short internment in Spain in April 1941, Harper managed to send a telegram to the British Naval Attaché in Madrid, Captain A.H. Hillgarth, who sent money and promised to get them released. They were eventually sent to Gibraltar, arriving there on 31st May.[7]

On 4th December *Ole Jacob* arrived at the 'neutral port' of Kobe with her cargo of 9,000 tons of aviation spirit, and sixty-four Norwegian sailors under a German prize crew led by Lieutenant-Commander Kamenz, and the secret documents from the *Automedon*. Even without the envelope in the green bag, it was a sensational haul, and Captain Rogge had every reason to be excited when he had gone through it with Commander Mohr prior to placing it aboard the tanker. They had captured copies of Admiralty decyphering tables nos. 7, 8, and 9, and new fleet cyphers, Merchant Navy codes, details of minefields and Admiralty sailing instructions, Admiralty Intelligence Summaries dating from September, and in bags marked 'Safe Hands, British Master Only', coded communications to British SIS stations in the Far East. But Rogge considered the most important document was the one in the green bag. It was addressed to Britain's Commander-in-Chief, Far East, Air Chief Marshal Sir Robert Brooke-Popham, and was a copy of the minutes of the British War Cabinet's deliberations of 15th August 1940. It summarised Britain's strategic policy in the Far East and basically said that Britain did not have the wherewithal to meet any major Japanese transgression in the area, and that open clashes must therefore be avoided, and that Britain would put up with a Japanese attack on Thailand or French Indo-China without going to war. There was much else besides on the defence of Malaya and the Netherlands East Indies. Hong Kong and Borneo were virtually written off as being indefensible.[8]

Rogge had ordered Kamenz on the *Ole Jacob* to make for Kobe, but during the voyage Berlin radioed the ship over Norddeutsch Radio and tried to divert her to the sheltering place code-lettered 'Y', which was the island of Lamotrek in the Japanese Caroline Islands; Berlin informed the German Naval Attaché in Tokyo of this in a cypher cable sent on 29th November, in which they also noted that the ship was carrying top-secret captured material. This proves that Rogge on *Atlantis* must have radioed Berlin about his intentions and also that he had indicated the importance of his haul. However *Ole Jacob* had not answered the diversion message and so Berlin was not sure whether it had been received. In fact Kamenz had received it, but had taken it upon himself to ignore the diversion for two reasons. Firstly, to have taken the Norwegians to sheltering place 'Y' would have compromised its location; and, secondly, with only six of his own men aboard, he needed the Norwegians to work the ship, and they had been promised release in Japan if they helped. He feared sabotage or mutiny if he acted otherwise.

Now began much German diplomatic activity in Tokyo. Admiral Wenneker, the Naval Attaché, approached the Japanese naval authorities over the impending arrival of the Norwegian ship, and found them unco-operative; they did not want the ship calling at any Japanese port as it could lead to international complications. Furthermore, the Germans wanted to spirit the Norwegians on to German vessels in port before they could be interviewed by the British SIS.

In the middle of all this activity in Tokyo, *Ole Jacob*, having made an excellent passage, arrived at Kobe two days earlier than expected and flying the German naval ensign. As a naval ship, under international law, she was obliged to leave again within twenty-four hours or be interned. Wenneker rushed his assistant Wigand to Kobe with orders to retrieve the secret documents and order the ship to proceed to 'Y' while meanwhile going himself to the Navy Ministry, where he was told that the ship must sail within twenty-four hours, that the Norwegians could leave the ship but must be allowed their freedom, and that if, to facilitate the vessel's sailing, German seamen from other ships in port were put on board – a move against international law – the Japanese would turn a blind eye. Wenneker noted in his diary for 5th December 1940 that the funeral of Prince Saionji took place on that day, and that both he and the British Naval Attaché were to be in attendance. Wenneker hoped this would show that he had no great interest in the prize.

Despite the Navy Ministry's insistence that the Norwegians be allowed their freedom, they were secretly taken off *Ole Jacob* before she sailed for 'Y' with a new German crew aboard. They were initially taken aboard a German ship in the harbour by Japanese secret police. Meanwhile the documents, now filling a trunk, were brought by two members of the German consulate at Kobe to Tokyo, where they were scrutinised by Wenneker who realised at once the significance to the

Japanese of the British War Cabinet report. He cabled a summary of it to Berlin and asked permission to give the Japanese a copy. Meanwhile, the trunk was sent with special couriers to Berlin by way of Russia.*

Permission was received on 10th December, but Wenneker was ordered to give Berlin as the source of the information, the Germans preferring the Japanese to think that the information had come as a result of the excellence of their intelligence system rather than as a result of a lucky chain of events involving one of their raiders. The Japanese Naval Attaché in Berlin, Captain Yokoi, was also given a copy which he relayed to Tokyo by radio. This message was probably contemporaneously intercepted by the Allies, but the copy of it found by James Rusbridger in the National Archives in Washington, DC, clearly shows that the American copy was not decyphered until 19th August 1945.[9] That does not prove of course, that the British had not decyphered it concurrently, but it seems unlikely that they had. Had the British decyphered it, it is unlikely that they would have passed such a decrypt to the Americans anyway. Although there was some exchange of intelligence information between Britain and the US, the United States, like Japan, were not yet in the war, and anyway, under no circumstances would evidence be passed on that could be construed as a British security cock-up.

Wenneker noted that when he handed the material to the Japanese on the following day, 'the contents were read with extraordinary interest'.

Despite Wenneker's efforts to keep the Norwegians under German control and away from contact with British Intelligence, the Japanese, who had been put under pressure by the British Naval Attaché about the presence of the *Ole Jacob* in Japanese waters and certain other matters of a similar nature, insisted on keeping to the letter of international law. On 10th December a party of forty of them was sent via Nagasaki to Shanghai at their own request. The remaining twenty-four were to travel home via Siberia. Berlin's insistence that the true source of the documents be kept from the Japanese, thus backfired on them. Had the Japanese known the truth, they would

* According to Enid Saunders Candlin, the journey from Shanghai to London – by sea to Darsen, than by the Trans-Siberian railway to Moscow, and on by rail and ferry from there – took sixteen days in 1938. This indicates that a journey from Tokyo to Berlin, including the sea passage from, say, Shimonoseki to Dairen, would have taken about ten days.

probably have been as keen as Wenneker to keep the Norwegians away from all outside contacts.

In an article published in *World War II Investigator* in 1988, James Rusbridger hinted that the secret papers might have been planted aboard a 'vulnerable' merchantman, the *Automedon*, as part of a clever ruse by Winston Churchill to encourage Japan to attack in the hope that this would bring America into the war. This does not stand up to examination. In the first instance there was nothing unique about placing secret documents in the care of the master of a British merchantship. It was a fairly common practice, though later in the war better ways were introduced for the destruction of such documents in case of an attack.* Furthermore, although *Automedon* was eighteen years old, for a merchantman she had a fair turn of speed at 14.5 knots, some four knots faster than the average merchant ship speed of those days. Again, how could anyone be certain that any particular British ship, out of all the other Allied ships plying the Indian Ocean, was going to be one of those captured by a German raider? That was a point made by Stanley Hugill in a newspaper feature in 1988; he had been at the ship's wheel during the attack on *Automedon*.

Rusbridger posed the question why a naval ship was not made available for this document-carrying task. In the first place, at that critical time in the war it is doubtful if one could have been spared for the purpose. In the second place, although the secret material was very important indeed, *none of it was of a particularly urgent nature*. The War Cabinet Report, the most important of the documents, was a top-level 'appreciation' of the Far Eastern situation, but it contained no instructions requiring immediate action by Brooke-Popham. Whether it took four weeks or six weeks to reach him, was of little consequence; and, in fact, no replacement copy was ever sent. (The document was arguably of more use to the Japanese than it would have been to its intended recipient.)

What is of consequence is whether the British knew that the documents and codes had fallen, or might have fallen, into enemy hands prior to Sam Harper reaching England and making his report

* These new methods did not prevent the capture of another haul of secret papers by the raider *Thor* on 10th May 1942 when, again in the Indian Ocean, the Australian steamer *Nankin* was intercepted. That haul included some papers from the Combined Intelligence Centre, Wellington, New Zealand, to the C-in-C, Eastern Fleet, in Colombo.

in June 1941. For as soon as they knew there was even the remotest possibility that this had happened, the British would have had to take corrective action.

The British were intercepting German and Japanese naval wireless traffic at this time but were able to decrypt only a few of the messages sucked in by the interception stations. Berlin knew of the capture for she had been informed by *Atlantis*, and the only way that could have been done was by radio, almost certainly using the German Naval Enigma machine. It may be that the British intercepted that message, but it is extremely doubtful that they could have read it at that early date. Professor F.H. Hinsley says in his introduction to *Code Breakers – The Inside Story of Bletchley Park*:

> Although decrypts from the German Enigma were obtained regularly from the spring of 1940, they were confined for the next twelve months to an Enigma key used only in the Norwegian campaign and to two keys used by the German Air Force.[10]

The same would have applied had the British intercepted the Berlin message to *Ole Jacob* ordering her to divert to 'Y'; anyway, it is unlikely that particular message would have contained specific mention of *Automedon*. The two-way flow of telegrams between Admiral Wenneker and Berlin were not open to the British; the cables used did not pass through British controlled territory.

What other ways and means were there for the British to have learned of the possible fate of the *Automedon* papers? Ways and means, that is, prior to Sam Harper reaching Spain in April 1941 and making contact with Captain Hillgarth, the British Naval Attaché; or Gibraltar on 31st May where he was interviewed by British Field Security; or prior to his being interviewed again and making his report in England on 27th June? It seems clear that the British must have known before any of those events that the papers had fallen, or might have fallen, into enemy hands for *at no time during those interviews, or subsequently, was Sam Harper ever asked whether he knew anything about the fate of the papers; they were not mentioned to him at all*. In fact Harper knew nothing of the papers' existence until he read about them many years later in a newspaper, but the interviewing officers could not have known that. Surely those officers would have been instructed to ask pertinent questions unless, of course, the probable fate of the papers was already known?

There is a possibility that the SIS in Japan were somehow able to interview some of the Norwegian sailors either at Kobe, or while they were on the way to Nagasaki, or at that port itself. There is also a possibility, more of a certainty in view of the British presence in Shanghai, that they were interviewed by British Intelligence when they arrived at that place in the second or third week of December 1940. As 'distressed seamen', the term given to merchant sailors who have lost their ship, they would have reported to the Norwegian consul in Shanghai. It is inconceivable that the consul would not have arranged for them to be interviewed by Allied Intelligence, for apart from anything they had to say about *Automedon*, they had information about the activities of a German commerce raider, and had travelled half-way across secretive Japan. They would have been a source of much interest to Harry Steptoe, the SIS man in Shanghai, and to Commander Woolley of Naval Intelligence. It is unlikely that the Norwegians knew anything about *Automedon*'s secrets, but they would have been able to report that many items from the ship had been transferred to the German raider.

We must now return to Sam Harper's report of 27th June 1941, remembering that he knew nothing of any secret papers at that time, and was asked nothing about them.

He reported: 'The Chief Engineer of the *Teddy* was very pro-British. He took messages from Mr Stewart, our Second Mate, *which messages have since come through safely from Japan.*' (Emphasis added.)

Harper was given this information about the prior safe arrival of Stewart's messages by one of the officers who interviewed him. He was also shown a photograph of *Atlantis* which he was able to identify although he did not know the name of it.

It seems certain, therefore, that from the reports of the Norwegians and/or the contents of Mr Stewart's messages, which one can assume were handed over in Shanghai, the British knew that *Automedon* had been captured and that at the very least there was a chance that her secrets had fallen into German hands. Even the suspicion that this might have happened should have set alarm bells ringing in London.*

* Donald Stewart cannot be asked now what the messages were that he sent, or to whom they were addressed, or what form they were in. He survived internment, rose to be a captain with Blue Funnel Line after the war, and died in the 1970s.

What effect did the capture of this hoard have on the immediate course of the war? Professor John Chapman, whose writings in *The Price of Admiralty* are based on German records, states:

> It is clear that a copy of the British NYKO Code, used for sea-air communication in the Mediterranean, which had been seized from the *Automedon* . . . was handed over to the Italian Navy Ministry in January and used with good effect by Italian forces and the German Air Force's Xth Air Corps, based on Sicilian airfields, and equipped with divebombers which successfully ambushed Force 'H' on 10 January, causing severe damage to the carrier HMS *Illustrious* and the loss of the cruiser HMS *Southampton*.[11]

Professor Chapman adds that the first recorded German resolutions of the British Military, Naval and Air Attaché codes came within two weeks of the receipt of the *Automedon* material. Then he says, 'changes introduced [by the British] in January 1941 slowed down resolution'. This seems to indicate that, by January 1941, Britain was aware that the papers might have fallen into German hands, and had taken steps to rectify the situation. However, to change codes and cyphers for a far-flung fleet is no easy matter and takes time. Furthermore, unless *all* units begin using new codes at the same time, any messages sent out in both the new and old codes gives cryptographers a wonderful opportunity with a process they very descriptively call 'cribbing'.

Admiral Wenneker noted the extreme interest shown in the British War Cabinet papers when he handed a copy over to his Japanese opposite numbers in December 1940. It seems however, that farther up the Japanese High Command the papers were initially treated with a pinch of salt. Had the Germans been open about where they had obtained them instead of trying to give the impression they had a mole in high places in London, the Japanese might at once have taken them more seriously. It is possible that some Japanese leaders might even have thought the papers to be a German forgery made to persuade Japan to come into the war on Germany's side.

The receipt of the papers had no immediate effect on Japanese strategic thinking. After all, the papers gave the British position on 15th August 1940, four months before they were handed over in Tokyo. Since August things had changed on the other side of the world for Britain had survived the worst of the Blitz, which reached a climax in September, and there was now no chance of Germany invading Britain in the immediate future. Much better, then, to treat the contents of the papers with caution.

The Commander-in-Chief of the Japanese fleet, Admiral Yamamoto, originally held pro-British and pro-American views but these had changed three months prior to the *Automedon* incident, a change brought about by the military successes of the Germans in Europe and by the huge rearmament policy adopted by the United States.[12] Even so, on 25th February Yamamoto wrote to the Japanese Naval Minister warning of a possible strong reaction from America and Britain should Japan use force in French Indo-China.[13]

But the information in the papers soon came to be regarded with more favour. The initial change in attitude may have been one result of Britain's failure to do anything about the border war between Thailand and Indo-China that began in November 1940 and went on until the Japanese-mediated settlement of 11th March 1941. Though the British knew that the Japanese had encouraged the Thais to attack and had not only supplied them with arms but had also trained them in their use, and that if French reports were to be believed, that Japanese pilots were manning Thai planes, during those four months the British lion sat back and did nothing. This tended to support the information in the Cabinet papers about Britain's inability to do much to protect its interests in the Far East.

What is clear is that from the early spring of 1941 the Japanese began in earnest to plan their move to the south. In a cypher message to Lord Halifax in Washington dated 5th February, Sir Robert Craigie, Britain's ambassador in Tokyo, said:

> Evidence is accumulating that the Japanese may already have decided to push on southward, even if this means war. Press reports indicate that Japan is using her position as mediator in between Thailand and Indo-China to gain . . . naval base at Camranh Bay, air bases in South Indo-China, and control of Indo-China customs. There is also reason to suppose that some military agreement with Thailand directed against our territories and the Netherlands East Indies is under consideration.[14]

This cementation of Japanese plans had much to do with the fact that, from early in 1941, Hitler was again calling the shots in the West. Although the British had successes against the Italians in East Africa, in February Rommel and his Afrika Korps landed in North Africa and by April had driven the British back to Benghazi. There were similar

German successes in the Balkans. All began to look rosy again from the Axis point of view, and the British position regarding the Far East must have seemed to the Japanese to have deteriorated even from the pessimistic summation given in the Cabinet papers. The Japanese were already well into the process of taking control of French Indo-China, and the Dutch in the East Indies were weak. With Britain embroiled in Europe and the Middle East, the main worries for the Japanese were the Russian Eastern Army and the United States Pacific Fleet at Pearl Harbor and the American outlying island strongholds of Guam, Wake and Midway. Concern over the Russians largely disappeared when the Germans attacked Russia in June.

On 15th July 1941 the Japanese informed the German embassy in Tokyo that the full occupation of Indo-China could be expected soon, and that they expected no serious repercussions from either Britain or the United States.[15] In fact there were grave repercussions, but they were not military ones. Ten days later President Roosevelt issued a freezing order on all Japanese assets in the United States, a move that was soon followed by Britain and by the exiled Dutch government in London.

One of the few documents of the *Automedon* haul that has survived post-war British Intelligence weeding of German archives, is a document dealing with the expertise of the Japanese in landing operations and their use of rubber boats for this purpose. The document, signed by Major L.F. Field in the Directorate of Military Operations in London, is reproduced in Professor Chapman's *The Price of Admiralty*.[16] Chapman notes that these Japanese skills 'remained unappreciated by Far East Command', probably basing that remark on the fact that the document never reached Singapore. However, as we have seen elsewhere, Japanese expertise in this direction had already been noted in the FECB document called *Japanese Army Memorandum*. Furthermore, Major Field, raised to Colonel and then to Brigadier, arrived in Singapore himself late in December 1941, and no doubt personally passed on any information he had. He was there well in advance of the Japanese landings on Singapore Island itself which took place on 8th February 1942.

Fifteen

Shanghai – September 1939 to December 1941

Following the so-called China Incident of 1937, the Chinese Nationalists (KMT) and Chinese Communists (CCP) formed a United Front against the Japanese. It was an ill-fated alliance, for 'from the beginning the Communists regarded it as nothing more than a means to carry out the orders of the Comintern, to be freed from Nationalist attacks, and to build up strength during the war'.[1] After some initial encounters with Japanese forces the communists concentrated most of their efforts on regrouping and expanding, aiming for Mao Tse-tung's oft-pronounced target of 'a million Red soldiers and a million Party members'.

Tension between the United Front partners grew against a background of rapidly shifting international alignments and changes of opinion. Germany, Japan's Anti-Comintern partner since 1936, was not in favour of the Japanese attack on China. She feared that such a commitment of troops might reduce Japanese pressure on Russia, and moreover, draw China into seeking Russian aid. Nor did Germany overlook the sensitive issue of her many advisers who were engaged in training Chinese troops.

China did indeed seek Russian aid; she sought it also from other nations but from most received little more than sympathy. The United States offered aid amounting to $170m most of it covered by the proviso that it was to be used for non-military purchases. At the same time Japan's access to the American market both directly and indirectly supported her war aims in China. The Russians, on the other hand, offered China a Non-Aggression Pact in August 1937 and supplied low-interest loans over the period 1937–39 amounting to $250m. In addition, by 1939 she had supplied China with 1,000 aircraft, 2,000 pilots and 500 military advisers. Among the latter were Marshal Voroshilov and General Zhukov, both to achieve fame during World War Two. But with the outbreak of war in Europe, this Russian assistance first slackened, then ceased altogether.

The British and French, preoccupied by the developing situation in Europe, and leaning over backwards to avoid irritating Japan in the east, did relatively little to help China. Britain's placatory attitude towards Japan in 1937 is perhaps best illustrated by the incident that occurred late that year in which Sir Hughe Knatchbull-Hugessen, the British ambassador to China, was seriously wounded by machine-gun fire from Japanese aircraft. Sir Hughe had left Nanking for Shanghai in a car convoy; the roof of his own vehicle being covered in a large Union flag for identification purposes. The flag could not have been unseen by the raiders who came down to within sixty feet of the ground, yet they strafed the convoy. Only a few decades earlier such an event would have caused the British lion to roar; now it brought forth little more than a whimper. London filed a note of protest with Tokyo, demanding an official apology, the punishment of the culprits, and assurances that similar attacks would not occur in future. The Japanese reply was deliberately offensive. It took four weeks to arrive and its contents fell far below London's demands. Nevertheless, the British government pronounced itself satisfied. Major-General F.S.G. Piggott, summed up the end of this affair in a rather abrupt fashion in his book, *Broken Thread*: 'The new Ambassador to Japan, Sir Robert Craigie, arrived on 3rd December, and it was largely through his patient and skilful handling, and his friendship with certain officials . . . that the question was disposed of.'[2]*

Later, in the spring and summer of 1939, Britain was made to suffer a series of humiliating incidents in and around its Tientsin Concession, provocations which led finally to the withdrawal of the British battalion from Tientsin during the winter of 1939–40.

There was an occurrence in Shanghai, also in 1939, which began

* Knatchbull-Hugesson was awarded a 'solatium' of £5,000 by the British government – not by the Japanese. It took him a year to recover from his injuries and then he became ambassador to Turkey from 1939 to 1944. His valet there, code-named 'Cicero', photographed many of his official documents and passed them to the Germans.

to assume the proportions of a major international incident. In June, Japanese marines landed to break up a strike of Chinese workers, and in the process surrounded a British-owned cotton mill. The mill's manager, Richard Maurice Tinkler from Lancashire, attempted to get in the way of the marines, drew his revolver and fired a shot. He was bayoneted several times and died after fifteen hours during which the Japanese refused him medical treatment. Tinkler had been a member of the Shanghai Municipal Police until 1930, and risen to the rank of acting Inspector. During his police years he had often been detailed for military intelligence work with the Shanghai Volunteers. His resignation from the police came about after disciplinary procedures were taken against him, which might have concerned his very racist attitudes. It is not known why the Japanese treated him so badly. It may just have been his 'effrontery' at getting in their way, or his racial attitudes, or his earlier association with intelligence.

The incident created headlines in the British press, caused questions to be asked in the House of Commons, and resulted in a two-way flow of protests between London and Tokyo. The Japanese protested as vigorously as did the British, and called Tinkler's action an affront. The matter was finally allowed to die away quietly as it became overshadowed by the events in Europe culminating in the war there in September.[3]

The year 1940 brought more pressure from the Japanese. The French were forced to discontinue the rail supply service from Indo-China to Yunnan in June 1940, and a month later Britain closed the Burma Road and the Hong Kong border, thus virtually isolating China from the rest of the world. In August 1940, the British withdrew their two infantry battalions from Shanghai. These troops were needed elsewhere, but Japanese pressure was another factor in the equation.

All these outside influences aggravated the 'inside' tensions that existed between the Chinese Nationalists and Communists. The signing of the German–Soviet Non-Aggression Pact in August 1939, followed by the Japanese–Soviet Neutrality Pact of April 1941, served to remove 'the doctrinal basis and expediency of the United Front. Conflict between the KMT and CCP became more serious.'[4] In fact it developed into a situation that was not resolved throughout World War Two.

* * *

The importance of Shanghai as a centre for intelligence, espionage, and subversion grew in direct proportion to the gravity of the Far Eastern situation.

In 1939, only a week before the outbreak of war in Europe, the British Naval Control Service (NCS) at Shanghai was resurrected by Major R. Neville, Royal Marines, the SO (I) there. At its head was Commander J.B. Woolley, the retired naval officer who had been involved in its earlier brief life. In 1940, when Neville was posted elsewhere, Woolley became SO (I), another retired officer, Lieutenant-Commander Gilmore, taking his place. The importance of Shanghai as a centre for naval intelligence-gathering is indicated by the number of naval personnel there. According to a consular report of 31st October 1940, the Royal Navy had the following staff in Shanghai at that date:

Naval Liaison Section:	1 Captain RN, 1 Lieutenant-Commander, 2 Clerks.
Naval Intelligence Office:	1 Commander, 1 Lieutenant-Commander, 2 Lieutenants RNVR, 3 Clerks, 5 Lady Cypher Clerks.
Resident Naval Officer:	1 Paymaster-Commander, 2 Clerks.
Naval Control Service:	1 Commander, 1 Lieutenant-Commander, 3 Lieutenants, 1 Clerk.

The NCS staff were based in the British consulate where they 'posed to the world' as civilian members of its staff.[5] As their true occupation was generally known this attempt at subterfuge seems hardly to have been necessary. Their quarters in the consulate, close by those of Naval Intelligence, were guarded by British soldiers until August 1940, when the troops involved sailed for Singapore, and then by SMP Sikhs and a body of British civilians specially recruited for the purpose. These precautions were necessary 'in view of the international nature of Shanghai . . . large Japanese and Italian colonies of doubtful neutrality, and no small number of Germans. Numbers of these spoke fluent English and were quite capable of trying to impersonate British [ship]masters', said the authors of an Admiralty report.

By this time Greater Shanghai was under the control of the Japanese army and navy. This included virtual control of the International Settlement, though the Municipal Council and SMP still continued to operate, and of the French Concession. The harbour remained open to ships of all nations.

The Naval Intelligence Staff, including the SO (I), were engaged in coding and decoding signals, and in collecting, receiving and collating intelligence reports from Reporting Officers at outports and from other sources. All this material was remitted to FECB, stationed at Singapore since August 1939. NCS staff, on the other hand, were involved in obtaining intelligence from masters of ships, keeping a check on shipping movements, anti-sabotage precautions, maintaining a watchful eye on the activities of German naval agents, and issuing routeing instructions to British masters. Inevitably there was some overlap in the responsibilities of the two organisations. For example, the Assistant SO (I) who, in 1941, was Lieutenant de Kermode, RNR, was in charge of recording the disposition of ships in the harbour, and he was assisted by Lieutenant Farmbrough, RNVR, of the NCS, who made daily launch trips up and down the river despite the fact that he was shadowed all the way by boats from Japanese warships moored in the river.[6]

The Germans had two undercover organisations in Shanghai. One of these, the Naval Supply Service (*Etappendienst der Kriegsmarine*), operated a Reporting Officer system similar to that run by the British, although its main functions were procuring fuel and provisions for German ships sailing to and from Japanese ports and purchasing materials for the German war effort. The British NCS paid particular attention to the activities of this organisation, and an example of the type of information it picked up is to be found in a message dated 29th April 1941 from the C-in-C, China Station, Admiral Sir Percy Noble, to the Foreign Office in London: 'It is reported that Germans propose to manufacture 200,000 pairs of boots in Shanghai and that a trial order for 40,000 has already been placed. Further enquiries being made.' As armies march in boots as well as on their stomachs, this information was considered important enough for someone in the Ministry of Economic Warfare in London to write on 7th May 1941: 'It is possible something might be done to impair the efficient completion of this order in the way of encouraging labour troubles or something of the kind.'[7]

The issue of routeing instructions was probably the most important of NCS's functions. These instructions were based on the latest intelligence reports received from FECB about the location of German naval units in the Pacific – mainly surface raiders – thus enabling British and Allied ships to avoid areas of particular danger. A measure of NCS's success in this is that, before the Japanese entry into the war in December 1941, only one Allied vessel routed from Shanghai was lost, the Norwegian *Ringwood* sunk by a German raider on 15th October 1941 en route to Nauru.[8] This was achieved despite the special difficulties posed by the de facto control of the port by the Japanese and the fact that Japanese warships lay in the river off the city as did an Italian sloop and a minelayer/gunboat. The Japanese regularly passed on shipping information to Tokyo where their Naval Staff handed it over to the German Naval Attaché, and no doubt the Italians were doing the same.[9] At sea Japanese merchant ships were reliably believed to be signalling the positions of any Allied ships they passed at sea.

Because the British consulate wireless systems, which included one used by the SIS, tended to be overworked, NCS organised a sub rosa, semi-official Admiralty wireless station out of the existing private stations run by Butterfield & Swire and Jardine Matheson & Co., two of the oldest of the 'taipan' companies in Shanghai. This station transmitted to ships under the acronym BUJAR, using official Admiralty codes. In some instances, where there was doubt over the allegiance of particular shipmasters, and their ships had not been provided with official code and decoding-books, company codes were used.[10]

The fleet of British gunboats that had operated on the Yangtze for many years, and whose continued presence annoyed the Japanese, was gradually withdrawn to Hong Kong, Singapore and the Mediterranean. By the summer of 1940 only one was still in Chinese waters. HMS *Peterel* remained in commission, moored in the river off Shanghai with a special complement of men, and was being used as a secure wireless telegraphy link.[11] Its boiler was kept permanently on 'flash' so that records and code books could be swiftly destroyed. It may have been the fact that the ship was a floating wireless station that led to the Japanese opening hostilities at Shanghai on 8th December 1941 by demanding her surrender. However, surrender she did not. Her commander opened fire on Japanese ships in the river and kept it up until the tiny vessel was sunk by gunfire from the shore and shells from the cruiser *Idzumo*. She became the first British naval victim of the Japanese war.[12] Petty Officer Telegraphist Jim Cummings of the *Peterel*, who was ashore at the time of the attack, managed to evade capture by the Japanese for the entire war. He joined a Chinese-American guerrilla group as its wireless man.[13]

NCS thought it likely that Shanghai would become a saboteur's paradise as the war in Europe progressed. However, only one attempt at sabotage against British property was ever established. Commander Woolley attributed this to the 800-strong anti-sabotage corps of British civilians he organised. These unpaid volunteers kept continuous watches aboard British vessels.

It is likely, of course, that the Germans and Italians did not contemplate widespread sabotage for fear of reprisals of a similar nature. The British Foreign Office had, in fact, vetoed any action against both neutral and enemy property in Shanghai. A Special Operations Executive (SOE) proposal to blow up the Italian sloop *Eritrea* in 1941, as she lay in the river sending out wireless messages regarding British shipping movements, was one of the plans vetoed. A factor in this affair seems to have been friction between the top SOE man in Shanghai and Harry Steptoe, the Special Intelligence Service officer there, who had seen incoming SOE signals. An SOE report says:

> *Eritrea* situation 'blew-up' apparently because 'C's'* man in Shanghai rushing round to Le Rougetel [later Sir John, a member of the British Embassy staff attached to the consulate] and suggesting that SOE were going to blow up a ship without consulting anybody. Actually Killery's [Head of SOE's Far East Mission] instructions were to examine urgently possibility of destroying or damaging Italian sloop.[14]

In fact the SOE had neither the explosives nor sufficient expertise to make such an attempt.

Masters of British and Allied ships arriving in the port were interrogated first by a Naval Control Officer and subsequently by the SO (I) if they had any special information. These reports provided valuable information about Japanese shipping movements in the area, any sudden change in pattern – i.e. the removal from normal routes of passenger liners capable of being converted to troopships – being especially watched for. To these reports were added others from Reporting Officers at Yokohama, Kobe, and Nagasaki in Japan, from Seoul in Korea, and from the Chinese ports of Tientsin, Chefoo, Weihaiwei, Tsingtao and Foochow. Some information was still being obtained from the Chinese Maritime Customs Service, although by

* 'C' was the code initial for the Head of SIS in London, Major-General Sir Stewart Menzies.

now it was under Japanese military domination, despite the fact that the Service was still headed by Inspector-General Sir Frederick Maze, and that no less than twenty of its forty-six commissioners were British. 'It was a question of getting what we could from well-disposed individuals.'[15]

According to a War Office paper headed 'Intelligence Organisation in the Far East' dated 4th April 1940 and updated in early 1941, the two Military Intelligence officers in Shanghai during that period – officially called Liaison Officers – were GS02 Major Gwyn, a Japanese interpreter, and GS03 Captain Dewar-Durie, a Chinese speaker. The latter, an Argyll & Sutherland Highlander, operated under cover of being an army recruiting officer. They were augmented by another Japanese-speaking GS02, Major Hunt, who was serving as the Consulate Liaison Officer.[16] Their tasks included obtaining information on Japanese troop dispositions and operations in their area and similar information on Chinese forces. However, the Japanese were making life steadily more difficult for these officers. A message to the War Office from the GOC Hong Kong reads:

> 8846 cipher 20/1 Desp. 20/1/41
> Situation in Western district [Shanghai] where Hunt and Dewar-Durie live has so deteriorated that Hunt has moved into the concession and Dewar-Durie will move at first opportunity.[17]

The situation worsened, and the consequent drop in both quality and quantity of reports from Shanghai caused the GOC Hong Kong to put forward an argument in May for reducing the number of Military Intelligence officers at Shanghai.

> To GSO1 Intelligence (Far East) Singapore
> 9744 cipher 17/5 Desp.17/5/41
> (a) information obtainable from scrutinising Chinese and Japanese Press in Shanghai is obtainable equally quickly or even better in Hong Kong. For example MLO Shanghai in his 8231 May 15th could only identify 2 of Japanese Divisions in present operations in North China whereas we have identified all 11 participating . . .
> (b) opportunities for travelling of Shanghai Staff Officers in interior are becoming daily more restricted and will probably soon cease altogether save to ports where information already obtainable from Consuls . . .
> (c) Owing to ever increasing Japanese and puppet [government] pressure

> in Shanghai, Chinese Military contacts there presumably reduced to a minimum as terrorist gangs now operating . . .

The message went on to point out that in the event of war with Japan the escape of these officers would be problematical.[18] In the event, both Hunt and Dewar-Durie got away from Shanghai before the start of hostilities. Disguised as peasants they made their way across China and eventually reached Chungking and safety.[19] Commander Woolley, on the other hand, and other members of the Naval Intelligence fraternity in Shanghai, became prisoners-of-war.

A Special Operations Executive team was formed in Shanghai, under the overall direction of the HQ in Singapore, in mid-1941. It consisted of eight people, and was led by W.J. Gande. Gande was the Chief Special Constable of the Shanghai Municipal Police, which was probably the reason he was selected for the post. Another Special Constable member was S.C. Riggs. The other members were J.F. Brister, H.G. Clarke (a one-time SMP officer and SIS operative), J.K. Brand, W.M. Reeves, E. Elias and G.D. Jack.

Only one of them received any training in subversive techniques. In September 1941, only two months before Japan struck, Brand was sent to Hong Kong to receive ten days' training in the use of explosives and incendiary devices from Major (later Major-General) J.M.L. Gavin. It was a pointless trip, for the Shanghai group had no explosives.

At the end of the day the group accomplished little apart from compiling a register of enemy goods in store in Shanghai and the destinations of these goods when shipped out. One of them, S.C. Riggs, was in an excellent position to obtain such information; an ex-master mariner, he was a partner in a firm of cargo and ship surveyors with access to many dockside warehouses.[20]

According to an SOE file recently made available at the Public Record Office, Kew, Gande was asked whether his organisation could interfere with the activities of an American journalist in Shanghai named Carl von Wiegand as there were 'reasonable indications' that he was a German agent. Wiegand's articles, which were syndicated throughout the United States by the anti-British and pro-isolationist Hearst newspaper group, were 'doing harm to the Allied cause'. In the same cable Gande was urged to use special caution, 'as even anti-Nazi journalists would resent interference with a fellow journalist'. Whether or not Wiegand was a German agent, his articles were strongly anti-British. However, in at least one respect Wiegand seemed not so opposed to the British, for his associate and long-time companion in Shanghai and elsewhere in the East, was the forty-six-year-old widow, Lady Grace Drummond-Hay.[21] Wiegand seems to have had some important Japanese sources. On 17th October 1941, seven weeks before the attack on Pearl Harbor, he met Rear Admiral William Glassford, USN, in Shanghai, and informed him that 'war in the Pacific will begin any hour after midnight on December 6th'. The attack came in the early morning hours of 7th December.

The friction between Gande's organisation and the SIS over the *Eritrea* matter did not result in the cessation of co-operation between them. SIS sought the aid of SOE in watching the movements of an Indian nationalist resident in the city, one A.M. Sahay, described as 'a Japanese Indian agent of extreme propaganda views'.

The existence of Gande's organisation was known to the Japanese through an agent whose loyalty they had probably bought, and who worked as chief book-keeper for Gande's firm, Gande, Price & Company. The agent's name was Kaman, and he carried a Rumanian passport. He had worked for Gande for many years. All the SOE members were arrested immediately after the outbreak of war and confronted with copies of messages exchanged with Singapore. This indicates either that there had been no time to destroy the files or that Kaman had made copies at an earlier stage. All the SOE men were brutally treated and, in April 1942, tried and sentenced to prison. Later that year some of them, including Riggs but not Gande, were released in an exchange of prisoners.[22] Riggs wrote a long report when he arrived home. In it he mentioned a conversation he had had on board the *Kamakura Maru*, the exchange ship, with a man who was convinced of Kaman's involvement. The report was 'doctored' by British 'weeders' before its recent release into the public domain in the Public Record Office; the name of the man Riggs had spoken to had been removed, the removal being endorsed as having taken place under Section 3(4) of the Public Records Act of 1958. The name was, in fact, that of the top SIS man in China, Harry Steptoe, who had been working under cover of being a British consul in Shanghai. He was an expert on all matters dealing with Russia and the Comintern. An SIS colleague, named Barton, seems to have specialised in Chinese matters.

° ° °

During the peacetime years the Germans set up units of their Naval Supply Service in various places throughout the world. In Japan and China the Service came under the charge of the German Naval Attaché in Tokyo. The members of it were mainly German civilians employed in shipping and commerce in the area, and it was their task in the event of war to service naval ships, armed raiders, and any merchant ships under the command of the German Navy, such as merchant blockade-runners.

Germany's Secret Military Intelligence Service (*Abwehr-Abteilung*) was also active in the Far East. In 1940 the *Abwehr* set up an intelligence office (*Nachrichtenstelle*) in Shanghai which by 1942 had been extended to cover all of China and many places throughout Southeast Asia. The overall organisation was called the War Organisation in China (*Kriegsorganisation China*). There was more than a degree of professional rivalry between this army organisation and the naval one, and Professor John Chapman records in the introduction to Volume One of his *The Price of Admiralty* that a division of labour had to be worked out in Berlin between them.

A week prior to Germany's attack on Poland on 1st September 1939, the Naval Supply Service was placed on a war footing. The Head of the Service in China, based in Shanghai, was Dr Adalbert Korff. At first, it seems, Korff was not highly regarded by the then German Naval Attaché in Tokyo, Captain Johannes Lietzmann. One of the reasons for this seems to have been that Korff had made errors in identifying British troopships in the Far East. Another reason was that Korff's man at Dairen, called Pansing, was not carrying out his duties to Lietzmann's satisfaction.

One of Korff's first reports to Lietzmann after war with Britain and France began on 3rd September 1939, concerned the departure from Shanghai of HMS *Dorsetshire*, a report soon confirmed by the Naval Attaché's contact on the Japanese Naval Staff, who added the information that HMS *Dainty* had arrived at Hong Kong. This shows that two years before Japan entered the war, there was close contact between the German and Japanese navies in the field of Naval Intelligence.

Over the following months Korff's organisation continued to report usefully. In October he reported the withdrawal of five British gunboats from Shanghai, and in mid-November sent in a report on the status of guns and guncrews aboard British merchant vessels. By January 1940 Korff was sending Tokyo photographs of Allied vessels in Shanghai, and in April of that year advised against the sailing of the German vessel *Ramses* which was bottled up in the port, as 'many of the [harbour] pilots were British', and 'to obtain the services of a pilot, 48 hours' notice was required', ample time for the British NCS to pass on the sailing information to Hong Kong.[23]

The later part of the *Ramses* saga illustrates German–Japanese Intelligence co-operation. On 27th March 1941 the German Naval Attaché in Tokyo sent Korff a message ordering him to sail *Ramses* immediately as 'British gunboat [HMS *Peterel*] out of commission at present because of engine repairs. Get in touch with Japanese Naval Attaché.' The message went on to give precise sailing directions, timings, etc., for the vessel's voyage to Kobe, on Japan's Inland Sea. *Ramses* arrived safely at Kobe on 3rd April where its master reported that, by taking special measures, he had managed to deceive the British Secret Service about his exact intentions. He had ordered sand ballast delivered in lighters, the transfer of which would have taken over a week; then instead, he filled his ballast tanks with water which took only a few hours. As his ship passed the moored *Peterel* he noted that there was lots of shouting and a general alarum aboard her.

Korff did not confine himself to naval matters. At one time he advised the Naval Attaché against using Carl Jochheim as an agent in Japan. But Lietzmann employed him anyway to squeeze information out of British and Allied seamen visiting Japanese ports and not only that, transferred him in June 1941 to Shanghai for the same purpose. Another agent likewise transferred from Japan to Shanghai was an engineer called Gustav Mand. He had worked for the Naval Supply Service in Japan where one of the matters he was concerned with was self-destruct mechanisms for blockade-runners and supply ships. However, in Shanghai he was part of the *Abwehr* War Organisation.

Perhaps the most important aspect of the supply side of Korff's task was in purchasing, or rather in attempting to purchase, diesel oil for ships. In this field the Germans did not get as much co-operation from the Japanese as they did in Intelligence. Korff found himself confronted with difficulties cooked up by the Japanese who were not keen to see stocks of precious fuel gobbled up by someone else. They raised difficulties over shipping such purchases to Japan in Japanese tankers, for with British warships perhaps lurking off the Chinese coast, German vessels could not be used for the purpose. Funds too, were a problem, for Japanese currency control regulations made it impossible to remit funds to Shanghai from Tokyo, so monies had to be sent to the German consulate-general's office from places as far afield as Mexico, sometimes in hard cash.

Despite Berlin's attempts to define the responsibilities of the two German Intelligence agencies in Shanghai, many difficulties existed between them. Korff was responsible to the Naval Attaché in Tokyo, whilst Lieutenant-Commander R. Schuler of the Secret Military Intelligence Service's War Organisation in Shanghai, was not. Admiral Wenneker, who became German Naval Attaché in Tokyo in March 1940, held a meeting with Schuler in August of that year about fixing areas of responsibility, but it led to nothing. Apparently Schuler was concerned about security in Korff's organisation, for he made that the excuse for not co-operating with it. In a message to Berlin Admiral Wenneker pointed out that exchange of information must continue to take place in Tokyo and that this entailed a duplication of effort and increased costs. In fact the situation was to grow even worse. Schuler left for Berlin shortly after the Tokyo meeting and his successor, Theodore Siefkin, managed to alienate everyone he came into contact with including the Gestapo officials in Shanghai. Admiral Wenneker seems to have taken against him too, not least, says Professor Chapman, because he saw the War Organisation as something of a threat to Dr Korff's Supply Organisation. 'Wenneker appears to have had a tendency to palm off many of the various rather shadowy characters who wound up in Japan on the . . . War Organisation at Shanghai.'[24] The rivalry between the two organisations was open.

The Gestapo was well represented in Shanghai and its officers were responsible to Meisinger, the head Gestapo man in Tokyo. Operating on the fringe of German Intelligence, the Gestapo was responsible for security, propaganda, and for ensuring the 'co-operation' of all German nationals in Shanghai. After the fall of France and the setting-up of the Vichy Government in June 1940, the Gestapo took upon itself the task of undermining the Free French organisation in the area. According to a message from the British ambassador in Tokyo, Sir Robert Craigie, to the Chief of Intelligence Staff, Singapore, in October 1941, the two Gestapo officers in Shanghai at that time were called Wiedemann and Gellert. It seems that Wiedemann was well known to British Intelligence authorities and was in Shanghai under an assumed name.[25]

The headquarters of the Free French organisation in China was at Chungking where it was headed by Dr Bechamp. The Shanghai section was headed at first by a merchant in his fifties called Roderick Egal and latterly by R. Pontet. (Egal was in Hong Kong at the start of the Japanese war and was interned there.) Two other prominent members of the organisation were J.E. Mercuse and a Belgian citizen Roger Pierard. Mercuse was Head of the Free French News Agency in Shanghai, and Pierard was its propaganda chief. Pierard, who was thirty years old, was also an operative of the Far East section of the British Ministry of Information. His work included broadcasting in French over the British-owned radio station with the call-sign XGDN, and over the American station, call-sign XMHA. As his work placed him in such jeopardy, from both German or Japanese agents, or from gangsters in the employ of Wang Ching-wei, the puppet ruler in north China, he was advised by the police always to carry a pistol.

One matter in which the Gestapo busied themselves was in trying to prevent Frenchmen in the city from leaving to join the Free French Forces. In this they reckoned without the efforts of the British Colonel, V.R. Burkhardt. Burkhardt, who until his retirement early in 1941 had been Military Attaché in Chungking, and before that GSO1 with FECB in Hong Kong, had been appointed Liaison Officer between the Free French Organisation in the Far East headquartered in Singapore, and the British Minister dealing with Free French matters in London. Very much a francophile, Valentine Burkhardt went far beyond his official remit. He turned himself into a sort of latterday Scarlet Pimpernel, and in concert with Commander Woolley and his organisation, assisted many French ex-servicemen and civilians to leave Shanghai and other places along the China coast on board British naval and merchant vessels, and sometimes across country. Several British civilian residents of Shanghai helped in this risky undertaking. They included Eric Davis, by profession a ship-broker, and a Mr and Mrs M. Raitson, who harboured some of the escapees in their bar called Gaby's on Broadway, off The Bund. Davis and the Raitsons were arrested by the Japanese for these 'offences' in December 1941.

When, in the late summer of 1942, arrangements were made with the assistance of the Swiss government for an exchange of internees, the British attempted but failed to get Davis, the Raitsons, Commander Woolley and his NSO staff, and Gande of SOE, included on the exchange list for Shanghai, together with Pontet and Pierard, and a German Jew called A. Peretiz who had been instrumental in aiding the head of the Free French News Agency, Mercuse, to hide and avoid arrest. Using a false name, Mercuse was 'exchanged' in September 1942 and spent the rest of the war working for the Free French organisation in New Delhi. Pierard was captured whilst attempting to pass through Japanese lines in early 1942 and was tortured by the Kempetai. He was finally tried for attempting to escape and sentenced to two years' imprisonment.[26]

Two other men who had been employed in undercover work of one form or another and whom the British attempted to have included in an exchange were a Dr Eric Vio and an SMP Inspector named A.R. Soohorukoff. Vio was an Italian working undercover for the British SIS. Against his name on a British document concerning the exchange appears the notation 'Most secret – confidential'. Inspector Soohorukoff was apparently working for H. Vere Redman, the man in charge of propaganda in the British embassy in Tokyo.

Japanese Intelligence Services remained extremely active in Shanghai throughout the 1939–41 period. Much intelligence regarding shipping and naval matters, obtained directly by the Germans, was confirmed by these Japanese sources acting through the Naval Staff in Tokyo. Such confirmation was extremely valuable, but it was far from being all that the Japanese supplied. In late December 1939, for example, Japanese Intelligence in Shanghai somehow obtained a copy of a secret document issued by Admiral Sir Percy Noble, C-in-C, China Fleet, entitled 'Instructions Regarding Recognition of British Aircraft'. It was sent to Tokyo where it was handed over to the German Naval Attaché with the expressed hope that the gesture would encourage an increase in exchange of intelligence, the Japanese especially requesting information from German experiences in the war against England.

A by-product of their taking control of the Chinese part of the city in 1938, was an increase in Japanese influence on the operations of the Shanghai Municipal Police. This influence grew stronger when, on the outbreak of the war in Europe many British SMP men left for England to join the armed forces. This egress took place despite a request from the Foreign Office in London urging them to stay as they would be far more useful in Shanghai.[27] During this period the Japanese also began a purge of anyone of their own nationality in the SMP who was of a pro-British persuasion. Superintendent Igaki, an extreme anglophile, was gunned down and killed outside his home. The precise motive for this killing and exactly who the assassins were was never established. Igaki lived in the Japanese controlled part of the city and the detectives involved in the unsuccessful investigation were Japanese themselves.

Two Europeans who had long been watched by SMP Special Branch as suspected Japanese sympathisers, were an Australian called Alan Raymond, leader of the 'Free Australia Movement', and a Briton called Notingham [*sic*] who was publisher of the *Shanghai Times*. The SMP were correct in having suspicions about the two for, after all other Europeans apart from neutrals had been interned by the Japanese, these two remained free in the city.[28] In 1937, as publisher of the *Shanghai Times*, Notingham had brought out in book form *Dawn or Doom of Humanity* by Trebistsch Lincoln who had become a Buddhist monk, and who, as Abbot Chao Kung, wrote this anti-communist evangelical sermon which was also hostile to European nationalism. As a critic has put it, it was stronger on 'doom' than 'dawn'.

The SMP, including its British members, continued to police the city for some months after the Japanese war began in December 1941 although the force was then placed under a Japanese Commissioner of Police. That was the situation until July 1942 when all British and Allied members were discharged from the Service and interned. Superintendent Fred West's Discharge Certificate is dated 24th July 1942. It notes that he had been in the service from 31st December 1921 to 31st July 1942, so effectively he was given one week's notice. The reason for his discharge was noted as 'service terminated as a result of re-organisation of the Force', a euphemism of the very highest order.

One hitherto unreported feature of the Shanghai situation in the period between September 1939 and December 1941, was that a number of British-owned firms carried on trading with Germany. On 17th May 1941, Colonel Grimsdale, the GSO (I) at Singapore, and the top military officer in the FECB organisation, wrote a 'secret and personal' letter to General Sir Hastings (later Lord) Ismay, Churchill's Chief of Staff as Minister of Defence. It contained the following paragraph:

> We get a constant supply of reports from censorship and other sources which show the large quantities of war materials still reaching Germany via Japan and USSR. A particularly dreadful aspect of the situation is

> the number of British firms in Shanghai and elsewhere which are not above turning a dishonest penny by trading with the enemy. I spoke frankly to Sir A. Clark-Kerr (thank God he encourages frankness) when he passed through here last month about this. He is fully alive to the truth of it, but failed to see what he could do in the absence of a proper MEW [Ministry of Economic Warfare] authority out here to make a full investigation and report to him about it.[29]

The fact that the British ambassador to China found himself unable to act against British firms in Shanghai who were actively trading with Germany is a measure of the strange, twilight sort of world the city became after the war in Europe began.

One British firm, Wheelock & Company, was described by the SO (I) as always being 'evasive and difficult'.[30] Wheelock's had several ships under charter to Japan and owned several dockside premises.

In the pre-Pacific War days, any cargoes and supplies the Germans managed to procure in Shanghai, or which they procured elsewhere by making use of the commercial services available in the city, were shipped to Japan in neutral, including Japanese, vessels. There they were either transferred to blockade-runners, or before Germany attacked Russia in June 1941, shipped to Vladivostok and taken across the USSR via the Siberian Railway.

In April 1942, four months after the Japanese took Shanghai, the British learnt from 'most secret sources', which meant a Sigint source, that the Germans were complaining that 'in Shanghai they [the Japanese] were treating all whites, whether enemies or friends, exactly alike, with the result that German interests were suffering.' The Japanese might have had cause to take such stance, for the British report went on: 'Japanese have demanded recall of German Consul-General in Shanghai because of his having set up an espionage organisation which is highly unwelcome to them.'[31]

When the Japanese took Shanghai, several British, American and other Allied ships in the harbour fell into their hands. The number might have been much higher had not some British shipping companies there shown considerable foresight, or perhaps been warned by Commander Woolley's organisation. In April 1941, for instance, Butterfield & Swire transferred six of their largest ships to the Indian coast. They also transferred part of the barge fleet belonging to their subsidiary, the Tientsin Lighter Company, to Singapore in September.[32]

Sixteen

Japan's Build-up to the Attack on the USA

Japanese subversion in the United States-held territories of the Philippine and Hawaiian Islands was no less effective and pervading than in other parts of the north Pacific region.

If sheer weight of numbers of a Japanese resident population is anything to go by, then subversive infiltration in the Philippines was probably worse than anywhere else in Southeast Asia, for there were over 29,000 Japanese resident in the islands prior to the war compared with fewer than 6,000 in Malaya and 6,300 in the Netherlands East Indies.[1] In the Hawaiian Islands there was an even greater number of Japanese, estimated at 160,000 of whom 40,000 were considered aliens, that is Japanese not born there. Many of the Japanese-Americans born in those islands, and known as Nissei, were loyal to their new homeland.

As in other countries in Southeast Asia there was a widespread nationalist movement in the Philippines. This first arose when the islands were under Spanish domination, a domination which ended when the United States took the islands by force in 1898. That takeover did not stop the movement, for its members had no desire merely to exchange one foreign colonisation for another. That the Americans very soon laid out plans for the eventual independence of the country does not detract from the fact that for forty-eight years the Americans had a Far Eastern colony, something that many American citizens tend to forget. As one Filipino historian has written, 'the colonial period under the United States saw the Philippines make remarkable strides in health, education . . . infrastructures, transportation and communications . . . the dark side . . . was the development of an economy that was, and remains to date [1990], overly dependent on the United States'.[2] Adjusting that statement for the fact that no country of the old British Empire, whose abolition the Americans actively sought during World War Two, was still 'overly dependent' on Britain in 1990, it would apply equally well to Britain.

Japanese influence in Filipino affairs began early. The Japanese Black Dragon Society was in contact with nationalist movements there from the 1890s. Early in this century came the Aguinaldo uprisings in which the Japanese supplied arms to the insurgents. One of the leading rebels, General Ricartez, subsequently took up residence in Japan. In 1930 a political party called Sakdalista was created by Benigno Ramos in central Luzon which received some Japanese encouragement. The Sakdalistas rebelled in 1935 but were eventually suppressed, only to rise again in 1939 and 1940. When Japan occupied the Philippines in 1942 Ramos was to emerge as a prominent member of the puppet government.

The Japanese were aided in their subversive efforts by German military personnel sent into the Philippines under the aegis of the German embassy in Tokyo. These agents taught espionage methods to native spy rings. German connections with Fascist Spain brought more benefits for the Japanese, for in 1940 the Falangist leader, José del Castano, was sent from Madrid to Manila. Castano formed a Falangist movement which infiltrated the ranks of the Civil Administration to such an extent that, when the Japanese attacked, administration broke down completely. Not only that, the movement was able to undermine morale generally by spreading subversive rumours.

Japanese companies and individuals infiltrated the islands. A doctor named Hara, a long-time resident of Palawan, acted as guide to Japanese troops when they invaded that island. Ota Yasiyiro, director of the Ota Hemp Spinning Company with offices in several places in the islands, is known to have acted for several Japanese *kikans*.

One of the most successful infiltrators, successful in that he managed to ingratiate himself with many top-ranking Filipino business leaders and officers of the Filipino army, was a man called Souy Shiko. He arrived in Manila early in the 1930s and set up the Triangulo Photographic Studio. Souy was a major in the Imperial Japanese army and one of Japan's most important agents in the country; he was far from being the only one. The pre-war President of the Philippines, Manuel Quezon, is quoted as saying that he discovered that both his gardener and his masseur were Japanese army officers.[3]

From these sources and many others, photographs and descriptions of possible landing beaches were relayed to Tokyo, together with reports on American defence establishments, including Nichol airfield and America's largest air base in the Far East, Clark Field, fifty miles north of Manila.

At the head of the American defence organisations in Manila were Admiral Thomas C. Hart and Lieutenant-General Douglas MacArthur.

Admiral Hart was a tough, stern little man who had been C-in-C, US Fleet since 1939. In 1941 he was sixty-three years old and close to retirement.[4] He was not above taking decisions on his own cognisance and without reference to Washington. In September 1940, the month that brought a rise in world tension with the signing of the Tripartite Axis Pact between Germany, Italy and Japan, he received orders that no more navy dependants were being sent to the Far East and so took it upon himself to expand that order by directing that navy dependants already in the east should be sent home. It was a tough and unpopular decision but one that in the event decreased the number of US civilians that were to fall into Japanese hands.

At several meetings held during 1941 Hart was authorised by his government to discuss joint co-operation plans with British and Dutch naval representatives in the event of war. But he was not authorised to commit the United States to such co-operation; that was a political decision that could be made only in Washington. The meetings did however, lead to an exchange of Liaison Officers, Lieutenant-Commander Wisden RN joining Hart's staff in Manila, for example. They also led to exchanges of intelligence information.

In his biography of Admiral Hart, Professor James Leutze states that in the spring of 1941 Hart received 'a decoding device known as a Purple machine which, installed in the Malinta Tunnel on Corregidor, allowed his team of code specialists to read certain Japanese messages'.[5] The Purple machine, duplicating others at Washington and elsewhere, facilitated the breaking of Japanese *diplomatic* messages, the resulting product going under the code-name 'Magic', much as the British used the words 'Special' or 'Ultra'. Thus Hart, unlike his opposite number at Pearl Harbor, Admiral Kimmel, did not have to rely solely on Sigint information sent to him by the Navy Department's cryptologic organisation in Washington (known as Op-20-G). Two of these Purple machines were handed over to the British by the Americans in London in late 1940, and one of them was probably sent to Singapore.

Captain William Purnell, Hart's Chief of Staff, made several visits to Singapore during this period, taking with him intelligence specialists. During one such visit, says Leutze, American cryptanalysts were provided by the British with 'complete information on the make-up of the Japanese Navy's code system that carried the heaviest volume, its idiosyncrasies, etc., and the keys they had thus far broken down'.

That passage seems to imply that the British in 1941 had JN-25, the name given by the Allies to the main Japanese Navy code, at its fingertips, but that is certainly an exaggeration. The passage needs to be compared with the statement made by Commander Rudolph J. Fabian, USN, at the Hewitt Inquiry into Pearl Harbor in 1945. As a lieutenant, Fabian had been in charge of the naval cryptanalytic group on Corregidor Island, and in his sworn testimony stated that his unit had, in late 1941, been working on the Japanese naval system known as JN-25, 'which was the system containing the greatest volume of Japanese despatches. They were . . . only in the initial stages of breaking the code, and were exchanging values, both code and cypher recoveries', with the British in Singapore, 'but we had not yet developed either to the point where we could read enemy intercepts'. Fabian's summation fits in well with the facts of the British situation as shown earlier. It also fits in with information from three first-hand sources quoted by Bruce Lee in his book *Marching Orders*. One of these was the radioman and cryptographer Duane Whitlock who was also at Corregidor. He told Lee that nobody, including the British 'with whom we worked closely', was reading JN-25 concurrently before the start of the Japanese war.[6] (Whitlock later received the Bronze Star for his role in breaking Japanese codes at the time of the Battle of Midway.)

Be all that as it may, with what he obtained from the Purple machine Admiral Hart was as well endowed with Japanese raw intelligence as was Washington, and, much better endowed than the commanders at Pearl Harbor.

Acting on intelligence received during the last week of November 1941 indicating the prospect of war, Hart had explosives, magazines and stocks of aviation spirit moved. In conjunction with the British and Dutch he authorised reconnaissance flights by PBY seaplanes personally instructing the aircrews to avoid detection if possible when Japanese convoys were sighted, but at all costs to avoid giving provocation. His PBYs did sight large numbers of cargo ships and troop transports both at sea and in Indo-Chinese ports. At Camranh Bay, north of Saigon, there were over twenty such ships together with auxiliary craft, all protected by air patrols. Convinced that an amphibious operation was soon to be mounted somewhere, Hart reported so to Washington.

In Manila meanwhile, on 28th November, Major Souy called together the members of the militant underground organisation called the *Legion del Trapajo*, a group made up of Japanese residents and Filipino fellow-travellers. He told them that Japanese ships and planes were massing on the island of Formosa and that the invasion of the Philippines was imminent. As soon as the meeting broke up, one of the Filipino attendees, Lorenzo Alvarado, an undercover US intelligence agent, reported the news to his American superior. It passed up the American chain of command to find a final resting place on the desk of a senior army officer, but it never reached General MacArthur.

General Douglas MacArthur had retired from the US Army in 1935 and was then appointed Field Marshal in the Army of the Philippines as well as military adviser to the government there. He was recalled to the US Army in July 1941.

At the end of September 1941, as a backdrop to the Anglo-American co-operation talks, MacArthur asked Air Chief Marshal Brooke-Popham, British C-in-C, Far East, to send an officer to Manila to receive an update on American defence plans for the Philippines and for a general exchange of information. Commander A.N. Grey of Brooke-Popham's staff was selected. Perhaps it was an indication of the importance placed on this contact that Grey voyaged to Manila aboard the cruiser HMS *Danae*.

In MacArthur's personal Dakota aircraft Grey was given a conducted tour of the United States Army Airforce bases on Luzon island. He concluded that the Philippines' air defences were much further advanced than the British ones in Malaya, but also got the impression that there was no appreciation among American officers of 'the realities of war'. At Clark Field, the largest airbase, he saw Flying Fortresses lying undispersed, and discovered that few arrangements had been made either for their dispersion or for operations from dispersed sites. The aircraft were still as pristine silver as on the day they were received from the manufacturer, and none of the aerodrome buildings had been camouflaged. (In fact, Major-General Lewis Brereton, commander of US air forces in the Philippines, did disperse some of his aircraft before the Japanese attack came.)

Grey was granted a meeting with the great man himself on 16th October. General MacArthur said that he would not transmit important information either by letter or by cypher telegram to Singapore because of the 'possibility of leakage'. Rather, he proposed a monthly interchange of visits between the two staffs. He told Grey to tell Brooke-Popham that the Japanese Cabinet under Tojo was not the Cabinet to make a sudden strike. 'They will have to re-organise their Government before any serious move can be made.' The General went on:

> I have other reasons to believe that the Japanese are not in a position to go to war at present. They have recently received models and plans of the latest German aircraft and are now commencing to manufacture them: this will take some time. They have also commenced to re-organise their Army . . . Finally they have decided to standardise the calibre of their small arms.[7]

This information on the calibre of small arms was new to Grey, so he took the matter up with Colonel (later Major-General) Charles Willoughby, MacArthur's Chief of Intelligence. Willoughby said he knew nothing about it and asked where Grey had got the information. When told it was from MacArthur, Willoughby said, 'Out of his head probably, straight out of his head.'

Grey's remarks on MacArthur's views on the improbability of Japan embarking on war almost on the eve of them actually doing so, provides some support for the views of Professor Arthur Marder – and others – that the Americans as well as the British underrated the Japanese ability to do the unexpected. It also seems that MacArthur had undergone at least a partial *volte-face* since December of the previous year when, according to the American journalist Theodore White, MacArthur 'insisted war was coming', going on to warn of the excellence of the Japanese navy and that 'Japanese carrier-based aviation was superb'.[8]

Grey wrote his report aboard *Danae* on the way back to Singapore in November 1941, by which time, he said, 'It was clear that they [the pages of his report] were already so much waste paper and that war was almost inevitable'. However, Brooke-Popham scribbled a few notes on the report and later, when most confidential papers were destroyed, Grey extracted this document and subsequently handed it to Brooke-Popham in London. 'He was grateful to have it as indication of MacArthur's views as expressed immediately prior to the outbreak of war, and he passed the document over for retention by the Cabinet Office.'

On 1st December Admiral Hart had received secret personal instructions from President Roosevelt to form a 'Defensive Information Patrol' of ships to be sent out into the South China Sea and Gulf of Siam to report on Japanese activities. Roosevelt was specific in his instructions. No existing US Navy vessel was to be used, but instead, three small vessels were to be chartered and manned and armed to meet 'no more than minimum requirements to establish their identity as US men-of-war'. Roosevelt also gave precise instructions on the positions the vessels were to take up, positions which lay astride the route of any south-moving Japanese force.

Professor James Leutze has posed the question whether by this device the President was trying to provoke an incident that would provide justification for a US declaration of war should the Japanese bypass US territories and attack only the British.[9] Lieutenant (later Rear-Admiral) Kemp Tolley, USN, commander of the inter-island trading schooner *Lanikai*, which was one of the chartered vessels involved, is certain that was exactly what Roosevelt intended.[10] Leutze, however, points out that more objective witnesses than Tolley contend that the *Lanikai's* mission was merely another reconnaissance and had no conspiratorial intent; but then goes on to point out that there are certain difficulties with that explanation. Admiral Hart's air patrols were already supplying detailed information which was being relayed to Washington. Furthermore, it was highly unusual for Roosevelt himself to give operational orders in such detail.

On 3rd December Hart, who considered Roosevelt's plan ill-advised, issued secret but unwritten instructions based on the President's orders, to the commander of one of the other craft involved, the two-funnelled yacht *Isabel*. Lieutenant John Walker Payne, Jnr, was told to take up his patrol position and to tell his crew only that they were searching for a downed plane. If necessary *Isabel* was to fight, but under no circumstances was she to fall into Japanese hands. Several extra lifeboats were placed on board before she sailed. On the 5th December *Isabel* was actually spotted by Japanese off

Camranh Bay but she was not engaged, and that same evening Hart recalled the craft to Manila.

It is not surprising that Japan made no attempt to interfere with *Isabel*. Though her fleets were everywhere on the move, Japan's grand strategy called for simultaneous, or almost simultaneous, attacks of one sort or another to be made all over the Pacific; on Pearl Harbor and the outlying fortress islands of Wake and Guam, on Malaya, Thailand, the Philippines and Hong Kong, and, give or take a few hours, they were eminently successful in this. They were not about to intercept some tiny American craft which could do them no harm, when such an interception might set off more alarm bells than were already ringing in the region. Their initial strategy was built around surprise, though in their wildest dreams they could not have envisaged that, due to inertia, incompetence and errors, the Americans at Pearl Harbor were to be taken so completely unawares.

In the case of *Isabel* and the other vessels of the Defensive Information Patrol, Admiral Hart himself was always sure that Roosevelt intended to provoke the Japanese, and said that the craft of the patrol were 'bait tossed into the sea of Japanese sharks'. In an interview after the war he said he could prove his contention but added that he would not. Roosevelt's provocative actions throughout 1940 and 1941 against the Germans in the North Atlantic and in support of the British, lend credence to the views of both Admiral Hart and Kemp Tolley.

That Roosevelt might well have been looking for ways to provoke Japan seems to be borne out by a passage from the diary of his Secretary of War, Henry Stimson. For on 25th November 1941, only six days prior to the President instructing Hart to set up the patrol, Stimson wrote:

> the President . . . brought up entirely the relations with the Japanese. He brought up the event that we were likely to be attacked perhaps as soon as next Monday [1st December], for the Japanese are notorious for making an attack without warning, and the question was what we should do. The question was how we should maneuver them into the position of firing the first shot without allowing too much danger to ourselves. It was a difficult proposition. [Cordell] Hull [Secretary of State] laid out his general broad propositions on which the thing should be rested – the freedom of the seas.[11]

Cordell Hull himself wrote of that meeting of 25th November in his memoirs, but perhaps because he was more careful about what he committed to paper, made no mention of the subject of provoking the Japanese into firing the first shot. But he did report that day that relations with Japan were critical, and 'the Japanese might make the element of surprise a central point of their strategy'.[12]

The British Secret Intelligence Service agent in Manila was Gerald H. Wilkinson, manager of the local branch of Theo H. Davies & Company, and a sugar-broker. Theo H. Davies & Co. was a Pacific-wide British trading company with headquarters in Honolulu. Major Wilkinson had married one of the nine granddaughters of Theophilus Davies, the founder of the firm, and his wife and family were with him in Manila.

Colonel Willoughby, MacArthur's Chief of Intelligence, had a file on Wilkinson. Willoughby, not known for his regard for things British, was disparaging of British Intelligence in general saying its agents were useful adjuncts to British commercial interests, and of Wilkinson in particular, being 'convinced that his main purpose was to ingratiate himself into some official [American] recognition'.[13] Willoughby also took exception to the fact that Wilkinson had not registered himself as a foreign agent, something which he was required to do under American law in the Philippines. (One wonders how many Japanese agents had registered themselves under that system.)

Towards the end of November 1941, ten days or so before the Japanese struck, Wilkinson warned Colonel Joseph K. Evans, one of MacArthur's senior staff officers who was about to return to the United States, that he had received information from SIS in Singapore that hostilities between Japan and America were imminent and that large Japanese naval forces were concentrating in the vicinity of the Caroline and Marshall Islands, a curtain of islands that lay across the direct route between the Philippines and Hawaii. Apparently this information was acted upon to the extent that the army transport ship on which Colonel Evans was travelling, the *H.L. Scott*, took a circuitous route to Honolulu to avoid any contact with the Japanese. The attack on Pearl Harbor took place during that voyage.

On 3rd December Wilkinson sent the following urgent cypher cable to the British SIS representative in Honolulu, Harry Dawson, who was also the British Vice-consul in the Hawaiian Islands:

> We have received considerable intelligence confirming following developments in Indo-China.

A. 1. Accelerated Japanese preparation of airfields and railways.
2. Arrival since Nov. 10 of additional 100,000 repeat 100,000 troops and considerable quantities fighters, medium bombers, tanks and guns (75mm).

B. Estimate of specific quantities have already been telegraphed Washington Nov. 21 by American Intelligence here.

C. Our considered opinion concludes that Japan envisages early hostilities with Britain and U.S. Japan does not repeat not intend to attack Russia at present but will act in the South.

You may inform Chiefs of American Military and Naval Intelligence Honolulu.[14]

Lieutenant-Colonel Henry Clausen, who in 1944 began investigating the circumstances behind the Pearl Harbor attack on behalf of Henry L. Stimson, US Secretary of War, found a copy of Wilkinson's cable at Honolulu, and the distribution list showed that copies went to the American army and navy, and to FBI agent, Robert Shivers. Clausen concludes that the message could only have been based on British 'Special' sources – 'Ultra'.

That part of the message which emphasised that Japan did not intend to attack Russia was indeed based on 'Special', for on 30th November the British intercepted a message from Prime Minister Tojo to the Japanese ambassador in Berlin, which included reference to the Russian situation. 'It is in the South . . . that we lay most emphasis, and . . . we propose to refrain from deliberately taking positive action in the North.'[15] This message had been decrypted and circulated by the British on 2nd December and would have been available in Singapore by the following day, the date of Wilkinson's message. However, as the British were not reading Japanese military and naval codes on any great scale at that time, only diplomatic ones, it seems likely that the information about the Japanese massing of troops and aircraft in Indo-China came from non-Special sources, possibly from SIS agents operating in the French territory. One is left with the thought that this 'ground' information might have been that to which Major John Westall of British Naval Intelligence had been referring (see page 318), when he said that 'further action would have been taken on these reports, had it not been for the fact that up-to-date information from "these particular sources" was treated as being so secret that no action on it could be taken'. Could the intermingling in intelligence summaries of various types of intelligence, including those derived from intercepts, have resulted in no action being taken on the intelligence as a whole, because it came under the strict Ultra rules? If so, this indicates an administrative cock-up.

It might have been as an indirect result of Wilkinson's message that General Willoughby bitched about British intelligence officers mixing intelligence business with commercial interests. John E. Russell, British consul in Honolulu, saw the message to SIS agent Dawson, whose cover was vice-consul. Russell also happened to be the President of the company for which Wilkinson worked, Theo H. Davies & Co., and on 4th December he telephoned C.V. Bennett, the manager of the company's San Francisco office, instructing him to cancel all shipments to the Philippines, to try to stop any shipments already en route, and also to cancel sugar contracts that were in the pipe-line.

In *Pearl Harbor, Final Judgement*, Colonel Clausen comments that the contents of Wilkinson's message should have received greater attention than they did from the combined American staffs in Hawaii, who ignored the implicit warning it contained just as they ignored other warnings of a similar nature. As it was, the only person there who seemed to take the message to heart was John Russell who no doubt saved his company a great deal of money.

Early in February 1942 Gerald Wilkinson, who had become the SIS representative on MacArthur's staff, escaped from the Philippines aboard an American submarine. He had been sent on a mission to General Wavell based in the NEI. He later rejoined MacArthur's staff in Australia before spending the rest of the war in the so-called British Security Co-ordination in New York run by William Stephenson, or 'Intrepid' as he was code-named. Wilkinson had to leave his family behind in the Philippines. In September 1942 British Intelligence authorities in London were attempting to extricate Mrs Wilkinson and her family from Manila as part of the diplomatic exchange process. Her name was put forward by Peter Loxley of the British Foreign Office who, seconded to the Cabinet Office from 1940, acted in a liaison capacity between the intelligence services and the British government.[16]* The attempt was not successful.

* Peter Loxley (1905–45), described by Harold Nicolson, MP, as 'one of the lights of the FO', was killed in a plane crash on 2nd February 1945 off the island of Pantelleria. He was then Personal Secretary to Sir Alexander Cadogan of the Foreign Office, and was on his way to attend the Yalta Conference. Loxley's earlier involvement with the intelligence services serves to illustrate the close links the British Foreign Office has always had with these services.

The SOE had an agent in Manila whose main task seems to have been liaison work with the American secret agencies. He was Henry Cecil Whittall, a 'retired business man of modest means well known in all circles of the Manila community'. Whittall had previously worked for the Shell Oil Company. Another SOE operative in Manila at the time of the Japanese occupation was Miss Yvonne Pollock. She had been on the way from Shanghai to Singapore to take up an SOE appointment when, on the outbreak of war, her ship had been diverted to Manila. Though the British had no reason to think that the covert work of either of them was known to the Japanese, the SOE attempted to have both placed high on the official repatriation list.[17]

In the course of 1940 Admiral Yamamoto Isoroku's thoughts had settled on a possible carrier-based assault on the American fleet at Pearl Harbor. Such thoughts were not new; the prospect of such a daring scheme had occupied the minds of Japanese naval staff officers for some years. The achievement of British carrier-based planes against the Italian fleet at Taranto during the night of 11th–12th November 1940 merely raised the chances of tactical success and did not much affect Japanese strategic thinking. Professor Chapman has pointed out that, 'although Taranto stands out as a model for the Pearl Harbor attack plan, its standing is more as a tactical element and to some extent as a negative example rather than the strategic basis of the Japanese war campaign'.[18] The strategic model that impressed Yamamoto more than Italian losses at Taranto was the German *Blitzkrieg* that resulted in the conquering of most of Europe. The knowledge gained in early December 1940 from the *Automedon* documents, which indicated that Britain could not send a fleet to the East, also would have played a part in his planning. He could concentrate his mind on one main enemy, the US Pacific Fleet in its base at Pearl Harbor, and had no need to worry much about a possible British fleet affecting the equation.

On 7th January 1941 Yamamoto submitted a report to the Navy Minister entitled *Views on Preparations for War* which included references to a Pearl Harbor attack. He noted that success would not be easy to achieve, but might be possible if all concerned pressed ahead with selfless determination. Even while yet being unconvinced that a war with America and Britain was inevitable or desirable, he set about honing the plan for an attack on Pearl Harbor, a plan code-named 'Operation Z' after

Admiral Togo's signal pennant flown at the Battle of Tsushima in 1904.

Surprise lay at the core of Japanese strategy; there was to be no prior declaration of war. President Roosevelt was to call the day of the Pearl Harbor attack 'a date which will live in infamy', and spoke of 'an unprovoked and dastardly attack'. They were fine and emotive words and just what the Americans needed to hear at the time, but they took no heed of the fact that throughout history few nations embarking on war give notice of their intent, and Japan never had, something Roosevelt himself knew very well.

The keys to a successful operation against Pearl Harbor were twofold. The first was strict secrecy. It was a long voyage from Japan and if during it any warning came of the approach of a Japanese fleet, the American ships at Pearl Harbor would sail and the Japanese might themselves be at risk from land-based bombers. For their part the Americans knew of the dangers from a carrier-based air strike for they had been graphically illustrated during their own naval manoeuvres in 1932 and again five years later when, under the direction of that great proponent of naval air operations, Admiral Ernest J. King, the carrier USS *Saratoga* had evaded the guard fleet and successfully launched a mock bombing raid on Pearl Harbor.

The second key, and of equal importance to secrecy, was good intelligence and as elsewhere, the Japanese were more than adequately supplied in this direction.

Because of his naval training probably the most important Japanese spy in Hawaii was ex-Ensign Yoshikawa Takeo of Japanese Naval Intelligence. Forced to resign from the navy through ill health he had been personally chosen for this task by Admiral Yamamoto. Under the false name of Morimura Ito, he was based at the Japanese consul-general's office in Honolulu with the official title of vice-consul. From the time of his arrival in mid-1941 he watched and observed the comings and goings of the fleet and just about everything else that went on in the area. His reports were detailed almost to the point of absurdity, but they enabled Yamamoto and his staff to build up an impressive file on the base, a file that was still being updated on the very day of the attack.

One of Yoshikawa's favourite vantage points was the Shuncho-ro Japanese restaurant high up in the Alewa Hills overlooking Pearl Harbor. He also took trips in tourist planes and went round the harbour in pleasure boats, managing to lose himself easily among the large Japanese-American population of the islands. He never drew attention to himself by carrying either camera or notebook. He was known to American Intelligence who even had his phone tapped, but they discovered nothing that warranted his arrest.

Yoshikawa relayed his coded messages through Kita Nagao, the consul-general. 'The FBI and US Army Intelligence knew that Kita dabbled in spying, but they respected his diplomatic immunity and considered him harmless.'[19] Kita was also in receipt of information passed to him by one Otto Kuhn (or Kuehn), a one-time officer of the German navy. Kuhn had arrived in Honolulu in October 1936 from Yokohama. According to Eric Nave some of the Japanese diplomatic traffic intercepted and decrypted by FECB in Hong Kong during that year referred to an agent who was soon to arrive in Hawaii with his family, an agent code-named 'Jimmy'. Using the sailing information contained in the messages the British Secret Service were able to identify Kuhn as the man involved and they passed this information to the FBI who apparently did nothing about the matter until 1939 when the war in Europe began. Even then Kuhn was not kept under continuous surveillance.[20]

Kuhn set up a furniture business as a front. He had sufficient funds to buy houses on the west coast of Oahu Island including one called 'Kalama' which not only offered fine views over the ocean but was conspicuous to any observer on a craft out at sea who may have been waiting for visual signals. Kuhn's wife Friedel, and daughter Ruth, were regular users of Honolulu's beauty parlours where they picked up much useful gossip from service wives. Ruth's marriage to an American opened the door to the acquisition of further information.

Through Yoshikawa, the Japanese Fleet Commander knew that the carriers of the US Pacific Fleet were not at Pearl Harbor as he made his approach, which must have been a grave disappointment. The *Enterprise* task force was in fact some 200 miles west of Oahu and steering for Pearl Harbor, whilst the *Lexington* force was 400 miles southeast of Midway. Yoshikawa's last updating message to Tokyo was relayed to *Akagi*, the flagship of the Japanese task force – which was observing radio silence but could receive messages – less than two hours before the strike began, this being very much in keeping with the efficiency of the entire operation. The message gave the latest details on warship sailings and arrivals.

Churchill called the fall of Singapore Britain's 'worst disaster'. The end-result of Admiral Yamamoto's planning, aided by the excellent intelligence received from Yoshikawa and to a lesser extent Kuhn, resulted in Pearl Harbor becoming the United States' worst disaster. In an attack lasting only two hours, eighteen ships of the US Pacific Fleet, including seven battleships, were sunk or seriously damaged, 183 planes destroyed and 2,375 servicemen killed. Against that the Japanese lost only five midget submarines and 29 aircraft.

Yamamoto's use of surprise had presented Japan with a great victory, but it was not a decisive one, for as Michael Handel has pointed out, surprise is rarely decisive in war and never decisive in and of itself.[21] Had the initial Japanese air strikes been followed up with others to take out the workshop and docking facilities at the Naval Station and on Ford Island, and the oil tank farms in the vicinity, Pearl Harbor could not have been used as a naval base for many months. Due to the long distances involved, replenishing the oil stocks alone would have taken several weeks. That would almost certainly have made it impossible for the US Navy to conduct any major operations in the western Pacific into 1943.

Yamamoto made a grave error in his appreciation of the objectives of those first raids. In Annex No. 3 of his Secret Operation Order No. 1 to the task force which was issued on 1st November 1941, he ordered: 'Targets for attack are airfields; aircraft carriers; battleships, cruisers and other warships; merchant shipping; port facilities; and land installations, in that order.'[22] It would have been much better for him to have concentrated on the airfields and installations first and to have come back to attack the ships later. Furthermore, the capital ships destroyed were battleships, and the war in the Mediterranean had already shown that the aircraft carrier had taken the pre-eminent place in a battle fleet. So, Yamamoto also erred in not ordering his task force to seek out and destroy the two American carrier task forces that were at sea in the vicinity. That mistake was even more glaring in that it is clear from the pecking order of ships in his list of targets that he knew which ones were more important.

The decision not to make a follow-up raid may have been one result of exaggerated reports by returning Japanese pilots. These reports were not made to trained interrogation officers, as was the proven British system, but rendered cumbersomely on standard forms that passed through the flight commander and others before reaching the top and then radioed to Yamamoto. This system almost certainly led to overestimates of successes being heaped on top of other overestimates.[23]

Even as the fires aboard the damaged ships in the harbour raged, Yoshikawa was picked up by American security. As a member of the Japanese diplomatic staff he could only be interned. Later in the war he was released in an exchange of diplomatic personnel, and after repatriation continued to serve in Japanese Naval Intelligence.

The Kuhns were picked up too. They enjoyed no diplomatic immunity and Otto was tried by military court and sentenced to death. The sentence was then commuted to thirty years' imprisonment. Mother and daughter were interned until deported to Germany in 1946. Kuhn left Leavenworth, the American military penitentiary, in 1948 and was also deported to Germany. He died there in 1956.

Several Pearl Harbor conspiracy theories have arisen since the war based around whether Roosevelt and/or others knew in advance from Sigint sources about the attack, but deliberately concealed this information from the two American commanders in Hawaii, Admiral Husband Kimmel and General Walter Short, in order to lure Japan into making the attack and thus get America into the war on Britain's side. Lesser conspiracy theories concern alleged falsifying of documents and log-books by Washington top-brass to cover their own failings in not properly warning the local commanders. James Rusbridger in *Betrayal At Pearl Harbor* also roped in Churchill, arguing that the British leader had foreknowledge of the attack but failed to warn the Americans because of his, undoubted, desire to get the Americans into the war.

All the theories had one thing in common; they thrived on the fact that both the United States and the British governments had refused to release into the public domain many of the decrypts of Japanese messages that were germane to the matter. Only recently has this situation started to be rectified.

The United States' 'worst disaster' has, like Britain's at Singapore, spawned a host of books the most recent major one being Henry Clausen's *Pearl Harbor, Final Judgement*, first published in 1992, the year of its author's death. It had the benefit of being written by an officer uniquely placed to write on the subject, as the man appointed in 1944 by Secretary of War Stimson to investigate the affair on behalf of the US army. It is based on Clausen's 800-page report to Stimson, which report, in toto, had been presented in 1946 as evidence to the American Joint Committee investigating the Pearl Harbor attack. Because some of what he discovered had been ignored by even the more responsible of the authors who have written about Pearl Harbor, Clausen felt obliged to write a book himself.

Clausen presents a persuasive case, and his book might well be the definitive one on the débâcle of Pearl Harbor, the only reservation being that Clausen, a professional lawyer, was working to a brief prepared by the US army, and kept to that brief sometimes to the detriment of the US navy. He went about his task armed with a letter from Stimson which directed US army personnel to give him the fullest co-operation, and that included access to all records and documentation. Although he also interviewed many US navy men, being himself an army man, albeit on an hostilities only basis, he did not have quite the same authority over them. In 1944 the men he interviewed were scattered far and wide, and he travelled extensively to see them.

Clausen was also armed with copies of about forty decrypts of Japanese messages including some from British sources, decrypts that gave clear warning that the Japanese were preparing something. 'Armed with' is an apposite phrase, for so secret was this material – if it had fallen into enemy hands in 1944 it would have given away the Allied ability to read Japanese codes – that he carried the documents in a booby-trapped bag that would have blown it and him to smithereens had he been captured.

As some of the material he had was British he was permitted to interview some Britons and was enabled, in his own words, 'to review the signals files at Bletchley Park'.

On the evidence only of the British decrypts which Clausen carried with him, and which are reproduced in his book, let alone any of those produced from their own Sigint sources, it is clear that the Americans in Washington had enough solid evidence to know that the Japanese were going to create some mischief in that first week of December 1941. Clausen set about trying to unravel what Washington had done with the intelligence at hand, especially how much of it had been passed to Honolulu (which, unlike Manila in the Philippines, had no Purple machine facilities of its own) and when it had been passed, and what actions the commanders there had taken upon that intelligence.

President Roosevelt, with his Defence Information Patrol in the South China Sea, may well have been seeking to provoke Japan into firing the first shot, but Clausen deduced no evidence that even remotely suggested that Roosevelt or anyone else knew of a *specific* attack against Pearl Harbor, let alone deliberately let it happen as a means of bringing the United States into World War Two. Clausen showed that there was certainly inertia and some incompetence in certain Washington departments. He showed that the method of handling decrypts left much to be desired, and pointed out the fact that no one on the restricted list of recipients was allowed to retain copies long enough to give them full attention. He mentioned the rivalry that existed between the Army and Navy Departments, and that there was not at that time any central intelligence advisory body in existence to take on the function of risk assessment based on the intelligence material that was available. One of Clausen's conclusions was that army code-breakers did not take seriously enough some of the intelligence they received, and that resulted in a final warning being delayed for a vital eight hours.

Despite all this the fact remains that Washington did conclude that war was imminent. In the last two or three weeks before the Japanese onslaught, Washington supplied the Pearl Harbor commanders with enough information that should have put them thoroughly on their guard. The argument used later by Admiral Kimmel's Fleet Intelligence Officer, Captain (later Admiral) Edwin Layton, that Washington had denied him a Purple machine and therefore the capability to do his job properly, does not really hold water, for nothing learned from Purple indicated any specific attack on Pearl Harbor.[24]

Clausen found that there had been many liaison problems between the Army and Navy Intelligence arms in Hawaii. Not only that, in the army's case at least, the man in charge of intelligence, Colonel (later General) Kendall Fielder seems to have thought that his principal mission was to safeguard against internal subversion among the 160,000 persons of Japanese ancestry who resided in the Islands. Fielder may not have been to blame for this, for it is clear that his superior, General Short, also thought that sabotage and other subversion was the main threat. Short just did not believe that there was any chance of the Japanese attacking Pearl Harbor, and based all his actions, in the final days before the attack – perhaps lack of action is a better description – around that premise.

On 5th November 1941, and without informing Washington, General Short reversed the long-standing alert procedures, so that when he later informed Washington that he had gone to Number 1 Alert this merely meant that he had instituted internal defence procedures against sabotage, and not what it had originally indicated, a state of maximum defence readiness, which was now Number 3 Alert. His command was still in Number 1 Alert state at the time of the Japanese attack, with the aircraft at both Wheeler and Hickam airfields tightly concentrated so that they could be adequately guarded against saboteurs. Of course, this presented a wonderful target for the Japanese aircraft. It also meant that most ammunition, including that for the anti-aircraft guns, was still in guarded arsenals rather than being available for immediate use.

So Short's belief that the Japanese would not attack Pearl Harbor resulted in disaster for his forces. That, and his failure to liaise properly with the navy, to conduct proper reconnaissance and to make effective use of the radar installation available to him, led to his dismissal and disgrace.

On his part, Admiral Kimmel had taken to heart the results of an intelligence coup by his Chief of Intelligence, Captain Layton, who in 1940 had established by wireless traffic analysis that the Japanese had created bases, contrary to international agreement, in the mandated Caroline and Marshall Islands. These bases posed a flanking threat to the Philippines and to Singapore, and led Captain Layton to believe that it would be from these bases that any attacks would emanate. Kimmel took that on board, and it was this belief that led him in late November 1941 to order air reconnaissance of the mandated islands, and around Wake and Midway Islands, and completely to neglect air reconnaissance around Hawaii. Kimmel afterwards argued that he lacked sufficient planes to conduct a comprehensive reconnaissance, but that does not absolve him from blame for not having conducted any at all. He too was dismissed and disgraced.

At one point in his book Clausen quoted from one of John le Carré's novels, in which one of the spy-novelist's characters poses the question, 'Which is it going to be, that's all. The conspiracy or the fuck-up?' Clausen added, 'I can only say that what I was uncovering was not a conspiracy.'

The attack on Pearl Harbor brought about some significant changes in US military institutions. Unified commands were in, and divided commands like that at Hawaii, were out. From now on, either a general or an admiral was given command of all forces within a specified area. This did not prevent other problems arising along the geographical boundaries between commands, or prevent clashes of personality between some commanders; nor did it end long-held rivalries between the army and the navy. But it was a move in the right direction. Steps were also taken to centralise intelligence activities, the final result of that centralisation being the creation of the CIA, the Central Intelligence Agency, in May 1947.

It is of interest to compare the British and US states of readiness at the time of the Japanese onslaughts, remembering that both had virtually the same forewarnings from decrypts of Japanese diplomatic messages. For several days beforehand the British in Malaya had been deployed to meet an *expected* attack with one of their own (into Thailand). They were not too surprised when the Japanese attack began and not at all surprised that it came at Kota Bharu. Yet the British were not sufficiently equipped, especially with aircraft, to withstand it. The Americans at Pearl Harbor, on the other hand, were equipped in numbers of planes and anti-aircraft guns – of the latter only four of the thirty-one available engaged the enemy for the others had no ammunition near at hand – to have at least dealt fairly adequately with the attack, had they not been taken completely by surprise.

It is also interesting to note what other US army commanders did upon receiving essentially the same pre-warnings of possible Japanese action as General Short received at Hawaii. General DeWitt at the Presidio in San Francisco and General Andrews in the Panama Canal Zone, both much farther away from Japan than Pearl Harbor, replied to the effect that they were on the fullest possible alert – then artfully used the occasion to complain about the limited forces available to them. General MacArthur in the Philippines, and therefore much nearer the sharp end than any other US commander except Admiral Hart, replied that he had expanded his air reconnaissance. Admiral Hart, as we saw, also took preparatory steps.

Seventeen

Countdown to the Japanese Victory in Malaya

By the time they made their attacks all over the North Pacific in early December 1941, the Japanese had done their intelligence homework well. In no place, perhaps, was this more evident than in Malaya.

Lieutenant-General Sir Lewis Heath, Commander of the 3rd Indian Army Corps which was at the sharp end of all the initial battles in Malaya, was to write:

> It would not be out of place to refer here to the striking advantage which before and during the campaign accrued to the Japanese through the superior facilities they enjoyed for obtaining accurate and timely information regarding all our military activities and for ingratiating themselves with, and for obtaining timely assistance from local inhabitants.

Heath went on to contrast this with 'the crabbed work of our Secret Service and counter-Intelligence services'. General Heath was almost certainly not privy to 'Special Intelligence' sources.[1]

Between them, Japanese 'sleeper' and visiting agents and paid informants from among the local population, had enabled the Japanese to build up an accurate picture of the British order of battle. Over the years several British servicemen had been suborned into supplying the Japanese with additional valuable information but by far the most important of their coups among those British serving in Malaya was the case of Captain P.S.V. Heenan of the Indian army.

Patrick Heenan was a man of complex character. Very good on

the sports field and in other physical occupations, he had been academically poor at school. He had managed to get selected for the Indian army with its very strict officer selection policy, by a rather back-door route, but ever since his arrival in India early in 1935 he had been a misfit among his fellow officers who felt he carried a great chip on his shoulder. Unknown to them, and to the Indian army who would never have employed him had it been known, such were the mores of the time, that chip was there largely because he was illegitimate.

In the Indian army he was moved around. His original regiment, the 2/16th Punjab, got rid of him and sent him to the Royal Indian Army Service Corps until, having blotted his copy-book with them, he was sent back. Although Heenan acquitted himself bravely during a campaign on the Northwest Frontier he could not shake off his great unpopularity, indeed he made little attempt to do so. There must have been a collective sigh of relief in the regiment when in 1938–39 he went off on long leave and spent six months in Japan.[2]

Back with the regiment but still causing problems, a golden opportunity to get rid of him arose when in 1940 a sister regiment, the 3/16th Punjabs, about to sail for Malaya, began crying out for officers. They, like all the other regiments of the Indian army which was being rapidly expanded, had been 'milked' of officers for the new battalions being formed. The opportunity not only to transfer Heenan, but to get him well away from India, was too good to miss, and the CO of the 2/16th obligingly supplied his 3/16th counterpart, Lieutenant-Colonel Frank Moore, with an officer of five years' seniority who, on the face of it, was quite an acquisition. Heenan duly arrived at Penang in Malaya with the 3/16th in October 1940. Coincidentally, the 2/16th was also to sail for Malaya a few months later. It was not long before Colonel Moore realised that he had been imposed upon. According to his namesake Captain D.J.R. Moore, an officer on the staff of 11th Indian Division in Malaya, Colonel Moore one day rang up in a fury and ordered that Heenan be posted away from the battalion immediately, saying he was unsuitable.[3] The next available posting came in March 1941; it was for an officer to go to Singapore to be trained as an Air Intelligence Liaison Officer (AILO). Heenan was duly selected for it; perhaps a better word would be elected. As it is almost certain that he had been suborned by Japanese secret agents during his leave in Japan, he could scarcely have been placed in a better position from their point of view. Furthermore, a later investigation threw up the fact that during his training time in Singapore he had several times there frequented Japanese social and sports clubs.

Three months later he returned to northwest Malaya as a trained AILO with the grade GSO3, as part of 300 Air Intelligence Liaison Section. Thereafter at various times Heenan was attached to one or another of the three RAF aerodromes – Alor Star, Sungei Patani, and Butterworth – in the northwest, one of his duties being to act as observer during military/air exercises.

A fellow AILO was another officer of the Indian army, Captain Harry Landray, Royal Garhwal Rifles. The exact sequence of events is unknown, but fairly soon Landray became suspicious of Heenan's actions. Heenan is known to have made several unauthorised visits to places close to the Thai border where he met someone who looked like a 'Dutchman', according to Private Fred Cox, the soldier who drove him there. On other visits Heenan took photographs of salient points along some of the many trails that crossed the mainly unmarked frontier. On two occasions he was known to have gained unauthorised access, on some pretext or other, to the Station Commander's safe at Alor Star airfield.

A Japanese cypher message intercepted and read by the British on 10th August 1941, may have referred to Heenan. The message was summarised in Admiralty Special Intelligence Summary No. 320, of 14th August: 'The Thai Consul-General at Penang informed Bangkok that a British Army Captain had told him on 10th August that British advance into South Thailand was imminent. This advance would be for defensive purposes only.' A note to that dycrypt stated, 'The identity of the British captain is unknown to the War Office'.[4]

Because of his position Heenan had legitimate access to the RAF recognition signals which were changed daily. He is known to have taken more than a passing interest in the RAF's secret SCI (Smoke Curtain Installation) equipment. The ostensible use for the equipment was to lay smoke screens from the air but, with a change of nozzle, it could be used to spread poison gas, stocks of which were held by both the RAF and the army in Malaya.[5]

Landray, obviously worried about the effect this might all have on the honour of the Indian army if his suspicions proved correct, telephoned the CO of his mother-regiment which at that time was stationed at Kuantan on Malaya's east coast, and asked for advice. This was in about October 1941, two months before the Japanese attack. He was told by Lieutenant-Colonel Guy Hartigan to report the matter to

Major James France, CO of the Liaison Section, 'especially if Heenan was behaving in a manner likely to be potentially dangerous'. Landray made his report shortly before he was killed when the private plane he was piloting crashed.

It is not known why Major France, or Captain Landray himself, did not bring the matter immediately to the attention of higher authority. There are several possible reasons. Britain was not yet at war in the Far East, and even at this late hour, many people much more senior than Major France, were still convinced that Japan would not attack. Unlike Heenan who was a regular officer, albeit of the Indian army, France was not a regular but a territorial officer. Furthermore, at this stage, there was no definite proof.

It is unlikely that France kept his suspicions entirely to himself. He must have discussed some of them with Wing Commander Forbes who knew about Heenan's visits to the Air Station safe. And who better to discuss it further with than the colonel who commanded the Indian troops that guarded the airfields? Especially as the officer concerned was Lieutenant-Colonel H.E. Tyrell, himself originally of the 2/16th Punjabis and who had known Heenan since 1935. If Tyrell was indeed approached for advice, one can imagine the news that a fellow officer of the regiment might be a spy would be almost too awful to bear. Pride in the regiment was everything, and Tyrell would have urged France to take more time to be sure the suspicions were justified.

Whatever the circumstance behind his decision, France waited for some firm evidence. Unfortunately that was not forthcoming until after the Japanese attacked.

In 1941 Malaya possessed the finest network of roads in Southeast Asia, but they were mostly on the west side of the country and in those days there was no road in northern Malaya linking the east and west coasts. Down the west coast too ran the Malayan railway, linking Singapore with Singora in Thailand. Another rail link ran northwards through central Malaya from Gemas, but it did not cross the frontier and terminated at Kota Bharu, the most northerly town on Malaya's eastern seaboard. To attack successfully down the Malay peninsula the Japanese needed to land troops in Thailand within striking distance of the British airfields that guarded the northern end of the road system. Once they had taken those airfields, the road to the south would be open to them.

The British also had plans for Thailand. In their case this was a pre-emptive strike into the country in order to take up positions at Singora and Patani on the east coast of Thailand where it was – correctly – forecast the Japanese would land. The British plan was code-named Operation Matador, but it was never implemented. Most of the British intelligence effort in the north had been centred around Matador, and the British forces stationed there had spent several months preparing and deploying for the strike and for precious little else. Thus the belated changeover, from the Matador deployment to that required for static defence created the circumstances for the first major defeat for the British in northern Malaya, the one that presaged all that followed.

Militarily, Matador made good sense, providing the troops could reach the landing beaches in time to dig in and be in position to annihilate the enemy as he landed. To accomplish this, about sixty hours would be needed after the troops crossed the frontier, that time including an allowance made for mopping up any Thai resistance met with on the way. This was approximately the same time the Japanese troopships needed to reach the Thai beaches from their bases in southern Indo-China.

It all looked good on paper, but the plan suffered from two significant drawbacks, one military, the other political. On the military side, Malaya Command did not have sufficient forces to guarantee success, given that a number of battalions had to be left in the south to protect not only Singapore and that part of Malaya closest to it, but also to protect strategic places on the east coast of Malaya.

The political drawback was that the plan entailed attacking a neutral country and the British were well aware of how this would look to the world in general and to the United States in particular. The United States' agreement to such a pre-emptive strike must therefore be sought.

The preparations for Operation Matador involved sending British officers into southern Thailand on reconnaissance and intelligence trips. Some of these trips came about in a rather strange way. In mid-1941 Sir Josiah Crosby, Britain's envoy, found occasion to complain to the Thai Prime Minister about the number of Japanese agents operating in the southern part of Thailand. He was told there was nothing to be done about it, but that if Britain should choose to do likewise, the Thais would turn a blind eye. As a result, and over a period of months, some thirty or so British officers were sent into Thailand in mufti and with false passports, which described them variously as accountants, lawyers, journalists and rubber traders. A measure of the lack of seriousness that some of these officers placed on these junkets is that the passport of one described its holder as a comedian, and of another, as an acrobat. One officer, Major S.P. Fearon of the 5/14th Punjabis, actually recorded that to him the episode was something of a lark.

Several of these officers reported meeting Japanese 'businessmen' on jungle paths, apparently doing the same thing for their army. One officer sent in late, almost too late, was Captain D.J.R. Moore, of 11th Indian Division Staff. Supplied with a radio, he was told that his recall signal would be the playing of 'Keep the Home Fires Burning' over the Malayan Broadcasting System. The signal was made, but only the tune and not the words, and Moore was tone deaf. He only just managed to escape the advancing columns of the Japanese army.

The British army and the Federation of Malaya Police had earlier set up joint patrols and a series of control stations along the Malayan border with Thailand, a border that runs for almost its entire length through thick jungle. Parts of the border area, especially that in the centre around the small towns of Grik and Kroh, were honeycombed with jungle tracks, making it virtually impossible to control passage across it. This had been brought home to Assistant Superintendent Harvey Ryves when, in June 1940, at the time Italy entered the war, he had been stationed on the border on intelligence work under cover of being an immigration officer. Several Italian escapees were known to have successfully made it across the border into neutral Thailand.[6]

This worked both ways, for members of the British army's Frontier Patrol were also able to cross over the border and bring back intelligence for the Matador planners. Some of the personnel in the patrol were officers of the Government Forestry Service on secondment, and others were volunteer planters, well versed in junglecraft. One of the former was Eric Robinson who, after managing to escape from Singapore in February 1942, spent the rest of the war in an intelligence capacity in New Delhi.[7]

British Admiralty summaries of 'Special' intelligence, which included reports derived from intercepting and reading Japanese diplomatic and consular messages, gave many clear indications of Japan's intentions over the months that preceded the opening of the Far East war. These summaries were sent out over the signature of Admiral Godfrey, Director of Naval Intelligence in London. Some of the messages summarised were obviously intercepts made by FECB, whilst others, for example those between the Japanese ambassador in Berlin and the Foreign Office in Tokyo, must have been intercepted by one or another of the UK based 'Y' stations that relayed information to Bletchley Park. Messages in the latter category were endorsed in the summaries, 'Far East Authorities informed'.*

One summary, No. 380 dated 28 October 1941, stated that:

> Japanese Consul-General, Singapore, has been instructed to send fishermen with a knowledge of surf conditions on the East Coast of Malaya, to Bangkok. He has also been instructed to report on training, air tactics organisation of the RAF in Malaya.[8]

Perhaps more ominous was a message No. 390 dated 7th November 1941: 'The [Japanese] Consul-General, Singapore has been informed that the *Asama Maru* leaving Singapore on 16th November, would be the last Japanese ship to call there.' Again, in No. 395 dated 11th November: 'Foreign Minister Tokyo told the Japanese Consul-General, Singapore to send TAHIRA back to Japan via Bangkok without relief.' This was noted as having come 'from COIS Singapore, 9th November', COIS being the head of FECB. Admiral Godfrey appended three notes to that particular summary:

> i. TAHIRA's official position is Counsellor in the office of the Japanese Consul-General.
> ii. He is almost certainly a military officer, as he has been receiving messages from the Vice Chief of the General Staff and recently, on request, rendered a report on the RAF in Malaya.
> iii. Grounds for preventing his departure are being sought by Singapore SB.

* Bletchley Park had its own 'Y' Station in 1938 which was codenamed Station X. Very soon it was decided that German radio tracking devices would be able to pinpoint it and, as even then Bletchley was becoming an important code-breaking centre, it was decided to move the station seven miles away to Whaddon Hall. As war approached other listening stations connected with Bletchley by direct teleprinter lines were established in other parts of Britain.

What is interesting is that Tahira's sending of the RAF information was not being used as reason for detaining him, for to have done so would have given away the fact that Japanese messages were being read.

Summary No. 400 of 14th November contained the following unattributed précis, important in that it indicated a possible lessening of tension with Russia over on Japan's western flank, a prerequisite for a safe move south for Japan: 'Japan and Russia in Far East were doing their best to prevent trouble and it might be possible to move Japanese troops, if necessary, from Manchuria to the South.'

Summary No. 404 of 16th November reported:

> Jap. Government has instructed their Ambassador at Vichy to press the Vichy Government to agree to a modification of the original NISHIMURA-MARTIN agreement in order that Japanese troops may operate on the south side of the Red River [in Indo-China].

Godfrey's comment on this was: 'The War Office view is that this increases the evidence in support of a movement against Thailand. Other recent reports tend to strengthen the argument in favour of such a movement'.

Summary No. 415 of 21st November:

> The Foreign Minister, Tokyo, in a circular message . . . stated . . . The Soviet, on the assumption that Japan is not going to attack them, have moved troops westward . . . Tension on Manchukuo-Soviet border has eased . . . In spite of French passive resistance, Japan's grip on Indo-China is becoming firmer . . .

Under the heading 'Japanese Fifth-Column organisation in Siam and Malaya', that particular summary went on:

> On the 8th November the Japanese Consul-General at Singapore, in reply to the Foreign Minister, Tokyo's instructions, suggests that the following organisation be put in force.
>
> The Young Men's Malayan League to be given the short title of KAME. This organisation, which appears to be a Fifth-Column organisation, to be divided into Thailand and Malayan Groups. Their function to be to act as guides for Japanese troops at landing places, spreading of propaganda, reporting military movements in unoccupied territory, surveillance of the populus [*sic*] after occupation, and to form the nucleus of Malaya's

administration after the war. The Group in Thailand to be armed, but the Malayan Group to operate unarmed.

Special Intelligence Summary No. 429, of the 25th November, referred to a message from the Minister of Foreign Affairs, Tokyo, to the Japanese Chargé d'Affaires, London, sent on 19th November giving certain code words that were to be used over the Japanese Overseas Broadcasting Service in the form of a weather report, to indicate that diplomatic relations were about to be severed. It was ordered that, on receipt of this message, all confidential books were to be destroyed. This message and the subsequent relay of the code words – indications of Japanese intentions that could scarcely be more plain – and the timing of their interception and reading by the Allies were to become central issues in the 'conspiracy theories' later raised to explain the United States' unpreparedness at the time of the attack on Pearl Harbor.

The code words, or rather phrases, to be used formed the now famous 'Winds messages' designed to indicate with which of Japan's major possible antagonists relations were about to be severed:

(i) With America, the words 'HIGASHI NO KAZE AME'
(Easterly wind, rain.)
(ii) With Soviet, the words 'KITA NO KAZE KUMORI'
(Northerly wind, cloudy.)
(iii) With Britain, including the invasion of Thailand, the words 'NISHI NO KAZE HARE'
(Westerley wind, fine)

The British Sigint summary of 2nd December included an intercepted message of 30th November from Tokyo to the Japanese ambassador in Berlin, which stated that the breakdown of the Japanese–American negotiations which had been going on in Washington for some months, 'is inevitable and Japan must take a serious decision'. The ambassador was to inform Hitler and Ribbentrop that 'armed collision with British and Americans is feared', and that 'this may happen sooner than expected'.

A summary issued on 3rd December stated that the cypher machine in the Japanese embassy in London had been destroyed as a result of instructions received from Tokyo two days earlier.

Examination of the Japanese messages, as given in these Admiralty summaries, shows that throughout 1941, and indeed up to January 1942, they contained mostly what were obviously intercepts of diplomatic and consular messages. Very few can be attributed to the interception of Japanese naval messages, which supports the case that Britain, though intercepting Japanese naval signals, was not able regularly to read them during 1941. Between 3rd August and 8th December 1941, a period in which there was intense activity going on in the Japanese navy as it reorganised itself for war, the summaries show only four signals that refer specifically to naval matters, and the information in three of these could have come from non-Sigint sources. As these signals appeared in summaries of Specials and were classified 'A1', the highest reliability rating given to intelligence information, it may be that information from non-Sigint sources, when confirmed by direction-finding and/or radio finger-printing, was thus converted into A1 graded Special intelligence. After February 1942, when it is reported that the Americans and British made their big-breakthrough with the Japanese naval codes and were able to read them fairly regularly, the number of naval messages in the summaries rises sharply.

These Admiralty summaries are not the only British source of 'Specials' now available to researchers. Recently the actual files of selected Specials which daily, sometimes twice a day, landed on Mr Churchill's desk have been made available at the Public Record Office at Kew. All intercepted and decrypted messages, whether from German, Italian or Japanese sources, were numbered consecutively, and originally all the Churchill files had cover sheets listing their contents by these numbers. It is clear from this methodology that some of the files are now no longer complete. Furthermore, a few cover sheets are noted as 'missing' which makes it impossible to check whether the contents of those files are still in the original state. Neither on the covers, nor inside the files, is there any indication of who did the 'weeding' of the documents or when it took place.[9]

The decrypts in the Churchill files include many that appear in the Admiralty summaries, but there are others that do not. As in the summaries, those relating to the Far East give clear indications of Japanese intentions. Only three of these will be discussed here, chosen because they reached Churchill's desk on 6th December 1941, the last date on which Operation Matador could have been implemented with any chance of success, although, of course, Churchill would not have known the exact timing of the coming Japanese onslaught.

The first message, numbered 849 by the Japanese and 098583 by the British, was sent by the Japanese ambassador in Bangkok, to the Foreign Ministry in Tokyo. It was sent, and intercepted, on 25th November; the delay in laying a copy of it before Churchill was possibly caused by decyphering difficulties.

The message concerned the necessity of defining the relationship between the rights of the Thais and the 'exercise of belligerent rights' by Japan, in the event of a southward advance that would pass through that country as a result of a Japanese attack on Malaya and Burma. Such an operation must, advised the ambassador, be carried out in such a way as to draw Thailand into the Japanese camp. He referred to talks which he had held some time earlier with Thai Prime Minister Pibul 'with this idea at the back of my mind', which he had recorded in a previous message to Tokyo. (That too, had been intercepted by the British – noted as 'our 098276' – but no copy has been found by this author.) It went on to suggest that in order to keep the Thais happy any encroachment on their territory should be temporary and Thai independence should be respected. Furthermore, that if Thailand should co-operate actively with the Japanese, guarantees should be given about the recovery of territory the Thais had lost over the years to the French in Indo-China, and to the British in Malaya and Burma.

In that same Churchill file was another decrypt, numbered 098603, and dated as having been sent from Tokyo on 2nd December, ordering the Japanese embassy in London to burn all their codes, and to telegraph the one word HARUNA when it had been done, and 'taking all possible care not to arouse outside suspicions, all secret documents to be treated in the same way'. The British decryptors noted at the end of this message, 'HARUNA sent 3rd December'.

British decrypt No. 098607 of a message dated 30th November from the Japanese Ambassador, Bangkok, to the consul-general, Singapore, was also in the file. It was annotated by the decryptors 'see our Nos. 098468 and 098490' (neither of which has been located by this author). It contained what virtually amounted to an immediate order to action stations for *Kame* members.

1. For KAIDE from OKAMOTO.

The instructions given below are to be passed by you to representatives of KAME organisation as soon as possible. After steps have been taken to see that preparedness for the activities are immediately completed,

WATANABE, ISHIKAWA and KUROIWA will leave for Bangkok or South Thailand by the quickest route accompanied by several reliable young Japanese. They should telegraph their proposed actions. We expect them to arrive here within the next ten days.

Besides the actions mentioned in your No. 690 [British note: our No. 097924] the KAME organisation is to undertake:

(a) the inciting of native soldiers to desert; the severance of lines of communications; the execution of preparatory measures for destroying Great Britain's [group corrupt] (mainly their important transport routes), and subversive activities designed to terrorise the British people.

(b) Attention is to be given to the immediate extension of the range of the KAME organisations activities in Kota Bharu and various important points in eastern Malaya . . . individuals to serve as guides and undertake intelligence work. Powerful points d'appui for these activities to be established at Alor Star, Kota Bharu, and Kuala Lumpur.

(c) The main objects of the movement are to stir up anti-British feeling and to undertake subversive propaganda on the outbreak of war. After the actual fighting begins, stress is to be laid on [corrupt group] plots.

(d) As regards liaison, the sign mentioned in my [Tokyo's] No. 365 [not read] is to be exhibited. Connection should be quickly established with the Japanese officer in command and his instructions followed.

(e) Guarantees for the future. When the time for co-operation arrives, the members of KAME organisation will be given special treatment. Their principles will be respected and every assistance will be given to carrying these into practice [group corrupt:?thereby?] raising the status of the Malayan peoples both socially and politically.

(f) The despatch of the Malayans referred to in my No. 36 (our No. 098468) [not found by author] is to be made at once.

2. For UCHIBOR, acting Consul-General. Please provide the representatives of the KAME organisation with any funds they may require to have in their possession.*

The messages transcribed or paraphrased above, and others in the files, could scarcely have provided Churchill and the British Chiefs of Staff, let alone the commanders in Malaya, a clearer indication of Japanese intent. Yet, in those critical weeks immediately preceding the Japanese attack Whitehall continued to hedge over granting Brooke-Popham the permission he sought to implement Operation

* Two of the persons mentioned in this message, Kaide and Ishikawa, had been responsible for recruiting the Malay nationalist Ibrahim bin Haji Ya'acob to the ranks of *Kame*.

Matador. Lord Halifax, the British ambassador in Washington, raised the question of the strike into Thailand with American Secretary of State Cordell Hull, on 30th November. On 1st December, Hull discussed the matter with Roosevelt, who agreed to meet with Halifax about it.[10] However it was not until four days later that Brooke-Popham was told by the British Chiefs of Staff that American support had been vouchsafed under certain conditions. He could now, from 5th December, order Matador himself without further reference to Whitehall should the Japanese violate any part of Thailand, or if there was good information that a Japanese expedition was actually advancing on that part of Thailand immediately adjacent to Malaya.

The British Official Historians of the Malayan Campaign, commenting on this eleventh-hour permission, noted that Brooke-Popham's instructions were worded in such a way that the chances of Matador succeeding were greatly reduced, for it would be too late to take action by the time he could be *certain* that a Japanese expedition was making for Thailand. 'This', they said, 'was to have serious consequences.' That was not the half of it. Those historians writing in 1957 – when any mention of 'Special Intelligence' was still not permitted – did not say that the *good information* Brooke-Popham must have, had to come from sources other than Special, because he, like all other British commanders, was forbidden to act on information received from that source *alone* for fear of compromising it. Brooke-Popham had to be certain from 'ground' sources of intelligence, or from air reconnaissance, that the Japanese were going to land in Thailand, but how could he be certain until the Japanese were actually landing on the beaches? Brooke-Popham's decision-making processes, which anyway were not very good at that late stage in his career, were made even more difficult by the content of a message to Tokyo from the Japanese Minister in Bangkok intercepted by the British on 29th November, which said that pro-Japanese elements in the Thai Cabinet hoped that Britain could be made to strike the first blow at Thailand in order that Japan could intervene 'legitimately'. As a result of this, any Japanese convoy sighted off the coasts of Malaya or Thailand could merely be part of a ruse to get Britain to act first. From whichever way the situation was seen, Brooke-Popham was on a hiding to nothing.

On top of all that, on 6th December he received an impassioned, almost hysterically phrased secret message from Sir Josiah Crosby in

Thailand, one that Brooke-Popham stated in his despatch he could not ignore, urging him not to be the first to attack Thailand.

Major J.C. Westall, the SO (I) Singapore, is a source not to be lightly regarded. Most of his career in the Royal Marines was in intelligence. Having arrived in Singapore in 1939, his continuity of office was longer than that of almost anyone else engaged in intelligence there. He remained in Singapore almost to the end for 'fear that if he had joined the prevalent exodus yet another brick would have been taken from that crumbling structure, Malayan morale'. Escaping from the Island in the final hours before it fell, he later held intelligence appointments in Ceylon and India and after that in London for the remainder of the war. By 1952 he was a Lieutenant-General and Commandant-General of the Royal Marines. He was promoted to full general and knighted in 1954.[11]

In a report made in India on 14th May 1942, Westall said that up until the last moment it was the considered opinion of the Malayan High Command that a landing on the east coast of Malaya was not possible during the monsoon, even though he and a fellow member of the intelligence staff had travelled down that coast during the monsoon and had reported that there would be no difficulty in landing on six days out of ten. It is not known whether this was the same traverse of the coast that Major Vinden made (see pp. 143–145), but Westall also pointed out that a warning to the same effect had been given earlier by Colonel Hayley Bell.

One phrase in Westall's report adds a new dimension to the problem confronting Brooke-Popham. He said:

> It is worthwhile confirming that warning was received of the departure of the convoy [sent to attack Malaya and Thailand] and of the actual point of attack. I am convinced that further action would have been taken on these reports if it were not for the fact that up to that date information from these particular sources was, quite incorrectly, treated as being so secret that no action could be contemplated on receipt of it.[12]

Two possible interpretations can be placed on this statement. The less likely of them is that Westall, who under the rules would not have been a recipient of 'Special' but who had been in intelligence in Singapore long enough to have gained some inkling of what was going on behind the scenes, thought that any information received should have been acted upon no matter what its source. That does not sound much like the opinion of a good intelligence officer. It seems more likely that Westall was saying that firm information was received from non-Special sources, but that it was placed under the 'Special' umbrella in error. If that is so, the mistake was a serious one, and as there was a Special Liaison Unit in Singapore involved in all matters of 'Special' the question arises, did the error occur with them?

Throughout the two months preceding the Japanese attacks on Pearl Harbor and Malaya, ground intelligence reports, including one dated 17th October from Captain D.N.C. Tufnell, the British Naval Attaché in Tokyo, and from 'Y' sources, had enabled the British to record, in the words of Captain A. Hillgarth and R.T. Barrett, the two men who compiled the unfinished *History of the Far East and Pacific War* in the Admiralty files in the British Public Record Office, that:

> NID [Naval Intelligence Department] knew all about the Japanese naval mobilisation, had a fair idea of the fleet's composition, organisation and movements, and were aware of the formation of five divisions of aircraft carriers and of a special task force.
>
> We did not know its purpose, against Pearl Harbor, but we had penetrated Japan's security screen by careful collation of every scrap of material from all sources, sufficiently to know that Japan was up to mischief, and that from the beginning of December a state of alert was necessary in all British and American possessions.[13]

However, Hillgarth's first paragraph does not fit squarely with a report made by Lieutenant-Commander E.G.P. Sandwith, an officer brought from retirement and sent to FECB in August 1941 to join that part of 'Y' dealing with D/F bearings. He was not impressed with either the quantity or the quality of the work the D/F operators were doing. The operators were, he said, poorly trained and lacked proper supervision. 'Call signs would be brought up on the same bearing for ten days at a time, though ships using the signs were known to have moved several hundred miles.' He did not explain how it was known that the ships had moved. He went on to say that the C-in-C's daily inspection of the plotted positions of the ships, was therefore misleading. He reported that the relations between the 'Y' Office and the rest of FECB were not good, and that in consequence the accuracy of the intelligence passed to the C-in-C suffered.

In their *History*, Hillgarth and Barrett quote a range of naval reports from the period October to early December 1941, received from both ground and 'Y' sources. The reports showed what at best can be described as a confused and generalised picture, and one which confirms that the British, and the Americans with whom information was being exchanged, could not then have been regularly reading intercepted Japanese naval messages. There were more than enough indications that the Japanese navy was up to something to put the whole region on alert, but no precise information about anything in particular. This tends to support Commander Sandwith's low opinion of the standard of D/F fixing at FECB at that critical time.

On 20th November W/T and Special traffic indicated that the Japanese had organised their aircraft carriers into five squadrons, a fact later proved to be correct, and that one of the ships in the 5th Squadron was a converted liner, which was wrong. A graph kept by FECB based on information supplied by Reporting Officers, showed that the ships of the Japanese merchant fleet were steadily returning to home waters, a sure sign of coming hostilities, and that most would be back by the first week in December. Towards the end of November FECB advised Admiral Layton's staff that reconnaissance by air and submarine should be undertaken to watch for a force approaching Malaya. On 28th November a message from the US Navy Department warned that an aggressive Japanese move directed at the Philippines, Malaya, Thailand, or possibly Borneo, could be expected within days. On the following day, with the few suitable aircraft available for the purpose, systematic American, British and Dutch air reconnaissance was put in hand over the South China Sea. Two Dutch submarines left Singapore on 6th December to patrol off the southern coast of Indo-China.

Heavy wireless traffic and other forms of intelligence indicated that naval ships were on the move from Japan to Hainan Island. Others, including troop transports, were leaving Shanghai for the south. Yet more transports were concentrating on Saigon and Haiphong. On 1st December, A1 graded intelligence caused the NID in London to report that a Special Task Force was estimated 'to have been organised to carry out an operation in the South. Indications are an attack on Siam, including possibly a landing on the Kra Isthmus.'

In the middle of all this activity, at 0000 hours on 1st December, it was noted that, 'all Japanese service radio calls for units afloat were changed'.

On 3rd December the Americans at Manila reported Japanese naval vessels arriving at Takao (now Kaohsiung) on the southern tip of Taiwan. 'The [U.S.] Navy Department safely diagnoses that this assembly of units in the Takao area is beginning to indicate a concentration in this area.'

During all this confusion, made worse by deliberate deception signals, and with all pointers indicating a southward thrust, around thirty ships of the Japanese navy began slipping out of port, to head north to converge on a planned assembly point at Tankan Bay in the Kurile islands. These movements were carried out under the strictest radio silence. Amongst the ships forming this Pearl Harbor Attack Force were three two-carrier squadrons. The task force sailed from Tankan Bay on 26th November and, still maintaining radio silence and taking a northerly route well clear of all shipping lanes, made for the Hawaiian Islands.

On 4th December, in a message which for some unexplained reason was not received in London until 0049 hours on 8th December, FECB reported that the Japanese 5th Aircraft-Carrier Squadron had 'recently arrived at Saipan' which is in the Mariana Islands. In fact on 4th December the two carriers forming the 5th Squadron, the *Zuikaku* and *Shokaku*, were with the Pearl Harbor Attack Force which at that time was 800 miles to the north of their intended target and some 3,000 miles east of Saipan.

The known southward movement of Japanese naval vessels and transports caused Air Chief Marshal Brooke-Popham to order British reconnaissance flights to be flown from Kota Bharu, a task made difficult by heavy monsoonal rains. On 6th December two Japanese convoys were sighted by Hudson aircraft flown by Royal Australian Air Force pilots. The first convoy was made up of twenty-two transports escorted by six cruisers and ten destroyers. Shortly afterwards, the second and smaller convoy was sighted. Both convoys at that time were headed west, and not south towards Malaya or southern Thailand. In other words, at that time, Brooke-Popham could not be certain that the Japanese intended to invade Malaya or Thailand.

After that, the monsoon closed in, and according to all official reports and unofficial published histories, no further sightings of the convoys were made by the British although planes were sent out to do so. However, according to Flying-Officer Basil Gotto, another sighting was made on 7th December.

Gotto's 100 Squadron RAF, stationed at Seletar airfield on Singapore Island, whose planes were obsolete Vildebeestes, had for some time been expecting them to be replaced by Bristol Beauforts, then considered the fastest medium bomber in the world, and equipped also for torpedo bombing and general reconnaissance. In preparation for the arrival of the Beauforts the squadron's pilots had been trained in reconnaissance, ground personnel had been increased from 100 to 300, and navigators and wireless operators for the Beauforts had arrived from Australia where the planes were being built. At 1500 hours on 6th December, 'slap on ETA six specks hove into sight and six really beautiful machines landed without mishap', says Gotto. The event was witnessed by the C-in-C, Far East and other dignatories.[14] The planes arrived unarmed and without torpedo racks fitted; this may have been in order to reduce weight during the long flight from Australia, or it may have been a concession to the 'neutral' Dutch in their colony to the south where the planes had to land for refuelling.

On the following day, 7th December, one of the Beauforts piloted by Flight Lieutenant Mitchell who had flown it in, was sent 'up to Kota Bharu with the job of photographing the [Japanese] convoy'. According to Gotto, Mitchell not only found it but took photographs of it, and the resulting photographs were flown down to Singapore in another aircraft.

In the process of taking the photographs, 'Mitchell . . . seeing Jap fighters climbing to attack him and thinking he had the fastest machine east of Suez, had not done much about it. However, they caught him on the level, out-climbed him, and out-dived him and when he tried manoeuvring, forced him into a spin. He recovered, and with the use of the wobble pump, reached Kota Bharu much shot about.' (The use of the hand-operated wobble-pump indicates that part of the plane's fuel system had been damaged.)

If Gotto, who was writing contemporaneously and from first-hand knowledge, had all his facts correct, then at some time on 7th December, when the Japanese were very much closer to the Malayan and Thai beaches than they had been when sighted on the previous day, Brooke-Popham must have known that an invasion was imminent and moreover, that the Japanese had committed an act of war by shooting up Mitchell's plane. On that date the Japanese carried out another act of war by shooting down a reconnaissance Catalina sent out from Singapore, but that fact was not known until after the war was over.*

Gotto's account must be compared with that given in the *Official History of the RAF in World War Two*. The authors of that history mention the Beaufort flight but state that it was made *after* the Japanese had landed. However, in their account, the official historians made an error in indicating that these landings took place on *the morning of 7th December* when in actual fact they took place *on the morning of 8th, local time* which was a Monday. They compounded this error earlier in their account by stating that 'as that Sunday dragged on, and no news of Japanese aggression arrived – Pearl Harbo[u]r was bombed that day but no report of this reached Singapore until the following morning'. In fact the Pearl Harbor attack occurred some *two hours after the attack on Malaya*, but because of the effect of the International Date Line and the resulting difference in time zones between Malaya and Hawaii, the date and timing of the Pearl Harbor attack is recorded as coming at dawn on 7th December.

It follows that, if the official historians were at least right about the date of the Beaufort flight, then it took place on the day before the Japanese landings, just as Gotto said it did.

This seems to make sense, for had the flight been made on 8th December with a shooting war already under way, one has to ask why an unarmed aircraft was used when an armed Hudson was available. For the Beaufort to have taken photographs, daylight was necessary, and by dawn on the 8th, those ships in the Japanese convoy which had escaped the night pounding by RAAF Hudsons, and having accomplished their task of landing the army, had already made off seawards, so an armed Hudson would certainly have been available to make any reconnaissance flight then required.

Gotto is adamant that his account is correct. He was there in the thick of things. He had written of these events within weeks of their occurrence. In a note made years later when he was typing up his contemporary memoir, he said, 'this incident is absolutely true, however, I understand that the close shadowing of this convoy has

* The other five Beauforts took no part in the Malayan campaign. Of no use without their armaments which had not arrived, they were soon flown out of Singapore and back to Australia. Mitchell's damaged craft was blown up by the RAF.

been very much played down in official history. This was probably due to some political whitewashing.'

There is supporting evidence for Gotto's case. Sergeant (later Squadron Leader) Dave Thomas was at Kota Bharu airfield on both 7th and 8th December. He remembers the Beaufort flying in on the first of those days. He says it was quite a sight, for it was the first one he had seen, and he recalls that it had been constructed in Australia and had an American engine. He remembers it taking off again on that reconnaissance trip, and believes that to have been on the day before the Japanese attack, which would have made it 7th December.

If Mitchell's flight did take place on the day before the Japanese landings, then we are faced with another twist in the extraordinary chain of events leading up to war. Not only had Brooke-Popham been given incontrovertible evidence of Japanese intentions by the attack they made on the Beaufort, but some of the photographs Mitchell took over Singora in Thailand, 'revealed the presence of sixty aircraft, mainly fighters, on Singora airfield', say the authors of the official history. This would indicate, apart from anything else, that the Japanese had already in effect forestalled any chance of Operation Matador being successful.

The arrival of HMS *Prince of Wales* and HMS *Repulse* and their escorting destroyers at Singapore on 2nd December made an impressive sight. Admiral Sir Tom Phillips, newly sent out from England as C-in-C, Eastern Fleet, was on the quayside to greet the ships, the first of which was to be his flagship. Phillips's new command was to swallow up that of Vice-Admiral Layton's, including FECB under Captain Harkness. On 8th December Phillips sallied forth with his fleet without adequate air cover to deal with the Japanese landings. It did not turn out like that. The two capital ships were sunk by air attack, and Phillips went down with his flagship.

Admiral Phillips had flown to Manila on 4th December with three naval staff officers to consult with his American opposite number, Admiral Thomas C. Hart. On the way his aircraft – a seaplane – made an overnight stop at Labuan and he stayed the night at Government House with Hugh Humphrey, the British Resident who, among his many other roles, held the post of Naval Reporting Officer. At dinner Humphrey asked Phillips whether there would be a war with Japan and received the answer, 'I don't think so.'[15]

In his *Old Friends, New Enemies*, Professor Arthur Marder, making use of 'extensive correspondence' with Captain Harkness in 1978/79, wrote:

> Phillips and his staff relied on getting the latest and best intelligence from [FECB], but unfortunately, the time between the arrival of the *Prince of Wales* at Singapore . . . and [her] departure on 8th was short. Phillips moreover, was away from the 4th to the 7th. He never asked the COIS [Harkness] for a personal briefing . . .

Is it possible that Harkness, after the passage of thirty-seven years could have forgotten that he was one of the three staff officers who had accompanied Phillips on that Manila flight? Would not he have remembered that trip, if for no other reason, than that, in Manila, one of the American officers who attended the talks held there was none other than General Douglas MacArthur, a once-seen-never-forgotten type of man? And is it likely that, stuck in a plane for hours on end with Phillips he did not give the Admiral the fullest possible briefing? Hugh Humphrey says, 'Captain Harkness and two other naval officers were with Phillips. I remember Harkness because he told a rather silly story. He said, in reference to the battleship *Prince of Wales*, that one had to be careful when ringing for a steward in the wardroom that the wrong button was not pressed, otherwise one could let off a broadside!'*

When Phillips took his fleet north against the Japanese without air cover he did so, according to Harkness, with the idea that Japanese naval air efficiency was slightly lower than that of the Italians. Harkness told Marder that FECB did not know of the Japanese efficiency in dropping torpedoes, and that they expected attacks by bombs, rather than by torpedoes.

This must be compared with the recollections of Air Commodore Roy W. Chappell as also told to Marder. Chappell, as a Group Captain, was head of FECB's RAF section in 1941, a post he doubled with that of being British Air Attaché in Bangkok. He had been a Language Officer in Japan and that was followed later with a stint as Air Attaché, Tokyo. If any British airman knew about Japanese army or navy air efficiency, then, it was he. (Like the Americans, the Japanese had

* The two other naval officers on the plane were Captain S.T. Beardsworth, secretary to Phillips, and Commander M. Goodenough, who was Staff Officer (Plans).

no separate air arm at this time.) He says that he was not consulted on enemy air capabilities by any member of Admiral Phillips's staff until after the capital ships had been lost. He remembers being sent for by Air Chief Marshal Brooke-Popham about two hours before the fleet sailed on 8th December, and being told to prepare an estimate of the amount of bombing the fleet could expect if attacked. Chappell produced an estimate which said that Phillips could expect an attack by at least 100 aircraft based in Indo-China and that the attackers would include torpedo-bombers as well as bombers. 'We expected attacks from high-level bombing and above all torpedo-bombing,' he said.

Marder states that there is no conclusive evidence that Chappell's appreciation reached Brooke-Popham, or that it reached Phillips before his fleet sailed. We do know, however, that Phillips had meetings and was in contact with Air Vice Marshal Pulford, the AOC in Malaya, before he sailed. Pulford, who had served in the Royal Naval Air Service during World War One, had always kept himself abreast of developments in naval air services, would no doubt have warned the Admiral of the dangers he faced by proceeding without air cover.[16]

In the very early hours of 8th December 1941, the Japanese launched their attack on Kota Bharu in Malaya and landed other waterborne forces at Singora and Patani in Thailand.

The Japanese were guided ashore at Kota Bharu by a light from the shore. It is possible that the section of the *Kame* message (see page 316, section 'd') which referred to a sign to be exhibited and ordering that 'connection should be quickly established with the Japanese officer in command', may have been in reference to this. General Heath has recorded that the invaders were guided ashore in this way, and that a Japanese agent, a Chinese, had been identified at Kota Bharu before the war, but that there had been insufficient evidence for the police to arrest the man.

In the dark, as the Australian pilots of the Hudsons stationed at Kota Bharu airfields roared in to attack the Japanese troopships off the beaches, they found the escort ships flashing the correct RAF recognition signal for the day, the letter 'K'.[17] It is possible that this signal was revealed to the Japanese by the Air Intelligence Liaison Officer, Patrick Heenan.

Over in the west, whilst these landings took place on the east coast, troops were still standing by for Matador. The last day to implement that operation with any chance of it being successful, in the opinion of General Heath, was 6th December, the day the convoys were first sighted by the Hudsons. But Brooke-Popham had made no move to cancel Matador on the 6th, nor on the day after when the existence of the convoys much closer to the landing places may have been confirmed by that Beaufort reconnaissance flight. It was something he did not do until well into 8th December.

By the 8th the troops of the 11th Indian Division on the west coast had been on standby for Matador for some days, and now they were required to stand down from an offensive stance and take up half-finished defensive positions along the so-called Jitra line that guarded the northern airfields. This change took place in driving rain and, as it turned out, there was no time to complete the defences before the Japanese, racing down the road from Singora, were upon them. To make matters worse, in preparation for Matador, wireless links had been switched to new frequencies and special codewords had been issued. Now there was confusion, as everything had to be changed back again.

Immediately upon the outbreak of war the military and police implemented 'Operation Collar and Trousers', designed to round up every Japanese in the country together with known sympathisers. Police Assistant Superintendent Harvey Ryves was in his bed at Kuala Kangsar when he got a phone call from his superior, C.W.D. Hall, ordering the operation.

Ryves wrote, 'So it was that the war in Malaya started for me at 1.55 a.m. on 8th December 1941, appropriately perhaps on a Monday morning to start off a new week and, indeed, a new life'. Ryves had been expecting such a call for several weeks, and the four Japanese living in the town had been kept under surveillance by selected police constables. After warning his outstations and sending a contingent of men to guard the nearby Iskandar Bridge on the route to the north, he then went round the shops where the four Japanese were, one of them a barber's. The Japanese gave no trouble and were allowed to pack a few things before being taken to the lock-up. It seems as if they too, had been expecting this to happen, at least for the past week. Ryves says, 'The morning was busy. A stream of orders came through while I was preparing the papers and particulars of the Japs to accompany them on the mid-day mail train for their journey to the internment camp at Port Swettenham. They had over $8,000 in cash among them, because they had been feverishly selling the goods in their shops over the previous week at greatly reduced prices.'

Ryves was pleased with the round-up; all had gone like clockwork. Then, half an hour before the train was due to leave an order came through that the Japs must not take rubber-soled shoes with them. After some frantic hurrying and scurrying, leather-soled shoes were found. Ryves later discovered the order was made because the internment camp was surrounded by electrified wire.

It is not known how successful Operation Collar and Trousers was overall. Certainly not everything went as well as Ryves's part of the operation. The Japanese at the iron mine near Dungun on the east coast were rounded up easily enough, but were released by a Malay police inspector the following day, and some of them were seen heading north in the direction of their landing forces. John Fletcher-Cooke, District Officer, Cameron Highlands in Pahang, went out with the police to round up the Japanese market gardeners and two photographers who resided in his district. Except for 'a couple of aged crones, all had slipped away'. In an outhouse belonging to one of the Japanese, the police found a well-fitted dark room, photographic equipment, and a large number of photographs of signposts, cross-roads, and of the approaches to the District Office.[18]

The operation seems to have involved at least one tragedy. Colonel R.R. Baily of the Malay Regiment says that a locked wagon of detainees, after it was shunted into a siding at Kuala Lumpur, was inadvertently left there. All the occupants succumbed to heat-stroke, and when Japanese troops later took Kuala Lumpur and discovered this, they went on a murderous rampage.

Throughout 8th and 9th December, RAF pilots returning from sorties to land at the airfields in northwest Malaya, found themselves time and time again being strafed by Japanese planes. This, according to the report on 'Operations in Singapore and Malaya' signed by General Wavell in June 1942, was due to 'information sent from the vicinity of the northern aerodromes. At least one European was detected using a secret transmitter for this purpose'.[19] The European referred to was, again, Captain Patrick Heenan. He was arrested at Butterworth Airfield near Penang, on the morning of 10th December, and at the time he had in his possession two radio transmitters, one which looked like a typewriter, while the other fitted into a leather case disguised as a field-communion set, like those carried around by army and RAF padres. Another ecclesiastical touch was a code-book disguised as a bible. He was also carrying military 'situation reports' he was not supposed to have. A contemporary source, written on the day of Heenan's arrest, says that he was in charge of the entire Japanese subversion network between Penang and the Thai border.[20]

Heenan was taken to Singapore with an escort under a captain of the Gordon Highlanders, possibly Captain Ivan Lyon who was then attached to the security services. A few days later an Inquiry into the Heenan affair was held at Taiping where Major James France and other members of the Air Liaison Section, together with RAF personnel, were interviewed. A court-martial which lasted two or three days was held at Singapore in January 1942. During the proceedings information about Heenan's contacts with some of the trouble-making officers of the 1st Bahawalpurs was produced in evidence, and the prosecution, according to Brigadier G. Qasim Gilani, endeavoured unsuccessfully to implicate one of those officers, Captain A.D. Jahangir.[21]* Heenan was sentenced to death, but for some reason the sentence was not carried out. Then, two days before Singapore surrendered, he was taken down to the harbour by Military Policemen, shot in the back of the head and his body pushed into the sea.

The first day's battle at Kota Bharu on the northeast coast brought the first wartime fruits for the efforts of the Indian Independence League (IIL). During the evening of that day, sepoys of the 1st Hyderabads of the Indian States Forces, engaged in protecting Kota Bharu airfield, shot and killed their commanding officer, Lieutenant-Colonel C.A. Hendricks, before fleeing into the night and making for the railway station. Those members of the regiment who managed to board a train were arrested and disarmed when they reached central Malaya, and were later used as part of a construction unit.[22]

Over on the west coast, as defeated troops fell into their hands, the Japanese began forming what came to be known as the Indian National Army, or INA, from among Indian prisoners-of-war. One of the first Indian officers to be captured was Captain Mohan Singh of the 1/14th Punjab Regiment. He had held nationalist views from way back, and in Malaya had come under the influence of the IIL. Within a short time of being captured he was interviewed by Major Fujiwara of *F-Kikan*, and the INA was born. Mohan Singh, until

* Jahangir, and Gilani himself, were to become senior members of the Japanese-sponsored Indian National Army.

his disillusionment with the Japanese, was to lead it with the rank of General, which must have been one of the fastest promotions in military history. As more Indians joined the ranks of the INA, some were used to infiltrate back behind British lines to disaffect other Indian units. Leaflets produced by *F-Kikan* and printed in both Urdu and English, urging Indians to defect, were dropped by aircraft and were otherwise distributed.

Exactly what each particular agent achieved in Japanese pre-war clandestine operations in Malaya and Singapore is, of course, unknown. But there are certain pointers. It seems likely, for instance, that an agent of either 'Shawan', the steward in the Officers' Club in the Naval Base, or of the 'photographer' Nakajima, working from his shop outside the Naval Base main gate, made a significant contribution when he was successful in sabotaging the steering gear of the cruiser HMS *Mauritius* immediately after the war began.

The Naval Base, around which the very concept of 'Fortress Singapore' was based, was a prime target for Japanese espionage activities. It was for this reason that Inspector-General Dickinson had in 1940 seconded one of his ablest officers to head the Naval Police. He was Assistant Superintendent A.V. Cockle, who took with him Chief Inspector R. Higgens as his number two.[23] The Detective Branch of the Singapore Police also had interests in the base. In the machine-shop, for example, they had a paid Cantonese-speaking Chinese acting as an informant.

HMS *Mauritius* (Captain W.D. Stephens), one of the Royal Navy's newest cruisers, was dubbed HMS 'X' by the Singapore newspapers when she arrived there on 6th November 1941 for a major refit necessitated by heavy war duty. She was due to stay for several months as all her fire-main piping had been found to be corroded; it was all to be ripped out and replaced. Her machinery was also to be stripped down. All this work necessitated the crew being housed ashore at night so making it relatively easy for any determined saboteur to go about his work.

When the Japanese first bombed Singapore on 8th December, 'there was a panic to get the ship to sea,' says Chief Engineer Artificer Bill Lewis. 'We were lucky to get away,* for most of the

* On 15th December (author's note).

dockside workers had disappeared.' Bill Lewis goes on, 'We were in a sorry state when we left, except for the main engines which were OK. Then, as we were racing up the Malacca Strait, one of the two hydraulic steering motors seized up. It had sand in it. So did the other one, but we noticed it in time to drain and clear it. The sand had been put into sealed units, so the act was done deliberately and with knowledge. I was in charge of the job of stripping the gear down, and I was sweating blood as we raced past Penang at 32 knots with the steering gear only half working.'[24] (The Japanese were close to Penang by then, and the place was evacuated by the British on 17th December.)

Bill Lewis says that whoever the dockside worker was who placed the sand in the machinery, knew exactly the best place to put it for maximum effect. In fact the trouble was not finally sorted out until the ship reached Devonport after having spent several weeks in the hands of engineers in Colombo and other places en route. The Japanese saboteur had managed to put one of the Royal Navy's best cruisers out of effective commission for a good many weeks.

Another act of sabotage was carried out by a British Leading-Aircraftsman of 34 Squadron RAF. It is not known for certain why this young man (he was about twenty-four) acted in the way he did, but it was rumoured that he was in the pay of the Japanese. He was caught putting soft soap in the fuel filter of a Blenheim aircraft at Tengah airfield on Singapore Island. Under close arrest, he was taken off the island by sea with the rest of the ground crew to Sumatra, and then to India. He was taken to Delhi, court-martialled and hanged.[25]

As the British retreated down the Malay peninsular there were many reports of fifth-columnists at work along the ever-changing front-line, and also from well behind the lines. A local man who may have worked with or for Patrick Heenan was arrested at Alor Star on 9th December after the freshwater pipeline feeding the airfield was blown up by saboteurs. On the following day, the very day Heenan was arrested, seven Malays were taken into custody at the airfield and, according to the War Diary of the General Staff, Singapore, it was 'directed that they be obtained from the police immediately and all of them to be disposed of as expeditiously as possible'.

Assistant Superintendent Harvey Ryves remembers that on 18th December his police station at Kuala Kangsar became the temporary

HQ for General Heath and his 3rd Indian Corps Staff. Ryves thought the visit might prove embarrassing if not dangerous, because of something Heath said. 'He said that all the way down the country Divisional and Brigade Headquarters had been systematically and effectively bombed soon after every move. He quoted the instance of Parit Buntar, where a conference was being held in Divisional Headquarters when a Jap bomber came over. It had scored a direct hit and killed a number of Indian soldiers.'

A report in British official archives says that fifth-column activity was rife, especially in the north, 'but this was undoubtedly the result of Japanese bribery and promises rather than a genuine desire to see the end of British rule in the country'.[26]

Throughout the campaign frequent reports came in of gun positions given away to aircraft by arrows made of various materials on the ground, and of jungle paths marked by strips of cloth. Some fifth-columnists were said to have arranged stocks of stores, and even bicycles, at strategic places. Harvey Ryves says that many of the Malays arrested in various parts of the country as established fifth-columnists were schoolmasters.

Field Security and Liaison officers were kept busy whenever locals were seen near the front-line. Several natives are known to have been shot, two of them by a young British officer of the 5/14th Punjab Regiment. Guy Madoc, the Officer Superintending the Police Circle (OSPC) at North Kedal and, after the war, during the Malayan Emergency, the top policeman on General Templar's staff, recalls one Chinese 'suspect' being brought into the High Street police station in Kuala Lumpur, where a Military Policeman shot him dead. Later, when Madoc was attached to the headquarters of a military unit in Johore, he saw a British NCO shoot a Chinese who was probably a vegetable gardener – there were many such in the area – and whose only crime was to be in the wrong place at the wrong time. Harvey Ryves also noted that a fifth-column mania seemed to beset the military.

In Singapore itself there seemed to be as many false reports of fifth-column work as there were real ones. One of the latter involved troops of the 2nd Loyals under Lieutenant-Colonel M. Shrimpton. On 2nd January he led some of his men on a hunt in the vicinity of Tengah airfield on Singapore Island for a radio known to be operating there. They raided 'a lair of enemy wireless operators . . . in a house on Sungei Buloh Estate', but failed to capture the quarry though they did find 1,000 rounds of ammunition. Two weeks later men of the same regiment brought in a suspected sniper, and he was shot.[27] Other reports by military intelligence officers of mysterious lights being flashed and the like, were demonstrated to be false.

Some police officers were critical of military action taken against suspects on the flimsiest of evidence. Had the police known about the military 'Death Squad' that operated on the island, they would have been even more critical. It was made up of officers from Field Security and other security services. At one time or another members of it included Colonel A.G. Warren of the Royal Marines, Captain Ivan Lyon, Captain Tyrwhitt and Captain E.M. Golder, the latter an ex-Sub-Inspector of the Shanghai Police. One officer is reported to have detected and executed no fewer than nine Malays in the week before Singapore fell. Such dreadful acts are done in war when there is no time for due process, and it is likely that innocent men were executed.

Some members of the police, too, seemed over-anxious to find traitors where none existed. One such case occurred at Kuantan, where at the instigation of Superintendent B.M. O'Connell, Lieutenant C.J. Windsor of the Malayan Navy Volunteer Reserve was arrested on suspicion of aiding the enemy. At Kuantan he had been in charge of two naval auxiliary craft, one of them owned by himself. Windsor, a local businessman and trader, had been born with the name Winckle, his grandfather having come to England from Germany. The second generation of the family in England had changed its name to Windsor during World War One. The official naval historian-authors of the recently published (1995) *War With Japan* – which since the war and up until 1995 was a document seen only by *restricted* Royal Navy personnel – had this to say about the Windsor affair: 'Unfortunately, he fell under suspicion of the civil administration, and was arrested and taken to Singapore, where he was cleared of all suspicion. But a local intelligence organisation he had created was broken up, and in the retirement [retreat] both the ships of his force were lost.' It is a pity the Royal Navy did not see fit to publish that account of Windsor many years ago, for there are old Malaya hands around who still think he was guilty. Windsor, who died in 1970, and his wife who died in 1993 in Kuantan, would have been mightily pleased to hear of this official naval exoneration. It would have been especially pleasing as it had been a naval ship, HMS *Hungjao*, that had been sent to Kuantan to take him to Singapore under arrest at the behest of the civil administration, which was something the naval historians did not mention.[28]

Neither the police nor the military confined their suspicions to the low-born. A report produced by the Singapore police indicates that there were worries about the loyalty to the British cause of the Sultan of Johore. The report indicated that HRH Major-General Sir Ibrahim, GCMG, GBE, had harboured anti-British sentiments ever since the British authorities had stepped in to prevent him marrying a lady called Lydia Hill in 1938. The report went on to say that the Sultan had returned to Malaya from England in January 1941, 'harbouring pro-Nazi sentiments'. If that was indeed true, it is difficult to reconcile it with the fact that the Sultan had given Britain a quarter of a million pounds towards the war effort in 1940. The report went on:

> Under these circumstances soon after his return the Japanese sought to contact him and his entourage. Japanese businessmen began to entertain prominent Malay personages of Johore, including personal friends of the Sultan and high-ranking officers of the Johore Military Force (JMF).[29]

The authors of the report said that in May 1941 certain JMF officers who enjoyed the Sultan's confidence, as well as his personal aide-de-camp, visited the Japanese consulate in Singapore. Singapore Special Branch were so concerned over this matter that three weeks after the Japanese attack they were urging the Governor of Singapore to request the Sultan to declare his loyalty. But it would seem that the Sultan, in his relations with the Japanese, was merely exhibiting a realistic stance based on the principle of the interests of Johore first, and everything else second. He was waiting to see which way the wind blew, and at that time it was blowing from the east.

The military and the police were perhaps on firmer ground over their suspicions regarding the Sultan's third son, Ahmad. Pre-war, on 2nd July 1941, the signals section of the 22nd Indian Brigade in Malaya had picked up transmissions from an unknown station using the call-sign BCA. The signallers were instructed not to contact the station. After the war began, Australian signallers under Lieutenant R.G. Wells picked up transmissions from a powerful radio situated in Johore Bharu, which lies close to the northern end of the causeway that links Singapore to mainland Malaya. This may or may not have been the same transmitter whose signals had been intercepted earlier. Using

D/F sets borrowed from Kranji and with the help of the engineers at the local power station who shut off the power in the town, sector by sector, Wells concluded that the transmitter was in close proximity to Ahmad's residence.[30]

That Ahmad was under suspicion is confirmed by the Malayan Security Officer, Johore, Assistant Superintendent H.B.J. Donaldson, who reported that Ahmad was known to have a transmitter and that he was being kept under police surveillance. Another man thought to be involved was an Englishman, H.M. Still, the secretary of the Royal Johore International Club, whose house lay close to Ahmad's residence. Although he was married with two children, Still was a notorious homosexual who featured on Special Branch's Black List. When he crossed over the causeway to Singapore on 27th January, he was arrested. It is not known whether he was charged with any crime, but he was still around in 1957.

So-called 'denial schemes' had been prepared pre-war, their purpose to deny the enemy, if ever he came, the use of strategic materials and facilities. Some of these schemes were successfully carried out, but others were not. Into the latter category fell some of the northern airfields, some of which such as those at Kota Bharu and Sungei Patani, were evacuated in a panic. Many boats were left intact in Penang harbour, and were used later in the campaign by the Japanese. It is perhaps not surprising that, during the rapid retreat of British forces down mainland Malaya, men left behind to carry out demolitions were sometimes rather more concerned about getting away ahead of the advancing Japanese than they were to carry out their allotted tasks effectively.

In at least two instances it seems that a denial scheme was halted by enemy agents. A small group left behind to blow up Sungei Patani airfield was interrupted in its work by two Europeans, one in the uniform of an officer, the other a civilian. The demolition squad was ordered on its way, an order they were only too pleased to obey. The other instance occurred on Singapore Island five days before it fell. An officer arrived at a civilian workshop which was busy repairing army vehicles, and gave instructions for all the motor transport to be destroyed. 'A start was made, but a countermanding order was received by telephone, and accepted. It was undoubtedly sent by a Japanese agent.'[31]

An example of an international and combined military, police and civilian denial operation was the scheme for destroying the British oilfields in Borneo, and the Dutch oil fields on the same island and on Sumatra. Although it was well planned, it was not very successful. Commander A.N. Grey, a member of Brooke-Popham's staff – who had been sent to see General MacArthur in September 1941 to receive a briefing on US defence plans for the Philippines – was given the task pre-war of ensuring that a correlated plan was prepared which would ensure that any machinery the Japanese might salvage from the various plants could not be brought together to get at least one of them back in operation quickly. When the Japanese attacks came the plan for the British oilfields was immediately implemented. Assistant Superintendent A.C. Cunnyngham-Perdriau was sent to Miri in Sarawak with a contingent of Sikh constables to guard the local management under Brian Parry as they went about the task. Oil borings were either plugged or blown up, and the three-mile long under-sea pipe-line to the tanker loading moorings was demolished. The plans of the field were sent out of harm's way to Australia. All key personnel, except for a few who were to stay until the last minute, and all important pieces of machinery were shipped to Singapore. When the *Lipis* carrying the men and machinery arrived back at Singapore docks, she was met by Commander Grey who had orders to ascertain that the demolition had gone satisfactorily. He was horrified to discover that Brian Parry, the man who carried in his head more information about the oilfield than anyone else, had stayed behind 'from a mistaken sense of duty . . . to look after those Asiatic operators who were left there'. Grey considered this 'most unpleasant information', for if Parry fell into Japanese hands he may have been forced to give vital information. In the event, Parry made good an escape from Miri, and after a crossing Borneo reached the port of Tarakan. There he did fall into Japanese hands, but he was beheaded before it was discovered who he was.

Not long after Singapore fell the Japanese had part of the Miri field working again anyway. Some of the evacuated Asiatic technicians fell into their hands at Singapore, and one of them was persuaded to tell where some of the machinery had been hidden. Not only that, the Japanese brought in French engineers from Saigon to reinstate the refinery at Lutong.

Little is known about the performance of British military intelligence in the field during the campaign. It is known that some intelligence and attached liaison officers were killed during the fighting in the performance of their duties. According to Captain Stanley Lemin, one of two intelligence officers attached to the British 53rd Brigade, his fellow intelligence officer, Captain Grevil Kerrison, was killed during fighting on the mainland. Lieutenant Vanya Ringer, the Japanese-speaking liaison officer serving with 5/14th Punjab Regiment, also lost his life in the jungle. A senior FMS policeman, L.H. 'Tam' Pearce, whilst serving in an intelligence capacity with the 4/19th Hyderabad Regiment, disappeared and was never seen again.

Major-General Gordon Bennett, commanding the Australian forces in Malaya, was a great proponent of ambushes, and his troops conducted a highly successful one at Gemas on 14th January. It can be assumed that he received timely and sufficient intelligence on the strength of the Japanese columns that marched into the ambush. Perhaps he tried the tactic out too often or sometimes without sufficient intelligence, for his Chief of Staff, Colonel J.H. Thyer was to say in 1953, 'Bennett had an ambush complex. If you could set ambushes right along your front it would fix everything.' Thyer was here criticising Bennett's troop dispositions near the Muar River.[32]

In some instances insufficient attention was placed on the importance of gleaning every scrap on intelligence from captured Japanese soldiers. Although the British forces were engaged in a retreat it seems odd that, during the fifty-five days of fighting on the mainland, only about a dozen prisoners were taken and sent back for interrogation, and some of those were pilots of downed aircraft. This is especially strange in view of the favourite Japanese tactic of sending out small flying columns of men to infiltrate behind British lines; surely some of these must have been captured? Lieutenant-Colonel H.C. Phillips, GSOI (Ops) Malaya Command, wrote, 'The conduct of the forces in this respect is still somewhat of a mystery. Units did not realise the importance of going out and getting information for themselves by sending out patrols, particularly by capturing prisoners. The reason for the lack of prisoners has been proved to be that units shot any prisoners taken in order to avoid the trouble of sending them back to the rear.' He went on, 'It is a matter of training until every officer and man down to the youngest realises that all information, however trivial, is important.'[33]

At least one British officer sent out on an intelligence-gathering patrol on Singapore Island came across something that astonished him. Captain W.V. Gurteen, 1st Cambridgeshires, scouting near the MacRitchie Reservoir on 12th February, three days before Singapore surrendered, 'was astonished to see between four and five hundred of the enemy relaxing by the water's edge. He noted that many Indian troops were with the Japanese.'[34]

Too late for it to do much good, a force of Chinese Irregulars was organised to fight the Japanese. The genesis of the force was 'Dalco' formed and named after John Dalley a policeman who was given the rank of Lieutenant-Colonel for this purpose. It was to consist of small groups of Chinese led by European officers for operations behind Japanese lines. This later developed into 'Dalforce', after many more Chinese joined including some communists who were let out of jail for the purpose.

As there were a vast number of Chinese in Malaya, and the great majority were violently anti-Japanese, it can be asked why such a force was not raised and trained far earlier. In the first place many Chinese were 'overseas Chinese', that is they had not been born and bred in Malaya and it was believed that their allegiances lay elsewhere. Secondly, some were communists, and the police had been waging an underground war against the most militant for many years. Thirdly, and perhaps most important, the Malay Sultans, who would have liked to have seen all Chinese removed from their lands, would have objected had the British taken this step in peacetime. Another reason was that the raising and arming of a large force would have required expenditure, and money and arms were in short supply.

Five Kuomintang Chinese officers had been sent to Singapore by Chiang Kai-shek at the outbreak of war as observers. They offered their services to help train the Dalforce guerrillas but this posed a problem as most of the Chinese volunteers came from among the ranks of the communists. The matter was left in abeyance, which itself caused another problem when in January 1942, Lieutenant-General Cheng Kai-Min passed through Singapore on his way to join General Wavell's staff on Java. He saw that the training of the communists was well advanced while that of the KMT Chinese had barely started, and kicked up a rumpus.

Although poorly armed and trained, Dalforce did put on an impressive show in the initial battles on Singapore Island, some units acting as scouting and intelligence-gathering parties for the army proper. But towards the end it was disbanded to give its members time to flee from possible Japanese retribution. Many were caught and executed; others disappeared into the jungle and were used later in the war by the SOE.

By the end of December 1941, the Admiralty decided it was time to transfer FECB from Singapore to Colombo. This transfer was not to be like the previous one from Hong Kong, however, for from now on FECB was to become a purely naval operation.

A secret message dated 27th December from the C-in-C, Eastern Fleet – a post taken over by Admiral Layton after Phillips had gone down with the *Prince of Wales* – to the Admiralty and copied to the Australian Naval Board, advised of the intention: '1. To transfer to Ceylon the naval section of FECB (including COIS, 'Y' and Special Intelligence) by transport returning from Singapore about 5th January. 2. Interpreters will be left to assist Army and Air Special Intelligence.'[35]

This meant that the army and air force members of FECB transferred to the intelligence arms of their respective forces with but one or two exceptions. Lieutenant-Colonel A.K. Ferguson, for example, joined the staff of the newly appointed Allied Supreme Commander in the area, General Wavell, at Bandung, Java. With this reorganisation, Brigadier L.F. Field arrived to take charge of the Intelligence Branch of Malaya Command, but he too, was shortly transferred to Java.[36]

The 'Bletchley Park party' or SLU, also left at this time. Marr-Johnson eventually ended up in India, and Stevens went to the States. It is not known what Webb did for the rest of the war. Wavell had a one-man SLU with him during his short spell as Supreme Allied Commander on Java. That man may well have been Marr-Johnson.

After fifty-five days of retreating down the Malayan mainland, the last British forces crossed the causeway to Singapore Island on 31st January, blowing up the causeway after them, though not very effectively. The Japanese invaded the island on 8th February.

It is not known how, or exactly when the Indian National Army sent representatives over to the island to subvert Indian troops, but send them they did. Amongst them, according to Major Fujiwara of *F-Kikan*, was Captain Allah Ditta. In his book called *F-Kikan*, Fujiwara tells how Ditta urged the men of one Indian Regiment to come over and join the INA. This Regiment may have been the 2/10th Baluch who left the front-line on 14th February to go behind Japanese lines.* Evidence that was not previously available now shows that it might equally well have been either the 4/19th Hyderabad or the 5/2nd Punjab Regiment of the 12th Indian Brigade, both of which disappeared even earlier than the Baluchis. In the *full* report of Australian Major-General Gordon Bennett, the most senior officer to escape from Singapore – of which this author previously had at hand only a summary as was sent to Britain in April 1942 – there appeared the following:

> Some units suffered heavy casualties by desertion. Many deserters were collected and returned to their units but towards the end when morale of some units was very low, it became difficult to bring deserters back to their units. For instance on 11th February the 12 Indian Brigade disappeared and only 70 men could be gathered by 15th February. This was not the only brigade that suffered severely from desertions.[37]

The exact role of INA on Singapore Island is not known, but there can be little doubt that members of it, or perhaps of the IIL, were involved in subverting Indian troops there just as they had been doing on the mainland.

The large scale of desertions at Singapore together with the consequences of it has been discussed at some length in *Singapore: The Pregnable Fortress*. That book also highlighted the many reasons for the incidence of desertions, which included lack of air support, poor leadership, lack of appropriate training, the poor quality of some of the reinforcements, two months of continuous retreat, no tanks, etc., etc. The morale of the troops on Singapore Island was abysmally low, and taking into consideration all the factors that led to that situation, it is not surprising that desertion, the dreadful end-result of low military morale, manifested itself in such large numbers. Another significant contributory factor was that, unlike at Dunkirk, it was obvious to the troops that there was going to be no major attempt to evacuate them. No overall desertion figure was presented in the book, though readers were enabled to reach their own conclusions, as the body of

* This incident is described in some detail in this author's *Singapore: The Pregnable Fortress* (1995).

official evidence from first-hand and other contemporary accounts concerned mainly Australian and Indian desertions; there was little firm evidence concerning British troop desertions, though it was obvious that some must have taken place for no disease spreads faster than low battlefield morale. Whatever the actual total figure was, it amounted to the highest number of desertions in British military history.

Additional information has come to light since that book was published, which shows that the desertion factor was even higher than indicated there. On the basis of the 'new' evidence of Major-General Gordon Bennett, the desertion figure can be increased by the number of 'lost' Indian troops of the 12th Brigade. Yet another contemporary source gives some indication of the scale of British desertions, as opposed to Australian and Indian, and permits the problem of the size of the deserter factor to be estimated in another way.

When the balance of the British 18th Division (one brigade had arrived earlier) landed at Singapore on 29th January 1942, less than three weeks before the island fell, it arrived complete with its own Intelligence and Field Security section. Although according to one of their number, Captain A.F.C. (later Sir Alexander) Barrington, none of the intelligence staff could speak Japanese and had scant knowledge of Far Eastern affairs for the Division had expected to go to the Middle East, all of them had received training in field intelligence.[38]

Another of those officers was Captain (later Sir) Harold Atcherley. He kept a diary in the Changi prison-of-war camp from May 1942, in which he also recorded his memories of his brief participation in the defence of Singapore. As an aside, but one which illustrates an extraordinary lack of urgency on the part of at least one senior member of General Percival's HQ staff, Atcherley wrote that on Friday 6th February he was sent to see the Brigadier, General Staff, but did not get to see him until the following Monday. The excuse given was that the BGS was out riding.[39]

Atcherley made other indictments. The Division arrived at Paya Lebar on 3rd February with orders to set up its HQ at precise co-ordinates:

> Paya Lebar HQ was not 100 yards from two important road junctions. Not content with that, our senior officers then proceeded to cover all the road junctions in the vicinity with MPs who were made to wear

red caps. We were staggered. Had the bloody army learnt nothing? Singapore was full of Jap agents and Fifth-Columnists.

But perhaps the most important passage in Captain Atcherley's diary concerns his abortive attempt to escape on 13th February as one of an officially arranged party of evacuees:

> Chaos in the streets, and through it all were the thousands of troops who had deserted. In the town there was, at a rough estimate, a division. Perimeter now held by a pathetically thin line. Nothing was being done to get these men back to their units. Many of them were drunk on liquor stolen from deserted bars and restaurants.

Before we discuss the contents of this passage, we should remember that, as a trained field intelligence officer, Atcherley would have been properly versed in estimating the size of any military group he came across, and also that he had trained with a division in England and travelled out with one from there. He would have known what a division of men looked like. It should also be remembered that his diary was written within three months of the event when everything was fresh in his mind.

To his estimate of the deserters in the town being 'a division in strength' on the 13th February, must be added the estimated 3,000 deserters who had already left the island by that date which Atcherley would have known nothing about. Nor would he have known of the two Indian army regiments that had already 'disappeared' on the 11th, and of course, nothing about the Baluchis who were to do something similar on 14th February.

But that passage from the diary contains another important sentence: 'Perimeter now held by a pathetically thin line'. The perimeter on 13th February, almost the final one, was a rough semi-circle, its two termini resting on the waterfront east and west of the city. It was then about thirteen miles long, of which the most northerly five miles had been allocated to the British 18th Division. Atcherley came down into the town from the 18th Division part of the perimeter, and – even given that one of its three brigades had arrived early, fought on the mainland and suffered casualties, and that further casualties must have been sustained in fighting on the island itself (though official figures show it was not many) – if all the remaining men of that division had been in the vicinity of the front-line, that five-mile stretch of the perimeter could not have been described as being held by a pathetically thin line. It can be taken therefore, that the ranks of the deserters in the town included many men of the British 18th Division.

As the end of the battle for Singapore drew near, attempts were made to evacuate many of the remaining women and children, officers and men with special qualifications, and others considered to be specially vulnerable to Japanese reprisals.

On 4th February, Wavell's intelligence staff in Java, working on information received from decrypts of intercepts picked up by FECB, now in Colombo, informed General Percival that the Japanese convoy previously identified as being anchored off the Anamba Islands north of Singapore, and which might have been expected to launch a sea-attack against the fortress, was instead destined for Palembang, the site of large oil installations in Sumatra. This was confirmed by additional messages sent to Percival on 7th and 9th February. This information, according to Major-General S. Woodburn Kirby, one of the British Official Historians, should have enabled Percival to reorganise his defences on the island early enough to have thrown the Japanese back when they attacked on 8th February, an opportunity he did not exploit to the full.[40]

Be that as it may, those earlier messages and an additional one on 10th February which indicated that the Japanese had issued definite orders for its convoy to rendezvous in the Banka Strait on the 13th for the attack on Palembang, should at least have been taken as a warning that the fleet of mainly little ships being organised for the partial evacuation, should avoid the Banka Strait like the plague. No such order was issued, and in the event most of the little ships were intercepted by the Japanese, many of the people on them perishing, or forced to spend the rest of the war in captivity.

One whole party of police officers considered to be at special risk from the Japanese left aboard a small diesel-engined boat called *Mary Rose* which sailed on the night of the 14th/15th February, the night before Singapore fell. Amongst them were Mervyn Wynne, head of Singapore Special Branch, and his FMS counterpart, H.B. Sym. Others were Major K.S. Morgan David Matheson, C.M.J. Kirke who like Morgan was a Japanese speaker, D.N. Livingstone who had run agents on the Thai border, and Colonel J.D. Dalley, the man behind the Dalforce guerrillas. With them went V.G. Bowden, the Australian Government Representative who had earlier worked in intelligence in Shanghai and elsewhere. *Mary Rose* ran into the Japanese fleet in the Banka Strait at dawn on 17th February and was captured and escorted into the small port of Muntok.

Almost immediately Bowden was executed by the Japanese after having been made to dig his own grave. Morgan was taken back to Singapore and there given an exceptionally hard time by his captors. He survived the war, as did Dalley. Matheson died in an internment camp on Sumatra at the end of 1944. Sym had died there some time earlier.[41]

Mervyn Llewelyn Wynne, the man whose warnings had been so often ignored, died at Pladjoe, near Palembang, Sumatra, on 4th April 1942.[42] A fellow policeman wrote of Wynne, 'a very fine man indeed, but he made many enemies in high places by his forthright and undiplomatic approach to problems.'[43]

In his memoir, Commander Grey, who escaped from Java himself on 26th February, wrote: 'Mervyn Wynne . . . died miserably in Sumatra . . . he was captured . . . by the Japanese who recognised him as one of their inveterate enemies, and his end was unpleasant.' Whatever the circumstances of Wynne's death, it was a wretched end for such a far-sighted man.

Eighteen

The Far East Intelligence War, 1942

The first months of 1942 brought with them major defeats for the Allies at the hands of the Japanese. At the same time the Allied intelligence services underwent considerable expansion.

General Sir Archibald Wavell was appointed Supreme Commander ABDA (American, British, Dutch, Australian) Command, Southwest Pacific, early in January 1942. At the end of February, with the fall of Java then imminent, ABDA was disbanded, and soon afterwards General Douglas MacArthur was made Allied Commander-in-Chief, Southwest Pacific, with Admiral Chester Nimitz becoming C-in-C of all Allied Forces in the remainder of the Pacific Ocean Area. The British were delegated command of the Indian Ocean area. This series of changes in command, together with the need to move Allied intelligence agencies further away from danger in the face of the Japanese onslaught, and the necessity for much closer international collaboration, resulted in many changes in the intelligence community and to intelligence systems. Unfortunately the collaboration between commands did not always work well, let alone collaboration between intelligence agencies.

General Wavell had set up his headquarters at Lembang, near Bandung on the island of Java. This made military sense rather than choosing Singapore even though that 'fortress' was the pivotal point in the defence of the island chain forming the Malay barrier, the barrier behind which lay Australia, for by the time of Wavell's appointment the writing was already on the wall for Singapore which was under regular air attack. Furthermore, the need to set up a Combined HQ with all the extra communications that entailed, would not have been possible on an island where the communications system was already dangerously overloaded.[1]

In January FECB transferred out of harm's way to Colombo, and in the process the organisation changed in nature. Only the naval personnel went to Ceylon, aboard the troopship *Devonshire* which sailed on 5th January. At Colombo FECB became an exclusively naval unit with the primary task of providing operational intelligence for the Eastern Fleet, the fleet which was to operate in the Indian Ocean, and when a little later Admiral Sir Geoffrey Layton was appointed C-in-C, Ceylon, to him also.

Some FECB Army and RAF officers proceeded to Java to form the nucleus of Wavell's intelligence staff, while others became part of their respective service intelligence organisations in Singapore, although officially remaining on the FECB establishment. One of the Army officers transferred to Java was Japanese-speaking Lieutenant-Colonel A.K. Ferguson, and one of those who stayed behind was Captain Peter Pender-Cudlip. One lady member of Wavell's intelligence staff, until she was transferred to FECB Colombo where she remained for the rest of the war, was Ursula Boxer, the estranged wife of Major Charles Boxer of FECB, Hong Kong.[2]

It seems likely that Wavell brought with him from India his own one-man Special Liaison Unit (SLU) to handle 'Special' intelligence. Either that or one of the three officers of the SLU in Singapore was sent to join him, the likely candidate in that event being Major P. Marr-Johnson, for his colleague Captain Stevens did not speak Japanese, and Lieutenant Webb would have been too junior and inexperienced. That there was such a man on Wavell's staff seems to be evidenced by the memoirs of the General's Dutch ADC, Captain the Baron Reinhard Mackay. Some time after 1974, when the secrets of 'Ultra' or 'Special' first became known to the general public, Mackay wrote:

> At Lembang on Java, February/March 1942, General Wavell had a functionary with quarters next to his own, who nobody knew nor his job, in uniform but without weapons or rank indications. Having access to General Wavell's private room I happened to come across this mysterious figure once or twice, closing his door when he saw me, and

> I wondered who or what he was. At the time I took him for a private secretary for secret correspondence . . . but now I am inclined to post him as Wavell's SLU . . . He was taken to safety from Java.[3]

On arrival at Colombo, FECB set up an operational centre in the Navy Office close to the port, with its 'Y' station situated some miles south of the city. The complement of the 'Y' station initially included 38 WRNS, Chief Petty Officer Telegraphists trained in Japanese W/T. Captain K.L. Harkness remained in charge of FECB in his capacity as Chief of Intelligence Staff (COIS) until he was replaced late in 1942 by Captain Stephen Barry.

The FECB cryptanalysis section was soon into its stride at Colombo, and shortly after its arrival it learnt from an intercepted message that the Japanese were aware of its moving from Singapore.

Ten days after Singapore fell on 15th February, and with the fall of Java so obviously imminent, ABDA Command was dissolved and General Wavell was flown out to Colombo and then on to India. Two days later, on 27th February, his British, American and Australian staff, but not the Dutch who elected to stay behind, also left Java from the southern port of Tjilajap on board HMS *Kedah*. The convoy of cars that conveyed the staff members across country was organised by ex-FECB officer Colonel Ferguson.[4]

The most senior officer to escape on *Kedah* was Lieutenant-General Sir Henry Pownall.* Of all the senior British military figures, except Major-General Piggott who spent many years as Military Attaché in Tokyo, Pownall was considered by the Japanese themselves to be the most knowledgeable about them and their country. Pownall, whose father had built the Japanese railways, had spent a large slice of his boyhood in Japan and learnt the language concurrently with English. It is therefore interesting to consider what he had to say about British underestimation of the Japanese. Writing in his diary on 25th February 1942, two days before his escape from Java, he said:

> There's no doubt that we've underestimated the Jap. He is far more efficient, a far better fighter than we ever thought. We thought (I

* General Pownall was lucky, for he had been designated to take over Brooke-Popham's role as British C-in-C, Far East, and but for the advent of ABDA Command under General Wavell which swallowed up Far East Command he would, in Churchill's words, 'have been called upon to bear the terrible load which fell upon the shoulders of General Percival'.

among them) that when they got up against something other than the Chinese they would begin to quail. Therein we underestimated the Chinese too.[5]

On the same day that Colonel Ferguson was extricating Wavell's staff and himself from Java, the so-called Allied Combined Fleet, made up of Dutch, American, British and Australian ships met with disaster at the Battle of the Java Sea, a battle in which the Japanese made good use of their Long Lance torpedo. The battle itself was presaged on 25th February by Allied interception of Japanese reconnaissance reports which indicated that the cruiser HMAS *Hobart* had been mistaken for a much larger ship, possibly a battleship. That, and other intelligence reports around the time, indicate that the Allies had made a start in reading concurrently some signals sent in the Japanese naval codes, a sign that the extra facilities and manpower poured into such cryptanalysis since Pearl Harbor and Malaya had begun to produce results. FECB was also able to give some forewarning based on wireless telegraphy traffic patterns of the impending Japanese landings on Java which actually took place on 28th February. They were able to name the *Natori*, perhaps by radio-fingerprinting, as one of the Japanese cruisers involved.

In March 1942, following the defeat at the Battle of the Java Sea, Vice-Admiral C.E.L. Helfrich of the Royal Netherlands Navy arrived in Colombo from Batavia by air with some of his staff including intelligence officers, and set up an organisation to work alongside the British.

Within days the Japanese onslaught in Decembeir 1941, the Allies began pouring extra men and resources into breaking the Japanese naval codes, and also began to sort out new priorities in assignments. The American unit at Pearl Harbor under Lieutenant-Commander Joseph Rochefort was taken off its pre-war task of trying to break the Japanese flag-officer's code, that job now being left to the section of the US Navy in Washington called OP-20-G. Rochefort was now to concentrate on JN-25, the most widely used of Japan's cryptosystems, already being worked on by the Corregidor unit in the Philippines under Lieutenant Fabian, by OP-20-G itself, and by FECB. By Christmas this combined effort began to produce results, though the readings were 'tantalisingly fragmentary, and much remained to be done'.[6] One indication of the new man-power effort was that

Rochefort at Pearl Harbor was allotted the entire band from one of the ships that had been damaged there, the USS *California*, an astute move as it turned out, for the bandsmen proved exceptionally good at their new work, probably because cryptanalysis, like music, is based on mathematics.

David Kahn has pointed out in *The Codebreakers* that, with the exchange of information going on, it is impossible to say which group deserves the major part of the credit for initially breaking the code, and afterwards for continuing to break it every time the Japanese made changes to it. Suffice it to say that the collaboration worked well, and that the fruits from it began to ripen in March 1942. According to Lieutenant Fabian the first JN-25 message his unit on Corregidor read was on 13th March, in which the Japanese designator letters for some target places in the Pacific area were identified, though by that time it seems that Fabian himself had already been evacuated from Corregidor by submarine.[7]

On 21st March FECB in Colombo identified more Japanese place designator letters, and all this 'recovered' material was pumped into the Allied exchange of information system which led to yet more recoveries. The small Royal Indian Navy W/T and Cypher Office at Bombay Fort, Colaba, also, it seems, made a contribution to the interception of Japanese signals. Stationed there were selected ratings trained in Japanese morse. At the outbreak of the war with Germany in 1939, officers' wives at Bombay had volunteered to act as cypher clerks, and several of them stayed on to join the Women's Royal Indian Naval Service when it was formed. From this station 'a steady stream of intercepted traffic was being forwarded to Naval HQ in Ceylon'.[8] At Delhi, from an earlier date, another interception centre had been set up under the cover name Wireless Experimental Centre, or WEC. The wireless receiving side of this centre was manned by operatives of the Royal Corps of Signals specially trained in Japanese morse.[9]

The FECB organisation was to undergo several more changes. At the end of March, Captain Harkness and other officers were relocated to Delhi to work principally on intelligence required for naval planning and 'combined appreciations'. What was called the Combined Intelligence Centre was set up in Colombo under Colonel Ferguson who had arrived there aboard *Kedah* on 7th March. The 'Y' operation, which about this time came to be called HMS *Anderson*, continued to operate on the site south of that city.

The authors of an official Admiralty report recorded that these changes proved to be a handicap to FECB. Quoting an unnamed source they recorded 'the disadvantage being "the separation of static and long term intelligence from operational intelligence, the advantages of a combination of the two have long been proved".' That may have been naval sour grapes over losing control over non-naval intelligence, for at this stage the new system seemed to be working well overall, especially that part involving collaboration amongst the Allies.[10]

This was demonstrated by a series of events before the Japanese air attacks on Colombo on 4th April 1942 and on the naval base of Trincomalee on 9th April. On 21st March the newly appointed C-in-C, Eastern Fleet, Admiral Sir James Somerville, had received intelligence from FECB gained from several Japanese messages intercepted between 13th and 17th March, that a Japanese fleet was about to enter the Indian Ocean and that an attack on Ceylon was expected on 1st April. The British Admiralty passed this information to the Americans who came back on 26th March with confirmation based on their own intercepts. FECB received further confirmation from intercepts on 28th March, again confirmed by the Americans, who provided the additional information that ships and not port installations were to be the primary targets of the attack. FECB and Allied Sigint collaboration seemed to be going well, and it is difficult to see where any handicap had arisen due to the organisational changes at FECB. In point of fact, FECB and the Americans had got the date of the Japanese attack wrong and had seriously underestimated the size of the naval force involved, but that can hardly be attributed to the changes at FECB.

With these changes having taken place, it is useful to summarise the strategic situation in the Indian and Pacific Oceans in April 1942, and the main events leading up to it. Guam had fallen on 10th December 1941, Wake on the 22nd and Hong Kong on the 25th. On 15th December the Japanese had crossed the Kra Isthmus in Thailand to attack and capture Victoria Point, the southernmost township in Burma and the site of a British airfield on the so-called Empire Air Reinforcement Route. Singapore fell on 15th February, and the Japanese force which had landed on the island of Sumatra on the 14th reached the Sumatran shore of the Sunda Strait a week later, thus threatening Java on which landings were made on the 28th. By March virtually the whole of the Philippines was under the control of the Japanese who had commenced landings in the islands on 10th December 1941, with only Bataan and Corregidor holding out until 9th April and 6th May respectively. Rangoon, the capital and chief seaport of Burma, fell to the Japanese on 8th March. On the following day the Allied forces on Java were compelled to surrender.

By April 1942, therefore, Japanese conquests stretched as far east as the western Solomon Islands, and they had made landings on New Guinea. They were now in a position to threaten Australia, having already made a carrier-based air attack on Port Darwin on 19th February. Their thrust into Burma was threatening India. In six months, which in a ratio of time involved and size of geographical coverage, completely outclassed the German *Blitzkrieg* in Europe, the Japanese had taken control of a vast area of the Pacific and, it seemed, were poised to wrest control of the eastern Indian Ocean. In reaching this position the largest naval unit the Japanese had lost was a destroyer.

Japanese command of all the straits leading from the South China Sea into the Indian Ocean and of bases along the Burmese coast, posed a threat to Ceylon which, situated in the centre of the Indian Ocean, had become a vital strategic point for the Allies. If the Japanese should take Ceylon it would undermine Britain's position in both the Middle and Far East. India would then be at risk from the south as well as from the advancing Japanese army in Burma. Everything the Allies had afloat in the Indian Ocean would be at risk – including ships on the all-important round-the-Cape supply route to Egypt and the British 8th Army there, and on the supply route via the Persian Gulf and Iran to the Russians, to say nothing of the oil tankers travelling in the reverse direction.

To combat this threat Britain began, in January 1942, to put together a scratch Eastern Fleet for service in the Indian Ocean under the command of Admiral Somerville. The fleet, when finally assembled, was to consist of the four World War One vintage 'R' class battleships *Revenge, Ramilles, Resolution* and *Royal Sovereign*, the battleship *Warspite*, which although equally as old had undergone an extensive modernisation programme, and three aircraft-carriers, *Formidable, Indomitable* and *Hermes*, the later being old and carrying few aircraft. The remainder of the fleet consisted of six cruisers and sixteen destroyers, among them the very few survivors of what had been the China Fleet, and two submarines. The Dutch added another cruiser, a destroyer, an anti-aircraft ship, and two more submarines.

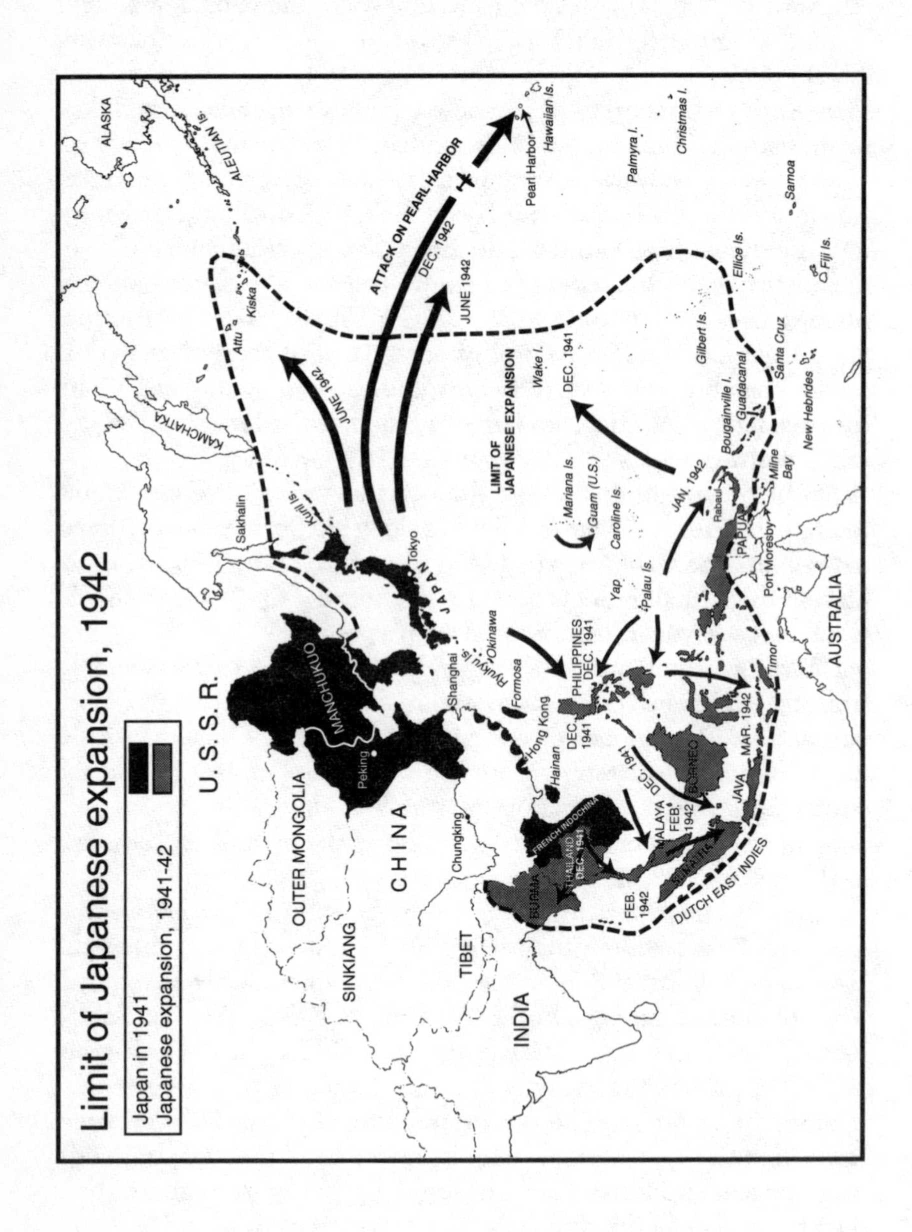
Limit of Japanese expansion, 1942
Japan in 1941
Japanese expansion, 1941-42
U. S. S. R.
ALASKA
ALEUTIAN Is.
Attu
Kiska
KAMCHATKA
Sakhalin
Kuril Is.
MANCHUKUO
Peking
OUTER MONGOLIA
SINKIANG
CHINA
TIBET
INDIA
Chungking
Shanghai
Hong Kong
Hainan
Formosa
Ryukyu Is.
Okinawa
JAPAN
Tokyo
JUNE 1942
ATTACK ON PEARL HARBOR
DEC. 1942
JUNE 1942
Pearl Harbor
Hawaiian Is.
Palmyra I.
Christmas I.
Samoa
Fiji Is.
Ellice Is.
Gilbert Is.
Santa Cruz
New Hebrides
Bougainville I.
Guadacanal
Milne Bay
LIMIT OF JAPANESE EXPANSION
Wake I.
DEC. 1941
Mariana Is.
Guam (U.S.)
Caroline Is.
Yap
Palau Is.
JAN. 1942
Rabaul
PAPUA
Port Moresby
AUSTRALIA
Timor
PHILIPPINES DEC. 1941
DEC. 1941
DEC. 1941
BORNEO
JAVA
MAR. 1942
MALAYA FEB. 1942
FRENCH INDOCHINA
THAILAND DEC. 1941
BURMA
FEB. 1942
SUMATRA
DUTCH EAST INDIES

Although it was called a 'fleet' there had been no opportunity for the ships to train together and furthermore it was 'composed almost exclusively of ships that had been engaged on independent duties or were newly commissioned'.[11] On top of that, the carriers had only 95 planes between them, and 58 of those were Swordfish and Albacore torpedo-bombers in no way comparable to the corresponding Japanese types. Admiral Somerville travelled out aboard *Formidable*, and to say that he was not impressed with the standard of expertise shown in exercises by his 'green' Fleet Air Arm pilots would be an understatement.

Nevertheless, by March 1942 a British fleet had been assembled in the East, one that in size at least resembled the one that the Singapore Naval Base – which by then had been in Japanese hands for over a month – had been constructed to accommodate. Furthermore it had been assembled at an extremely difficult time for the Royal Navy. Only four months previously, in November 1941, the aircraft-carrier *Ark Royal* and the battleship *Barham* had been lost. That was followed by a body blow on 10th December when the Japanese sank *Prince of Wales* and *Repulse*. Then in January Italian frogmen had partially avenged Taranto by damaging the battleships *Valiant* and *Queen-Elizabeth* in Alexandria harbour with limpet mines.

The primary function of Admiral Somerville's Eastern Fleet was to secure Allied sea communications in the Indian Ocean; given that the fleet was in no way comparable in power to the fleet the Japanese could muster, just about the only card the admiral had up his sleeve, and that was no ace, was that some work had been going on in secret to build a fleet base at Addu Atoll, the southernmost of the Maldive group. This hideaway was known as 'Port T' and was one British secret the Japanese had not broken.

Somerville took his fleet to sea on 30th March in the knowledge that whatever the strength of the Japanese fleet of which he still had no exact knowledge, it was likely to be greater than his own, and that a direct confrontation must be avoided at all costs, it being vital to keep his fleet in being. Indeed, the Japanese fleet under Admiral Nagumo Chuichi which had entered the Indian Ocean was significantly more powerful than the British one, consisting of five fast carriers, four fast battleships, three cruisers, eight destroyers and six support tankers. As a reconnaissance patrol ahead of this task force were the eight boats forming the 2nd Submarine Flotilla.

Admiral Somerville divided his fleet into two, the fastest ships in Force A and the slowest in Force B, and then lay in wait some eighty miles south of Ceylon. He knew that his only chance of success against superior naval aircraft was to launch a night torpedo-bomber attack against the carriers, so on the night of 31st March–1st April he swept towards the enemy's probable line of attack but, sighting nothing, withdrew at daybreak to the westward. Either the Japanese had somehow learned that he had put to sea and postponed their attack on Ceylon, or the original intercepts had been read wrongly.

By the night of 2nd April, with no further intelligence forthcoming to indicate a later attack on Ceylon, and with his older battleships running out of fuel and water, Somerville decided to withdraw the bulk of his fleet to the secret 'Port T' to which most of the fleet's auxiliary ships, including tankers, had already been despatched. But he sent the carrier *Hermes* with her attendant destroyer *Vampire* to Trincomalee where they were to prepare for Operation Ironclad, the proposed occupation of Madagascar, in part to protect the round-the-Cape route to the Middle East. He also sent two cruisers, *Dorsetshire* and *Cornwall*, back to Colombo, the first to resume an interrupted refitting programme, the second to escort Convoy SU 4, which was taking Australian troops back home from the Middle East. Somerville arrived at 'Port T' with Force A at noon on 4th April and his ships began refuelling. Force B followed him into port a few hours later.

But the Japanese commander, Admiral Nagumo, who had been Commander-in-Chief of the fleet that attacked Pearl Harbor on a Sunday, the day of the week when defenders were likely to be less on the *qui vive*, had but been biding his time; he was one old sea-dog who did not need to learn new tricks and it was his intent to attack on 5th April, which was Easter Sunday. Late in the afternoon of 4th April Nagumo's fleet was spotted some 360 miles southeast of Ceylon by a Catalina operating out of Colombo. The flying-boat just had time to report her find, but not the strength of the force, before she was shot down. Somerville sailed with his Force A at midnight to be followed seven hours later by Force B, though there was no hope of them getting to a position where they could intervene in time. Meanwhile, Admiral Layton, C-in-C, Ceylon, ordered *Dorsetshire* and *Cornwall* away from Colombo.

The Colombo raid lasted less than two hours, and thanks to an earlier dispersal of merchant ships after the initial warning from

FECB, British losses were much lower than they might have been. The destroyer *Tenedos* and the armed merchant cruiser *Hector*, both refitting, were sunk, and two other ships were damaged. Hurricanes and Fulmars, the latter badly outclassed by escorting Japanese Zeros, brought down nineteen of the enemy and AA defences a further five, but British air losses equalled those of the enemy.

At about noon on 5th April the two British cruisers racing to link up with Force A were attacked by Japanese bombers, and in less than fifteen minutes, first *Dorsetshire* and than *Cornwall*, were sunk.

That afternoon Somerville received conflicting reports which caused him to turn northwest to keep within night-striking distance of the enemy; then during 6th April he turned east, then southeast for much the same reason. But with air reconnaissance showing no sign of the enemy he returned to 'Port T' on 8th April. He had in fact been operating too far west, for after sinking the two cruisers Nagumo had turned northeast to attack Trincomalee.

Early on the morning of the 8th, the 'Y' installation at Colombo drew a D/F bearing on a call-sign identified as that of Nagumo's flagship *Akagi*, its position indicating a possible attack on Trincomalee. As in Colombo, the harbour there, one of the finest natural harbours in the world, was cleared as best possible of ships, the *Hermes* and *Vampire* making to the south, the former having had to leave her aircraft behind.

The attack on Trincomalee came on 9th April, but as at Colombo, British shipping losses were small, and the Japanese lost another twenty-four aircraft in the process. However, unfortunately for the British, *Hermes* and her escort were spotted by a Japanese aircraft. The aircraft's sighting report was intercepted by the British but because of damage caused by Japanese bombs to communications ashore, the order for fighters to be sent out to cover the carrier did not reach the aerodromes in time. At 1100 hours the carrier was sunk, with one of her 4-inch guns still firing defiantly as she went down. She was soon followed to the bottom by the destroyer.

Meanwhile submarines of the Japanese 2nd Flotilla had sunk five Allied ships aggregating 32,000 tons, and in the Bay of Bengal another Japanese force led by the carrier *Ryujo* sank a total of eighteen merchant ships and the Indian navy sloop *Indus*.

No doubt Admiral Nagumo was pleased with the haul from his sortie into the Indian Ocean although, had it not been for the Sigint warnings from FECB and the Americans, it is likely that British losses would have been far higher. Even so, Nagumo's expedition caused Somerville to decide for the immediate future not to use any base in the north Indian Ocean for his fleet, and withdrew to Kilindini on the Kenyan coast. Work was even stopped on 'Port T' in case the Japanese discovered and captured it to use as an advance base of their own. For fear that Nagumo's raid might presage an all-out invasion of Ceylon, FECB's operational and cryptanalysis centre in Colombo was also moved to Kilindini where it was called HMS *Alidina*, being housed, along with Somerville's HQ, in a requisitioned Indian girl's school of that name. HMS *Anderson* continued to operate as Colombo's 'Y' station. The Kilindini operation was to stay in situ until September 1943 when it was considered that all danger from a Japanese attack was over.

The British move to Kilindini, and the importance of the Cape route to and from the Middle East, enhanced the strategic standing of the French-held island of Madagascar. For fear that the Japanese might create bases there and that, with the connivance of the Vichy-French, Germany and Japan might join hands there, the Allies decided on an expedition to forestall this. British commando and army units were landed at the main port of Diego Suarez on 5th May, and despite opposition from the French including an attempted submarine attack on the carrier HMS *Illustrious*, the port was in British hands by 7th May. Complete occupation of the island was deferred in the hope that General de Gaulle might persuade the French commanders to come into the Allied fold, a hope that proved vain, and after more fighting complete occupation was achieved in September.

During February and early March 1942 a series of raids by American carrier task forces on Japanese-held islands in the Pacific, and the build-up of American ground and air forces in that area, especially in Australia, demonstrated to the Japanese that the US Pacific Fleet was still a force to be reckoned with. The Japanese High Command saw two immediate needs: a way must be found to bring the American fleet to battle, and further action in the south was necessary to protect the 'Empire's' southern flank. The need for these actions was reinforced in the most dramatic way when, on 18th April, at President Roosevelt's instigation, a force of sixteen B.25s flown off the USS *Hornet*, raided

Tokyo. The material damage done was negligible, but the effect on the Japanese – to say nothing of the way the raid uplifted American morale – was far-reaching; the motherland was not inviolate.* Not only that, that raid set Admiral Yamamoto on the path of attempting to take the strategically placed island of Midway which, if successful, would serve to prevent any further carrier raids on the homeland for its airfield would be on the flank of any attacking force.

A week after the raid on Trincomalee, and the day before the US raid on Tokyo, American cryptanalysts achieved further successes. On 17th April they gleaned from intercepts the gist of a Japanese plan to attack and capture Port Moresby on the south coast of New Guinea. It was now part of Japanese strategy to take Port Moresby and make it a southern outpost of their defensive perimeter, a perimeter they seemed not to realise was already too large for their naval and military strength and national economy to support. However, taking Port Moresby would not only threaten northern Australia, but would offer a threat to all the communication links between Australia and the United States.

The Americans sent two task forces, led by the carriers *Yorktown* and *Lexington*, on a spoiling mission, and the subsequent Battle of the Coral Sea became the first battle in naval history in which the issue was decided without surface ships exchanging a shot, the entire action being carried out by carrier-based aircraft. Both prior to the battle, which took place on 7th/8th May, and during it, the Americans' ability to read certain Japanese signals concurrently, and their growing experience in the use of wireless traffic analysis, were to prove crucial.

However, it was one thing to know about Japanese intentions and quite another to defeat them, and the United States navy's official history has dubbed this engagement, 'the Battle of Naval Errors', for it was characterised by blunders on both sides.[12] One blunder was *Yorktown*'s initial strike against Japanese ships which were engaged on only a secondary operation, the invasion of the harbour at Tulagi in the Solomons, for by the time the carrier's planes reached the target only a handful of Japanese ships remained there. For a disproportionate expenditure of torpedoes, bombs and 83,000 rounds of ammunition,

* The B.25 Flying Fortresses were too large to land back on *Hornet*, so they overflew Japan and made for China. Some crew members whose aircraft landed in Japanese occupied territory were executed.

the Americans bagged a destroyer and three small auxiliary vessels. Admiral Chester Nimitz, American Commander-in-Chief, Pacific, thought the swap 'disappointing'.

The next mistakes were made by the Japanese. Had the commander of the main Japanese task force ordered air searches to the southeast on 6th May, the combined American carrier forces would have been discovered only seventy miles away in the process of refuelling from tankers. After that refuelling the American tanker *Neosho* and its attendant destroyer *Sims* were detached to the south, a move that unintentionally provided a perfect decoy, for on the following day the two ships were spotted by a Japanese reconnaissance plane which reported them as a carrier and a cruiser. That resulted in these minor targets being attacked by seventy-eight aircraft. *Sims* was sunk immediately, and *Neosho* was so badly damaged she had later to be sunk by an American destroyer.

There were other mistakes, but suffice it to say that, by the end of the final engagement, the Japanese had lost the carrier *Shoho* with damage to another, the *Shokaku*. Against that the Americans had lost *Lexington*, as well as *Neosho* and *Sims*, and the *Yorktown* was damaged. Tactically, and measured only by the vessels sunk on both sides, it can be regarded as a Japanese victory – they certainly regarded it so. But strategically it was an American one for, although it did not prevent the Japanese from later making an attempt to take Port Moresby in the rear by landing a force on the other side of the island, they called off a sea expedition against the port for good. Not only that, although the Americans had lost many planes, the enemy had lost sixty-nine, bringing the total number of Japanese navy aircraft lost since the beginning of the war to over six hundred. Those losses in aircraft, and more especially of trained pilots, were losses that the Japanese, unlike the Americans, were never able to make up. In addition the Americans had gained valuable battle experience and learnt many lessons, not least in the immediate use of operational intelligence.[13]

Soon after his escape from the Philippines, General Douglas MacArthur had been appointed Supreme Allied Commander, Southwest Pacific. He set up his headquarters first at Melbourne, South Australia, and then at Brisbane in Queensland, much nearer to the scene of action. Australia thus became the centre of Allied intelligence operations in the Southwest Pacific, and before the war was over there were at least a score of separate intelligence organisations operating there. Over fifty years on it is difficult to sort out the precise functions of these different organisations or how they worked with each other; an added difficulty is that all worked on the 'need to know' principle with the heads of some of the organisations not even knowing of the existence of others. This sometimes led to a duplication of effort and to associated inefficiencies.

Tom Harrisson, an anthropologist and co-founder (with Charles Madge) of the Social Research organisation 'Mass Observation', who was later to win world renown as the Director of the Kuching Museum, Sarawak, was a section leader in one of these organisations. He wrote in his *World Within* about the stringent application of the need to know principle:

> There were several units responsible for what are nowadays known as cloak-and-dagger works in this theatre. True to the mood of the business, the secrecy they valued above all other was among themselves. Each unit appeared more concerned with preventing its 'operatives' from knowing about or being in contact with any other unit, than anything else. It was a heinous sin to be found in possession of knowledge of or contact with a closely related body operating in parallel with you – or, often, in conflict. One of the ultimate effects of this was that units with the best salesmanship, warmanship and political savvy tended to get the plum jobs . . . A[n] important effect . . . was that . . . things which should have been done never got done properly.[14]

There certainly seems to have been an over-provision of intelligence organisations, with demarcation lines between them indistinctly drawn. However, MacArthur's disparate command was the first major attempt of the war to draw together the intelligence services of several nations, intelligence services which, by the very secrecy under which they operated, themselves had indistinct boundaries. On top of that each service and each nation did its best to preserve control over what it considered to be its own patch. An official US source, referring only to American organisations, noted:

> An artificial barrier existed between the intelligence services of the Army and Navy. Throughout the war, lacking unified command in the Pacific, we operated without an intelligence system capable of meeting the requirements of co-ordinated land, sea and air warfare . . . a system was not established during the war which insured the

timely production of balanced, objective intelligence and the timely dissemination of that intelligence for all those who needed it in the performance of their tasks.[15]

If the Americans could not solve the problem of co-ordination between their own Army and Navy Intelligence Services, it is not surprising that there were problems at international level.

At the hub of MacArthur's intelligence organisation was Colonel (later Major-General) Charles Willoughby. Born Karl Weidenbach in Germany, Willoughby spoke English with a thick accent and was known to his men as the 'Prussian Drillmaster'. He was tough and lacked certain diplomatic skills which, had he possessed them, might have made his control over an international staff much better. He was very loyal to his commander, but 'his loyalty was not matched by his ability', says one commentator.[16] Rather old-fashioned over intelligence matters, he seemed never to trust fully information that came from Sigint sources, and his use of such material was often ineffective. It was probably Willoughby's lack of diplomacy as much as MacArthur's own failings in this department, that led to MacArthur being unpopular with many non-American members of his staff. In point of fact, he also had difficulty in getting on with some of his own people, especially with the navy.

On the naval Sigint side, and already operating in Melbourne long before MacArthur's arrival there, was the group of cryptographers led by Commander Eric Nave who worked from HQ, Australian Naval Intelligence, in St Kilda Road. This Melbourne unit was in fact an important cog in the Commonwealth Sigint system. When newly promoted Commander R.J. Fabian, USN, and his cryptographic team arrived in Australia from the Philippines in February 1942, he too set up shop in Melbourne, in his case in the Monterey Building. Fabian's unit was known as FRUMEL, short for Fleet Radio Unit, Melbourne. Both groups were latterly responsible to MacArthur's HQ through the Allied Naval Forces HQ.

Attached to the HQ of the Director of Australian Naval Intelligence in Melbourne, were a Dutch liaison officer, Commander Salm, and a Chinese liaison officer, Captain Chik Kway-way. It may have been Captain Chik's presence that paved the way for the Australian Intelligence Services throughout the war always being on better terms with their Chinese counterparts than were the British Intelligence Services. The British were strongly of the opinion that, whatever intelligence was passed to the Chinese would eventually and inevitably end up in the hands of the Japanese.* Although Australian Naval Intelligence placed the whole of its resources at the disposal of General MacArthur, it preserved its identity and remained a link in the world-wide British Admiralty Naval Intelligence organisation.

The Australian Military HQ was also at Melbourne. It too had certain Sigint operations, including a diplomatic cryptographic section to which Professors A.D. Tyndall and T.G. Room of Sydney University were attached. This section had decyphered a message of 4th December 1941 from Tokyo to the Japanese consul-general in Sydney, ordering him to destroy all codes and cyphers.[17] The bulk of the Australian Military Intelligence branch was transferred to Brisbane when MacArthur's HQ moved north, leaving behind only the Internal Security Branch which controlled, amongst other bodies, the Northern Australia Observer Unit, whose personnel, equipped with teleradios, kept watch along the vital area between the Gulf of Carpentaria in the east to the township of Broome in the west.

In April 1942 MacArthur set up his own signals intelligence operation in Melbourne. It moved north to Brisbane in September, into premises close to the Ascot racetrack, at 21 Henry Street, said to have been a former brothel. It was the direct, though greatly expanded, successor to the Sigint organisation MacArthur had had in the Philippines. Indeed, its first head was Lieutenant-Colonel Joe Sherr, who had commanded the earlier unit. After Sherr was killed in an aircraft accident in India, the command went to one of the fathers of American cryptology, Colonel Abraham Sinkov. No expense was spared in setting up the operation. The unit had two banks of IBM computers for use in decryption and analysis, and had a large staff. The personnel included Australians and Britons from Special Wireless Units that had served in Singapore – including one officer and twelve

* The British attitude towards the Chinese is well illustrated by the case of Herbert Yardley. Yardley was the father of American cryptography, having created the US War Department cryptologic service in 1917. After 1918 he worked in the so-called 'Black Chamber' of the State Department, engaged in the same kind of work. That was closed down in 1929 by Secretary of State Henry L. Stimson on the basis that 'gentlemen do not read each other's mail' – a decision that Stimson must have come to regret by the time of Pearl Harbor when he was Secretary for War. After that Yardley had a varied career and in 1938 was employed by the Chinese Nationalist Secret Service to break Japanese military codes. In 1941 the Canadians employed him in Ottawa to oversee their own cryptanalytical team until Britain asked for his removal, a request no doubt at least partly due to Yardley's Chinese connections.

other ranks who had served with FECB – and had been brought out before Singapore fell. This set-up was the intercept arm of a much larger organisation known as the Central Bureau, or CB for short, which controlled intelligence from US Army, Australian Army and Royal Australian Air Force sources.

The British had their own quite separate Sigint operation at Brisbane, which was an arm of Bletchley Park. Attached to it was a Special Liaison Unit. Over on the other side of the Tasman Sea at Wellington, New Zealand, the Combined Operational Intelligence Centre (COIC), which had been set up in October 1941 under Lieutenant-Commander F.M. Beesley, was the centre from which British Naval Intelligence in the South Pacific was directed. Although it had officers attached from the other services, it was mainly a naval operation. It had it own 'Y' and W/T operation but did not have a decyphering unit. There was a subsidiary 'Y' unit at Suva, Fiji Islands. In May 1942 D/F fixes from the Wellington and Suva stations, combined with callsign identification, gave warning of the presence of Japanese submarines off the east coast of Australia. Melbourne was warned before the midget submarine attack on Sydney took place – on the night of 31st May/1st June – and the withdrawal of the mother submarines concerned to their base in the Japanese Mandated Islands to the north was clearly followed by D/F.[18]

Aside from the Central Bureau itself, MacArthur's intelligence organisation consisted of three main bureaux, each with several important offshoots. The Combined Operational Intelligence Centre, COIC (which, with the same name as the British organisation in Wellington, New Zealand, adds to the difficulties in sorting out the general situation), was by the end of 1942 under Group Captain Malloy, RAAF, and engaged in collating and recording intelligence and issuing bulletins. Amongst those bulletins were Daily Situation Reports which included intelligence from all sources except 'Special', and a Daily Review of Intelligence which did include 'Special', and which had a much more restricted circulation. It also produced a Daily Naval Appreciation, the only document to give the complete disposition of all Allied naval units together with estimates of enemy naval dispositions in the area. Situated at Brisbane and reporting to COIC was the US Naval Intelligence Section under Captain Hudson, USN; the Australian Military Intelligence Section which was part of the staff of the Commander Allied Land Forces, General Sir Thomas Blamey; and the Air Intelligence Directorate. The latter, under Air

Commodore J. Hewitt, RAAF, was the largest and best equipped of all the intelligence organisations, and owed its relative importance and rapid development to a war in which, due to the great distances involved, air played the dominant part.

The second of the main intelligence bureaux was called the Allied Intelligence Bureau, or AIB. This was set up in June 1942 to co-ordinate the activities of a number of disparate intelligence agencies engaged in activities behind enemy lines and other activities of a 'most secret' nature. AIB was headed by Colonel C.G. Roberts, formerly Director of Australian Military Intelligence, a consummate professional but chosen for the job largely because he was more likely to get the full co-operation of Australian government and military leaders than an American. However, MacArthur placed Captain Allison Ind, US Army, in charge of AIB finances which effectively ensured that nothing much went on that did not meet with MacArthur's approval.[19]

AIB had several sections, its Section C taking over the existing Coastwatchers Organisation which – building upon an organisation code-named 'Ferdinand' created after World War One – had been set up, organised and trained by Captain R.B.M. Long of the Australian navy in September 1939.

The legendary coastwatchers comprised some 800 members, the majority local officials such as District Officers and police, but also planters, traders, and even missionaries; they were spread all over the island chain lying to the north of Australia and along the north Australian coast itself. It is not known how the coastwatchers on the north coast fitted in with the Army observer units which, as mentioned, were engaged in much the same sort of activity there. Some coastwatchers were given ranks in the RANVR. They had been trained to report on enemy shipping movements, and about one hundred of them, based in the more remote places, had been supplied with teleradios – small radio instruments resistant to damp, heat and rough handling which had been developed by Australian scientists.[20] A number of coastwatchers had volunteered to remain behind in the Solomons and other islands overrun by the Japanese, and the accuracy of their identifications of enemy aircraft and warships and their reports on movements of hostile forces were considerably better than those obtained by air reconnaissance. Many of these men had hair-raising experiences when their radio transmissions were pinpointed by Japanese direction-finders, some being saved only by the bravery of islanders who acted as scouts. Caches of food and arms had been hidden pre-war, and from these hideaways some coastwatching groups developed into guerrilla bands. One such group, led by Nick Waddell, a future Governor of Sarawak, once 'took out' a party of sixteen Japanese soldiers.[21] Waddell's group was also instrumental in saving the lives of a number of downed Allied airmen. Another coastwatcher, New Zealander Donald Kennedy, operated his own private navy from a remote bay on New Georgia. In his schooner he occasionally sallied forth to give battle to Japanese patrol boats. The coastwatchers, say the authors of the Official Royal Navy History of the Japanese war, 'made a contribution to the Allied arms out of all proportion to their numbers'.

AIB's Section 'A' was responsible for 'unconventional operations', and took over an existing unit known as SOA, or Special Operations Australia, which was a branch of Britain's SOE. Section 'B', headed by Captain R. Kendall, RNR, was responsible for the bureau's 'Special' Intelligence, and had its own cryptographic unit. Under its aegis came a Dutch intercept station which had transferred to Darwin after the Japanese invasion of Java. Section 'D' was responsible for propaganda, although the Political Warfare and Propaganda Division of the Australian Department of External Affairs remained completely independent of MacArthur's command.

The third main intelligence bureau was called the Allied Geographical Section, a body of Australian and US officers and civilians with particular knowledge of areas where operations were being planned. They produced 'Terrain Studies' based on all manner of sources, but including the proceeds from aerial reconnaissance, information from coastwatchers, and interrogation of people with local knowledge. Associated with that body was the Allied Translator and Interpreter Section. This was based at Indoroopilly, a suburb of Brisbane. It made use of a number of Japanese language scholars, and translated captured enemy documents and interrogated the comparatively few Japanese prisoners-of-war who allowed themselves to be captured alive.

With all the effort now being put into cryptography by the Allies, giant strides were being made daily. Within two weeks of the Battle of the Coral Sea (7th-9th May 1942), Allied listening posts which now ringed the Pacific picked up an extremely long Japanese message, its length indicating that it was important and probably an operations order. With the aid of previous retrievals stored in the IBM machines at Pearl Harbor, a part solution was soon achieved, and within a week cryptanalysts had cracked what turned out to be Admiral Yamamoto's order for a main attack, backed by a diversion, designed to suck in the three carrier task forces that now made up the major part of the US Pacific Fleet. Japan would then finish the job she had begun at Pearl Harbor. However, the most important parts of the message – containing the date-time information and the places to be attacked – remained unsolved for these had been 'superenciphered' in a system that had been observed only rarely before, allowing small chance of reconstruction. A message to the US Navy from FECB Colombo on 22nd May indicated that it, too, had picked up the same transmission and although it could not confirm the target, thought it might be Midway.[22]

Admiral Chester Nimitz set the Navy's Combat Intelligence Unit to work, and on the basis of ship locations and speeds, contextual evidence and earlier decryptions of messages that suggested that the code letters AF denoted Midway Island – the westernmost but one of the Hawaiian Islands which acted as a sentry for Pearl Harbor – they came up with the probability of that island being the main target and with a date of 3rd June. By use of a deception device they were soon able to get the target confirmed. The Midway garrison sent a message in plain language indicating that their distillation plant had broken down, and shortly afterwards a Japanese coded message was intercepted and read, which stated that AF had a fresh water problem. Now the only matter outstanding for Nimitz, but an extremely weighty one on which might depend the fate of his fleet, was the timing of the attacks, the 3rd June date being an educated guesstimate, but a guesstimate nevertheless.

On a night late in May, Lieutenant-Commander Joseph Finnegan, who had spent three years as an American language officer in Tokyo, and a cryptanalyst, Wesley Wright, set about the superenciphered portions of Yamamoto's message. In a lengthy bout of hard work mixed with brilliant inspiration based on experience, and no doubt with some of those flashes of good luck that all good codebreakers must have, they came up with a solution. Though it contained 'a certain amount of slack', they 'regarded it as essentially sound'. The solution in fact confirmed the date of the attack on Midway as 3rd June and of a feint attack on the Aleutians on 2nd June. With this confirmation under his belt, Admiral Nimitz laid plans for the battle that was to turn the tide of the war in the Pacific.[23]

In the Battle of Midway the Japanese pitted four carrier task forces against three of the Americans, although in reality the Americans had a fourth and unsinkable 'carrier' in the island of Midway itself which had been reinforced to bring the number of planes there up to the strength of a carrier force. The three American carriers were the *Yorktown*, which after the damage sustained in the Coral Sea battle had been patched up in a record two days, *Enterprise* and *Hornet*.

On 2nd June the Japanese attacked Dutch Harbor in the Aleutians, and attacked and subsequently captured a couple of insignificant islands there. (Because of the intervention of the International Date Line, some books give the date of these initial attacks as 3rd June, but in fact they began a day earlier than the one on Midway.) The loss of those islands was a small price to pay for what was to come, and Nimitz did not commit any part of his main force in trying to prevent their loss.

On 3rd June reconnaissance planes from Midway picked up the so-called Japanese Occupation Force consisting of transports, seaplane carriers, a tanker, and their cruiser-led escorts. Nine Flying Fortresses based on Midway made an attack on it that afternoon, the attack coming as a complete surprise to the Japanese who had no radar. But despite some exaggerated claims made by returning American pilots, they achieved no hits, demonstrating the ineffectiveness of high altitude bombing against moving targets. That night, four torpedo-carrying Catalinas from Midway had better luck, one torpedo damaging the tanker.

At dawn the following morning the Japanese carriers began flying off their strike forces, with neither side having located each other's carriers and the Japanese quite unaware of the strength the Americans had been able to concentrate in the area. At 0545 a reconnaissance aircraft sighted the approaching Japanese planes when they were still one hundred and fifty miles off the island, and a few minutes later another sighting was made, this time of two carriers and supporting ships. Every serviceable aircraft on the island was scrambled, including twenty-five marine fighters. These fighters proved no match for a superior number of escorting Zeros, and the Japanese strike aircraft managed to get through to the island. In a seventeen-minute attack, most of the structures above ground were either destroyed or damaged, including the aircraft refueling system.

Less than an hour later the American strike aircraft from Midway attacked the Japanese carriers, but in an engagement lasting over an

A major diplomatic incident arose in January 1940, before Japan entered the war. (*Above*) The crack Japanese liner *Asama Maru* is stopped and boarded by an armed British boat party. (*Below*) The Germans, having taken off the *Asama Maru* by force, are now climbing up the side of the cruiser HMS *Liverpool*.

SS *Automedon* (*above*) in her Blue Funnel peacetime livery and (*below*) the German raider *Atlantis* in her wartime livery, which captured and sank *Automedon* in November 1940 in the Indian Ocean. In the process *Atlantis* made one of the most dramatic hauls of secret documents in the Second World War. (*Automedon, courtesy John Clarkson*)

The attack on Pearl Harbour, 7th December 1941. This Japanese photograph shows the tracks of torpedoes launched from aircraft and heading for US vessels.

Admiral Yamamoto Isoroku, famed commander-in-chief of the Imperial Japanese Navy (*top, left*); (*right*) Tojo Hideki, the Prime Minister of Japan during the Second World War. (*Below*) General Douglas MacArthur, Supreme Allied Commander, Southwest Pacific with the outspoken Australian General Sir Thomas Blamey at Port Moresby, Papua New Guinea, in November 1942.

(*Above, left*) General MacArthur has said: 'I have had to barter like a rug merchant throughout the war to get the intelligence I have needed from the Navy'. (*Above, right*) Brigadier-General C. A. Willoughby, MacArthur's chief of intelligence, considered they needed 'a completely joint, interlocking concept and cryptological service – on the highest level'. (*Right*) Gerald Wilkinson worked with MI6 in the Philippines but Willoughby had scant regard for him.

'Twenty-one curves,' part of the Burma Road (in Annan, China) over which Allied supplies were carried to Chiang Kai-shek and the Kuomintang. (*US Army photograph*)

(*Above*) HMS *Formidable*, a British aircraft-carrier, is crashed by a Japanese kamikaze aircraft on 4th May 1945. (*Left*) A group of kamikaze, or 'divine wind', pilots.

(*Above*) Signals Intelligence officers at the Wireless Experimental Centre (WEC), Delhi, July 1944. In the front row, seventh from left, is Major Peter Marr-Johnson of the Bletchley Park Special Liaison Unit formerly in Singapore. Third from left, front row, is Wilfrid Noyce, the climber and writer. (*Courtesy Alan Stripp*)

(*Below*) US Airways Listening Station, near Harrogate, Yorkshire. Compare the earlier picture of Stonecutters Island, Hong Kong. (*Author's photograph*)

hour not a single hit was achieved. The outlook for Midway at that point looked very serious, for although the Japanese force of some eighty ships, including the aircraft-carriers, had been attacked by the full strength of shore-based aircraft, it was still converging on the island. However, aircraft from the American carriers were about to enter the fray, although not before there was a great hiccup. The Japanese fleet altered course, a change which, although reported to the American carriers, they did not relay to their aircraft strike forces because that would have necessitated breaking wireless silence. This resulted in the first wave of aircraft, those with fighter escorts, missing the target altogether, and a search having to be made for the target by the second wave, *Hornet*'s torpedo squadron.

The *Hornet*'s squadron came upon the Japanese carriers at a time when their decks were full of aircraft already loaded with bombs and torpedoes and ready to take off. Although unsupported by fighters the squadron reported their find and then roared in. Not one of the fifteen aircraft survived against heavy fighter opposition and anti-aircraft fire, but this brave attack bought time for the strike aircraft from *Enterprise* and *Yorktown* to arrive. Though many more American aircraft were brought down, all four Japanese carriers were eventually sunk. In return Japanese aircraft managed to sink *Yorktown*. But with the loss of the four carriers and, of course, their full complements of planes, the Japanese had suffered a huge naval defeat, and Admiral Yamamoto, who had been in command of the Combined Fleet, retired back to base. But even though the Americans had the benefit of knowing just what the Japanese were up to, it had been a close run thing.

An American scholar has noted the impact that the Battle of Midway had on the course of the war. It was he said, 'the first irreversible Allied victory of the Second World War'.[24] It provided the opening for an Allied counter-offensive in the Solomon Islands which kept the Japanese busy for the remainder of 1942. It also had the spin-off result of preventing another Japanese excursion into the Indian Ocean as part of a Grand Scheme to support and perhaps link up with the Germans coming from the other direction.

Admiral Nimitz, in a generous tribute to his codebreakers, later wrote, 'Midway was essentially a victory of intelligence.' He also reported that 'Pearl Harbor has been partially avenged.' The American Chief of Staff, General George C. Marshall, was even more specific when he recorded in his papers that, as a result of cryptanalysis, it had been possible to concentrate all the limited forces available to meet the Japanese off Midway. However, General Marshall was also acutely concerned lest the comprehensiveness of the victory and the surprise that led to it, might cause the Japanese to suspect their codes were being read, and he advised caution in any press briefings given.[25]

Despite Marshall's cautionary advice, on 7th June an article appeared in the Washington *Times-Herald* under the title 'US Navy Knew In Advance All About Jap Fleet'. Quoting 'reliable sources in Naval Intelligence' it said that the strength of the Japanese forces at Midway had been known in advance. It went on:

> The information in the hands of the Navy Department was so definite that a feint at some American base, to be accompanied by a serious effort to invade another base, was predicted. Guesses were even made that Dutch Harbor in the Aleutians and Midway . . . might be targets . . . by last Tuesday [2nd] the Americans were able to conclude that a feint was to be made at Dutch Harbor.

It is small wonder that American security over the operational handling of 'Special' was to be a constant worry to the British throughout the war. The British operational handling of 'Special', through its system of Special Liason Units, worked extremely well, although there was at least one cock-up in the administrative handling of it, a cock-up that might have had serious results, and knowledge of which was kept from the Americans.

The value placed on intelligence received from coastwatchers demonstrates that static or ground intelligence agents still had a major part to play in the overall intelligence picture of the war. In some instances information received from them served to confirm material from Sigint sources, but in some areas ground agents were the only source of information.

One such was the tiny Portuguese colony of Macau, some thirty miles west of Hong Kong. Portugal was a neutral country and Japan had not attacked the colony although they stationed some troops and intelligence officers there soon after Hong Kong had fallen.* As the

* The Japanese did attack and occupy the Portuguese colony of East Timor. Against Portuguese protests it had, on 17th December 1941, been occupied by Dutch and Australian troops. The Japanese landed on 20th February 1942 and the Allied forces capitulated three days later except for those who made for the centre of the island from where they conducted guerrilla operations until they were taken off in the following December.

war went on and the Portuguese governor had to rely more and more on Japanese goodwill for food supplies, it came increasingly under Japanese control. Lying at the mouth of the Pearl River, it was an excellent place for observing Japanese shipping arriving at or leaving Canton, as well as being a contact point for agents being run by the British and Chinese in occupied Hong Kong and elsewhere. Weather reports from there were also useful for Allied pilots.

The British consul in Macau, John Reeves, remained free for the whole of the war although he and his wife and family were kept under observation by Japanese intelligence officers based in the town.[26] His official work was to look after the interests of the British residents in Macau and also, because they had no official representative of their own, of American residents too. Undercover he worked for both the British SOE and SIS. SOE papers recently released in the British Public Record Office confirm his secret relationship with that organisation, and amongst the papers is one that contains mention of a denial by SIS that Reeves had any connection with them. However, that is par for the SIS course, and the denial seems to have been doubted even at the time.[27]

Reeves was collecting information from neutral travellers including members of what he called his 'Portuguese Group', who passed through Macau to China, Hong Kong and elsewhere. He reported on conditions in the prisoner-of-war and internee camps in Hong Kong, on Japanese defence plans in the area, and boat-building. He was asked to obtain samples of Japanese 'type and print', presumably to be used for forging papers, and to obtain the wavelengths of Japanese radio stations.

Unfortunately John Reeves was a man rather inclined to bravado, and like many such men, could be indiscreet. A Danish operative of SOE, F.A. Olsen – the Danes, being considered neutral by the Japanese, were permitted to travel on business more or less freely around occupied territory – wrote a report on 4th August 1942 after completing a 'business' tour of places in southern China. In it he was critical of Reeves' too-open attitude and lack of security. Olsen had smuggled in two codes, but after meeting Reeves gave him only one. Olsen subsequently discovered that, against advice, Reeves had taught his wife how to use it, Mrs Reeves being considered even more indiscreet than her husband.

Olsen looked for someone to whom he could entrust the second code, and found Mrs Joy Wilson whose husband, Superintendent

Geoffrey Wilson of the Hong Kong Police, was interned in the British colony. He co-opted her as an agent, gave her the second code, and also recruited two other Britons in Macau, one of them a man called 'Fletch' Fletcher, the manager of the Macau Electric Company. Before Olsen left he had overseen arrangements for the carriage of written messages by crew members of Portuguese and French ships trading between Hong Kong, Macau and Kwangchowan – the latter a French-leased territory on the Chinese mainland just north of Hainan Island, and another excellent place for observing shipping movements.

As a result of Olsen's visit funds were smuggled into Macau for the local purchase of equipment to construct a wireless station with which to communicate directly with Chungking, the capital of free China where the Asian headquarters of several Allied intelligence agencies, including SIS, were now situated. Prior to that all reports from Macau were by telegraph via Lisbon before they got to London and then Chungking, a route the Japanese were surely monitoring. Full details of what information was passed to Chungking is not known. What is known is that, from 1943 onwards, Chungking was receiving much information from Stanley Camp, the main prisoner-of-war centre in Hong Kong, not only about the terrible conditions that existed there, but also valuable information on shipping and troop movements in the area. Geoffrey Wilson has written that his wife Joy 'was certainly in touch with me in Stanley Camp, but this was very dangerous'.[28]

Joy Wilson's undercover work was not confined to working with SOE. A Hong Kong escapee, Lieutenant-Colonel (later Sir) Leslie Ride, had set up an organisation in China called the British Army Aid Group, or BAAG, which became part of MI9, the section of Military Intelligence in London that dealt with escapes. Ride interpreted his remit rather widely, which brought him into conflict with the British SIS in the area, who considered he was trespassing on its preserves. His forward posts rescued shot-down Allied pilots, produced weather reports, and picked up intelligence. In one operation his men managed to smuggle out of occupied Hong Kong a number of top bankers, and some valuable dockyard foremen. Ride found the communist Chinese much more reliable and efficient than the Nationalists, and perhaps made this known in the wrong quarters. In 1943 Tai Li, the anti-British head of Chiang Kai-shek's secret service, made him close down his forward post overlooking Hong Kong harbour which was manned by 'Reds'. Ride also had difficulties with the American

Office of Strategic Services, OSS, who bribed his runners in order to get information first.

In Edwin Ride's book called *B.A.A.G.*, he notes that 'as its official representative in Macau, the BAAG appointed Mrs J. Wilson, who was on the staff of the Consulate. Joy Wilson was in charge of all codes and communications and was the main point contact for the various agents in the colony. Chief among these was Y.C. Liang, of Wang Tai Compradores, who operated under the codename "Phoenix".'

Joy Wilson and her two young sons, together with Mr and Mrs Fletcher, in a party totalling thirty-seven, made good an escape from Macau in April 1943. To do so they had first to pass through Japanese picket boats, then through Japanese occupied territories, then through others controlled by Chinese guerrillas who were not always friendly. During part of the journey the children in the party were drugged to keep them quite. This remarkable lady and her party eventually reached Chungking and safety, then went on to India.[29]

Admiral A. Andrade e Silva was a young boy in Macau during those years, his father being commander of the Portuguese naval base. He says:

> It was generally suspected that John Reeves was somehow getting information to the Allies. One day some American fighters flew over and strafed the Japanese HQ buildings, one of which was an hotel. The pilots obviously knew the exact targets.
>
> The Portuguese authorities in the city were also attempting to swap some gasoline oil with the Japanese in exchange for some much needed rice, for the colony was suffering from severe food shortages. No sooner had the deal been struck than a flight of American planes strafed the hangers in which the gasoline was stored, blowing it up. The planes then went on to strafe the Portuguese naval units in the harbour, probably from fear they might be taken over by the Japanese.[30]

Back in Delhi Captain Harkness was relieved of his command of FECB in late 1942. It is possible that this may have been due to a 'zealous but indiscreet report' he produced after making an extensive tour of the Eastern and Pacific theatres of war.

In that report Harkness commented on the difficulties experienced with working with Chiang Kai-shek's Secret Service, run by General Tai Li at Chungking, who would only work on a *quid pro quo* basis, the objection to that being that it was considered that any information given to the Chinese would eventually filter through to the Japanese, so bad was Chinese security. On the other hand, Harkness pointed out that only Orientals had much chance of obtaining intelligence from conventional means in the East, and he thought the Chinese would be better at selecting such agents than any Western agency.

Harkness in fact gathered little of value from his tour, but did make contact with a number of British SIS agents, and his report mainly consisted of his impressions of the men he contacted. He gave their names and addresses. When the report reached the Naval Intelligence Department (NID) in London, one of these personal impressions, which was in fact an appreciation of the man involved, was sent to Stewart Menzies, the head of SIS who was known as 'C'. Someone in NID endorsed the report with the comment that 'C' would not appreciate Harkness visiting his agents and giving their addresses even in a most secret report. That writer added:

> *Moral.* Avoid putting on paper remarks about 'C's' agents and representatives, particularly anything which would be of use if the document got into the wrong hands, as documents occasionally will.[31]

Although by June 1942 the Japanese navy had sustained defeats at Coral Sea and Midway, the Japanese army had yet to suffer any reverses. By then the Japanese had completed their occupation of both Burma and the Philippines, and the Allies assumed this would release additional troops for use elsewhere.

The 'Europe First' strategy of the Allies, with the Americans committed to building up forces in Britain, meant that only enough American reinforcements could be sent to the South Pacific for a holding operation against further major disasters, to make up for losses, and perhaps, hopefully, to give the Japanese a few jolts.

The Japanese had begun to build a 'secret' airstrip on the northern side of Guadalcanal in the Solomon Islands, an operation that was spotted by coastwatchers on 20th June. The Solomons were of significant strategic importance to both sides, for the islands formed the extreme southeasterly corner of the Japanese defence perimeter and were possible bases for attacks on the Allied line of communication between Australia, and Hawaii and the United States.

It was as well the coastwatchers on Guadalcanal, under Captain M. Clemens, were in position to spot the construction of the airstrip and to send in further reports. Information from Sigint cryptanalysis had virtually dried up when, some three weeks previously, on 28th

May, the Japanese navy had made a major change in its codes; the near-stoppage of information from that source was to last for almost the entire Guadalcanal campaign which began in August 1942. Fortunately the Allies had made further strides in traffic analysis, which although a less productive and dramatic part of the Sigint effort, and with results that could only be confirmed by events, did help to fill the gap. Then, late in July, the Japanese Navy changed their callsigns, a move that was taken to indicate an impending operation and probably one in which the new airfield would play a principal role. General MacArthur took the decision to invade the island of Guadalcanal.

In the middle of planning the operation the General was buoyed up with news from the Philippines. On 10th July a secret 'left-behind' Dutch monitoring post on Java picked up a weak radio signal from Lieutenant-Colonel Guillermo Nakar of the Filipino 14th Infantry Regiment, stating that he was leading a combined Filipino-American force that was conducting guerrilla war in central Luzon. This was the first firm indication MacArthur had received that resistance to the Japanese was continuing in some parts of the island archipelago, and Nakar's was to prove to be the first of many such messages.* Later, a monitoring post on the north Australian coast picked up a message from Major Macario Peralta, of the 61st Division. He reported that he was in control of the interior of the island of Panay with a force of 8,000 men. Then Captain Ralph Praeger, US Army, radioed from northern Luzon that he was organising a 5,000-strong guerrilla force. Such resistance, MacArthur knew, would not only be holding down Japanese forces, but if properly armed and supplied the guerrillas were a potentially powerful force behind enemy lines.

On 7th August 10,000 men of the US 1st Marine Division landed on the beaches of Guadalcanal and Tulagi – the latter being an island to the north of Guadalcanal which guarded the channel between them – in Operation Watchtower. They were covered by planes from *Enterprise* and the two recently arrived carriers *Saratoga* and *Wasp*. So began the offensive which in three years was to carry the Allies to the shores of Japan, but not without many a hitch in the meantime. The Guadalcanal operation itself was to last six months.

The Japanese were taken completely by surprise, and by the

* Colonel Nakar was captured and beheaded by the Japanese within weeks of sending that first message.

following day the airstrip, to be called Henderson Field, was in American hands. But on Tulagi, in a foretaste of savage fighting to come, the Americans met with fanatical resistance.

On the day before the landings Admiral Nimitz at Pearl Harbor sent a warning based on traffic analysis that Japan had considerable cruiser strength in the area, commanded by Admiral Mikawa in his flagship *Chokai*. On 7th August, after the Americans had landed, Mikawa informed Tokyo that his two cruiser divisions were making for Guadalcanal. The message was intercepted by the Americans but because of the earlier change in code it was not decrypted until the 23rd. Had it been decrypted in time the forthcoming naval disaster off Savo Island might have been averted.

The first of several Allied errors occurred when on 8th August the report of a sighting of the Japanese force made by an Australian Hudson aircraft was somehow delayed in getting to the American fleet commanders. According to Samuel Eliot Morison in his Official History of US naval operations in World War Two, the Australian pilot concerned completed his patrol, landed, and had his tea before reporting, but even if true that hardly accounts for a delay of some six hours.[32] But not only that, the report greatly underestimated the composition of the force. When the message did arrive the Americans decided the Japanese ships were too far away to be an immediate threat to their forces on Guadalcanal.

Meanwhile a reconnaissance aircraft flown off one of the Japanese cruisers had returned with precise information on what opposition Admiral Mikawa might expect off the island. His attack began at 0145 hours on 9th August and, when his ships retired half an hour later, they had sunk three American cruisers, the *Astoria*, *Quincy* and *Vincennes*, and so damaged HMAS *Canberra* that she had to be despatched later by an American torpedo. In the process of retiring they also badly damaged the destroyer *Ralph Talbot*. It could have been much worse for the Allies had Mikawa got amongst the troop transports before retiring, which he did out of fear of being caught by aircraft from the three-carrier force under Admiral Fletcher. Fletcher, with his ships short of fuel, had in fact left the scene. The only consolation the Allies had was that one of the retiring Japanese cruisers was sunk by the American submarine S-44.

Believing there to be a risk of further attacks all the Allied transports were withdrawn from the landing beaches that afternoon, leaving the US Marines ashore with less than half of their ammunition and food for only thirty days. None of the 5-inch coastal defence guns nor the long-range radar warning sets for use ashore were landed. Without air cover, for the Americans feared jeopardising their aircraft carriers which formed the principal defence of the Australian line of communications with the US, and without other naval support, the Marines were virtually a besieged garrison until 20th August when two squadrons of aircraft were flown off to them by the light carrier *Long Island*.

By now some progress was being made in decyphering the new Japanese naval code, which the Americans called JN-25c, an exercise made easier by the capture at Guadalcanal of a complete codebook and supporting additive tables. However, any joy felt in Allied cryptanalysis circles was soon to evaporate, for on 14th August the Japanese changed the code once more. This change – to JN-25d – so soon after the one made on 28th May, might have been the result of that indiscreet article about Midway in the Washington *Times-Herald* in June. But there is another possibility; the change may have come about because of a gross administrative mistake made by the British Combined Operations Intelligence Centre at Wellington, New Zealand. Like the *Automedon* incident of November 1940, it involved secret mail placed aboard a merchant vessel.

The British-registered *Nankin* had sailed from Wellington in April 1942 bound for Colombo via Fremantle. She left Fremantle on 5th May, and on the 10th, when about a third of the way along the 3,100-mile route to Colombo, she was spotted by a plane launched by the German raider *Thor* (Captain G. Gumprich). The plane attempted to destroy *Nankin*'s wireless aerial by the usual practice of diving between the masts with a trailing hook, but missed. The steamer was able to send off a distress message complete with position (26–43′S, 89–56′E) before *Thor* hove up and attacked. *Nankin* put up a short fight, during which Captain Stratford threw overboard the ship's code-books and other papers, before surrendering.* Unbeknownst to Stratford or anyone else on board, amongst the 120 bags of ordinary mail the ship carried, was some secret mail from COIC, Wellington, to FECB, Colombo.

* According to the Merchant Navy Memorial, Tower Gardens, London, two *Nankin* crew members lost their lives in this engagement. Some authorities show the ship to be Australian, but her port of registry was Greenock, Scotland. She was built in 1912.

Almost certainly this mail had been inadvertently included with the ordinary mail, but however it happened it was an appalling breach of security.

A prize crew was put on board with the intention of sailing *Nankin* to Yokohama. In close proximity to *Thor* at the time was the German blockade-runner *Regensburg*. That ship had been in Japan at the outbreak of the European war but had successfully run the British blockade and reached Bordeaux in 1941. Now she was on her way back again, and had rendezvoused with *Thor* on 4th May to restore and refuel, and did so again on 13th. The three ships remained in company until 28th May when the two cargo vessels left to make their separate ways to Yokohama. James Rusbridger, in an article in *Encounter*, says that the mail bags were transferred to *Regensburg*, but gives no authority for the statement.[33] Anyway, both ships eventually arrived at Yokohama, the *Regensburg* on 18th July.*

When in July Admiral Wenneker, the German Naval Attaché in Tokyo, examined the *Nankin* mail he discovered a package containing four COIC Intelligence Summaries. As well as summarising intelligence from 'normal' sources these also gave information that could only have come from the breaking of Japanese codes. Wenneker relayed the details to Berlin in late July, but it took a month for authorisation to come back for him to show the reports to the Japanese which he did on the 29th August. It must be considered highly likely, however, that Wenneker gave the Japanese a much earlier intimation than this. Unlike the *Automedon* incident, which took place when Japan was still at peace, she was now fighting alongside Germany and surely Wenneker would not have waited for confirmation from home but would have acted on his own authority and told the Japanese at the earliest opportunity that it appeared that their codes were being read.

* Whilst attempting to run the blockade yet again, *Regensburg* was torpedoed by an American submarine in the Sunda Strait on 12th October 1942. She was beached and subsequently repaired by the Japanese. At Yokohama *Nankin* was renamed *Leuthen* by the Germans. *Thor* herself arrived at that port on 9th October. On 30th November the German fleet tanker *Uckermark* blew up there, taking *Leuthen* with her. *Thor* was damaged beyond repair, and British merchant seamen prisoners-of-war aboard the captured *Speybank* in the harbour watched and cheered as a southeast wind fanned the flames which threatened to engulf all Yokohama. However, the Japanese managed to confine the fire to the warehouse area.

Like the German High Command itself, which at various times during the war received indications that their Enigma codes were being read but refused to believe it, it appears that the Japanese High Command, too, did not believe this evidence. Nevertheless the mere possibility that it was true might have resulted in that change of code on 14th August.

The British never told the Americans of the *Nankin* affair. Furthermore, several mysteries have arisen since the war that might be indications of a cover-up process by the Allied intelligence agencies who took control of German records at the end of the war. According to Rusbridger, the log of the raider *Thor* seems to have been retyped at some subsequent time, and the incoming signal-log of Naval HQ in Berlin for the period is missing. One thing is certain; the parts of the diary of the German Naval Attaché in Tokyo covering the period May to November 1942 are missing, although this may be a coincidence.[34]

The change in the Japanese naval code on 14th August was followed shortly afterwards by a total change of ship callsigns, and there were indications that the Japanese were using radio deception techniques, probably in an attempt to cover the build-up of a major operation. Once again the Allies were having to rely heavily upon traffic analysis, the main worry now being to locate the Japanese aircraft carriers.[35]

Between the 17th and 19th August the Japanese, running down a channel known as 'The Slot' between two lines of islands in the Solomons, landed reinforcements on Gaudalcanal, the first run in a Japanese operation the Americans came to dub the 'Tokyo Express'. However, Japanese intelligence had grossly underestimated the size of the American marine force on shore and in bitter fighting the Japanese landing force was virtually exterminated.

On 21st August Allied traffic analyists concluded that a three-carrier task force was in existence, though its destination was unknown. In fact on that date the carriers and other vessels were rendezvousing at sea between Truk in the Caroline Islands and the Solomons, with the dual objectives of finding and destroying Admiral Fletcher's carrier force, which was now back at sea and positioned southeast of the Solomons, and of ensuring that the so-called Japanese Occupation Force which was being formed was safely landed on Guadalcanal. On 23rd August Pearl Harbor sent Fletcher, flying his flag on *Saratoga*, a message which incorrectly indicated that there were no Japanese carriers south of Truk, in consequence of which he detached the carrier *Wasp* with three cruisers and their destroyer escorts southward for refuelling. Before making this move Fletcher had the advantage in numbers over the enemy.

On the morning of 24th August a shore-based American plane spotted the light carrier *Ryujo* and escorts, but the message to Fletcher was so delayed and so confusing that early in the afternoon he ordered *Enterprise* to send up a search-and-find group of twenty-nine bombers and torpedo planes, followed by a similar force from *Saratoga* itself. Planes of the first group sighted *Ryujo* and twenty minutes later also spotted the heavy carriers *Shokaku* and *Zuikaku*, and attacked all three. They inflicted slight damage on *Shokaku*. Bad communications prevented Fletcher from directing *Saratoga*'s planes at the larger and more important targets, and they attacked and sank *Ryujo*, the lesser target. Meanwhile Fletcher stacked his fifty-three fighter aircraft above his task force and waited for the expected Japanese counter-attack which, when it came, was made by eighty aircraft. The Japanese managed to hit *Enterprise* with three bombs, but in the process lost seventy planes to fighters and ships' guns.

As the surviving Japanese planes flew away, Admiral Fletcher's ships retired southwards. The battle had been a Japanese reverse, but the Americans had missed a golden opportunity of making it a resounding Japanese defeat.

Despite these events the Japanese Occupation Force continued to close on Guadalcanal. On 25th August, Marine Corps aircraft from Henderson Field found and damaged one of the troopships and its cruiser escort. The trooper was finished off by eight Flying Fortresses from the New Hebrides, who also sank a destroyer. The rest of the expedition turned back, and by the afternoon of that day all Japanese surface forces were retiring northwards.

From then until the final Japanese evacuation of Guadalcanal in February 1943, the island and the seas around it became the scene of battles of attrition, with the Japanese continuing their 'Tokyo Express' by night, and with land- and carrier-based American aircraft ruling the roost by day.

By 12th September the Japanese had managed to get sufficient reinforcements ashore to launch another attack on Henderson Field. Traffic analysis showed that Admiral Yamamoto had assembled another fleet to back up the attack, but when the Japanese land forces were defeated in a bloody battle, Yamamoto's task force retired.

As a result of the various setbacks the Japanese navy had suffered, in August Yamamoto decided to relocate the submarines he had sent to the western Indian Ocean earlier in the summer, an allocation made under an agreed joint strategy with the Germans. Between 5th June and 8th July in the Mozambique Channel, on the all-important Allied Middle East supply line, these Japanese submarines had sunk twenty Allied ships totalling nearly 100,00 tons.[36] Now Yamamoto brought them back east in an endeavour to improve his position in the Pacific. It is clear, therefore, that the American Guadalcanal campaign had positive implications on the Middle East campaign at a time when the British were reforming and rearming with their backs almost against the Suez Canal, in preparation for the Battle of El Alamein that was to come in the fourth week of October. For the same reason Guadalcanal had implications on the northern campaign where the Russians were fighting to prevent the Germans breaking across the Caucasus; they needed the essential supplies reaching them via the Indian Ocean route.

The increased submarine activity in the South Pacific brought dividends to the Japanese. During the three weeks beginning 31st August, the *Saratoga* was torpedoed and put out of action till the end of the year, the carrier *Wasp* and destroyer *O'Brien* were sunk, and the battleship *North Carolina* damaged.

At the end of September the Japanese once more changed their code and on top of that made so many changes to their communications system that it rendered most of the Allied database, to use a modern word, of Japanese radio traffic, obsolete overnight. For the time being even greater reliance had to be placed on traffic analysis, which itself was not unaffected by the changes.

From early October it became evident that the Japanese were planning another attempt to drive the Americans off Guadalcanal. The sea battle called the Battle of Esperance Bay took place on 11th and 12th October when the Americans intercepted a Japanese fleet bringing in planes and reinforcements. On the basis of number of ships sunk it was an American victory, but the Japanese did manage to land men and guns, and that occasioned renewed heavy fighting ashore.

By 23rd October American cryptanalysts had made some headway in breaking the new codes and reported that a major naval offensive against Guadalcanal could be expected within days in support of yet another land attack. Admiral Yamamoto's fleet lay waiting north of the Solomons with the two-fold objective of annihilating the American fleet if and when it came within range, and of flying in aircraft from three carriers as soon as the ground forces had taken Henderson Field. But as the Japanese fleet waited with fuel running out, the Americans around Henderson held firm. In addition, the Americans had time to build up their own naval forces, most notably with the carrier *Enterprise* which had raced across the Pacific from Pearl Harbor after completing repairs.

The Battle of Santa Cruz which followed on 26th October, was unsatisfactory for both antagonists. In a day of air strikes and counter-strikes the Americans lost the carrier *Hornet* which they could ill spare, whereas the Japanese had a carrier, *Zuiho*, badly damaged and lost ninety-seven planes together with about one hundred and fifty irreplaceable aircrew.

Despite another Japanese callsign change at the beginning of November, traffic analysis and a growing ability to read the new codes gave warning of another Japanese attempt to retake Guadalcanal, one that was to result in one of the biggest and bloodiest battles of the entire war.

On 8th November Admiral Yamamoto issued orders to his fleet, and unknowingly also to American cryptanalysts who, by the following day, were able to present the American commanders with an outline of the enemy's plans. On the 10th confirmation of a build-up of troop transports and escorts was received from a coastwatcher based in the Shortland Islands, south of the large Japanese base on Bougainville Island. The Americans landed 6,000 infantry reinforcements on Guadalcanal over 11th and 12th November in the face of several enemy air attacks. On that second day, air reconnaissance located Japanese transports with an escort including battleships approaching from the north.

Hurriedly leaving Noumea where she was undergoing further repairs, *Enterprise*, the only American carrier now in the South Pacific, raced for the area. The Japanese had two carriers, *Junyo* and *Hiyo*, but with fewer than fifty planes apiece they were not the danger they would have been fully planed up, although at the time this was not known to the Americans. The respective fleets took up positions for the Battle of Guadalcanal that was to last into the early hours of 15th November.

A US cruiser and destroyer division under Rear-Admirals Callaghan and Scott made the first radar contact with a Japanese force under Vice-Admiral Abe which included two battleships, a little after one o'clock in the morning on 13th November. The two fleets were then about seventeen miles apart and closing rapidly. Before Callaghan, the senior US commander, could get a clear picture of the situation, the destroyers in his van became mixed with the enemy, and even before firing began confusion reigned. In the following melee, in which most of the American ships were hit, it is thought that the light cruiser *Atlanta* might have suffered from what is nowadays called 'friendly fire', and Admiral Scott was killed when *Atlanta* was struck by torpedoes from enemy destroyers. Then the Japanese battleships arrived. One of them, the *Hiyei*, was repeatedly hit by gunfire from the American cruisers and was forced to withdraw to the west. Aboard the American flagship *San Francisco* Admiral Callaghan was killed. By the time that action was broken off at 0230 the Americans had suffered severely; five ships of the thirteen engaged were lost either at the time, or soon afterwards from damage suffered. Only one ship was undamaged. The Japanese lost two destroyers with three damaged, and the battleship *Hiyei* had later to be scuttled.

The long-running battle continued, for that engagement had not discouraged the Japanese from their plan to bombard Henderson and to land reinforcements. On the night of 13th/14th November a bombardment force of Japanese cruisers was approaching Guadalcanal, as was a separate force of eleven troopers and an oiler escorted by destroyers. The Americans had organised a strike force of two battleships, *Washington* and *South Dakota* and four destroyers to intercept the bombardment force but due to a communications fault it failed to arrive in time, so that when the Japanese cruiser group arrived in the early hours of 14th November the naval defence of Guadalcanal devolved upon six Motor Torpedo Boats. After a bombardment lasting a little over an hour, the Japanese retired having done only minimal damage to the airfield and the planes there.

Meanwhile *Enterprise* had closed within two hundred miles of the island and had flown off her attack planes. As she was far too valuable to risk, she then withdrew to the south, and her planes throughout the remainder of the battle worked from Henderson. The two Japanese carriers sent off planes to look for *Enterprise* but did not find her, and that abortive effort was almost the only part the Japanese carrier planes were to take in the battle.

The first wave of planes from *Enterprise* arrived over the retiring bombardment force at 0800 just as a strike force from Henderson was retiring after attacking the same target. At the end of these combined attacks one Japanese cruiser had been sunk, and three other ships damaged. Then, half an hour later, the force of eleven Japanese troopships with their escorts was spotted. Aircraft from Henderson, and from the New Hebrides operating close to the limit of their range, and the second wave of bombers from *Enterprise*, came into attack. The Japanese had little in the way of air cover to retaliate with as the American aircraft attacked, flew to Henderson to refuel and be bombed up, and attacked again and again, all that day and well into the night. About that action the authors of the Official British Naval History had this to say:

> The lesson that it was tantamount to suicide for a surface force lacking control of the air or at least adequate fighter cover, and with no better screen than lightly gunned destroyers, to remain within range of an airfield in active operation, was demonstrated that day by the slaughter.[37]

Seven transports were set on fire, but with fanatical resolution Japanese destroyers went alongside the burning ships to take off troops and head with the surviving transports for the landing beaches. Dawn on the 15th saw four transports beached and landing troops, although little was landed in the way of stores and equipment. Air attacks went on all day, with guns from the American garrison ashore and others from the destroyer *Meade* joining in. By the end of that day of carnage, and for the loss of only five aircraft, the Americans had destroyed all eleven transports. It was reported that the sand along a ten-mile stretch of coast in the vicinity was bloodstained and strewn with human remains.

Late on 14th November the battleship-led American task force, which had arrived too late to intercept the first Japanese bombardment force, fell in with a hastily formed and heavier second bombardment force. That night in one of the rare battleship engagements of the war, *Washington* battered the *Kirishima* into such a wreck that she had later to be scuttled.

All in all, in over two days of fighting the Americans lost two cruisers and seven destroyers, with eight more vessels damaged. The Japanese had lost two battleships, a heavy cruiser, three destroyers and eleven transports. In that battle of attrition the Americans had come off better.

The Japanese were still not quite finished with Guadalcanal. A decrypted Japanese message of the 29th November indicated further 'Tokyo Express' runs. Armed with this foreknowledge the Americans formed a cruiser strike force and sent it out to intercept a force of eight Japanese destroyers each with its deck crammed with troops. Once again the Japanese navy was able to demonstrate its excellence, whilst once again an American Sigint-created chance to inflict severe damage on the enemy was spoilt by bad operational command decisions. Using their excellent Long Lance torpedoes the Japanese inflicted damage on four of five American cruisers, one of which later sank. In return the Japanese lost one destroyer. However, they were prevented from landing troops.

Throughout December the Japanese made further desperate attempts to reinforce and supply their forces on the island, but each attempt was revealed by Sigint and very little got through. In a final act of desperation the Japanese began running in supplies by submarine. Forewarned by Sigint two PT boats lay in wait on 9th December and sank the submarine I-3.

During December Allied naval reinforcements arrived in the South Pacific, amongst them three battleships and six cruisers, one of the latter being HMNZS *Achilles* of Battle of the River Plate fame. Unable to match this build-up with one of their own, the Japanese decided to evacuate Guadalcanal. Under a smokescreen of naval activity which led the Americans to believe that yet another counter-attack was coming, by early February 1943 the Japanese effected the evacuation of the island right under the noses of the unsuspecting Americans.

The Guadalcanal campaign was not only the most important one taking place in the South Pacific in the latter part of 1942, but the Sigint background to it illustrates well the changing fortunes of the Allied cryptanalytic effort during those months.

However, Guadalcanal and the waters around it were not the only places which were to witness tough fighting. On 18th May 1942, Allied intelligence sources revealed the possibility of a Japanese overland advance on Port Moresby in New Guinea. Then, early in July, enough of an intercepted message was decyphered to indicate a possible landing on the 21st of that month, which is exactly what

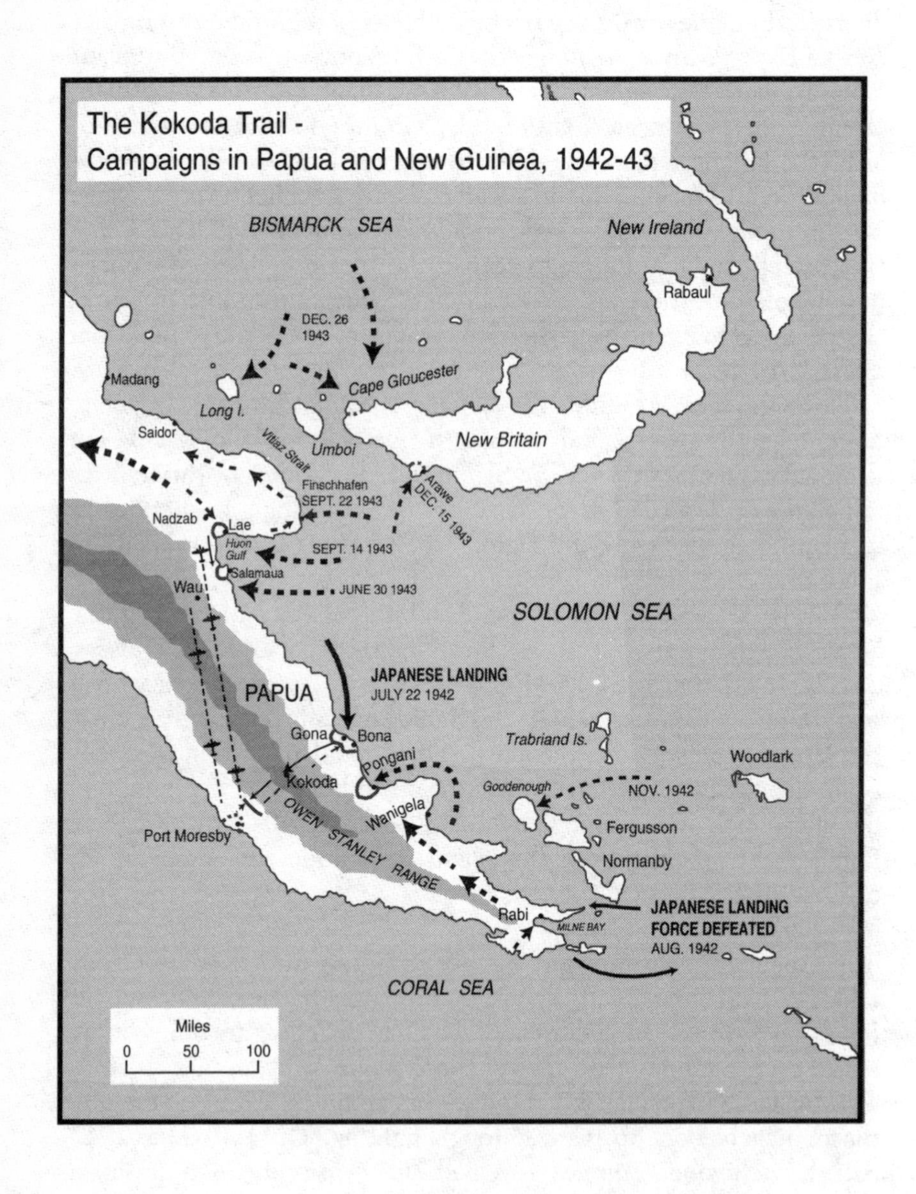
The Kokoda Trail -
Campaigns in Papua and New Guinea, 1942-43
BISMARCK SEA
New Ireland
Rabaul
DEC. 26
1943
Madang
Long I.
Cape Gloucester
Saidor
Vitiaz Strait
Umboi
New Britain
Finschhafen
SEPT. 22 1943
Arawe
DEC. 15 1943
Nadzab
Lae
Huon
Gulf
SEPT. 14 1943
Salamaua
Wau
JUNE 30 1943
SOLOMON SEA
JAPANESE LANDING
JULY 22 1942
PAPUA
Gona
Bona
Trabriand Is.
Woodlark
Pongani
Kokoda
Goodenough
NOV. 1942
Wanigela
Fergusson
Port Moresby
OWEN STANLEY RANGE
Normanby
Rabi
MILNE BAY
JAPANESE LANDING
FORCE DEFEATED
AUG. 1942
CORAL SEA
Miles
0
50
100

happened, but for some reason General MacArthur's intelligence staff failed to recognise the threat in time.

The reason for this involved what were called 'some pitfalls in the interpretation of Japanese Special' by the authors of an official British file.[38] American intelligence bulletins attempted to collate 'Special', both with other forms of intelligence and with deduction, but without making it clear which was which. In British 'Special' bulletins deductions, for example, were placed under 'comments', so that they could easily be distinguished from material obtained directly from intercepts. Whenever FECB received American bulletins, therefore, which contained deductions that differed from FECB's own, it was impossible to trace the source of the discrepancies; they could have been from mistakes in reception and decoding, or mistranslation and incorrect identification of codenames, or collation of Special with other information, or simply speculation and conjecture. One such conjecture, which was not clearly segregated from conclusive intelligence, occurred on 21st March and concerned the identification of the Japanese code letters for Port Moresby. The Americans had reported that RZQ *is* Port Moresby and that RR *is* Rabaul. By 5th June they had 'flatly contradicted' the second identification and, in fact, they were wrong on the first, which FECB had correctly identified as RZP.

This mistake in code letter identification may have been one reason why the Australian force available to confront the Japanese overland thrust against Port Moresby was of insufficient strength. The Japanese landed a force at Buna on the northeast coast of New Guinea where the island is at its narrowest with only 150 miles separating it from Port Moresby on the south coast. But it happened to be 150 miles of some of the most horrendous terrain in the world, with only the first third of it, from Buna to the Owen Stanley Range of mountains, being made slightly easier of passage by the so-called Kokoda trail, a jungle path no more than a couple of feet wide in places. The Japanese proceeded to push back the defending Australians who, on top of everything else, were not provided with sufficient air support. The Japanese crossed the mountain range and had reached within thirty miles of Port Moresby before the Australians managed to halt their advance on 17th September. Then, when almost in sight of their objective and certainly in sight of the sea, under attack from the reinforced Australians and from the air, and weakened by the terrible terrain and by tropical disease, and with no sign of their own promised reinforcements from the Solomons, the Japanese began to withdraw.

Many of them never saw Japan again. Indeed after Guadalcanal and New Guinea, the Japanese were rarely off the defensive.

Nineteen

The Far East Intelligence War, 1943–1945

The different turnings of the tide – on the North African front at El Alamein in October 1942, on the Russian Caucasus front in November/December, and at Guadalcanal in January/February – ensured that the Allies entered 1943 with new heart. The Axis partners were far from beaten yet, but the ebb had begun to flow for them.

The first few months of the new year brought the Allies several intelligence coups. The network of D/F stations in New Zealand had been augmented by a Radio Finger-Printing (RFP) organisation 'manned' by local Wrens. The authors of an official British report noted that, 'RFP results on Japanese submarine transmissions proved extremely valuable'.[1] Alerted by these stations, two trawlers of the Royal New Zealand Navy's 25th Minesweeping Flotilla, the *Kiwi* and *Moa*, lay in wait for Japanese submarines running in supplies to Guadalcanal on 29th February. After making asdic contact they went in with a depth-charge attack that blew submarine I-1 to the surface, and subsequent ramming and gunfire caused it to ground on a reef. Gutted by fire, she ended up with only her bow section above water. I-1 had been carrying thirty tons of stores and sixty troops. According to the Official British Navy History, 'Only one prisoner [the wounded navigating officer] was picked up, but important confidential documents were recovered, for the Japanese failed to complete their destruction'. (Other survivors managed to reach the shore and escape.)[2]

As well as her own code-books the submarine had been carrying a quantity of code-books for other vessels, which was why the Japanese attempted unsuccessfully to destroy the wreck by using another submarine and by bombing. They also brought in a major change to their codes on 15th February, so that, by the time the captured material reached Pearl Harbor, it was out of date. Nevertheless, the Americans were able to verify from it previous decryptions and to correct many mistakes. However, Allied cryptographers estimated it would take four weeks to bring an equal degree of decypherability to the new system.

These difficulties did not prevent the Allies from discovering that a Japanese convoy was being formed to reinforce their New Guinea garrisons. The convoy comprised eight transports with the same number of destroyers, and was given air cover. It was intercepted in the Bismarck Sea on 3rd and 4th March by American and Australian aircraft and by patrol torpedo (PT) boats. All eight transports and four of the destroyers were sunk, and about 4,000 Japanese troops were lost, many of them in the terrible aftermath of the battle. It may be a truism that it pays to be on the winning side of a war, but it is one well illustrated by the post-battle events of 5th March, which Rear-Admiral Samuel Eliot Morison, the official American naval historian, has described:

> Meanwhile planes and PTs went about the sickening business of killing survivors in boats, rafts or wreckage. Fighters mercilessly strafed anything on the surface. On 5 March . . . two PTs . . . put out to rescue a downed pilot . . . came upon an enemy submarine receiving survivors from three landing craft. The PTs turned their guns on and hurled depth charges at the three boats – which, with over a hundred men on board, sank. It was a grisly task, but a military necessity since Japanese soldiers do not surrender and, within swimming distance of the shore, they could not be allowed to land.[3]

Despite what Morison wrote about the Japanese refusal to surrender – later in the war, many did – it is a very generalised statement and does not excuse the fact that in this case they were given no chance to do so. The commander of the PT boats involved, Lieutenant-Commander Barry Atkins, USN, could thank his lucky stars that he was on the side that won the war. He was acting under orders, but the Allied War Tribunals and other courts since the war have never taken that to be an acceptable defence in similar cases.

The Battle of the Bismarck Sea was a great victory for land-based aircraft against ships, as had been the Japanese sinking of the two British capital ships off the east coast of Malaya at the very start of the Far Eastern War. But it is one that leaves a bad taste in the mouth especially when one remembers that the Japanese flyers had not attacked the survivors from *Prince of Wales* and *Repulse* when they were in the water, or the ships that were picking them up.

The Bismarck Sea battle brought the Allies an intelligence bonzana. A lifeboat from the encounter was found washed up on the shore of an island off the southern end of New Guinea. Aboard were Japanese documents that, when translated by the Allied Translation Service at Indooroopilly near Brisbane, were found to include the complete Japanese Army List, containing not only the names of 40,000 officers, but also their units.[4]

These achievements of the Allied intelligence community came about despite a lack of frank and full co-operation between agencies, between various commands, and between countries. MacArthur's Central Bureau, working mainly on low-level Japanese army and air force codes, received little help from other agencies. In March they broke into the Water Transport Code, of particular importance because it carried information on logistics and orders of battle, and they did it without much help from anyone, and certainly with none from Admiral Nimitz's Pacific Ocean Area Command. Central Bureau's relationship with the US Navy's cryptanalysts were 'not just difficult, they were non-existent', claimed American Colonel Sinkov. However, it is possible that this lack of co-operation may have been due 'to MacArthur's unwillingness to tolerate signals intelligence personnel not under his complete command'.[5]

About this time Admiral Somerville, C-in-C, British Eastern Fleet, sent his SO (I), Captain H.R.M. Laird, RN, on a crucial 'Special Intelligence' mission to promote a greater exchange of information with the American navy cryptanalysts in Melbourne. Laird did not find things easy. 'Fabian [Commander Rudy Fabian, USN, in charge of the unit] was friendly, but when it came to producing a practical solution of our mutual problem he raised every sort of objection.' In view of earlier British hesitancy on the other side of the world, over handing to the Americans intelligence gained from the reading of German Enigma traffic, this American attitude in the Pacific area where they held most of the cards is perhaps hardly surprising. Laird also commented, on 15th March, on the relations within and between the various intelligence agencies in Australia. 'I have endeavoured not entirely with success to keep out of the continual quarrels and bickers which go on apparently in every Special Intelligence Centre among the personnel. Everybody is telling tales about the next one.'[6]

April brought with it an event that was the equivalent of a major victory for the Allies. It began with the successful decryption at Pearl Harbor of a series of Japanese messages giving details of Admiral Yamamoto's personal tour of air and naval bases in the northern Solomons. Although the decryptions were incomplete, there was enough information to show that Yamamoto would be flying to Ballale Island, off the southeastern tip of Bougainville, at 1000 hours on 18th April which would bring him within range of fighter aircraft from Guadalcanal. Admiral Nimitz at Pearl Harbor gained President Roosevelt's consent before authorising Admiral Halsey, in whose 'bailiwick', to use Nimitz's own word, Bougainville fell, to go ahead with Operation Vengeance, as it was to be called. To avoid betraying the fact that Japanese codes were being read, everyone concerned, including the pilots, were told that the information on Yamamoto's whereabouts had come from Australian coastwatchers.

At 0725 hours on 18th April, sixteen P-38 Lightnings, specially fitted with long-range fuel tanks, took off from Henderson Field, Guadalcanal. The squadron was led by Major John Mitchell, USAAF, who was told that Yamamoto was a stickler for being on time; in his younger days he would have been brought up to relieve ship watches punctually – to be late was to give grave offence. Mitchell was given a precise time and a precise interception point, and both proved to be just that, for Yamamoto's flight of two Betty bombers with six protective Zeke fighters were spotted dead on time. Both Bettys, in one of which was Yamamoto, were shot down together with three of the Zekes at the cost of only one Lightning.

At Halsey's HQ, and at Pearl Harbor and Washington, all those in the know were cock-a-hoop, although nothing could be published about Yamamoto's demise until the Japanese announced it. In fact, only intervention from the US Joint Chiefs of Staff prevented General MacArthur, whose command Admiral Halsey at that time came under, from making Yamomoto's death a well-publicised triumph for his command.

Yamamoto's death was a severe blow to the Japanese Navy, for there was no admiral of equal calibre to replace him. It was also a severe blow to the Japanese public who held him in esteem second only to the Emperor. The Admiral's ashes were taken back to Tokyo where a state funeral took place on 5th June.

By the summer of 1942 the Japanese had completed their occupation of Burma, in as far as any mountainous and jungle-clad country can be said to be truly occupied. They had begun to moot 'Operation 21', a three-pronged drive across the border into India. Had they attacked into Assam then, there would have been little to stop them, but the project was shelved because of the difficulties of the terrain to be crossed and supply problems, for the Japanese army in the north was at the end of a very long line of communications which was constantly under threat from Chinese troops led by the American General Stilwell from Yunnan in the east.

One of the officers who initially voiced opposition to such an operation, though his objections had nothing to do with either terrain or supply problems, was the intelligence officer, Major Fujiwara Iwaichi. He, who had raised the Indian National Army (INA) from among the thousands of Indian troops captured in Malaya and Singapore, attempted to dampen enthusiasm for the plan, judging that Gandhi and other Indian leaders would likely urge their people to oppose any purely Japanese invasion of their country. He was firmly of the opinion that the training and equipping of the INA was a prerequisite for any entry into India, a view that was not shared by all his superiors.

In February 1943 a British force called Chindits, headed by General Orde Wingate, entered Burma from India over the very terrain the Japanese thought difficult to cross, albeit that he came in the opposite direction. This first of Wingate's Long Range Penetration Group's incursions had three main purposes, to upset enemy morale, to raise that of the British, and to provide what would nowadays be called training on the job. To be effective the Chindits must learn to be better jungle fighters than the Japanese, to become expert in demolition and in jungle radio communications, and there was no better place to learn than behind enemy lines.

The Japanese first received intimation of Wingate's incursion from Burmese spies, news soon followed by the Chindits' successful ambush of a battalion of the Japanese 33rd Division. It fell to Major Fujiwara's lot to attempt to discover the intent behind the incursion. On elephant-back he followed in Wingate's tracks, picking up prisoners whenever he could. In a jungle trek lasting forty days he gathered in over three hundred, but the only important thing he learnt was the name of the leader of the British expedition. Fujiwara concluded that the British expedition which, after cutting railway lines, blowing bridges, and conducting ambushes, was back in India by mid-April – having lost a third of its men – showed a new strength in the British army.

General Mutaguchi, GOC 18th Division in north Burma, who had no high opinion of the British, did not much care for that interpretation. He preferred to think that the incursion was made to set up an intelligence network that would spy on Japanese preparations for an offensive against Assam, in which he was partly correct. Soon promoted GOC of 15th Army, Mutaguchi began to plan the invasion anew. Not only had Wingate shown that the terrain could be crossed by a large force, but Mutaguchi was receiving reports of massive Allied preparations for a counter-offensive and of airborne troops being trained in India. Immediately across the border, at Imphal, the British were strengthening their base there. The General, who had been closely involved in the 'China Incident' and in the fall of Singapore, saw more glory ahead for himself. He would capture Imphal and use it as a base for the INA in the hope that that would create an anti-British rising in Bengal, much as Fujiwara had advised.

In April and May Fujiwara and a dozen or so graduates of the Nakano Espionage School were sent on a reconnaissance to check terrain, river-crossing points and, on the side, to conduct propaganda amongst the border tribes. They came back with favourable reports; the area could be crossed during the dry season. In consequence the Japanese spent the remainder of 1943 in planning and training for the attack.

Meanwhile Subhas Chandra Bose, the ardent Indian nationalist, arrived in Singapore from Tokyo in June to organise a congress of the Indian Independence League (IIL). Bose had been arrested by the British for sedition in India in 1940 but had escaped via Afghanistan and Russia to Germany, using an Italian passport issued to him by Mussolini's ambassador in Kabul. In Berlin Bose busied himself broadcasting anti-British propaganda and in building up the so-called Indian Legion from Indian troops captured in North Africa. After contacting the Japanese ambassador, Oshima, in Berlin, in 1943 Bose left Germany by U-boat which rendezvoused with a Japanese submarine off Madagascar on 26th April. He arrived in Tokyo in May.

By the time Subhas Chandra Bose arrived in Singapore, 'General' Mohan Singh was no longer in command of the INA. Dissension between Singh and Rash Behari Bose, the Indian nationalist who had spent many years in Japan (there was no relationship between the two Boses), had resulted in Singh's arrest by the Japanese and much wrangling within INA ranks.

At Singapore Subhas Chandra Bose was told of the Japanese plans to attack Assam, and in November he was given assurances that the INA would be treated as an autonomous army of an ally by the Japanese in return for it taking part in the Assam campaign. Bose himself was convinced, and managed so to convince the Japanese that when he appeared in Bengal the whole of the Indian Army would desert the British and join him.

Bose did not get the opportunity to prove his case because the British and Indian forces in Assam held the Japanese advance at Imphal and Kohima. The INA did operate in Burma but was not a success, and it suffered from desertions. When Bose refused to sanction use of the INA against its Burmese equivalent, the Burmese National Army, after it had revolted against its Japanese masters, the Japanese became disillusioned with both the INA and Bose himself. He slipped into the sidelines, and on 12th August 1945 was killed in a plane crash on Formosa on his way to Tokyo. He had had it in mind to make for Russia where he hoped to find sanctuary.

At his Brisbane HQ General MacArthur was planning the first moves in the island-hopping campaign that was eventually to take him all the way to Japan. One of his first priorities was to obtain better information on the strength of the guerrilla movement in his beloved Philippines, and to that end a group code-named 'Planet' was formed in December 1942 from the ranks of Filipinos who had managed to escape from the islands. The seven men selected, led by Major Jesus Villamor who had served with the US Army Air Corps, underwent a brief but rigorous training programme before being taken by the submarine *Gudgeon* to the island of Negros in the central Philippines. The group had orders to make contact with guerrillas, establish intelligence networks, set up a chain of radio communications which, via a relay station, was to be in contact with Darwin, and to form organisations for subversion and sabotage. Other native-born agents were infiltrated into Sarawak and North Borneo with similar remits.

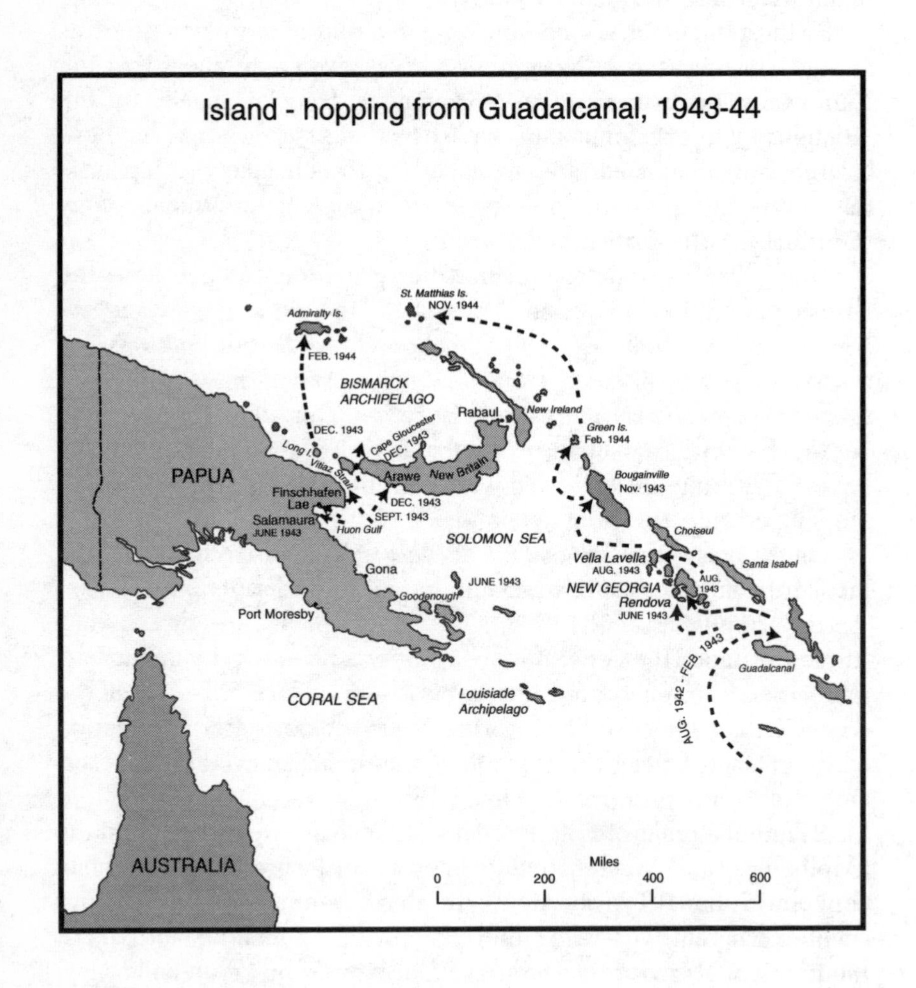
Island - hopping from Guadalcanal, 1943-44
St. Matthias Is.
NOV. 1944
Admiralty Is.
FEB. 1944
BISMARCK
ARCHIPELAGO
Rabaul
New Ireland
Green Is.
Feb. 1944
DEC. 1943
Long I.
Vitiaz Strait
Cape Gloucester
DEC. 1943
Arawe
New Britain
PAPUA
Finschhafen
Lae
Salamaura
JUNE 1943
DEC. 1943
SEPT. 1943
Huon Gulf
Bougainville
Nov. 1943
Choiseul
SOLOMON SEA
Vella Lavella
AUG. 1943
Santa Isabel
Gona
JUNE 1943
NEW GEORGIA
AUG. 1943
Rendova
JUNE 1943
Goodenough
Port Moresby
AUG. 1942 - FEB. 1943
Guadalcanal
CORAL SEA
Louisiade
Archipelago
AUSTRALIA
Miles
0
200
400
600

As the Allied counter-offensive against Japan began to develop momentum, Bletchley Park sent more trained people out east. Among the three sent to Kilindini in April 1943 to augment the cryptanalysis section at HMS *Alidina*, was Hugh Denham, aged just nineteen, who had been dragged away to Bletchley for training from Cambridge where he had been reading Classics.

By then the much travelled Captain Shaw, RN, from FECB Hong Kong, Singapore and Colombo, had been relieved by Commander (later Captain) Bruce Keith, who came from the Japanese Section at Bletchley. Other members of the staff included two former members of the British consular staff in Japan,[7] a Dutch naval officer called Brouwer and, as translators, Lieutenant-Commanders Barham and Curnock who had once been naval language officers in Tokyo.

Hugh Denham has given the following description of the HMS *Alidina* operation:

> The 'front line' of the unit was the wireless operators, who intercepted the enemy messages; then the analysts and their staff stripped off the additive key;* the linguists established the meanings of the code-groups and translated the texts for prompt reporting to COIS at Naval HQ.[8]

Denham says that his team received ever-growing assistance from Hollerith punched-card machinery, and acknowledges the extensive retrieval input passed to Kilindini from OP-20-G in Washington, which he knew under the cover-name of 'Susan'. He describes particularly the care in which those parts of the translated decrypts passed to the COIS, which could be categorically guaranteed, were clearly distinguished from those based on garbled intercepts or uncertain meanings.

Kilindini exchanged all key and code recoveries with Bletchley, Melbourne and Washington, by signals encyphered 'by the secure but cumbersome Typex system', the Typex being the standard British cypher-machine with teleprinter attached. On a less regular basis the station was also in direct touch with Brisbane and Pearl Harbor.

The man at Kilindini who appears to have had most of that spark of

* In cryptographic terms a key is a random numerical text which has no meaning of its own but is used as a second stage to disguise further a crypto-text by non-carrying addition, non-borrowing subtraction, substitution, or other methods; hence an 'additive' or 'subtractor' key. The author is grateful to Alan Stripp for this definition.

imaginative genius required of people successfully engaged in Sigint, was Lieutenant-Commander George Curnock, He had spent three years as a language officer in pre-war Tokyo, and served with FECB in Colombo before coming to Kilindini. He was a gin-before-breakfast man but, once so fortified, his knowledge of the Japanese language enabled him quickly to scan the most fragmentary of texts and assign meanings to corrupt or unsolved code-groups; he seemed to be able to feel his way into the Japanese mind.

In September 1943, by which time it was considered that all danger to Colombo had passed, HMS *Alidina* was closed down and the staff transferred to HMS *Anderson*, the shore establishment in Colombo.

The Sigint operation at New Delhi, known as the Wireless Experimental Station (WEC), also received a new input of cryptanalysts from Bletchley in 1943. They joined WEC's Section C, under Lieutenant-Colonel Peter Marr-Johnson, who in 1940 had been attached to FECB in Hong Kong in a capacity considered so secret that his colleagues in that organisation did not know about it. Then in 1941 he had headed the Special Liaison Unit in Singapore, handling 'Special' for the C-in-C there. For a very brief period he may later, as we have seen, have been General Wavell's one-man SLU in Java. He then spent a period as liaison officer in Washington, before arriving at Delhi to take charge of the WEC'C' Section, which was engaged in breaking and translating Japanese army and army airforce codes.

The other four WEC sections were concerned with administration, collating and evaluating signals intelligence, traffic analysis, and radio interception. The entire establishment was commanded by an RAF Group Captain. The officer commanding the signals section was Colonel Aldridge, and part of his command was the No. 5 Wireless Detachment, Royal Corps of Signals.[9]

WEC was situated in Ramjas College, formerly part of the Delhi University campus, perched atop a hill called Anand Parat – 'the hill of happiness' – some miles outside the city and difficult to reach even by pony-driven gharri. The place was thus easy to make secure. Several other intercept stations in India, including a large one at Bangalore, reported to WEC.

Perhaps because of the secretive nature of Marr-Johnson's tasks in recent years, most of his staff found him to be distant and inaccessible. It may have been this that earned him the reputation of being snobbish. He ran a tight ship and did not much care for anyone of independent thought although, at Hong Kong, he had been rather given to independent action himself. A regular army officer, he had little time for war-commissioned officers, branding one of them who had been in business before the war as a 'Bombay carpet-bagger'. Nevertheless Marr-Johnson ran a successful operation, albeit run on too rigid lines. In the spring of 1943, for instance, two of his team, an Oxford don, Maurice Allen, and a Classics scholar and mountaineer, Wilfrid Noyce, achieved the first significant penetration into high-level Japanese Army codes.[10]

Bletchley Park-trained Alan Stripp arrived at WEC in June 1943 to find the difference between it and the parent organisation in England quite striking. WEC, with a staff numbering something over a thousand, made up of Army, RAF, Indian and West African service personnel, was only a fifth of the size of Bletchley Park, but the differences were more profound than just size. At BP, says Stripp, 'the Japanese section had been a small exotic plant grafted on to a large and vigorous German parent. Here everyone was concerned with Japanese codes or cyphers'. He goes on:

> Moreover, the presence in the next building of 'B' section, which passed the tactical and strategical assessments straight on to various headquarters, and the fact that we all lived and messed together, should have given a sense of immediacy. It was possible to visualise our individual jobs as part of the whole and not just as separate chores on some vast assembly line.
>
> Nevertheless in our daily affairs there were closed doors between one section and another . . . Communications between 'B' and 'C' sections took place only at the top . . . Hence needless inaccuracies and time wasted: security turned into absurdity . . . The informality praised . . . as contributing to Bletchley's success could not survive in the hierarchy of WEC.[11]

In March 1943 intercepts decyphered at Pearl Harbor revealed that the Japanese were about to reinforce the two islands in the Aleutians that they had captured the previous June. Pearl Harbor gave an estimate of the size of the Japanese cruiser force involved and the Americans sent a matching one to intercept. Unforunately, Sigint sources did not pick up in time the fact that, at the last moment, the Japanese doubled the number of cruisers to four, so American Admiral Charles McMorris found himself outnumbered. Despite these odds he managed to turn the Japanese fleet away from its target, an achievement which led to the recapture by the Americans of one of the islands in May, and of the other in August.

Another aspect of Signals Intelligence is graphically illustrated by the action between an American fleet under Rear-Admiral 'Pug' Ainsworth, consisting of three cruisers and four destroyers, and a Japanese force of nine destroyers, on 5th/6th July. Ainsworth was not aware of the exact make-up of the Japanese fleet, and in the action one American cruiser and two Japanese destroyers were sunk. Ainsworth, however, claimed he had sunk two cruisers and other destroyers which he reported as having disappeared from his radar screens during the action, making a total of six. The action was made much of, despite Pearl Harbor intelligence pointing out that Sigint showed that no Japanese cruisers had been involved in the action, known as the Battle of Kula Gulf. This led to an acerbic row between Ainsworth and Captain Layton, Admiral Nimitz's chief of intelligence at Pearl Harbor but it was not many days afterwards when a top-secret document taken from an officer-survivor from another Japanese destroyer confirmed that, indeed, no Japanese cruisers had taken part.

As 1943 wore on and the Allies poured more and more resources into Sigint, the cryptanalysts grew in competence as well as experience. Allied forces began clearing the Solomons and adjacent islands and more Japanese documents, situation reports and code-books were captured, thus further easing the intelligence task. Now, no matter how many times the Japanese changed their codes, callsigns, or communications procedures, it was rare for there to be any long gaps in 'Special' knowledge, although mistakes still sometimes occurred in the operational use made of it.

Mistakes still occurred in the administration of 'Special', too. One American indiscretion was spotted in London in November 1943. Late in that month, the Admiralty in London received through Rear-Admiral Pott, British Naval Attaché in Washington, a report made by Commander B.V. Wilson, the British Liaison Officer based at San Francisco. The report concerned an attack by aircraft from the US carriers *Saratoga* and *Princetown* on Rabaul, New Britain, on 11th November, and it 'showed throughout the unmistakable colour of Special intelligence'.[12] The report, after listing the numbers and types of Japanese ships sunk or damaged which, of course, could have been observed by US aircraft during the battle, went on to name surviving ships, the exact extent of damage to them and their current position. Neither Pott nor Wilson was 'in Special' and neither seemed to have noticed anything unusual about the information. 'Both were accustomed to the cocksure claims of US airmen and submarine officers, from whom the information could have been gained', said the authors of an Admiralty report. But, 'had the report got into enemy hands in itself it might have conveyed little, except that Allied Intelligence was remarkably accurate. Collated with similar "leakages" it might have helped to fill in the picture. Inquiry as to how the information got out might have pointed in one direction.' Commander Leggatt of British Navals Intelligence, who was 'in Special', wrote:

> This is an alarming document as it seems to contain nothing but Special Intelligence. As a first step the docket should be graded MOST SECRET. The fault is evidently with the Americans who have blabbed to Wilson, but if Wilson or any other British officer were heard repeating it, we should probably be blamed.

The matter was referred back to the American authorities, 'and the risk taken of damaging Commander Wilson's valuable connections'.

This British criticism of American security over 'Special' does not sit comfortably with the efforts made earlier in that year by Commander R.B.M. Long, Director of Australian Naval Intelligence in Melbourne, who, on behalf of the British and in the face of American intransigence, 'Had to obtain . . . Special Intelligence information by underhand means, which must make it very difficult for him'.[13]

Brigadier Jolly a Royal Marine in British Naval Intelligence did a round of the Pacific region in early 1943. On co-operation in general and the demarcation between the American zones of command, he reported the following:

> The most noticeable feature was the inability of the Americans to appreciate the full meaning of the word 'co-operation'. The atmosphere was 'What is yours is mine, and what is mine is my own'.
>
> Secondly, the absolute control assumed by the Americans over all islands and military forces is remarkable.
>
> Thirdly, the arbitrary line of demarcation between Southwest Pacific and South Pacific is a firm boundary. Senior officers declared it was 'flexible', junior officers with more candour assured [me] it was rigid, and one aviator said he had instructions not to cross into the next area, 'no matter what the reason'.

> The South Pacific is under Admiral Halsey and the Southwest Pacific is under General MacArthur. Thus the time-worn antipathy between the Army and the Navy of the USA comes into play.[14]

A symptom of this inter-service rivalry is that, at one stage, Admiral Halsey threatened to put everyone under his command, both navy and army, with attached air services, into the same uniform.

Most, but not all, Japanese merchant ship names ended, and still end, with the affix 'Maru', which is a kind of blessing. The so-called 'Maru' convoy code was used by the Japanese for communicating with their merchant ships. The Americans cracked this in January 1943, and although it was changed from time to time thereafter, it usually took only a few days to crack it again. Messages sent in this code gave convoy and escort strengths, routes and destinations, together with noon positions, and the decrypts should have been like manna from heaven to American submarine commanders. Unfortunately, sometimes due to shortage of submarines, or to the vast distances involved in the Pacific when measured against a submarine's operational range, or to bad communications over such long distances, and often to the unreliability of American torpedoes at this time, comparatively few of the large number of potential targets identified by 'Special' were sighted by American submarines and successfully attacked. During the first four months of 1943, for example, well over two hundred targets were reported – a target sometimes being more than one ship if individual members of a convoy could not be identified – but only ten ships were sunk.

On the unreliability of their torpedoes, the Americans sometimes intercepted and decrypted Japanese messages that reported hits but no explosions. Other torpedoes exploded before contact, and this resulted in false claims being made of sinkings. It was not until more reliable torpedoes became available at the end of 1943 that the situation improved and more benefit was obtained from the ability to read the Maru code.

When the Oriental Mission was set up by Britain's Special Operation Executive in Singapore in 1941, SOE also set up at about the same time an India Mission (IM) which after March 1944, came to be known as Force 136. The head of India Mission throughout the war was Colin Mackenzie. Like Valentine Killery of the ill-fated Oriental Mission, Mackenzie had few obvious qualifications for the job, having been a director of the textile firm J. & P. Coates Ltd pre-war, but one qualification he did have – he knew the Far East well. Several of the Oriental Mission people who escaped from Singapore were to join him in India.

With the passage of time India Mission's territory expanded to cover not only India, but Afghanistan, Tibet, China and Burma, the sheer size of its theatre of operations imposing its own special difficulties. Also, special operations in the countries making up Southeast Asia – namely Malaya, Thailand, Netherlands East Indies, and French Indo-China – were up for grabs, with India Mission and Special Operations, Australia (SOA) free to operate there provided they kept each other informed of their activities. Just to complicate the situation a little more, the American Office of Strategic Services (OSS) was also able to join in on the same basis. When in early 1943 the American Lieutenant-General Joseph Stilwell was appointed Chief of Allied Staff to Generalissimo Chiang Kai-shek, who had troops fighting in the eastern border areas of Burma, the special operations situation in Burma became confused, too. The OSS had an outfit in India under Colonel Eifler who was supposed to co-ordinate anything he planned in Burma with the SOE, but often did not do so. An SOE Report dated 26th July 1943, is critical of Eifler: 'It is clear . . . he [Eifler] has no political sense, and that his people are developing into Suicide Squads, since he puts them in daylight and some have been quickly rounded up.' On Eifler's reluctance to discuss much in advance with SOE, the report goes on:

> He had so far refused to submit his operational plans in advance . . . and maintains this attitude on two grounds.
> (i) That he is answerable only to General Stilwell. Every American soldier abroad, be he OSS or not, is subject to the orders of the US Theatre Commander.
> (ii) Burma is a country in which both parties can operate.[15]

A major difficulty was that the C-in-C, India, Field Marshal Wavell, and General Stilwell who had no time for each other, were unable to agree a demarcation line between their operations. This situation was only marginally improved when Admiral Lord Louis Mountbatten was appointed Allied Supremo in Southeast Asia, with Stilwell as his Deputy.

Another difficulty was that SOE was a subversive organisation, with only peripheral intelligence-gathering functions, whereas OSS was engaged in subversion and intelligence conjointly, and the Americans were not about to impart all their intelligence to SOE; in fact, not even the British Secret Service did that.

SOE's activities in China were greatly affected by the attitude of General 'Wild Bill' Donovan, Head of OSS in the States, who was 'very jealous of his position in China and has aimed at excluding SOE if possible'. SOE had set up a small Adviser's Office at Chungking at the request of Chiang Kai-shek. It worked closely with the Chinese secret organisation euphemistically called the Institute of International Relations, or IIR, which under General Wang Peng-son was charged with all anti-Japanese activity other than sabotage, which was the responsibility of Tai Li, the chief of all the Chinese secret services. The SOE office in China was under Findlay Andrew, whose relationship with Wang was excellent, the one known exception to the fact that the Chinese and British Secret Services did not get on. Chiang Kai-shek seems to have been playing both ends against the middle, for he had requested SOE 'not to allow or invite American participation' in its activities, with a similar request to OSS, who worked closely with Tai Li, not to invite British participation. 'This may have been due to a desire of the Chinese to get what they can out of each organisation separately and to play one Ally off against the other.'[16]

It is apparent from reading many SOE files, that in addition to working towards the defeat of Japan, OSS was also working to a long-term, and hidden political agenda designed to preclude the former colonial powers in the area, Britain, France and Holland, from regaining their erstwhile colonies. On top of that, China had irredentist notions particularly with regard to Hong Kong, their ambition to take it back after the war receiving a lot more than a nod and a wink from the Americans. During a meeting with his Secretary of State at the White House on 5th October 1943, President Roosevelt said that 'the British might, as a gesture of generosity, return Hong Kong to China', a notion that for such an experienced statesman was rather naive.[17] All these political angles served sometimes to entangle SOE in matters quite outside its remit.

One of SOE's most remarkable 'dirty-tricks' campaigns took place in China in 1944; it was one which was concerned less with waging war against Japan than with saving British funds. The scam was organised by Walter (later Sir Walter) Fletcher – once described by British Minister Hugh Dalton as 'a thug with good commercial contacts' – and by Edward Wharton-Tigar, both British businessmen, and aided and abetted by Frank Shu, a Chinese from Manchuria. This trio set about exploiting the Chinese black markets in currency and high value goods to help pay for the British war effort. Called Operation Remorse (an indication of sorrow *before* the event perhaps?), it used Indian rupee notes, pounds sterling, diamonds, gold watches and jewellery, motor bikes and sulpha drugs, which were exchanged for Chinese dollars at between six and twenty times the official rate of exchange. The operation netted Britain some £77 million (nearly a billion pounds at 1997 prices) which was used as official remittances to British organisations operating in China. Senior Chinese officials knew what was going on and some of them profited from the scheme themselves. Remorse has been called the biggest black market operation in history.*

Amongst the India Mission's earlier operations was one that involved the recruitment of tribesmen in Burma who, after the Japanese occupation, joined road gangs engaged in repairing roads and tracks. They had orders to effect demolitions whenever they could and for that purpose explosives had been planted at various locations. In Burma, as in Singapore, though not quite on the same scale, SOE was the recipient of some animosity from the British army. SOE was allowed to control native guerrillas fighting behind enemy lines but the responsibility for them, including training, came under the army.

In the early days, when under pressure from its superiors in London to make itself felt, India Mission produced a plan of action against four Axis merchant ships, three Germans and one Italian, that since early in the European war had taken refuge in the small Portuguese colony of Goa on the Indian west coast south of Bombay. As with most India Mission operations, due to the need to consult with various commands and with other subversive organisations, the time-span between the conception of the plan and its implementation was very long. In this case, because neutral Portugal was involved, the Foreign Office had to be consulted as well. Conceived early in 1942, the plan was not put into operation until March 1943. Operation Longshanks, as it was called, was designed to capture one of the German ships, *Ehrenfels*,

* Another British black market operation, but *not* one authorised by London, took place under the British Military Administration (BMA) which controlled Malaya and Singapore for several years after their liberation from the Japanese. Black market dealings were so rife, with so many Britons and Chinese involved, that BMA was frequently, and not so jokingly, taken to stand for Black Market Administration.

which was suspected of relaying by wireless, to German submarines information about British shipping movements on the Indian coast. As intelligence had discovered that the German ship could not move under her own power, IM chartered a dredging vessel at Calcutta to be used to tow her away after first getting a raiding party aboard; the raid being planned around a not-a-shot-to-be-fired stipulation insisted on by the Foreign Office. Despite this stipulation, the raiders were armed to the teeth. They were led by Lieutenant-Colonel Lewis Pugh and other IM operatives, the numbers being made up by veteran volunteers from the Calcutta Light Horse, which was essentially a military and sporting and drinking club, but one which took its military commitments very seriously indeed.[18] Operation Longshanks had all the attributes needed to produce a fine Hollywood script, as so it later proved.*

The attempt to board the vessel by surprise was spoilt by an alert German watchman, and the boarding party met with resistance during which five German crew members were killed. The crew also detonated demolition charges and opened sea-cocks. The other Axis vessels also scuttled themselves. In that the Axis lost the possible services of four ships, including one that may have been supplying radioed intelligence to submarines, the raid must be considered a success, especially as no British lives were lost and the dredger got safely away. However, in view of the broken stipulation, the Foreign Office in London did not think so, and many were the shenanigans that went on to placate Lisbon and the local Portuguese governor. The governor was somehow finally persuaded to believe that the long-hemmed-in Axis crews had mutinied, and that in an effort to save themselves from possible later retribution from the Gestapo they had invented the story of a ship full of masked and armed men coming at them out of the dark.

By far the most successful of IM's operations was Operation Jaywick. This was conceived by Captain (later Lieutenant-Colonel) Ivan Lyon after his escape from Singapore. He first proposed the project, a raid on Singapore harbour, in June 1942 and though it was approved in the following month it did not take place until September 1943. It was an IM project, but training and preparations for it took place under the aegis of Special Operations, Australia.

* *The Sea Wolves*, 1980, starring Gregory Peck, David Niven, Trevor Howard and Roger Moore.

Lyon sailed from Exmouth Gulf on the northwest coast of Australia aboard an ex-Japanese fishing vessel, *Krait*, with a party of thirteen most of whom were Australians. On 18th September 1943, Lyons and five others were put ashore with three folboats (light canvas boats) on an island in the Rhio Archipelago opposite Singapore. On the night of 26th/27th they made for Singapore Roads, limpet-mined three large cargo vessels, and made good their escape. They had blown up 50,000 tons of enemy shipping. Lyon was awarded the DSO for what many commentators have said should have been a VC operation, but unfortunately, during the training and planning period in Australia, he managed to rub some Australian army brass up the wrong way, and this probably had a bearing on the grade of award.

The end of this story is a grim one. In September 1944 Lyon and a mixed party of Australians and Britons tried to emulate Jaywick in Operation Rimau against Singapore, but all lost their lives in one way or another. Ten who were captured were beheaded by the Japanese only a month before the end of the war. Some of the deaths have been attributed to the fact that the submarine HMS *Tantalus*, which had been designated to pick up any surviving members of the expedition from an island called Merapas, which lies about sixty miles southeast of Singapore, arrived late because its commander, Lieutenant-Commander (later Vice-Admiral Sir) H.S. Mackenzie 'considered that his first priority was to hunt and attack enemy shipping so long as his torpedoes lasted'.[19] In his autobiography, and during a conversation with the present author in early 1996, the late Admiral Mackenzie saw the need to present more facts because of certain statements made in a recent Australian book on this subject which blamed him for some of the deaths. Mackenzie said that his patrol orders specifically gave as his primary aim the destruction of enemy shipping, with the secondary task of closing Merapas on some date between '8th November and 8th December, depending on circumstances and the submarine's safety', to land a two-man reconnaissance party, Major Chapman and Corporal Croton of SOA, and on the following night to pick up the two together with any members of the expedition they had found there. Mackenzie said that 'quite rightly and correctly', he had not been made privy to the details of Rimau. 'There was no indication of any urgency for the pick-up and to confirm this I signalled operational headquarters in Australia saying that I intended to remain on patrol for about another week before carrying out the special operation. This received immediate approval.' Chapman and Croton were in fact landed on the night of 21st/22nd November, and retrieved the following night. No members of Rimau had been found, but there were indications that some had occupied the base camp earlier. After discussions with Chapman, Mackenzie reluctantly decided to withdraw and sail for Fremantle.

All the evidence assembled since the war shows that those members of the expedition who reached Merapas had been discovered there by the Japanese, and had immediately evacuated the base camp, or been killed, and that this happened four days prior to the earliest pick-up date. Even had *Tantalus* been off the island on the 8th, it would already have been too late. Mackenzie added, for the benefit of what he called the 'anti-Pom lobby' in Australia, that his submarine would have been endangered had he stayed to search the numberless islands in the vicinity, 'particularly in the light of the unusual anti-submarine activity we had experienced off Merapas', which probably indicated that the Japanese had a special interest in the island.[20]

For months after the fall of Singapore little was known of the fate of the few British left-behind parties in Malaya, or of the Chinese who had been trained in the SOE school in Singapore for the same purpose, nor indeed, of those Chinese members of Dalforce who had escaped into the Malayan jungle. As it happened, few of the Europeans involved managed to survive long in the jungle.

In May 1943 in Operation Gustavus, Force 136 operatives began a series of visits to the west coast of Malaya by submarine. Gustavus had the twin objectives of making contact with guerrillas and setting up an intelligence network including wireless links with the outside world. John Davis, a Singapore policeman who had escaped from the island, made the initial landing on 23th May together with five Chinese. To-ing and fro-ing of men, mainly Chinese but with Europeans and others amongst them, went on between Ceylon and Malaya over succeeding months. One of the Chinese guerrilla members contacted was Wong Man-wa, more generally known by his codename, Chen Ping, who in the communist-inspired 'Malayan Emergency' which began in 1948, was to become Malaya's Public Enemy No. 1. Through Chen Ping and others, SOE learnt of the extent of the guerrilla movement in Malaya. Though this movement consisted mainly of communists whose political aims were much wider, it was presently only interested in getting rid of the Japanese. On behalf of the various guerrilla movements the main negotiator with the British – the guerrillas wanted arms, ammunition, medical supplies and money in return for their co-operation – was a man called Chang Hung.

Chang Hung was better known as Loi (or Lai) Tek, but during his career was also known as 'Mr Wright' or 'The Plen' – for plenipotentiary. An Annamese by birth, he had arrived in Singapore in 1933 from French Indo-China where he had been a police informer. In Singapore, and Malaya, and 'run' by Singapore policeman René Onraet, he worked in the same capacity for the Malayan authorities. He joined various Communist organisations including the Seamen's Union, and after claiming friendship with Ho Chi Minh was voted in as secretary-general of the Malayan Communist Party. Loi Tek was arrested by the Japanese when Singapore fell, but managed to save himself from death by undertaking to work for them, thus becoming a triple agent. Some of his information resulted in the Japanese ambushing a section of communist guerrillas and wiping them out near the Batu Caves. He also divulged enough information about SOE activities to keep the Japanese happy.*

Force 136, as it had come widely to be known, accomplished some comparatively minor feats against the Japanese in Malaya and, had the country to be taken back by force in 1945 under the planned Operation Zipper, no doubt the organisation it had set up would have operated to advantage in the Japanese rear. As it happened, before the Zipper forces landed the atom bombs dropped on Hiroshima and Nagasaki had compelled the Japanese to surrender. Without any disrespect to the efforts of the brave men of the several nations involved, it must be said that Force 136 in Malaya accomplished little apart from arming the communists. Unfortunately those arms were to be used to deadly effect during the post-war Malayan Emergency.

Another fertile sphere for disagreement between SOE and the OSS, was Thailand. There were difficulties over the respective areas of operations in that country. On a higher plane than that however,

* Post-war Loi Tek returned for a short time to being a double-agent; despite their knowledge of his wartime activities, the British employed him again. Then one day in September 1945 he disappeared from Singapore taking most of the Communist Party funds with him, an act likely to have been carried out with the connivance of the Singapore police. A year or two later Loi Tek is known to have visited the Singapore home of a senior police officer. It seems likely that Loi Tek was up to his old tricks, perhaps in another part of Southeast Asia, and had come back to report.

Thailand had declared war on Britain in 1942, albeit under pressure from the Japanese, but had not done the same with the USA. Consequently the British War Cabinet, and especially the Foreign Secretary, Anthony Eden, was opposed to making promises to the resistance movement in Thailand in return for them acting against the Japanese, whereas the Americans had no such qualms. Eden is on record as saying that collaboration with the Thais is 'hard for us all to swallow and the British public to understand'. As the British public was unlikely to find out about any such collaboration for many years under the government's secrecy rules, it is likely that the real reason for Eden's antagonism lay in the fact that, in pre-war years, the Thai Prime Minister, Pibul, had been so successful in hiding his pro-Japanese views from Sir Josiah Crosby, the British envoy that he had led the British up the garden path. On top of that, as a sop to Thailand's irredentist ambitions, Japan had 'given' back to the Thais certain British colonial territories in Malaya and Burma. Eden's uncompromising stand, one that somewhat smacks of vindictiveness, is summed up in the text of a message delivered to the US State Department by the British ambassador to Washington on 26th February 1944. The message is schoolmasterish in tone which perhaps indicates that Sir Josiah Crosby, who arrived back in England in late 1942 after an exchange of diplomatic personnel and who no doubt would have been used by the Foreign Office as an adviser on Thai matters, had a hand in it for he always tended to treat the Thais as children.[21]

> A country with a long traditional friendship with us has, though admittedly under pressure from Japan, betrayed that friendship . . . For these acts Thailand is already paying the price and will undoubtedly pay a yet heavier price as the war reaches her territories. It is still possible for the people of Thailand to do something to save themselves from the worst consequences of their betrayal, and they will be judged by the efforts that they make to redeem themselves from the position in which the actions of their present regime has placed them. Like other countries in like case, 'They must work their passage home'.[22]

Despite this, SOE did make contact with Luang Pradit, a pro-British and pro-communist Thai ex-minister. To get him out of the way, Pibul had kicked Pradit upstairs and made him Regent, the nominal Head of State, the young king being at school in Switzerland. Pradit organised a Thai resistance movement and became its leader. Pradit, who was also known as Pridi, was soon in regular contact with OSS agents by whom he was given the codename 'Ruth', and with SOE who knew him as 'BB855'. SOE agents opened up a line of communications between Admiral Mountbatten and Pradit, and over it there was a regular exchange of information and ideas. There existed, therefore, a unique situation in which 'the Supreme Allied Commander was exchanging vital military plans with the Head of a State technically at war with us'.[23]

Under agreed arrangements SOE smuggled some 'overseas' Thais into the country, and yet others were smuggled out to bring intelligence information. One party which arrived in Ceylon in February 1945 included General Nakrop of the Thai Army who brought with him much military intelligence including details of Japanese troop dispositions and airfields, and even copies of Japanese military manuals. However, it was the American OSS that got closest to Pradit. Two OSS majors, Richard Greenlee, who had been an associate in Bill Donovan's pre-war law firm, and John Wester, a businessman who knew Thailand well, were flown in by seaplane and then travelled upriver to Bangkok in a Thai Customs launch right under the noses of the Japanese. Greenlee left the country again after five days, carrying with him not only more information on Japanese troop dispositions, but also Pradit's plans for a guerrilla force. Wester remained behind to help train the Thai underground in more effective intelligence-gathering and to become the main link in the information channel between Thailand and the Allies. Thus it was that the OSS, by being the first to place western agents in Thailand, stole a march on the British who had always considered Thailand to be in their field of special influence. Nevertheless, the British were initially the main suppliers of arms and equipment to the Thai underground movement.

By the beginning of 1945, over 5,000 trained guerrillas, organised by Pradit and supplied by Allied air drops, were in control of a large portion of the northern part of the country. It seems that all sections of the community there were involved in one way or another. A force of 3,000 villagers carved an airstrip out of the jungle which the British nicknamed 'Heston'. But Pradit's movement was not only active in the north; on a smaller scale there was subversion in other parts of the country. Police vehicles were used to move arms and equipment. Thai Highway Department equipment was used to build jungle camp sites. Some units of the Thai army wanted to join the guerrillas but were ordered to stand-fast for fear that the Japanese would react even more strongly than they had. By August 1945 the total strength of the guerrilla movement throughout the country has been estimated at 90,000, a figure that would have been even higher had the war gone on, for the Thai army had become ever more restive under the stand-fast order.[24] The guerrillas stole gasoline, weapons, equipment and vehicles from the Japanese for their own use, guarded the secret airstrips being constructed, blew bridges, and attacked small and isolated Japanese patrols. They rescued downed Allied pilots, and members of the Thai underground often risked their lives in contacting Allied prisoners-of-war in Japanese controlled camps in Thailand. They tied down thousands of Japanese troops and wreaked more than a little havoc with Japanese lines of communication. The Thais were indeed working their passage home.[25]

John Haseman in his book on Thai resistance to the Japanese, says that 'by 1945 the two agencies [OSS and SOE] were willing to put aside parochial concerns and co-operate in future endeavours in Thailand'.[26] This is perhaps overstating the rapprochement, for SOE files indicate how worries over American involvement in Thailand continued to occupy British minds until the end of the war, and even later. Certain ventures, however, were Anglo-American planned and implemented. When, in December 1944, Admiral Mountbatten required better intelligence on Japanese activities in southwestern Burma, the Americans set up a base on the Thai-owned Chan Island which lies a few miles off the coast and just south of the Burmese border. It was in a dangerous location, not too far from Japanese strongpoints, so perhaps inevitably it became known as 'Chance Island'. The mission, under Lieutenant John Calhoun of the American Navy, supplied Mountbatten with much information, and the island soon became a major transhipment point for stores and arms for guerrillas, with supplies coming in by Catalina flying boats and going out by small craft. However, in the spring, when the parachutes of two downed Allied aircrew were spotted hanging in the trees by Japanese planes, the island had to be evacuated.[27]

After the war Mountbatten wrote a warm letter of appreciation to Pradit for his war work, and in the immediate post-war years the British and Americans supported his bid for power in Thailand. All that changed when Pradit's known communist leanings burst forth, especially after twenty-year-old King Ananda's assassination by gunshot in 1946. The exact circumstances behind this event remain a mystery, but Pradit was almost certainly involved in it. He later fled the country and ended up in communist China.

Yet another area for dispute between the British and American subversive organisations was French Indo-China. There, as in other Southeast Asian territories, the root of the dispute lay in a series of political problems. The country's leadership was pro-Vichy; there was a Free French element but it was small, and anyway, neither the Americans nor the British trusted General de Gaulle overmuch. President Roosevelt had no wish for Indo-China to return to French domination after the war, whereas Britain did, if for no other reason than that any alteration in the colonial structure in the area might affect its own position. Britain's proposal and preparations for a major French-led resistance movement in Indo-China did not have the President's backing.

Roosevelt's antipathy towards the French over Indo-China was based on two premises other than his antipathy for de Gaulle. First, according to US Secretary of State Cordell Hull, Roosevelt put some of the onus for the original Japanese attacks of the war squarely on France:

> He . . . [Roosevelt] entertained strong views on independence for French Indo-China. That French dependency stuck in his mind as having been the springboard for the Japanese attack on the Philippines, Malaya and the Dutch East Indies. He could not but remember the devious conduct of the Vichy Government in granting Japan the right to station troops there, without any consultation with us but with an effort to make the world believe we approved.

Second, Roosevelt considered France to be a very bad colonial power. Quoting Roosevelt directly, Hull recorded: 'France has had the country [Indo-China] – thirty million inhabitants – for nearly one hundred years, and the people are worse off than they were in the beginning.'[28]

It is therefore not surprising that, when the British began to staff SOE's 'country section' with French officers under Captain de Langlade in 1943, and in 1944 added a French Mission to Southeast Asia Command Headquarters, Roosevelt became restive. And when, in October 1944, Hull sent Roosevelt a memo relating to an OSS proposal to assist resistance groups in Indo-China, he received the following answer: 'In regard to the Indo-China matter, it is my judgement on this date that we should do nothing in regard to resistance groups or in any other way in relation to Indo-China.'

Subsequently he seems to have changed his mind, for by the end of 1944 SOE and OSS were squabbling over the country, with the Chinese joining in for good measure. The Americans argued that the country fell within China Command, virtually under their control despite the fact that Chiang Kai-shek was the nominal Allied Supreme Commander there.

The build-up of Allied interest in Indo-China was not lost on the Japanese. With more and more intelligence reports coming in of actual or planned Allied subversion operations, in March 1945 the Japanese launched a successful military coup and took complete control of the country. Some French garrisons fought the Japanese who took the ultimate reprisal against many prisoners. Some units of the French Foreign Legion, after a fighting two-month retreat managed to reach China. One of these legionnaires was a Briton, Edmund Murray, who in 1950 became Winston Churchill's personal bodyguard and confidant.[29]

This take-over effectively put paid to any attempt by the Allies to send in major resistance forces; although some agents were air-dropped in from time to time and guerrillas conducted some sabotage, it was on a small scale.

In relation to their fellow Allies the Dutch were in a far stronger bargaining position over special operations which concerned their occupied colonies than were the Free French. Furthermore, unlike with Burma and Indo-China, the Chinese had no common border with the Netherlands East Indies, and so were not directly involved in policy decisions.

Admiral Helfrich, based in Ceylon, commanded all Dutch forces in the area, including the *Korps Insulinde*, a commando unit specially trained in India. He wished to use his commandos for special operations in spite of having been told that there was a difference between subversive tactics and commando raids and that the two required quite different characteristics in the men involved. In fact the *Korps'* first operations, in Sumatra, were special operations in the accepted sense, and proved to be unsuccessful.

SOE set up its own Dutch Country section, but its first operation in Sumatra was not a success either, and for much the same reason; the Sumatrans were not keen to collaborate with anyone who might eventually bring back the Dutch colonisers. In fact the Anglo-Dutch unit involved in this operation, whose objective had been to set up a resistance organisation, walked into a Japanese ambush almost certainly connived at by the Sumatrans, and its members only just managed to escape with their lives. There were other attempts at the same sort of action, but none met with much success. SOE met with similar problems in Java. Throughout what is now known as Indonesia, and unlike the other countries of Southeast Asia, there was no resistance movement seeking active outside help against the Japanese; what the Allies had to face there was militant anti-Dutch nationalism. At the war's end when British forces took temporary control of the Dutch islands they found themselves fighting a war against nationalists, a war on such a scale that they had to rearm captured Japanese troops who then fought on the British side. (Much the same situation arose in Indo-China.)

By the end of 1943 twin lines of assault on Japanese-held islands in the Pacific had begun, primarily by American forces. In certain areas, and especially at sea, the Japanese had been experiencing reverses and it was essential to keep them on the defensive for fear that, given half a chance, they would make such strongholds out of some of the islands they might prove extremely difficult, even impossible, to dislodge.

One of the twin thrusts came from MacArthur's command, which included Australians, driving on after their initial victories in New Guinea and the Solomons. The other came from the US Navy and Marine operations under Admiral Halsey against the islands of the Central Pacific. Although it was essential to keep up the momentum against the Japanese, the build-up of the land and sea forces required to do so was slow because of the Allies' 'Germany first' agreement.

The commanders of the twin thrusts gained significant aid from Signals Intelligence, though the handling of this material by MacArthur's chief of intelligence, General Willoughby, sometimes left much to be desired. Willoughby's intense loyalty towards MacArthur was reciprocated and then some, for although prior to several actions Willoughby grossly underestimated Japanese strengths, MacArthur does not seem to have called him to account.

One example of Willoughby's neglect of Sigint occurred when on 8th January 1945 the US 6th Army landed on Luzon Island in the Philippines. The Americans expected to meet 152,000 troops under General Yamashita, but in truth the 'tiger of Malaya' had in excess of 280,000 men at his disposal, the higher figure having been indicated by decrypts. Willoughby's handling of ordinary intelligence was also sometimes at fault. This was evidenced by the neglect of terrain intelligence prior to the landings on Leyte in October 1944, inexcusable on two counts: the island had been under American control for decades, and in the months before the attack MacArthur's HQ had been in contact with Leyte guerrillas. One of MacArthur's reasons for choosing Leyte as the site of the first landings in the Philippines was because he assumed airfields could be constructed in the centre of the island to support following operations, an erroneous assumption because of the nature of the terrain which Willoughby and his staff should have known about. Another example was in the clearance of Manila in February, where the tenacity of the Japanese defenders came as a hideous surprise to the Americans. In house-by-house and street-by-street fighting, 12,000 Americans and 16,000 Japanese died, in addition to countless Filipinos. The American Professor Gerhard Weinberg has written: 'the use of signals intelligence by MacArthur's headquarters was not as fruitful as the navy's, though the army air force appears to have been more consistent in its use. Certainly in the bitter fighting on Leyte . . ., the neglect of signals intelligence . . . was a serious error.[30]

General Willoughby also receives some criticism in a document in the British Public Record Office. In reference to the situation prevailing in the first months of 1944, 'the idea was that as the battlefront was pushed further north, advanced echelons [of the Central Bureau] would radiate out to the various combat areas'. But, said the authors of the document, 'politics were behind much of the intrigue and manoeuvring then in progress. General Willoughby . . . was thought to be heavily involved in the political side of General MacArthur's activities, and in the various plans for boosting the claims and reputation of his chief.'[31]

MacArthur's initial thrusts were in New Guinea and over on the wing, in the islands surrounding Rabaul, New Britain, which was Japan's most important base in the Southwest Pacific. By the beginning of 1944 MacArthur was by-passing Japanese strongholds, a technique which, together with control of the air and sea, virtually neutralised the by-passed garrisons. This happened with Rabaul itself, where 100,000 Japanese became a wasting liability for most of the rest of the war. This policy of 'leap-frogging', which MacArthur later claimed was his own invention, was in fact born at the Allied Conference held in Quebec in August 1943, where the outline plan for it was codenamed 'Reno'.[32]

Farther north, the so-called Atoll War across the islands of the Central Pacific began with the battle for Tarawa in the Gilberts, an island that had to be taken because of its excellent airfield. As with many of the outlying islands, it was defended not by the Japanese army but by naval special units using naval communications and naval codes, the latter being more easily read by the Allies than those of the army. Sigint was thus able to estimate the size of the Japanese garrison at Tarawa, 4,820 men, to within a hundred or two. Reconnaissance aircraft and submarines supplied more intelligence, so that the Americans had a thorough and complete picture of the defences awaiting them, which were formidable. One of the reconnaissance submarines, the *Nautilus*, whose presence in the area was somehow not known to the American task force commander, was actually attacked by a US cruiser and destroyer. It sustained damage but managed to escape this friendly fire.

The assault on Tarawa, which was made on 20th November 1943 after a three-hour aerial and naval bombardment, showed that even when an attack is based on the best of intelligence, things can still go badly awry. The communications system aboard HQ ship *Maryland* was damaged by her own first salvo; troop transports arrived in the wrong lowering position and when moved, lost some of their boats; wind and sea conditions and a stronger than expected ebb-tide caused landing craft to arrive on the beaches late. On top of all that many more Japanese survived the initial bombardment than had been thought possible.

In three days of fighting against an enemy ordered to fight to the last man, and to take an island not much more than a mile in length and a quarter of a mile wide, the Americans lost over three thousand dead and wounded. Only seventeen Japanese and 129 members of a Korean labour company survived. Of the 125 landing craft used in the assault, ninety were lost.

After the fall of Tarawa the Japanese assumed that the Americans would make their next move against one or more of the outlying islands in the Marshall group to the north. They began reinforcing some of these islands, a fact soon picked up by Allied listening posts. When decrypts of these messages were handed to Admiral Nimitz, he decided to go instead for Kwajalein Island, in the centre of the group, and where the Japanese were constructing an air strip. The lessons of Tarawa were taken to heart and even more thorough preparations were put in hand. Reconnaissance intelligence showed that the Japanese had neither mined nor placed obstructions in the lagoon or its entrances. To reconnoitre the beaches, advance parties of Underwater Demolition Teams were used for the first time in the Pacific. From Sigint sources the Americans estimated the strength of the garrison to be 3,800, which proved to be correct to within a few dozen; Sigint was showing its worth.[33] The island fell on 5th February 1944, and this time American losses were much smaller, though again the Japanese fought almost to the last man.

One problem that came to light early in the islands' campaign was the serviceman's penchant for collecting souvenirs including, it seems, important intelligence material. A Japanese code-book was discovered in the messdeck of a ship when it arrived back at Pearl Harbor, by which time the code was out of date. Nevertheless, much invaluable intelligence material, including charts of minefields, was captured as various islands fell.

After Kwajalein it was Eniwetok Island's turn, the Americans by-passing a smaller island that lay between them that was in later years to achieve much fame, called Bikini. Eniwetok fell on 24th February and within days the Americans were building an advanced naval base there and a bomber strip. Lying some five hundred miles to the northeast of Eniwetok was Wake Island and over to the west was Guam in the Marianas; the Americans were drawing nearer home ground.

Truk Island in the Carolines was attacked conjointly with Eniwetok. The Japanese called Truk the 'Gibraltar of the East' with about as much justification, as it turned out, as the British had once done with Singapore. American reconnaissance flights showed a mass of naval targets in the area, but forewarned by these flights, the Japanese sent most of their naval units west. Nevertheless, in a night-raid on 17th February followed by more sorties on the following day, aircraft from American carriers turned the Truk lagoon into a maritime scrapyard. For an expenditure of twenty-five aircraft and twenty-nine aircrew, the Americans sank a cruiser, two armed merchant cruisers, a submarine tender, three destroyers, and no fewer than twenty-nine merchant ship auxiliaries, including three of the largest Japanese tankers afloat.* Not far short of a quarter of a million tons of shipping littered the bottom of the lagoon, to say nothing of the 250 Japanese aircraft destroyed in the air or on the ground, and the destruction of military installations ashore. To this day Truk remains a scrapyard.

Two air crashes off the central Philippine island of Cebu on 31st March 1944 provided the Americans with another intelligence bonanza. The planes, one of which carried Admiral Koga Mineichi, who had become Commander-in-Chief of the Japanese Combined Fleet after the death of Yamamoto, and his Chief of Staff, Rear-Admiral Fukudome Shigeru, crashed into the sea during a midnight electric storm, the crashes being witnessed by Filipino guerrillas. Ten injured Japanese survivors from one of the planes were eventually brought ashore by local fishermen. During the pick-up one of the Japanese tried to sink a briefcase, but it was retrieved. The guerrillas carried their prisoners by stretcher to the mountain hideaway of James Cushing, the leader of the Cebu resistance who had earlier received a radioed commission as lieutenant-colonel from General MacArthur. On the way to the hideout one of the prisoners identified himself as Koga.

Colonel Cushing radioed Brisbane with news of the prisoners and of the capture of the briefcase and received instructions to rendezvous off an adjacent island with a submarine which would take prisoners and case away. Meanwhile the commander of the Japanese troops out looking for the survivors threatened to massacre Filipino villagers unless all the Japanese were handed over. Cushing informed MacArthur that in the circumstances he had no option but to accede to this demand, but sent the briefcase to the submarine by messenger. An apoplectic MacArthur reduced Cushing to the ranks, a move which made no difference at all to his status with his guerrillas. Still believing that his principal prisoner was Koga, Cushing handed them all over to the Japanese.

When the contents of the briefcase were examined and translated at AIB in Brisbane, amongst them was a Fleet Secret Order 'Z' detailing Japanese deployment plans in the face of the encroaching American fleet, which was to prove of great value to American commanders over

* One of these, the *Tonan Maru*, had seven months earlier survived an attack by the US submarine *Tinosa*. Although the tanker was damaged, eight of the torpedoes fired at her bounced off her side without exploding.

succeeding months. AIB's examination of the documents also led them to the conclusion that Cushing's main prisoner survivor had been Real Admiral Fukudome rather than Koga, and that seems to be borne out by a Japanese announcement of Koga's death a little later. Fukudome, on the other hand, after a Board of Enquiry in Tokyo had acquitted him of dishonourable conduct in not having committed *hara-kiri* on being captured in compliance with the unwritten but powerful code of *sen-jin-kun* – his defence was that his captors were not military but mere guerrillas – went on to become a fleet commander.[34] Cushing, happily reinstated in his rank at war's end, and his Filipinos remained convinced always that they had captured Koga.

General MacArthur, acting on knowledge from intercepts that Japan was reducing her forces at Hollandia, the capital of what had been Dutch New Guinea, and by using deception techniques which persuaded the Japanese that he meant to attack elsewhere, took that town in late April 1944. MacArthur's success also owed something to radioed information from two Dutchmen who had earlier been set down in the vicinity of Hollandia, Jean de Bruijn previously a colonial administrator in the Dutch territory, and Rudy Grout, a radio operator. Ground intelligence still had an important part to play in the war.

Planned to support MacArthur's attack on Hollandia by keeping Japanese naval units based in Singapore occupied, Admiral Seymour's British Eastern Fleet, temporarily reinforced by an American carrier and its escorts, launched Operation Cockpit on 19th April, an aerial attack on the harbour and oil installations at Sabang, an island off the coast of Sumatra. Around this time FECB at HMS *Anderson* in Colombo devised several W/T deception plans to fool the Japanese over Allied intentions. False information was passed through 'certain channels' earlier built up by intelligence. In keeping with the practice of secret agencies to make positive use whenever possible of catastrophes that happen to one's own side, FECB used the accidental explosion of the ammunition ship *Fort Stikine*, in Bombay harbour on 14th April, as part of one of the deception plans. When the *Fort Stikine* blew up, fourteen merchant ships and two small naval ships were destroyed, as was a great part of the port including a landing craft base and the many craft in it.[35] FECB planted airwaves information that the loss of the landing craft meant that no sea raid could now be made on Port Blair in the Andamans, but that a carrier-based plane raid would instead be made on that port in mid-May. That false trail was to cover an actual raid in mid-May on the naval base at Surabaya and the Wonokrono oil refinery in eastern Java, made by aircraft from the American carrier as it was detached from the British Fleet to make its way home to the USA.*

Other deception messages were used prior to Operation Pedal in June, in which planes from a British carrier actually did attack Port Blair, and also before a second and larger attack on Sabang in July, both attacks designed to keep up pressure on the Japanese western front as the Americans attacked in the east.

The loss of many of their outlying bases and the problem of oil supplies for ships guarding those that remained, caused the Japanese to change their strategy. Their Empire had begun to implode, and instead of holding an outer perimeter of islands they were forced into trying to hold an inner barrier. Fleet operations were hampered by losses of tankers due to the growing success of US submarine operations and air attacks such as those on Truk, added to the fact that the programme of tanker construction the Japanese had implemented in May 1943 had as yet had little effect. From February 1944, many Japanese ships began to fall back on Singapore where they were in closer proximity to the oilfields of Balik Papan, Miri, and Palembang.

To bolster defence of the inner barrier the Japanese took many submarines away from offensive operations and made floating pickets of them, their principal job now being to scout and report Allied movements. Sigint revealed this plan, and over the succeeding weeks seventeen of the submarines were sunk.

The Marianas Group of islands, forming part of the inner barrier, was of crucial importance to both Japanese and Americans. The two most important of the islands, Saipan and Guam, were keys to the

* The *Fort Stikine* was carrying a dangerous cocktail of ammunition and cotton, for under certain circumstances cotton is liable to spontaneous combustion. She should never have been berthed alongside, but discharged instead at the dangerous goods anchorage. A fire was discovered when the hatches were opened, and despite the efforts of the port fire service the ship blew up in what has been described as the largest explosion of the war before Hiroshima. There is a story that the ship was also carrying seven tons of gold bullion and that it rained gold in certain parts of the city. This author has not been able to authenticate that part of the story. Suffice it to say that the Bombay Port Commissioners have no record of any gold being handed back to the authorities.

back door to the Philippines over to the west. Both had airfields within long-range aircraft reach of Formosa and even of Japan itself. Moreover, the American fleet's own line of communications with its main base at Pearl Harbor was growing ever longer, and Saipan and Guam would provide superior advance bases to that on the coral atoll of Eniwetok.

For the attack on Saipan, American intelligence, combining Sigint with photo-reconnaissance and reports from Underwater Demolition Teams, provided much information, but this time managed to underestimate the size of the Japanese garrison there by about fifty per cent. The garrison actually numbered 27,700, three-quarters of them army, the rest navy. On 15th June, nine days after D-Day in Normandy, the most massive amphibious landing in history, Americans began storming ashore on Saipan from the largest fleet so far assembled in the Pacific. Fighting went on until 7th July by which time no fewer than 25,914 Japanese were dead, many of them by suicide. Amongst those who died were the Japanese army and navy commanders who committed ritual suicide, the latter being Admiral Nagumo of Pearl Harbor, Colombo and Trincomalee fame.

The attack on Saipan brought out the Japanese Fleet under Admiral Ozawa, its main body from the Philippines linking up with a force from the south. The fleet maintained strict radio silence, but American Naval Intelligence, combining submarine sightings with a coastwatcher's report from the Philippines, and Admiral Koga's 'Z' order captured earlier by the guerrillas on Cebu, was able to provide a largely accurate prediction of the composition of the Japanese fleet and of the intentions of its commander. In the Battle of the Marianas that took place on 19th/20th June, the Japanese lost two carriers, a cruiser, and almost five hundred irreplaceable planes. The American fleet under Admiral Spruance sustained minor hits on two ships and lost one hundred and thirty planes. So many Japanese planes were shot down on the first day of the battle that it came to be called the 'Great Marianas Turkey Shoot'.

Landings on Guam began on 21st July and the island was declared secured on 10th August. Even before the occupation was complete the Americans began using Apra harbour there, the site of the former US naval base, and before long a base with the capability of supporting one-third of the Pacific Fleet was made available.

According to American official records over fifty tons of Japanese documents were captured at Saipan and Guam. Some of these proved useful in checking past decryptions, but others, including Japanese Army orders of battle, were extremely valuable for future operations.

Sigint played a role in several all-submarine operations in eastern waters. Ten months after the operation on 12th November 1943, when the British submarine *Taurus*, after being ordered to lay in wait at a specific time and place in the Malacca Strait, sank the Japanese submarine I-34, another British submarine, *Trenchant*, commanded by Lieutenant-Commander A.R. Hezlett, RN, and patrolling off the Sumatran coast in September 1944, was suddenly ordered to proceed with all speed to a position north of Penang. This is an instance when the British ability to read German Enigma codes and the U-boat code in particular, played a part in the eastern war. *U-859*, one of five U-boats operating in the Indian Ocean in 1944, was due to arrive at Penang for refitting after a six-month operational cruise. Its exact time of arrival was signalled to Hezlett who sighted the U-boat on the surface at the precise time indicated and at a range of 2,700 yards. One of the salvo of three torpedoes fired by *Trenchant* sank the U-boat.[36]

The Japanese used some submarines as blockade-runners between Europe and the homeland, and Sigint enabled the Allies to track most of them. The I-29, which a year earlier had been the submarine that rendezvoused with the U-boat bringing the Indian nationalist Subhas Chandra Bose back east, left L'Orient on the French coast in April 1944. Allied listening posts intercepted messages first from Berlin about her voyage, then later from a Japanese station at Singapore. They not only indicated her track, but also gave full details of what she was carrying. On board were seventeen technicians, including four Germans, and some highly specialised equipment including radar. Also aboard were plans for a new high-speed submarine and certain bacteriological warfare material. Not least in importance, she also carried twenty Enigma coding machines. She got as far as the Luzon Strait before being sunk by the US submarine *Sawfish* on 26th July.

By October 1944 Allied forces had occupied a ring of islands stretching from the Moluccas in the south round to the Marianas and were poised for an attack on the Philippines. Throughout the summer the British Eastern Fleet over on the western flank in the Indian Ocean had continued its diversionary operations in an attempt to draw Japanese forces away from the Pacific, but Sigint sources revealed that the enemy had not reacted; the threat of an attack on the Philippines was of much greater import to the Japanese than anything going on in the west, for the loss of the island group would threaten the supply of oil to Japan from Sumatra and Borneo.

The American build-up for the initial attack on the central Philippine island of Leyte began on 10th October with carrier-based attacks on targets stretching almost a thousand miles from Okinawa in the Ryukyu Islands in the north down to the Philippines. The Japanese Imperial Navy, proving it was not finished yet, sent three task forces, one from the homeland, one from Singapore, and the other from the Philippines itself, to confront the danger. Meanwhile, Japanese land-based aircraft made sorties against American ships, their returning pilots claiming eleven carriers and two battleships sunk and many other units damaged, when in fact the sum total of their successes was hits on two cruisers. The extravagant claims were used in Tokyo to boost public morale, and although the Imperial Naval Command assessed the losses at a more reasonable level, Sigint revealed that Japanese officialdom still believed grossly overestimated figures. That belief may be the reason why, to follow up on the perceived success, Tokyo prematurely activated plans for the defence of the Philippines, with hundreds of planes being committed to stop an invasion that had not yet begun. No firm figure can be given of the losses of Japanese aircraft at this time, but it is likely to have been around five hundred.

The first American landings on Leyte came on 20th October, and the sea battle that signalled the end of the Japanese Imperial Navy as an effective fighting force, which was to be called the Battle of Leyte Gulf, took place between the 23rd and 26th. It was an overwhelming victory for the Americans but one marred by wrong tactical decisions, a divided naval command with one admiral reporting to Nimitz in Pearl Harbor and another reporting to MacArthur, and bad communications. But against a loss of three light carriers and three minor ships, the Americans sank four Japanese carriers, three battleships, ten cruisers and nine other vessels. After Leyte the worst threats to the United States navy came from land-based planes, especially those turned into piloted bombs, the famous kamikaze.

* * *

The Japanese invasion of India began on 15th March 1944, an attack indicated in advance by Allied Sigint which also provided information on the four Japanese divisions involved and on the reorganisation of the Japanese command. During that same month General Wingate made his second excursion behind enemy lines in Burma, his brigades this time being flown in to an area south of Myitkyina where they were a threat to the Japanese lines of communications. In India the Japanese had some initial successes but then magnificent holding actions by the British and Indian Armies at Imphal and Kohima, assisted by Allied command of the air and information from Sigint sources, ensured that the danger was over by June. The Japanese withdrew in disorder, and despite the monsoon, the British began to pursue them.

It was in March 1944 that Lieutenant-Colonel H.P. Seagrim of Force 136 (SOE), who had in the previous year volunteered to stay behind enemy lines to organise guerrilla activity among the Karen tribesmen, gave himself up to the Japanese who had threatened to massacre Karen villagers unless he did so. A tall, thin man known to his beloved Karens as 'Grandfather Longlegs', Seagrim was later executed by the Japanese. After the war he was awarded a posthumous George Cross.

The operations of Force 136 in Burma at this time were sometimes jeopardised by the attitude towards them of the British Army. General Wingate, for example, 'disliked and suspected' the organisation even though in 1943 more than a few wounded and stragglers from his original expedition in 1943 had been saved by Force 136 trained natives.

Even General Bill Slim, GOC 14th Army, seemed against the organisation, complaining in June that neither Force 136 nor the army's own armed 'Z' Force patrols were bringing in enough intelligence. Here Slim was being unfair, for it was not Force 136's remit to supply intelligence, except as an adjunct to its main sabotage and guerrilla functions. In fact, in his book about the Burma campaign, which was written in 1956, eighteen years before the secret of Allied code-breaking was revealed and when he could not even hint of its existence, General Slim wrote what seems to be a blanket criticism of all sources of intelligence available to him, including Sigint.[37] Certainly, Louis Allen in his *Burma, the Longest War*, took this to be an overall criticism. However, as Alan Stripp, one of the cryptographers engaged in supplying Slim with Sigint, has pointed out, Slim's criticism was almost certainly confined to ground intelligence sources. Why otherwise would the

General have expressed satisfaction with the Sigint information he was receiving when he was visited during the campaign by Group Captain F.W. Winterbotham from Bletchley Park?

Winterbotham wrote in his own book *The Ultra Secret*:

> General Slim . . . [was] well satisfied with the information which was being received . . . [including] a complete order of battle of the Japanese forces. Some of the most interesting signals had been those showing the shortages of rations and equipment.[38]

It would seem that General Slim's problems lay with ground intelligence sources, and especially with intelligence concerning Japanese lines of communications, best discovered by ground sources. Some of these problems were caused by the sheer number of British security services involved, by the failure to co-ordinate their operations with military operations, and by the extreme secrecy measures adopted by some of them. The British SIS, which in India and Burma went under the name Inter-Service Liaison Department, or ISLD, has been singled out in this latter respect. Squadron Leader Terence O'Brien – who as a Dakota pilot with RAF 357 Squadron was engaged during 1944–45 in many clandestine operations involving ISLD and Force 136 – has recorded that the title Inter-Service Liaison Department was a misnomer 'for an organisation renowned for its lack of liaison with anyone or anybody, let alone just the services'.[39] ISLD was run from Calcutta by Colin Tooke who 'was reluctant to put anything on paper, kept all his agents separated from one another, and even his second-in-command was ignorant of many of the operations Tooke arranged'. The local SIS officer O'Brien dealt with at Jessore airfield north of Calcutta, was a namesake, Charles O'Brien. Of his namesake and the organisation for which he worked, Squadron Leader O'Brien wrote, 'like most of his fellows in that service, he considered his work far more important than the fighting war, and far too secret to be shared'.*

As a result of General Slim's concerns, in July 1944 Admiral Mountbatten ordered a review of British secret services in the area with the idea of perhaps cutting out some of the confusion

* The cloak of ultra-secrecy in which the SIS has wrapped itself, and its refusal to co-operate with other British intelligence organisations, is possibly the principal reason why some of their senior operatives were able to get away with being traitors for so many years. Secrecy is a double-sided dagger.

in functions and the overlapping of responsibilities. At that time, apart from Force 136, 'Z' Force, and ISLD, there were working in the area a Psychological Warfare Division, an organisation called 'D.Div.' which was engaged in deception, the Combined Operations Pilotage Parties (COPP) engaged in marine sabotage and surveying enemy-held coasts, a prisoner-of-war escape organisation, and several others, about a dozen in all.

The review did not bring about immediate changes, and Slim continued to inveigh against what he called the deplorable state of the clandestine forces. He compared the amount of intelligence coming from Force 136 detrimentally with that coming from OSS. This was rather harsh in that not only was OSS constitutionally an intelligence-gathering body which Force 136 was not, but OSS in fact obtained much of its material from Force 136 sources. In the end it was decided to combine Force 136 with 'Z' Force, with the new main function of collecting intelligence from behind enemy lines. For technical reasons the amalgamation was not fully a success, but Slim had got his way in the change of function of Force 136 and in the exercise of military control over it in battle zones.

General Slim's criticisms were not the only ones concerning the intelligence community in Burma. The OSS, backed by General 'Vinegar Joe' Stilwell, did not much care for Force 136 operatives working in its area of responsibility despite the fact that British-organised units had been in those areas for a long time.

A more significant problem for Force 136 was a political one. It concerned its use of Burmese nationalist groups against the Japanese. There were two main nationalist factions, both having originated pre-war. One faction was communist-inspired which, after Russia entered the war, thrust its anti-British propensities into the background and decided to aid the Allies. The other faction was under Aung San who, after being trained in Japan, had returned to Burma to join the Japanese-sponsored Burmese National Army. Very soon Aung San became disillusioned with the Japanese and sent out feelers to the Allies, and it was then that political difficulties arose. Force 136, which had been arming tribesmen in Burma, ran into opposition when it proposed to arm Burmese nationalists now prepared to fight the Japanese. Opposition came from the organisation known as the Civil Affairs Service (Burma), (CAS(B)), which used the argument that short-term military advantage was no proper trade-off for possible long-term problems when the civil administration regained control of the country. CAS(B) fought against such rearmament, and in the end there was a sort of compromise which came about more from the unrolling of events as Burmese everywhere began to rise against the retreating Japanese, than it did from the implementation of any British decisions.

The British Combined Operations Pilotage Parties (COPP) upon which the US Underwater Demolition Teams had been partly based, had been formed earlier in World War Two and had conducted many successful operations in Europe and North Africa. The first COPP teams, consisting mainly of navy personnel, had arrived in the Far East in 1943. They engaged in beach reconnaissance and surveying, occasional sabotage, and landing and picking up agents. They operated in tiny two-man canoes off-loaded from submarines and, in missions ranging geographically from the Burmese Arakan coast down to Morib Beach in Malaya and to the island of Sumatra, they brought back valuable intelligence about prospective landing beaches, including tidal data that had sometimes to be gathered under the very noses of the Japanese. Sometimes they managed to bring back prisoners for interrogation. Some COPP operatives were captured and at least two were executed by the Japanese. One of COPP's few failures occurred in June 1945 when parties were landed at Morib Beach on the west coast of Malaya, which was to be the site for the landing of Operation Zipper for the retaking of Malaya. They failed to learn the true nature of the beaches there. On the other hand, that was something that would have been known to several members of the pre-war Malayan Civil Service who were serving in India after having escaped from Malaya. Had anyone on Mountbatten's Zipper planning staff bothered to ask these men, they would have discovered that Morib Beach was not a good landing site. Under a thin layer of sand which seems firm enough to the naked eye, and feels firm enough to a walking man, there lies a belt of thick mud. It is fortunate indeed, not least for Mountbatten's reputation, that by the time Operation Zipper forces were landed at Morib, the dropping of the atom bombs on Japan in August 1945 had forced her to surrender. Zipper was thus an unopposed landing, which was just as well. Although troops got ashore in good order, their heavy equipment did not; trucks, tanks, and guns sank through the sand and disappeared into the deep mud below.

* * *

Admiral Sir Bruce Fraser, who had relieved Somerville as C-in-C Eastern Fleet in August 1944, was given command of the British Pacific Fleet in November. On its way to Australia this fleet, which eventually comprised four large carriers, two battleships, five cruisers, sixteen destroyers, and a 'fleet support train' of over fifty vessels including eight tankers, made two major air strikes against the oil installations at Palembang.

Left behind in the Indian Ocean was a fleet, newly designated the East Indies Fleet, under Vice-Admiral Sir Arthur Power whose main tasks were to support the British army in Burma and wherever possible to prevent the Japanese evacuating their garrisons from the Nicobar and Andaman Islands or from any other islands in Southeast Asia Command's area. Over succeeding months the 'Y' installation at HMS *Anderson* kept special listening watch for any sign of Japanese evacuation operations, the *Anderson* operation being backed by small 'Y' groups which included Japanese-speaking operators, embarked aboard naval vessels.

Power's fleet used radio deception, and diversionary air attacks and bombardments on the Andaman and Nicobar Islands, to cover military landings made near Rangoon, that port-city falling to British forces on 3rd May 1945 with hardly a shot being fired. A week later Sigint revealed that the Japanese were about to evacuate their Andaman and Nicobar garrisons using the cruiser *Haguro*, a destroyer, and two smaller vessels. A British fleet sailed to meet the Japanese ships off the northern entrance of the Malacca Strait but Sigint soon discovered that the British ships had been spotted by Japanese land-based air reconnaissance and that, in consequence, the cruiser and destroyer had turned back towards Penang. Meanwhile the smaller Japanese units had somehow managed to reach Nancowry in the Nicobars and took off 450 troops.

On 14th/15th May British 'Y' units picked up and read several messages that indicated that *Haguro* and her consort were about to try again to reach the Andamans, and the British 26th Destroyer Flotilla was detached to intercept. At 0200 hours on 16th May, after a running gun and torpedo attack, the cruiser was sunk. The Japanese destroyer, called *Kamikaze*, was damaged but managed to reach Penang. The two smaller vessels, which had successfully eluded the British to bring troops away from Nancowry, did not last long, for a month later both were sunk by British destroyers off Sabang.

The sinking of the *Haguro* left the cruiser *Ashigara* as the only major Japanese naval unit left in the south. Then, in June, Lieutenant-Commander A.R. Hezlett, aboard H.M. submarine *Trenchant*, received contact reports from two American submarines that a Japanese heavy cruiser had entered Batavia harbour. With indications from Sigint that the cruiser was embarking troops for Singapore, the submarine lay in wait for her prey on the usual route taken by ships sailing between the two ports. At about noon on 8th June *Trenchant* sighted the cruiser and fired its full broadside of torpedoes. Its decks crammed with troops, *Ashigara* attempted to 'comb' the torpedo tracks but being in restricted waters could turn only one way and not quickly enough. Struck by five torpedoes, smoke and flame engulfed the cruiser which sank within half an hour, taking many men with her including Vice-Admiral Hashimoto Shintaro. *Ashigara* sank in the Banka Strait where three years and three months previously so many of the fleet of small vessels fleeing from Singapore had met their fates. Hashimoto, who had commanded the Imperial Navy's 1st Escort Force in the invasion of Malaya, and who came from a nation renowned for its meticulous attention to detail as in their tea-making ceremonies, might have had time to appreciate the dreadful symmetry of it all as his ship went down in that same place.

The Japanese naval forces in the area were now reduced to a point where the largest ship they had was the destroyer with the ominous name, *Kamikaze*.

For the remainder of the war Sigint continued to reveal Japanese plans, including their use of that weapon of last resort, the kamikaze plane.* By this time no matter what changes the Japanese navy made to their code-books and cyphers, they were being quickly broken and being read concurrently by, at the latest, the second day after the change.

What Sigint could not reveal was the fanatical resistance offered by most Japanese garrisons as the Americans continued their island-hopping campaign, nor how many Japanese were able to survive the pre-landing air attacks and naval bombardments. The island of Iwo Jima, halfway between Saipan and Tokyo, underwent six months of air attacks and several bombardments before American marines landed there on 19th February 1945. The Americans found themselves

* The word 'kamikaze' is honoured in Japanese legend. It refers to the 'Divine Wind' which was said to have destroyed Kublai Khan's invasion fleet of 1281 – rather like the wind-driven fate of the Spanish Armada against England in 1588: 'God blew with his wind, and they were scattered'.

fighting troops occupying a maze of strongpoints connected by underground passages which had been impossible to spot by air reconnaissance. The epic story of the month-long battle for the island is one of hand-to-hand fighting that went on as much under the ground as on it.

In February 1945 in preparation for Australian troop landings at Tarakan on the northeast coast of Borneo in May, a small force of men known as 'Z Special' under Tom Harrisson was parachuted into Borneo. They were to make contact with native inhabitants, set up guerrilla units, radio back information on Japanese depositions, dislocate enemy communications and supply routes, and to 'deal with' any enemy troops who fell back into the interior after the Australians had landed. Harrisson's success with the native chieftains was helped by the fact that some of them took him to be Anthony Brooke, nephew of the Third White Rajah of Sarawak. Anthony, whom Harrisson somewhat resembled in build, had at one time been designated Rajah Muda, next in line to rule Sarawak. Although Harrisson did not directly lie, he did nothing to correct the chieftains' misapprehension, the Brooke name being held in high esteem by the natives. Some chieftains even tried matchmaking, attempting to get Harrisson to wed a comely maiden. He always maintained that he did not, in any way, succumb to these blandishments.[40]

Harrisson did not have to try too hard to persuade the chiefs to inflict damage on the Japanese. Indeed, he reported that 'the clamour for [firearms] could practically be heard in Brunei Bay, if not Tokyo'. The tribesmen saw in the situation a way to return to the good old days of head-hunting, a practice which the White Rajahs in Sarawak and the government of British North Borneo had more or less eliminated in pre-war days.

Arms were air-dropped in, an air-strip built, and marauding bands of guerrillas organised. Now Harrisson's major problem lay in getting ancient grudges between various tribes of now well-armed natives shelved for the duration. Much information was radioed out, which Harrisson later recorded 'had been helpful in the [Australian] landings'.

Other Z Special groups dropped near the west coast of Borneo supplied information about the proposed landing sites around Brunei Bay and Miri, the sites of major oil installations. Ambushes were set for Japanese patrols at various places and these always tended to be a bit one-sided for, said Harrisson, not one of the local guerrillas would consider being left out. The problem was to prevent the guerrillas 'by a combination of over-enthusiasm and the automatic lever on a carbine or Sten gun', from killing each other instead of the enemy. The native penchant for the more ancient but equally deadly blow-pipe with its *upas* tipped dart was an additional hazard to friend and foe alike in these close contact ambushes, especially early on before firearms were generally available.

It cannot be said that Z Special operations were crucial to the reconquest of Borneo. The chapter in Harrisson's book dealing with the actual operations is entitled 'impact of ants', and that probably best sums up the situation. The Japanese certainly found them to be a biting nuisance, and this author can personally vouch for the fact that more than a few Japanese lost their heads.

Operation Iceberg, the first assault on Japanese home territory, the island of Okinawa, was made on 1st April. It was made against a garrison of 100,000, twice the number estimated by Allied intelligence. Here, as throughout all their amphibious campaigns in the central Pacific, the Americans had to live with the problem that the operations were undertaken beyond the normal range of their shore-based airforces; at Okinawa the problem was accentuated by the proximity of the island to Japanese airfields on Formosa to the south and those on Kyusho, the southernmost of the main Japanese islands, to the north. The British carrier task force operating with the Americans was given the task of neutralising the airfields of the Sakashima group lying between Formosa and Okinawa, which the Japanese were to use as staging fields for their aircraft.

Opposition to the American landings was at first surprisingly weak, but the Japanese were merely saving themselves for what for many of their pilots was to be the supreme sacrifice. Although forewarned by Sigint of a counter-attack to be launched on 6th April, American fleet defences were overwhelmed by the sheer numbers of aircraft sent against it on the 6th and 7th, especially as over half of the nearly seven hundred Japanese aircraft involved were from kamikaze special attack forces. For the loss of almost four hundred planes, the Japanese sank six US ships and damaged a further twenty, including a carrier.

Meanwhile decrypts indicated that a Special Attack Force of ten ships led by the huge battleship *Yamato* had left the Inland Sea for Okinawa hell-bent on a suicide mission to create whatever havoc it could upon the Allied Fleet before beaching on the island where survivors would join the garrison. Alerted by Sigint, by submarine patrols, and by air reconnaissance, American carrier-based planes attacked the force on 7th April, sinking the battleship, a cruiser, and four destroyers in the Battle of the East China Sea.

Over succeeding days kamikaze planes kept on coming, and although most of the attacks were pre-revealed by Sigint, there was little defence possible against any plane that managed to penetrate the Allied aerial screen and massive anti-aircraft fire put up. On 9th April, the two British carriers, *Formidable* and *Victorious*, sustained hits from kamikazes, and that was followed by damage to the American carriers *Bunker Hill* and *Enterprise*, to other capital ships, and to a host of smaller craft. But heavy as was the damage inflicted, the kamikaze tactic suffered from the inherent defect of giving ever diminishing returns as losses of both aircraft and pilots rose. On top of being a wasting asset, the kamikaze tactic, given the limited penetration power of the bombs the aircraft carried, could not sink but only temporarily put out of action their primary targets, the Allied carriers.

What of the ominously named destroyer *Kamikaze*? She had survived the actions that resulted in the sinking of the cruisers *Haguro* and *Ashigara* to both of which she had been escort. Like some stormy petrel roaming the seas in the vicinity of Singapore, her signals continued to warn the Allies of what she was about. On 15th June her messages from off the coast of Malaya brought an Allied air attack on the convoy she was escorting, with the result that a large tanker was sunk. She herself had the luck of the devil, and survived the war.

The Japanese submarine blockade-runner I-29 was sunk by the Americans on 25th July 1945 as a result of Allied Signals Intelligence, some three weeks before the end of the war (see page 421). Her cargo included certain biological warfare material. A considerable body of evidence has been uncovered in recent years about the activities of the Japanese Army Unit No. 731 which, hidden away in a remote corner of Manchuria, had been conducting experiments in various forms of biological warfare from the 1930s. Over the years Germany and Japan had exchanged information on this, the I-29 episode being the latest and last of such exchanges.[41] Under Lieutenant-General Ishii Shiro, Unit 731 used prisoners-of-war and internees for experimental purposes, and some three thousand individuals probably met their ends in this way. Amongst those experimented on were Americans and Britons, although the majority were Chinese and Russians. Allied Intelligence, or more specifically American Army Intelligence, played a part in covering this up after the war.

British and American intelligence organisations had known from before the war that Japan was experimenting with biological warfare (BW), just as British, American, Canadian, German and other nations' scientific establishments were doing. During the fighting in China from 1940 onwards, there were a number of reports that the Japanese had scattered BW material of one sort or another from the air against civilian targets. In America these reports were investigated and evaluated by the intelligence arm of the US army's Chemical Warfare Service (CWS) under Lieutenant-Colonel Howard Cole. By early 1944 the Allies were convinced that Japan had such weapons and had used them. In fact British intelligence sources had identified the Pasteur Institute in Rangoon as another centre for Japanese BW experiments, and later evidence indicated that live human prisoners had been used there as well. The British also had some doubts about the exact role of the Japanese biological and vaccine establishment in Singapore; enough doubts to cause a major investigation to be held. The findings of the investigation have never been released.

A week after Japan's surrender on 15th August 1945, and a week before General MacArthur's own triumphal arrival there, the American ship *Sturgis* arrived in Yokohama with intelligence officers and other specialists aboard. Amongst them was Colonel Murray Sanders of CWS who had been given the task of uncovering what the Japanese had achieved in the field of biological warfare, and especially what had been going on at Unit 731 in Manchuria, under its euphemistic title, Water Purification Unit. Within a short time Sanders met one of the senior scientists of the unit and obtained an outline of what had been achieved there, enough to make him very excited. He asked for and obtained from the scientist a declaration that no prisoners had been used in the experiments; the mere fact that he asked such a question must indicate that Sanders and his superiors suspected that such experimentation had gone on.

Using that declaration, which forty years later he was to say he believed only 'for a very short time', Sanders met with General MacArthur and Major-General Willoughby, MacArthur's chief of intelligence, and it was agreed that no one from the unit would be prosecuted as a war criminal providing they divulged everything they knew. The upshot was that there is not a single mention of

Unit 731 in the vast records of the Tokyo War Crimes Commission. Justice was corrupted by this deal made by MacArthur and his intelligence advisers, while many of the scientists involved went on to have distinguished careers. It is believed that some even assisted in American, Canadian and British chemical research defence establishments, including Porton Down, Britain's top-secret facility hidden away in a village on Salisbury Plain.

Twenty

Conspiracy Theories

Several 'conspiracy theories', perhaps several variants on one basic theory would be a better way to describe them, have surfaced since the end of the war centred around the attack on Pearl Harbor and about what prior knowledge President Roosevelt had of Japanese intentions and what information was passed or not passed on to Pearl Harbor from Washington. These theories fed on the secrecy procedures adopted by the British and the American authorities who did not release into the public domain all the relevant material involved.

Then, in 1991, James Rusbridger in his *Betrayal at Pearl Harbor* added a new dimension by theorising that Winston Churchill had prior knowledge of the Pearl Harbor attack but failed to pass this on to the Americans because he wanted them to come into the war on the Allied side. Rusbridger based his theory on an alleged British ability to read concurrently, or almost concurrently, the Japanese naval code JN-25 prior to the attacks on Pearl Harbor and Malaya in December 1941. He used the alleged recollections of Captain Eric Nave, one of the British cryptographers involved in the breaking of Japanese naval codes, but which later, in an interview with Japanese television, Nave largely repudiated. If Nave did tell Rusbridger that the British were able to read JN-25 during 1941, then his memory was at fault. There is little doubt that the British had made some headway in reading that code up to 1st December 1940, but on that date the Japanese made significant changes to it, and neither the British, nor the Americans who were also working on it, made much headway in breaking the new one, which they called JN-25b, until the early months of 1942, well after the attack on Pearl Harbor.

Since Rusbridger wrote his book there have been significant, if still incomplete, releases of previously classified material into the public domain in Britain, some of which has been used in this book. This, and similar material from American archives, clearly shows that both the Americans and the British had sufficient warnings from Sigint based on sources other than a reading of the Japanese naval codes to have put the whole of the Pacific on alert in the days immediately prior to the Japanese attack. Indeed, the Americans, through their ability to read Japanese diplomatic codes with the aid of the Purple machine, were even able to follow the secret side of the Japanese 'peace' negotiations going on in Washington immediately pre-war, which gave indications of the 'final' attitudes for Japanese negotiators to adopt.

Even British leaders in the Middle East who were 'in Special' knew something dramatic was about to happen in the Far East before it actually did. According to Colonel Bonner Fellers an American liaison officer at RAF Headquarters in Cairo – who was recalling the episode twenty-five years later – Air Chief Marshal Sir Arthur Tedder told him on 7th December 1941 that he had seen a secret signal which indicated that Japan would strike at the USA within twenty-four hours. Tedder went on to say that this was in Britain's interest, and he was happy about it.[1]

Throughout the Pacific region in those last tense days, and in one way or another, British and American commanders placed their commands on a war footing. However, the commanders at Pearl Harbor reacted least. US records show that those commanders were provided with sufficient warnings by Washington, though some delays and errors did occur. All the evidence points to there having been cock-ups rather than conspiracies, and to the fact that had the Pearl Harbor commanders acted properly on the information passed to them, the débâcle might have been avoided.

On the American side we are still left with the mystery of whether or not President Roosevelt did deliberately attempt with his Defence Patrol to sucker Japan into firing the first shot on the small ships of the patrol. It is a sobering thought that had the Japanese taken the bait, the war sirens would have sounded loud enough to awaken the two commanders at Pearl Harbor.

* * *

On the British side there remain several outstanding questions which have already been touched upon in this book.

On 5th December 1941, three days before the Japanese landed in Thailand and Malaya, London sent to the Commander-in-Chief, Air Chief Marshal Sir Robert Brooke-Popham, orders that he could implement Operation Matador on his own initiative under certain conditions; conditions that in fact effectively meant he could not make a move until the Japanese threat had actually manifested itself, that is when they were already on the beaches. By that time it would be too late anyway, for Matador had been designed to forestall Japanese landings in Thailand: it had not been designed for attacking them after they had landed. Churchill, who had been behind the approaches made since 1st December by Halifax, the British ambassador in Washington to get President Roosevelt's support for such a move, and his Chiefs-of-Staff in London, must have known that these conditions tied Brooke-Popham's hands. Could it be that it was Churchill's intent to make absolutely certain that the Japanese attacked neutral Thailand, so bringing America into the war? An early British forestalling operation might have put the Japanese off making such landings.

If Flight-Lieutenant Gotto is correct in reporting that the pilot of an RAF Beaufort aircraft had sighted the Japanese convoys close to Thai and Malayan beaches on 7th December – he was writing contemporaneously and was on the spot – that still was not evidence of an actual attack. And if on that same date the Beaufort pilot had taken photographs of Japanese aircraft already at Singora airfield, then it was already too late for Matador anyway, for those aircraft could be used against any invading British force; and if in the process of taking those photographs the Beaufort pilot had been shot up in an overt act of war, that made no difference to the overall picture.

Winston Churchill needed America in the war on Britain's side. From the time he became Prime Minister in May 1940, his prime concern was to get the United States into the fight against Germany. A second concern was to keep Japan from going to war on the Axis side but, as 1941 wore on, and although Churchill continued to initiate and support actions to placate Japan, this grew a more and more remote hope in the face of provocative Japanese actions throughout the Far East.

Churchill's excellent grasp of world war strategy, as opposed to his curious flights of fancy in the tactical field where he often chased after will-o'-the-wisps, has been noted by many commentators. Why then, on the face of it, does he appear to have had such a blind spot over the Far East?

During 1940 and 1941 Churchill downgraded the importance of Singapore to some kind of second eleven status in Imperial defence a decision which he cloaked from the prime ministers of the two antipodean dominions, and more specifically Australia by resorting to outright deceit.[2]

Major-General (later Sir) John Kennedy, Director of Military Operations at the War Office throughout the war years, noted that the 'Prime Minister had always fiercely opposed any attempt to rob our Middle East Peter to pay our Far East Paul.' He also wrote:

> October, 1940. The Chiefs of Staff recommended a garrison [in Malaya] of 26 battalions . . . and 336 aircraft. Commenting on this in January 1941 the Prime Minister had minuted: 'I do not remember to have given my approval to these very large diversions of force. On the other hand, if my minutes are collected they will be seen to have the opposite tendency'.[3]

This downgrading of Singapore did not meet with the approval of Field Marshal Sir John Dill, the Chief of the Imperial General Staff. According to Lieutenant-General Sir Henry Pownall:

> Dill . . . always regarded the Middle East as less vital than Malaya. But Winston had the priority of these two the other way round. He didn't believe that the Japs would come into the war – not yet at any rate. For once his long range vision was at fault and badly. As a rule his hunches (as distinct from his day to day strategy) are pretty good. Not this time. I only hope we shall not pay dearly for the mistake. Singapore has *got* to be held, for to lose it may well mean losing Australia, if not New Zealand. I don't mean losing them to the Japanese, but to the Empire, for they will think themselves let down by HMG at home.[4]

It is more than possible that this particular divergence of view between Churchill and Dill (there were others) may have led to Dill being replaced as CIGS. According to Lord Wavell, the field marshal's son, writing in 1953:

> In dealing with the responsibility before the outbreak of the Japanese War and leaving Malaya so bare, I wonder if full justice is done to Sir

> John Dill. One of his [military adjutants] told me and General Pownall confirmed it, that there was a severe disagreement in the War Cabinet or Defence Committee some time about November 1941, when Dill wished to reinforce the Far East with aircraft at the expense of the Middle East, but the P.M. over-ruled it. Among Dill's papers, which I have been through, there is a pencilled note which he wrote to the Secretary of State for War – presumably while the meeting was going on – indicating that he would resign at once, and the Secretary of State [David Margesson, later 1st Viscount] scribbled that he would do the same.[5]

(In the event Dill did not resign but shortly afterwards was replaced as CIGS and sent to Washington.)

The fact remains that Churchill, in the face of criticism from the CIGS and from other senior military figures including General Kennedy, continued a policy of downgrading any threat from Japan, and did so almost to the outbreak of fighting even though he was getting information from many sources, including Sigint, which signalled Japanese intentions. Even in August 1941 he was expressing the view that there would be at least three months' warning of any serious explosion in the Far East, and in his almost dictatorial position of being Prime Minister and Minister of Defence, it was his view that counted. Churchill's 'conviction' that there would be ample warning of a Japanese attack was expressed on the authority of General Ismay, Churchill's link with the Chiefs of Staff, in a letter dated 1st August 1941 from Air Marshal John Babington in London to Air Chief Marshal Sir Robert Brooke-Popham in Singapore.[6]

The image of Churchill having a blind spot over such an important area neither fits in with his undoubted strategic genius, nor with much of the advice and information being passed to him. Is it possible that the Far East was not a blind spot, but that instead he was using a variant of the Nelsonian blind eye as he worked towards some secret agenda? Many commentators have made the point that Churchill's strategic interests were in places he had visited, and that, as he had never travelled further east than Calcutta, he had a blind spot as far as Japan was concerned. Can this be true? Despite his lack of personal knowledge of Japan, he had at his disposal what is arguably the finest body of advisers ever available to a wartime leader, some of whom did have knowledge of the Far East. Yet, largely, he chose to ignore their advice.

Late in 1940 the British Assistant Naval Attaché in Washington was shown certain US navy defence plans 'in confidence' but on the tacit understanding that he would pass them back to London. The plans indicated that a war between the USA and Japan would at that time take up most of America's resources which would reduce the help being given to Britain. If it came to war, the plans – which were held to reflect the views of Admiral H.R. Stark, the US Chief of Naval Operations – went on to say that it would at first be waged by the Americans on a strictly defensive basis and this might lead to the loss of all the colonial empires in the Far East, including the Philippines and Singapore.[7] This came at about the time when Churchill's attitude began the process of downgrading the defence of the so-called 'impregnable fortress' of Singapore which had previously been regarded as second only in importance to Britain's own home defence.

Then in November 1940 came the interception of the British ship *Automedon* (see Chapter 14) by a German raider which gave the Japanese the priceless information that because it had no fleet available, Britain could not defend Singapore. At some time during the next month or two, the British must have learnt that there was, at the very least, a strong likelihood that the Chiefs-of-Staff document containing this information had fallen into enemy hands.

Could Japanese knowledge that Britain was not able to defend Singapore properly be turned to Britain's advantage? Someone in Churchill's immediate coterie, which included a personal adviser on security matters, SIS man Desmond (later Sir Desmond) Morton, perhaps even Churchill himself, might have decided to make use of the possibility. Japan was an Axis partner of Germany's and if America went to war with Japan that might bring about a German/American war by the back door. A Japanese attack on Malaya through neutral Thailand, or on any other part of the Far East, might be an event enough to damp down the isolationist cause in America, a cause partly backed by internal sympathisers for Germany who would not have the same sympathy for Japan. Policy in the Far East must continue to be, if at all possible, to prevent war with Japan, but if the Japanese did attack in that area, then they must directly attack British interests which would bring America into the war. Japan now knew that Britain could not protect Singapore with a fleet, and if army and air force reinforcements were kept to the barest minimum, Japan would not be put off from making such a move. Such a hidden agenda could account for Churchill's 'blind spot', and would not have required much in the way of conspiratorial endeavour; all he had to do as Minister of Defence was to maintain his present stance over reinforcements for Malaya. In fact, as a conspiracy requires the involvement of more than one person, there need have been no conspiracy element at all. He did not have to voice such a hidden agenda to anyone.

All, of course, depended on the attitude of the United States. The far-sighted President Roosevelt saw from the start of the war in Europe that there was small chance of his country being able to stay out of it. Also from the start, the powerful and vociferous isolationist movement in his country thought that nearly every move he made was intended eventually to carry the United States into the war.

As Churchill used all his persuasive skills in the background, Roosevelt embarked on a policy of aiding Britain whenever he could, a policy that by late 1941, resulted in the United States being in what was virtually a state of undeclared war with Germany in the Atlantic. But it was not all-out war; and that was what Churchill and Britain needed.

Roosevelt's aid began with the breaches he permitted the Royal Navy to get away with in the conditions of the Declaration of Panama of 23rd September 1939, three weeks after the war in Europe started. This Declaration asserted the right, though there was no precedent for it in international law, for the twenty-one American republics to set up a no-go zone for belligerent navies, westward of a line running down the Atlantic from the Canadian border and stretching out from the various American seaboards some 300 to 1,000 miles into that ocean. Britain, in the form of the then First Lord of the Admiralty, at that time none other than Churchill himself, had no great objection to this, providing British ships were not cut off from the British Central American colonies and the West Indies. Roosevelt interpreted the declaration in favour of the British although occasionally and mainly for the record, he dished out admonitions for transgressions of it, the gravest transgression being the *Graf Spee* incident at Montevideo. (Churchill rather cleverly sent Roosevelt a complete report of this action and received back a letter of thanks containing plaudits for the actions of the British cruisers involved.)

In fact, with this vast zone of the Atlantic effectively being patrolled by the US Navy, it relieved the Royal Navy of that duty. On top of that, almost from the start, the Royal Navy began to receive intelligence from ships of the American patrols. One such report led to the scuttling of the German liner *Columbus* by its crew on 19th

December 1939 and the interception of the *Asama Maru* a month later off the coast of Japan because she was carrying *Columbus* crew members.[8*]

In June 1940 Churchill made a request for fifty World War One vintage American destroyers and a deal was struck exchanging them for the use by the US Navy of certain British bases in the West Indies and Bermuda.

March 1941 brought the unique and hugely important Lend-Lease Agreement under which American equipment began pouring into Britain. In the following month, on 9th April, the United States, under the terms of a formal agreement with the Danish Ambassador in Washington, was granted landing and other facilities in Greenland which gave them a mid-Atlantic base from which to protect those shipments. Two days later Roosevelt informed Churchill that he was moving the north-south 'quarantine' line eastward to Longitude 25° West; US naval vessels would now patrol within that new boundary and supply the British with any intelligence on Axis ships they spotted. This meant, says Professor Bradley F. Smith, 'that the American patrols in the central and western Altantic would function not only as thinly disguised associates of the Royal Navy anti-submarine operations, but also would be close partners of Britain in operational intelligence collection'.[9]

Despite all this aid, and there was yet more to come, the Americans were still not in the war. Even the Germans had not taken offence enough to declare war on them. However, over on the other side of the world lay another possible route to get the Americans to declare war. So, could Churchill's refusal to sanction proper and timely reinforcements for the Far East have been part of a scheme to entice a Japanese attack on Thai or British territory that would bring America in?

There can be little doubt that Churchill was temperamentally equipped to take the huge strategic risk of losing Singapore for the duration of the war in order to get the Americans into it. His whole life from the time of his escape from the Boer prisoner-of-war train, had been a sort of training ground for the position he held during the war. If F.W. Winterbotham, in his book *The Ultra Secret*, is correct, it was Churchill who, with Ultra foreknowledge of the great bombing attack on Coventry in 1940, decided not to reinforce the

* See Chapter 13, page 246.

anti-aircraft batteries, or evacuate the city, for fear that that might give the Ultra game away. During that raid 554 people were killed and 836 seriously injured. Furthermore, once the Americans were in the war Churchill was convinced that it would be only a matter of time before the Allies were victorious on all fronts. There can be little doubt also, that Churchill was quite capable of hiding such a decision from posterity. He had a reputation to protect, a reputation arguably second to no other in modern history, and historians in the last twenty years or so have shown that he was not above telling, to use a euphemism Churchill himself concocted in 1906, 'terminological inexactitudes' to protect it. Furthermore, in the scenario being laid out here, there was no need for lies; all he had to do was not submit to paper anything about it and keep his mouth shut. He was a man much given to risk-taking especially when he was convinced that all would turn out well in the end; and he was also given to deception, even to deceiving close Allies.

In order to cover the chance that, even if Japan attacked British and American interests in the Far East the United States would still not declare war on Germany, the British Intelligence organisation in America known as British Security Co-ordination (BSC) initiated an elaborate deception plan. In the days immediately preceding the Japanese attack on Pearl Harbor, according to the author of *A Man Called Intrepid* which was written with the full co-operation of BSC's head, Sir William Stephenson, Stephenson had a document planted on Senator Burton Wheeler, the noted isolationist, in late November 1941. Such were the ramifications of the deception that it would not have been carried out without Churchill's knowledge and consent. The document was called the 'Victory Program' which purported to be a forecast of the US Government's plans to enter the war. Wheeler passed it on to the *Chicago Tribune* which plastered it all over its front page on 4th December under banner headlines which called it 'a blueprint for total war'. (At least part of the document seems to have been authentic, which might indicate some high-level American connivance; the authentic part had been embellished with 'misleading information'.) According to British sources the primary aim of the deception was to use isolationist channels as a means of revealing to Hitler a secret plan designed to provoke him into a declaration of war. A secondary aim was to 'plant the notion that Anglo-American planners of a massive assault upon Europe had set Invasion Day for July 1, 1943'. This would force Germany into maintaining large armies in the West and so reduce the pressure on Russia.[10]

It may be significant that Gerald Wilkinson, the SIS officer in Manila who had been supplying secret warning information to the Americans in the weeks before the Japanese onslaught, knew Churchill. Wilkinson's wife, Lorna, was the niece of Sir George Davies, a Conservative Member of Parliament and a lord commissioner of the Treasury. Through this connection Wilkinson had come enough to the attention of Churchill to have lunched with him.

Wilkinson later joined Stephenson's BSC organisation in New York, heading its Chinese section. At one stage there was even talk of replacing Stephenson by Wilkinson. Wilkinson's SIS designation was 48982–48 for the United States, 982 being his personal number. (Stephenson was 48000.) Like Malcolm Kennedy in pre-war Japan, Wilkinson was a great diarist. His papers are now in the Churchill College Archive in Cambridge.

The follow-up to the question of whether Churchill's refusal to sanction timely reinforcements for the Far East was a device to get the United States into the war is this. Had Churchill been of such a mind, could timely reinforcements have been sent, say, in the late summer or early autumn of 1941?

The authors of the official British naval history *War with Japan* state that, at the time *Prince of Wales* was ordered to Singapore – she arrived there on 2nd December 1941 – there was no hope for another three or four months of despatching a fleet to the area, 'save only in the unlikely event of Australia or New Zealand being invaded, when the government was prepared to abandon the Mediterranean in order to come to their assistance'. Quite apart from the preposterousness of the idea of the Royal Navy being ordered to abandon all the British forces in North Africa – which would anyway have caused ructions in both Canberra and Wellington because the vast bulk of the fighting men of those two Dominions were part of the North African forces – that statement does not tie in with the facts of the naval situation that existed in the autumn of 1941.

The second half of 1941, up to the time of the loss of *Ark Royal* and *Barham* in November, brought with it significant improvements in the position of the Royal Navy compared with earlier in the year. By June the Battle of the Atlantic had turned temporarily in favour of the British partly because Winston Churchill had given it his special attention. Then in July, at La Pallice, RAF bombers had seriously damaged *Scharnhorst*, one of the perceived German threats to British North Atlantic convoys. From July, US Catalina flying boats, protected by P-40 fighters, had begun operating convoy protection patrols from Iceland, thus releasing British resources for other purposes. British ability to read German naval codes through 'Enigma', sometimes concurrently, had significantly reduced the number of ship losses to U-boat attacks. In September, after an incident involving the USS *Greer* and a U-boat, and although America was not in the war, President Roosevelt ordered a 'shoot-to-kill' policy, which strengthened the British position again. Later in the year the German Naval Command ordered the transfer of some U-boats from the Atlantic to the Mediterranean and to Norway which again contributed substantially to the improved British situation. In those months the only British capital ship put out of commission by enemy action was the battleship *Nelson*, damaged by a torpedo in the Mediterranean on 27th September. (On 3rd November the aircraft-carrier *Indomitable*, which was to have accompanied *Prince of Wales* to Singapore, was also out of commission due to running aground off Kingston, Jamaica.)

The authors of *War With Japan* went on to say that the ships of the envisaged Eastern Fleet would need refitting before they could be sent, and to be fitted with 'modern radio direction finders' – by which they probably meant radar – and that some required war damage repairs. Even this statement does not stand up to close scrutiny. Any refitting and repair work required, remembering that we are talking about the situation in the autumn of 1941, could have been done in Far Eastern ports. In fact, *Revenge* did arrive at Bombay for a refit on 20th November and *Hermes* was refitting in Simonstown at about the same time. Had the fleet been sent to the East at this time, the naval facilities at Singapore, Colombo, Trincomalee, Bombay, Simonstown, and even Australia, could have been used for most of the refitting required and the modern equipment needed could have been shipped out. The presence of the ships in the near vicinity would have been felt by Japan, even when they were under refit.

In the event, in January 1942, just a month after the Japanese attack on Malaya, Britain began to raise its Eastern Fleet and by March, a month after the fall of Singapore, most of the ships forming it had been assembled in the Indian Ocean. How is it that in March 1942 Britain could assemble such a fleet when it could not do so six months earlier? In September 1941 Britain was better off by one aircraft-carrier (*Ark Royal*), four battleships (*Barham, Prince of Wales, Valiant*, and *Queen Elizabeth*, in the order of their loss or incapacitation) and the battle-cruiser *Repulse*, than it was at the beginning of the following year. Of course, by March 1942, the crucial reinforcing and oil routes to and from the Middle East were under threat and had to be protected at all costs, but that situation may never have arisen had the *Prince of Wales* and *Repulse* been accompanied by the ships (three carriers, five battleships, six cruisers, and sixteen destroyers) or even the better part of them, that Britain now found could be made available; and such a fleet, if formed earlier, could have been even larger, for Britain's China Fleet was then still afloat instead of being mostly at the bottom of the Java Sea. The fleet would also have been augmented by the ships of the Dutch fleet.

In December 1941, Japanese naval air power and tactics proved to be decisive off the coast of Malaya and at Pearl Harbor, but no one before then could have been sure of that, not even the Japanese themselves. Prior to hostilities they were secretly confident of the expertise of their naval air arm, but it had yet to pass the acid test of combat. On the Allied side the expertise shown by the Japanese came as a complete and shocking surprise, which means that prior to those first battles they did not know of it either. With hindsight it is clear that, had a British Fleet similar in make-up to the March 1942 one, with its old, slow ships and poor aircraft, been sent out in November 1941, it would have been no match in battle for a Japanese force of comparable size. Even so, it must be questioned whether the Japanese would have dared attack southward had such a fleet been in the vicinity, and at the very least its presence would have required a radical re-think of the Japanese overall strategic plan, which the presence of only *Prince of Wales* and *Repulse* did not. Why then was such a British Fleet not sent at a time when the naval situation had improved from earlier in the year?

The facile answer to that question is that, prior to 8th December 1941, Britain was not at war with Japan, and that to have sent such a large number of ships east then would have been a waste of scarce resources. However, by the autumn of that year it was clear to most observers that unless the Japanese were successfully deterred from their plans by a strong show of force, then war with them was inevitable. All the relevant Sigint decrypts pointed in that direction. Indeed, even earlier than the autumn, when on 26th July President

Roosevelt froze all Japanese assets in America in retaliation for their occupation of Indo-China, a move immediately followed by similar ones by Britain and the exiled Netherlands government in London, it was clear that the Japanese must either fight or suffer an ignominious climbdown, and the latter was something it was not in their national character to do.

The British ambassador to Tokyo, Sir Robert Craigie, had pointed out almost two months earlier, to Anthony Eden, the British Foreign Secretary, that: 'To extend restrictions on Japanese imports to an extent that would force Japan to draw on her reserves on any considerable scale would at present be liable to produce those very actions we wish to avoid.'[11]

Although Craigie was at first in favour of the July freezing of assets as having 'the merit of removing from the minds of the more responsible Japanese leaders the lingering hope that any further southward advance could be made without the *virtual certainty* [author's italics] of war with the United States', in September he began to express doubts. By then it was clear that Washington was not prepared to reward Japan with any easement of the ban in return for 'minor' concessions – what Washington required was the virtual complete abandonment by Japan of all the advantages she had gained by armed force since 1935. He shared the view with the US ambassador to Tokyo, Joseph Grew, that the lack of any desire to compromise by Washington, would make war more likely, not deter it.[12]

After his repatriation to England in the diplomatic 'exchange' made in late 1942, Sir Robert Craigie produced his official 'Final Report', in which he castigated the British War Cabinet for its acquiescence in what turned out to be the road to war. What Mr Churchill wrote to Anthony Eden about Craigie's report after ordering that the report must not be published, is especially interesting:

> It was . . . a blessing that Japan attacked the United States and thus brought [her] into the war. Greater good fortune has rarely happened to the British Empire than this event which has revealed our friends and foes in their true light.[13]

In view of all the above, and leaving aside the actions of President Roosevelt, the question is posed again. Could it be that Churchill's adamant refusal to reinforce the Far East was coloured by the hope that Japan would attack Malaya – Japan was more likely to attack a weak Malaya than a strongly defended one – and thus draw America into battle? That it was virtually on his orders alone – for most of the admirals were against the move as being too small a gesture – that the 'deterrent' force made up of the *Prince of Wales* and *Repulse* was sent to Singapore, does not of itself obviate that possibility. With danger looming north of their homeland the Australians were rightly kicking up so much fuss towards the end of the year, and even threatening to take their army divisions in the Middle East back home, that for that reason alone Churchill had to make some such gesture. On the face of it, it was a grand gesture. Only two ships perhaps, but one of them the pride of the Royal Navy in which he himself had voyaged when he met President Roosevelt off Newfoundland! And, after the deterrent effect this ship and her mighty battle-cruiser consort would have on the scene, in Churchill's own words he thought they 'should disappear into the immense archipelago'.[14]

Instead of sending a fleet, could Britain have reinforced Malaya in the autumn of 1941 with sufficient additional troops and air forces strong enough to deter the Japanese or push them back? If the political will had been there, the answer to that seems to be 'yes'. The argument used by most historians, that the Middle East had to be given the utmost priority, does not of itself mean that no additional troops could have been spared for the Far East. It is known now that the Middle East commanders were vastly over-insuring in the build-up for the North African campaigns. In February 1942, as soon as it became clear that Singapore was about to fall, the Australians pulled away two of their three divisions in the Middle East, the 6th and 7th AIF, and brought them homeward. (It had been the original intent to send the 7th AIF to Singapore, but Churchill insisted it go to North Africa.) So the crucial battles that followed in North Africa were fought, and in the end successfully, without them. With the benefit of hindsight it is clear that had these two divisions, for example, been stationed in Malaya early – early enough to get the men acclimatised and appropriately trained (one authority gives two months as the minimum period necessary for acclimatisation) – they would have given General Percival the depth in forces he so lacked throughout the campaign. Indeed, the Japanese might never have tried it on in the first place. The British 18th Division was sent in much too late, partly as a sop to the Australians, and Churchill conveniently passed the onus for sending that on to the Chiefs-of-Staff.

General Percival, after a review of his command when he arrived in

Malaya, asked for an extra division, plus an additional brigade to make up the 'short' 9th Indian Division already in Malaya, and two extra battalions to protect Penang. He got some modest reinforcements, but not what he asked for, and those two Australian divisions would have fitted that part of his bill very nicely. He also asked for two tank, and two anti-aircraft artillery regiments. No doubt his planners based their figures, amongst other considerations, on estimates of the likely strength of a Japanese army sent against him, bearing in mind Japan's commitments in China and Indo-China, the need to protect her long lines of communications, and that if she attacked Malaya she would also probably need to attack the Philippines on her seaward flank and Burma, where there was a British army, on her landward flank. In the event the Japanese used three divisions. (In his Official Despatch of 26th February 1948, which he must have written without the benefit of seeing Japanese records, General Percival estimated the force sent against him as being 'five, perhaps six divisions'.)

Two extra Commonwealth divisions sent to Malaya early enough, in addition to the troops already stationed there, should have been enough, providing Malaya Command had been given the support regiments of tanks and anti-aircraft guns that a modern army needs to support infantry. Percival's demands were not excessive, and even in those difficult days, surely to have reduced Middle East supplies by say fifty tanks, would have made no difference to that theatre of war. It might have made the world of difference in Malaya.

What of planes? Between the time of the German invasion of Russia in June 1941, and December of that year, some two hundred Hurricanes were sent to Russia in the face of the British Chiefs-of-Staff arguments to the Defence Committee 'that they would pay a better dividend if sent to the Far East and to the Middle East'. Since the CIGS himself, Sir John Dill, who would have had all available planning and supply information at his fingertips, was prepared to resign on the issue of planes for Malaya, he must have thought that some could be safely spared for that purpose.

British, Australian and New Zealand pilots in the mainly obsolete or obsolescent aircraft that were available to them in Malaya, fought bravely, but most of them had very little battle experience. A few dozen battle-hardened veteran pilots from Britain, flying some of those two hundred Hurricanes right from the start of the Malayan campaign, might also have made all the difference. In good machines, veteran pilots tend to treat bad odds not as a handicap so much as a target-rich environment. And, of course, had such planes and men been there in the autumn of 1941, given the excellence of Japanese ground intelligence sources in Malaya, Japan may not have attacked anyway.

It was probably Churchill's sense of guilt over his part in what he called the worst disaster in British military history, that caused him to look at the commanders at Singapore with a more benevolent eye than those involved in far lesser débâcles. His treatment of the commanders in Crete, which fell six months earlier than Singapore, is a case in point. Crete fell on 31st May 1941, Churchill ordered an Inquiry into the loss in early June, and the committee reported in July. The full report of that Inquiry was suppressed, but it is known to have contained harsh criticisms of some of the commanders involved.

Churchill's conscience over Singapore also caused him to dissimulate on certain matters. For instance, the statement in his *The Second World War* that he never knew that the island of Singapore had no northern defences, has been disputed by Lieutenant-General Sir Ian Jacob, Military Assistant Secretary to the War Cabinet, 1939–45. 'How is it that he did not know when we all did?'

During the war Churchill promised that there would be an Official Inquiry into the fall of Singapore after hostilities were over, but one was never held.

Until the spring of 1995 when the present author requested and obtained early release of it into the public domain, a Cabinet Office file dating from 1946 entitled 'Implications of an Inquiry into the Fall of Singapore' lay closed in the British Public Record Office. It did not contain much information on the reasons leading up to Churchill's worst disaster; it was, instead, a report containing a list of reasons compiled for the Chiefs-of-Staff Committee about why no Inquiry into the matter should be implemented, this despite Churchill's promise.[15]

Amongst the catalogue of reasons given was that 'important witnesses would have to be called, the summoning of whom might be very embarrassing. For example, the presence of Mr Churchill and Lord Wavell would be essential.' On intelligence, the authors of the document noted that 'the inquiry would have to consider our assessments of the timing, method and scale of Japanese attacks. This might well involve a general inquiry into our intelligence system, including methods of collection.' Other points to be answered were 'whether we over-insured in other theatres at the expense of the Far East', and 'whether all possible steps were taken to provide the aircraft necessary'.

One of the members of the Defence Committee which considered the report on 15th May 1946, was Marshal of the Royal Air Force, Lord Tedder, who had been Allied Deputy Supreme Commander under General Eisenhower. In what turned out to be a consensus that nothing should be done on the matter of an Inquiry, he suggested 'that the Committee need only take note of the report as interest in this matter had lessened'. One wonders if Tedder was casting his mind back eight years, and was concerned that such an Inquiry might investigate why, at that time, a string of airfields had been built in Malaya without consultation with the army whose job it was to defend them, and so which in most cases were built in indefensible positions. The Air Officer Commanding, Malaya, when those decisions were taken, was Tedder himself.

One last wrinkle. Was there, as with the Crete campaign, some sort of secret war-time Inquiry into the fall of Singapore? Brigadier F.H. Vinden, who had been on General Dobbie's staff in pre-war Malaya, says in his memoir that there was. In 1942, he says, he was brought back from India, where he was serving, to be questioned about the pre-war appraisal he had written on the defence of Malaya. This suggests that, whatever the nature of the investigation, it had a wide remit. Vinden said that the investigation was conducted by Lord Hankey.[16]

Vinden told this same story to a post-war colleague, Brian Cane, who writes, 'Jo Vinden told me there was an Inquiry held in secret during the war, ordered by Churchill. Vinden . . . was ordered home for a period to give evidence . . . he did not know the outcome. . . but surmised that the results were embarrassing to those in high places.'[17]

If there was such an Inquiry then, like the Crete one, its findings have been suppressed.

Christopher Hankey, writing to this author in September 1995, said that he did not remember his father mentioning any report on the fall of Singapore. He added that his memory might be at fault.

Notes

CHAPTER ONE – The Rise of Japan (pages 7–22)

1. P.G. Rogers, *The First Englishman in Japan*, Harvill, London, 1956. This book tells the story of Will Adams who arrived in Japan aboard a Dutch ship in April 1600. James Clavell's novel *Shogun* is based on Adams's life.
2. Saburo Ienaga, *Japan's Last War*, Blackwell, Oxford, 1979. Originally published under the title *Taiheiyo Senso*, Tokyo, 1966.
3. Ibid.
4. R.W.E. Harper and H. Miller, *Singapore Mutiny*, OUP, Oxford, 1984.
5. Richard Storry, *A History of Modern Japan*, Penguin, Harmondsworth, 1982.
6. Peter Calvocoressi, Guy Wint and John Pritchard, *Total War*, Penguin, Harmondsworth, 1989.
7. Ibid.
8. Ibid.
9. Storry, op. cit.
10. Lord Chatfield, *It Might Happen Again*, Heinemann, London, 1947.
11. Frederick Moore, *With Japan's Leaders*, Chapman & Hall, London, 1925.

CHAPTER TWO – Supreme in Eastern Asia (pages 23–33)

1. David Bergamini, *Japan's Imperial Conspiracy*, William Morrow, New York, 1971.
2. Saburo, op. cit.
3. Major-General F.S.G. Piggott, *Broken Thread*, Gale & Polden, Aldershot, 1950.
4. Joseph C. Grew, *Ten Years in Japan*, Hammond, Hammond, London, 1944.

CHAPTER THREE - The Japanese Secret Services (pages 34 to 51)

1. *Jane's Dictionary of Military Terms*, Brigadier P.H.C. Hayward, Macdonald and Jane's, London, 1975.
2. Sun Tzu, *The Art of War*, translated by Brigadier Samuel B. Griffith, OUP, Oxford, 1963; Sun Tzu, *The Art of War*, translated by Yuan Shibing, Wordsworth, Ware, 1993.
3. 'Japanese Secret Intelligence Services, Part 1', prepared by General Staff (Intelligence), Australian Military Forces. AL1351, Imperial War Museum, London.
4. 'C's War', Robert Cecil, *Journal of Intelligence and National Security*, Vol. 1, No. 2, May 1986. See also *SOE – An Outline History, 1940–1946*, M.R.D. Foot, BBC, London, 1984, especially Chapter One.
5. Papers of Captain Malcolm Kennedy, OBE (1895–1984), Kennedy Collection, Sheffield University.
6. Saburo Ienaga, *Japan's Last War*, Blackwell, Oxford, 1979.
7. 'Lessons of the Russo-Japanese War', article by Lt-Col. Picard, 1905. Translated from the French by Lt-Col. W. Malleson of British Military Intelligence, and published in Britain and India. Copy in Oriental & India Office Collections, British File, File L/MIL/17/20/22.
8. Saburo Ienaga, op. cit.
9. Major-General F.S.G. Piggott, op. cit.
10. 'Japanese Secret Intelligence Services', Part 1. Produced by General Staff (Intelligence), Australian Military Forces, p. 27.

11. Eric Robertson, *The Japanese File*, Heinemann Asia, Hong Kong, 1979.
12. René Onraet, *Singapore – a Police Background*, published by D. Crisp, London, n.d., but 1945. In old times 'ronin' were warriors of the samurai class temporarily unattached to an overlord. Being unattached made them even more prideful than usual, and they were easily upset. Their modern-day descendants gloried in the spirit of Old Japan and considered themselves the spiritual descendants of the seventeenth-century Kyokaku, stout-hearted plebeians who banded together to protect themselves and to right the wrongs, real and imaginary, inflicted on them by the swaggering Natamoto, personal followers of the Shogun.
13. ADM178/178. PRO, Kew.
14. From part of an unpublished manuscript by Herbert Greene entitled 'A Page of History', sent to journalist and publisher Dorothy Crisp in 1947. From the Crisp/Becker Collection in the hands of Hugh Becker. (This author has been unable to trace the remainder of the manuscript.)
15. Letter from Herbert Greene to Dorothy Crisp dated 19th August 1947. In Crisp/Becker Collection held by Hugh Becker. Lt-Col. John Travers de Saulez Washington, Royal Marines, was seconded to British Naval Intelligence from 1st October 1931. Captain (later Admiral) Arthur L. Bristol, USN, was the US Naval Attaché in London from 1932.
16. See James Rusbridger and Eric Nave, *Betrayal At Pearl Harbor*, Michael O'Mara Books, London, 1992.
17. Lt-Col. Cecil L'Estrange Malone, 1889–1968. Malone was shunted into a job in World War Two in which he could do little harm, had he any mind to do so by then. He was placed in charge of the Admiralty Small Boat Pool.
18. ADM178/178. PRO, Kew.
19. Summary of Japanese Intelligence Activities, in papers of Captain Malcolm Kennedy, Sheffield University.
20. 'Japanese Secret Intelligence Services', Part 1. General Staff (Intelligence), Australian Military Services.
21. Netherlands Forces Intelligence Service Bulletins.

CHAPTER FOUR – Undercover Operations in China in the 1930s (pages 52–68)

1. 'Report on Japanese Secret Intelligence Services', Part 1. Produced by General Staff (Intelligence), Australian Army HQ.

2. Mikhail Borodin was a Latvian Jew, born in 1884. Educated in the USA, he became a Comintern agent in Britain and other European countries before going to China. He left China in 1927.
3. Richard Deacon, *History of the Chinese Secret Service*, Frederick Muller, London, 1974.
4. Charles Drage, *Two-Gun Cohen*, Cape, London, 1954. Cohen died in 1970.
5. Oliver J. Caldwell, *A Secret War: Americans in China*, South Illinois University Press, 1972.
6. Han Suyin, *The Morning Deluge*, Cape, London, 1972.
7. Deacon, op. cit.
8. Han Suyin, op. cit.
9. Immanuel C.Y. Hsu, *The Rise of Modern China*, OUP, Oxford, 1975.
10. Edward Behr, *Hirohito – Behind the Myth*, Random House, New York, 1989.
11. Saburo, Ienega, op. cit..
12. Sir Edward Johnston (1874–1938). Hong Kong Civil Service, 1898. District Officer and Magistrate, 1906–17. Tutor to Pu Yi, 1918–25. Professor of Chinese, London University, 1931–37.
13. See Amleto Vespa, *Secret Agent of Japan*, Gollancz, London, 1938; Ronald Seth, *Secret Servants – The Story of Japanese Espionage*, Gollancz, London, 1957.
14. Mark Gayn, *The Fight for the Pacific*, Bodley Head, London, 1941.
15. David Bergamini, op. cit.
16. Diary of Captain Malcolm Kennedy. Kennedy Collection, Sheffield University.
17. Sir Robert Scott, GCMG, CBE (1905–82).
18. See the unpublished biography of Scott (67/194/6) in the Harry Miller collection of papers, Imperial War Museum, London.
19. Historical Record of the Tientsin Section, at Royal Corps of Signals Museum, Blandford Forum.
20. Information received from the family of Mrs Wilkins.
21. Major-General F.S.G. Piggott, op. cit.
22. 'Radio Intercept & Strategic D/F History' by Lieutenants Lyon and Daniels, USN: memorandum sent to Captain L.F. Stafford, USN, on 24 October 1934, as quoted by Hugh Skillen in *Spies of the Airwaves*, Skillen, Pinner, 1989.

CHAPTER FIVE – Hong Kong, 1930–1941 (pages 69–97)

1. S. Woodburn Kirby and others, *The War Against Japan* Vol. 1, HMSO, London, 1957. The 'Official' History.
2. A.G. Denniston, 'The GC&CS Between the Wars', *Journal of Intelligence & National Security*, Vol. 1, No. 1, 1986.
3. F.H. Hinsley and others, *British Intelligence in the Second World War*, HMSO, London, 1979, Vol. 1.
4. Leon Comber in *Asian Studies Review*, Vol. 18, No. 3, April 1995, Melbourne, Australia, in a review of *Signals Intelligence in the Post-Cold War Era*, by Desmond Ball.
5. See ADM 233/494. Public Record Office, Kew.
6. Patrick Beesly, *Very Special Admiral*, Hamish Hamilton, London, 1980. This book is a biography of Admiral J.H. Godfrey who was DNI for two years from 1939. The book is based on Godfrey's personal records.
7. Beesly, op. cit.
8. Vice-Admiral John William Ashley Waller, CB (1892–1975). Entered navy, 1909. Served in Grand Fleet, 1914–18. COIS, Far East, 1935–36. Commanded HMAS *Sydney* 1937–39. Rear Admiral, 1944. Served in Washington 1945–46 on Lend-Lease Administration. Retired as Vice-Admiral 1947. Information about the confidentiality of the COIS title is to be found in the 'Most Secret' memorandum, NID 001262/40, from the Admiralty to the Foreign Office in FO371/24715, PRO, Kew.
9. Colonel Valentine Rodolphe Burkhardt, DSO, OBE (1884–1967). Entered Army 1903, Royal Artillery. Staff Captain, RA, 28 Div., 1914. British Mission with French HQ, 1918–19. GSO2 and Brigade Major, North China, 1923–28. GSO1 China Cmd, 1936–39. Retired 1939. Military Attaché China, 1939. Employed Admiralty 1943–46. Author of three volumes of *Chinese Creeds and Customs*. He lived his last years in Hong Kong.
10. Captain Charles Ralph Boxer, later Major. Born 1904. PoW of the Japanese in Hong Kong, 1942. Commissioned Lincolnshire Regt, 1923. Post-war was Camöens Professor of Portuguese, London University. Many other academic positions, including (Emeritus) Professor of History, Yale, from 1972. Author of several books on Portuguese, Japanese and Dutch history. Married in 1945 American writer Emily Hahn.
11. The incorrect information is contained in file ADM 223/494 at the PRO, Kew. The correct information, and much else, was supplied to the author by Group Captain H.T. 'Alf' Bennett during an interview in 1995 and in subsequent correspondence and telephone conversations.
12. ADM233/494, PRO, Kew.
13. ADM233/494, PRO, Kew.

14. Wesley K. Wark, *The Ultimate Enemy – British Intelligence and Nazi Germany 1933–1939*, Oxford, OUP, 1986.
15. Brigadier E.E. Mockler-Ferryman, 'Military Intelligence Organisation'. This document appears to be an internal service one. It is quoted from in Hinsley's official history *British Intelligence in the Second World War*. Eric Edward Mockle-Ferryman (b. 1896) was 'attached' to the American Forces in North Africa as Eisenhower's Chief of Intelligence. He was sacked after the Kasserine Pass débâcle in Tunisia in February 1943 for 'over-dependence upon a single source of information'. (See Eisenhower diaries for February and April 1943 in Eisenhower Library, Abilene.)
16. ADM233/494, PRO, Kew.
17. Captain Eric Nave, RAN (1899–1993).
18. ADM233/494, PRO, Kew.
19. James Rusbridger and Eric Nave, op. cit. See also, 'Timewatch Special', BBC2 television documentary, 5th April 1989: Editor, Roy Davies.
20. See Vice-Admiral M.E. Miles, USN, *A Different Kind of War*, Cave Books, Taipei, 1967.
21. ADM 233/494. PRO, Kew.
22. Rusbridger and Nave, op. cit.
23. A.G. Denniston, op. cit.
24. Diary entry of Captain Malcolm Kennedy for 15th February 1938. Kennedy Collection, Sheffield University. Kennedy knew Boxer from his days as a language officer in Japan.
25. Emily Hahn, *China To Me*, Blakiston, 1944. Reprinted by Virago, London, 1993. Emily Hahn (1905–97) was also the biographer of the Soong sisters – one of whom was Madame Chiang Kai-shek; Sir Stamford Raffles; and Rajah Sir James Brooke. In China in 1935 she created a scandal by becoming the concubine of the Chinese poet, Sinmay Zao. Emily Hahn was the longest-serving contributor to the *New Yorker*, having written for it for sixty-eight years. She was survived by her husband Professor C. R. Boker, and two daughters.
26. WO193/913. Collation No. 27, Far East Espionage, Cable No. GHFE 138. PRO, Kew.
27. See Professor John W.M. Chapman, *Price of Admiralty*, Vol. 4, Saltire Press, 1989, p. 1019 n.4; and, 'Tricycle Recycled: Collaboration among the Secret Intelligence Services of the Axis States', 1940–41, in *Journal of Intelligence and National Security*, Vol. 7, No. 3, 1992.
28. Vice-Admiral Edmund Gerard Noel Rushbrooke, CBE, DSC (1892–1972). COIS, Far East, 1937–39, then sea service to 1941. Promoted Commodore 1942; DNI, 1942–46. Retired 1948. He married in 1937 (probably in Hong Kong) his second wife, Marjorie Foster.

29. George Wright-Nooth, *Prisoner of the Turnip Heads*, Leo Cooper, London, 1994.
30. Charles Drage, *The Amiable Prussian*, Anthony Blond, London, 1958.
31. Information supplied to the author by Group Captain H.D. 'Alf' Bennett, and confirmed by an officer who served in Singapore Special Branch pre-war.
32. Kennedy Collection, op. cit.; Japanese Secret Services, Part 1, Australian Army Handbook, AL1351 IWM, London, p. 49.
33. S. Woodburn Kirby and others, op. cit., p. 110.
34. See secret telegram from GOC, Hong Kong, to War Office and Military Attaché, Tokyo, No. 8258, dated 23/10/40. In WO193/913, PRO.
35. Letter from Lord Zetland to Lord Linlithgow dated 9th May 1940. File L/WS/1/391, Oriental and India Office Collections. See also Chapter 10, pages 194–195.
36. The Hong Kong and Singapore Royal Artillery was a regular unit of the British army raised to man certain coastal, anti-aircraft and mobile units in Hong Kong and Singapore. Officers and some NCOs were British and there were Indian Viceroy Commissioned Officers. Other ranks were Indians recruited in India by special arrangement with GHQ, India, and some Chinese locally enlisted. The artillery batteries in Hong Kong were all HK&SRA manned (there were no RA regiments there), and two of them were 'mountain batteries', i.e. their guns and equipment were hauled around by mules.
37. See file L/WS/1/391, Oriental and India Office Collections, London.
38. Wright-Nooth, op. cit.
39. Cypher Message No. 17299 dated 28/3/1941. Copy in file L/WS/1/391, op.cit.
40. From an interview and subsequent telephone conversations with Bill Wiseman during 1995–96.
41. Files HS1/111, HSI/205, PRO, Kew. Swettenham, whose peace-time job was with Butterfield & Swire, was killed in the battle for Hong Kong. See also Charles Cruickshank, *SOE in the Far East*, OUP, Oxford, 1986.
42. 'Report on the Canadian Expeditionary Forces to the Crown Colony of Hong Kong', Ottawa, 1942. See also, Anthony Hewitt, *Children of the Empire*, Kangaroo Press, Kenthurst, NSW, Australia, 1995, p. 92.
43. S. Woodburn Kirby and others, op. cit.
44. Tim Carew, *The Fall Of Hong Kong*, Anthony Blond, London, 1960.
45. S. Woodburn Kirby and others, op. cit.
46. Letter from Anthony Hewitt to the author, dated 3rd October 1995.
47. ADM223/494, PRO, Kew.
48. ADM223/494. Undated note by a Mr Barrett on Fall of Hong Kong. PRO.

49. Anthony Hewitt, letter to the author dated 3rd October 1995.
50. 'Japanese Secret Intelligence Services', Part 1, *Australian Army Handbook*, AL1351. IWM, London.

CHAPTER SIX – 'The Paris of the East' (pages 98–121)

1. See *All About Shanghai*, Shanghai University Press, 1934/35.
2. R.M. Tinkler letters. File 'P'8, Imperial War Museum, London, with notes by Dr Robert Bickers. Tinkler was born in 1898, and became a constable in the SMP in 1919 after war service. He was killed by the Japanese in June 1939.
3. See Ted Quigley, *A Spirit of Adventure*, Book Guild, Lewes, 1994. One of these criminals was 'King Jack' Riley, who controlled most of the slot machines in the city. After it was discovered that he had escaped from gaol in America, he was deported.
4. Charles Willoughby, *Sorge: Soviet Master Spy*, William Kimber, London, 1952. (Published in USA under the title *The Shanghai Conspiracy*.)
5. Figures from Shanghai Municipal Council Report for 1938, published by *North China Daily News & Herald*, 1939.
6. See Quigley, op. cit.
7. Information from Stanley Knowles of the Shanghai Municipal Police who now lives in Australia and was interviewed on the author's behalf by Walter Scragg, a retired senior officer of the Royal Hong Kong Police (RHKP). Other information on the SMP has come from: a) the author's interview and correspondence in 1995/96 with Superintendent Frederick West who joined the force in 1922. Now in his mid-nineties, Fred West is probably the oldest surviving SMP member; b) the data base kept by David Deptford, QPM, CPM, a recently retired senior officer of the RHKP.
8. Luft was born in Zurich in 1898. In Basle in 1922 he became a member of the Swiss Communist Party. He then spent five years in the USSR. He was in Brussels in 1929 where he acquired the passport that got him into China.
9. Agnes Smedley (1894–1953). Born in Missouri. Arrested in USA in 1918 along with Salandranath Ghose, an Indian political agitator, for actions that violated the Espionage Act. Case never went to trial. She was in Berlin in 1920 living with another Indian agitator. In 1921, visited

Moscow. Arrived on China in 1929 as correspondent for *Frankfurter Allgemeine Zeitung*. She used several aliases at this time. Returned to US in 1941. 1950, left USA for London on eve of summons from Un-American Activities Committee. Died in London in 1953 and, in accordance with her will, her ashes were taken to China.

10. Thomas Patrick Givens, born 1888, was an Irishman from Tipperary. He joined the SMP in 1907, and was Deputy Commissioner when he retired in 1936. For many years he had been in charge of Special Branch, and was given credit for the handling of the Noulens case. He was MI6's man in Shanghai. On retirement he received several Chinese awards. One commendation noted that in the course of his duties in securing evidence against communists, he frequently worked in close co-operation with the Chinese Public Security Bureau. At the time this caused some outrage among the more radical editors of Shanghai newspapers. It was also said of Givens that he was in the pockets of the Japanese.

    Henry Nathaniel Steptoe (1892–1949). Student Interpreter China Consular Service, 1919. Vice Consular positions in the 1920s at Chenghui, Shanghai, Chinkiang, and Peking. HM Vice Consul Grade I, 1931 and Grade II, 1935. HM Consul in China, 1936. He was part of the 'exchange' of diplomatic personnel at Lorenço Marques in September 1942, and served at that place until March 1943 before going to Foreign Office, London. Acting Consul Basra then Tehran in 1945. Consul-General at Leopoldville, April 1946. Later Envoy Extraordinary and Minister Plenipotentiary, San Salvador. Died in this post 1949.
11. Philip Knightley, *Philby, KGB Masterspy*, André Deutsch, London, 1988.
12. See Willoughby, op. cit.
13. See Mark J. Gayn, *The Fight for the Pacific*, Bodley Head, London, 1941. According to Willoughby, op. cit. p. 204, Gayn was implicated in 'the mysterious "Amerasia" case of wartime theft of secret State Department documents'. In 1949, Gayn was a contributor to the American communist front publication called 'Far East Spotlight'.
14. ADM233/494, XC 23805, P.2B. PRO, Kew.
15. The Shanghai Club, a British institution, was famous not only for its exclusitivity, but also for having the longest bar in the world. That it was an exceedingly long bar this author can vouch for. He visited it several times in the late 1950s by which time it had become the much more prosaic 'Shanghai Seamen's Club'. Pre-war it had been the second office for Shanghai taipans, and many were the business deals finalised behind its magnificently pillared façade. Gaining membership was not easy, but members of the almost equally prestigious Bengal, Singapore, and Hong Kong Clubs, had visitors' privileges.

16. ADM233/494 XC23805, PRO, Kew.
17. From information provided by Colonel Hayley Bell's daughter, Mary, Lady Mills.
18. Roger Faligot and Remi Kauffer, *The Chinese Secret Service*, Headline, London, 1989.
19. Later Major-General Augustus Klingner Ferguson (1898–1965). Japanese speaker who had been a language officer in Japan in the 1920s. A GSO2 in China, he was later, in 1941, GSO1 Malaya Command. He transferred to General Wavell's Staff in January 1942. In March that year it was he who organised the evacuation of ABDA Staff from Java. He then became Director of Intelligence, India. After the war he was Military Adviser to the UK Liaison Mission, Tokyo.
20. The Hawker Report is in Australian Archives A901, Far East Reports 10, Section VI. See also V.G. Bowden, 'Annual Report on China' in *Commonwealth of Australia Parliamentary Reports*, 1937–1940, Vol. 2.
21. See 'Japanese Secret Intelligence Services, Part 1', prepared by General Staff (Intelligence), Australian Military Forces. Copy in the archive of the Imperial War Museum, London, under reference 'Japanese AL Series'.
22. See *Policing Shanghai 1927–1937*, Frederic Wakeman, Jr, University of California Press, 1995. This book is an excellent survey of the policing of Shanghai and of the background to this policing over the decade mentioned.
23. Percy Chen, *The Sino-Japanese War, 1937*, Shanghai, 1938. A barrister, Chen was Editor-in-Chief, China Information Service, Shanghai.

CHAPTER SEVEN – Singapore, Malaya and British Borneo, 1930–1939 (pages 122–152)

1. Sir Richard Winstedt, *Malaya and its History*, Home University Library, London, 1948; G.P. Dartford, *A Short History of Malaya*, Longmans, Green & Co., London, 1956.
2. Captain Russell Grenfell, RN, *Main Fleet to Singapore*, Faber, London, 1951.
3. Major-General F.S.G. Piggott, op. cit., p. 196.
4. For a description of the experiences of these language students, see 'Student Days in Old China', by A.W. Hamilton, *Malayan Police Magazine*, 1952.

5. H. Fairburn and A.H. Dickinson, 'A Survey of the Colonial Police', *Malayan Police Magazine*, 1953.
6. CO717/133/11. 'Javanese Immigration into FMS'. PRO, Kew.
7. For a full account of the Ducroux case, see Laurent Metzger, 'Joseph Ducroux, a French Agent of the Comintern in Singapore (1931–32)', *Journal of the Malayan Branch of the Royal Asiatic Society*, Vol. LXIX, Part 1, 1996.
8. Joseph Ducroux (1904–80). After release from Outram Jail Ducroux was banished and sent to Indo-China where he was arrested by the French and sentenced to a year's imprisonment for possessing a false passport. He served this sentence in France.
9. Fairburn and Dickinson, op cit.
10. A.H. Dickinson papers in the BEAM Collection, Royal Commonwealth Library, now at Cambridge.
11. Eric Robinson, *The Japanese File*, Heinemann Asia, Hong Kong, 1979, p. 128.
12. Sir David Petrie (1879–1961). Indian Police from 1900. Special Mission to Singapore, 1922–23. Director Intelligence Bureau, Government of India, 1924–31. Headed MI5 in London, 1940–45.
13. WO32/5628. PRO, Kew.
14. WO32/5628. PRO, Kew.
15. The Russian light-cruiser *Jemtchug* was one of the few survivors of the ill-fated Baltic Fleet which was destroyed by the Japanese in the battle of Tsushima in 1904. She was at Penang in October 1914 when what at first was taken to be a British cruiser appeared from seaward and approached without challenge. Reaching within a mile range, the ship, which proved to be the *Emden*, hoisted the German ensign and fired a torpedo. She finished off the *Jemtchug* with shellfire and another torpedo, killing 91 and wounding 108 of the crew of 340.

    The French destroyer *Mousquet* entered the fray but was destroyed by the much larger German raider. However, the gallant French action undoubtedly saved other ships and the port itself from destruction. The *Emden* made off but not before rescuing 36 of the Frenchman's crew.
16. FO371/22173/532. PRO, Kew.
17. René Henri de Solminihac Onraet, CMG (1887–1952). Born in Mauritius. Cadet, Straits Settlements Police, 1907. Language officer, Amoy, 1908–9, where he learnt Hokkien. Chairman Sikh Advisory Board, 1930. Director, CID, 1931. IGP Singapore, 1935–39. British Army with rank of Major, 1939–41. Police Adviser to British Military Administration, Malaya, 1945–46. Died at Burley, Hampshire, 8th March 1952.
18. René Onraet, *Singapore, A Police Background*, Dorothy Crisp, London, 1946.

19. Kenneth Sayce Morgan (1895–1960). Commissioned British Army, 1915, Indian Army, 1917. 3/23 Sikh Infantry, then 19th Hyderabads. Captain 1919, Major 1933. Officiated as second-in-command of his regiment in 1933. Became CO, Territorial Hyderabads, then on Special Unemployed List from 23rd February 1936 when he transferred to the Singapore Police. Died at Lavenham, Suffolk, 16th August 1960.
20. Letters from Barbara Herdman, née Brown, to H.P. Bryson, dated March and April 1972. BEAM Collection, XII 26, Royal Commonwealth Library (now at Cambridge).
21. Enid Saunders Candlin, *The Breach in the Wall – A Memoir of Old China*, Cassell, London, 1974.
22. Colonel Frank Robert Rennick (1866–1915). 40th Pathans (later called 5/14th Punjab Regiment, also known as the 'Forty Thieves'). Rennick was one of the many fine officers of the Indian army who came from an Anglo-Indian background. He made an extensive study of Japan and the Japanese, and the Indian army considered him their expert on the subject. He was killed at Neuve Chapelle on 26th April 1915.
23. Information from letters to the author from Mary, Lady Mills, during 1993. She wrote plays under her maiden name Mary Hayley Bell. The actresses Hayley Mills and Juliet Mills are the granddaughters of Colonel Hayley Bell.
24. Letter to author from Anthony Hewitt dated 3rd October 1995.
25. Correspondence and telephone conversations between the author and Mrs Wyn Steel during 1995/1996.
26. Brigadier H. Vinden, CIE (1895–1977). Commissioned Suffolk Regiment. Served in France, 1914–18. Later served in Ireland, Middle East, India. Shanghai, 1927–28. Staff College, 1930–32. In 1934 was responsible for selecting Bren Gun as standard light machine-gun for British army. After his period on Malaya Command Staff, 1937–40, was attached to War Office and responsible for developing War Office Selection Board Interview techniques known as WOSBI. In 1942–45 he introduced WOSBI system into the Indian army.
27. FO371/22173/532. PRO, Kew.
28. FO371/22174. PRO, Kew.
29. CO717/127/7 'Japanese Settlement at Cameron Highlands'. PRO, Kew.
30. From a copy of Brigadier H. Vinden's unpublished memoirs kindly supplied to the author by the brigadier's widow, Madame Rose Vinden, and his daughter-in-law, Mrs Winnie Vinden. A copy of the memoir is now lodged at the Imperial War Museum, London. The quotations on succeeding pages come also from Vinden's unpublished memoir.
31. WO106/2430. PRO, Kew.
32. Speaking to a reporter of the *Singapore Free Press* after the war,

on 29th March 1947, Becker said of his times in Thailand in 1937 and 1938, 'through no fault of my own I became deeply involved in Siamese politics,' adding that he often travelled dressed as a native. In Malaya, well ahead of his contemporaries, he tended to support those Malays who wanted independence from Britain. Despite this, he had no hesitation in passing on intelligence information to Hayley Bell. For the full story of John Becker, see Chapter 7 of this author's *Singapore: The Pregnable Fortress*, Hodder & Stoughton, London, 1995.

33. Elizabeth Hewitt, née Hayley Bell, is almost certain the name was Bavier.
34. See correspondence between Brigadier Ivan Simson and A.H. Dickinson in BEAM Collection of papers, Royal Commonwealth Library.
35. From interviews and correspondence with Guy Madoc, 1994–96.

CHAPTER EIGHT – The Far East Combined Bureau moves to Singapore (pages 153–172)

1. ADM233/494. PRO, Kew.
2. Major J.G. Ewens had been commissioned into the Dorset Regiment. It is believed that he was killed in 1942 whilst taking part in the Burma campaign.
3. Information from J.S.A. Lewis to the author, 6th May 1996. John Lewis returned to Malaya after five months' leave on 17th July 1941. He found himself an internee of the Japanese in February of the following year. Post-war he became Deputy Controller of Customs.
4. ADM233/494. PRO, Kew.
5. Strangely, neither Professor A.C. Hardy nor his invention are mentioned in the standard book on British Scientific Intelligence in World War Two, *Most Secret War*, by R.V. Jones, Hamish Hamilton, London, 1978.
6. ADM233/494. PRO.
7. Information from letters to the author from Lt-Col. P. Pender-Cudlip during 1995 and 1996 and from a meeting with him on 26th October 1995.
8. Japanese Army Memorandum, March 1941. Copy in Oriental and India Office Collections, File reference, L/MIL/17/20/24.
9. For a list of some of FECB's non-'Y' sources of information, see FO371/24715, p. 127. PRO, Kew.
10. File No. 1937/2/159. Australian Archives Victorian Regional Office:

Accession Series MP1185/8. Department, of Navy, Secret and Confidential Correspondence Files. Australian archives contain 'open' copies of many British documents not in the public domain in Britain. It is a matter of interest that, ever since World War Two, British officials have weeded through the Australian files and removed many documents pertaining to Far Eastern intelligence. This process was still going on in 1995.

11. This information comes from Mrs Beatty Rose Thompson, private secretary to Inspector-General of Police, A.H. Dickinson, from 1940. See File CO980/217, PRO, Kew.
12. See Arthur Cramsie, *Guest of an Emperor*, William Trimble Ltd, Enniskillen, 1987.
13. WO208/78. PRO.
14. WO208/1925. PRO.
15. Air Chief Marshal Sir Robert Brooke-Popham, GCVO, KCB, CMG, DSO, AFC (1878–1953). Retired from the RAF in 1937 and became Governor-General and C-in-C, Kenya. Rejoined RAF active list, 1939. The title of his job in the Far East is a misleading one. He was responsible for the operational control of the British land and air forces in Malaya and the adjacent territories, but not of the navy. Even the GOC and AOC remained in charge of their own administrative and financial responsibilities, and reported on those directly to their respective ministries in London.
16. Dennis Richards and Hilary St G. Saunders, *Royal Air Force, 1939–1945*, 3 vols, HMSO, London, 1953–54. See Volume 2, pp. 10–11.
17. Arthur J. Marder, *Old Friends, New Enemies*, Part 1, OUP, Oxford, 1981, p. 308.
18. ADM199/1472B. 'Supplementary Report on Events in the Far East 1940/5', Admiral Sir Geoffrey Layton, p. 3. PRO.
19. Letter from Dr Toby Carter to the author dated 29th September 1996.
20. Air Vice-Marshal Sir Lawrence Darvall, KBE, CB, MC (1898–1968). After Singapore and Java, Darvall served in Burma where he became well-known for sporting an Australian bush hat. Later in the war, he was in command of that part of RAF Transport Command involved with the airborne landings at Arnhem. It may be that he was not too proud of his Singapore days. His entries in both *Who's Who* and *Kelly's* make no reference to his time on the staff there.
21. Letter from Colonel Grimsdale to General Ismay, 8th March 1942. Ismay Archive, IV/Gri, LA7/2d, Liddell Hart Centre, King's College, London.
22. Joseph C. Grew, *Ten Years in Japan*, Hammond, Hammond & Co., London, 1944, p. 355.

23. *War With Japan*, Vol. II, p. 22, HMSO, London, 1995.
24. Captain Kenneth Lanyon Harkness, CBE, DSC, (RN 1900–1990). COIS until 1942. Deputy Director Naval Ordnance, Admiralty, 1943–44. Retired 1949.
25. Prem3/168/3. Summary of Air Chief Marshal Sir Robert Brooke-Popham's Despatch, July 1942. PRO.

CHAPTER NINE – 'Special' Intelligence (pages 173–186)

1. See F.W. Winterbotham, *The Ultra Secret*, Weidenfeld & Nicolson, London, 1974. A good description of the work of the SLUs is to be found in Chapter 5 of Ronald Lewin's *Ultra Goes to War*, Hutchinson, London, 1978.
2. See file WO193/920, PRO, Kew. Message 21487 DDMS Far East to War Office, 30/7/41.
3. WO193/920, PRO. Message 21079/G from C-in-C, India, to C-in-C, Far East 17/12/41.
4. Dickinson papers in BEAM Collection, Royal Commonwealth Society.
5. 1954 report by H.B.J. Donaldson in BEAM Collection, Royal Commonwealth Library. Made in answer to a questionnaire sent him by Dickinson.
6. Report by SO (I) Singapore, dated 14/5/42. In WO106/2550A, PRO.
7. Letter to the author dated 20th November 1996 from an ex-senior officer of the Singapore Police who does not wish to be identified.
8. From A.H. Dickinson papers, courtesy of his daughter, Mrs Pauline Ashbury. From papers written in 1946 at the request of Lt-Gen. A.E. Percival to help him write his Official Despatch.
9. WO193/913. Collation No. 27 Far East Espionage, 23/10/40–18/12/41. PRO, Kew.
10. Most Secret Telegram 59/3 of 16th May 1941, C-in-C Far East to War Office. File WO193/920. PRO, Kew.
11. WO193/920. Page notated '18'. PRO.
12. MP1185/8, 1935/2/415, Australian Archives, Victoria Regional Office, Melbourne.
13. See HS1/185. PRO.
14. H.P. Bryson, MCS. Letter to A.H. Dickinson in 1972. In BEAM Collection, Royal Commonwealth Library.
15. Letter dated 6th November 1995 from R.W.E. Harper to the author. Harry Harper co-authored *Singapore Mutiny* with Harry Miller.

16. See the Memoir written by Captain A.N. Grey, DSO, RN. IWM, London.

CHAPTER TEN – Japanese Infiltration and Indian Nationalism (pages 187–204)

1. For a fuller discussion of the Shinozaki Case, see Brian Bridges, 'Britain and Japanese Espionage in Pre-War Malaya: the Shinozaki Case', *Journal of Contemporary History*, SAGE, London, Vol. 21 (1986). See also Shinozaki's own story in his *Syonan, My Story*, Times Books International, Singapore, 1975.
2. WO193/913, PRO.
3. C.E. Collinge correspondence, BEAM collection, Royal Commonwealth Library. See also this author's *Singapore, The Pregnable Fortress*, pp. 55–57.
4. AL 1351 Part II. AL Japanese Series. IWM.
5. Letter from Colonel R.R. Baily to the author dated 12th September 1995.
6. L/WS/1/391, WS4367. 'Discipline of Indian Troops in Singapore'. Oriental and India Office Collections.
7. Lt-Col. Sir Geoffrey Betham, *The Golden Galley – the Story of the 2nd Punjab Regiment, 1761–1947*, OUP, Oxford, 1956.
8. Foreign Secretary's note in FO371/28126, PRO.
9. Letter from Michael Keon to the author dated 5th March 1996.
10. Lionel Wigmore, *The Japanese Thrust*, Australian War Memorial, Canberra, 1957.
11. HS1/332. PRO.
12. Giles Playfair (1910–96). Author of *Singapore Goes Off the Air*, 1943. See obituary in *The Times*, 24th January 1996.
13. HS1/339. SOE documents, Far East. PRO.
14. Walter Gibson, *The Boat*, W.H. Allen, London, 1952.
15. HS1/226. SOE Far East Reports. PRO.
16. Notes on the Free French Movement in the Far East. ADM199/1472, PRO.

CHAPTER ELEVEN – Subversion in the South (pages 205–218)

1. WO193/917. PRO.
2. AL338. Japanese AL Series. IWM.
3. Mark J. Gayn, *The Fight for the Pacific*, Bodley Head, London, 1941.
4. FO371/28108. PRO.
5. FO371/28111. PRO.
6. FO371/28110, '1941 Siam'. (File was closed until 1992.) PRO.
7. FO371/28153, 'Far East, Siam, 1941'. (File was closed until 1992.) PRO.
8. AL1351, Part II, Japanese AL Series, IWM. See also FECB Report 5401, Appendix E. p. 28, in WO208/1915, PRO.
9. FO371/28123. PRO. The relevant paper F7375/210/40 was missing from this file when it was made public in 1992. Reinstated 17th July 1995 after application from this author under the new 'Open Government' policy.
10. FO371/28125. PRO. This was one of several messages that were missing in the file when it was originally opened to the public in 1992. After representations by this author it was reinstated in the file on 12th July 1995, but noted as 'reinstated by blanking'.
11. Louis Allen, *Burma: The Longest War*, Dent, London, 1984.
12. Ba Maw, *Breakthrough in Burma*, Yale University, New Haven, 1968.
13. Lieutenant-Colonel Anthony Mains, *The Retreat From Burma: An Intelligence Officer's Personal Story*, Foulsham, London, 1973.
14. AL 1351. Part II. Japanese AL Series. IWM.
15. HS1/96. SOE. French Indo-China. PRO.
16. HS1/70. SOE.PRO.

CHAPTER TWELVE – Australian Diplomatic Intelligence in the Far East (pages 219–227)

1. David Day, *The Great Betrayal*, Angus & Robertson, London, 1988, p. 7.
2. See 'Strategic Concentration Plan 1937' AWM 51 (158), Australian War Memorial, Canberra.
3. See Wayne Gobert, *The Origins of Australian Diplomatic Intelligence in Asia, 1933–1941*, Strategic & Defence Studies Centre, Australian National University, Canberra, 1992.
4. See article 'Singapore Was a Fatal Posting' by P. Hastings in *Sydney Morning Herald*, 31 August 1989.
5. Lionel Wigmore, *The Japanese Thrust*, Australian War Memorial, Canberra, 1957, p. 57.
6. Charles A. Willoughby, *Sorge: Soviet Master Spy*; William Kimber;

London, 1952; Gobert, op. cit.; Richard Deacon, *Spyclopedia*, William Morrow, New York, 1987; G.W. Prange, *Target Tokyo*, McGraw-Hill, New York, 1985.

7. See this author's *Singapore: The Pregnable Fortress*, Hodder & Stoughton, London, 1995 p. 163.
8. See William H. McDougall Jr, *By Eastern Windows*, Arthur Barker, London, 1951. McDougall was an American and the Far East correspondent for United Press. After escaping the clutches of the Japanese at Shanghai, he ended up an internee in Sumatra. He records the death of Bowden as told to him by men who had been there at the time. Apparently Bowden remonstrated in Japanese with his captors regarding their treatment of him and his companions. He was taken away and forced to dig a grave in the sand with his hands. He was then ordered to pick a handful of flowers growing nearby and stand in the grave. Then he was shot.
9. 'Japanese Secret Intelligence Services Part II', Australian Military Forces. Copy in Imperial War Museum, London, ref. AL1351. The passages quoted in the rest of this chapter come from this document, except for that from the Report on Ross (note 10).
10. Report on Ross, letter dated 30th July 1942. Item No. 1942/2/2948, Series A433, Australian Archives, Dickson, ACT.

CHAPTER THIRTEEN – Inside Japan Pre-war (pages 228–254)

1. Major-General F.S.G. Piggott, op. cit., p. 167..
2. Cecil Bullock, *Etajima: The Japanese Dartmouth*, London, 1942.
3. ADM1/11326. Dreyer memorandum dated 10th February 1939. PRO. Rear-Admiral Victor H. Danckwerts, the man most responsible for this denigration of Dreyer's views, was not in good health. Described by Air Vice-Marshal J.C. Slessor as having 'a first-class mind and wide experience', he has also been described as 'ponderous and lacking in humour'. He died in 1944 of tuberculosis.
4. ADM116/3682. PRO.
5. Report of 1st May 1941. JIC(41)175. CAB79/11. PRO.
6. ADM223/347, NID Reports, 1941–44.
7. See Marder, op. cit, for a full description.
8. Chapman, Volumes II & III, op.cit. See also J. Rohwer & G. Hummelchen, *Chronology of the War at Sea*, Volume I, Ian Allan, London, 1972.
9. See FO371/247241. PRO.

10. Copies of Attachment Reports and other documents and information kindly supplied to the author by Lieutenant-Colonel Peter Pender-Cudlip in 1995–96.
11. Professor Gordon W. Prange, *Target Tokyo*, McGraw-Hill, New York, 1984.
12. Professor John W.M. Chapman, *The Price of Admiralty – The War Diary of the German Naval Attaché in Japan, 1939–1943*', Volume 1, Saltire Press, Ripe, 1982, p. 209.
13. WO106/129. PRO.
14. Sir Herbert Vere Redman (1901–75). After he was 'exchanged' with other interned British diplomats in late 1942, Redman spent the remainder of the war as Director of the Far East Division, Ministry of Information, in London. He was back in Japan after the war as an adviser to the British Commonwealth Occupation Force. He was knighted in 1961.
15. Sir Hubert Ashton Graves, KCMG, CMG, MC (1894–1972). Served in British Consular Service, 1924–41. After being 'exchanged' with other diplomats in 1942, was on 'special duties' in Australia 1941–45. Counsellor at British embassy in Washington 1946–50. Minister to Associated States of Cambodia, Laos and Viet Nam, 1951–54. Ambassador to Viet Nam 1954–55.
16. Information received in correspondence from Michael Keon, who knew Graves in those war years in Australia and who served in the same intelligence organisation.
17. Chapman, op. cit., Vol. I, p. 35.
18. From an unpublished and previously unrecorded memoir of Vanya Ringer written in 1940. Copy kindly supplied to the author by his daughter, Mrs Virginia Valpy.
19. See Volumes I and II, *War With Japan*, Ministry of Defence Naval Historical Branch, HMSO, London, 1995.
20. Information kindly supplied by Reg Eddington and John Waters of the HMS *Liverpool* Association, and based on a record of the incident researched and compiled by Professor G.R. Steele, whose father was a Chief Telegraphist aboard the vessel.
21. Chapman, op. cit.
22. David Dilks, editor, *The Diaries of Sir Alexander Cadogan, 1938–1945*, Cassell, London, 1971.
23. Chapman, op. cit., Volume I, p. 170.
24. FO371/24740. F4318, 20th September 1940. PRO.
25. WO32/14550. Prisoner-of-War Reports. PRO.
26. HS1/332. Copy of file F11671/137/23. PRO.
27. HS1/204. PRO.
28. John (C.J.) Morris, *Traveller From Tokyo*, Cresset Press, London, 1943.

CHAPTER FOURTEEN – SS *Automedon* (pages 255–267)

1. Alan Stripp, *Code Breaker in the Far East*, OUP, Oxford, 1995.
2. From copies of papers and reports kindly supplied by Samuel Harper to the author in 1996, and from telephone conversations and correspondence thereafter.
3. Ulrich Mohr and Felix Sellwood, *Atlantis*, London Press, London, 1955, p. 127.
4. Captain S.W. Roskill, *A Merchant Fleet At War*, Collins, London, 1962. Roskill had been commissioned by Blue Funnel owners, Alfred Holt & Co., to write this war history of the line.
5. Information from Sam Harper and Frank Walker. Confirmed by Charles Metcalf who worked in the Blue Funnel personnel department during the war.
6. See *War With Japan*, Vol. II, op. cit., note, p. 34.
7. Captain A.H. Hillgarth, CMG, OBE, RN. Born 1899. Naval Attaché, Madrid 1939–43. Afterwards Chief of British Naval Intelligence, Eastern Theatre. Co-author of the Naval Intelligence Department internal history, ADM223/494. PRO.
8. A summary of the British communication as sent to Berlin by Admiral Wenneker, the German Naval Attaché, Tokyo, can be found on pp. 332–4, of Chapman, op. cit.
9. See Chapman, ibid., note 6, p. 584. The Washington reference is given as Records Group 457, National Security Agency, SRNA No. 0020.
10. F.H. Hinsley and Alan Stripp, *Code Breakers – The Inside Story of Bletchley Park'*, OUP, Oxford, 1993, p. 2.
11. Chapman, op. cit., pp. xxxix, xl.
12. Chapman, ibid.
13. Marder, op. cit., p. 157.
14. F0371/27962. Japan File 523. Cypher No. 693. PRO.
15. Chapman, op. cit. Vol. I, p. 476.
16. Chapman, op. cit., p. xxv.

CHAPTER FIFTEEN – Shanghai – September 1939 to December 1941 (pages 268–284)

1. Immanuel C.Y. Hsu, *The Rise of Modern China*, OUP, Oxford, 1975.
2. Major-General F.S.G. Piggott, op. cit.

3. R.M. Tinkler file, 'P'8, Imperial War Museum, London.
4. Hsu, op. cit.
5. ADM223/494. 4552. PRO, Kew.
6. ADM199/607A. PRO, Kew.
7. HS1/340. SOE Operations. PRO, London.
8. The raider involved was the *Komet*, a ship of many names. Originally the North German Lloyd vessel *Ems*, the German codename for her was 'Schiff 45' while the British called her 'Raider B'. The *Komet* entered the Pacific via the North East Passage (which she navigated with the help of three Russian ice-breakers) and the Bering Strait in August 1940. She linked up with another raider, the *Orion*, and the tanker supply ship *Kulmerland*. After *Ringwood* she sank eight more vessels totalling 50,000 tons and bombarded oil installations at Nauru. She reached Hamburg after an eighteen-month voyage in November 1941. She was sunk by a British force of destroyers and MTBs off Flushing on 14th October 1942 along with three vessels of her escort. See *War With Japan* – Vol. 1, MoD Naval Historical Branch, HMSO, London, 1995; Charles Hocking, *Dictionary of Disasters at Sea*, Lloyds, London, 1969.
9. See *The Price of Admiralty – The Diary of the German Naval Attaché in Japan, 1939–1943*, four volumes, edited by Professor John Chapman, Saltire Press, 1982–89.
10. HS1/340. SOE operations. PRO, Kew.
11. *War With Japan* – Vol 1, op. cit.
12. HMS *Peterel* (the second 'e' is often omitted in error) under Lieutenant Stephen Polkinghorn, RNR, fought the gallant action (the first naval action of the war with Japan) against overwhelming odds, her light armaments being dwarfed by the 8-inch and 6-inch guns of *Idzumo*. *Peterel*'s survivors were thus treated with great honour by the Japanese. Commander J.B. Woolley's post-war report on the action caused Polkinghorn, a New Zealander, to be awarded the DSC. Polkinghorn reached the grand age of ninety-nine before dying in the Ranfurley War Veterans Home, Auckland, New Zealand, in the 1980s.
13. Information supplied to the author by J. Mariner, himself a *Peterel* survivor.
14. HS1/340. SOE Operations. PRO, Kew.
15. ADM233/494. PRO, Kew.
16. WO193/920. 10682, 'Intelligence Organisation in Far East, 4th April 1940, together with changes made as at February 1941'. PRO, Kew.
17. WO193/920. 10682. PRO, Kew.
18. WO193/920. 10682. PRO, Kew.
19. CO980/217. No.161. Report of Mr J.F. Brister. PRO, Kew.
20. See S.C. Riggs Report in HS1/181. PRO, Kew.

21. Wiegand papers in US Army Military History Institute, Carlisle, Pennsylvania.
22. See Charles Cruickshank, SOE in the Far East, OUP, Oxford, 1983, pp. 76–77, and Riggs Report, op. cit.
23. Chapman, op. cit.
24. Chapman, op. cit., Vol. 3, p. 984, note 5.
25. HS1/204, SOE Operations, PRO, Kew. Message No. 2418 Craigie to COIS, Singapore.
26. FO916/433 and FO919/434. PRO, Kew.
27. Ted Quigley, *The Spirit of Adventure*, Book Guild, Lewes, 1994.
28. HS1/205. SOE Operations. From information supplied from a passenger on diplomatic exchange ships at Lourenço Marques. PRO, Kew.
29. HS1/339. PRO, Kew.
30. ADM223/494. PRO, Kew.
31. HS1/344. SOE AD/SI File, Far East. PRO, Kew. Information contained in a paper dated 29th April 1942 and entitled, 'German–Japanese Relations', prepared by ad hoc Committee on Intelligence for Propaganda in the Far East.
32. Zhang Zhongli and others, *The Swire Group in Old China*, Shanghai People's Publishing House, China, n.d. but c. 1990.

CHAPTER SIXTEEN – Japan's Build-up to the Attack on the USA (pages 285-304)

1. *Japanese Secret Intelligence Services*, Part I. Prepared by Australian Military Forces. AL1352, IWM. p. 52.
2. Ramon Ma Zaragoza, *Old Manila*, OUP, Oxford, 1990.
3. John Toland, *But Not in Shame*, Random House, New York, 1961.
4. Admiral Thomas Charles Hart, USN (1877–1971). Submarine officer during World War One; C-in-C, US Asiatic Fleet, 1939–42. Senator for Connecticut 1945–46.
5. James Leutze, *A Different Kind of Victory*, Naval Institute Press, Annapolis, 1981.
6. Bruce Lee, *Marching Orders*, Crown, New York, 1995.
7. Papers of Captain A.N. Grey, DSO, RN (1898–1994). Imperial War Museum.
8. Theodore H. White, *In Search of History: A Personal Adventure*, London, 1979.
9. Leutze, op. cit.

10. Kemp Tolley, *Cruise of the Lanikai*, US Naval Institute, Annapolis, 1973.
11. As quoted by Charles A. Beard in his *President Roosevelt and the Coming of the War, 1941*, Yale University Press, New Haven, 1948.
12. Cordell Hull, *Memoirs*, Vol. 2, Hodder & Stoughton, London, 1948, p. 1080.
13. (a) Major-General C.A. Willoughby's written testimony to Lt-Col. H.C. Clausen during the latter's Pearl Harbor investigation for the American War Department. Appendix A to Willoughby's testimony concerned British Intelligence and Gerald Wilkinson. See Henry Clausen and Bruce Lee, *Pearl Harbor, Final Judgement*, Leo Cooper, London, 1993. (b) Gerald Wilkinson (1908–1965). After war service he returned to his pre-war company position in Manila. In 1961 he became chairman of the company in Honolulu, and died there aged 56.
14. This message, held in official US government files, is reproduced in Clausen and Lee, op. cit.
15. HW1/288. PRO. Message No. 985, from Tojo to Berlin, 30th November 1941. Decrypt numbered by the British 098452.
16. FO916/433. PRO. This file contains some information about the build-up to the diplomatic exchange that took place at Lourenço Marques in the late summer of 1942. Other files on this subject appear not to have been released into the public domain (1996).
17. HS1/339. PRO.
18. John W.M. Chapman, 'Tricycle Recycled: Collaboration among the Secret Intelligence Services of the Axis States, 1940–41'. Article in Vol. 7, No. 3 (1992), *Intelligence and National Security*, published by Frank Cass, London.
19. Stanley Weintraub, *Long Day's Journey Into War*, Dutton, New York, 1991.
20. James Rusbridger and Eric Nave, *Betrayal at Pearl Harbor*, Summit Books, New York, 1991.
21. Michael Handel, 'Military Deception in Peace and War', in his *War, Strategy and Intelligence*, London, 1989.
22. See Appendix H, *War With Japan*, Vol. II, HMSO, London, 1995.
23. See *War With Japan*, Vol. II, HMSO, London, 1995.
24. E.T. Layton, with R. Pineau and J. Costello, *And I Was There*, New York, 1985.

CHAPTER SEVENTEEN – Countdown to the Japanese Victory in Malaya (pages 305–344)

1. Unpublished papers of Lt-Gen. Sir Lewis Health. Imperial War Museum.
2. For the full Heenan story, see Peter Elphick and Michael Smith, *Odd Man Out – the Story of the Singapore Traitor*, Hodder & Stoughton, London, 1993. There is additional information in this author's *Singapore, the Pregnable Fortress*, op. cit.
3. Memoirs of Lt-Col. D.J.R. Moore. EUR226, IO1R/E/1/311, 0 & 10 Collections, London.
4. ADM223/321 PRO.
5. See this author's *Singapore, the Pregnable Fortress*, pp. 198–205.
6. See *Seventy Days*, a memoir of Harvey Ryves, 84/30/1, Imperial War Museum.
7. Post-war, Eric Robertson joined the BBC, and ended his career with them as Deputy Managing Director, External Broadcasting.
8. ADM223/321. Special Intelligence No. 380, 28 October 1941. PRO. The run of Summaries in this file is incomplete; that a few are missing is evidenced by the consecutive numbering system.
9. HW1/303, PRO.

10 *The Memoirs of Cordell Hull*, Vol. 2, Hodder & Stoughton, London, 1948.

11. General Sir John Westall, KCB, CBE (1901–1986). Born in New Zealand. Educated at Dulwich. Joined Royal Marines, 1919. Died in New Zealand 30 September 1986. See obituary in *The Globe & Laurel* (Journal of the Royal Marines) Sept/Oct. 1986.
12. WO106/2550A. 23A. PRO.
13. Captain D.N.C. Tufnell's report on the mobilisation of the Japanese navy is in FO371/279064, PRO. Captain Hillgarth's remarks are in ADM233/494. PRO.
14. '100 Squadron versus Japan', unpublished memoir by Basil A. Gotto. It was written in exercise books within three months of the events described in it, and was secreted until after the war. Copy kindly supplied to the author by Basil Gotto.
15. Information from A.H.P. Humphrey, CMG, OBE, PMN, at a meeting with the author in November 1995 and in subsequent correspondence. Humphrey had been private secretary to Sir Shenton Thomas, 1936–38. At Labuan on 16th December 1941 he reported to Singapore by radio a sighting made by the Coastwatch of Japanese ships. Subsequently he and the Cable & Wireless manager destroyed the island's communications centre. Captured by the Japanese, he was kept in solitary confinement by the Japanese for six months, a period made a little more bearable by the drinks the Sultan of Brunei sent down to him each evening. After the war he became Defence Secretary, Singapore.
16. See article by J.R. Munday on Air Vice-Marshal C.W.H. Pulford

entitled 'An Inspiration To All', in *Flight Deck, Journal of Naval Aviation*, no.2, 1993.

17. Dato H.L. Wrigglesworth, '*The Japanese Invasion of Kelantan in 1941*', privately published in Kuala Lumpur in 1991.
18. Sir John Fletcher-Cooke (1911–89). Malayan Civil Service from 1937. Attached RAF in January 1942 as intelligence officer. Captured by Japanese in Java. After the war held various posts in Colonial Service. MP for Test division of Southampton, 1964–66. Wrote of his wartime experiences in *The Emperor's Guest*, Hutchinson, London, 1971.
19. 'Operations in Malaya and Singapore', WP(42)314, signed by General A.P. Wavell, 1 June 1942. PREM 3/168/3, PRO.
20. *Great Was the Fall*, by 'An RAAF Officer', Patterson's Press Perth, Australia, 1945. This book is in the form of letters that the officer sent home to his daughter in Australia. As the letters had obviously not been censored, the present author assumed that they had been written by someone acting as squadron censor! Research showed the RAAF officer to be Flight Lieutenant A.D. Elson-Smith, and this was later confirmed in Australia by Mrs May Elson-Smith, his widow.
21. See *Live and Let Live, the Life and Times of Brigadier G. Qasim Gilani*, as told to Ziaul Haque, published in Singapore, n.d. but c. 1980, with a foreword by Tunku Abdul Rahman Putra.
22. For further details see Peter Elphick and Michael Smith, *Odd Man Out*, op. cit.
23. Captain Albert Victor Cockle, MC. He had joined the police from the army about the same time as Major K.S. Morgan.
24. Information received from CERA Bill Lewis, 23rd June 1996. The author is grateful to the following ex-crew members of HMS *Mauritius* for their help in tracing Bill Lewis and in piecing together this story: Admiral of the Fleet Sir Henry Leach (then a midshipman and whose father was captain of HMS *Prince of Wales* and went down with her), Captain R.I.A Sarell (then the gunnery officer), George Crane, Len Furness and Johnnie Hunter.
25. Information from Squadron Leader 'Fiery' Phillips, MBE, who was a sergeant with the squadron at the time.
26. HS1/185. 'Far East – Japan,' SOE file. PRO.
27. WO172/147. War Diary 2nd Loyals. PRO.
28. See *War With Japan* MOD Naval Historical Branch, HMSO, London, 1995, Vol. 2, p. 53; Elphick and Smith, op. cit., contains more details of the Windsor affair.
29. A copy of this report is to be found in file WO106/2579C. PRO.
30. CAB106/153, PRO. Wells's report was appended to the Report of the 8th Australian Division.
31. ADM233/494. Section on Fall of Singapore. PRO.

32. From transcript of conversation between Colonel Thyer and Major-General S.W. Kirby, Adelaide, 19th January 1953. In CAB106/151. PRO.
33. WO208/1529. PRO. Malayan Campaign and Fall of Singapore. Extracts of Report from Lieutenant-Colonel H.C. Phillips, RA.
34. From accounts written by officers of 1st Cambridgeshires, edited by Dennis Hutt.
35. File No. 1937/2/159. Australian Archives Victorian Regional Office, Department of Navy.
36. Brigadier Leonard Frank Field, CBE, born 1898. Commissioned into RASC. Attached to directorate of Military Operations, 1940. Director of Intelligence, SW Pacific 1942. Escaped from Sumatra with other members of General Wavell's Staff in March 1942 aboard HMS *Kedah*. Chief Chinese Liaison Officer, Burma 1942. Military Attaché, China 1945–49.
37. Major-General Gordon Bennett's full report can be found in file WO32/11749, PRO.
38. From interview with and letters from Sir Alexander Barrington in 1995.
39. From excerpts of his diary kindly supplied by Sir Harold Atcherley to the author, and from notes taken during an interview on 26th September 1995.
40. See S. Woodburn Kirby, *Singapore, The Chain of Disaster*, Cassell, London, 1971. This book, published after Kirby's death, contained many criticisms of the way the Malayan campaign was fought which did not appear in the same author's volume of the British Official History. General Percival, who died in 1966, had threatened to take action if anything critical of him or his senior officers appeared in the History. (See the present author's *Singapore*: *The Pregnable Fortress* for details of this threat.)
41. For details of the *Mary Rose* escape see report made by Major K.S. Morgan in file ADM199/622A, PRO.
42. See file CO980/234 for date of Wynne's death. File CO980/238 contains details of Wynne's will and the personal effects he left. Both files at PRO.
43. Forbes Wallace, *War-time Interlude of a Temporary Soldier*, privately published, Norwich, 1980.

CHAPTER EIGHTEEN – The Far East Intelligence War, 1942 (pages 345–386)

1. A fuller discussion of the communications situation in Singapore can be found in this author's *Singapore, The Pregnable Fortress*, op. cit.
2. Ursula Churchill-Dawes, née Tulloh (1909–96). At the time of her marriage to Charles Boxer she was described as the most beautiful woman in Hong Kong. After returning to England from Ceylon at the end of the war she married I.A.R. Peebles, the Middlesex and England cricketer who became a journalist with the *Sunday Times*. Ian Peebles died in 1980, and she married, thirdly, Montague Churchill-Dawes in 1984. He predeceased her.
3. From the memoir of Baron Reinhard Alexander Mackay (1903–90). Copy kindly supplied to the author by H.W.B. Croiset van Uchelan, husband of the Baroness Sonja Gratia, the baron's daughter. With the family's permission a copy has been lodged with the Imperial War Museum, London.
4. See Memoirs of Captain A.N. Grey, RN. Imperial War Museum, London.
5. Brian Bond, editor, *Chief of Staff, the Diaries of Lieutenant-General Sir Henry Pownall*, Vol. II, Leo Cooper, London, 1974. Pownall was born in 1887 and died in 1961.
6. David Kahn, *The Codebreakers*, Weidenfeld & Nicolson, London, 1973.
7. Kahn, op. cit.
8. See chapter 15 by H.C. Bird and others in, *Bombay Buccaneers*, edited by Commander D.J. Hastings, RINVR, BACSA, London, 1986.
9. Hugh Skillen, *Spies of the Airwaves*, self-published, London, 1989.
10. ADM223/494. PRO.
11. *War With Japan*, Vol. II, op. cit., p. 121.
12. Samuel Eliot Morison, *Coral Sea, Midway and Submarine Actions, May–August 1942*, Vol. IV in the monumental *History of United States Naval Operations in World War II*, OUP, Oxford, 1949.
13. For a month-by-month listing of Japanese naval aircraft losses, see Appendix Q, Vol. III, *War With Japan*, HMSO, London, 1995.
14. Tom Harrisson, *World Within*, OUP, Oxford, 1984. Thomas H. Harrisson (1911–76). Director of the Kuching Museum (which had been created by the Third White Rajah of Sarawak), 1947–66. Harrisson was killed in a plane crash in Southeast Asia. See also Note 40 to Chapter 19.
15. *Air Campaigns of the Pacific War*, US Strategic Bombing Survey Report, US Government Printing Office, Washington, 1946, p. 62.
16. Professor Gerhard L. Weinberg, *A World At Arms*, CUP, Cambridge, 1994, p. 553.
17. Geoffrey Ballard, *On Ultra Active Service*, Spectrum, Richmond (Victoria), 1991, p. 145.

18. ADM223/494. New Zealand section, page marked 'E'. PRO.
19. Allison Ind, *Spy Ring Pacific*, Weidenfeld & Nicolson, London, n.d.
20. See ADM223/494. PRO.
21. June Knox-Mawer, *Tales From Paradise*, BBC Publications, London, 1986. Sir Alexander (Nick) Waddell, KCMG, DSC (b. 1913). Entered Colonial Service 1937, and served as Cadet & District Officer, Solomon Islands. Malayan Civil Service 1946. Service in Gambia and Sierra Leone before becoming Governor and C-in-C Sarawak, 1960–63.
22. The summary of the Sigint aspects of the Battle of Midway is based on 'The Role of Radio Intelligence in the American–Japanese War', SRH-012, US National Archives, Washington, D.C.
23. David Kahn, *The Codebreakers*, Sphere, London, 1973.
24. H.P. Willmott, *The Barrier and the Javelin: Japanese and Allied Pacific Strategies, February to June 1942*, Naval Institute Press, Annapolis, 1983.
25. Larry I. Bland (ed.), *The Papers of George Catlett Marshall*, Vol. 3, Johns Hopkins University Press, Baltimore, 1991, pp. 227–28.
26. John Pownall Reeves, b. 1909. Student interpreter China Consular Service, 1932. Vice-consul at various places including Hankow and Mukden before becoming consul at Macau in June 1941.
27. HS1/339 & HS1/176. PRO.
28. Information contained in letters from Geoffrey Wilson to the author during 1996. Sadly, Joy Wilson died in 1978.
29. From a written description of that escape, called 'Escape from Macau to India', later written by Mrs Fletcher.
30. Information from Admiral A.M. Andrade e Silva in conversations and correspondence with the author during 1996. Of a total population estimated at 300,000, two hundred persons per day are said to have died in Macau of starvation or disease during the last months of the war.
31. ADM223/494. NID Far East History, 1942. PRO.
32. Samuel Eliot Morison, op. cit., Vol. V.
33. James Rusbridger, 'The Sinking of the *Automedon* and the Capture of the *Nankin*', *Encounter*, May 1985.
34. See John Chapman, *The Price of Admiralty*, op. cit., p. xxxiii, Vol. I.
35. The information on Sigint in the Guadalcanal campaign is based on American Special Research History, *The Role of Radio Intelligence in the American-Japanese Naval War*, Volume III, SRH -012, US National Archives, Washington, DC.
36. *War With Japan*, op. cit. Vol. II, p. 11.
37. *War With Japan*, op. cit., Vol. III, p. 85.
38. ADM223/494. 'Jan–June 1942', pp. 1–3. PRO.

CHAPTER NINETEEN – The Far East Intelligence War, 1943–1945 (pages 387–433)

1. ADM223/494. PRO.
2. *War With Japan*, op. cit., Vol. III, 1995.
3. Samuel Eliot Morison, op. cit., series from 1947.
4. Allison Ind, *Allied Intelligence Bureau*, David McKay, New York, 1956.
5. Gerhard L. Weinberg, op. cit.
6. ADM223/494. PRO.
7. The two members of the consular staff were Dudley Cheke and Edward Biggs. Cheke (born 1912) was a vice-consul in Japan 1936–1942. He was part of the diplomatic exchange made in late 1942, as was Biggs. After the war Cheke became successively first secretary, Singapore 1950; consul-general, Osaka 1956; minister, British embassy, Tokyo, 1963–67; ambassador to Ivory Coast, 1967–70. From 1979 to 1982 he was Chairman of the Japan Society in London.
8. Hugh Denham, 'Bedford, Bletchley, Kilindini, Colombo', in *Code Breakers, The Inside Story of Bletchley Park*, edited by F.H. Hinsley and Alan Stripp, OUP, Oxford, 1993.
9. Hugh Skillen, *Spies of the Airwaves*, self-published, London, 1989.
10. Bradley F. Smith, *The Ultra-Magic Deals*, Airlife, Shrewsbury, 1993, p. 146.
11. Alan Stripp, *Code Breaker in the Far East*, OUP, Oxford, 1995.
12. ADM223/494. PRO.
13. ADM223/494. PRO.
14. ADM223/494. PRO.
15. HS1/341. SOE – Far East General Policy and Planning. PRO.
16. Ibid.
17. Cordell Hull, op. cit., Vol. II, p. 1596.
18. Roger Perkins, *Regiments of the Empire*, privately published, Newton Abbot, 1989.
19. ADM199/1884, PRO. Quoted by Charles Cruickshank, *SOE in the Far East*, OUP, 1983.
20. Vice-Admiral Sir Hugh Mackenzie, *The Sword of Damocles*, RN Submarine Museum, Gosport, 1995, pp. 151–52, and in a conversation with Peter Elphick in January 1996. Admiral 'Rufus' Mackenzie, KCB, DSO, DSC was born in 1913 and died on 9th October 1996.
21. For a pen-portrait of Sir Josiah Crosby, see this author's *Singapore, The Pregnable Fortress*, op. cit.

22. US State Department Records, 1945. Foreign Relations 1944, Volume V, Washington. 5:1312.
23. Andrew Gilchrist, *Bangkok Top Secret*, Hutchinson, London, 1970.
24. James V. Martin, 'Thai-American Relations in World War II'. Article in August 1963 edition of the *Journal of Asian Studies*.
25. John B. Haseman, *The Thai Resistance Movement During the Second World War*, Chalermnit Press, Bangkok, n.d. but probably late 1980s. The author's thanks to Major-General Clifford Kinvig for drawing this book to his attention.
26. Haseman, op. cit.
27. Richard M. Kelly, 'The Chance Island', in *Blue Book Magazine*, March 1946.
28. Cordell Hull, *Memoirs*, Volume II, op. cit., pp. 1595–97.
29. Sergeant Edmund Murray (1917–96). Murray, like Churchill, was an amateur painter. When Murray had some of his paintings turned down by the Royal Academy, Churchill commiserated with him. 'You know,' he said to Murray, 'your paintings are much better than mine, but yours are judged on their merit'. See Murray's autobiography, *I Was Churchill's Bodyguard*, published in 1987.
30. Gerhard L. Weinberg, op. cit., p. 554.
31. ADM223/494. PRO.
32. *War With Japan*, op. cit., Vol. III, p. 202.
33. *War With Japan*, op. cit., Vol. IV, p. 72.
34. Richard Fuller, *Shokan*, Arms & Armour, London, 1991.
35. *War With Japan*, op. cit., Vol. IV, p. 180.
36. *War With Japan*, op. cit., Vol. IV, p. 199.
37. Field-Marshal Viscount Slim, *Defeat Into Victory*, Macmillan, London, 1956.
38. F.W. Winterbotham, *The Ultra Secret*, Weidenfeld & Nicolson, London, 1974.
39. Terence O'Brien, *The Moonlight War*, Collins, London, 1987.
40. From Tom Harrisson, *World Within*, OUP, Oxford 1959, and from talks between Harrisson and this author and his wife who was a secretary to Tom Harrisson in Kuching, 1961–63.
41. The revelation of this Axis exchange of information comes from Major Karasawa Tomio who was a production chief with Unit 731. He is quoted in *Unit 731*, by Peter Williams and David Wallace, Hodder & Stoughton, London, 1989.

CHAPTER TWENTY – Conspiracy Theories (pages 434–450)

1. Reported in Stanley Weintraub, *Long Day's Journey Into War*, op. cit.
2. See David Day, op. cit.
3. John Kennedy, op. cit.
4. Brian Bond (editor), *The Diaries of Lieutenant-General Henry Pownall*, Volume 2, op. cit.
5. CAB103/340. PRO. Letter from 2nd Earl Wavell to Major-General S.W. Kirby, the Official Historian, dated 13th October 1953.
6. Brooke-Popham Papers, V/II/I. Liddell Hart Centre, King's College, London.
7. Roger Parkinson, *Blood, Toil, Tears and Sweat*, Hart-Davis, London, 1973. This book is based on British War Cabinet Papers.
8. For a full discussion see Joseph P. Lash, *Roosevelt & Churchill, 1939–1941*, André Deutsch, London, 1977.
9. Bradley F. Smith, *The Ultra-Magic Deals*, Airlife, Shrewsbury, 1993.
10. William Stevenson, *A Man Called Intrepid*, Macmillan, London, 1976.
11. FO371/27895. Craigie to Eden, 3rd June 1941. PRO.
12. (a) FO371/35957, Craigie's Final Report, 4th February 1943. (b) See also, Joseph C. Grew, op. cit.; and W. Heinrichs, *American Ambassador: Joseph C. Grew and the U.S. Diplomatic Tradition*, OUP, New York, 1966.
13. FO371/35957. PRO.
14. Winston S, Churchill, *The Second World War*, Vol. III, Cassell, London, 1950.
15. CAB119/208. PRO.
16. Memoir of Brigadier F.H. Vinden, CIE. Copy kindly supplied to the author by Mrs Winnie Vinden.
17. Letter dated 22nd August 1995 from Brian Cane to the author.

Bibliography

Official Publications

British

War With Japan, Volumes I to VI (in four books) with four packets of maps, Ministry of Defence Naval Historical Branch, HMSO, London, 1995.

The War Against Japan, Volume 1, Major-General S. Woodburn Kirby and others, HMSO, London, 1957.

Royal Air Force 1939–1945 Volumes I-III, Denis Richards and Hilary St George Saunders, HMSO, London, 1953–54.

Grand Strategy II, in two parts, James R.M. Butler, HMSO, London, 1957 and 1964.

British Intelligence in the Second World War, Volumes 1–4 (in five). F.H. Hinsley and others, HMSO, London, 1979–90.

British Intelligence in the Second World War, Volume 5, Michael Howard, HMSO, London, 1990.

British Intelligence in the Second World War, abridged volume, F.H. Hinsley, HMSO, London, 1993.

Merchant Shipping and the Demands of War, C.B.A. Behrens, HMSO, London, 1955.

The War at Sea, Captain Stephen Roskill, HMSO, London, 1954–61.

SOE Operations in the Far East. Introductory Guide to Newly Released Documents, Louise Atherton, PRO Publications, London, 1993.

American

The Campaigns of the Pacific War, United States Strategic Bombing Survey (Pacific), Washington, DC, 1956.

Role of Communications Intelligence in the Japanese Naval War, 4 Volumes J.V. Connorton, SRH 012, Washington, DC.

Australian

Greece, Crete and Syria, Australia in the War 1939–1945 Series, Volume II, Gavin Long, Australian War Memorial, Canberra, 1953.

The Japanese Thrust, Australia in the War 1939–1945 Series, Volume IV, Lionel Wigmore, Australian War Memorial, Canberra, 1957.

Royal Australian Navy 1939–1943 and *1943–1945*, 2 volumes, Hermon G. Gill, Australian War Memorial, Canberra, 1957 and 1968.

Royal Australian Air Forces 1939–1943, Douglas Gillison, Australian War Memorial, Canberra, 1962.

Royal Australian Air Forces, 1943–1945, George Odgers, Australian War Memorial, Canberra, 1957.

Official Reports

British

Operations of Malaya Command 8th December 1941–15th February 1942, 2nd Supplement, The London Gazette 20th February 1948. Despatch by Lieutenant-General A.E. Percival.

Air Chief Marshal Sir Robert Brooke-Popham. Despatch on the Far East. 8th July 1942 (PREM3/168/3, PRO).

General Sir A.P. Wavell. Report on Operations in Malaya and Singapore, 1st June 1942 (PREM3/169/3, PRO).

Air Vice-Marshal Sir Paul Maltby, *Report on the Air Operations during the Campaign in Malaya and the Netherlands East Indies from 8th December 1941 to 12 March 1942*, Supplement to *The London Gazette* 26th July 1947.

Australian

Major-General Gordon Bennett, Report on the Malayan Campaign, March 1942 (WO32/11749, PRO).

Canadian

Report on the Canadian Expeditionary Forces to the Crown Colony of Hong Kong, Ottawa, 1942.

Articles

Bridges, Brian, 'Britain and Japanese Espionage in Pre-war Malaya: the Shinozaki Case', *Journal of Contemporary History*, Vol. 21, Sage, London, 1986.
Cecil, Robert, 'C's War', *Journal of Intelligence and National Security*, JINS, Vol. 1, No. 2, Frank Cass, London, May 1986.
Chapman, John W.M., 'Tricycle Recycled: Collaboration among the Secret Intelligence Services of the Axis States, 1940–41', JINS, Vol. 7, No. 3, 1993.
Denniston, A.G., 'The GC&CS Between the Wars', JINS, Vol. 1, No. 1, 1986.
Kelly, Richard M., 'The Chance Island', *Blue Book Magazine*, March 1946.
Martin, James V., 'Thai-American Relations in World War II', *Journal of Asian Studies*, August 1963.
Metzger, Laurent, 'Joseph Ducroux, a French agent of the Comintern in Singapore, 1931–1932', *Journal of the Malayan Branch of the Royal Asiatic Society*, Volume LXIX, Part 1, 1996.
Munday, J.R., 'An Inspiration To All', *Flight Deck Journal of Naval Aviation*, No. 2, 1993.
Rusbridger, James. 'The Sinking of the *Automedon* and the Capture of the *Nankin*', *Encounter*, May 1985.

Unpublished Manuscripts and Papers

Becker, John and Crisp, Dorothy. Papers and Memoirs.
Gotto, Basil A. *100 Squadron versus Japan*.

Mackay, Baron. Papers and Memoirs.
Ringer, V., Memoir.
Rivers, P.J. *Clipped Wings: The Collapse of British Air Defence, Malaya, 1941–1942.*
Vinden, Brigadier H. Papers and Memoirs.

Guide Book

All About Shanghai, Shanghai University Press, 1935. Reprinted by Oxford University Press, Oxford, 1981.

Books

'An RAAF Officer' (A.D. Elson-Smith), *Great Was The Fall,* Patterson's Press, Perth, Australia, 1945.
Abkhazi, Peggy, *Enemy Subject*, Alan Sutton, Stroud, 1995.
Allen, Charles (editor), *Tales From The South China Seas*, André Deutsch/BBC, London, 1983.
Allen, Louis, *Burma – The Longest War*, 1941–1945, J.M. Dent, London, 1984.
——, *Singapore 1941–1942*, Davis-Poynter, London, 1977.
Ballard, Geoffrey, *On Ultra Active Service*, Spectrum, Richmond (Victoria), 1991.
Ba Maw, *Breakthrough in Burma*, Yale University Press, New Haven, 1968.
Barber, Noel., *Sinister Twilight*, Collins, London, 1968.
——, *Tanamera,* Hodder & Stoughton, London, 1991.
Barnett, Correlli, *Engage The Enemy More Closely – The Royal Navy in the Second World War*, Hodder & Stoughton, London, 1991.
Beesly, Patrick, *Very Special Intelligence*, Hamish Hamilton, London, 1977.
——, *Very Special Admiral*, Hamish Hamilton, London, 1980.
Behr, Edward, *The Last Emperor*, Futura, London, 1988.
——, *Hirohito – Behind The Myth*, Vintage, New York, 1990.

Bennett, General H. Gordon, *The Fall of Singapore*, Natraj, Dehra Dun, 1990.
Bergamini, David, *Japan's Imperial Conspiracy*, William Morrow, New York, 1971.
Betham, Sir Geoffrey, *The Golden Galley – the Story of the 2nd Punjab Regiment 1761–1947*, Oxford University Press, 1956.
Bland, Larry I. (Editor), *The Papers of George Catlett Marshall*, Volume 3, Johns Hopkins University Press, Baltimore, 1991.
Bond, Brian (Editor), *Chief of Staff, The Diaries of Lieutenant-General Sir Henry Pownall*, Volume II, Leo Cooper, London, 1974.
Brewer, William B., *MacArthur's Undercover War*, John Wiley, New York, 1995.
Brice, Martin H., *The Royal Navy and the Sino-Japanese Incident, 1937–1941*, Ian Allan, Shepperton, 1973.
Brown, Anthony Cave, *The Secret Servant, the Life of Sir Stewart Menzies*, Michael Joseph, London, 1988.
Bryant, Arthur, *The Turn of the Tide, 1939–1943* (Diaries of Field Marshal The Viscount Alanbrooke), Collins, London, 1959.
Bulloch, John, *MI5*, Arthur Barker, London, 1963.
Bullock, Cecil, *Etajima: The Japanese Dartmouth*, London, 1942.
Caldwell, Oliver, *A Secret War: Americans in China 1944–1945*, South Illinois University Press, 1972.
Calvocoressi, Peter, Wint, Guy and Pritchard, John, *Total War*, 2 Volumes, Penguin, London, 1989.
Candlin, Enid Saunders, *The Breach in the Wall – A Memoir of Old China*, Cassell, London, 1974.
Carew, Tim, *The Fall of Hong Kong*, White Lion, London, 1976.
Chapman, F. Spencer, *The Jungle Is Neutral*, Chatto & Windus, London, 1949.
Chapman, John W.P., *The Price of Admiralty* Volumes I to IV (in three books), Saltire Press, Ripe, 1982–89.
Chatfield, Lord, *It Might Happen Again*, Heinemann, London, 1947.
Chen, Percy, *The Sino-Japanese War 1937*, Shanghai, 1938.
Churchill, Winston S., *The Second World War*, Volumes II and III, Cassell, London, 1950, 1951.
Clausen, Henry C., and Lee, Bruce, *Pearl Harbor, Final Judgement*, Leo Cooper, London, 1993.
Colledge, J., *Ships of the Royal Navy*, David & Charles, Newton Abbot, 1969.
Collis, Maurice, *Last and First in Burma*, Faber, London, 1956.
Cook, Haruko Taya and Cook, Theodore F., *Japan At War – An Oral History*, New Press, New York, 1992.
Costello, John, *The Pacific War*, Collins, London, 1981.

——, *Ten Days that Shaped the West*, Transworld, London, 1991.
Craig, William, *The Fall of Japan*, Weidenfeld & Nicolson, London, 1967.
Cramsie, Arthur, *Guest of an Emperor*, William Trimble, Enniskillen, 1987.
Cruickshank, Charles, *Deception in World War II*, OUP, Oxford, 1979.
——, *SOE in the Far East*, OUP, Oxford, 1986.
Dartford, G.P., *A Short History of Malaya*, Longmans Green & Co., London, 1956.
Daws, Gavan, *Prisoners of the Japanese*, Robson, London, 1994.
Day, David, *The Great Betrayal*, Angus & Robertson, London, 1988.
Deacon, Richard, *Chinese Secret Service*, Frederick Muller, London, 1974.
——, *A History of the British Secret Service*, Granada, London, 1980.
——, *'C' – Biography of Sir Maurice Oldfield*, Macdonald, London, 1984.
——, *A History of the Russian Secret Service*, Grafton, London, 1987.
——, *Spyclopedia*, Silver Arrow, New York, 1987.
——, *Kempetai*, Tuttle, Tokyo, 1990.
Dilks, David, *The Diaries of Sir Alexander Cadogan*, Cassell, London, 1971.
Drage, Charles, *Two-Gun Cohen*, Cape, London, 1954.
——, *The Amiable Prussian*, Anthony Blond, London, 1958.
Eade, Charles (Editor), *Secret Session Speeches* (W.S. Churchill), Cassell, London, 1946.
Edwards, Bernard, *Blood and Bushido*, SFA, Upton-upon-Severn, 1991.
Elphick, Peter, *Singapore: The Pregnable Fortress*, Hodder & Stoughton, London, 1995.
Elphick, Peter and Smith, Michael, *Odd Man Out, The Story of the Singapore Traitor*, Hodder & Stoughton, London, 1993.
Enever, Ted, *Britain's Best Kept Secret: Ultra's Base at Bletchley Park*, Alan Sutton, Stroud, 1994.
Faligot, Roger, and Kauffer, Remi, *The Chinese Secret Service*, Headline, London, 1989.
Farrell, J.G., *The Singapore Grip*, Weidenfeld & Nicolson, London, 1978.
Felix, Christopher, *The Spy and his Masters*, Secker & Warburg, London, 1963.
Finkemeyer, Gunner, *It Happened to Us*, self-published, Melbourne, Victoria, 1994.
Fletcher-Cooke, John, *The Emperor's Guest*, Hutchinson, London, 1971.
Flynn, John T., *The Truth about Pearl Harbor*, Strickland Press, Glasgow, 1945.
Foot, M.R.D., *SOE, 1940–1945*, BBC Publications, London, 1984.

Foot, M.R.D. and Langley, J.M., *MI9 Escape and Evasion, 1939–1945*, Bodley Head, London, 1979.
Frei, Henry, *Japan's Southward Advance and Australia*, Melbourne University Press, Melbourne, 1991.
Frisch, Colin, *Heroes Denied, The Malaya Harrier Conspiracy*, Marlin, Wheelers Hill, Australia, 1990.
Fujiwara Iwaichi, *F-Kikan*, Heinemann Asia, Hong Kong, 1983
Fuller, Richard, *Shokan – Hirohito's Samurai*, Arms & Armour, London, 1992.
Gayn, Mark J., *The Fight for the Pacific*, Bodley Head, London, 1941.
Gibson, Walter, *The Boat*, W. Hallam, London, 1952.
Gilbert, Martin, *Finest Hour – Winston Churchill, 1939–1941*, Heinemann, London, 1983.
——, *Road to Victory – Winston Churchill, 1941–1945*, Heinemann, London, 1986.
Gilchrist, Sir Andrew, *Bangkok Top Secret*, Hutchinson, London, 1970.
——, *Malaya 1941*, Robert Hale, London, 1992.
Glaskin, G.M., *A Many Splendoured Woman – A Memoir of Han Suyin*, Graham Brash, Singapore, 1995.
Gobert, Wayne, *The Origins of Australian Diplomatic Intelligence, 1933–1941*, Australian National University, Canberra, 1992.
Goodwin, Ralph, *Passport to Eternity*, Arthur Barker, London, 1956.
Gough, Richard, *SOE, Singapore 1941–1942*, William Kimber, London, 1985.
Grenfell, Captain Russell, *Main Fleet To Singapore*, Faber, London, 1951.
Grew, Joseph C., *Ten Years in Japan*, Hammond, Hammond, London, 1944.
Griffith, Samuel B., (trans.), *Sun Tzu, The Art Of War*, OUP, Oxford, 1963.
Hahn, Emily, *China To Me*, Blakiston, New York, 1944.
Han Suyin, *A Many Splendoured Thing*, Jonathan Cape, London, 1952.
——, *Destination Chungking*, Penguin, London, 1959.
——, *The Morning Deluge*, Jonathan Cape, London, 1972.
Handel, Michael J., *War Strategy & Intelligence*, Frank Cass, London, 1987.
Haque, Ziaul. *Live and Let Live: The Life and Times of Brigadier G. Qasim Gilani*, Singapore, n.d. but c. 1980.
Harper, R.W.E. and Miller, H., *Singapore Mutiny*, OUP, Oxford, 1984.
Harper, Stephen, *Miracle of Deliveries*, Sidgwick & Jackson, London, 1985.
Harris, Robert and Paxman, Jeremy, *A Higher Form of Killing*, Chatto & Windus, London, 1982.

Harrison, H.L.H., *The Sarong and the Kris*, Nautical Publishing Co., Lymington, 1969.
Harrisson, Tom, *World Within*, OUP, Oxford, 1984.
Haseman, John B., *The Thai Resistance Movement During the Second World War*, Chalerminit Press, Bangkok, n.d. but c. 1989.
Hastings, D.J. (Editor), *Bombay Buccaneers*, BACSA, London, 1986.
Hayley Bell, Mary, *What Shall We Do Tomorrow?* Cassell, London, 1968.
Hayward, Brig. P.H.C., *Jane's Dictionary of Military Terms*, Macdonald & Jane's, London, 1975.
Heinrichs, W. *American Ambassador: Joseph C. Grew and the U.S. Diplomatic Tradition*, Oxford University Press, New York, 1966.
Hewitt, Anthony, *Children of the Empire*, Kangaroo Press, Kenthurst, NSW, 1995.
Hinsley, F.H. and Stripp, Alan. *Code Breakers – The Inside Story of Bletchley Park*, OUP, Oxford, 1993.
Hocking, Charles, *Dictionary of Disasters at Sea, 1824–1962*, Lloyds, London, 1969.
Holmes, Richard and Kemp, Anthony, *The Bitter End*, Antony Bird, Chichester, 1982.
Hoyt, Edwin P., *Davies: the Inside Story of a British-American Family in the Pacific*, Topgallant, Honolulu, 1983.
Hsu, Immanuel C.Y., *The Rise of Modern China*, OUP, New York, 1975.
Hull, Cordell, *Memoirs*, Volumes I & II, Hodder & Stoughton, London, 1948.
Hyde, H. Montgomery, *The Quiet Canadian*, Hamish Hamilton, London, 1962.
Ind, Alison, *Allied Intelligence Bureau*, David McKay, New York, 1956.
——, *A History of Modern Espionage*, Hodder & Stoughton, London, 1965.
——, *Spy Ring Pacific*, Weidenfeld & Nicolson, London, 1959.
Ismay, Lord, *Memoirs*, Heinemann, London, 1960.
Jones, R.V., *Most Secret War: British Scientific Intelligence, 1939–1945*, Hamish Hamilton, London, 1978.
Jowitt, The Earl, *Some Were Spies*, Hodder & Stoughton, London, 1954.
Kahn, David, *The Codebreakers*, Sphere, London, 1977.
Kennedy, John, *The Business of War*, Hutchinson, London, 1957.
Kirby, S. Woodburn, *The Chain of Disaster*, Cassell, London, 1971.
Knightley, Philip, *Philby, KGB Masterspy*, André Deutsch, London, 1988.
Knox-Mawer, June, *Tales from Paradise*, BBC Publications, London, 1986.
La Forte, Robert S. and Marcello, Ronald E., (Editors), *Remembering Pearl Harbor*, SR Books, Wilmington, Delaware, 1991.

Lamb, Richard, *Churchill as War Leader – Right or Wrong?* Bloomsbury, London, 1991.
Lash, Joseph P., *Roosevelt and Churchill, 1939–1941*, André Deutsch, London, 1977.
Layton, E.T. with Pineau, R., and Costello, J., *And I Was There*, William Morrow, New York, 1985.
Leasor, James, *War At The Top – Experiences of General Sir Leslie Hollis*, Michael Joseph, London, 1959.
Lee, Bruce, *Marching Orders*, Crown, New York, 1995.
Lee, Geok Boi, *Syonan – Singapore Under the Japanese, 1942–1945*, Singapore Heritage Society, Singapore, 1992.
Leon, R.W., *The Making of an Intelligence Officer*, Dale Luce Press, London, 1994.
Leutze, James, *A Different Kind of Victory*, US Naval Institute, Annapolis, 1981.
Lewin, Ronald, *Ultra Goes To War*, Hutchinson, London, 1978.
——, *The Other Ultra*, Hutchinson, London, 1982.
Lewis, G.E.D., *Out East in the Malay Peninsula*, Penerbit Fajor Bakti Sdn Bhd, Petaling Jaya, Malaya, 1991.
Lucas, Celia, *Prisoners of Santo Tomas*, David & Charles, Newton Abbot, 1975.
McDougall, William H., *By Eastern Windows*, Arthur Barker, London, 1951.
Mackenzie, Hugh, *The Sword of Damocles*, Royal Navy Submarine Museum, Gosport, 1995.
Mains, A.A., *The Retreat from Burma: An Intelligence Officer's Personal Story*, Foulsham, London, 1973.
——, *Field Security – Very Ordinary Intelligence*, Picton, Chippenham, 1992.
Marder, Arthur J., *Old Friends, New Enemies*, OUP, Oxford, 1981.
Marder, Arthur J., Jacobsen, Mark and Horsfield, John, *Old Friends, New Enemies*, Volume II, OUP, Oxford, 1990.
Marshall, G.K., *The Changi Diaries*, self-published, 1988.
Masterson, J.C., *The Double-Cross System*, Yale University Press, 1972.
Menezes, Lieutenant-General S.L., *The Indian Army – Fidelity and Honour*, Viking, New Delhi, 1993.
Middlebrook, Martin and Mahoney, Patrick, *Battleship*, Allen Lane, London, 1977.
Miles, Vice-Admiral M.E., USN, *A Different Kind of War*, Cave Books, Taipei, 1967.
Mohr, Ulrich, and Sellwood, Felix, *Atlantis*, Werner Laurie, London, 1955.
Montgomery, Brian, *Shenton of Singapore*, Leo Cooper, London, 1984.

Moore, Frederick, *With Japan's Leaders*, Chapman Hall, London, 1930.
Moore, Michael, *Battalion at War*, Gliddon Books, Norwich, 1988.
Morison, Samuel Eliot, *History of United States Naval Operations in World War II*, 15 volumes, Little, Brown, Boston, Mass., 1947–62.
Morris, John, *Traveller From Tokyo*, Cresset Press, London, 1943.
Morrison, Ian, *Malayan Postscript*, Faber, London, 1942.
Nicolson, Harold. *Diaries and Letters 1939–1945*, 2 volumes, Collins, London, 1967.
Nish, Ian (Editor), *Britain and Japan, Biographical Portraits*, Japan Library, Folkestone, 1994.
O'Brien, Terence, *The Moonlight War*, Arrow, London, 1989.
Onraet, René, *Singapore – A Police Background*, Dorothy Crisp, London, n.d. but c. 1946.
Paneth, Philip, *Chiang Kai-shek*, Alliance Press, London, n.d. but c. 1944.
Parkinson, Roger, *Blood, Toil, Tears and Sweat*, Hart-Davis, London, 1973.
Patterson, George, *A Spoonful of Rice With Salt*, Pentland Press, Bishop Auckland, 1993.
Pearce, Bill Channing, *Indian Copper*, Bert Gold, Lewes, 1990.
Perkins, Roger, *Regiments of the Empire – A Bibliography*, privately published, Newton Abbot, 1989.
Piggott, F.S.G., *Broken Thread*, Gale & Polden, Aldershot, 1950.
Playfair, Giles, *Singapore Goes off the Air*, Jarrolds, London, 1944.
Prange, Gordon W., *Target Tokyo*, McGraw-Hill, New York, 1984.
Quigley, Ted, *A Spirit of Adventure*, Book Guild, Lewes, 1994.
Ranelagh, John., *CIA – A History*, BBC Books, London, 1992.
Robinson, Eric, *The Japanese File*, Heinemann (Asia), Hong Kong, 1979.
Rocker, George, *Escaped Singapore, Heading Homewards*, Graham Brash, Singapore, 1990.
Rogers, P.G., *The First Englishman in Japan*, Harvill, London, 1956.
Rohwer, J. and Hummelchen, G., *Chronology of the War at Sea*, Volume I, Ian Allan, London, 1972.
Roskill, Stephen, *A Merchant Fleet at War*, Collins, London, 1962.
——, *Churchill and the Admirals*, Collins, London, 1977.
Rusbridger, James and Nave, Eric, *Betrayal at Pearl Harbor*, Summitt Books, New York, 1991.
Russell of Liverpool, Lord, *The Knights of Bushido*, Cassell, London, 1958.
Saburo, Ienaga, *Japan's Last War*, Blackwell, Oxford, 1979.
Seth, Ronald, *Secret Servants – The Story of Japanese Espionage*, Gollancz, London, 1957.

Sherwood, Robert E., *The White House Papers of Harry L. Hopkins*, Volumes I & II, Eyre & Spottiswoode, London, 1948.
Shinozaki, Mamoru, *Syonan, My Story*, Times Books International, Singapore, 1975.
Shuttle, Jack, *Destination Kwai*, Tuccan, Lincoln, 1994.
Sidhu, H., *The Bamboo Fortress*, Native Publications, Singapore, 1991.
Sillitoe, Sir Percy, *Cloak without Dagger*, Quality Book Club, London, 1955.
Simpson, Michael (Editor), *The Somerville Papers*, Scholar Press for Navy Records Society, London, 1995.
Skillen, Hugh, *Spies of the Airwaves*, Skillen, Pinner, 1989.
——, *The 'Y' Compendium*, Skillen, Pinner, 1990.
Slim, Field Marshal Viscount, *Defeat into Victory*, Cassell, London, 1956.
Smith, Bradley F., *The Ultra-Magic Deals*, Airlife, Shrewsbury, 1993.
Stevenson, William, *A Man Called Intrepid*, Macmillan, London, 1976.
Stilwell, Joseph W., *The Stilwell Papers*, Macdonald, London, 1949.
Storry, Richard, *A History of Modern Japan*, Penguin, London, 1982.
Stripp, Alan, *Codebreaker in the Far East*, OUP, Oxford, 1995.
Strutton, Bill and Pearson, Michael, *The Secret Invaders*, Hodder & Stoughton, London, 1961.
Thomas, David A., *Japan's War At Sea*, André Deutsch, London, 1978.
Thorn, Christopher, *The Far Eastern War, States and Societies, 1941–1945*, Counterpoint, London, 1986.
Toland, John, *But Not in Shame*, Random House, New York, 1961.
Tolley, Kemp, *Cruise of the Lanakai*, US Naval Institute, Annapolis, 1973.
Trager, Frank N., *Burma: Japanese Military Administration Selected Documents, 1941–1945*, University of Pennsylvania Press, 1971.
Trenowden, Ian, *Operation Most Secret*, William Kimber, London, 1978.
Tsuji, Masanobu, *Singapore*, Constable, London, 1962.
Tuchman, Barbara W., *Sand against the Wind*, Futura, London, 1981.
Van der Post, Laurens, *The Night of the New Moon*, Hogarth, London, 1970.
Van der Vat, Dan, *The Pacific Campaign*, Grafton, London, 1992.
Vespa, Amleto, *Secret Agent in Japan*, Victor Gollancz, London, 1938.
Wakeman, Frederic, *Policing Shanghai 1927–1937*, University of California Press, Berkeley, 1995.
Wallace, Forbes, *War-Time Interlude*, privately published, 1980.
Ward, Ian, *The Killer They Called God*, Media Masters, Singapore, 1992.
Wark, Wesley K., *The Ultimate Enemy*, OUP Oxford, 1986.
Weinberg, Gerhard. L., *A World At Arms*, CUP, Cambridge, 1994.
Weintraub, Stanley, *Long Day's Journey into War*, Dutton, New York, 1991.

West, Nigel, *MI5 – British Security Service Operations, 1909–1945*, Bodley Head, London, 1981.

——, *A Matter of Trust – MI5, 1945–1972*, Weidenfeld & Nicolson, London, 1982.

Wheatley, Dennis, *The Deception Planners*, Hutchinson, London, 1980.

White, Theodore H., *In Search of History: A Personal Adventure*, London, 1979.

Whitehead, John and Bennett, George, *Escape to Fight On*, Robert Hale, London, 1990.

Whymant, Robert, *Stalin's Spy*, I.B. Tauris, London, 1996.

Williams, Peter and Wallace, David, *Unit 731*, Hodder & Stoughton, London, 1989.

Willmott, H.P., *The Barrier and the Javelin: Japanese and Allied Pacific Strategies, February to June 1942*, US Naval Institute, Annapolis, 1983.

Willoughby, Charles A., *Sorge – Soviet Master Spy*, William Kimber, London, 1952.

Winstedt, Sir Richard, *Malaya and its History*, Hutchinson University Library, London, 1956.

Winterbotham, F.W., *Secret and Personal*, William Kimber, London, 1969.

——, *The Ultra Secret*, Futura, London, 1974.

——, *The Nazi Connection*, Weidenfeld & Nicolson, London, 1978.

Winton, John, *Ultra in the Pacific*, Leo Cooper, London, 1993.

Wrigglesworth, Dato H.L., *The Japanese Invasion of Kelantan*, Kuala Lumpur, 1991.

Wright, Peter, *Spycatcher*, Viking, New York, 1987.

Wright-Nooth, George, *Prisoners of the Turnip Heads*, Leo Cooper, London, 1994.

Wynne, Mervyn Ll., *Triad and Tabut: A Survey of the Origin and Diffusion of Chinese and Mohammedan Secret Societies in the Malay Peninsula, 1800–1940*, Singapore Government Printer, 1941.

Yuan, Shibing (trans.), *Sun Tzu, the Art of War*, Wordsworth, Ware, 1993.

Zaragoza, Ramon. *Old Manila*, OUP, Oxford, 1990.

Zhongli, Zhang, Zengnian, Chen and Xinrong, Yao, *The Swire Group in Old China*, Shanghai People's Publishing House, n.d. but c. 1990.

Abbreviations Used

ABDA	American, British, Dutch, Australian Command, Southwest Pacific
ADC	Aide-de-camp
ADNI	Assistant Director of Naval Intelligence, British Admiralty
AEM	Australian Eastern Mission
ADNI	Assistant Director of Naval Intelligence, British Admiralty
AIB	Allied Intelligence Bureau, Melbourne
AIF	Australian Imperial Force. That part of the Australian army specially raised for service overseas
AILO	Air Intelligence Liaison Officer
AOC	Air Officer Commanding
BAAG	British Army Aid Group. Escape and intelligence-gathering organisation in China
BGS	Brigadier, General Staff
BMA	British Military Administration in post-war Singapore and Malaya
BNA	Burmese National Army
BP	Bletchley Park, war-time home of GC&CS
BSC	British Security Co-ordination. British Intelligence organisation in USA
BW	Biological Warfare
'C'	The codename of successive heads of the British SIS (MI6)
CB	Central Bureau. Melbourne intelligence centre for the US and Australian armies and the RAAF
CCP	Chinese Communist Party, led by Mao Tse-tung

CIA	Central Intelligence Agency, USA
CID	Committee of Imperial Defence, London. Also, in police context, Criminal Investigation Department
CIGS	Chief of the Imperial General Staff, London
C-in-C	Commander-in-Chief
CIE	Companion of the Indian Empire
CMCS	Chinese Maritime Customs Service
COIC	Combined Operational Intelligence Centre; the Allied organisation at Brisbane; there was a British organisation of the same name at Wellington, New Zealand
COIS	Chief-of-Intelligence-Staff. Confidential title of Chief of British Naval Intelligence in a given theatre of war
COPP	British Combined Operations Pilotage Parties
CWS	US Army's Chemical Warfare Service
DDNI	Deputy Director of Naval Intelligence, British Admiralty
D/F	Direction Finding, radio
DNI	Director of Naval Intelligence, British Admiralty
DSO	Defence Security Officer, a MI5 appointment. A DSO was stationed in many British colonies
ERB	Economic Research Bureau. Propaganda arm of the Oriental Mission
FBI	Federal Bureau of Investigation, USA
FCP	French Concession Police, Shanghai
FEB	Far Eastern Bureau. The British propaganda organisation in the Far East. (Not to be confused with FECB.)
FECB	Far East Combined Bureau (Hong Kong, Singapore, Colombo, Kilindini)
FESS	Far Eastern Security Section, a branch of FECB
FIC	French Indo-China
FMS	Federated Malay States
GC&CS	(British Government) Code & Cypher School, forerunner of GCHQ
GCHQ	British Government Communications Headquarters, successor to GC&CS, now at Cheltenham
GOC	General Officer Commanding
GRU	The Russian army's principal intelligence agency
GSO	(British) General Staff Officer, in various grades GSO1, GSO2, GSO3
H/F-D/F	High frequency wireless direction finding ('Huff-Duff')
HK&SRA	Hong Kong & Singapore Royal Artillery
HMG	His Majesty's Government
HQ	Headquarters
IGP	Inspector-General of Police

IIL	Indian Independence League
IIR	Institute of International Relations, a Chinese secret agency
IM	India Mission. The SOE organisation in India, Burma and surrounding areas
INA	Indian National Army
ISLD	Inter-Service Liaison Department. Cover name for the British SIS in India and Burma
IWM	Imperial War Museum, London
JIB	Joint Intelligence Bureau in Malaya
JIC	Joint Intelligence Committee of Joint Chiefs-of-Staff, London
JMF	Johore Military Force, personal army of the Sultan
JN-25	The codename given by the Allies to the main Japanese Naval Code. As it was changed it became known as JN-25b, etc
KGB	Soviet State Security organisation
KMM	*Kematuan Malaya Muda*, a Malayan nationalist and subversive organisation
KMT	Kuomintang. Chinese Nationalists led by Chiang Kai-shek
MCS	Malayan Civil Service
MEW	(British) Ministry of Economic Warfare, parent organisation of the SOE
MI5	British Internal Security Service. (Also operated within British Colonial Territories)
MI6	British Secret Intelligence Service (SIS)
MI9	British Secret Escape Organisation
NA	Naval Attaché
NCO	Non-commissioned officer
NCS	(British) Naval Control Service
NEI	Netherlands East Indies
NID	Naval Intelligence Department, London
NKVD	Forerunner of the KGB
OCPD	Officer Commanding Police Department, Malaya
OM	Oriental Mission. The SOE organisation in the Far East, with its headquarters at Singapore
Op-20-G	US Navy cryptographic section in Washington
OSS	Office of Strategic Services, USA. Forerunner of the CIA
PM	Prime Minister. In the context of this book, Mr Winston Churchill
PSB	Public Security Bureau. The Nationalist Chinese police force in Shanghai
PT	Patrol torpedo (boats)
'Q'	Q Station was the original codename for the 'Y' Station on Stonecutters Island, Hong Kong
RAN	Royal Australian Navy

RFP	'Radio finger-printing'. A British invention for identifying any particular radio transmitter
RM	Royal Marines
RNZN	Royal New Zealand Navy
SB	Special Branch
SCI	Smoke Screen Installation
Shaforce	Shanghai Defence Force
Sigint	Signals Intelligence. The product of this was known to the Allies under several codenames e.g. Special, Ultra, Magic, Zymotic
SIS	(British) Secret Intelligence Service (called MI6 after 1942)
SLU	Special Liaison Unit. Bletchley Park controlled units serving on the staffs of British Cs-in-C, and who handled all matters dealing with 'Special' intelligence
SMP	Shanghai Municipal Police
SMR	South Manchurian Railway Company. Japanese commercial undertaking which was also a front for an intelligence-gathering and subversive organisation
SOA	SOE branch in Australia
SOE	(British) Special Operations Executive. See also OM and IM
SO (I)	British Naval Staff Officer, Intelligence
UMS	Unfederated Malay States
WEC	Wireless Experimental Station. A Sigint operation near New Delhi
WRNS	Colloquially 'Wrens'. Women's Royal Naval Service
W/T	Wireless Telegraphy
Y	Signals Interception

Index

Index

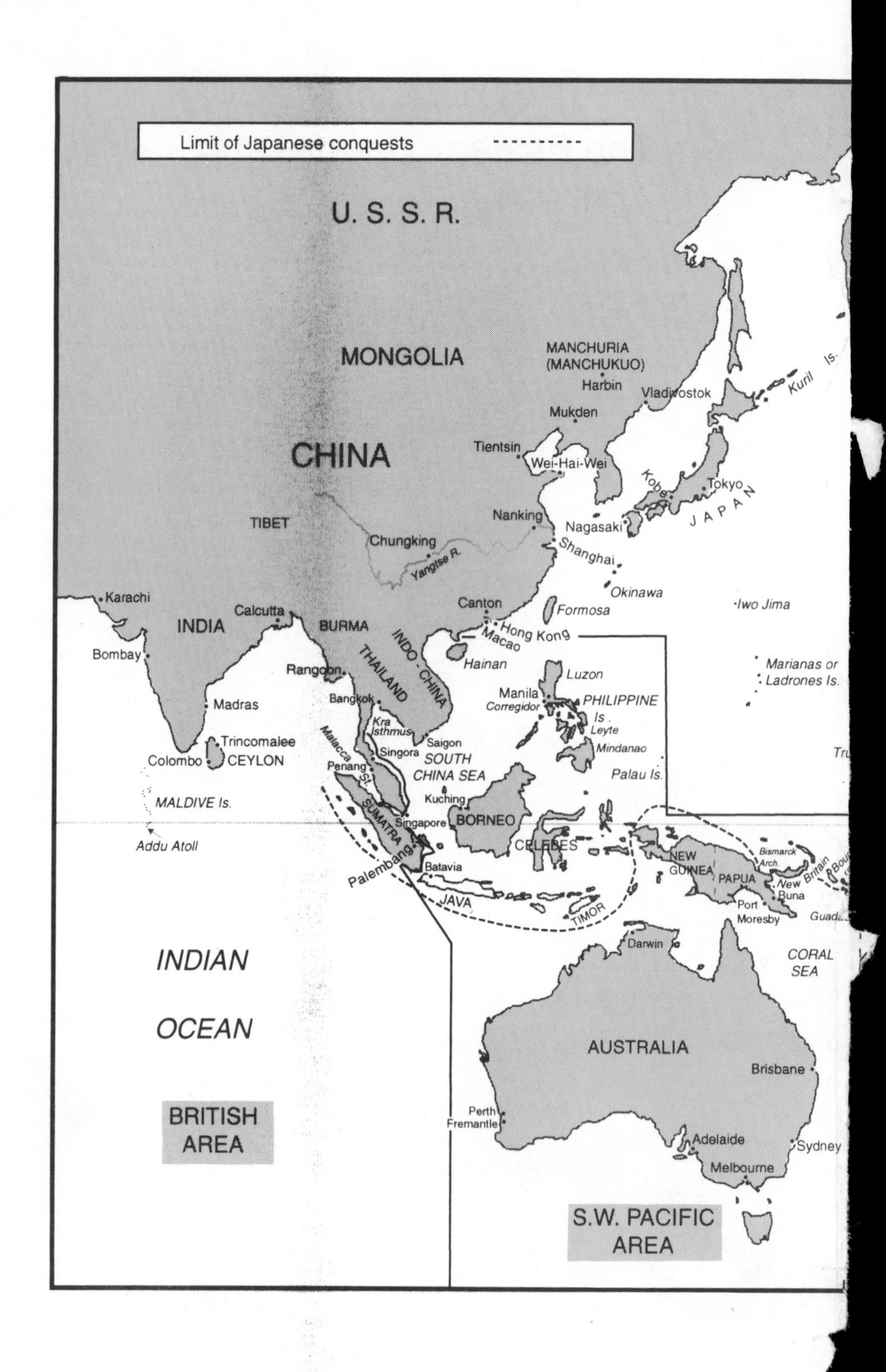

Limit of Japanese conquests
U. S. S. R.
MONGOLIA
MANCHURIA
(MANCHUKUO)
Harbin
Vladivostok
Mukden
Kuril Is.
CHINA
Tientsin
Wei-Hai-Wei
Kobe
Tokyo
JAPAN
TIBET
Nanking
Nagasaki
Chungking
Yangtse R.
Shanghai
Okinawa
Karachi
Calcutta
INDIA
BURMA
Canton
Formosa
Iwo Jima
Hong Kong
Macao
Bombay
INDO-CHINA
THAILAND
Hainan
Marianas or
Ladrones Is.
Rangoon
Luzon
Bangkok
Manila
Corregidor
PHILIPPINE Is.
Madras
Leyte
Kra Isthmus
Saigon
Trincomalee
Mindanao
Colombo
CEYLON
Singora
Malacca St.
SOUTH
CHINA SEA
Penang
Palau Is.
Kuching
MALDIVE Is.
SUMATRA
Singapore
BORNEO
Addu Atoll
CELEBES
Palembang
Batavia
NEW GUINEA
PAPUA
Bismarck Arch.
New Britain
Buna
JAVA
TIMOR
Port Moresby
Darwin
INDIAN
OCEAN
CORAL
SEA
AUSTRALIA
Brisbane
Perth
Fremantle
Adelaide
Sydney
Melbourne
BRITISH
AREA
S.W. PACIFIC
AREA